THE FRENCH SCHOOL OF CLASSICAL BALLET

UNIVERSITY PRESS OF FLORIDA

Florida A&M University, Tallahassee
Florida Atlantic University, Boca Raton
Florida Gulf Coast University, Ft. Myers
Florida International University, Miami
Florida State University, Tallahassee
New College of Florida, Sarasota
University of Central Florida, Orlando
University of Florida, Gainesville
University of North Florida, Jacksonville
University of South Florida, Tampa
University of West Florida, Pensacola

François Aulibé, photographed by Sébastien Mathé.

THE FRENCH SCHOOL

of Classical Ballet

THE FIRST YEAR OF TRAINING

Vanina Wilson

Photographs by Dorothée Lindon

UNIVERSITY PRESS OF FLORIDA

Gainesville · Tallahassee · Tampa · Boca Raton · Pensacola · Orlando · Miami · Jacksonville · Ft. Myers · Sarasota

This book may be available in an electronic edition.

18 17 16 15 14 13   6 5 4 3 2 1

A record of cataloging-in-publication data is available from the
Library of Congress.
ISBN 978-0-8130-4451-4

The University Press of Florida is the scholarly publishing agency
for the State University System of Florida, comprising Florida
A&M University, Florida Atlantic University, Florida Gulf Coast
University, Florida International University, Florida State University,
New College of Florida, University of Central Florida, University
of Florida, University of North Florida, University of South Florida,
and University of West Florida.

University Press of Florida
15 Northwest 15th Street
Gainesville, FL 32611-2079
http://www.upf.com

CONTENTS

♡♡♡♡♡♡♡♡♡♡♡♡

PREFACE

This book was born out of a need that I felt when I first began teaching ballet. The instruction I had received had been in the French method of classical dance; but as I sought to impart my knowledge to students, I noted the absence of literature on French ballet training or, for that matter, on any kind of ballet training program based on that school. The guide I needed had to be flexible, logical, realistic, and orderly—yet still had to reflect the pure style of the French school of classical ballet. This unmet need resulted in this manual. It reflects my quest for safety, precision, and simplicity in approaching ballet basics *à la française*, while also incorporating my personal touch, which sometimes changes traditional approaches as a result of my own teaching experiences.

The genesis of this manual comes from my instruction by some extraordinary and inspiring French dancers: Gilbert Mayer, Raymond Franchetti, and Claire Motte, to name the most memorable, for whom teaching ballet was truly an art in itself. Their pedagogical talent and their thorough knowledge of French style ballet technique and artistry has been a never-ending source of admiration and inspiration.

I hope this insight into ballet technique, French style, will inspire ballet instructors and ballet students alike on their quests for beauty.

I would like to thank my husband and daughter for their patience and contributions to what appeared sometimes as an insurmountable task. I also wish to thank photographers Sébastien Mathé and Dorothée Lindon, my patient models, and all the staff of the University Press of Florida for giving me the opportunity to make this book come true.

Introduction

§

Like other performing art forms, ballet cannot be learned from a book—and neither can the teaching of ballet. Why, then, a manual of ballet instruction? This book's purpose is to guide ballet instructors to teach students the basic components of ballet technique. The program is designed primarily to teach first-year students in a pre-professional program. The elements of the program, however, can be applied easily to students who take ballet classes just for fun. The manual also seeks to familiarize readers with the characteristics of the French school of training, inspired by the *danse d'école* as first developed in France in the seventeenth century, and today epitomized by the Paris Opera Ballet School.

Unlike the Cecchetti, Vaganova, or Royal Academy of Dance schools of training, which use formal and written syllabuses, French-trained dancers follow an oral tradition passed on from one generation of dancers to another, seeking to ensure the continuity of their art. It is, therefore, the teacher, not a syllabus, who sets the pace and the progression of learning. There is no clear-cut rule as to when to do this and when to do that. If the use of an oral tradition allows flexibility and adjustment in teaching, it is also less accessible and exportable. Teachers who are not French-trained will have difficulty understanding and emulating the characteristics of the French school in their own teaching. This manual seeks to remedy that situation and to facilitate the incorporation of French tenets in ballet training, even for teachers who were not trained in France. This manual, however, cannot, nor does it seek to, replicate the material or training used at the Paris Opera Ballet School. The School's training can only inspire, for its standards and physical requirements are so exacting that it cannot be copied.

This manual presents a daily regimen for the first year of ballet training of a contemplated six-year training program. This first year is often long and difficult, but it is almost certainly the most important year of a student's training. Habits acquired during this first year are particularly long-lived and resistant to change. Instilling good habits requires accuracy, slowness, and *repetition*, *repetition*, and more *repetition*, all under careful supervision by knowledgeable instructors who should make students work to their utmost capability without exceeding their limitations. Only when the basics of ballet can be performed properly and automatically, without the need for conscious reflection, can the student be introduced to more advanced and difficult moves and steps. This book seeks to make this training as efficient and logical as possible to enable students to acquire a solid technical foundation.

Unlike other books on ballet training that offer just a description of the ballet vocabulary, a few sample classes, a syllabus, or yet another teaching method, this manual provides complete coverage of the key elements that beginners need to learn. It progressively sets forth the precise exercises that they must perform to make ballet steps and moves preprogrammed, automatic, multi-neuromuscular patterns, and to acquire good habits from the beginning of training. This manual is not, however, a recipe for success, for many other variables are involved in the successful completion of a pre-professional program. The harsh reality is that relatively few students have the physical and mental abilities, determination, discipline, and interest to complete a program of pre-professional ballet training. Physical capability plays a large role in what is obviously a physical activity; so does the ability to assimilate intellectually all the material taught and focus relentlessly, sometimes monomaniacally, on improvement. Raw physical talent, however, coupled even with artistic ability, will not suffice. Good training is essential. This manual seeks to ensure that ballet students get the best start possible on the long path of a ballet professional program.

The French School of Classical Ballet

Because cultural and national characteristics give particular flavors and different approaches to the art of ballet, dancers' performances tend to reflect the school of their training. Therefore, while many exercises in this manual are standard for beginning students in any school, others reflect the particularities of the French school of classical ballet.

The Emphasis on Footwork and the Rapidity of Lower Leg Movements

The French school emphasizes the importance of footwork. The foot is not just a pretty extension of the leg; rather, it carries the leg by strongly brushing out and in to give it momentum and vivacity. This use of the foot minimizes the work of the quadriceps and gives airiness and lightness to the technique. The foot is so important that it tends to steal the leg movement. French-trained dancers learn to show off their pointed foot with the heel strongly pushed forward.

The dexterity of the French dancer's lower leg and the rapidity of the footwork can be quite impressive: a holdover from the Italian dancers who performed in Paris in the nineteenth century. All this work makes the quality of attack among French dancers quite strong. Therefore, classes for beginners include many exercises to: (1) develop the flexibility of the foot and to strengthen it; (2) enable dancers to bend their knees sharply; and (3) strengthen and improve the work of the adductors. For instance, the practice of quick and low (no higher than 25°) battements jetés, which develops the strength of the adductors, is very common in a French ballet class. The application of different musical accents is also worked on in many battements tendus, battements frappés, and petits battements exercises. Finally, the depth of the plié is emphasized throughout to assure softness in landings and allow smooth transfers of weight from one leg onto another.

Elegance and Charm

Ballet's deep historical roots in France add weight and density to the country's interpretation of the art form. Even though we are more than three centuries away from Louis XIV's era, during which the art of ballet developed as a royal court dance, nobility and elegance highlight the style of French-trained dancers. French dancers hold their heads with soft angles and incline their chin upward so that their gaze includes spectators in the balcony. The carriage of the upper body conveys dancers' self-confidence and elegance, with the shoulders pushed down to make the neck more visible and projecting the chest forward from the upper back. Overall, there is a unique sense of aesthetics and appearance—grounded in the origin of ballet as court dance—in which one has to look as majestic and as eye-pleasing as possible. The épaulement and arm movements are more discrete and of a more reserved grace than the flamboyant and dramatic Russian ones. The ballerina adds charm to her dance, conscious of her own artistry and theatrical presence, sometimes with alluring undertones, whether her movement is a simple entrance or a feat of ballet technique. Such *savoir-être* is cultivated early on in the studio, even in a beginner class, where a simple walk, run, pose, or the end of a port de bras—all moments where students do not have to be preoccupied with the technical aspect of ballet—are opportunities for students to feel and pretend they are all ballet stars facing an audience.

Purity, Precision, and Simplicity

The Paris Opera Ballet School was the first school to teach ballet. The strict adherence to classical ballet technique in France has assured the continuity of the *danse d'école*, in its purest form, through generations of dancers. The teaching of ballet is viewed as constructing a building: without a proper foundation, the structures resting on it will be neither stable nor aesthetically pleasing. This approach is also common in the world's other top ballet schools. But in France, the demands for precision and cleanness of movement are particularly strong. Even in more advanced levels of training, French ballet instructors favor series of exercises calculated to work a specific part of the body or a particular movement, not to do pretty choreography. In general, class combinations tend to be short and simple so that students can concentrate on perfecting a specific movement one at a time.

The 5th Position as a Hub

In all ballet schools, the 5th position is a crucial component of the technique. For French dancers, however, it is not just a starting and closing position but a hub that allows dancers to re-center themselves, on both legs, ever so briefly, before initiating another step. The program described in this manual seeks to make students sensitive to the transfer of weight from one foot to another or from both feet onto one, for this sensitivity to weight transfers allows quick and light transitions from one step to another, without losing balance or disrupting the flow of the movement. French ballet dancers make considerable use of their adductors for quick closings in 5th. Out of this hub, the foot, again, initiates the opening of the leg as triumphantly as possible.

Pointe Work

Pointe work is usually introduced later in France's ballet classes than in other countries' ballet schools, the philosophy being that the demi-pointe must be sufficiently high and strong to make the introduction of pointe work easier. Repetitive drills of all kinds of relevés during the first year prepare students for later pointe work.

When You Become a Teacher, by Your Students You'll Be Taught

Teaching ballet is itself a constant source of learning, always challenging familiar ways of instruction. Keeping this in mind, while I have remained faithful to the roots of my training, my experience as a teacher has caused me to depart from certain traditions in order to facilitate the process of assimilation and learning in the safest manner possible. Adopting safe practices early on, such as keeping the knees above the toes in plié, avoiding over turning, and pushing the heels down in the demi-plié, is important in the evolution not only of the training, but also in limiting the number and gravity of injuries, and contributing to the longevity of a dancer's professional life. However, such safe practices should not keep students from working to the maximum of their capability. In other words, students must be pushed, but not beyond what they can accomplish.

1. The parallel position (the 6th position) is used extensively at the beginning of the year to help true beginners make the transition to all turned-out. The use of the 6th allows students, especially those with less than perfect turn-out, to concentrate on their posture, footwork, port de bras, et cetera, without having the extra burden of using the turn-out right away.

2. Exercises of battements tendus take a large portion of class time in order to perfect the work of the foot and to develop its interior musculature.

3. Exercises in the more demanding 4th and 5th positions tend to come after the ones using the easier 6th, 2nd, and 1st positions.

4. The deep plié exercises at the barre usually start in 2nd, the easiest turned out position.

5. In the first lessons, the introduction to the 1st position is done by opening the legs together simultaneously without adjustment, to avoid the tendency to open the feet beyond the level of turn-out from the hips.

6. Throughout the year, the first battement tendu exercise at the barre is done in 1st to allow the hips to warm up gradually before moving to the more difficult 5th position.

7. The barre is performed without slippers so that students better feel the grabbing of the toes and the flattening of the feet on the floor.

8. Almost all exercises at the barre end with a relevé to work balance and strength of the feet and ankles.

Application to a Recreational Ballet Program

Very few ballet schools offer a pre-professional training program of daily lessons for young (pre-teen) students. Many more dance schools offer classes two or perhaps three times a week for beginners in a more casual setting. These schools are a rich ground for acquainting children with the art of ballet. While most students in these schools do not pursue a career in dance, some whose talent becomes apparent in these recreational ballet programs may pursue the activity more intensely. In fact, many successful American professional dancers started ballet training in a local dance school, first becoming acquainted with ballet training casually and then moving on to more intense training.

Whether teaching students to dance just for fun, or training them with a future professional life in mind, ballet teachers can easily incorporate elements described in this manual into their own program. They will appreciate the simplicity and clarity of the exercises and will be able to adapt most of the contents to their own classes. This manual is a practical teaching aid for all levels and abilities. Instructors will benefit particularly from understanding how steps are broken down into their constituent parts and how some specific exercises prepare for others. For instance, introducing a certain step or movement (for example, a glissade), is made easier by following the precise mechanisms of the step as described in this manual, regardless of a student's age or level of talent. Students, whether or not they aspire to becoming professional, will also appreciate this broken down approach that allows them to understand the mechanisms involved in different ballet steps. (Students who consult this manual should do so, however, as part of an instructed ballet program; it is not intended as a self-teacher). If teachers wish to improve their students' ability to acquire rapidity in the lower leg, they can include exercises that require bending the working leg sharply against the supporting leg, as described in several exercises of this manual. In addition, the particular carriage of the upper back and head of the French school of classical ballet will be eye-pleasing, when properly applied even by recreational students.

The progression of exercises in the class and the order of learning ballet vocabulary, as described in this manual, change very little for recreational students—even those who may take ballet as infrequently as once a week. Demands on the muscles increase gradually throughout the dance class, no matter how advanced students are, and during the course of training students learn the simplest steps and movements before advancing to more complicated ones. For instance, a soubresaut is introduced before

a changement de pied, and a battement comes before a développé.

However, since this manual describes a pre-professional program aimed for students taking daily ballet classes and meeting minimum requirements for physical and mental ballet abilities, as well as commitment and motivation, applying it to students who may be taking ballet only two or three times a week will acquire adjustment. Most of the adjustment will be in the *pacing and progression of instruction,* for two reasons: (1) since most recreational students are not selected for their natural aptitude for this art form, they will have difficulty in acquiring the proper placement and posture required to learn and master the steps and movements quickly; and (2) recreational students will not repeat exercises often enough to allow rapid acquisition of technique. As a general rule, the less time a student spends practicing ballet, the slower the pacing of introducing new elements will be.

One challenge for the child starting a rigorous and highly structured ballet training program, such as this one, is to be able to release energy. The much-used application of holding must not totally frustrate the need for movement during this first-year program. Skipping, ballet runs and walks in class, for example, are welcome opportunities for children to release pent-up energy; so are cross-training classes in character dance, mime, and conditioning. The need to release energy is even greater for recreational students. Instructors, facing the realities of teaching ballet in a commercial school heavily dependent on tuition revenue for economic survival, must present the class material in such a way as to provide more immediate gratification to their students: perhaps more movement and less position holding, since usually the last thing a child expects to do in a ballet class is to hold still! Students in a pre-professional program are more likely to understand the ultimate goal of their instruction: dancing in a professional company. They are more likely to accept the grind necessary to develop the level of skill to merit consideration for such employment. Students in a recreational program have no such expectation; consequently the instruction itself, coupled perhaps with the recreational school's performances, must be their own reward.

Throughout this manual, I have incorporated some explanations (the first one being at the end of the First Class of the First Week) when describing a certain pose or movement for students who do not follow a daily regimen of classes. This is an effort to account for the variability in the different levels that exist in ballet training.

Terminology

Ballet teachers in the United States come from many backgrounds and receive their training in many different schools. The terminology of the ballet vocabulary in these different schools, while remaining French, has known wide variations and inconsistencies in both the name of the steps and what they represent, which at times creates confusion among ballet teachers and students. The manual closely follows the traditional French ballet vocabulary. While this manual does not compare different styles of training, it does include the equivalent terminology of the Vaganova and, to some extent, the Cecchetti schools of ballet, when their terminology differs from the one used in the French school.

Content

The amount of material learned in the first year is limited to the most basic steps and combinations, for the focus of the first year is mainly to teach students correct placement and posture. The coverage of the program of this manual reflects the following important goals to be achieved during the first year of a pre-professional program:

1. Correct placement and posture, especially of the back and pelvis, without pushing the ribs out or tucking the pelvis under
2. Holding of a pulled-up back
3. Holding still before and after each exercise with the correct alignment
4. Control of the turn-out of the whole legs and feet in the elements introduced throughout the year
5. Precise carriage of the arms, hands, shoulders, and head

6. Simple coordination of the arms and head accompanying the leg movement
7. The pulling up of the quadriceps on the kneecap when the legs are in stretched position
8. Correct application of the mechanisms of the plié, keeping the heels on the floor and the knees above the toes, and its different qualities whether it is used in allegro or adagio
9. Pointing of the whole foot—without sickling—and the flexibility of the ankle
10. In the jump, stretching the knees and toes in the air and a soft landing with the whole foot down into plié
11. In the relevé, keeping the instep part of the foot as much as possible above the toes—without any sickling—while keeping the knees taut

By the end of the year, students are also expected to perform certain basic steps correctly, which are the core of the ballet vocabulary, such as the battement tendu, the battement jeté, the rond de jambe, the simple relevé, and the soubresaut. Other more complex steps, like the pas de basque, the pas de bourrée, or the détourné can be introduced later at the teacher's discretion. The instructor may decide that some steps need not be introduced during the first year, if students are not progressing as planned, or if more time is needed on some elements and not others. In other words, the content of this program need not be followed to the letter. The fact that this manual is not a syllabus means that it is flexible in the *amount* of material introduced.

The *order* of the steps, by contrast, is not as flexible, because they are presented in a logical path. A petit jeté dessous, a jump finishing on one foot, is not taught before an assemblé, which is landed on both feet. A développé, physically more complex and demanding, does not precede the introduction of lifting the stretched leg in the air. To make assimilation as easy, efficient, and logical as possible, the program is based on two important concepts: (1) the simpler movements and positions precede the more complicated ones and must be mastered before the more complicated movements are introduced; and (2) the simpler movements and positions should prepare students for the more complicated ones.[1] For instance, the study of the battement tendu takes a large part of the daily lessons, for it is the root of many more complex moves in ballet technique. These concepts, as logical as they seem, appear to be falling out of favor with increasing numbers of ballet teachers, whose approach is to expose students to more difficult moves before they have mastered simple ones. There are five possible explanations for this phenomenon: (1) pressure for young ballet dancers to acquire complex technique quickly (often disguised rhetorically as a need to challenge students); (2) genuine belief among pedagogues that exposure to more difficult technique facilitates learning simpler technique; (3) instructor's boredom with teaching basic technique; (4) overall declining attention span and the need for immediate gratification; (5) too much room for improvisation and no coherent program toward a set goal. Whatever the reason, this book rejects this approach to teaching ballet.

The composition of each class also follows a logical order that should not be the subject of much variability. Certain exercises should precede others so that the body is properly conditioned. For example, in each lesson, the battement tendu precedes the battement jeté. A small jump exercise on both feet, such as the changement de pied or the soubresaut, comes before the more demanding jumps landing on one foot such as the jeté.

No area of the student's body is neglected and the instructor should avoid focusing on some areas while ignoring others. There is no pet body area in ballet, for ballet's beauty lies in movements and positions of the whole body from head to toe. If areas of the body are ignored during the first year, students will have a hard time developing those areas later in their training. Even the expression of the face is important for the beginner; it must not reflect any tension or boredom. A pasted-on smile is also unasked for

during class. The eyes are alert and there is no biting of the lips or any other tic that would be hard to eradicate.

Each class is approximately ninety minutes. A longer class may be acceptable only if students get a small break, for their level of concentration and overall fatigue may impede the benefits of the longer class. The program is the same for boys and girls in their first year of training.

Photos

The reliance on photographs has deliberately been kept to a minimum. Even though ballet is a very visual art, this manual is not a book for the eyes but for the mind. By reading and carefully considering the text, images should form in the reader's mind of how a step or position should appear. This intellectual process is essential before either performing or instructing ballet. Moreover, ballet is movement; photos and images can capture only tiny parts of movement and freeze it. They cannot express ballet's flow and continuity, whereas the mental images formed by words can actually better acquaint the instructor with the nature of movement. Even moving pictures are almost always taken from one angle, whereas an instructor must necessarily view students from different angles. The instructor who has a mental image of how a position, move, or step should appear knows that appearance from every conceivable angle.

The positions illustrated by the models in the photos are not always perfect, since they are young students still in the early process of learning. They do not, nor are they able to, show the ideal positions, especially the more demanding ones. They represent, however, realistic representations of what instructors of students of this age, in a pre-professional program, are likely to encounter in their classes and may be more useful to the reader, therefore, than professional or more advanced dancers illustrating perfect positions. If the reader can spot the flaw in the photograph, he or she may truly understand the text!

---

1   Attikov, *La voie du Perfectionnement en Danse Classique*, 16.

Music

Music accompaniment is an intrinsic part of the students' training in the dance class. It must be able to trigger the emotional and physical responses that the dancer needs to become an accomplished artist.[2] The first year is often very repetitive and slow for the beginning student. The instructor must make sure that the choice and the quality of music help students learn not only the proper automatisms that the body needs to acquire for ballet technique, but also to motivate and inspire them through the daily class.

When appropriate, the manual suggests a choice of music (a tango, a waltz, et cetera) for a particular exercise, but the suggestions are in no way exclusive. Especially in the beginning of the year, each movement is broken down, sometimes taking a whole eight-count to be completed. The instructor should work with the accompanist so that the musical phrasing and rhythm and melody choices help students keep the movement from becoming sleepy, heavy, boring, or just off the beat. Melodies should remain simple for beginners so that they can easily coordinate the movement with the music. The quick movements required in the lower legs—a trademark of the French school—should be matched by an appropriately snappy and crisp musical choice. The music for exercises in the French school, such as the battement tendu, battement jeté, and battement frappé, tends to be sharper (with perhaps fewer notes), and with a clearer beat, than in other ballet schools. This helps to convey and develop briskness, precision, and crispness in the movement.

For practical purposes, the breakdown of the music accompanying the movement is done with full counts, except when parts of a particular movement are on musical upbeats. In such a case, the term "and" is noted to show that a certain portion of a movement needs to be done at a certain time of the counting. The term "and" is otherwise omitted, except when a certain quality of performance of a particular exercise would require the instructor to hum the "and," like to accompany a particular extension of the

leg or arm, the brush of the foot on the floor, or the depth of a plié. Except for the very beginning exercises, which are preceded by an eight-count preparation, students will perform a four-count preparation before each exercise.

Organization

The program is divided into thirty-three weeks. Each week is then divided into five daily classes. In most weeks, two or three classes are fully laid out, subsequent classes merely repeating earlier classes. Exercises introducing new elements are fully described. These exercises are then subsequently repeated a number of times. If such an organization seems cumbersome, it gives the necessary background to facilitate the understanding of the progression involved, starting with the simplest positions and movements and then increasing the level of difficulty. Such a structure also offers an orderly approach for introducing new material and sets the pace of learning throughout the year. The program is followed by a section describing some conditioning exercises pertinent to the training. Finally, an index that shows the progression of the steps introduced during the year is included at the end of the manual.

The size of this manual, with a limited number of visuals, may seem overwhelming, and the prospect of reading it in its entirety at once a daunting task. The manual should be treated as a textbook, with the reader approaching the material in stages: trying parts in class, understanding their purpose and logic, and evaluating their use for a particular class or program. If the reader has difficulty understanding a particular exercise, he or she should consult the "rules" as stated at the beginning of the manual. Moreover, the fundamentals of ballet basic technique that all beginners need to apply throughout the year are introduced in the first lessons of the present program. To understand the subsequent lessons, it is important to have read and understood the explanation of these fundamentals. Instructors must exercise a wholesome discretion in applying the exercises set forth in this manual, and in supervising students performing these exercises. The progress and safety of the students

---

2   Cavalli, *Dance and Music*, 20.

are dependent on many variables, one of them being the interaction between the instructor and students, and the author makes no guarantee that the use of the manual will prevent injuries, or result in a particular amount of progress. In any case, the author hopes that this manual can enlighten readers, whether they apply all or parts of it to their teaching or training.

The Beginning for the Beginner

§

To help students keep their feet flat—without the toes curling up and the feet rolling to one side or the other—students will wear just a pair of thin socks for barre work. They will wear ballet slippers for center work.

Unless otherwise specified, the following rules should be observed:

1. When working one leg, students start each exercise with the right leg and then repeat the exercise with the left leg.

2. Students start an exercise sideways at the barre, working the right leg and holding the barre with the left hand. After turning toward the barre, they repeat the exercise on the other side, working the left leg and holding the barre with the right hand.

3. The working arm or arms are in 2nd position.

4. Exercises start with a preparatory port de bras and end by bringing the arms into the preparatory position.

5. Students practice center exercises facing the front of the studio.

6. When in 5th position, students start each exercise with the right foot front.

7. The exercise is done en croix (in the shape of a cross) en dehors (outward).

8. Students hold still in the preparatory position for a few seconds before and then after each exercise, when the music stops.

9. A plié is a demi-plié. Unless it is a grand plié, a plié is a demi-plié with the knees bent at about 90°.

10. In the battement frappé and the petit battement sur le cou-de-pied (neck of the foot), the working foot is in a wrapped position.

11. Exercises of petits battements are on the cou-de-pied.

12. The échappé is an échappé sauté (jumped).

13. Exercises are performed in 5th position.

14. The expressions arms in preparatory position and arms down are used interchangeably.

15. The legs are in a stretched position. Stretching the legs and the knees means that students pull the quadriceps on the kneecap for a full extension of the leg.

16. Expressions devant and front, and derrière and back, respectively, are used interchangeably.

17. At the end of each exercise, students close their feet into the same position as the one in which they started the exercise.

18. When the arms are in 1st position or low 1st position during an exercise, the arms open 2nd and come down into preparatory position at the end of the exercise.

19. Each class starts with barre work, followed by work in the center. The part of the class that is performed in the center will be specified; without such a specification, the exercise described should be done at the barre.

THE FRENCH SCHOOL OF CLASSICAL BALLET

First Week

§

FIRST CLASS

Exercise 1

Preparatory port de bras (port de bras préparatoire; préparation) [position de repos normale—Cecchetti], plié and stretch (tendu) in 6th position (parallel), port de bras to 2nd, four counts, facing the barre.

Stand in 6th facing the barre, at about one foot distance between the toes and the barre, arms in preparatory position with the proper body alignment.

Preparatory port de bras on four counts: on 1, hold; on 2, bring the arms in 1st; on 3, turn the palms down and bring the hands gently and gracefully to rest on the barre, with relaxed elbows and the head and eyes directed de face; on 4, hold the position. From now on, when starting an exercise facing the barre, students will execute this preparatory port de bras.

On 1 and 2, plié, keeping the heels down; on 3 and 4, stretch both knees; on 5 and 6, plié; on 7 and 8, stretch both knees; on 1, students release the arms from the barre and bring them to 1st; on 2, hold the position; on 3 and 4, open the arms 2nd; on "and," turn the palms down, bringing the forearms slightly higher than the elbows; on 5 and 6, bring the arms in preparatory position; on 7, bring the arms in 1st; on 8, rest the hands on the barre. Repeat the whole exercise one more time, with the arms remaining in preparatory position at the end of the port de bras.

Explanation. The barre should be at a suitable height (usually at the level of the rib cage), and students must stand at a proper distance from it so that their arms are at a comfortable angle (no less than 120°) when the hands rest on the barre, with the elbows relaxed. The 6th position, in which the legs are parallel and the feet side by side, is not considered one of the main ballet feet positions. It is a neoclassical variation of the first position. It existed as far back as the eighteenth century; however, Serge Lifar first codified it in his *Traité de Danse Académique* while serving as the master of the Paris Opera Ballet.[1]

In this exercise, students become acquainted with many aspects of ballet placement and posture that should be mastered during the first year. The following explanation, therefore, applies not

---

1   Lifar, *Traité de Danse Académique*, 31.

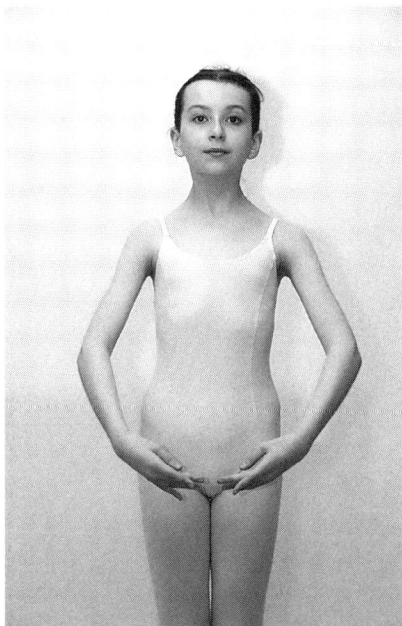

Arms in preparatory position.

Hands resting on the barre.

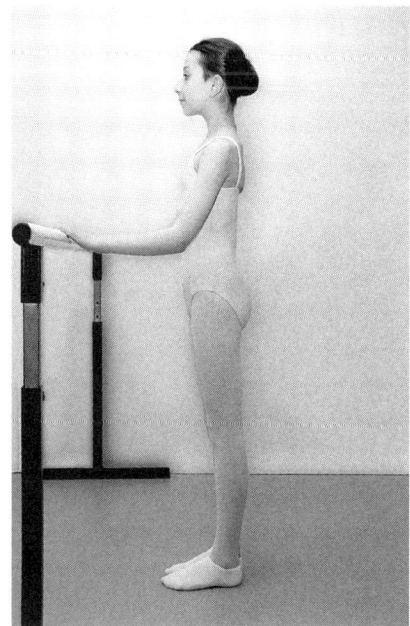

Hands resting on the barre, side view.

only to this exercise but also to the rest of the program.

This simple exercise of plié and stretch introduces students to the basic ballet posture with the different parts of the body aligned like building blocks balanced one on top of the other.[2] It involves the most basic movements in ballet: the plié and the stretch of the legs. They act as a hinge and an essential spring for a whole range of ballet moves. The plié itself is performed smoothly so that the dancer develops elasticity and strength in the legs. The plié also strengthens the Achilles tendon and the ligaments of the ankles and the knees. Students do not sit in the plié, but straighten the legs as soon as they reach the lowest level that they can achieve without lifting their heels off the floor.

The following parts of the body need to be monitored carefully and physically adjusted by the instructor.

The upper body: the back is erect and the chin held slightly upward. The shoulders are pushed down. Many students tend to tense up their arms when holding them in ballet positions. One of the instructor's most difficult tasks is to make students understand that it is in fact the upper back that is fully engaged to hold the arm positions, so that there is no tension in the arms themselves or in the upper part of the shoulders. In holding the upper back, students do not stick out their rib cage and close their shoulder blades. Doing so would bring the arms too close to the torso, whether they are in preparation or in 1st, and cause the shoulders to rise.

The pelvis: since the correct placement of the pelvis is not a natural position, the instructor has to adopt a hands-on approach to teach students this position. Another useful manner to introduce this difficult position is to show the contrast between the correct alignment and the position of the hips out of alignment so that students can visualize the difference between both positions. The pelvis must be slightly tilted, keeping the hip bones lifted in front, while the lowest part of the spine is directed downward. The spine remains elongated without the pelvis tucking under. The abdominal and buttock muscles are tensed sufficiently to hold the pelvis in the proper alignment. Some students can achieve this position relatively easily, while those who have a sharply curved back may need extra work. In aligning the pelvis correctly, the upper torso is ideally pulled up and held as if it were suspended and in isolation from the rest of the trunk, with the lower abdomen lifted.

The knee: another part of the body that requires careful monitoring from the beginning of training is the knee, since it allows both the plié

---

2   Grieg, *Inside Ballet Technique*, 26.

Plié in 6th position.

Arms in 2nd position.

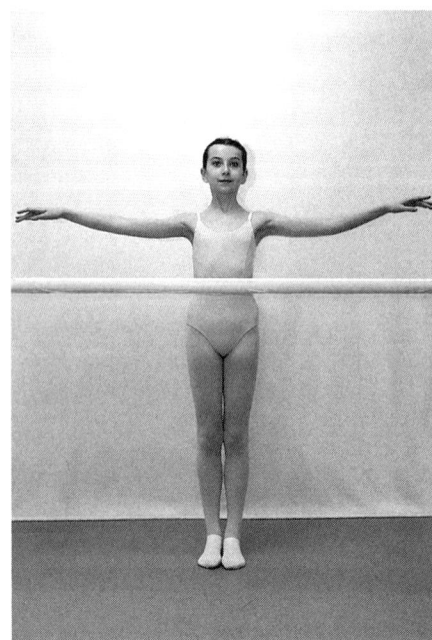

Arms turning to close in preparatory position.

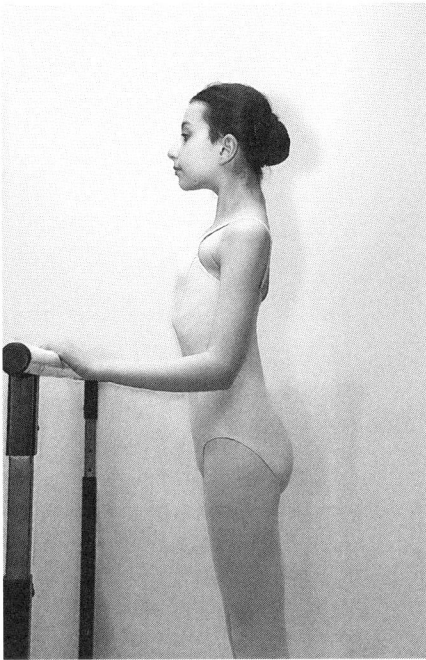

The rib cage is pushed out.

The pelvis is out of alignment.

and the stretch of the legs. The knee is a wonderfully hinged tool that is, unfortunately, relatively fragile and prone to disabling injuries. Some of these can be avoided by adopting safe practices early on. One good rule to follow is to *keep the knees above the toes in the plié*. Any deviation from this close partnership could be disastrous. Executing the plié and the stretch of the knee in 6th position facilitates the introduction of this practice. In the stretching, students must feel the pull of the quadriceps on the kneecap while lengthening the back of the legs, not only for aesthetic reasons but also for the knees to be safely in place in ballet moves.[3] The stretching should be done by pushing the heels onto the floor and standing as tall as possible. The bending and stretching of the knee must always be done with proper alignment. Unless the leg is in plié, it is stretched. Note that the stretching of the knees in a French ballet class is called tendu, not to be confused with the tendu like in battement tendu!

The feet: for French-trained dancers, the floor is their best friend! Resistance work against the floor builds up energy and strength to perform ballet technique. The first approach to this natural and close relationship is for the feet to be

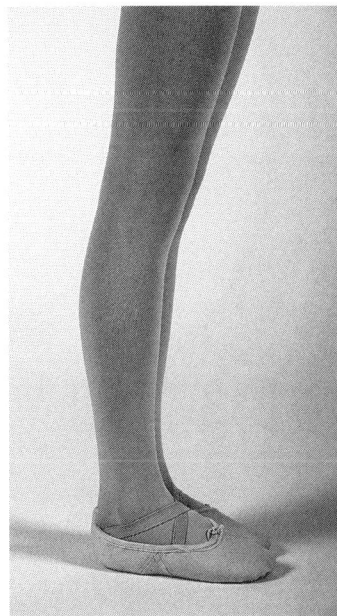

The quadriceps is pulled on the knee cap.

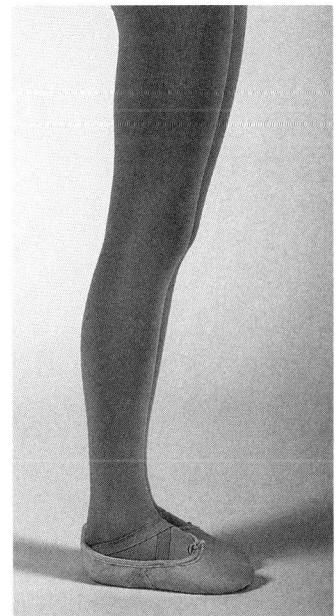

The quadriceps is released.

---

3   Grieg, *Inside Ballet Technique*, 90.

completely flat on the floor and pressed down with the toes elongated, especially in the plié, in which the heels are pressed onto the floor while going down and coming back up. This practice will increase balance and strength in the legs.

The arms and hands: the preparatory arm position is the arm position that starts and ends each ballet exercise. In the French school, this position is called commonly bras en préparation or more simply préparation. The large upper back muscles (latissimus dorsi) should be very active in holding the arms in position while avoiding putting tension in the shoulders, which remain low. The arms are softly curved without sticking the elbows out. To do so, one slightly rotates inward the lower arms. The palms of the hands are turned toward the upper torso. The angles of the elbows are as soft as possible, and the shoulders are pushed back without throwing the upper torso back and sticking the rib cage out. The middle fingers are held about an inch or two apart. The fingers are not touching but are held slightly together with the thumb directed toward the middle finger, which is moved slightly forward. Certain conditions may make the symmetry of the arms in ballet positions difficult to achieve: one arm is longer than the other; the torso is not held entirely straight; the weight is not distributed equally on both legs; or there is too much tension in one arm. It is the role of the instructor to catch any asymmetry early on to apply proper corrections.

Arms in preparatory position are held low in front of the body, but not so low that the arms are hanging down with the hands held against the upper thighs. And the arms should not curve around against the side of the thighs, a position which makes it impractical when moving the arms from one position to another (like from preparatory position to 1st). The space between the hands must be consistent in both the preparation and the 1st positions, the logic being that the arms should not have to move closer to each other when coming to 1st. The same curve is found in the preparatory and the 1st positions. In the preparatory port de bras, the arms are brought to 1st (or to a low 1st, if the barre is an obstacle), the palms rotate downward, and without flexing the wrists, the hands gracefully rest on the barre, with all the fingers on the barre

Arms in preparatory position, with the left shoulder lower than the right one, and a slight asymmetry between the right arm and the left arm.

and the elbows relaxed. The barre must not be an obstacle so that students have to shorten the curve of the arms and stick their elbows out to be able to raise their arms. In 1st position, the arms are raised to the level of the lower level of the rib cage, keeping the shoulders back. Holding the arms too high tends to hide the chest area and pull the shoulders forward, while holding them too low prevents the arms from lining up to open 2nd in a straight line.

In 2nd position, the arms are at the level just below the shoulders, with the elbows slightly bent and the hands prolonging the line of the arms and facing forward. The hands and the fingers must not fall or contract. Like in the preparatory position, the fingers are close to one another but are not touching. The elongated thumb is inside the hand pointing toward the middle finger.

Closing the arms in this exercise occurs in the following succession of movements: students

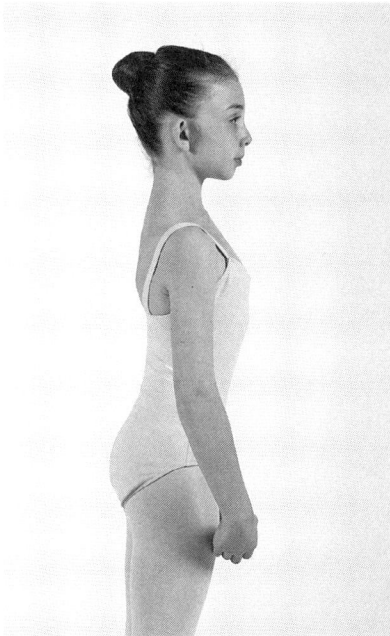

Arms in preparatory position, hands against the thighs.

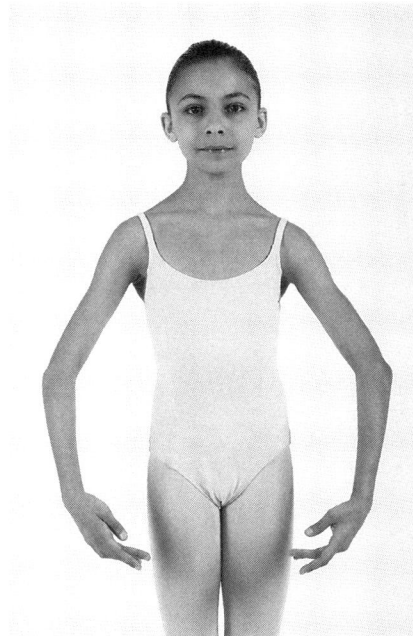

Arms in preparatory position, hands around the thighs.

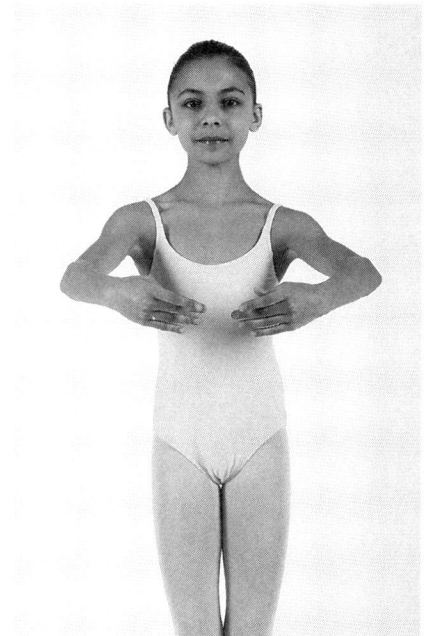

Arms in 1st position held too high.

first bring their arms in 1st, open them in 2nd, and then turn their palms down, raising the fingers slightly, lowering the arms with the elbows initiating the descent but keeping the arms in a soft curve. About halfway down, the upper arms stop moving, while the forearms continue to curve in. When the forearms stop their movement, the hands continue to curve, bending slightly at the wrists, with finally the fingers completing the curving movement. Some students tend to raise their forearms too high (flapping the arms like in Swan Lake!) when bringing their arms into preparatory position. Any extra or exaggerated movement during the port de bras (such as the flexing of the wrist in the first phase of the port de bras) should be discouraged. Such closing port de bras will be done following an exercise facing the barre, unless otherwise specified.

Breathing: because students are asked from the beginning to control and keep many parts of their body still, they also tend to block or just forget breathing. Thus the importance of breathing in ballet exercises must be emphasized from the beginning. It is unfortunate that the role of breathing is hardly mentioned in even prestigious ballet schools. Yet, learning to breathe properly should be a systematic part of the ballet dancer's training. Among other things,

Arms in 2nd position, with one hand facing down.

Arms closing, with the wrists bending excessively.

it increases the dancer's stamina during dancing, helps to oxygenate muscles for better performance, makes the dancing look lighter and effortless, and gives a deeper artistic dimension to each movement.

The breathing sequence of this exercise is as follows: inhale when bringing the arms in 1st, in the preparatory port de bras, and exhale when extending the arms and resting the arms on the barre. Since the plié and stretch is at a fairly slow tempo, normal breathing is required, still coordinating the exhaling part with the lowest part of the plié. Inhale before closing the arms, when turning the palms down, and exhale when closing the arms down.

Students should often be reminded of a few general rules on breathing: exhale in the actions of plié, stretching (such as in bending forward), closing a port de bras, and any landing; inhale in the actions of jumping, relevé, starting a port de bras, and the first part of a battement tendu.

Music. A slow to medium 3/4 waltz would be an appropriate musical choice for this first exercise.

Exercise 2

Battement tendu à terre devant (in front), broken down, in 6th, eight counts, facing the barre.

On "and" 1, brush the right foot devant, stretching the instep of the foot up still with the toes on the floor; on 2, hold the position; on 3, point the toes on the floor without moving the foot off the floor; on 4, hold the position; on 5, bring the toes down; on 6, hold the position; on "and" 7, brush the foot into 6th; on 8, hold the position. Repeat the whole exercise one more time.

Explanation. This is the very first approach of working one leg independently of the other, with the weight remaining on the supporting leg (la jambe de terre) and the working leg (la jambe qui travaille) executing the movement. By breaking down the brushing action of the foot, starting first with the instep and then the toes, students are forced to maximize the stretching of the instep on the way out before actually pointing the toes. Over time, such action will strengthen all the intrinsic muscles of the foot. Students must transfer their weight onto the supporting leg as the leg comes out, keeping just enough weight on the working leg to apply downward pressure to brush the foot out and in of position. Both knees are fully taut throughout the exercise. To work the intrinsic muscles of the feet thoroughly, students must press down the feet onto the floor, with the toes acting as a magnet onto the floor. When the foot points on the floor (except when the foot points 4th derrière, as we will see later), only the longest toes (the big toe and possibly the second toe, depending on the length of the toes and of the metatarsals) touch the floor. Students keep their hips and torso straight without sagging on the supporting hip. The hip of the working leg does not come forward when the leg comes out. When closing, the same brushing action is performed as on the way out, to finally bring the whole foot flat into 6th, without pushing the pelvis backward. Even though this exercise does not involve any turn-out, the main principles of the battement tendu apply: the brushing of the foot on the floor, the gradual pointing of the foot, the stretching of the knees throughout the exercise, and the transferring of weight from both feet onto one.

Music. Even though the movement is highly broken down, the music must be fairly sharp and energetic with clear counts. A moderato 4/4 or a 3/4 waltz would be an appropriate musical choice.

The foot is pointed, except for the toes.

The foot is fully pointed off the floor.

The arms are in 5th position.

Exercise 3

Lifting of the foot, in 6th, port de bras to 5th position, 5th position of the arms (bras en couronne), facing the barre.

On 1, lift the heel of the right foot with the foot resting now on its ball and toes, stretching the instep up; on 2, hold the position; on 3, point the toes with the foot now slightly above the floor; on 4, hold the position with the foot very still; on 5, bring the toes down, next to those of the supporting foot; on 6, hold the position; on 7, bring the heel down into 6th position; on 8, hold the position. Repeat the whole exercise. Bring the arms in 1st, open the arms 2nd, and then bring them up to 5th. Hold the position for a few counts before opening the arms 2nd and closing.

Explanation. Students are introduced to pushing the instep up and lifting the pointed foot off the floor in a broken down manner to understand the different parts of the foot involved in this particular movement. By pushing the toes down and the instep up, students are getting acquainted with the position of the foot when it is on demi-pointe without putting much weight on the foot. When lifting the heel, the pressure exerted on the second and third metatarsals is similar to the pressure on the foot when it is on demi-pointe. Students keep their foot straight without sickling out or rolling in. When pointing, the toes must actively push off the floor, and the pointed foot must hold still. The hips remain straight. Coming down, the toes do not flex prematurely but are kept pointed until they touch the floor, then come down, before the heel is pressed down onto the floor to bring the foot back to its starting place next to the other foot. The work of the foot in this exercise also prepares it for its major role in ballet jumps, as we will discuss later.

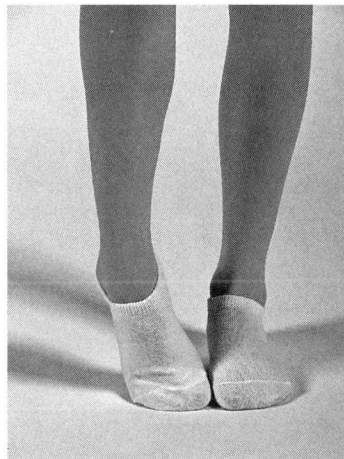

The foot is sickled.

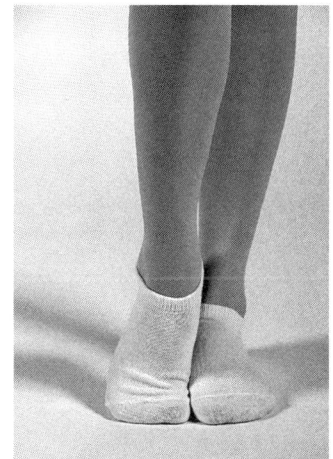

The foot rolls in.

Students are introduced to the 5th position of the arms, which is also called en couronne. When bringing the arms in 5th, students do not raise their shoulders. The arms are curved above and slightly forward of the head. The vision test for the correct position of the arms is to check whether one can see the little fingers by raising the eyes alone. If one can see the whole hand, the arms in 5th are too far forward; and if one cannot see even the little fingers, the arms are too far back. The elbows do not stick out, and the palms face down. Another useful test to check the symmetry of the arms is to have students touch both middle fingers slightly to see if they are lined up. The fingers do not drop but remain elongated. When the arms come down from the 5th to 2nd, the elbows start the movement, turn about halfway for the inside of the arms to face forward, keeping the arms slightly forward. As the arms start opening, students breathe in and very slightly raise their head a notch to give amplitude to the movement at the beginning of the opening of the arms.

Music. A medium tempo 4/4 would work well for the first portion of this exercise involving the feet.

Exercise 4

Preparation for the 1st position of the feet, start in 6th, facing the barre.

On 1, raise the balls and the toes of the feet slightly off the floor, transferring the weight onto the heels, open the feet simultaneously into 1st, and bring the feet flat on the floor without further adjustment; on 2, hold the position; on 3, raise the balls and the toes of the feet again and close the feet in 6th; on 4, hold the position. Repeat three more times. A small plié and stretch ends the exercise before closing the arms.

Explanation. This is the first exercise to acquaint students with the concept of turn-out. Without such an exercise, beginners, when asked to position themselves into 1st position, tend to place the feet in sequence (first one foot, then the other), with the risk of turning out the feet beyond what the hips permit or of turning out

The arms turn about halfway down between 5th and 2nd positions.

The arms are closer to the 2nd position, front view.

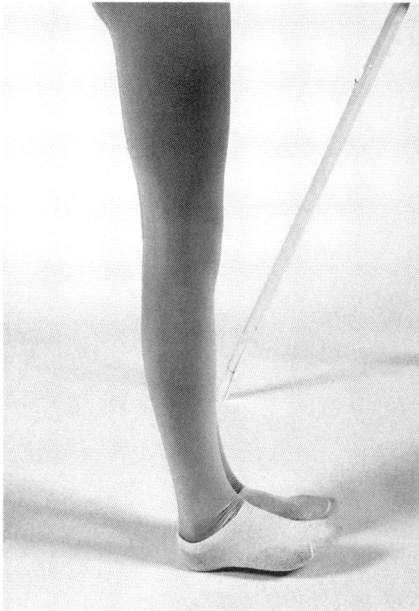

Above: The weight is transferred onto the heels.

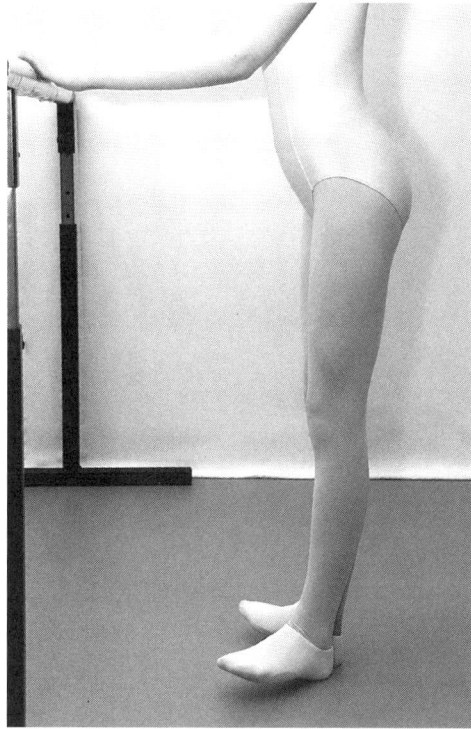

Right: As the feet open, the pelvis comes out.

one leg more than the other. The movement presented in this exercise forces students to open their feet symmetrically so that the turn-out is equal on both legs, and both legs open at the same time within the limits of their natural turn-out. For this exercise to be beneficial, students must not push back and stick their buttocks out in the opening of the feet. Once in place, the feet do not move. The knees remain as taut as possible.

How much turn-out? Turning out the legs is to rotate them outwardly from the hips, along with the feet, 90° each. But it also involves the active participation of the leg and feet muscles. It is the basis for classical ballet technique. The turn-out of the legs comes essentially from the hips, and its natural range is mostly predetermined. It depends on the shape of the femoral neck and the angle at which the femoral head is inserted into the hip socket, the orientation of the hip socket, the elasticity of the iliofemoral ligament, and the flexibility of the hip and thigh muscles.[4] The turn-out is a matter of degree. There is clearly a minimum amount of turn-out needed to follow and succeed in a professional

program, but it need not be the perfect 180° rotation. This minimum is not only a matter of aesthetics but also a question of safety. Lacking this minimum becomes crucial when it is time to be in the center, as students have to perform increasingly difficult moves requiring balance and strength, while keeping both legs turned out. A lack of hip turn-out must not be compensated for by turning out the legs from the feet. The dangers of turning out the feet beyond what the hips permit cannot be underestimated. As early as the sixteenth century, Jean-Georges Noverre warned against trying to turn the feet beyond the range of turn-out of the hip joints.[5] He further recommended the application of moderate but regularly practiced ballet exercises for working on turn-out. Several variables have to be taken into consideration in assessing the amount of turn-out that can be gained. Much depends on the quality of training, how well students apply it, and their physical ability. Certainly many professional ballet dancers have succeeded in their career despite the lack of a perfect turn-out. Before students swear at their parents (or God!) for not having given them the ideal hip design

---

4   Grieg, *Inside Ballet Technique*, 51.

5   Noverre, *Lettres sur la Danse et sur les Ballets*, 20.

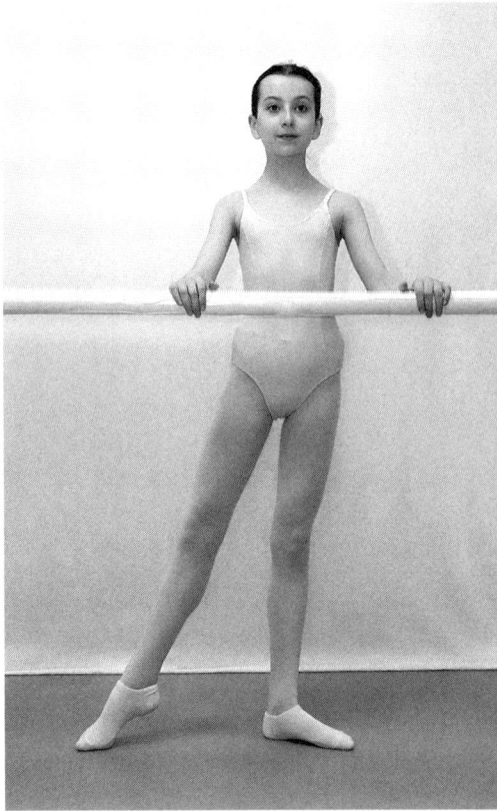

The foot is pointed, but for the toes, 2nd position.

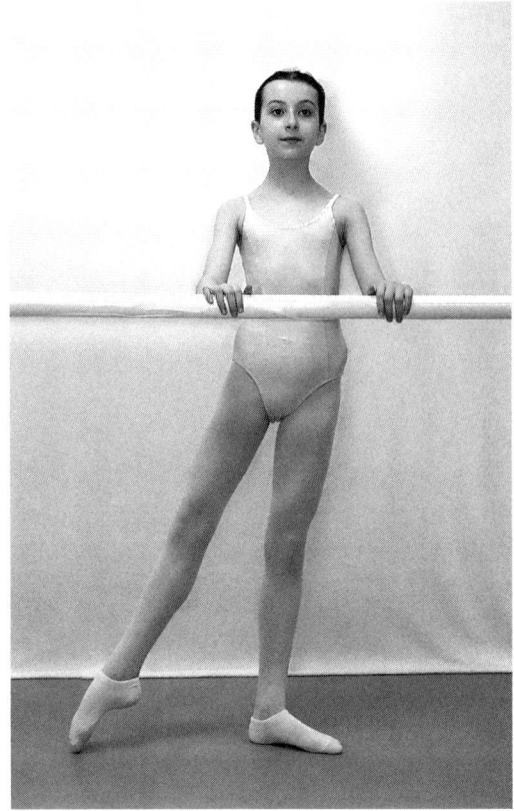

The whole foot is pointed.

for turn-out, they have to know the good news: they have an important role in gaining perhaps a slightly wider range of rotation, in using their turn-out properly and safely, and in developing the muscles of the legs as fully as possible to at least enable them to use and control the turn-out they do have to its full extent.

It should be noted that students' amount of turn-out could be somewhat misleading to the untrained eye, especially when they stand in 1st or 5th. It will be assessed preferably by having the students lie on the back with the whole body aligned as learned in Exercise 1 of the First Class of the First Week. Keeping the legs together and the feet flexed, they will open the legs in 1st, keeping the pelvis aligned and the lower back from curving. In this position, which replicates the one students have when standing in 1st position, the hips are extended without the possibility of using the friction of the feet on the floor to cheat, that is, to open the feet at a wider angle than the one permitted by the turn-out of the hips. Despite common practice, using the different frog positions will not give a realistic assessment of the true amount of hip outward rotation.

A complete discussion on the subject is beyond the scope of this book. Suffice it to say that this manual's program emphasizes safety practices to alleviate the risk of injuries, and the use of the turn-out muscles (such as the hip rotators, the gluteus, and the adductors) throughout to be able to improve and to control the amount of turn-out.

Music. The music is a medium tempo 4/4 with clear counts.

Exercise 5

Battement tendu 2nd, broken down, start in 6th, in 1st, eight counts, facing the barre.

Following the preparatory port de bras, open both feet into 1st simultaneously, as done in the previous exercise.

On "and" 1, brush the right foot 2nd, stretching the instep of the foot, still with the toes on the floor; on 2, hold the position; on 3, point the toes on the floor without moving the foot off the floor, with the toes resting lightly on the floor; on 4, hold the position; on 5, bring the toes down; on 6, hold the position; on "and" 7, brush the foot into 1st; on 8, hold the position. Repeat the whole exercise.

Explanation. Students are introduced to the battement tendu 2nd with turn-out. For the reasons set forward in the previous exercise, students start in 6th to open the legs and feet in 1st position. Students must draw the working foot along a straight line out from the supporting leg. Those who do not have the ideal turn-out, with both legs achieving a position close to 180° when in 1st position, must draw their foot along the same line as the one the foot was on when in 1st position. Trying to draw beyond this line would cause the turning in of the working leg or the supporting leg, or the turning of the hips toward the working leg. Shoulders remain straight, and the torso does not lean away from the working leg. The knees are fully stretched in this exercise. As soon as the foot disengages, the weight of the body is transferred onto the supporting foot; and as soon as the foot closes, the weight is transferred onto both feet. When extending the leg, the foot does not sickle with the heel pushed back. When pointing the toes, the foot is not raised at all off the floor.

As in other ballet schools, the battement tendu is considered the most important step, since it is the beginning and the end of many others. French dancers' training includes many small exercises to brush their feet, causing them to be well grounded. The friction they apply with their feet onto the floor gives them a unique strength in the legs and feet. Therefore, the battement tendu is given considerable attention in this manual. Students must apply downward pressure with the whole foot, including the toes, onto the floor on the way out and in without rolling in. This pressure activates the deep and inside muscles of the legs and those of the working foot to the maximum. It builds up strength and resistance. It is comparable to the tire of the Formula One car gripping the surface of the track to gain momentum and speed.

Music. The music is a 4/4 with clear counts and a slow-to-medium tempo.

Dégagé or battement tendu à terre? In France, the terms battement tendu à terre and dégagé are often used interchangeably to describe the same step. However, technically both names do not describe the same movement. In fact, they

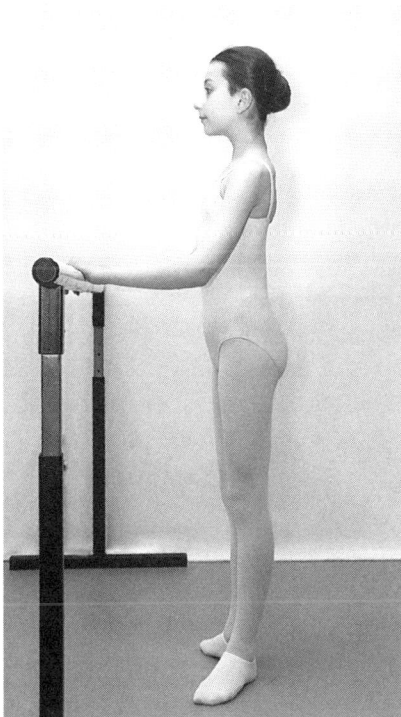

The feet are in 1st position (at an angle of about 150°).

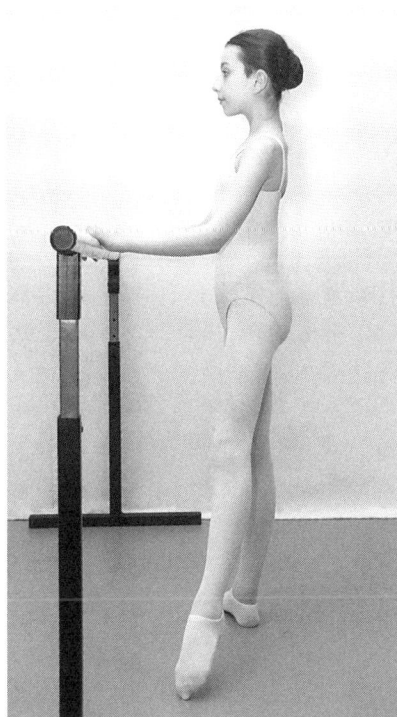

The foot is drawn out on the same line in 2nd position.

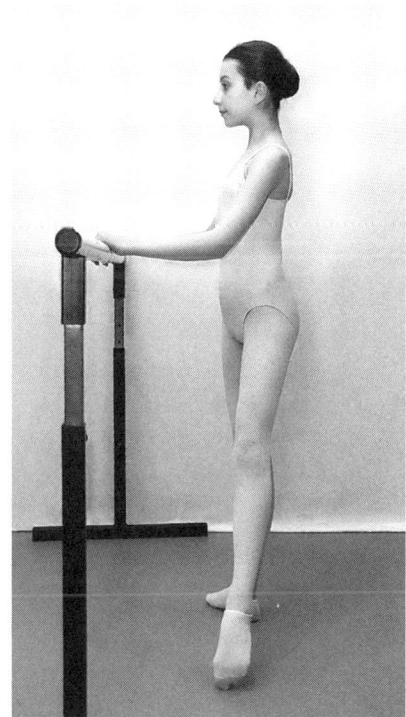

The hips are turned outward in an effort to open the leg more to the side.

The head is bent
to the side.

describe opposite actions! A battement is a closing movement, beating one leg against the other, with the accent on the closing. By contrast, the action of the dégagé means to disengage or to release, with the accent when the foot is pointed. Ideally, depending on the accent of the movement, one or the other should be used.[6] Since the term battement tendu is widely used in the United States, and the author does not wish to add more confusion to that faced by American ballet students already exposed to a myriad of names for this ballet step, the term battement tendu will be used in this manual.

Exercise 6

Preparation for spotting (head rotation) and stretching of the neck, in 6th, facing the barre.

On 1, turn the head sharply to the right side, with the eyes focusing on a particular point at eye level; on 2, straighten the head; on 3, turn the head to the left; on 4, straighten the head. Repeat three more times, alternating right and left sides. On 1 and 2, bend the head toward the right side, the ear directed toward the shoulder; on 3 and 4, straighten the head. Repeat three more times, alternating right and left sides.

Explanation. Besides preparing for the spotting of the head, this exercise helps to alleviate the tension and stiffness that tend to concentrate in the upper body, especially when it remains very static at the beginning of the barre. In the first part of the exercise, the rotation is sharp and

controlled but not too fast. The shoulders remain still and the eyes focused on a particular spot each time the head turns. This exercise is also a useful practice to fight the dead eyes common among ballet students. It helps for later spotting exercises to keep a sharp focus of the eyes with head rotation. In the second part of the exercise, students stretch their side neck muscles keeping the shoulders level. Unlike the turning of the head performed in the first part, the stretching of the neck is performed smoothly.

Music. The music should reflect the two different dynamics of the movement in this exercise. Whereas the first part of the exercise is sharper, the music should slow down for the second part of the exercise, which is smoother.

Exercise 7

Preparatory port de bras, eight counts, plié in 6th, four counts, battement tendu devant, broken down, head rotation, in 6th, eight counts.

Stand perpendicular to the barre, about one foot away from it, with the arms in preparatory position, turning the head slightly away from the barre at about a 45° angle toward the outside shoulder.

On 1 and 2, bring the arms in 1st; on 3 and 4, open the left arm 2nd, with the head following the left hand, and rest the hand gently on the barre, resting on the barre a little bit forward of the shoulders; on 5 and 6, open the right arm 2nd, with the head following the right hand; on 7 and 8, the head straightens and hold the position.

On 1 and 2, plié; on 3 and 4, stretch both knees; from 5 to 8, repeat. On "and" 1, brush the right foot devant, stretching up the instep of the foot, still with the toes on the floor; on 2, hold the position; on 3, point the toes without the foot going off the floor; on 4, hold the position; on 5, bring the toes down; on 6, hold the position; on "and" 7, brush the foot in 6th; on 8, hold the position.

On 1, release the barre with the left hand to have both arms now in 2nd; on 2, hold; on "and," turn the head toward the right arm and turn the palms down, with the eyes focused on the right hand; on 3 and 4, lower the arms, with the head following the movement of the outside hand; from 5 to 8, hold the position, keeping the head angled away from the barre, like at the beginning.

---

6   De Soye, *Les Verbes de la Danse*, 191.

Explanation. Students are introduced to working sideways at the barre, which is the position in which students stand perpendicular to the barre to work one leg at a time with one hand on the barre. The distance between the barre and the student is important. If too close, students bend the arm excessively, causing their shoulder to rise. If too far, the arm is overstretching, forcing students to shift their weight and pull the barre. Many schools have students start the barre with the arm already holding the barre. It is better practice to start with both arms in preparatory position to make sure that students are balanced on both legs, even before holding the barre. It is also more graceful to have the arm reaching for the barre with a soft port de bras and musical accompaniment than just grabbing the barre before the music even starts.

The preparatory port de bras is performed slowly (eight counts) so that students understand the different parts of it. It is done cleanly and elegantly. Generally, the French school does not start the preparation with an allongé (a slight lift of the forearms and the hands, before bringing the arms in 1st) of the lower arm like the one executed in many schools in the United States and elsewhere. The allongé may increase the risk for superfluous hand mannerisms in arm movements, especially at the beginning of training. This exercise includes two movements that have already been practiced in this lesson.

In the closing port de bras, students bring their arms down into preparatory position smoothly, starting by turning the palms down, the elbows initiating the descent, and the eyes following the working hand during the descent. To hold the arms symmetrically in preparatory or 1st position, students can test the alignment of the arms by touching both middle fingers, like they did for the 5th position of the arms. In the preparatory position, the head is held at about a 45° angle, with the chin slightly lifted and the eyes gazing in a diagonal direction. From now on, students will apply the same head positions and movements in the preparatory and closing ports de bras when performing exercises sideways at the barre.

The position of the head is very important in ballet and should not be underestimated. The various inclinations and positions of the head give the finished look to the many positions of the ballet dancer. From the beginning, students must learn to adopt a certain head pose, with the chin raised slightly to lengthen the neck. No trace of physical exertion or tension, often reflected by convulsive twitchings of the face muscles, must show on their face. The eyes must be engaged at all times during exercises. Unfortunately, under the effort of concentration and exertion, students tend to neglect this part of the body. Teachers also tend to focus more on the legs rather than on what is going on above the

The first part of the preparatory port de bras, bringing the first arm on the barre.

The second arm opens 2nd position.

At the end of the preparatory port de bras, the head straightens.

shoulders. Yet, the upper body, and especially the face, is the focal point for the audience when watching a dancer on stage. Without upper body, there is no expression, life, or soul to the dance.

When not carefully monitored, working sideways at the barre can cause bad habits that impede students' balance and the overall quality of their dancing. If unchecked, these bad habits (such as holding a crooked torso, putting more weight onto one leg than the other, or pulling the barre when working on one leg at the barre) can impact center work. To minimize these risks, students will be asked to release the barre very often when performing any exercise at the barre—especially sideways—to check balance.

Unlike some schools in which students alternate starting on the left or the right side, traditionally in France, students consistently start with the left hand at the barre to work the right leg. Always starting on the same side may be a good practice for beginners, sparing them confusion about which side they are going to start for each exercise. They have enough to think about!

Music. A slow and flowing 3/4 waltz would be a good musical choice.

Exercise 8

Roll-up relevé, in 6th, eight counts, facing the barre.

Stand at about one and a half feet away from the barre with the legs in parallel and the feet about one-half inch apart.

On 1 and 2, roll up both feet onto demi-pointes; on 3 and 4, hold the position; on 5 and 6, roll both feet down; on 7 and 8, hold the position. Repeat three more times, with a small plié and stretch at the end of the last roll-down to release tension in the calves.

Explanation. Students are introduced to the relevé. A staple of ballet training, the relevé increases strength in the feet and in the calf muscles. It must be practiced very regularly, from the earliest beginning and throughout training. It is recommended that students start the study of relevé with the roll-up to gain strength and greater control in the ankles and an overall better stability on demi-pointes. For now, it is performed slowly so that students can focus on the proper placement of the feet and use the

A correct position on demi-pointes, where the instep is above the toes.

The demi-pointe is too low.

resistance to develop strength to go up and down from demi-pointes.

Students are standing a little further away from the barre since they have to shift their weight forward onto the balls of their feet when on demi-pointes. The barre should not be an obstacle. As with all the previous exercises, students must apply the proper placement and posture. In the roll-up of the feet, students must keep their feet very straight and in parallel position. The small space between the feet in 6th allows the head of the first metatarsal of the big toes sufficient room so as not to press against each other when coming onto demi-pointes. It also gives room to keep the feet straight. Both knees are very taut. In the roll-up, the weight is transferred forward being mostly placed on the second and the third metatarsal heads with some support from the first and the fourth toes and the fifth toe only just touching the floor.[7] On demi-pointes, the instep should be above the toes. When coming down, the feet also stay straight and roll down with control. Students must be balanced at all times.

Music. A sharp 4/4 would be an appropriate choice.

A Ballet foot: pre-professional students must show a sufficient natural cou-de-pied, that is, an arched instep and at least adequate foot flexibility. It is especially important in the French school, which puts so much emphasis not only on the function of the foot but also on its

---

7   Howse and Hancock, *Dance Technique and Injury Protection*, 188.

aesthetics. The sufficiency of a cou-de-pied is a matter of degree, and a full discussion of this issue does not belong here. Suffice it to say that the lack of a cou-de-pied may cause different problems in more advanced training. For girls, the problem becomes very obvious when it is time to start pointes: it is likely to lead to difficulty balancing, thus forcing students to bend knees to stay up; this practice may in turn lead to a lack of balance and the development of bulking thighs.

Exercise 9

Plié in 2nd, start in 6th, four counts, facing the barre.

Following the preparatory port de bras, on 5, open both feet in 1st; on 6, hold the position; on "and" 7, brush the right foot 2nd, stretching up only the instep; on 8, bring the heel down, sliding the hands onto the barre so that the hands remain in front of the shoulders.

On 1 and 2, plié; on 3 and 4, stretch both knees; on 5 and 6, plié; on 7 and 8, stretch; on 1, stretch the instep of the right foot, sliding the hands onto the barre; on 2, hold the position; on 3 and 4, close in 1st; on 5, hold the position; on "and" 6, brush the left foot, stretching up only the instep; on 7, bring the heel down; on 8, hold the position. Repeat the plié exercise one more

The body is correctly aligned in 2nd position.

The pelvis is incorrectly tucked under.

The pelvis is incorrectly tilted backward.

time. At the end, bring both arms in 1st, open them to 2nd, and close.

Explanation. This exercise introduces the plié with turn-out in 2nd position. This is clearly a departure from tradition and common practice, which is to start with a plié in 1st, whereas, after the 6th, the 2nd is the simplest ballet position, since it requires less demand on the hip joints. The distance between the feet in 2nd is approximately one to one and a half times the length of the dancer's foot. In the opening of the position, the brushing out of the working foot does not involve the pointing of the toes in this case, since the foot comes down flat in 2nd between each of its rises. By properly executing the brushing 2nd and bringing the foot down without adjusting it, the distance between both legs will retain the proper width. The body's weight must be centered in the middle of both legs. The body is pulled up without sticking the ribs out. The pelvis is not tucked under or tilted backward. The lower abdomen is lifted.

In the plié, the knees remain above the toes. The heels stay firmly on the floor during the plié. When the lowest point of the plié is reached, students must not sit but straighten up right away smoothly, pushing the heels down, until the knees are fully stretched. Each plié and stretch must fill the four musical counts.

To remain in front of the shoulders, the hands have to slide along onto the barre when bringing the foot down in 2nd and when closing since the weight of the body shifts each time.

Music. The music is a slow and flowing waltz or a not-too-slow adagio.

Exercise 10

Pointing of the foot against the ankle and the side of the knee, in 6th, eight counts, facing the barre.

On 1, sharply bring the right foot fully pointed against the left ankle; on 2, hold the position; on 3, slide the working foot along the supporting leg so that it is now at the level of the supporting knee; on 4, hold the position; on 5, lower the leg to the level of the ankle; on 6, hold the position; on 7, bring the toes down, still holding the instep up, the working foot being next to and lined up with the other in 6th; on 8, bring the rest of

The foot is against the side of the knee.

the foot down in 6th. Repeat three more times, alternating legs.

Explanation. This is a very basic exercise to work the sharpness and control of the articulation of the knee so essential in the performance of many ballets steps (such as the coupé, the retiré, and the small jeté) studied later in the training. The development of this quality is found in many barre exercises throughout the year.

In the bending, the lower leg must be immobilized as quickly as possible for the exercise to be most beneficial. When bending the leg, the working foot does not wobble but holds still against the other leg, as if it is ready for a photo to be taken. As soon as the foot comes up, students should be balanced on their supporting leg, with the back pulled up. The working foot remains straight and touches the supporting ankle, with the side of the working big toe pressing above the talus of the supporting foot. The hips are straight, without the supporting hip sinking in.

The action of retirer (to pull out) is also introduced in parallel. The working foot slides against the side of the supporting leg, which remains stretched, to knee level. In this position, the thigh is almost perpendicular to the torso. In the closing, the toes come down first, with the instep stretching up, to have the heel coming down last.

The height of the barre must not impede the lifting of the working leg.

Music. A sharp rag or 2/4 tango would be good musical choices for this exercise.

CENTER (MILIEU)

Exercise 11

Adagio (adage): preparatory port de bras, four counts, in 6th, port de bras to 2nd.

Students are facing the front of the room (position de face), arms in preparation. The preparation is as follows: on 1 and 2, bring the arms to 1st, with the head inclining slightly toward the left shoulder and the eyes directed toward the right hand, keeping the shoulders level; on 3 and 4, open the arms 2nd, with the head straightening and following the right arm.

On "and," turn the palms down; on 1 and 2, bring the arms down, with the eyes following the right hand; on 3, bring the arms in 1st, slightly tilting the head toward the left shoulder, with the eyes focused on the right hand; on 4, open the arms 2nd, with the head straightening and following the right hand; from 5 to 8, repeat. Repeat the whole exercise one more time, with the head and eyes following the movement of the left arm. In the last port de bras, the arms come down in preparatory position to finish the exercise, with the head straightening at the end.

Explanation. Students are introduced to the position de face, which is the position of the dancer facing the audience. They are also introduced to the preparatory port de bras and the port de bras to 2nd. A port de bras designates a particular movement of the arm performed gracefully, sometimes independently, or in coordination with a leg movement. There are several basic ports de bras that are mostly practiced independently, often in adagio, to perfect the movement of the arms, the softness of the curves, the harmony of the lines, and the synchronization of both arms. These should be practiced very regularly by beginners. The first port de bras is the preparatory port de bras to place the arms where they should be to start

the exercise. Unless otherwise specified, from now on students will execute this preparatory port de bras on four counts. The port de bras to 2nd, which is similar to the introductory one, is then repeated several times, alternating the head movement following first the right arm and then the left arm.

Shoulders do not come forward when the arms come to 1st position. Both arms open and close at the same time. The arms are soft and rounded. Even though the head moves during the port de bras, the torso remains straight. When the head inclines in the 1st position of the arms, it does so very slightly. Even though the focus of the exercise is on the arms, students must be reminded to keep the proper alignment and their knees taut during the exercise.

Music. The music is adagio-like.

Exercise 12

Plié and battement tendu devant, broken down, in 6th.

On 1 and 2, plié; on 3 and 4, stretch the knees; on 5 and 6, plié; on 7 and 8, stretch the knees. On "and" 1, brush the right foot devant to stretch the instep up, with the toes still on the floor; on 2, hold the position; on 3, point the toes without moving the foot; on 4, hold the position; on 5, bring the toes down, still holding the instep up; on 6, hold the position; on "and" 7, brush the foot in 6th; on 8, hold the position. Repeat the exercise one more time performing the battement tendu with the left foot.

Explanation. This exercise combines the plié and the battement tendu devant in 6th, as performed at the barre. Students remain balanced on their supporting leg during the battement tendu. The arms are 2nd, and the back is erect. Students may find holding the arms in 2nd position tiresome, especially by the time they repeat the exercise. In this first class, the instructor may decide to divide the exercise in two parts to allow students to release their arms in between, especially if students start scooping their elbows, raising their shoulders, or releasing their back. As said earlier, the holding of the arms should originate in the upper back, not at the top of the shoulders.

Music. A medium-tempo waltz would be appropriate.

Exercise 13

Soubresaut (temps levé) [temps levé—Vaganova], in 6th, two counts, one count to stretch, one count to hold, facing the barre.

On "and," plié; on 1, jump off the floor equally with both feet, stretching the knees and pointing the feet; on 2, land into plié; on 3, stretch the knees; on 4, hold the position. Repeat three more times. After a pause, repeat the exercise.

Explanation. Students are not yet done with the barre in this first class. They will go back to it for this first jump exercise so that they can apply the mechanisms of the jump more easily with some support. However, this does not mean that they treat the barre as a vault for taking off!

The back is straight in the plié with the weight being on the entire feet. Students push off the floor with their whole feet and point them in the air. During the jump they do not bring their torso forward or backward, but jump straight up, with both knees remaining taut during the jump. To land, the toes of the feet touch the floor first, then the balls of the feet second, with the heels landing third into a deep plié. This is the basic shock absorber of ballet jumps. Under no circumstances should the heels hit the floor first. In the plié of the takeoff and the landing, the heels do not come off the floor. Students stretch their knees completely between each jump at this stage. Unlike the soft plié studied at the beginning of the barre, the plié for the takeoff is sharper, to allow students to reach the maximum point of the jump as quickly as possible. For this kind of plié, students are introduced to the concept of the musical "and," so they actually have to perform the plié on the upbeat. Too slow of a plié would impede the spring that gives the momentum necessary to jump as high as possible. It is the quality of the plié that contributes to the development of the ballon, which is the faculty to elevate oneself in the air with stretched legs and feet. When landing, students must not straighten out their knees too rapidly, but with control, to push the limits of the plié and stabilize the landing while keeping the heels down. Some students who have a shallow plié are likely to push back and land off balance in an effort to bring the heels down. For those students, more work on the plié at the barre may be necessary to achieve the correct landing. In the plié, stu-

A jump in 6th position.

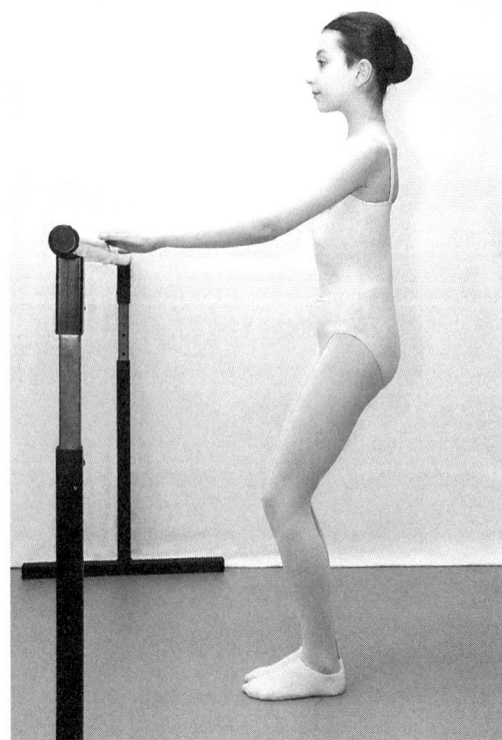

The plié is too shallow and the weight is too far back in this landing.

dents exhale, and when jumping, they inhale. A soubresaut is sometimes called temps levé.

Music. Usually for small jumps, the music accompaniment is often a 4/4. However, at the beginning of the year, to be introduced to the ballet jump, which requires more time in plié, a slow-to-medium tempo 6/8 or even a 2/4 march should be used.

Exercise 14

Preparation for spotting, with body rotation, without travel (sur place).

Legs are in parallel and hands are on the waist. Using small shuffling steps to turn around, students keep their head looking across the shoulder in the direction opposite of that in which they are turning, with the eyes focused on a definite spot de face, the head being the last to turn. As they complete the turn, the head precedes the body with the eyes still focused on the same point. Repeat four times, turning to the right, and four times, turning toward the left. Repeat the whole exercise one more time.

Explanation. This is an informal exercise solely to introduce the movement of the head, without which ballet dancers would feel dizzy in performing turns. This rapid snap of the head gives the impression that the dancer's eyes are always facing the audience. A good rule for students to remember is that the head is the last part of the body to turn and the first part to arrive. The spot at which the eyes are directed must be at eye level to make the turn more stable. Students usually spot themselves in the mirror, which is not the best spot. The image reflected by the mirror is not static for one thing (since students move), and students may also lack focus when trying to spot their own face; they are likely to switch their attention to the movement of their body instead. Therefore, to make the spotting of the eyes more precise and involved, students may be better off not facing the mirror.

Students must not bend their head while the body starts turning and the head has not yet turned. Shoulders remain straight and low.

Even if they cannot yet practice the formal ballet pirouette, students can only benefit from practicing this type of exercise early on in training so that they get used to the particular difference between the head and the body rotations.

Music. A tarantella would be an appropriate choice of music.

Exercise 15

Curtsey (révérence).

In this day and age, the whole concept of the révérence has become an anachronism in many ballet schools. Fortunately, it still prevails in others. The révérence shows consideration, deference, and respect for the teacher. Such respect is essential to the carrying out of the class and the progress of the students. There is a master and pupil relationship throughout the class that must be maintained up to the end of practice. The révérence is also an opportunity to review, in a quiet way, the basic alignment and bearing of the body, as it is done at the beginning of class, before going off to the outside world in which more natural and relaxed positions prevail. It can be more or less elaborate, but it should be included at the end of each class. Nothing new should be introduced; the exercise will be fairly slow, short, and simple.

Application. This introductory class is recommended for any beginner's first class. The very basic movements introduced during class are brought about so gently that most beginners will be able to practice them without becoming intimidated or frustrated in the process. The movement in each exercise is kept to a minimum to allow focus on the proper alignment and position of the whole body, head to toes. Some exercises, in fact, are so simple (such as the plié in 6th, the spotting exercise, and the soubresaut in 6th) that they can be introduced to a pre-ballet class, assuming that the barre is at the proper height or that the exercises are practiced in the center. However, the battement tendu 2nd, which is more difficult, especially for students lacking turnout or foot flexibility, will come a bit later. The level of absorption of students taking classes less frequently will certainly not be the same than that expected of students committed to taking daily lessons. Especially in a recreational program, the instructor will gauge the number of corrections that students can stand without becoming utterly bored or overwhelmed. In such programs, students will welcome some skips, light stretching, or ballet runs as diversions between exercises or toward the end of class.

SECOND CLASS AND THIRD CLASS

Students should not be introduced to anything new for the second and third classes of the week; they will repeat the First Class.

FOURTH CLASS

Exercise 1

Plié in 6th, 2nd, 1st, four counts, facing the barre.

In 6th: on 1 and 2, plié; on 3 and 4, stretch both knees; on 5 and 6, plié; on 7 and 8, stretch both knees; on 1, open the feet simultaneously in 1st; on 2, hold the position; on "and" 3, brush 2nd with the right foot, stretching the instep up and keeping the toes on the floor; on 4, hold the position; on 5, bring the foot down in 2nd; from 6 to 8, hold the position.

In 2nd: on 1 and 2, plié; on 3 and 4, stretch both knees; on 5 and 6, plié; on 7 and 8, stretch both knees; on 1, stretch up the instep of the right foot; on 2, hold the position; on 3 and 4, close in 1st; from 5 to 8, hold the position.

In 1st: on 1 and 2, plié; on 3 and 4, stretch; on 5 and 6, plié; on 7 and 8, stretch; on 1 and 2, bring the arms in 1st; on 3 and 4, open the arms 2nd; on 5 and 6, bring the arms 5th; on 7 and 8, hold the position.

Explanation. Students are introduced to the plié in 1st. Since the demand on the turn-out is higher in 1st than in 2nd, the plié in 1st follows the pliés in 6th and 2nd. As in the first three classes of this week, students must be at the proper distance from the barre and hold the correct posture. Students keep their back pulled up and their knees above the toes in the plié. When stretching from each plié, students push down onto the floor with their heels, keeping a pulled-up back. At the end of the stretching, the knees are fully taut and the back of the legs stretched and lengthened to the maximum. The heels remain down, even in the lowest part of the plié. The feet are flat on the floor without rolling or turning out excessively. Like in the plié in 2nd, the knees remain above the toes without over turning the feet. When brushing their foot out and in to change position, students keep their foot straight without sickling.

Application. For recreational students, this exercise will come later, depending, of course,

Plié in 1st position, front view.

Plié in 1st position, side view.

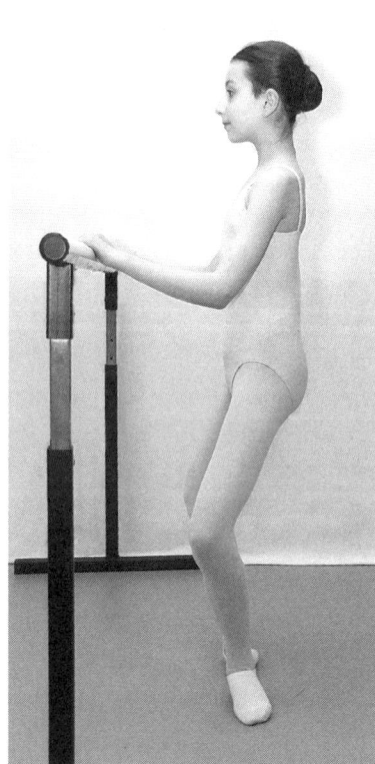

Plié in 1st position, with the feet over turning and rolling in.

on how often students come to class each week. Such students will benefit from repeating the plié in 6th for at least a few lessons before practicing it with turn-out.

Exercise 2

Battement tendu devant, broken down, in 6th, eight counts, facing the barre, increased repetitions.

On "and" 1, brush the right foot devant, stretching up the instep of the foot, still with the toes on the floor; on 2, hold the position; on 3, point the toes; on 4, hold the position; on 5, bring the toes down, with the instep still up; on 6, hold the position; on "and" 7, brush the foot in 6th; on 8, hold the position. Repeat three more times, alternating legs. After a pause, repeat the whole exercise.

Explanation. The number of battements tendus has increased in this review exercise.

Music. A 4/4 is appropriate with a slightly accelerated tempo.

Exercise 3

Preparation for battement tendu 2nd, start in 6th, in 1st, eight counts, broken down, facing the barre.

Students repeat Exercise 5 of the First Class of this week.

Exercise 4

Pointing of the foot against the ankle, extension of the leg devant, in 6th, eight counts, facing the barre.

On 1, bend the knee sharply and bring the foot pointed against the supporting ankle; on 2, hold the position; on 3, extend the right leg forward with the pointed toes touching the floor; on 4, hold the position; on 5, bring the toes down, keeping the instep of the foot up; on 6, hold the position; on 7 and 8, brush in and close in 6th. Repeat the exercise one more time with the right foot. Repeat the whole exercise one more time. At the end, bring the arms to 1st, 2nd, and 5th, and hold the position.

Explanation. Instead of closing directly into 6th, the working leg extends forward, pointing the foot onto the floor before closing. When extending out, the working leg stretches with en-

ergy and control, but without kicking, with the foot pointing directly at the floor.

Music. a tango with sharp counts is an appropriate choice of music for this exercise.

Application. this is another exercise that can be introduced early on in any beginner or intermediate class to work on the sharpness of the knee articulation.

Exercise 5

Preparation for spotting and stretching of the neck, facing the barre.

Students repeat Exercise 6 of the First Class of this week.

Exercise 6

Roll-up relevé, plié, in 6th, eight counts, facing the barre.

On 1 and 2, roll up both feet onto demi-pointes; on 3 and 4, hold the position on demi-pointes; on 5 and 6, roll down; on 7, plié; on 8, stretch. Repeat three more times.

Explanation. This exercise is similar to Exercise 8 of the First Class, except a small plié follows each relevé.

CENTER

Exercise 7

Adagio, preparatory port de bras, four counts, in 6th, port de bras to 2nd.

Students repeat Exercise 11 of the First Class of this week.

Exercise 8

Plié and battement tendu devant, broken down, in 6th.

Students repeat Exercise 12 of the First Class of this week.

Exercise 9

Battement tendu 2nd, broken down, start in 6th, in 1st, eight counts.

Following the preparatory port de bras, open the feet in 1st.

On "and" 1, brush the right foot 2nd, stretching the instep of the foot up, still with the toes on the floor; on 2, hold the position; on 3, point the toes; on 4, hold the position; on 5, bring the toes down; on 6, hold the position; on "and" 7, brush the foot into 1st; on 8, hold the position. Repeat the exercise one more time with the right foot.

Explanation. Students are now practicing the battement tendu 2nd in the center, still starting in 6th. As when performed at the barre, the weight must be transferred from both feet onto their supporting leg when the foot brushes out of position; when the foot is fully pointed on the floor, the working leg must be very light on the floor. The foot brushes out of the 1st, pressing firmly against the floor. The back is pulled up without leaning the torso away, and the elbows do not scoop or overstretch. The working foot does not sickle.

Music. The tempo is slightly increased for this exercise in the center.

Application. Practicing this exercise in the center comes later for recreational students. More practice at the barre is required before being able to balance while keeping the turn-out.

Exercise 10

Soubresaut, in 6th, two counts, one count to stretch, one count to hold, facing the barre.

Students repeat Exercise 13 of the First Class of this week.

Exercise 11

Preparation for spotting, without travel.

Students repeat Exercise 14 of the First Class of this week.

Exercise 12

Curtsey.

FIFTH CLASS

Students repeat the material of the Fourth Class of this week.

Application. Most exercises in the First Week material will benefit students taking ballet on a recreational basis. Some exercises (such as the sharp bending of the knee in bringing the foot against the ankle or the broken down battement tendu) can even be added to a class of students at more advanced levels to improve their foot work and the rapidity in the flexion of the knee. The tempo of the music can then be adjusted accordingly.

Battement tendu 2nd position.

Second Week

§

Students should not be introduced to anything new for the first and second classes of the week; they repeat the material of the First Week.

THIRD CLASS

Exercise 1

Plié in 6th, 2nd, 1st, four counts, facing the barre.

Students repeat Exercise 1 of the Fourth Class of the First Week.

Exercise 2

Battement tendu devant, broken down, in 6th, four counts, facing the barre.

On "and" 1, battement tendu devant, stretching the instep up; on 2, point the toes; on 3, bring the toes down; on "and" 4, close 6th. Repeat the exercise three more times, alternating legs.

Explanation. Each battement tendu is now on four counts, with less holding following each movement of the foot. Students must still focus on pressing down onto the floor with their working foot out and in of the battement tendu. The movement is still performed evenly with the same amount of time required to disengage and to close.

Music. The music is a 4/4 with clear counts and a slow-to-medium tempo.

Application. Once the exercise has been practiced on eight counts for just a few classes, the same exercise at a quicker pace should not pose any problem.

Exercise 3

Battement tendu 2nd, broken down, start in 6th, in 1st, four counts, facing the barre.

Following the preparation, open the feet in 1st.

On "and" 1, battement tendu 2nd with the right foot, stretching the instep up; on 2, point the toes; on 3, bring the toes down; on "and" 4, close in 1st. Repeat the exercise three more times, alternating legs. A small plié and stretch follows the last battement tendu.

Explanation. Students are repeating the exercise in 2nd on four counts. A small plié precedes the closing port de bras to alleviate tension in the legs.

Exercise 4

Battement tendu devant, in 6th, and battement tendu 2nd, broken down, start in 6th, in 1st, four counts.

On "and" 1, battement tendu devant with the right foot, stretching the instep up; on 2, point the toes; on 3, bring the toes down; on 4, close 6th; from 5 to 8, repeat the battement tendu devant. Open both feet in 1st.

On "and" 1, battement tendu 2nd with the right foot; on 2, point the toes; on 3, bring the toes down; on 4, close 1st; from 5 to 8, repeat the battement tendu 2nd. At the end, a small plié and stretch follows the closing of the last battement tendu.

Explanation. Students are combining the battement tendu devant in 6th and the battement tendu 2nd in 1st performed sideways. The preparatory port de bras, introduced in Exercise 7 of the First Class of the First Week, precedes the exercise, and the closing port de bras, also learned in the same exercise, ends the exercise. Since students are already familiar with the movement itself, the tempo is slightly accelerated.

Music. A not-too-fast rag or a 4/4 polka would work well for this exercise.

Exercise 5

Battement tendu 2nd, broken down, turn the leg in and out, start in 6th, in 1st, eight counts, facing the barre.

Following the preparatory port de bras, open both feet in 1st.

On "and" 1, battement tendu 2nd; on 2, point the toes; on 3 and 4, turn in the working leg; on

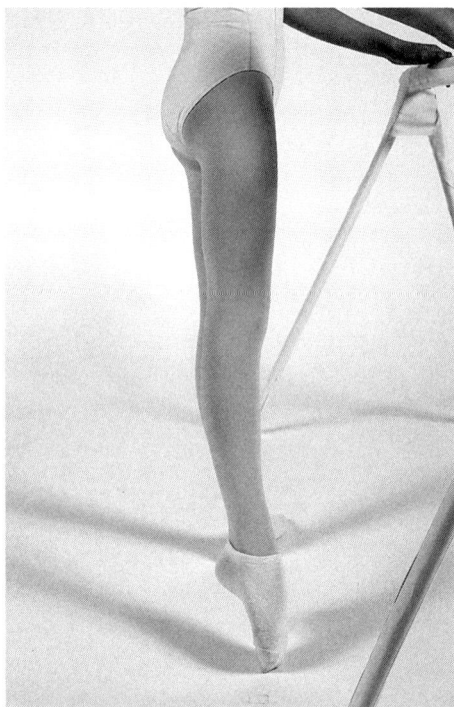

The working leg is turned in.

The working leg is turned out.

5 and 6, turn out the working leg; on 7, bring the toes down; on 8, close in 1st. Repeat the exercise three more times, alternating legs.

Explanation. Students are still breaking down the battement tendu. It is a good exercise for students to feel the range of rotation of the hip joint. The turning in and out of the working leg is mainly to acquaint students with the concept of turn-out coming from the hips. During the rotation, the hips do not swing at all; the main rotation occurring is the one of the head of the femur in the working hip socket. While turning in the leg, students do not sickle the working foot. This exercise also helps students to feel the turn-out muscles at work, which should rotate forward.

Music. A medium-tempo waltz would work here, for the turning in and out movement needs a softer music.

Exercise 6

Battement tendu devant, broken down, flexing the foot, in 6th, eight counts, facing the barre.

On "and" 1, battement tendu devant with the right foot; on 2, point the toes; on 3, flex the toes; on 4, flex the rest of the foot; on 5, stretch the instep out, still keeping the toes flexed; on 6, point the toes, lowering the toes onto the floor; on 7, bring the toes down; on 8, close 6th.

Repeat the exercise one more time. At the end, a small plié and stretch follows the closing of the last battement tendu.

Explanation. Students are introduced to the flexion of the foot off the floor. Both knees are fully stretched at all times. The flexion is broken down to a maximum: first the toes and then the rest of the foot, so that the articulations of the foot work independently. The working leg does not come down nor otherwise move when the foot flexes. The hips remain straight.

Music. The music is a medium tempo 4/4.

Application. This exercise for foot flexibility, with no demand on the turn-out, can be practiced early on by any beginner or others even at the beginning of the barre.

Exercise 7

Preparation for spotting and stretching of the neck, facing the barre.

Students repeat the spotting exercise performed in Exercise 6 of the First Class of the First Week, on a quicker tempo.

Exercise 8

Preparation for battement jeté devant [demi-position—Cecchetti; battement tendu jeté 45°—Vaganova]: battement tendu devant in 6th, bring the leg à la demi-hauteur (half-height), eight counts, broken down, facing the barre.

On "and" 1, battement tendu devant out of 6th; on 2, point the toes; on 3, lift the leg with vigor freezing it à la demi-hauteur; on 4, hold the position; on 5, lower the leg, and point the foot onto the floor; on 6, bring the toes down; on 7, close 6th; on 8, hold the position. Repeat the exercise one more time with the right leg. Repeat the whole exercise one more time. A small plié and stretch follows the last battement tendu and lift.

Explanation. Students are introduced to the battement of the leg à la demi-hauteur, which is a height inferior or equal to the middle of the calf of the supporting leg (when measured with the pointed working toes).[8] This broken down version precedes the execution of the direct battement jeté so that the working foot lifts only when the battement tendu is fully completed with the foot pointed on the floor. In some aspect, the battement jeté should be considered as an extension of the battement tendu, for the working foot must be fully pointed on the floor before the leg rises off the floor. The lifting is performed sharply and with control. The height of the barre or the wall against the barre should not impede the lifting of the leg forward. Using a portable barre is ideal here. The height can be lower than 45°, as long as the working foot is at least a few inches off the floor. The height of the lifting must be precise and consistent without the leg wobbling. Students must neither sit nor sag on the supporting leg. They hold the body erect at all times. The hips remain straight and the knees taut. Students should be asked to release the barre several times when balancing on one leg.

Music. A 2/4 tango with a sharp rhythm would work well.

Application. Any beginner can benefit from this exercise, as long as they are able to properly brush their foot out first in the battement tendu.

Exercise 9

Roll-up relevé, plié, in 6th, eight counts, facing the barre.

---

8   Guillot and Prudhommeau, *Grammaire de la Danse Classique*, 26.

Students repeat Exercise 6 of the Fourth Class of the First Week.

CENTER

Exercise 10

Adagio: plié in 6th and 1st, four counts, port de bras performed separately.

On 1 and 2, plié in 6th; on 3 and 4, stretch both knees; on 5 and 6, plié; on 7 and 8, stretch both knees; on 1, open the feet in 1st; on 2, hold the position; on "and," turn the palms down; on 3 and 4, bring the arms down; on 5 and 6, bring the arms 1st; on 7 and 8, open the arms 2nd, with the head following the right hand and straightening the head at the end of the port de bras.

On 1 and 2, plié in 1st; on 3 and 4, stretch both knees; on 5 and 6, plié; on 7 and 8, stretch both knees; on 1, close feet in 6th; on 2, hold the position; on 3 and 4, bring the arms down; from 5 to 8, hold the position.

Explanation. Students are performing the plié in 6th and 1st in the center. The exercise is done only one time.

Music. A slow 3/4 waltz is appropriate for this exercise in which students must seek a deep plié.

Exercise 11

Battement tendu 2nd, broken down, start in 6th, in 1st, four counts.

Following the preparatory port de bras, open the feet in 1st.

On "and" 1, battement tendu 2nd; on 2, point the toes; on 3, bring the toes down; on "and" 4, close 1st. Repeat the battement tendu one more time with the right foot. Repeat the whole exercise one more time. A small plié and stretch ends the exercise.

Explanation. Students are repeating the battement tendu 2nd on four counts performed earlier at the barre. The back is pulled up.

Exercise 12

Soubresaut in 6th, two counts, one count to stretch, one count to hold, facing the barre.

Students repeat Exercise 13 of the First Class of the First Week.

Exercise 13

Soubresaut in 6th, two counts, one count to stretch, one count to hold, hands on the waist.

The preparation is as follows: on 1, bring the arms in 1st; on 2, hold the position; on 3, bring the hands on the waist; on 4, hold the position.

On "and," plié; on 1, jump off the floor equally with both feet; on 2, land in plié; on 3, stretch both knees; on 4, hold the position. Repeat three more times. After a pause, repeat one more time.

Explanation. For this first jump exercise in the center, students keep their hands on the waist and concentrate on the legs and feet. The placement of the hands on the waist in the preparatory port de bras is now done elegantly and formally. During the jump, the hands do not slide up and down but remain firmly pressed on the sides of the waist without the shoulders coming forward or rising. Students push off the floor with their whole feet and point them in the air with the knees stretched. In the landing, the heels press onto the floor following the touch down of the rest of the foot. Students must avoid stumbling in the landing by allowing a deep plié once the feet touch ground.

Music. As for the small jump at the barre, a 6/8 or a march is used. The tempo is slightly faster so that students do not sit in the plié.

Application. This first jump exercise is recommended for any beginner before any other jump with turn-out is practiced, both at the barre and in the center.

Exercise 14

Preparation for déboulés [tours chaînés—Vaganova], in 2nd, hands on the waist, two half turns on four counts.

Students turn sideways facing the left side of the studio.

As in the preceding exercise, students place their hands on the waist. The feet are in loose 2nd (for the purpose of stability, students should keep their feet open to less than 180°), the head is turned toward the right shoulder, with the eyes focused on a particular spot at eye level.

On 1 and 2, transfer the weight onto the right foot, then rotate a half turn, slightly raising the left foot and pushing the heel of the right foot outward toward the right for the first half turn, with the head, by the end of the half turn, turned

Preparation for the introduction to déboulés.

toward the left shoulder, the body facing the right side of the studio, and the eyes focused on the same spot; on 3 and 4, transfer the weight onto the left leg, lifting the heel slightly, and rotate toward the right side, raising the right foot, keeping the eyes still focused on the particular spot as the body starts rotating; the head snaps so that it precedes the end of the rotation of the body with the eyes still focused on the same spot. Repeat the exercise several times. Repeat the exercise facing the right side of the studio and turning toward the left in each half turn.

Explanation. Students are not ready to perform the final version of the déboulé, since they have not yet done any relevé in the center; but they can prepare for it with this simple exercise that introduces them to spotting with travel. Students will study déboulés later on more formally on demi-pointes. For now, students try to keep spotting the same direction to avoid deviating from the projected line. Each half turn is performed along a straight line so that it is precise and sharp. Each half turn is performed evenly. Students must transfer the weight each time before the rotation. The feet do not adjust once they turn. The distance between the legs does not change as students rotate. Except for the head, the body moves as a block, keeping the same position of the feet. The head turns sharply so that the eyes stay focused on a spot; it remains erect and does not bend to the side during spotting. The spotting exercise without travel, mentioned earlier, should already have been practiced a few times.

Music. A medium tempo 4/4 (such as the one used for a battement tendu exercise) or a 2/4 march would be appropriate, since the rotation is fairly slow.

Application. Beginners tend to be confused about which way to turn. The instructor may help them by physically pushing lightly on their upper back toward the direction they need to take. In any case, much practice is likely to be required to get the movement right. This exercise is recommended for beginners, even those taking ballet as little as once a week. It is yet another exercise to acquaint them with rotation. The more rotation, even as simple as this one, they can perform early on, the easier the introduction of the pirouette or other turns will be later on.

Exercise 15

Curtsey.

FOURTH CLASS

Students repeat the material of the Third Class of this week.

FIFTH CLASS

Exercise 1

Plié, two counts, battement tendu devant and 2nd, broken down, in 6th and 1st, four counts, facing the barre.

In 6th: on 1, plié; on 2, stretch; on 3 and 4, repeat; on "and" 5, battement tendu devant with the right foot; on 6, point the toes; on 7, bring the toes down; on 8, close in 6th. Repeat the plié and the battement tendu devant with the left foot. Open the feet in 1st.

In 1st: on 1, plié; on 2, stretch; on 3 and 4, repeat; on "and" 5, battement tendu 2nd with the right foot; on 6, point the toes; on 7, bring the toes down; on 8, close in 1st. Repeat the plié and the battement tendu 2nd with the left foot in 1st.

Explanation. Students are mixing the plié and the battement tendu in 6th and 1st in this exercise. Even though each is on two counts, the plié is deep and controlled.

Music. A moderato 4/4 or a slow and flowing 3/4 waltz would fit this exercise.

Exercise 2

Battement tendu devant, in 6th, and battement tendu 2nd, broken down, start in 6th, in 1st, four counts, facing the barre.

Students repeat Exercise 4 of the Third Class of this week.

Exercise 3

Battement tendu 2nd, broken down, turn the leg in and out, start in 6th, in 1st, eight counts, facing the barre.

Students repeat Exercise 5 of the Third Class of this week.

Exercise 4

Battement tendu devant, in 6th, broken down, flexing the foot, eight counts, facing the barre.

Students repeat Exercise 6 of the Third Class of this week.

Exercise 5

Battement tendu devant, broken down, bring the pointed foot against the ankle, extend the leg, in 6th, eight counts, facing the barre.

On "and" 1, battement tendu devant; on 2, point the toes; on 3, bend the knee sharply and bring the working foot against the side of the supporting ankle; on 4, hold the position; on 5, extend the leg devant, with the pointed toes touching the floor; on 6, hold the position; on 7, bring the toes down; on 8, close 6th. Repeat the whole exercise three times, alternating legs. A small plié and stretch ends the exercise. Bring the arms 2nd and 5th and hold the position for a few counts.

Explanation. This is another exercise to develop the sharpness and control of the knee articulation. In this exercise students bend their knee and bring their working foot sharply against the ankle of the supporting leg without wobbling. The thigh remains as still as possible. The practice of sharply adducting the lower leg will benefit students later on when it is time to perform steps such as the frappé, the jeté, and the ballonné. They must extend the leg with control, without throwing it, placing the pointed foot onto the floor. The exercise is performed in parallel so that students can focus on the sharpness and control of the bending and of the extension.

Music. A 4/4 polka or even a medium-tempo 2/4 tango would work well here.

Application. This is another exercise that can be applied to any beginners' class to develop the speed of the articulation of the knee.

Exercise 6

Preparation for spotting and stretching of the neck, facing the barre.

Students repeat the spotting exercise performed in Exercise 6 of the First Class of the First Week.

Exercise 7

Preparation for battement jeté devant: battement tendu devant, in 6th, broken down, bring the leg à la demi-hauteur, eight counts, facing the barre.

Students repeat Exercise 8 of the Third Class of this week.

Exercise 8

Roll-up relevé, plié, in 6th, eight counts, facing the barre.

Students repeat Exercise 6 of the Fourth Class of the First Week.

CENTER

Exercise 9

Adagio: plié in 6th and 1st, four counts, port de bras performed separately.

Students repeat Exercise 10 of the Third Class of this week.

Exercise 10

Battement tendu 2nd, broken down, start in 6th, in 1st, four counts.

Students repeat Exercise 11 of the Third Class of this week.

Exercise 11

Preparation for battement jeté devant: battement tendu devant, in 6th, broken down, bring the leg à la demi-hauteur, eight counts.

On "and" 1, battement tendu devant; on 2, point the toes; on 3, battement à la demi-hauteur; on 4, hold the position; on 5, bring the pointed foot onto the floor; on 6, hold the position; on 7, bring the toes down; on 8, close in 6th. Repeat one more time with the right leg. Repeat the whole exercise one more time. A small plié and stretch ends the exercise.

Explanation. Students should have already practiced this exercise at the barre. The torso remains still while performing the exercise. The shoulders are pushed down, and the back is held very erect. Students do not sag onto their supporting hip. The leg is lifted sharply à la demi-hauteur, holding it still in the air. The supporting foot does not wobble.

Music. The tempo is brisker for this exercise done in the center, since students must hold balance on one leg each time without the help of the barre.

Application. This is a good exercise for all beginners to check balance with the proper alignment and to keep the knees and the feet stretched.

Exercise 12

Pointing of the foot against the ankle, in 6th, four counts, arms in 1st.

The preparatory port de bras is as follows: on 1, bring the arms in 1st; on 2, open them 2nd, with the head following the movement of the right hand; on "and" 3 and 4, bring them down into preparatory position, still with the head following the movement of the right hand, hold the position and straighten the head.

On 1, bring the right foot sharply against the side of the supporting ankle, bringing the arms in 1st; on 2, hold the position; on 3, bring the foot down, toes first; on 4, put down the rest of the foot in 6th position, stretching the working knee. Repeat one more time with the right foot. Repeat the whole exercise one more time. In the last of the series, as the foot comes down in 6th, the arms open 2nd and then close, accompanied by a small plié and stretch.

Explanation. In this exercise, not only do students have to hold on one leg but they also must find their balance very quickly, holding their back erect without wobbling. The rocking of the supporting foot is kept to a minimum, and the supporting knee stays taut. This is a good exercise to balance on one leg with a sudden motion of the working leg. As they have practiced at the barre, the position of the working foot along the supporting leg must be very sharp and precise. The closing is still broken down to make sure the foot stays pointed as long as possible before putting the toes down. Notice the preparatory port de bras that brings the arms down, since the arms are in 1st position throughout the exercise. At the end, the arms open 2nd to be able to come down into the preparatory position properly.

Music. A crisp 4/4 would be appropriate music for this exercise.

Application. This exercise will benefit any beginner student to develop not only sharpness of the knee but also the sense of balance on one foot.

Exercise 13

Soubresaut in 6th, two counts, one count to stretch, one count to hold, facing the barre.

Students repeat Exercise 13 of the First Class of the First Week.

Exercise 14

Soubresaut in 6th, two counts, one count to stretch, hands on the waist.

Students repeat Exercise 13 of the Third Class of this week.

Exercise 15

Preparation for déboulés, in 2nd, hands on the waist, two half turns on four counts.

Students repeat Exercise 14 of the Third Class of this week.

Exercise 16

Curtsey.

Third Week

§

FIRST CLASS

Students repeat the material of the Fifth Class of the Second Week.

SECOND CLASS

Exercise 1

Plié, battement tendu devant and 2nd, in 6th and 1st, four counts, facing the barre.

Students repeat Exercise 1 of the Fifth Class of the Second Week.

Exercise 2

Battement tendu devant, in 6th, battement tendu 2nd, broken down, start in 6th, in 1st, four counts, facing the barre.

Students repeat Exercise 4 of the Third Class of the Second Week.

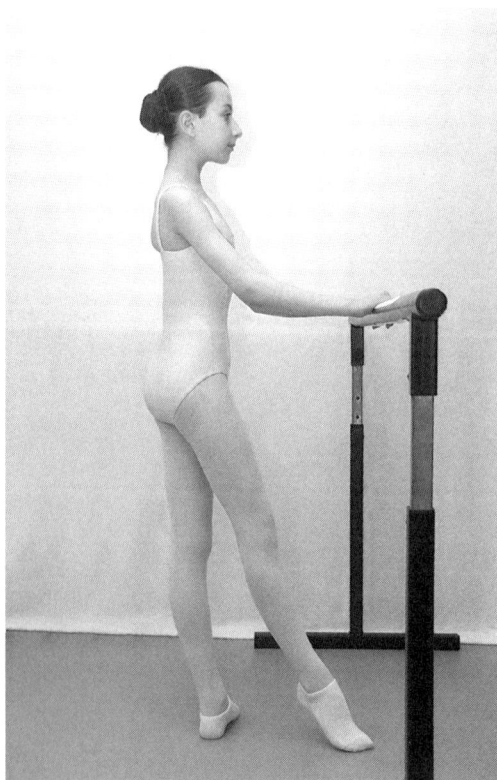

Exercise 3

Battement tendu 2nd, broken down, turn the leg in and out, eight counts, in 1st, facing the barre.

Students repeat Exercise 5 of the Third Class of the Second Week.

Exercise 4

Battement tendu 4th position devant, broken down, start in 6th, in 1st, eight counts, facing the barre.

Following the preparatory port de bras, open the feet into 1st.

On "and" 1, brush the right foot devant, pushing the heel forward and stretching up the instep of the foot, still with the ball of the foot and the toes on the floor, with the head slightly turned toward the right; on 2, hold the position; on 3, point the toes; on 4, hold the position; on 5, bring the toes down; on 6, hold the position; on

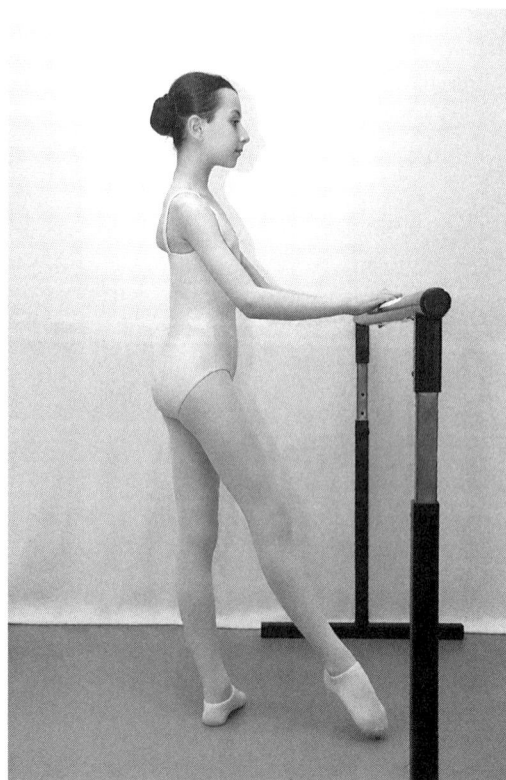

The foot is pointed forward, except for the toes. The head is held straight.

The foot is pointed 4th position devant, with the working leg slightly open. The head is held straight.

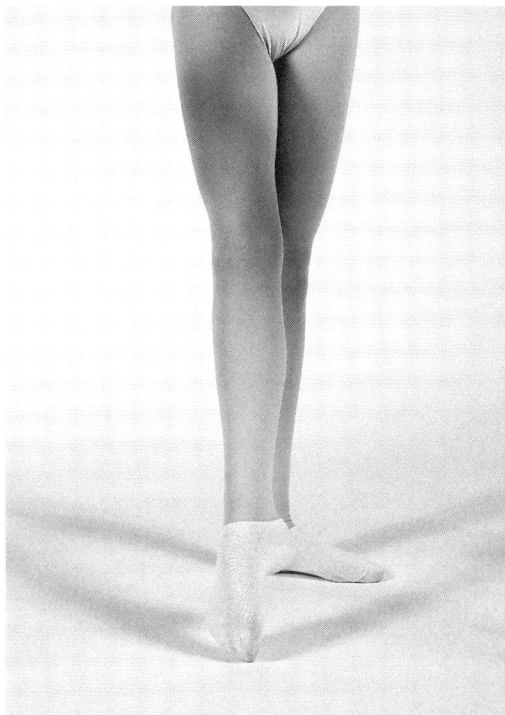

The toes are lined up with the heel of the supporting foot.

The working hip is lower than the other.

"and" 7, brush the foot in and close 1st, starting with the toes, straightening the head; on 8, hold the position. Repeat the exercise one more time with the right foot. The head turns slightly toward the left side when performing the exercise with the left foot.

Explanation. This exercise introduces the battement tendu devant with turn-out, on eight counts since it is new. It is a good idea to introduce the battement tendu 4th devant after the battement tendu 2nd, which involves a more natural trajectory, because the foot slides along the line it already has in 1st position. Since the exercise is done in 1st, the working foot, when pointing, slides slightly inside of the line that the toes would otherwise draw if they brushed out in a straight line. When performing the exercise in 5th, students will push their foot forward in a straight line out of the 5th position, where the toes of the working foot ideally line up with the edge of the heel of the supporting foot. Bringing the toes inside of that line, as favored by some teachers, tends to bring the working hip forward with a risk to turn in the working leg. The foot must brush the floor while both hips remain straight without turning out one leg more than the other. When brushing, the working toes adhere firmly to the floor.

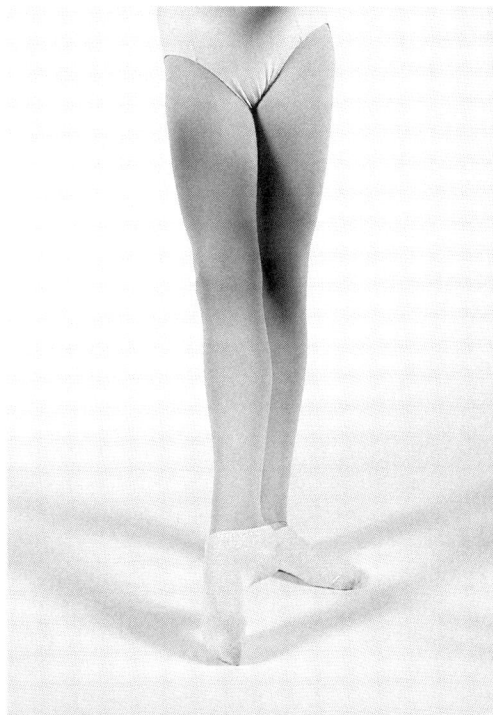

The toes are fully stretched in the pointed position without being crushed on the floor. The center of the body's weight is transferred onto the supporting leg as soon as the foot disengages. On the way out, the heel must be moved forward strongly, like pushing something with resistance with the heel alone, in order to maintain the turn-out position of the foot. The toes initiate the closing by pulling back, with the heel still pushed forward. The ankle gradually bends to return the foot flat into 1st. Students do not bring the supporting hip down or bend the supporting leg in an effort to turn out the working leg. The head turns at about a 45° angle toward the side of the working leg when it is stretched out forward. From now on, the same angle will be observed when the head is turned to the side.

Application. First year beginner students, again depending on their capability and the number of ballet classes they take, will start these battements tendus later. The alignment of the toes of the foot with the supporting heel need not be achieved right away, especially for students whose turn-out capability is low. It needs to be worked in gradually.

Exercise 5

Preparation for battement jeté devant: battement tendu devant in 6th, broken down, bring the leg à la demi-hauteur, eight counts, facing the barre.

Students repeat Exercise 8 of the Third Class of the Second Week.

Exercise 6

Battement tendu devant, broken down, bring the foot against the ankle, extend the leg, in 6th, eight counts, facing the barre.

Students repeat Exercise 5 of the Fifth Class of the Second Week.

Exercise 7

Roll-up relevé, in 1st, eight counts, facing the barre.

Following the preparatory port de bras, open the feet in 1st.

On 1 and 2, roll up the feet onto full demi-pointes; on 3 and 4, hold the position; on 5 and 6, roll down the feet; on 7 and 8, hold the position. Repeat three more times. A small plié and stretch follows the last of the relevé.

Explanation. So far students have performed the relevé with parallel feet. Here they are performing the relevé with turned out legs. This exercise is appropriate if the previous roll-up exercise in 6th is done correctly. As in the roll-up in 6th, the feet must not sickle but remain straight.

When coming down, students do not roll in or sickle their feet. The knees are fully taut throughout the exercise, but a small plié accompanies the closing of the arms to relax the leg muscles at the end of the exercise. Students must keep the proper placement and posture in the roll-up in 1st without letting their pelvis or abdomen out. Students do not adjust the landing in the attempt to turn out their feet: once their feet are down, they keep them where they are. This is a good habit to develop, to avoid any unnecessary small shuffling steps that ballet students often tend to include in their dancing. This practice makes the dancing cleaner and sharper looking.

Application. This more demanding relevé exercise will come generally later for the recreational student. Practicing the roll-ups more in parallel may be needed to gain strength in the ankles and keep the feet straight on demi-pointes. Notice the progression that applies to all beginners: first the roll-up in 6th, then in 1st. The relevé starting with a plié will come later.

CENTER

Exercise 8

Adagio: plié in 6th and 1st, four counts, port de bras performed separately.

Students repeat Exercise 10 of the Third Class of the Second Week.

The feet roll in, in 1st position on demi-pointes.

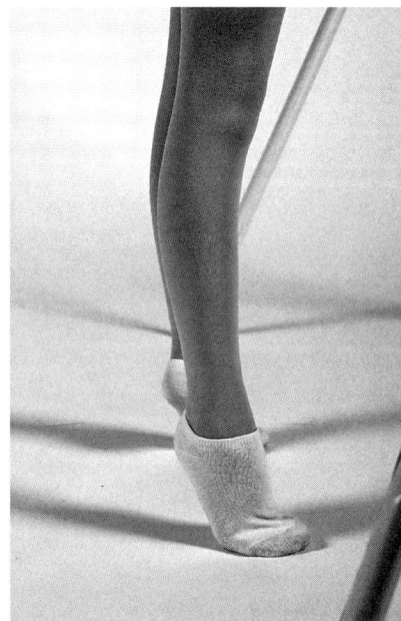

The feet sickle out in 1st position on demi-pointes.

Exercise 9

Battement tendu 2nd, broken down, start in 6th, in 1st, four counts.

Students repeat Exercise 11 of the Third Class of Second Week.

Exercise 10

Preparation for battement jeté devant: battement tendu devant in 6th, broken down, bring the leg à la demi-hauteur, eight counts.

Students repeat Exercise 11 of the Fifth Class of the Second Week.

Exercise 11

Pointing of the foot against the ankle, in 6th, four counts, arms in 1st.

Students repeat Exercise 12 of the Fifth Class of the Second Week.

Exercise 12

Soubresaut in 6th, two counts, one count to stretch, one count to hold, hands on the waist.

Students repeat Exercise 13 of the Third Class of the Second Week.

Exercise 13

Small bouncing jumps in 6th, on the count, hands on the waist.

The preparation is as follows: on 1, bring the arms in 1st; on 2, hold the position; on 3, bring the hands onto the waist; on 4, hold the position.

On "and," push off the floor; on 1, land in plié. Repeat three more times (counts 2 through 4), landing on the count each time without traveling; on 5 and 6, stretch the knees; on 7 and 8, hold the position in 6th. Repeat three more times.

Explanation. This exercise is an informal introduction of landing a jump on the count. For this type of jumps, the plié is sharper and the jump is on the musical upbeat, with the landing falling on the downbeat. Unlike the previous exercise, this is a bouncing exercise in which students jump just high enough to extend the toes and stretch the knees without pausing between jumps. Students push off vertically without pushing their torso backward. Shoulders remain low with no jerks in the upper body while jumping. The torso stays as straight as possible in the jump

and the plié. Students must avoid traveling. To bring their arms onto the waist, students repeat the preparatory port de bras as performed in Exercise 13 of the Third Class of the Second Week.

Music. A 4/4 is an appropriate musical choice. In this informal exercise, students are introduced to a quicker attack than in the other jump exercises done so far. The plié actually starts at the end of the preparation; but for the sake of simplicity, the "and" is shown in the main body of the exercise, with the landing falling on the count.

Application. All beginners will welcome this exercise, which allows them to release some energy without holding between each movement. At this stage, what is expected is the coordination of the jump with music, a good attack in the takeoff, the control of the plié at the end of each series, and at least the effort to stretch the feet and knees in the jump. Like the next skipping exercise, this kind of informal jumping exercise should be practiced along with the more formal kind of jump exercise performed with a hold between each jump to improve strength and precision.

Exercise 14

Skipping forward (sautillement en avant), around the room and in diagonal, hands on the waist.

Even though the action of skipping is not a ballet move and belongs more to a pre-ballet level, skipping is a wonderful exercise to get students to move around the room during early training of ballet, which is quite static, tense, and tedious. The hopping action involved in skipping also introduces students to jumping on one leg. While skipping, the shoulders do not move and the chin remains high. Students must point their feet and bring the working knee to the hip level at each hop. The hands are on the waist or the arms are in 1st. Performing the skipping around the room and in diagonal also introduces students to different spatial orientation, which usually comes later in ballet training.

Music. A coda-like tarantella, or other lively music for this exercise would be appropriate.

Application. Like the previous exercise, skips can be regular additions to a beginner class, no matter how often it meets.

A jump with one leg against the knee.

Exercise 15

Preparation for déboulés, in 2nd, hands on the waist, two half turns on four counts.

Students repeat Exercise 14 of the Third Class of the Second Week.

Exercise 16

Curtsey.

THIRD CLASS

Students repeat the material of the Second Class.

FOURTH CLASS

Exercise 1

Plié in 2nd and 1st, start in 6th, four counts, facing the barre.

Following the preparatory port de bras, open the feet in 1st.

On "and" 1, brush the right foot; on 2, point the toes; on 3, bring the toes down; on 4, bring the rest of the foot down in 2nd; on 5 and 6, plié; on 7 and 8, stretch; on 1 and 2, plié; on 3 and 4, stretch; on 5, transfer the weight onto the left leg, stretching the instep of the right foot up; on 6, point the toes; on 7 and 8, bring the toes down and close 1st.

On 1 and 2, plié in 1st; on 3 and 4, stretch; on 5 and 6, plié; on 7 and 8, stretch; on "and" 1, battement tendu 2nd with the left foot; on 2, point the toes; on 3, bring the toes down; on 4, bring the rest of the foot down; on 5 and 6, plié; on 7 and 8, stretch; on 1 and 2, plié; on 3 and 4, stretch; on 5, transfer the weight onto the right leg, stretching the instep of the left foot up; on 6, point the toes; on 7, bring the toes down; on 8, close 1st.

Explanation. Students are already familiar with the plié in 2nd and 1st. In this exercise they do not perform the plié in 6th, as they did last week. The pointing of the foot out and in to change position is still broken down and is now done by pointing the whole foot.

Exercise 2

Battement tendu 2nd, broken down, start in 6th, in 1st, four counts, increased number of repetitions, facing the barre.

Following the preparatory port de bras, open the legs in 1st.

On "and" 1, battement tendu 2nd; on 2, point the toes; on 3, bring the toes down; on 4, close 1st. Repeat twice more. On 5 and 6, plié and stretch, on 7 and 8, hold the position. Repeat the whole exercise one more time.

Explanation. Students are increasing the number of battements tendus 2nd with each leg in this exercise.

Exercise 3

Battement tendu devant, broken down, start in 6th, in 1st, eight counts, facing the barre.

Students repeat Exercise 4 of the Second Class of this week.

Exercise 4

Battement tendu devant, broken down, bring the foot against the ankle, extend the leg, in 6th, eight counts, facing the barre.

Students repeat Exercise 5 of the Fifth Class of the Second Week.

Exercise 5

Preparation for battement jeté 2nd, broken down, start in 6th, in 1st, eight counts, facing the barre.

Following the preparatory port de bras, open the feet in 1st.

On "and" 1, battement tendu 2nd in 1st; on 2, point the toes; on 3, sharply bring the leg à la demi-hauteur; on 4, hold the position; on 5, bring the pointed foot down onto the floor; on 6, bring the toes down; on 7, close 1st; on 8, hold the position. Repeat the exercise with the right foot.

Explanation. So far students have practiced the preparatory exercise for the battement jeté devant with the legs in parallel. Here, the exercise is done 2nd with turned-out legs. The dancer's hands must not move away from each other when performing the exercise in 2nd. The weight remains on the supporting leg. The hips are parallel to the barre. Students bring their leg energetically à la demi-hauteur and hold it still in the air.

Music. A 2/4, tango–type musical selection works well for this exercise.

The leg is in 2nd position à la demi-hauteur.

Application. The quality of the movement here that requires a sharp hold in the air is applied to increase the vivacity of the working leg. Students must freeze the working leg in position in the air.

Exercise 6

Pointing of the foot against the ankle, without and with plié, direct closing, in 6th, facing the barre.

On "and," bend the knee sharply and bring the foot against the side of the supporting ankle; on 1 and 2, hold the position; on 3, close the foot in 6th; on 4, hold the position; on "and," bring the foot against the side of the supporting ankle with a sharp plié of the supporting leg; on 5 and 6, hold the position in plié; on 7, close in 6th still in plié; on 8, stretch both knees. Repeat the exercise one more time with the right foot, alternating without and with plié of the supporting leg.

Explanation. This is another exercise to develop the sharpness of the knee articulation. When pointing the foot against the ankle, the working foot must not wobble but freeze in position. When it is performed in plié, both knees must bend at the same time with sharpness. Students press their working foot down in plié when closing 6th. The side of the big toe presses against the supporting ankle. The back remains straight. The closing is direct without breaking down the movement of the foot.

Music. A 2/4 tango with sharp beats works well for this exercise.

Application. This is another exercise accessible to any beginner class. The instructor may want to emphasize sharpness by clapping hands or making a sharp sound when students bring their foot against the ankle.

Exercise 7

Roll-up, in 1st, eight counts, facing the barre.

Students repeat Exercise 7 of the Second Class of this week.

CENTER

Exercise 8

Adagio: port de bras to 3rd and 4th, in 1st, eight counts.

Preparatory port de bras: on 1, bring the arms

1st, on "and" 2, open the arms 2nd; on "and" 3 and 4, bring the arms down and open the feet in 1st.

Port de bras to 3rd position: on 1 and 2, the arms are raised to 1st, with the head slightly inclined toward the left shoulder; on 3 and 4, the right arm goes to 5th while the left arm opens 2nd, and the head straightens and turns toward the right arm; on 5 and 6, open the right arm 2nd, with the eyes focusing on the right arm; on "and" 7, bring the arms down, with the eyes still on the right hand; on 8, straighten up the head. Repeat the exercise switching arms for the 3rd position. The head follows the left arm this time.

Port de bras to 4th position: on 1 and 2, the arms are raised to 1st, with the head slightly inclined toward the left shoulder; on 3 and 4, the right arm goes to 5th while the left arm remains in 1st, and the head straightens and turns toward the right arm; on 5 and 6, open the right arm 2nd, with the eyes focusing on the descent, while the left arm opens 2nd; on "and" 7, bring the arms down, with the eyes still focused on the right hand; on 8, straighten up the head. Repeat the exercise switching arms.

Explanation. Students are introduced to the 3rd and 4th positions of the arms. The trajectory of the arms is quite precise. It is more than for aesthetic purposes: the arms in a proper position are a crucial tool for ballet technique, especially in the turns and the allegro. Students are reminded of the proper breathing.

Application. Port de bras exercises such as this one, can be introduced early on even for recreational ballet students. Exercises made up solely of ports de bras tend to be discarded in many ballet schools. However, the study of ports de bras must be part of the class on a regular basis, regardless of the students' level and ability.

Exercise 9

Battement tendu 2nd, broken down, start in 6th, in 1st, four counts.

Students repeat Exercise 11 of the Third Class of the Second Week.

Exercise 10

Preparation for battement jeté devant: battement tendu devant, broken down, bring the leg à la demi-hauteur, in 6th, eight counts.

Students repeat Exercise 11 of the Fifth Class of the Second Week.

Exercise 11

Pointing of the foot against the ankle, in 6th, arms in 1st, four counts.

Students repeat Exercise 12 of the Fifth Class of the Second Week.

Exercise 12

Small bouncing jumps in 6th, on the count, hands on the waist.

Students repeat Exercise 13 of the Second Class of this week.

Exercise 13

Soubresaut in 2nd and 1st, two counts, one count hold, facing the barre.

Following the preparatory port de bras, open the feet 1st from 6th, on "and" 5, brush the right foot 2nd, on 6, pointing the toes; on 7, bring the toes down; on 8, bring the rest of the foot down.

On "and," plié; on 1, push off the floor with both feet, keeping the legs 2nd, and pointing both feet and stretching the legs; on 2, land in plié in 2nd; on 3, stretch both knees; on 4, hold the position. Repeat three more times. Point the right foot and close 1st. Repeat the exercise in 1st. Repeat the exercise starting with a battement tendu of the left foot.

Explanation. Students are already familiar with the technique of the jump introduced in the soubresaut in 6th. The introduction of the soubresaut in 2nd and 1st is thereby facilitated. The present program follows a logical order to introduce and practice jumps: first with jumps starting with both feet in the takeoff and the landing, then jumps starting on one foot and landing on both feet, and next jumps starting on both feet and landing on one, and finally jumps starting and landing on one foot that will be studied later in more advanced levels. Failure to follow this logical progression can lead to bad technique (for example, lack of height and sloppy and unbalanced landings) but also serious injuries.

In the starting and the finishing pliés of the jump, the knees must not come forward, but remain above the toes. The entire feet, including the heels, solidly push off the floor to spring up. In landing, the exact reverse occurs, with the

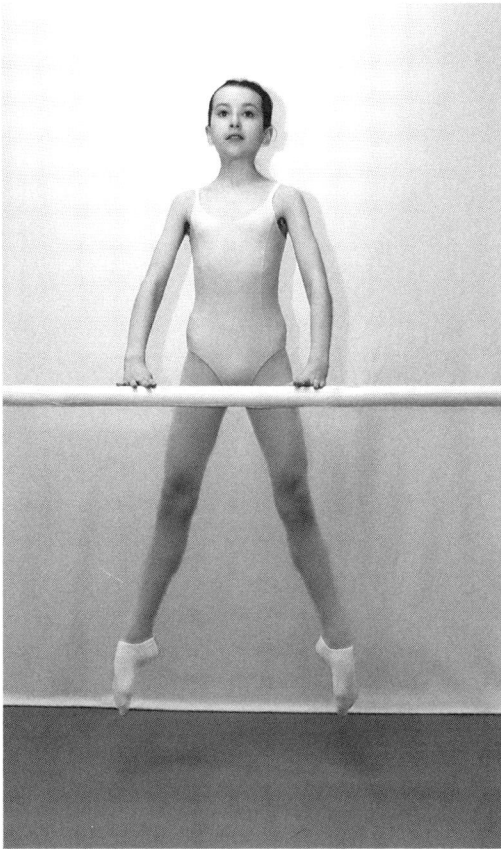

Soubresaut in 2nd position.

toes first touching the floor, and then the weight is taken through the whole foot onto the sole, coming down into plié, with the heels touching the floor last. It is this quasi-mathematical order that assures softness, lightness, and safety in the jumping exercises. Students do not widen or bring the legs closer while in the air. The toes must be pointed and the knees taut during the jump. Pressing the heels in the takeoff and the landing parts of the jump cannot be overemphasized. It gives greater stability and more surface from which to push off, and therefore produces a higher jump; it also engages the Achilles tendon in the plié to produce a stronger takeoff and thus a higher jump. The stretching of the knees and the holding between each jump help students keep their knees to the sides in the plié and control the plié in the landing.

Application. The introduction of jumps with turn-out does not mean that students should stop practicing those in parallel to perfect the quality of the plié in the takeoff and the landing, especially for those who practice ballet on a recreational basis. Regardless, the instructor has to

gauge students' readiness to start the jumps with legs turned out.

Exercise 14

Skipping forward, around the room and in diagonal, hands on the waist.

Students repeat Exercise 14 of the Second Class of this week.

Exercise 15

Curtsey.

FIFTH CLASS

Students repeat the material of the Fourth Class of the Third Week.

Fourth Week

§

Exercise 1

Bring the toes and ball up, plié, in 6th, rotation of the head, facing the barre.

On 1, bring the toes and the ball of the feet up, transferring the weight onto the heels with the knees stretched; on 2, bring them down; repeat on 3 and 4; on 5, plié; on 6, stretch; on 7, plié; on 8, stretch. Repeat one more time.

On 1, turn the head to the right; on 2, turn the head de face; on 3, turn the head to the left; on 4, turn the head de face. Repeat the head rotation one more time. Repeat the whole exercise one more time.

Explanation. This exercise involves stretching the calf muscles by bringing the toes and the ball of the feet up. Students must remain balanced on their heels and not push their buttocks out. Both feet remain straight when the toes are up. The rotation of the head is performed smoothly and without moving the shoulders or the upper back.

Music. The music is a slow flowing waltz.

Application. Most beginner students can perform this exercise relatively easily.

Exercise 2

Plié in 2nd and 1st, start in 6th, four counts, facing the barre.

Students repeat Exercise 1 of the Fourth Class of the Third Week.

Exercise 3

Battement tendu 2nd, broken down, start in 6th, in 1st, four counts, increased number of repetitions, facing the barre.

Students repeat Exercise 2 of the Fourth Class of the Third Week.

Exercise 4

Battement tendu devant, broken down, pointing of the foot against the ankle, extend the leg, with port de bras, in 6th, eight counts.

On "and" 1, battement tendu devant; on 2, point the toes; on 3, bring the working foot against the side of the supporting ankle, bringing the arm in 1st; on 4, hold the position; on 5, extend the leg with the pointed toes touching the floor, opening the arm 2nd with the head following the right hand; on 6, hold the position; on 7, bring the toes down; on 8, close 6th, straightening the head. Repeat three more times. At the end, bring both arms in 5th and hold the position.

Explanation. Students are now performing the exercise sideways with a port de bras. This is the first exercise in which students have to coordinate the arm and the leg movements. Such coordination should be introduced fairly early on in the training in a simple exercise such as this one, with both the arm and leg logically bending and stretching at the same time. When extending, the foot aims directly at the floor, with the toes touching the floor by the time the leg is stretched, not after. Notice the head following the opening of the arm 2nd.

Application. Even beginners taking ballet in a recreational environment should be exposed regularly to harmonizing the movements of the arm and the leg, even if it seems at first overwhelming. It is unfortunate that ballet instructors sometimes forego this aspect of training altogether under the pretext that it confuses students. Students, no matter how often they take ballet, should practice such coordination—for such an omission would be difficult to make up later on in training.

Exercise 5

Battement tendu devant, broken down, start in 6th, in 1st, eight counts, facing the barre.

Students repeat Exercise 4 of the Second Class of the Third Week.

Exercise 6

Preparation for battement jeté 2nd, broken down, start in 6th, in 1st, eight counts, facing the barre.

Students repeat Exercise 5 of the Fourth Class of the Third Week.

Exercise 7

Pointing of the foot against the ankle, without and with plié, direct closing, facing the barre, in 6th.

Students repeat Exercise 6 of the Fourth Class of the Third Week.

Exercise 8

Roll-up, in 1st, eight counts, facing the barre.

Students repeat Exercise 7 of the Second Class of the Third Week.

CENTER

Exercise 9

Adagio: port de bras to 3rd and 4th, in 1st, eight counts.

Students repeat Exercise 8 of the Fourth Class of the Third Week.

Exercise 10

Battement tendu 2nd, broken down, start in 6th, in 1st, four counts.

Students repeat Exercise 11 of the Third Class of the Second Week.

Exercise 11

Soubresaut in 2nd and 1st, two counts, one count hold, facing the barre.

Students repeat Exercise 13 of the Fourth Class of the Third Week.

Exercise 12

Marche (step march) in retiré in 6th, in diagonal, arms in 1st.

Start in the left upper corner of the studio to travel to the right lower corner. Following the preparatory port de bras, bring the arms down as performed in Exercise 8 of the Fourth Class of the Third Week.

On 1, bring the right leg against the supporting leg at knee level, with the arms in 1st, and

Holding with one leg against the knee.

hold the position; on 2, hold the position; on "and" 3, extend the working leg forward and step directly onto the right foot, bringing the left leg against the supporting leg at knee level still with the arms in 1st; on 4, hold the position. Repeat enough times to travel through the diagonal. Repeat the exercise from the right upper corner to the left lower corner.

Explanation. This exercise introduces students to traveling in diagonal. This is a simple march in which students raise one leg into retiré. They must be able to balance on one leg with a strong back and erect upper body. When extending, the supporting leg stretches before the student steps onto it. The position of the working leg bent with the foot against the side of the knee of the supporting leg must be as precise as the one already practiced at the barre. The toes of the working leg must not stick out beyond the back of the supporting leg, and the foot does not sickle. There is a slight freeze in the position of the working leg.

Music. A 2/4 march is, of course, appropriate for this exercise.

Application. Most beginners will appreciate this diversion and new exposure to working in a diagonal. The work in parallel will facilitate balancing on one leg in each step. Students keep their chin slightly raised. Besides working balance, this exercise also helps to bring about the good habit of stretching the leg before stepping onto it, like it is done in the chassé sauté, for instance.

Exercise 13

Curtsey.

SECOND CLASS

Students repeat the material of the First Class of this week.

THIRD CLASS

Exercise 1

Bring the toes up, plié, in 6th, rotation of the head, facing the barre.

Students repeat Exercise 1 of the First Class of this week.

Exercise 2

Plié in 2nd and 1st, four counts, facing the barre.

Students repeat Exercise 1 of the Fourth Class of the Third Week.

Exercise 3

Battement tendu devant, broken down, pointing of the foot against the ankle, extend the leg, with port de bras, in 6th, eight counts.

Students repeat Exercise 4 of the First Class of this week.

Exercise 4

Battement tendu devant and 2nd, broken down, directly in 1st, four counts, facing the barre.

For the first time, students are starting the exercise directly in 1st. Students' turn-out is equal in both legs.

On "and" 1, battement tendu devant, with the head turned slightly toward the right side; on 2, point the toes; on 3, bring the toes down; on 4, close 1st, straightening the head; on "and" 5, battement tendu 2nd; on 6, point the toes; on 7, bring the toes down; on 8, close 1st. Repeat the exercise three more times, alternating legs. A small plié and stretch ends the exercise.

Explanation. The battement tendu devant is performed on four counts, and both battements tendus devant and 2nd are performed together in this exercise. The breaking down of the foot is smoother and more flowing. From now on, students will start directly in 1st position.

Exercise 5

Preparation for battement jeté 2nd, broken down, in 1st, eight counts, facing the barre.

Students repeat Exercise 5 of the Fourth Class of the Third Week.

Exercise 6

Demi-rond de jambe à terre en dehors [rond de jambe par terre—Vaganova], in 1st, eight counts, bending to the side (penché sur le côté), facing the barre.

On "and" 1, battement tendu devant, turning the head slightly toward the right; on 2, point the toes; on 3 and 4, the working foot draws a

Bending to the side with the arm in 5th position.

Bending to the side with the weight carried over one leg.

Bending to the side with the arm too close to the head.

quarter of a circle to the 2nd position, straightening the head; on "and" 5, bring the toes down; on 6, close 1st; on 7 and 8, small plié and stretch. Repeat the exercise one more time with the right leg. Repeat the whole exercise one more time.

On 1, bring the left arm in 1st, with the head slightly inclined toward the right shoulder; on 2, bring it to 5th, with the head straightening and turning slightly toward the arm; on 3 and 4, once the arm is in 5th, turn the head toward the right, and bend the torso toward the right side; on 5 and 6, straighten up the torso, with the head turning de face; on 7 and 8, bring the arm forward to 1st with the head inclining again toward the right shoulder, and extend the arm to rest the hands on the barre, straightening the head. Repeat the exercise to the other side, bringing the right arm 5th, bending toward the left side.

Explanation. This exercise introduces students to the rond de jambe à terre. Notice that, in the demi-rond de jambe, the working leg actually draws only a quarter of a circle and not half of one. Since students have not practiced yet the battement tendu 4th position back, the rond de jambe is done only en dehors (traveling from

front to side). The main purpose of the rond de jambe is to develop the turn-out from the hips, a fact often lost on many ballet instructors.[9] When done properly, it also activates the turn-out of the foot and the inside muscles of the working leg. Students must consequently strive to maintain the turn-out of both legs at all times, especially as the working leg travels from one direction to another, while keeping the hips parallel to the barre. Students must not swing or wobble any part of their torso during the exercise.

Students are also introduced to bending sideways. Students must keep their weight spread out on both feet and in no way put more on one leg. To initiate the bending, students pull up and lengthen their back while inhaling and keeping the abdominal muscles fully active. The arm in 5th must remain exactly in the same 5th position during the bending and not come closer to the head. The shoulder of the arm in 5th remains low. Notice the port de bras en dedans from the 5th to the 1st position at the end of the bending. The head is turned toward the bending side

---

9   Grieg, *Inside Ballet Technique*, 56.

without dropping the chin down. The head can be kept de face as well. However, the showing of the face's profile in such movement is more aesthetically pleasing.

Music. A flowing waltz would be a good musical choice.

Application. The elements starting and finishing the rond de jambe must have already been practiced. The exercise of bending, to stretch the side muscles of the torso, must involve the activation of the abdominals. The bendings on the sides may have to wait for students who do not have enough upper body flexibility and control of their back.

Exercise 7

Pointing of the foot against the ankle, without and with plié, direct closing, in 6th, facing the barre.

Students repeat Exercise 6 of the Fourth Class of the Third Week.

Exercise 8

Adagio: port de bras to 5th, battement tendu 2nd, broken down, in 1st.

On "and," turn the palm down; on 1 and 2, bring the arm into preparatory position; on 3, bring the arm in 1st, with the head slightly inclined and the eyes focused on the right hand; on 4, bring the arm to 5th, with the head straightening and turning at a soft angle toward the right arm; on "and" 5, battement tendu 2nd; on 6, point the toes; on 7, bring the toes down; on 8, close 1st, opening the arm to 2nd, with the eyes following the descent of the hand. Repeat the exercise one more time.

Explanation. Students are introduced to bringing one arm in 5th from the 1st with the head turning toward the arm in 5th, performed sideways. They coordinate the head with the movement of the arm in each port de bras. When closing the foot in 1st, the arm opens 2nd.

Application. This simple exercise of port de bras can be introduced to most beginners. While most exercises are still done facing the barre, all beginners must also get acquainted to working on the side so that they practice moving and holding the arm through different positions to prepare for exercises in the center.

Exercise 9

Roll-up relevé, in 6th and 1st, four counts, three repetitions, facing the barre.

On 1 and 2, roll up in 1st; on 3 and 4, roll down; on 5 and 6, roll up; on 7 and 8, roll down; on 1 and 2, roll up; on 3 and 4, roll down; on 5, plié; on 6, stretch; on 7 and 8, open the feet 1st and hold the position. Repeat the exercise in 1st. After a pause, repeat the exercise one more time.

Explanation. Students are performing the roll-up in 6th and 1st on four counts, instead of eight counts.

Application. All beginners should be exposed to drills of relevés such as these to gain strength in the ankles. For those who do not practice ballet very often, careful monitoring is required so that the relevé is done properly with straight feet and taut knees.

CENTER

Exercise 10

Adagio: port de bras to 3rd and 4th, in 1st, eight counts.

Students repeat Exercise 8 of the Fourth Class of the Third Week.

Exercise 11

Battement tendu devant, broken down, pointing of the foot against the ankle, extend the leg, with port de bras, in 6th, eight counts.

On "and" 1, battement tendu devant; on 2, point the toes; on 3, bring the working foot pointed against the side of the supporting ankle, bringing the arms in 1st; on 4, hold the position; on 5, extend the leg, pointing the foot onto the floor, opening the arms 2nd; on 6, hold the position; on 7, bring the toes down; on 8, close 6th. Repeat one more time with the right foot. Repeat the whole exercise one more time.

Explanation. Students are repeating Exercise 4 of the First Class of this week in the center.

Exercise 12

Soubresaut in 2nd and 1st, two counts, one count hold, facing the barre.

Students repeat Exercise 13 of the Fourth Class of the Third Week, with a slightly faster tempo.

Exercise 13

Skipping forward and backward (en arrière), around the room and in diagonal, with hands on the waist.

Students are performing six skips forward and two skips backward. The quick change of direction must be met with a strong attack, especially when going forward after going backward, with students propelling their upper body forward and pushing hard on the back leg on the last skip going backward.

Exercise 14

Marche in retiré in 6th, in diagonal, arms in 1st.

Students repeat Exercise 12 of the First Class of this week.

Exercise 15

Curtsey.

FOURTH CLASS

Students repeat the material of the Third Class of this week.

FIFTH CLASS

Exercise 1

Bring the toes up, plié, in 6th, rotation of the head, facing the barre.

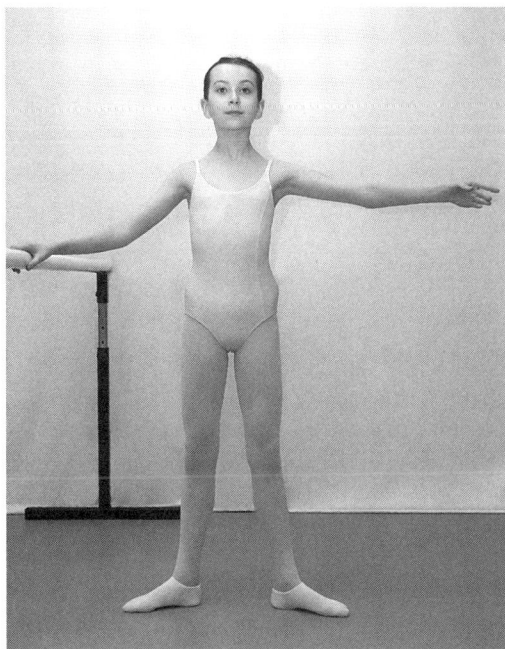

Correct distance between the body and the barre.

Students repeat Exercise 1 of the First Class of this week.

Exercise 2

Plié in 2nd and 1st, arm 2nd.

Start in 1st: following the preparation on eight counts, on 1, battement tendu with the right foot in 2nd; on 2, point the toes; on 3, bring the right foot down, with the weight in the middle of both legs; on 4, hold the position; on 5, transfer the weight onto the right leg and brush the left foot out in 2nd; on 6, point the toes; on 7, bring the foot down as well, with the weight in the middle of both legs; on 8, hold the position.

On 1 and 2, plié; on 3 and 4, stretch; on 5 and 6, plié; on 7 and 8, stretch; on 1, point the right foot, with the toes still on the floor; on 2, point the toes; on 3, bring the toes down; on 4, close; on 5, point the left foot, with the toes still on the floor; on 6, point the toes; on 7, bring the toes down; on 8, close in 1st. On 1 and 2, plié; on 3 and 4, stretch; on 5 and 6, plié; on 7 and 8, stretch, bringing the arms 5th and hold the position for a few counts.

Explanation. Students are performing the plié in 1st and 2nd sideways. In most ballet schools, students, when asked to open their legs in 2nd sideways, simply do a battement tendu with the outside leg and bring the foot down. Unfortunately, this practice brings students too far from

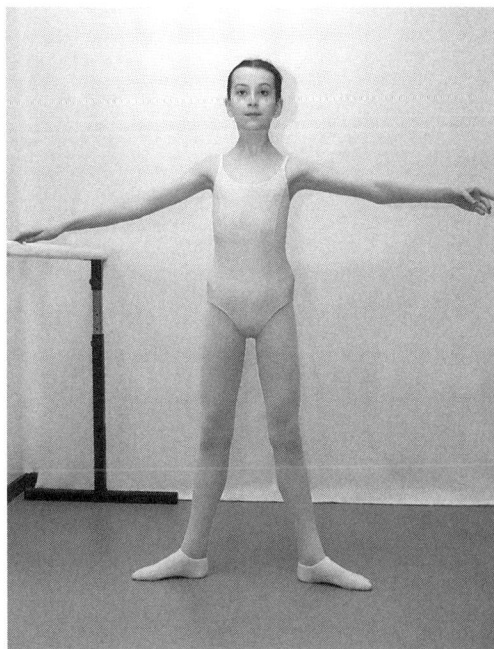

The body is too far from the barre.

the barre, forcing them to overstretch their arm to be able to hold it. In order to keep the proper distance from the barre, students need to move both feet equally away from the 1st so that they remain comfortably centered. Similarly, when closing in 1st, students bring one foot after the other so that they do not adjust their distance from the barre. The opening and closing of the legs to change position is performed as precisely as any other part of the exercise.

Application. Beginners in a recreational program will perform this type of plié still facing the barre to keep the whole body straight. Once students are exposed to this type of exercise sideways, the instructor will be vigilant to have students keep the body straight and the weight equally distributed on both feet.

Exercise 3

Battement tendu devant, broken down, pointing of the foot against the ankle, extend the leg, with port de bras, in 6th, eight counts.

Students repeat Exercise 4 of the First Class of this week.

Exercise 4

Battement tendu devant and 2nd, broken down, in 1st, four counts, facing the barre.

Students repeat Exercise 4 of the Third Class of this week.

Exercise 5

Battement tendu 2nd [battement tendu relevé—Cecchetti; double battement tendu—Vaganova], bring the foot down in 2nd, point the foot and close, broken down, in 1st, eight counts, facing the barre.

On "and" 1, battement tendu 2nd; on 2, point the toes; on 3, bring the toes down; on 4, bring the rest of the foot down, thus transferring the weight to the middle of both legs; on 5, stretch the instep of the right foot up, transferring the weight back onto the left leg; on 6, point the toes; on 7, bring the toes down; on 8, close 1st. Repeat the exercise three more times, alternating legs.

Explanation. The articulation of the foot is particularly demanding in this exercise. It is very broken down so that each part of the foot moves at a time. This is a good exercise to feel the several shifts of weight occurring in this otherwise simple exercise. Students should never crush their toes onto the floor, meaning that the weight should always be on the supporting leg with the pointed working foot light on the floor, keeping just enough weight on the working leg to apply downward pressure on the floor to brush out and in. Students must slide their hands along the barre during each transfer so that the arms remain in front of the shoulders.

Music. A medium-tempo waltz works well for this exercise.

Application. This simple exercise will be beneficial to all beginners to sense the different transfers of weight. But the instructor must monitor the transfer of weight and the pointing of the foot carefully, especially for students who take ballet recreationally.

Exercise 6

Preparation for battement jeté devant and 2nd, broken down, in 1st, eight counts, facing the barre.

On "and" 1, battement tendu devant, the head turned slightly toward the right; on 2, point the toes; on 3, lift the leg à la demi-hauteur with vigor; on 4, hold the position; on 5, bring the pointed foot down onto the floor; on 6, bring the toes down; on 7, close 1st, straightening the head; on 8, hold the position.

On "and" 1, battement tendu 2nd; on 2, point the toes; on 3, lift the leg à la demi-hauteur; on 4, hold the position; on 5, bring the pointed foot down onto the floor; on 6, bring the toes down; on 7, close 1st; on 8, hold the position. Repeat the whole exercise. A small plié and stretch follows the last closing.

Explanation. Students are performing the preparatory exercise for the battement jeté devant with turn-out, in 1st position. Like in practicing the battement jeté in 6th, students should have room to lift their leg à la demi-hauteur. The lifting of the leg is sharp and precise. The working leg quickly comes up, freezes à la demi-hauteur, and comes down quickly. Like in the exercise for the battement tendu devant, the head is turned at about a 45° angle to the side of the working leg.

Exercise 7

Demi-rond de jambe à terre en dehors, in 1st, plié, eight counts, bending to the sides, facing the barre.

Students repeat Exercise 6 of the Third Class of this week.

Exercise 8

Adagio: port de bras to 5th, battement tendu 2nd, in 1st.

Students repeat Exercise 8 of the Third Class of this week.

Exercise 9

Roll-up relevé, in 6th and 1st, four counts, three repetitions, facing the barre.

Students repeat Exercise 9 of the Third Class of this week.

CENTER

Exercise 10

Adagio: port de bras, all positions, in 1st, four counts each.

Port de bras to 2nd: on "and" 1, bring the arms down, with the head and the eyes following the right hand; on 2, bring the arms 1st, with the head slightly inclined toward the left shoulder and the eyes are directed toward the right hand; on "and" 3, open the arms 2nd with the head straightening and following the right hand; on 4, hold the position.

Port de bras to 3rd: on "and" 5, bring the arms down, still with the head focused on the right hand; on 6, bring the arms 1st, with the head inclined toward the left shoulder; on 7, bring the arms in 3rd position with the right arm going to 5th and the left arm opening 2nd, and the head straightening and turning slightly toward the right arm; on "and" 8, the right arm opens 2nd, with the head still following the right hand.

Port de bras to 4th: on "and" 1, bring the arms down, with the head and eyes following the right hand; on 2, bring the arms 1st; on 3, bring the arms in 4th position with the right arm going to 5th and the left arm remaining in 1st, and the head slightly turned toward the right arm; on "and" 4, the right arm opens 2nd, with the head following the movement of the right hand, while the left arm opens 2nd.

Port de bras to 5th: on "and" 5, bring the arms down, with the eyes focused on the movement of the right hand; on 6, bring the arms 1st, with the head slightly inclined toward the left shoulder;

on 7, both arms come to 5th, with the head straightening; on "and" 8, both arms open 2nd. Repeat the whole exercise with the left arm going up into 3rd and 4th arm positions, with the head turned toward the left arm and the left hand each time.

Explanation. In this exercise, students are practicing all the arm positions. The head accompanies each port de bras.

Music. A particular legato adagio music is used for this exercise, since there are four counts for each port de bras.

Application. This type of exercise should routinely be practiced by all beginners.

Exercise 11

Battement tendu devant, broken down, pointing of the foot against the ankle, extend the leg, in 6th, with port de bras, eight counts.

Students repeat Exercise 11 of the Third Class of this week.

Exercise 12

Battement tendu devant and 2nd, broken down, in 1st, four counts.

On "and" 1, battement tendu devant, turning the head slightly toward the right; on 2, point the toes; on 3, bring the toes down; on 4, close 1st, straightening the head; on "and" 5, battement tendu 2nd; on 6, point the toes; on 7, bring the toes down; on 8, close 1st. After a pause, repeat the whole exercise. A small plié and stretch follows the last closing.

Explanation. Students are repeating the exercise done at the barre. Students must make sure to engage the whole foot in the pointing and the flattening of the working foot, without the toes rising off the floor.

Exercise 13

Soubresaut in 2nd and 1st, two counts, one count hold, facing the barre.

Students repeat Exercise 13 of the Fourth Class of the Third Week.

Exercise 14

Preparation for the petit (small) échappé 2nd [pas échappé—Vaganova], broken down, in 1st, eight counts, facing the barre.

On "and," plié in 1st; on 1, push off the floor

with pointed toes and straightened knees and immediately open the legs 2nd in the air; on 2, land in plié in 2nd; on 3, stretch the knees; on 4, hold the position. On "and," plié in 2nd; on 5, push off the floor with pointed toes and straightened knees; on 6, land in plié in 1st; on 7, stretch both knees; on 8, hold the position. Repeat three more times.

Explanation. The échappé sauté consists of two jumps with no hold between them. In this introduction, however, students stretch the knees between both jumps so that the landing of the first jump can be done properly. Both legs must open and close at the same time. Students must not open the legs wider than the 2nd position in either jump. The legs open directly 2nd in the first jump without holding the legs together. The takeoff and the landing should be performed equally from and on both feet.

Music. A march, like one used for a grand battement exercise, would work well here.

Application. The soubresaut in 1st and in 2nd must be performed properly before this exercise is introduced.

Exercise 15

Skipping forward and backward, around the room and in diagonal, hands on the waist.

Students repeat Exercise 13 of the Third Class of this week.

Exercise 16

Marche in retiré in 6th in diagonal, arms in 1st.

Students repeat Exercise 12 of the First Class of this week.

Exercise 17

Preparation for déboulés, in 1st, arms in low 1st, each half turn on one count, hold one count.

Start the exercise in the back of the studio, facing the left side of the studio. Following the preparatory port de bras, bring the arms down. The head is directed toward the right shoulder, and the eyes are focused on a specific spot.

On "and" 1, transfer the weight onto the right foot, raising the right heel very slightly and rotating it outward toward the right, turn a half turn

toward the right holding the arms in low 1st in front of the torso, and turning the head so that, by the end of the half turn, it is now toward the left shoulder with the eyes focused on a particular spot; on 2, hold the position; on "and" 3, transfer the weight onto the left foot and rotate a half turn toward the right, keeping the eyes focused on the particular point as the body starts rotating, and the head snapping so that the head precedes the end of the rotation of the body with the eyes still focused on the same spot. Repeat six more times. Repeat the exercise facing the right side of the studio and rotating toward the left.

Explanation. Students are practicing the spotting exercise now in 1st. The closeness of the feet in 1st helps students keep a straight line but is more difficult for balance. To keep the legs together, the adductors are actively involved. The arms remain as still as possible and in front of the torso. It is the transfer of the weight onto the ball of the foot and the turning toward the direction of travel of the first heel that allow the rotation and thus the travel. The rotation is done more rapidly. The arms are in low 1st, which is a position between the preparatory and the 1st positions. In some exercises that require holding the arms statically for some time while the legs are in action, as in this one, it is preferable to hold the arms not as high as the 1st so that the arms are not as heavy to hold and do not compromise the rotating movement. At the end of the exercise, the arms are brought to 1st, they open 2nd, and come down in preparatory position. From now on, the same port de bras will apply when the arms are in low 1st throughout the exercise.

Application. For recreational students who take ballet once or twice a week, keeping the alignment of the body in this exercise, while trying to rotate in the proper direction, may be challenging. For these students, the opening of the legs in 1st should remain comfortable so that they can keep balance in the half turns.

Exercise 18

Curtsey.

Fifth Week

𝄞

FIRST CLASS

Students repeat the material of the Fifth Class of the Fourth Week

SECOND CLASS

Exercise 1

Battement tendu devant, in 6th, battement tendu 2nd, broken down, in 1st, facing the barre, review.

On "and" 1, battement tendu devant; on 2, point the toes; on 3, bring the toes down; on 4, close 6th. Repeat the exercise with the left leg. Open the legs in 1st. Repeat the exercise with a battement tendu 2nd. Close 6th. Repeat the whole exercise. A small plié and stretch follows the last closing. At the end, bring both arms in 5th.

Explanation. Students are reviewing the battement tendu exercise performed in Exercise 4 of the Third Class of the Second Week.

Exercise 2

Plié in 2nd and 1st, arm 2nd.

Students repeat Exercise 2 of the Fifth Class of the Fourth Week.

Exercise 3

Battement tendu devant and 2nd, broken down, in 1st, four counts, facing the barre.

Students repeat Exercise 4 of the Third Class of the Fourth Week.

Exercise 4

Battement tendu 2nd, broken down, bring the foot down in 2nd, point the foot and close, in 1st, eight counts, facing the barre.

Students repeat Exercise 5 of the Fifth Class of the Fourth Week.

Exercise 5

Preparation for battement jeté devant and 2nd, broken down, in 1st, eight counts, facing the barre.

Students repeat Exercise 6 of the Fifth Class of the Fourth Week.

Exercise 6

Demi-rond de jambe à terre en dehors, in 1st, plié, eight counts, bending to the sides, facing the barre.

Students repeat Exercise 6 of the Third Class of the Fourth Week.

Exercise 7

Position on the cou-de-pied (wrapped) devant, in 1st, eight counts, facing the barre.

On 1, bring the right foot on the cou-de-pied, the sole of the foot wrapping around the area of the supporting leg between the ankle and the lower calf, with the heel in front and the toes pointed down behind the ankle; on 2 and 3, hold the position; on 4, extend the working leg 2nd, pointing the foot with the toes touching the floor; on 5, hold the position; on 6, bring the toes down; on 7 and 8, close 1st. Repeat one more time with the right foot.

Explanation. This position prepares for the exercises of battement frappé and petits battements sur le cou-de-pied introduced later on in this manual. The term cou-de-pied and what it designates can cause great confusion for non-French dancers. Literally the expression means the neck of the foot. In fact, when the foot is wrapped around the cou-de-pied, it touches a larger area with the heel positioned against the inner aspect of the lower shin, the arch resting around the Achilles tendon, and the tips of the toes tautly stretched, aiming for the upper part of the calcaneus (heel bone). The ankle of the working foot is slightly bent so that it is able to fully wrap around the ankle. This slight bend of the foot around the ankle, allowed in the French school, permits students to turn out their working foot more, with the heel really pushing forward. The full grasp of the foot around the ankle is almost impossible for beginners if they do not bend the ankle. This bend also facilitates the brushing of the toes of the working foot in the frappé, when the tips of the toes graze the floor before extending the leg out. However, the bending of the working ankle occurs only when the foot is at the ankle, for the working foot must be fully pointed when the leg extends out. The thigh of the working leg should not move much while the knee bends and must stay open throughout the exercise. The hips remain parallel to the barre and do not turn toward the working leg.

There are three possible positions of the foot on the cou-de-pied: wrapped, pointed, and flexed. It is a good idea to start with the foot in a wrapped position around the ankle to emphasize the turn-out of the foot and the pushing of the heel forward. The flexed and the pointed positions are introduced later.

Music. The music is a sharp 4/4.

Application. Most beginners may be acquainted with this position fairly early in the training. It needs to be mastered before the battement frappé and the petits battements sur le cou-de-pied are introduced.

Exercise 8

Roll-up relevé, in 6th and 1st, four counts, three repetitions, facing the barre.

Students repeat Exercise 9 of the Third Class of the Fourth Week.

Exercise 9

Bending forward (penché en avant), in 6th, back to the barre.

Stand a short distance from the barre, the back facing the barre. Following the preparatory port de bras, rest the hands on the barre, keeping the elbows relaxed.

On 1 and 2, bend forward keeping the back as flat as possible, remaining balanced on the legs, still holding the barre; on 3 and 4, relax the back and the head to bring the torso closer to the knees for further stretching, without tensing the shoulders; on 5 and 6, with the head leading the movement, flatten the back again; on 7 and 8, straighten up while lengthening the back, bringing the pelvis aligned as soon as possible when reaching the upright position. Repeat three more times.

Explanation. Students are introduced to a stretching exercise for hamstrings and the back performed with legs in parallel. The barre must be at an adequate height. Students must be balanced at all times. A common error is to shift the weight of the body backward during the bending. Another one is to arch the lower back to initiate the bend. Before straightening up, students must lengthen their back so that the back is not rounded during the ascension. It is crucial

Bending forward, back to the barre.

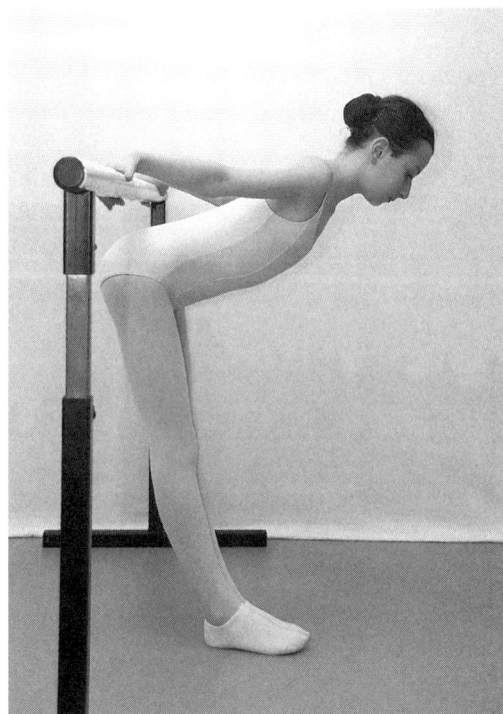

Bending forward with the weight too far back.

Bending forward initiated by curving the lower back.

that students work regularly on stretching the hamstrings, which, when tight, limit the range of extension in the legs and the flexion at the hips while bending forward. Legs do not bend during the exercise.

Music. An adagio music is used.

Application. This is a good stretching exercise for ballet dancers. But the instructor must watch the straightening of the back on the way up carefully to avoid any strain in the lower back. The back must be lengthened at all times.

CENTER

Exercise 10

Adagio: port de bras, all positions, in 1st, four counts each.

Students repeat Exercise 10 of the Fifth Class of the Fourth Week.

Exercise 11

Battement tendu devant, broken down, bring the foot against the ankle, extend the leg, in 6th, with port de bras, eight counts.

Students repeat Exercise 11 of the Third Class of the Fourth Week.

Exercise 12

Battement tendu devant and 2nd, broken down, in 1st, four counts.

Students repeat Exercise 12 of the Fifth Class of the Fourth Week.

Exercise 13

Demi-rond de jambe à terre en dehors, plié, eight counts, in 1st.

On "and" 1, battement tendu devant, with the head turning slightly toward the right; on 2, point the toes; on 3 and 4, demi-rond de jambe en dehors, straightening the head; on 5, bring the toes down; on 6, close 1st; on 7 and 8, small plié and stretch. Repeat the exercise one more time with the right foot.

Explanation. Students are repeating Exercise 6 of the Third Class of the Fourth Week, performed this time in the center without a port de bras for now.

Application. A good balance and control of the turn-out are required to practice this exercise in the center, abilities that may still be lacking in beginners of recreational programs.

Exercise 14

Preparation for battement jeté 2nd in 1st, broken down, eight counts.

On "and" 1, battement tendu 2nd in 1st; on 2, point the toes; on 3, battement à la demi-hauteur; on 4, hold the position; on 5, bring the pointed foot down onto the floor; on 6, bring the toes down; on 7, close 1st; on 8, hold the position. Repeat the whole exercise one more time.

Explanation. Students are practicing the exercise in the center. The working hip remains down. The turned-out muscles are fully activated to help keep balance. The back is erect, but the arms do not tense. The torso does not lean away from the working leg.

Music. A 4/4 polka with a fairly quick tempo is used to help students perform the exercise.

Application. This is a challenging exercise, especially for those who lack turn-out. For these students, the lifting of the leg remains low (around 25°) and the working leg is brought slightly forward. A strong back is necessary to keep balance. The lengthening of the torso, especially the side opposite of the working leg, is important to compensate for the lifting of the

The leg à la demi-hauteur is brought slightly forward in 2nd position.

working leg. In an effort to keep balance, the arms do not tense.

Exercise 15

Soubresaut in 2nd and 1st, two counts, one count hold, facing the barre.

Students repeat Exercise 13 of the Fourth Class of the Third Week.

Exercise 16

Preparation for the petit échappé 2nd, broken down, in 1st, eight counts, facing the barre.

Students repeat Exercise 14 of the Fifth Class of the Fourth Week.

Exercise 17

Skipping forward and backward, around the room and in diagonal, with hands on the waist.

Students repeat Exercise 13 of the Third Class of the Fourth Week.

Exercise 18

Preparation for déboulés, in 1st, arms in low 1st, each half turn on one count, hold one count.

Students repeat Exercise 17 of the Fifth Class of the Fourth Week.

Exercise 19

Curtsey.

THIRD CLASS

Students repeat the material of the Second Class of this week.

FOURTH CLASS

Exercise 1

Battement tendu devant in 6th, battement tendu 2nd in 1st, broken down, facing the barre.

Students repeat Exercise 1 of the Second Class of this week.

Exercise 2

Plié in 2nd and 1st, arm 2nd.

Students repeat Exercise 2 of the Fifth Class of the Fourth Week.

Exercise 3

Battement tendu devant and 2nd, no breaking down, in 1st, four counts.

On 1 and 2, battement tendu devant, the head remains slightly angled away from the barre; on 3 and 4, close 1st, straightening the head; on 5 and

Battement tendu in 4th position devant.

6, battement tendu 2nd; on 7 and 8, close 1st. Repeat three more times.

Explanation. From now on, students will not break down the battement tendu, but they still brush the foot thoroughly before pointing the toes. They execute the battement tendu exercise sideways with the head movement particular to this exercise. The head movement with the change of direction of the working leg has already been introduced in some exercises facing the barre. As a general rule, for a movement executed in 4th devant or when the working leg comes forward, the head is turned away from the barre (or toward the side of the working leg when facing the barre), at about 45° between the 4th and the 2nd positions without moving the torso or the shoulders. For the leg movement performed 2nd, the head is held straight. From now on, these particular head movements will be applied.

Music. A slow-to-medium tempo waltz works here.

Application. As said before, the different positions of the head must be applied during the training, whether students take ballet once or five times a week.

Exercise 4

Battement tendu 2nd, bring the foot down in 2nd, point the foot and close, in 1st, eight counts, facing the barre.

Students repeat Exercise 5 of the Fifth Class of the Fourth Week, except the battement tendu is not broken down.

Exercise 5

Preparation for battement jeté devant and 2nd, in 1st, eight counts, facing the barre.

Students repeat Exercise 6 of the Fifth Class of the Fourth Week, except the brushing out and in of the foot is not broken down.

Exercise 6

Demi-rond de jambe à terre en dehors and en dedans, start 2nd, plié, in 1st, eight counts, facing the barre.

On 1 and 2, battement tendu devant; on 3 and 4, the working foot draws a quarter of a circle to the 2nd position; on 5 and 6, close 1st; on 7 and 8, plié and stretch.

On 1 and 2, battement tendu 2nd; on 3 and 4, the working foot draws a quarter of a circle to the 4th position devant; on 5 and 6, close 1st; on 7 and 8, plié and stretch.

Repeat one more time with the right foot. To finish, bring both arms to 5th and hold the position.

Explanation. This exercise introduces students to the rond de jambe en dedans. Since they have not yet practiced the battement tendu back, they are performing only the rond de jambe en dedans from side to front. The working leg stays turned out as it comes forward, and the hips in no way move along with the working leg or swing around. Throughout the rond de jambe, the supporting leg keeps the turn-out. Students must respect the precise trajectory of the rond de jambe. As learned earlier in this class, the head will turn slightly to the side whenever the working leg is devant.

Exercise 7

Position on the cou-de-pied devant, in 1st, eight counts, facing the barre.

Students repeat Exercise 7 of the Second Class of this week.

Exercise 8

Adagio: lift the leg 2nd à la demi-hauteur, [battement lent 45°—Vaganova], in 1st, eight counts, facing the barre.

On 1 and 2, battement tendu 2nd; on 3 and 4, lift the leg à la demi-hauteur; on 5 and 6, lower the leg, and bring the pointed foot onto the floor; on 7 and 8, close 1st. Repeat the exercise three more times, alternating legs. At the end, roll up in 1st and hold the position.

Explanation. Students are introduced to lifting the stretched leg slowly and smoothly in the air. Notice that it is not called a battement, for the quality of the movement demanded in this type of exercise does not fit the sharp and vigorous character of the battement. Unlike the preparation for the battement jeté, which involves sharpness and quickness of execution, this exercise should be performed flowingly. For now the tempo is even, with the same amount of time spent lifting and lowering the leg. Students must be balanced and must not sit on their supporting leg. Both knees are taut, and the torso is straight without leaning away from the working leg. Unless students have a perfect turn-out, their leg in 2nd has to come slightly forward of the 180° line to be able to balance. The hips do not turn toward the working leg when the leg is off the floor. The back is lengthened throughout the lift. Notice the roll-up in 1st to end the exercise. Now that students are familiar with the roll-up movement of the feet, they should end many exercises at the barre with such relevé to balance on demi-pointes and to gain strength in their ankles.

Application. This exercise introduces the simplest form of lifting the leg in adagio. It precedes the more complicated développé for all ballet students.

Exercise 9

Roll-up relevé, in 6th and 1st, four counts, three repetitions, facing the barre.

Students repeat Exercise 9 of the Third Class of the Fourth Week.

Exercise 10

Bending forward, in 6th, back to the barre.

Students repeat Exercise 9 of the Second Class of this week.

CENTER

Exercise 11

Adagio: port de bras, all positions, in 1st, four counts each.

Students repeat Exercise 10 of the Fifth Class of the Fourth Week.

Exercise 12

Battement tendu devant and 2nd, in 1st, four counts.

Students repeat Exercise 12 of the Fifth Class of the Fourth Week, except the battement tendu is not broken down.

Exercise 13

Demi-rond de jambe à terre en dehors, plié, in 1st, eight counts.

Students repeat Exercise 13 of the Second Class of this week, except the brushing out and in of the working foot is not broken down.

Exercise 14

Preparation for battement jeté 2nd, in 1st, eight counts.

Students repeat Exercise 14 of the Second Class of this week, except the brushing out and in of the working foot is not broken down.

Exercise 15

Preparation for the petit échappé 2nd, broken down, in 1st, eight counts, facing the barre.

Students repeat Exercise 14 of the Fifth Class of the Fourth Week.

Exercise 16

Soubresaut in 2nd and 1st, two counts, one count hold.

In the preparation, on 1 and 2, bring the arms in 1st; on 3 and 4, battement tendu 2nd with the right foot, opening the arms 2nd; on 5, bring the foot down, on 6, hold the position; on 7 and 8, bring the arms down.

On "and," plié; on 1, jump straight up in the air keeping the legs 2nd; on 2, land into plié; on 3, stretch both knees; on 4, hold the position. Repeat the exercise twice more. Point the right foot and close 1st. Repeat the exercise in 1st. Repeat the whole exercise with a battement tendu of the left foot.

Explanation. Students are performing the exercise in the center. In the plié, the knees do not come forward. The arms should be held still without jerking throughout the exercise. It is common to see beginners' classes in which students hold their hands on the waist regularly for jumping exercises. Holding the hands on the waist must not become a lingering practice, for students need to get used to holding their arms in position early on in the training. While the feet and legs play an important role in the jump, a strong back is essential to the stability and quality of the overall exercise. A strongly held back does not mean that students push their torso backward, like some students tend to do. An image of absolute verticality must accompany the jump. Instructions such as touching the ceiling with the head may help students to gain this sense of verticality. Abdominal muscles should also be very involved in the effort to gain height in the jump, with the lower abdomen being lifted in the takeoff.

Music. The tempo of the musical introduction is slowed down so that students have time to perform the preparatory port de bras and the battement tendu 2nd correctly.

Exercise 17

Preparation for déboulés, in 1st, arms in low 1st, each half turn on one count, hold one count.

Students repeat Exercise 17 of the Fifth Class of the Fourth Week.

Exercise 18

Curtsey.

FIFTH CLASS

Exercise 1

Battement tendu devant in 6th, battement tendu 2nd in 1st, facing the barre.

Students repeat Exercise 1 of the Second Class of this week.

Exercise 2

Preparatory port de bras, four counts, plié in 2nd and 1st, port de bras performed separately.

Start in 1st; on 1, bring both arms in 1st; on 2, open the left arm and rest the hand on the barre; on 3, open the right arm 2nd, with the head following the movement of each arm; on 4, turn the head de face. From 5 to 8, battement tendu with both feet, bringing them down in 2nd.

On 1 and 2, plié; on 3 and 4, stretch both knees; from 5 and 8, repeat the plié and stretch; on "and" 1 and 2, bring the arm down; on 3, bring it 1st; on "and" 4, open it 2nd and straighten the head; on 5, point the right foot; on 6, close; on 7, point the left foot; on 8, close it 1st as well.

On 1 and 2, plié; on 3 and 4, stretch; from 5 and 8, repeat the plié and stretch; on "and" 1 and 2, bring the arm down; on 3, bring it 1st; on "and" 4, open it 2nd; from 5 to 8, release the left arm and bring both arms down with the head still turned slightly away from the barre and hold the position.

Explanation. From now on, the preparatory port de bras is performed on four counts for each exercise sideways of the barre. Both feet open 2nd as students learned in Exercise 2 of the Fifth

Class of the Fourth Week. At this stage, the arm is still 2nd during the plié, and the port de bras is performed independently at the end of each series of plié. The shoulders, especially the shoulder of the working arm, must not come forward during the port de bras, which is a common error among ballet students. When coming down, the arm curves slightly without the elbows scooping down. The arm is soft and rounded. Even though the head moves during the port de bras, the torso remains straight.

Music. As for other plié and port de bras exercises, an adagio-like music is appropriate here. But a slow-to-medium tempo waltz or even a barcarolle may also be good musical choices for these types of exercises.

Exercise 3

Battement tendu devant and 2nd, no breaking down, in 1st, four counts.

Students repeat Exercise 3 of the Fourth Class of this week.

Exercise 4

Battement tendu 2nd, bring the foot down in 2nd, point the foot and close, in 1st, eight counts, facing the barre.

On 1 and 2, battement tendu 2nd; on 3, bring the foot down; on 4, hold the position; on 5, point the right foot; on 6, hold the position; on 7 and 8, close 1st. Repeat with the right foot. At the end, roll up and hold balance.

Explanation. Students are repeating the same exercise as performed in Exercise 5 of the Fifth Class of the Fourth Week, except the tempo is accelerated and the whole exercise is done with more fluidity and continuity.

Exercise 5

Preparation for battement jeté devant and 2nd, in 1st, eight counts, facing the barre.

On 1 and 2, battement tendu devant; on 3, battement à la demi-hauteur; on 4, hold the position; on 5, bring the pointed foot down onto the floor; on 6, hold the position; on 7 and 8, close 1st.

On 1 and 2, battement tendu 2nd; on 3, battement à la demi-hauteur; on 4, hold the position; on 5, bring the pointed foot down onto the floor; on 6, hold the position; on 7 and 8, close

1st. Repeat the whole exercise. A small plié and stretch follows the last closing. At the end, roll up in 1st and hold the position.

Explanation. Students are repeating Exercise 6 of the Fifth Class of the Fourth Week, but this time the tempo is accelerated.

Exercise 6

Demi-rond de jambe à terre en dehors and en dedans (start 2nd), plié, in 1st, eight counts, facing the barre.

Students repeat Exercise 6 of the Fourth Class of this week.

Exercise 7

Position on the cou-de-pied devant, in 1st, eight counts, facing the barre.

Students repeat Exercise 7 of the Second Class of this week.

Exercise 8

Adagio: lift the leg 2nd à la demi-hauteur, in 1st, eight counts, facing the barre.

Students repeat Exercise 8 of the Fourth Class of this week.

Exercise 9

Relevé in 1st, start and end with plié, eight counts, facing the barre.

On 1, plié; on 2, relevé directly from the plié; on 3 and 4, hold the position; on 5, roll down; on 6, bring both legs down into plié; on 7, stretch the knees; on 8, hold the position. Repeat three more times. At the end, hold the last relevé and balance releasing the arms in 1st.

Explanation. Students are introduced to the relevé starting and ending with a plié. Whereas students must control the ascent and descent of the feet evenly in the roll-up, in the relevé with plié, students bring their feet onto demi-pointes sharply. The landing is performed more smoothly. In the relevé, students must not bring their feet closer (as in trying to touch the heels). The plié before the relevé, in this introductory exercise, takes a full count to get a good push onto the floor. The instructor will check for potential sickling, rolling on the big toe, or clawing of the toes (which must be elongated and pressed firmly on the floor). Students must

refrain from looking down at their feet. When coming down, the feet first roll down, and, without pause, once the heels touch the floor, the knees start bending. This is to avoid having the plié occurring too soon, when the heels are still up. The practice of bending the knees prematurely, if unchecked, may become a habit that could create unnecessary bulk on the thighs. It also tends to weaken the work of the adductors.

Music. A sharp 4/4 works well.

Application. This relevé demands a good control of the position of the foot on demi-pointe. More roll-ups should still be practiced, especially for students taking ballet once or twice a week.

Exercise 10

Bending forward, in 6th, back to the barre.

Students repeat Exercise 9 of the Second Class of this week.

CENTER

Exercise 11

Adagio: plié in 1st, port de bras performed separately.

On 1 and 2, plié; on 3 and 4, stretch both knees; on "and" 5 and 6, bring the arms down; on 7, bring them to 1st; on 8, open them 2nd, with the head following the right arm, and straighten the head. Repeat three more times, alternating turning the head toward the right arm and the left arm.

Explanation. This exercise is similar to the one practiced at the barre, except the tempo is a bit faster than the one used for the first plié exercise at the barre.

Exercise 12

Battement tendu devant and 2nd, in 1st, four counts.

On 1 and 2, battement tendu devant; on 3 and 4, close 1st; on 5 and 6, battement tendu 2nd; on 7 and 8, close 1st. Repeat one more time with the right foot. Repeat the whole exercise one more time.

Explanation. Students repeat Exercise 12 of the Fifth Class of the Fourth Week, except the tempo is a bit faster. Students are reminded of the different head positions that were learned at the barre, when the working leg is 4th devant and when the leg is 2nd.

Music. A more energetic 4/4 can be used here.

Exercise 13

Preparation for battement jeté 2nd in 1st, eight counts.

Students repeat Exercise 14 of the Second Class of this week.

Exercise 14

Demi-rond de jambe à terre en dehors, plié, in 1st, eight counts.

Students repeat Exercise 13 of the Second Class of this week.

Exercise 15

Soubresaut in 2nd and 1st, two counts, one count hold.

Students repeat Exercise 16 of the Fourth Class of this week.

Exercise 16

Small bouncing jumps, in 6th, on the count, review.

Following the preparatory port de bras, bring the arms down.

On "and," push off the floor; on 1, land in plié. Repeat three more times, landing on the count each time, without traveling. On 5 and 6, stretch the knees; on 7 and 8, hold the position in 6th. Repeat three more times.

Explanation. Students are reviewing this exercise with the arms down this time. The arms do not bounce, and the heels come down each time in the plié.

Exercise 17

Curtsey.

Sixth Week

§

FIRST CLASS

Students repeat the material of the Fifth Class of the Fifth Week.

SECOND CLASS

Exercise 1

Battement tendu 2nd, bend to the side, in 1st, facing the barre.

On 1 and 2, battement tendu 2nd; on 3 and 4, close 1st; from 5 to 8, repeat; on 1, bring the left arm to 1st; on 2, bring it to 5th; on 3 and 4, turn the head to the right and bend toward the right side; on 5 and 6, straighten up, bring the head de face; on 7, bring the arm down to 1st; on 8, turn the hand facing down and rest the hand on the barre. After executing the battement tendu 2nd with the left leg, bring the right arm to 5th and bend toward the left side. Repeat the whole exercise one more time. At the end, both arms are brought to 5th and held in position.

Explanation. Students are reviewing the battement tendu 2nd and the bending to the side.

Music. The tempo is fairly slow for this first exercise of the barre, especially for the bending.

Exercise 2

Preparatory port de bras, four counts, plié in 2nd and 1st, port de bras performed separately.

Students repeat Exercise 2 of the Fifth Class of the Fifth Week.

Exercise 3

Battement tendu devant and 2nd, in 1st, four counts.

Students repeat Exercise 3 of the Fourth Class of the Fifth Week.

Exercise 4

Battement tendu 2nd, bring the foot down in 2nd, point the foot and close, in 1st, eight counts, facing the barre.

Students repeat Exercise 4 of the Fifth Class of the Fifth Week.

Exercise 5

Battement tendu 4th position derrière (back), broken down, in 1st, eight counts, facing the barre.

On "and" 1, brush the right foot derrière, stretching the instep of the foot up, still with the big toe on the floor, the head turning slightly toward the left; on 2, hold the position; on 3, point the toes, with only the big toe resting on the floor; on 4, hold the position; on 5, bring the big toe down, still holding the instep up; on 6, hold the position; on "and" 7, brush the foot into 1st, re-aligning the pelvis and straightening the head; on 8, hold the position. Repeat the exercise one more time with the right foot. When performing the exercise with the left foot, the head turns toward the right side. At the end, roll up and hold balance.

Explanation. Students are introduced to the battement tendu derrière performed facing the barre to help them keep the back and torso straight. For this introduction, students have eight counts to perform each battement tendu. Like for the battement tendu devant, the toe should ideally be aligned with the edge of the supporting heel. In order to do so, students must draw their foot slightly inside of the line of the toe when the foot is in 1st. Realistically, a slight deviation is preferable if students do not have the turn-out to achieve this alignment while being balanced. The big toe must initiate the drawing out of the foot, while the thigh remains turned out and the heel of the working foot is lowered. In the battement tendu devant and 2nd, the pelvis is slightly lifted to allow the weight to remain on the supporting leg. However, in the battement tendu derrière, the pelvis not only lifts but also slightly swings backward so that the turn-out of the working leg is maintained with the knee facing sideways.[10] However, in pivoting the pelvis to

---

10   Hertsens, *Ballet Technique*, 79.

maintain the turn-out, students must not bring the hip of the supporting leg forward and open the pelvis on the side of the working leg too much; doing so would make them lose balance. When closing, it is important to re-align the pelvis into proper position as soon as possible. The weight of the body stays on the supporting leg. Students must really pull up their torso as they start drawing out their working leg. Unlike in the battements tendus 4th devant and 2nd, only the upper side of the big toe, resting lightly on the floor, remains in contact with the floor in the battement tendu derrière, so that the foot remains turned out when viewed sideways. Notice the position of the head, which is turned at about a 45° angle toward the side of the supporting leg.

Application. Because of the particular position of the pelvis, the turn-out is always more difficult to perform when the working leg is back. For students taking ballet once or even twice a week, this exercise will come later.

Exercise 6

Preparation for chassé à terre 2nd, without transfer, in 1st, four counts, facing the barre.

On 1, plié; on 2, slide the right foot on the floor to 2nd position while in plié; on 3, without stretching the legs, slide the working foot toward the supporting foot into 1st; on 4, stretch both knees. Repeat one more time with the right foot. At the end, plié, relevé and hold balance.

Explanation. This is only a preparatory exercise for the chassé à terre, in which the working foot slides onto the floor to an open position (in 2nd in this particular exercise) while remaining in plié, and slides back into 1st. The working foot does not slide beyond the 2nd position. When sliding out, the weight is transferred to the center of both legs in 2nd, and coming back, the weight is transferred onto the supporting leg first (just enough to be able to slide the working foot) before shifting it onto both legs in 1st. The hips do not turn toward the working leg but remain parallel to the barre.

Music. A medium-tempo waltz would work well here.

Application. This exercise can be practiced by most beginning students in a recreational program. It familiarizes students more with the transfer of weight from the 1st to the 2nd

position and vice versa. Dragging the foot along the floor as done in this exercise may seem inelegant; however, this friction of the foot on the floor pays off later when such action is needed in allegro or pointe combinations.

Exercise 7

Preparation for battement jeté devant and 2nd, in 1st, eight counts.

On 1 and 2, battement tendu devant; on 3, battement à la demi-hauteur; on 4, hold the position; on 5, lower the leg, bringing the pointed foot down onto the floor; on 6, hold the position; on 7 and 8, close 1st. Repeat in 2nd. Repeat the whole exercise one more time.

Explanation. This time students are performing the exercise sideways with the arm 2nd. As in the battement tendu exercise done sideways, the head is slightly away from the barre for the battement devant and straight for the battement 2nd. Students do not pull the barre, especially when they perform the battement in 2nd.

Music. The tempo is slightly accelerated.

Application. For students taking ballet fewer times a week, this exercise should be practiced while still facing the barre.

Exercise 8

Demi-rond de jambe à terre en dehors and en dedans (starting 2nd), plié, in 1st, eight counts, facing the barre.

Students repeat Exercise 6 of the Fourth Class of the Fifth Week.

Exercise 9

Position on the cou-de-pied derrière, in 1st, eight counts, facing the barre.

On 1, bring the right foot on the cou-de-pied in the position derrière; on 2 and 3, hold the position; on 4, extend the working leg 2nd, with the foot pointed onto the floor; on 5 and 6, hold the position; on 7 and 8, close 1st. Repeat three more times with the right foot.

Explanation. Students have been introduced to the position of the cou-de-pied position devant. Here they are performing the exercise with the working foot on the cou-de-pied derrière. The working knee is firmly pulled to the side and the foot derrière is not sickled. On the cou-de-pied derrière, the foot has the same shape

The foot is on the cou-de-pied derrière.

that it has when it is on the cou-de-pied devant. The inside face of the heel is against the outside face of the ankle with the forefoot pointed and lifted. The bending movement of the leg is brisk but controlled. In the extension 2nd, the thigh remains as still as possible. Students must be able to release the barre at any time to make sure their weight is on the supporting leg. Students will avoid stretching the leg in the air, then lower the leg to point the foot onto the floor; the pointed toes touch the floor directly at the end of the extension of the leg. The back thigh muscles of the supporting leg must be kept tight.

Application. When asked to bring their foot on the cou-de-pied derrière, beginner students tend to turn in their foot, pointing their toes down instead of up. The instructor of recreational students must be particularly careful that students always push their heel forward, both on the cou-de-pied devant and derrière. When extending the leg out, the foot adjusts so that it is fully pointed by the time the toes touch the floor.

Exercise 10

Adagio: lift the leg 2nd à la demi-hauteur, in 1st, eight counts, facing the barre.

Students repeat Exercise 8 of the Fourth Class of the Fifth Week.

Exercise 11

Relevé in 1st, start and end with plié, eight counts, facing the barre.

Students repeat Exercise 9 of the Fifth Class of the Fifth Week.

Exercise 12

Bending forward, in 6th, back to the barre.

Students repeat Exercise 9 of the Second Class of the Fifth Week.

CENTER

Exercise 13

Adagio: plié in 1st, port de bras performed separately.

Students repeat Exercise 11 of the Fifth Class of the Fifth Week.

Exercise 14

Battement tendu devant and 2nd, in 1st, four counts.

Students repeat Exercise 12 of the Fifth Class of the Fifth Week.

Exercise 15

Soubresaut in 2nd and 1st, two counts, one count hold.

Students repeat Exercise 16 of the Fourth Class of the Fifth Week.

Exercise 16

Small bouncing jumps, in 6th, on the count, review.

Students repeat Exercise 16 of the Fifth Class of the Fifth Week.

Exercise 17

Curtsey.

THIRD CLASS

Students repeat the material of the Second Class of this week.

FOURTH CLASS

Exercise 1

Battement tendu 2nd, bend to the sides, in 1st, facing the barre.

Students repeat Exercise 1 of the Second Class of this week.

Exercise 2

Plié in 2nd and 1st, port de bras performed separately.

Students repeat Exercise 2 of the Fifth Class of the Fifth Week.

Exercise 3

Battement tendu 2nd, bring the foot down in 2nd, point the foot and close, with transfer, in 1st, eight counts, facing the barre.

On 1 and 2, battement tendu 2nd; on 3, bring the foot down in 2nd; on 4, hold the position; on 5, point the left foot, transferring the weight onto the right leg; on 6, hold the position; on 7 and 8, close 1st. Repeat one more time with the right foot.

Explanation. Students are switching supporting legs in this exercise, while sliding their hands along the barre to accommodate the lateral travel from one leg onto another. Both feet should be lined up in 2nd when the foot comes down. If they are not, that means that the trajectory of the working foot is off, and one leg was turned out more than the other.

Application. All beginners will benefit from this exercise to feel the transfer of weight from one leg to another.

Exercise 4

Battement tendu derrière, broken down, in 1st, eight counts, facing the barre.

Students repeat Exercise 5 of the Second Class of this week.

Exercise 5

Preparation for chassé à terre 2nd, without transfer, in 1st, four counts, facing the barre.

Students repeat Exercise 6 of the Second Class of this week.

Exercise 6

Preparation for battement jeté devant and 2nd, in 1st, eight counts.

Students repeat Exercise 7 of the Second Class of this week.

Exercise 7

Demi-rond de jambe à terre en dehors and en dedans (starting 2nd), plié, in 1st, eight counts, facing the barre.

Students repeat Exercise 6 of the Fourth Class of the Fifth Week.

Exercise 8

Position on the cou-de-pied derrière, in 1st, eight counts, facing the barre.

Students repeat Exercise 9 of the Second Class of this week.

Exercise 9

Adagio: lift the leg 2nd à la demi-hauteur, in 1st, eight counts, facing the barre.

Students repeat Exercise 8 of the Fourth Class of the Fifth Week.

Exercise 10

Relevé in 1st, start and end with plié, eight counts, facing the barre.

Students repeat Exercise 9 of the Fifth Class of the Fifth Week.

Exercise 11

Bending forward, in 6th, back to the barre.

Students repeat Exercise 9 of the Second Class of the Fifth Week.

CENTER

Exercise 12

Adagio: plié in 1st, port de bras performed separately.

Students repeat Exercise 11 of the Fifth Class of the Fifth Week.

Exercise 13

Battement tendu devant and 2nd, in 1st, four counts.

Students repeat Exercise 12 of the Fifth Class of the Fifth Week.

Exercise 14

Battement tendu 2nd, bring the foot down, point the foot and close, without transfer, with port de bras, in 1st, eight counts.

On 1 and 2, battement tendu 2nd; on 3, bring the foot down, bringing the arms in 1st; on 4, hold the position; on 5, point the right foot, opening the arms 2nd; on 6, hold the position; on 7 and 8, close 1st. Repeat one more time with the right foot.

Explanation. This exercise is similar to Exercise 5 of the Fifth Class of the Fourth Week, this time performed in the center, accompanied with a simple port de bras. They must shift their weight properly from one foot onto two feet, and back again onto one before closing.

Exercise 15

Soubresaut in 2nd and 1st, two counts, one count hold.

Students repeat Exercise 16 of the Fourth Class of the Fifth Week.

Exercise 16

Échappé 2nd, in 1st, four counts, facing the barre.

On "and," plié; on 1, spring off the floor opening the legs 2nd; on 2, land in plié in 2nd; on "and," directly out of the plié, spring off the floor; on 3, land in plié in 1st; on 4, stretch both legs. Repeat three more times. After a pause, repeat the exercise.

Explanation. The échappé 2nd is now performed without holding between both jumps. The turn-out of the legs is maintained throughout. The second jump is performed more quickly and is not as high as the first one, since it starts with the legs spread out, which makes the takeoff more difficult. Like in other jump exercises, the heels do not rise in the plié and the legs are fully stretched in the air. The instructor will particularly pay attention to those students who tend to turn in their legs just as they stretch them out of the plié in the takeoff (the "kissing of the knees" condition). This bad habit can be difficult to catch because of the speed of motion. In any case, once identified, it must be corrected right away, for, otherwise, it will impede the progression of the allegro, especially in the performance of batterie (beating) where utmost turn-out is required. It could also lead to injuries to knees and ankles.

Music. A medium-tempo 6/8 or a 2/4 march for this exercise would work well so that students jump as high as they can in the first jump.

Application. For many beginners in a recreational program, the practice of the échappé broken down at the barre may last longer to get the movement right.

Exercise 17

Small bouncing jumps, in 6th, on the count, review.

Students repeat Exercise 16 of the Fifth Class of the Fifth Week.

Exercise 18

Preparatory exercise for the marche with battement tendu devant, close after each step, in 1st, with port de bras.

Start at the back of the studio and travel forward. Following the preparatory port de bras, bring the arms down.

On 1 and 2, battement tendu devant with the right foot, bringing the arms in low 1st; on "and" 3, open the arms 2nd with the head following the movement of the right arm; on 4, step forward onto the right leg and close 1st, straightening the head and closing the arms down.

On 5 and 6, battement tendu devant with the left foot, bringing the arms in low 1st; on "and" 7, open the arms 2nd with the head following the movement of the left arm; on 8, step forward onto the left leg and close 1st, straightening the head and closing the arms. Repeat several times, alternating legs.

Explanation. This is a very basic version of the standard ballet march. The closing after each step is done informally, since students have not yet been introduced to the brushing of the working foot through the 1st. Students must keep a very erect back and torso and raise their chin slightly upward. Here the head remains straight when the leg brushes out devant (unlike in the regular battement tendu exercise in which the head usually turns to the same side of the working leg), since students coordinate the movement of the head, starting with the position de face, with the opening of the arms 2nd.

Music. A largo waltz would be suitable here.

Application. This is another exercise for beginner students to carry themselves with elegance and majesty. This exercise can even be practiced with legs in parallel for a pre-ballet or beginner class in a recreational program.

Exercise 19

Curtsey.

FIFTH CLASS

Exercise 1

Battement tendu 2nd, bend to the sides, in 1st, facing the barre.

Students repeat Exercise 1 of the Second Class of this week.

Exercise 2

Plié in 2nd and 1st, port de bras performed separately.

Students repeat Exercise 2 of the Fifth Class of the Fifth Week.

Exercise 3

Battement tendu 2nd, bring the foot down in 2nd, point the foot and close, with transfer, in 1st, eight counts, facing the barre.

Students repeat Exercise 3 of the Fourth Class of this week.

Exercise 4

Battement tendu en croix en dehors (devant, 2nd, derrière, 2nd), in 1st, four counts, facing the barre.

On 1 and 2, battement tendu devant, turning the head slightly toward the right; on 3 and 4, close 1st, straightening the head; on 5 and 6, battement tendu 2nd; on 7 and 8, close; on 1 and 2, battement tendu derrière, turning the head slightly toward the left side; on 3 and 4, close straightening the head; on 5 and 6, battement tendu 2nd; on 7 and 8, close. Repeat the whole exercise one more time. At the end, roll up and hold balance.

Explanation. This exercise introduces students to the concept of executing an exercise en croix (that is, in the shape of a cross). It describes an exercise executed 4th devant, 2nd, and 4th derrière, or vice versa. Students are facing the barre to help keep the body straight. Students are reminded of the different head positions when the working leg changes direction. When students perform the exercise sideways, they will be introduced to yet another head position accompanying the battement tendu derrière.

The head is turned away from the working leg in the battement tendu derrière.

Application. As mentioned earlier, the alignment of the working toes with the heel of the supporting foot may need slight adjustment for students who lack turn-out, especially in a recreational program. In this case, the working foot is to draw along a line that is slightly outside of the line of the supporting heel.

Exercise 5

Battement tendu 2nd, in plié, stretch the leg after pointing, in 1st, four counts, facing the barre.

On 1, plié; on 2, battement tendu 2nd directly out of the plié; on 3, stretch the supporting knee; on 4, close in 1st. Repeat the exercise three more times, alternating legs. At the end, roll up and hold balance.

Explanation. Students are now starting the battement tendu in plié. Performing such an exercise is a useful practice, since many steps start with the working foot extending out of the closed position in plié. It is also a wonderful exercise to develop the turn-out of the lower leg and the foot.

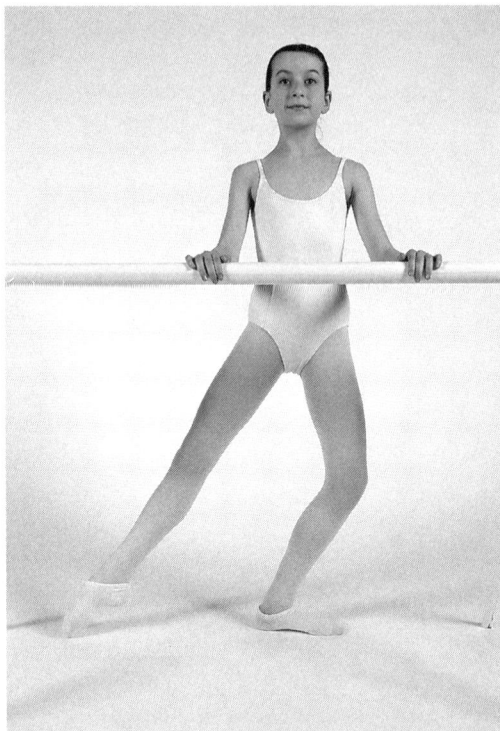

The working leg is extended 2nd position with a plié on the supporting leg.

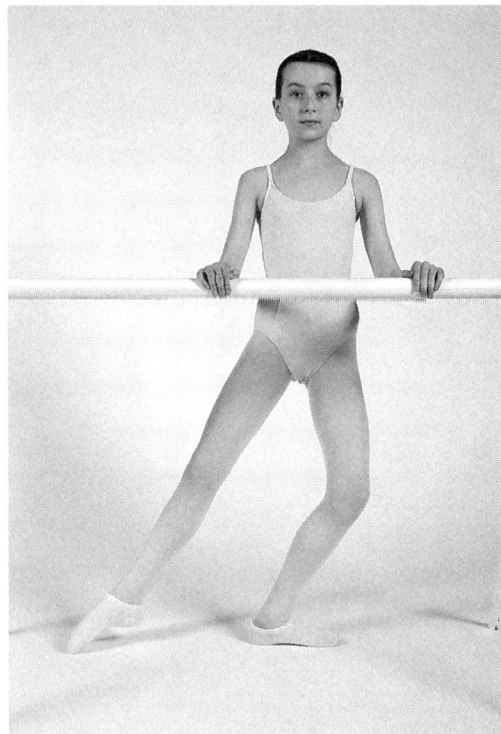

The working foot sags when pointing 2nd position.

In this exercise, students keep their foot fully pointed throughout the battement tendu. In the first part of the battement tendu, the working leg extends directly from the plié, pointing the foot with energy. For this reason, students must have already achieved a good control of the foot muscles, otherwise the working foot may sag as they perform the battement tendu in plié. When sliding out of the plié, the foot is still flat through the half 2nd. In other words, to get most benefit from the exercise, the heel, always pushed forward, remains on the floor as long as possible, but without transferring the weight off the supporting leg. The toes slide in when stretching the supporting knee, since the toes come closer to the supporting heel. Students do not move their supporting hip or leg forward in trying to achieve more turn-out of the working leg.

Music. A 2/4 tango, medium tempo, would work well here.

Application. This exercise is recommended for all beginners, as long as their feet have acquired enough strength to keep pointing throughout the exercise.

Exercise 6

Preparation for chassé à terre 2nd, without transfer, in 1st, four counts, facing the barre.

Students repeat Exercise 6 of the Second Class of this week.

Exercise 7

Preparation for battement jeté devant and 2nd, in 1st, eight counts.

Students repeat Exercise 7 of the Second Class of this week.

Exercise 8

Preparation for battement jeté derrière, in 1st, eight counts, facing the barre.

On 1 and 2, battement tendu derrière, turning the head slightly toward the left; on 3, bring sharply the leg à la demi-hauteur; on 4, hold the position; on 5, lower the leg, bringing the toes down; on 6, hold the position; on 7 and 8, close in 1st, straightening the head. Repeat three more times, alternating legs.

Explanation. To keep the torso as straight as possible, students face the barre in this exercise. They lift their lower abdomen and keep their shoulders straight when lifting the leg. As discussed in the exercise of battement tendu derrière, the position of the leg requires a slightly lifted pelvis with a pivot to keep the leg turned out. The position of the head is the same as the one in the battement tendu 4th derrière.

Exercise 9

Demi-rond de jambe à terre en dehors and en dedans (start 4th derrière), in 1st, eight counts, facing the barre.

On 1 and 2, battement tendu devant; on 3 and 4, demi-rond de jambe en dehors; on 5 and 6, close 1st; on 7 and 8, hold the position. On 1 and 2, battement tendu derrière; on 3 and 4, demi-rond de jambe en dedans to 2nd position; on 5 and 6, close 1st; on 7 and 8, hold the position. Repeat the exercise one more time, alternating en dehors and en dedans. At the end, roll up in 1st, hold balance.

Explanation. Here the rond de jambe en dedans starts with a battement tendu 4th position derrière. The toes then draw an arc to the 2nd position. In both kinds of ronds de jambe, the maximum turn-out and tautness of the whole leg are maintained throughout. The rotation of the head of the femur in the hip socket required in the demi-rond de jambe en dedans can be tricky for beginners. Its timing can present an even greater challenge. As soon as the leg moves away from the back position, it must start rotating so that, by the time it arrives 2nd, the leg has achieved the desired turned-out position.

Exercise 10

Position on the cou-de-pied derrière, in 1st, eight counts, facing the barre.

Students repeat Exercise 9 of the Second Class of this week.

Exercise 11

Relevé in 2nd and 1st, four counts, facing the barre.

Following the preparatory port de bras, battement tendu with the right foot 2nd, and bring the foot down.

On 1, plié; on 2, relevé; on 3, come down in plié; on 4, stretch both knees. Repeat twice more. Point the right foot and close 1st. Repeat the exercise in 1st. Repeat the exercise starting

The working foot slides through 2nd position, with the lower leg pushed forward.

with a battement tendu 2nd with the left foot and closing with the left foot. At the end, hold balance on demi-pointes in 1st position holding the arms in 1st.

Explanation. Students are introduced to the relevé in 2nd. Each relevé is now on four counts. The coming down into plié is performed directly, still without the knees bending before the heels touch the floor. No adjustment is made once the feet come down into plié. The feet in 2nd are not wider than one foot apart so that the insteps are as much as possible above the toes. A correct placement and a pulled up back are maintained.

Application. When students in a recreational program are introduced to the relevé with plié, they would benefit from starting first with parallel feet to maintain their feet very straight on demi-pointes.

Exercise 12

Bending forward, back to the barre, cambré (bend backward) facing the barre, in 6th.

Stand a short distance from the barre, the back facing the barre. Following the preparatory port de bras, rest the hands on the barre, keeping the elbows relaxed.

On 1 and 2, bend forward, keeping the back as flat as possible without pushing the weight back and keeping the weight on the legs, still holding the barre; on 3 and 4, relax the back and the head, to bring the torso closer to the knees for further stretching; on 5 and 6, with the head leading the movement, flatten the back again; on 7 and 8, straighten up to the upright position, lengthening the back, and aligning the pelvis as soon as possible. Repeat three more times. Turn to face the barre. From 1 to 4, lift the upper back and bend the back, keeping the head straight; from 5 to 8, straighten up. Repeat three more times.

Explanation. Students are repeating the bending forward in 6th position. Students are also introduced to the cambré. Note that the term cambré in the French school means only bending backward. Its practice must be carefully monitored, for an incorrect move or position is aesthetically unappealing and can lead to injuries, especially in the lower back. At this stage, students must learn *how* to initiate the bend and should not be expected to fold their back at a sharp angle, even those whose back is flexible. The first rule to follow is to pull up the lumbar spine when initiating the cambré, without raising the shoulders. It is like trying to curve the back around an imaginary bar at the level of the thoracic spine. Students must not bend their neck or let the head collapse back from the pull of gravity. The side muscles of the neck must be activated to keep the neck controlled. Keeping the pelvis placed correctly, the abdominal muscles tight for the safety of the extension, and the proper return to the upright position are equally important.[11] Students must not stick their buttocks out or bend their knees. Overall, in learning the cambré, students must not let the pull of gravity lead the movement; they should be able to control the bending by using the right muscles. The head is held straight, for rotating it at this stage could cause the shoulders to be uneven and the back to bend askew.

Music. A slow waltz is an appropriate musical choice.

Application. This approach to learning the cambré is the same, whether students take ballet recreationally or more seriously.

11   Grieg, *Inside Ballet Technique*, 24.

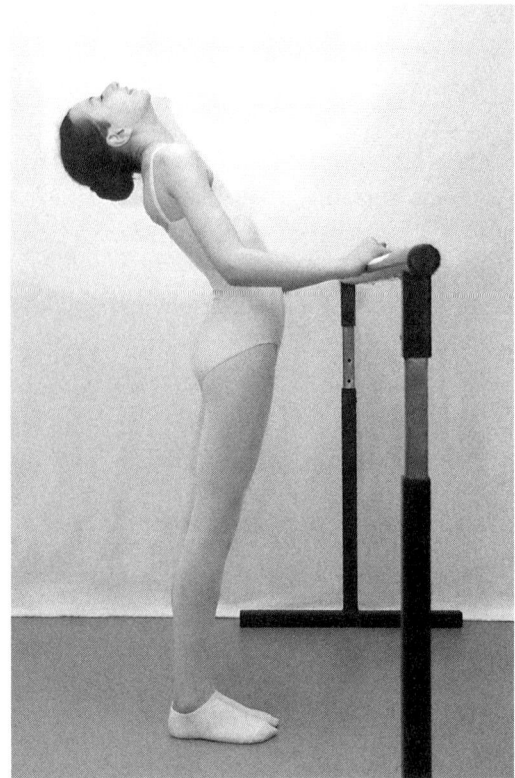

The neck is incorrectly bent and the back is not lengthened.

CENTER

Exercise 13

Adagio: plié in 1st, port de bras performed separately.

Students repeat Exercise 11 of the Fifth Class of the Fifth Week.

Exercise 14

Battement tendu 2nd, bring the foot down, point the foot and close, without transfer, with port de bras, in 1st, eight counts.

Students repeat Exercise 14 of the Fourth Class of this week.

Exercise 15

Demi-rond de jambe à terre en dehors and en dedans (start 2nd), in 1st.

On 1 and 2, battement tendu devant; on 3 and 4, draw a quarter of a circle to the 2nd position; on 5 and 6, close 1st; on 7 and 8, hold the position. On 1 and 2, battement tendu 2nd; on 3 and 4, draw a quarter of a circle to the 4th position devant; on 5 and 6, close 1st; on 7 and 8, hold the position. Repeat the exercise one more time with the right foot.

Explanation. Students are performing the rond de jambe en dehors and en dedans in the center.

Music. The tempo is slightly faster than the one used for the same exercise at the barre.

Application. Again this type of exercise may still be too challenging for recreational students, who are unlikely to have enough control of their turn-out to keep proper balance during the exercise.

Exercise 16

Soubresaut in 2nd and 1st, two counts, one count hold.

Students repeat Exercise 16 of the Fourth Class of the Fifth Week.

Exercise 17

Échappé 2nd, in 1st, four counts, facing the barre.

Students repeat Exercise 16 of the Fourth Class of this week.

Exercise 18

Preparatory exercise for the marche with battement tendu devant, close after each step, in 1st, with port de bras.

Students repeat Exercise 18 of the Fourth Class of this week.

Exercise 19

Introduction to balancé in 6th [pas balancé—Vaganova], traveling forward, flat-footed, four counts, hands on the waist.

In the preparatory port de bras, bring the arms in 1st, and then bring the hands onto the waist, as performed in Exercise 13 of the Second Class of the Third Week.

On 1 and 2, battement tendu forward with the right foot; on 3, step onto the right foot in plié, bending the left leg and bringing the left foot pointed next to the right ankle; on 4, transfer the weight onto the back leg, flat-footed, stretching both legs and pointing the front foot; on "and," step onto the right foot; on 5 and 6, brush the back foot forward, pointing the foot; on 7, step on the left foot in plié, bending the right leg and bringing the right foot next to the left ankle; on 8, transfer the weight onto the back leg, flat-footed, stretching both legs, and pointing the front foot. Repeat several times traveling forward. After a pause, repeat the exercise.

Explanation. This is the most basic and easiest introduction of the balancé. It is a kind of waltz, the difference being one of quality of the movement. Unlike the waltz (pas de valse), which involves a flowing and smooth motion with an emphasis on the upward part of the movement, the balancé has a more detached aspect, with a regular pattern of coming down and going up. It is also easier to learn for beginners. This pattern will appear more sharply when the balancé is practiced on demi-pointe. The step can be practiced even by pre-ballet students.

Music. The music, a medium-tempo waltz, of course, will have clear beats to help define each movement.

Exercise 20

Curtsey.

Seventh Week

§

FIRST CLASS

Students repeat the material of the Fifth Class of the Sixth Week.

SECOND CLASS

Exercise 1

Battement tendu 2nd, flex the foot, battement tendu 2nd, turn the leg in and out, in 1st, facing the barre.

On 1 and 2, battement tendu 2nd; on 3, flex the toes; on 4, flex the rest of the foot; on 5, stretch the instep out; on 6, point the toes, bringing the pointed foot onto the floor; on 7 and 8, close 1st.

On 1 and 2, battement tendu 2nd; on 3 and 4, turn in the leg; on 5 and 6, turn out the leg; on 7 and 8, close 1st. Repeat the whole exercise one more time.

Explanation. Here students are combining two kinds of joint movements in this battement tendu exercise: the first involving the foot, and the second involving the hip. The hips are maintained parallel to the barre, and the torso is kept straight and pulled up throughout the exercise.

Exercise 2

Plié in 2nd and 1st, port de bras performed separately.

Students repeat Exercise 2 of the Fifth Class of the Fifth Week.

Exercise 3

Battement tendu 2nd, bring the foot down in 2nd, point the foot and close, with transfer, in 1st, eight counts, facing the barre.

Students repeat Exercise 3 of the Fourth Class of the Sixth Week.

Exercise 4

Battement tendu en croix en dehors (devant, 2nd, derrière, 2nd), in 1st, four counts, facing the barre.

Students repeat Exercise 4 of the Fifth Class of the Sixth Week.

Exercise 5

Battement tendu 2nd, in plié, stretch the leg when pointed, in 1st, four counts, facing the barre.

Students repeat Exercise 5 of the Fifth Class of the Sixth Week.

Exercise 6

Preparation for battement jeté devant and 2nd, in 1st, eight counts.

Students repeat Exercise 7 of the Second Class of the Sixth Week.

Exercise 7

Preparation for battement jeté derrière, eight counts, facing the barre.

Students repeat Exercise 8 of the Fifth Class of the Sixth Week.

Exercise 8

Demi-rond de jambe à terre en dehors and en dedans (start derrière), in 1st, eight counts, facing the barre.

Students repeat Exercise 9 of the Fifth Class of the Sixth Week.

Exercise 9

Preparation for battement frappé 2nd, in 1st, four counts, facing the barre.

On 1, bring the foot on the cou-de-pied devant, turning the head slightly toward the right; on 2, hold the position; on 3, extend the leg in 2nd, pointing the foot onto the floor, straightening the head; on 4, close in 1st; on 5, bring the foot on the cou-de-pied derrière, turning the head slightly toward the left; on 6, hold the position; on 7, extend the leg in 2nd, straightening the head; on 8, close in 1st. Repeat the exercise one more time with the right foot devant and derrière. At the end, bring the working foot on the cou-de-pied devant and hold balance on one foot, with the arms in low 1st, and the head held straight. To close, extend the leg 2nd.

Explanation. Students are introduced to the basic movement of the battement frappé in which the working foot strikes the supporting leg (at the cou-de-pied level) and the leg extends out forcefully. The battement frappé prepares for the vivacity and energy needed in the small allegro. In this preparatory exercise, students extend their leg 2nd like shooting an arrow, yet without kicking the leg out (this is not soccer!), with the knee stretching with control at the end of the extension. Notice the position of the head changing, whether the foot is on the cou-de-pied devant or on the cou-de-pied derrière.

Exercise 10

Adagio: lift the leg in 4th position devant and 2nd, in 1st, eight counts, facing the barre.

On 1 and 2, battement tendu devant; on 3 and 4, lift the leg à la demi-hauteur; on 5 and 6, lower the leg, and point the foot onto the floor; on 7 and 8, close 1st. Repeat the exercise in 2nd. At the end, roll up on demi-pointes and hold the position.

Explanation. Students are now performing lifting the leg devant and 2nd. If space allows, the exercise is done facing the barre. The hips are parallel to the barre. The turn-out is not sacrificed to height. Students line up their working leg devant with the supporting leg, keeping their hips straight. When lifting the leg forward, the hips remain level, and the working hip does not come forward.

Exercise 11

Preparation for the 5th position: battement tendu 2nd, close 5th devant and derrière, start in 1st, four counts, facing the barre.

On 1 and 2, battement tendu 2nd; on 3 and 4, close 5th devant, with the weight on *both* legs, turning the head slightly to the right; on 5 and 6, battement tendu 2nd, straightening the head; on 7 and 8, close 5th devant, turning the head slightly to the right; on 1 and 2, battement tendu 2nd, straightening the head; on 3 and 4, close 1st; on 5 and 6, plié and stretch; on 7 and 8, hold the position.

On 1 and 2, battement tendu 2nd; on 3 and 4, close the foot into 5th derrière, turning the head

slightly to the left; on 5 and 6, battement tendu 2nd, straightening the head; on 7 and 8, close 5th derrière, turning the head slightly to the left; on 1 and 2, battement tendu 2nd, straightening the head; on 3 and 4, close 1st; on 5 and 6, plié and stretch; on 7 and 8, hold the position. At the end, roll up and hold balance.

Explanation. This is the first introduction of the 5th position of the feet. It comes at the end of the barre, when students' hips have had a good warm up. It is the most demanding position for the turn-out of the hips. Notice that the exercise starts in 1st position to avoid the risk of over turning the feet before even starting. It is better for students to experience this position first by actively closing the working leg into 5th and not just planting their feet into it. Students have been using the 1st position for a few weeks. They should be quite comfortable in performing most exercises in 1st and should be able to control the turn-out of both legs with an angle range of no less than 150°. Such control must also include the correct posture of the pelvis and the back.

At this stage of training, most ballet students are not able to achieve the ideal 5th position and should not be forced into it. For this first introduction of crossing the legs, a 3rd position or a not fully closed 5th, with a correct alignment, is more realistic.

Since ballet involves movement, the difficulty of the 5th position is not so much the position itself, but the opening and the closing of the working leg and foot out of and into that position. A large part of the training of the first year is dedicated to perfecting just such actions. In this exercise, when closing the 5th, the leg in 2nd should deviate as little as possible from the 2nd position, as the working foot gets closer and closer to the supporting foot. It should not describe any kind of curve toward the front or the back before closing 5th. Students slide the foot either in front or in the back of the supporting foot with, ideally, a trajectory as parallel as possible to the position of the supporting foot. In doing so, the hips do not turn, the pelvis does not go out of alignment, and the feet do not roll in. As soon as the closing is completed, the whole weight is transferred onto *both* legs. As with the battement tendu in 1st, in the battement tendu in 5th, the toes must not go off the floor when the working foot is drawn out,

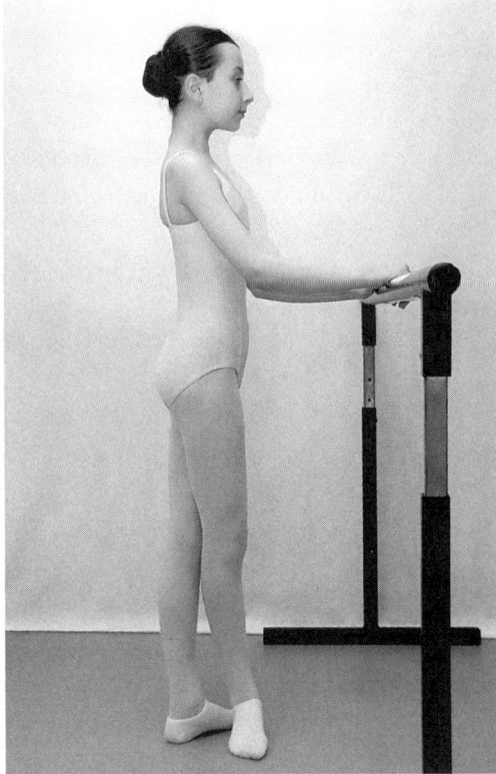

The front leg is more turned out than the back leg in 5th position.

The front knee is bent and the hips are not aligned with the torso.

and students must completely stretch the instep and the toes at the end of the dégagé. When disengaging, the working foot must brush along the same line that the foot had when closing in 5th. It is frequent for ballet students to have more turn-out in one hip than in the other, thus favoring the opening of one foot over the other. However, students must aim to keep the turn-out equal in both legs without adjusting their feet.

Since this manual is aimed for the instruction of students who aspire to become professionals, these students should have by the end of the first year, if not perfect, at least sufficient turn-out to achieve a crossed position that is at least close to the 5th, with the proper alignment, the knees tight, and without rolling in. In any case, the instructor must pace the demands of the turn-out in the 5th position. In no case should the instructor force a tighter feet position than students can achieve from the hips. As said before, turning the feet beyond what the hips permit, besides not improving the turn-out, can cause a wide range of problems, especially in the knees and the ankles. The closing of the 5th must not be done at the expense of bending the knees (especially the

front one). Such bending must be minimized, if not eliminated, not only for the safety of the knee but also to keep the adductors active. It is also important that the closing be done without pushing the pelvis backward. Placement and alignment are more important than tight closing at this stage. In any case, close supervision is needed to implement this increased demand on students' turn-out. Notice the movement of the head as the working foot closes front or back. As a general rule in ballet, the head turns at a 45° angle toward the side of the front foot when the feet are in 5th, and, when the feet are in 2nd, the head is straight. From now on, when students work in 5th, these rules will apply.

Application. Most students in a recreational program, who take ballet classes once or twice a week, are better off practicing the 1st position for a while before they start crossing their feet. They will feel more comfortable and stable while avoiding potential injuries. In fact, it may be realistic to wait a year or even two, especially when students come only once a week, before starting to cross the legs into 3rd or 5th. Many other students, lacking natural hip rotation, are better off to avoid it altogether: They still can enjoy their ballet practice and perform quite a few movements using the 1st position.

Exercise 12

Relevé in 2nd and 1st, four counts, facing the barre.

Students repeat Exercise 11 of the Fifth Class of the Sixth Week.

Exercise 13

Bending forward, back to the barre, cambré, facing the barre, in 6th.

Students repeat Exercise 12 of the Fifth Class of the Sixth Week.

CENTER

Exercise 14

Battement tendu 2nd, bring the foot down, point the foot and close, without transfer, with port de bras, in 1st, eight counts.

Students repeat Exercise 14 of the Fourth Class of the Sixth Week.

Exercise 15

Demi-rond de jambe à terre en dehors and en dedans (start 2nd), in 1st.

Students repeat Exercise 15 of the Fifth Class of the Sixth Week.

Exercise 16

Preparation for battement jeté devant and 2nd in 1st, in 1st, eight counts.

On 1 and 2, battement tendu devant; on 3, battement devant à la demi-hauteur; on 4, hold the position; on 5, lower the leg, bringing the pointed foot down onto the floor; on 6, hold the position; on 7 and 8, close 1st.

On 1 and 2, battement tendu 2nd in 1st; on 3, battement à la demi-hauteur; on 4, hold the position; on 5, lower the leg, bringing the pointed foot down onto the floor; on 6, hold the position; on 7 and 8, close 1st. Repeat exercise one more time with the right foot.

Explanation. Students are repeating the exercise done earlier at the barre.

Exercise 17

Échappé 2nd, in 1st, four counts, facing the barre.

Students repeat Exercise 16 of the Fourth Class of the Sixth Week.

Exercise 18

Introduction to balancé in 6th, traveling forward, flat-footed, four counts, hands on the waist.

Students repeat Exercise 19 of the Fifth Class of the Sixth Week.

Exercise 19

Preparatory exercise for the marche with battement tendu devant, close after each step, in 1st, with port de bras.

Students repeat Exercise 18 of the Fourth Class of the Sixth Week.

Exercise 20

Curtsey.

THIRD CLASS

Students repeat the material of the Second Class of this week.

FOURTH CLASS

Exercise 1

Battement tendu 2nd, flex the foot, battement tendu 2nd, turn the leg in and out, in 1st, facing the barre.

Students repeat Exercise 1 of the Second Class of this week.

Exercise 2

Plié in 2nd and 1st, port de bras performed separately.

Students repeat Exercise 2 of the Fifth Class of the Fifth Week.

Exercise 3

Battement tendu en croix en dehors (devant, 2nd, derrière, 2nd), in 1st, four counts, facing the barre.

Students repeat Exercise 4 of the Fifth Class of Sixth Week.

Exercise 4

Battement tendu 2nd, in plié, stretch the leg when pointing, in 1st, four counts, facing the barre.

Students repeat Exercise 5 of the Fifth Class of the Sixth Week.

Exercise 5

Preparation for battement jeté en croix en dehors, in 1st, eight counts, facing the barre.

On 1 and 2, battement tendu devant; on 3, battement à la demi-hauteur; on 4, hold the position; on 5, lower the leg, bringing the pointed foot onto the floor; on 6, hold the position; on 7 and 8, close 1st. Repeat the exercise 2nd, derrière, and 2nd again. At the end, plié and relevé, balancing with both arms in low 1st.

Explanation. Students are performing the preparatory exercise for battement jeté en croix en dehors. The working leg derrière remains aligned with the supporting leg and does not sway sideways. The knees are very taut throughout the exercise. Students must bring their leg sharply up and down, with a freeze in the air. The head rotates according to the different directions of the working leg when it is extended out.

Exercise 6

Demi-rond de jambe à terre en dehors and en dedans (start derrière), with port de bras, in 1st, eight counts.

Following the preparatory port de bras, bring the arm down.

On 1 and 2, battement tendu devant with the arm coming 1st; on 3 and 4, demi-rond de jambe en dehors while the arm opens 2nd; on 5 and 6, turn the palm down, bring the arm down as the leg closes 1st; on 7 and 8, straighten the head and hold the position.

On 1 and 2, battement tendu derrière with the arm coming to 1st; on 3 and 4, demi-rond de jambe en dedans to 2nd position, with the arm opening 2nd; on 5 and 6, turn the palm down, bring the arm down as the leg closes 1st; on 7 and 8, straighten the head and hold the position. Repeat the exercise one more time. At the end, roll up and hold balance.

Explanation. Both ronds de jambe are performed sideways with a standard port de bras. In stretching the leg backward, the toe initiates the movement until the foot points fully. The arm and leg coordination in this exercise follows a logical pattern: the arm closes when the leg closes and opens when the leg moves 2nd. The

head follows the arm movement as students have learned to practice so far.

Exercise 7

Preparation for battement frappé 2nd, 1st, four counts, facing the barre.

Students repeat Exercise 9 of the Second Class of this week.

Exercise 8

Preparation for the 5th position: battement tendu 2nd, start in 1st, close 5th devant and derriére, four counts, facing the barre.

Students repeat Exercise 11 of the Second Class of this week.

Exercise 9

Preparation for the 5th position: preparation for battement jeté 2nd, start in 1st, close 5th, eight counts, facing the barre.

On 1 and 2, battement tendu 2nd; on 3, battement à la demi-hauteur; on 4, hold the position; on 5, lower the leg, and point the foot onto the floor; on 6, hold the position; on 7 and 8, slide the foot and close 5th devant. Repeat the exercise one more time, closing 1st. Repeat the whole exercise closing derrière.

Explanation. This time students are performing the preparatory exercise for battement jeté 2nd in 5th. Like for the battement tendu, the same attention is given to the opening and the closing of the foot brushing out and in before and after it is in the air. Students apply the same head movement learned in Exercise 11 of the Second Class of this week.

Exercise 10

Adagio: lift the leg devant and 2nd, in 1st, eight counts, facing the barre.

Students repeat Exercise 10 of the Second Class of this week.

Exercise 11

Relevé in 2nd and 1st, four counts, facing the barre.

Students repeat Exercise 11 of the Fifth Class of the Sixth Week.

Exercise 12

Bending forward, back to the barre, cambré, facing the barre, in 6th.

Students repeat Exercise 12 of the Fifth Class of the Sixth Week.

Exercise 13

Battement tendu 2nd, bring the foot down, point the foot, with transfer, with port de bras, in 1st, eight counts.

On 1 and 2, battement tendu 2nd; on 3, bring the foot down in 2nd, bringing the arms in 1st; on 4, hold the position; on 5, point the left foot, while transferring the weight onto the right foot, opening the arms 2nd; on 6, hold the position; on 7 and 8, close 1st. Repeat the whole exercise one more time.

Explanation. Students are switching supporting legs in this exercise, like they have done at the barre earlier. The exercise is also accompanied by a simple port de bras.

Exercise 14

Demi-rond de jambe à terre en dehors and en dedans (start 2nd), in 1st.

Students repeat Exercise 15 of the Fifth Class of the Sixth Week.

Exercise 15

Preparation for battement jeté devant and 2nd, in 1st, eight counts.

Students repeat Exercise 16 of the Second Class of this week.

Exercise 16

Échappé 2nd, in 1st, four counts, facing the barre.

Students repeat Exercise 16 of the Fourth Class of the Sixth Week.

Exercise 17

Introduction to balancé in 6th, traveling forward, flat-footed, four counts, hands on the waist.

Students repeat Exercise 19 of the Fifth Class of the Sixth Week.

Exercise 18

Preparation for déboulés, in 1st, arms in low 1st, each half turn on one count, hold one count, review.

Students repeat Exercise 17 of the Fifth

Class of the Fourth Week, except the tempo is accelerated.

Exercise 19

Curtsey.

FIFTH CLASS

Exercise 1

Battement tendu 2nd, flex the foot, battement tendu 2nd, turn the leg in and out, in 1st, facing the barre.

Students repeat Exercise 1 of the Second Class of this week.

Exercise 2

Plié in 2nd and 1st, separate port de bras.

Students repeat Exercise 2 of the Fifth Class of the Fifth Week.

Exercise 3

Battement tendu en croix, in 1st, four counts.

On 1 and 2, battement tendu devant, keeping the head turned slightly toward the right; on 3 and 4, close 1st, straightening the head; on 5 and 6, battement tendu 2nd; on 7 and 8, close; on 1 and 2, battement tendu derrière, tilting the head very slightly toward the left shoulder, while turning it toward the right arm so that the eyes are focused on the right hand; on 3 and 4, close, straightening the head; on 5 and 6, battement tendu 2nd; on 7 and 8, close. Repeat the exercise one more time.

Explanation. Students are practicing the exercise sideways. They are introduced to another head position in the battement tendu derrière. This particular position used to be much more common; turning the head toward the barre at a 45° angle, when the battement tendu derrière is performed sideways, is now favored, even by the Paris Opera Ballet School. Yet students should be familiar with both positions. The shoulders remain straight as they turn their head to different directions. Only the head moves, and not the torso.

Exercise 4

Preparation for chassé à terre 2nd, with transfer, stretch the legs, in 1st, four counts, facing the barre.

On 1, plié; on 2, slide the right foot on the floor to 2nd position while in plié; on 3, stretch both legs, transferring the weight onto the right leg, while pointing the left foot 2nd; on 4, close 1st. Repeat three more times, alternating legs. At the end, plié, relevé, and hold balance.

Explanation. Unlike in the previous preparatory exercise for chassé à terre, students are switching supporting legs following the plié. This exercise is one step closer to the real chassé, in which the first leg is like being pushed away and the second leg takes the place that the first leg had at the beginning of the exercise. The hands move along the barre so that they are in front of the shoulders. The toes remain on the floor when the foot is fully pointed.

Music. A medium-tempo waltz works well for this exercise.

Application. This exercise can be practiced by most beginners.

Exercise 5

Battement tendu 2nd, start and close in plié, in 1st, four counts, facing the barre.

On 1, plié; on 2, battement tendu 2nd, staying in plié; on 3, close in 1st still in plié; on 4, stretch the knees. Repeat the exercise three more times, alternating legs. At the end, roll up and hold balance.

Explanation. Students remain in plié all the way through the exercise, instead of stretching after the first part of the battement tendu. The working hip must not come down. The brushing in is as close to the floor as the brushing out. Even though the working foot is sliding out close to the floor, the extension is done with vigor without the heel sagging when pointing the foot out. To avoid the twisting of the knees in the stretching after closing, students do not over turn when closing their foot in 1st and keep the knee of the supporting leg above the toes in the plié.

Application. This exercise is highly recommended for all beginners. It is a good exercise, especially to prepare for glissades.

Exercise 6

Preparation for battement jeté en croix, in 1st, eight counts, facing the barre.

Students repeat Exercise 5 of the Fourth Class of this week.

Exercise 7

Demi-rond de jambe à terre en dehors and en dedans (start derrière), with port de bras, in 1st, eight counts.

Students repeat Exercise 6 of the Fourth Class of this week.

Exercise 8

Preparation for battement frappé 2nd, in 1st, four counts, facing the barre.

Students repeat Exercise 9 of the Second Class of this week.

Exercise 9

Adagio: lift the leg devant and 2nd, in 1st, eight counts, facing the barre.

Students repeat Exercise 10 of the Second Class of this week.

Exercise 10

Petits battements sur le cou-de-pied, in 1st, one count hold after each movement, facing the barre.

On 1, bring the right foot to cou-de-pied devant, turning the head slightly toward the right side; on 2, hold the position; on 3, unbend the lower leg halfway to 2nd with the foot pointed, straightening the head; on 4, hold the position; on 5, transfer the foot to cou-de-pied derrière, turning the head toward the left side; on 6, hold the position; on 7, unbend the leg, straightening the head; on 8, hold the position; on 1, bring the foot on the cou-de-pied devant, turning the head toward the right; on 2, hold the position; on 3, unbend the leg, straightening the head; on 4, hold the position; on 5, bring the foot on the cou-de-pied derrière, turning the head toward the left; on 6, extend the leg 2nd, the toes pointing onto the floor, straightening the head; on 7 and 8, close 1st. Repeat the exercise one more time. At the end of the exercise, bring the right foot on the cou-de-pied devant and hold balance with the arms 2nd and the head held straight.

Explanation. Students are introduced to the petit battement sur le cou-de-pied. This is an exercise of preparation for batterie and requires that the foot changes position with clarity and precision. The position of the working foot around the ankle is the same as the one used for the battement frappé. It is only the lower part

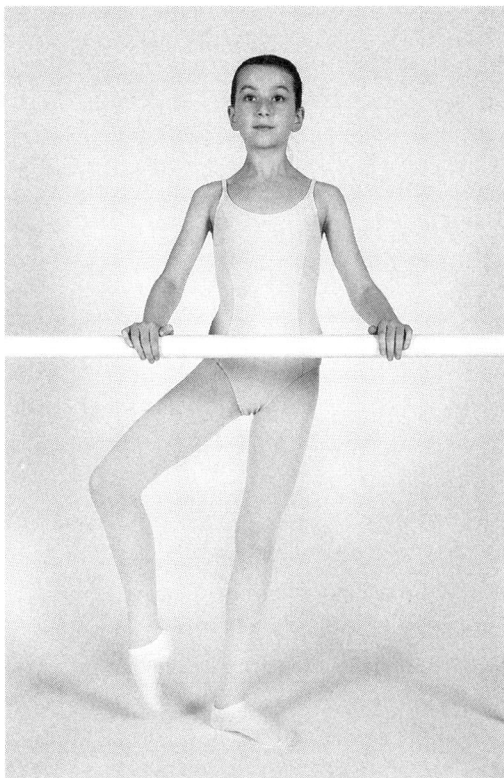

The leg is bent in 2nd position.

foot moves from front to back and back to front in the petits battement sur le cou-de-pied.

It is an excellent exercise to strengthen the adductors. This exercise develops mostly the very rapid contracting and releasing of the knee required for exercises in which the lower leg moves in a pendulum-like motion.

Unlike many of their American counterparts, French ballet students tend to be initiated to the petits battements exercise early in their training to acquire the proper leg reflexes for the speed and precision of the batterie work when the legs cross in the air. As soon as the students are familiar with the position of the foot on the cou-de-pied, they should be introduced to the petits battements exercise. The exercise must be practiced regularly.

Music. A coda music works well for this type of exercise.

Application. The lower leg working independently from the upper leg can be difficult for many students, especially for those who take ballet once or twice a week. For these students, the introduction of this exercise will be done later. A good position on the cou-de-pied is required first.

Exercise 11

Preparation for the 5th position: battement tendu 2nd, start in 1st, close 5th devant and derrière, four counts, facing the barre.

Students repeat Exercise 11 of the Second Class of this week.

Exercise 12

Preparation for the 5th position: battement tendu devant, start in 1st, close 5th, four counts, facing the barre.

On 1 and 2, battement tendu devant with the right foot, turning the head slightly toward the right; on 3 and 4, close 5th, keeping the head turned to the right; on 5 and 6, battement tendu devant; on 7 and 8, close 5th; on 1 and 2, battement tendu devant; on 3 and 4, close 1st, straightening the head; on 5 and 6, plié and stretch; on 7 and 8, hold the position. At the end, roll up and hold balance.

Explanation. The principles of the battement tendu devant performed in 1st apply here: the foot slides out with the heel pressed forward to the fully stretched position; coming back, the big

of the working leg that moves while the thigh remains as still as possible and fully turned out. The knee must be relaxed to allow the bending and unbending of the lower part of the working leg halfway to 2nd without moving the thigh. Imagining the knee being held by a thread attached to the ceiling may help convey the movement required. A common error is for students to move the upper part of the working leg when they switch front and back or back and front. Requiring students to hold, even briefly, the leg halfway to the 2nd position ensures that the battement goes actually through the 2nd position, thus avoiding the common error of moving the lower limb front and back in a flapping-like motion. This is important so that students do not flap their feet front and back while executing beatings in the air later on.

The movement is even; with each transfer of the working foot being timed equally. After each movement, there is a slight freeze. Notice the different positions of the head, whenever the foot changes positions.

The petit battement sur le cou-de-pied must not be confused with the battement frappé.

Unlike in the battement frappé, the working leg does not stretch 2nd completely while the toe initiates the return by pulling back, with the heel held high and forward; the ankle bends so that the foot comes down into a small 4th, and slides into 5th while maintaining the turn-out. Students must keep pulled up knees when closing, even if it means not closing the 5th completely. In the effort to push the heel forward, the supporting hip does not move forward when drawing the foot out.

Exercise 13

Preparation for the 5th position: battement tendu derrière, start in 1st, close 5th, four counts, facing the barre.

On 1 and 2, battement tendu derrière with the right foot, turning the head slightly toward the left side; on 3 and 4, close 5th; on 5 and 6, battement tendu derrière, keeping the head to the left; 7 and 8, close 5th; on 1 and 2, battement tendu derrière; on 3 and 4, close 1st, straightening the head; on 5 and 6, plié and stretch; on 7 and 8, hold the position. At the end, roll up and balance.

Explanation. In the battement tendu derrière, the big toe initiates the move by drawing backward to a fully stretched position, keeping the heel pressed down. To return, the heel initiates the movement, with the ankle bending gradually to lower the foot and slide it into 5th. Students hold the turn-out of the leg during the movement of the foot on the floor with a very slight opening of the working hip.

Exercise 14

Preparation for the 5th position: preparation for battement jeté 2nd, start in 1st, close 5th, eight counts, facing the barre.

Students repeat Exercise 9 of the Fourth Class of this week.

Exercise 15

Roll-up and relevé in 1st, plié, four counts, facing the barre, review.

On 1 and 2, roll up; on 3 and 4, roll down. Repeat three more times. On 1, plié; on 2, relevé; on 3, come down in plié; on 4, stretch the knees. Repeat three more times, holding the last relevé. Repeat the whole exercise.

Explanation. Students are reviewing this relevé exercise, mixing the roll-up and the relevé with plié.

Exercise 16

Pied sur la barre (jambe sur la barre) in 2nd, plié, facing the barre.

Stand facing the barre, lift the leg 2nd so that the right foot (at the level of the ankle) rests on the barre.

On "and" 1, plié; on 2, stretch; on "and" 3 and 4, repeat; on 5, bring the arms in 1st; on 6, open the arms 2nd; on 7 and 8, hold the position; hold the position for eight more counts.

Explanation. This is a very brief introduction to the pied sur la barre also called jambe sur la barre. It is a staple of the French ballet class, one that traditionally ends the barre. For this introduction, the height of the barre should be comfortable so that students can stretch both knees easily. Both hips remain parallel to the barre, and both legs are turned out. In order to execute this exercise properly, students must have a certain amount of flexibility, especially in the hamstrings and the adductors. Since students do not have to hold their working leg, they can relax their working hip and apply the full extension of its turn-out. The supporting knee is above the toes during the plié. The torso is erect, the elbows are

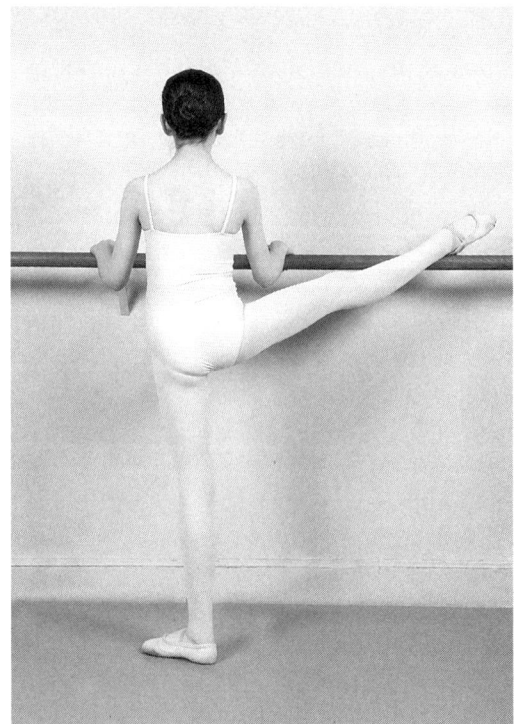

Pied sur la barre in 2nd position.

relaxed, and the shoulders are straight during the exercise. This is a good exercise to feel the turn-out of both legs without the stress of holding the working leg in the air.

Music. An adagio music is appropriate for this exercise.

Application. Students must be flexible enough to benefit from the exercise. They must be able to stretch both knees and bring their working hip down when the leg is on the barre. Assuming that students have enough flexibility to hold their leg on the barre with both knees taut, this is an excellent exercise that should be a staple of a ballet class, even for recreational students.

CENTER

Exercise 17

Battement tendu 2nd, bring the foot down, point the foot, with transfer, with port de bras, in 1st.

Students repeat Exercise 13 of the Fourth Class of this week.

Exercise 18

Battement tendu devant, 2nd, derrière, plié, in 1st, four counts.

On 1 and 2, battement tendu devant, with the head slightly turned toward the right; on 3 and 4, close, straighten the head; on 5 and 6, battement tendu 2nd; on 7 and 8, close; on 1 and 2, battement tendu derrière, with the head slightly turned toward the left; on 3 and 4, close, straighten the head; on 5 and 6, plié and stretch; on 7 and 8, hold the position. After a pause, repeat the whole exercise one more time.

Explanation. This is a similar exercise to the one practiced facing the barre. For the battement tendu derrière, students must avoid to tilting their pelvis excessively backward, transferring their weight onto the back leg, and crushing the big toe. They must pull up the lower abdomen, lift their back, and bring the arms 2nd very slightly forward so that students can better balance with the leg in the back. In addition, at this stage, students may have to turn their supporting foot inward ever so slightly to keep better balance. In any event, the turn-out will remain equal on both legs. Students are reminded of the different head positions.

Application. Balancing on the supporting leg with the working leg in the back, even in a simple battement tendu like in this exercise, while maintaining the turn-out, can be challenging for many beginners, more so for beginners in a recreational program. Its introduction in the center may have to wait for students who are not able to hold their pelvis and back correctly.

Exercise 19

Preparation for battement jeté devant and 2nd, in 1st, eight counts.

Students repeat Exercise 16 of the Second Class of this week.

Exercise 20

Adagio: lift the leg 2nd, in 1st, eight counts.

On 1 and 2, battement tendu 2nd; on 3 and 4, lift the leg; on 5 and 6, lower the leg, and point the foot onto the floor; on 7 and 8, close 1st. Repeat the whole exercise one more time.

Explanation. Students are practicing the exercise in the center. Again, the height of the working leg is not so much the goal that the control of the turn-out of both legs. Students keep their working hip down when raising their leg.

Standing on one leg while holding the working leg off the floor presents real challenges to the beginner ballet student, especially in an adagio-like exercise requiring the holding of the working leg 2nd. The challenge is particularly acute for those who have less than ideal turn-out and for those who do not know how to use their turn-out muscles. Because of the slow and controlled speed of the whole movement, this is the kind of exercise that tests not only the natural amount of turn-out from the hip but also the proper use of the turn-out muscles to be able to maintain balance while keeping the turn-out in both legs. The possibility of cheating in this type of exercise is basically limited to turning in the supporting leg to be able to keep balance. Obviously, this needs to be kept at a minimum.

Control of the turn-out: there are disagreements in the ballet teaching world as to which turn-out muscles must be activated. One school of thought advocates the use of the gluteus muscles to be able to control and maintain the turn-out, especially when one leg is off the floor like in the current exercise. Other ballet pedagogues have argued that the hip rotator muscles, in contrast to the gluteus, should be contracted.[12] In truth, all these muscles should be activated in the holding of the turn-out, especially when the demand on the turn-out, such as in lifting, is high. The gluteus muscles are larger and more apt at holding the turn-out. Another problem with solely using the hip rotator muscles is that they are more difficult to isolate for ballet students, especially beginners, whereas the tightening of the gluteus (achieved by tightening the buttock muscles) is much easier to feel and control. However, in tightening the gluteus muscles, one has to be careful to avoid tucking the pelvis under.

The back also plays a major role in the control of the whole movement. Pulling up is a must, especially the side of the supporting leg.

Exercise 21

Soubresaut in 2nd and 1st, two counts, one count hold, review.

In the preparation, on 1 and 2, bring the arms in 1st; on 3 and 4, battement tendu 2nd with the right foot, opening the arm 2nd; on 5, bring the foot down; on 6, hold the position; on 7 and 8, bring the arms down.

On "and," plié; on 1, jump straight up in the air keeping the legs 2nd; on 2, land into plié; on 3, stretch both knees; on 4, hold the position. Repeat three more times. Point the right foot and close 1st. Repeat the exercise in 1st. Repeat the exercise with a battement tendu of the left foot.

Explanation. Students are reviewing this simple soubresaut exercise.

Application. The exercise can also be practiced at the barre.

Exercise 22

Échappé 2nd, in 1st, with port de bras, four counts.

Following the preparatory port de bras, bring the arms down.

On "and," plié; on 1, spring off the floor, bringing the arms 1st, open the legs and the arms 2nd; on 2, land in plié in 2nd; on "and," directly out of the plié, spring off the floor, with the palms of the hands facing down, slightly raising the fingers; on 3, land in plié in 1st, the arms closing in preparatory position; on 4, stretch both legs.

Repeat three more times. After a pause, repeat the exercise.

Explanation. Students are now introduced to the échappé in the center performed with a port de bras.

Like with other jumps, the back remains straight during the whole exercise. For the successful completion of the jump, the coordination between arms and legs is important. At the highest point of the jump, the arms are still in 1st and open only in the descending part of the jump, when the legs open 2nd. In both jumps of each échappé, the knees are taut and the feet pointed, and the students must not open the legs wider than the 2nd position. The arms follow a precise trajectory without going off course, like it is often seen in ballet students: the arms must not open before they are brought to 1st and must not go higher than the 1st before they open. To help sustain the second spring, the arms in 2nd turn, palms down, with the fingers slightly raised (the same movement that is involved in the closing of the arms 2nd before bringing them down in preparatory position). The overall arm movement in the échappé is designed to help reach a higher height than the dancer would otherwise reach with the legs alone. This is one of the best examples of the arms directly contributing to the leg movement in ballet technique.

Music. Since the first part of the jump is done on two counts and the second one is done on the count, the choice of music will have to accommodate this difference so that students do not sit in the plié. A medium-tempo march could work well here.

Application. In a pre-ballet class or even a beginner class, the exercise can be done with legs in parallel to learn the coordination between the legs and arms early on.

Exercise 23

Preparation for déboulés, in 1st, arms in low 1st, each half turn on one count, hold one count, review.

Students repeat Exercise 17 of the Fifth Class of the Fourth week.

Exercise 24

Curtsey.

---

12   See Grieg, *Inside Ballet Technique*, 55–56.

Eighth Week

§

Students repeat the material of the Fifth Class of the Seventh Week.

SECOND CLASS

Exercise 1

Battement tendu 2nd, bring the foot down in 2nd, battement tendu 2nd, turn the leg in and out, in 1st, eight counts, facing the barre.

On 1 and 2, battement tendu 2nd; on 3, bring the right foot down in 2nd; on 4, hold the position; on 5, point the left foot while transferring the weight onto the right leg; on 6, hold the position; on 7 and 8, close in 1st.

On 1 and 2, battement tendu 2nd; on 3 and 4, turn in the working leg; on 5 and 6, turn out the working leg; on 7 and 8, close 1st. Repeat the whole exercise.

Explanation. This is essentially review material.

Exercise 2

Plié and grand plié in 2nd and 1st, four counts, facing the barre.

Following the preparatory port de bras, battement tendu with the right leg and bring the foot down.

On 1 and 2, plié; on 3 and 4, stretch; on 5 and 6, deeper plié, keeping the heels down; on 7 and 8, come back up into demi-plié and stretch; on 1, point the right foot; on 2, hold the position; on 3 and 4, close 1st; from 5 to 8, hold the position.

On 1 and 2, plié; on 3 and 4, stretch; on 5 and 6, deep plié, at the end of which the heels go off the floor to allow the bending of the knees further into a grand plié; on 7 and 8, bring the heels down first into a demi-plié and stretch the legs; on 1 and 2, roll up on demi-pointes; on 3 and 4, come down; from 5 to 8, battement tendu 2nd with the left foot and bring the foot down. Repeat the whole exercise one more time.

Explanation. In this first exposure to the grand plié, students will be facing the barre to keep the hips and the back straight, performing no more than one grand plié in each position at a time. Grands pliés in 5th and 4th positions will come later in the training. Unlike in the grand plié in 1st, in which the heels have to be lifted off the floor, the heels stay on the floor in the grand plié in 2nd. At this stage, students are not expected to go down so much that their thighs are horizontal in the grand plié in 2nd; they only slightly deepen the demi-plié while keeping their whole feet down. In the grand plié 2nd, it is important that students do not open their feet too wide. There is indeed a tendency to open the legs very wide in 2nd and to go down too much in the grand plié, sometimes to the extent that the pelvis is lowered below the level of knees. This habit may form bulky thighs by stressing the quadriceps unnecessarily, since a lot of strength is required to come up from this kind of grand plié. It is also aesthetically inelegant. Finally,

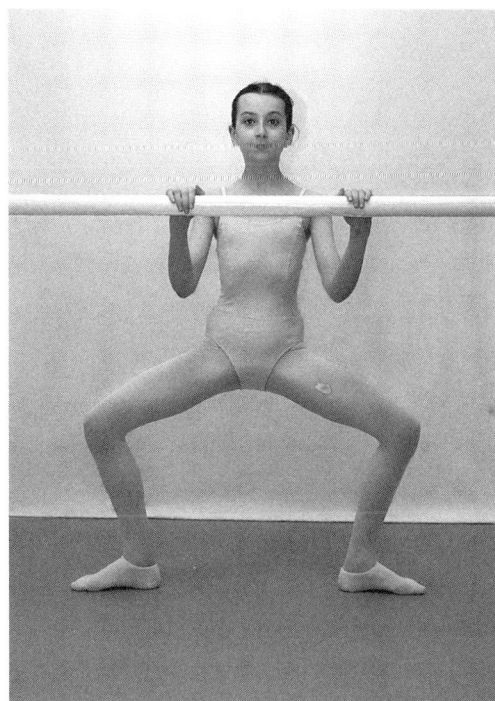

The legs are too wide in this plié in 2nd position.

widening the feet too much in the grand plié 2nd does not stretch the calve muscles like it should. In all the grands pliés, students must have a total control of the back, keeping an uplifted torso at all times.

For the grand plié in 1st, students start with a demi-plié, pressing their heels down. When they reach the deepest level of the demi-plié, without pausing, they release their heels just sufficiently to allow a full bend of the knees. Without sitting in the plié or releasing their thigh muscles, students straighten both legs, with the heels pressing down onto the floor as soon as possible into a demi-plié, and keep pressing onto the floor to stretch both knees thoroughly. The bending and stretching of the legs must be even throughout the grand plié.

The practice of the grands pliés in ballet training, especially at the beginner's level, is not to be taken lightly. There has been controversy about its overall usefulness in ballet technique and its potential effect on knees and feet articulations, with some ballet teachers advocating its total ban from ballet training. Because of the grand plié's high demands on the leg's articulation, especially the knee joint, there is room for injury to occur. However, if carefully and correctly executed, the grand plié, especially when performed in the less demanding 2nd and 1st positions, should be a welcome addition to barre work, for it stimulates the leg's articulations smoothly and gradually.

Focusing on the pressure of the feet on the floor while keeping a correct alignment and a consistent turn-out position throughout the descending and ascending parts of the grand plié, will help students to stay away from trouble. One common problem is for students to turn out their feet more than they should as the plié progresses to a grand plié, especially in 1st, where the heels are allowed to rise; when bringing their heels down and stretching the knees, this adjustment can have a disastrous effect on the knee joints, since students try to rotate their feet beyond what the turn-out of their hips allows them to achieve. This practice is often caused by an instructor who recommends that students push their heels forward in the grand plié. Another incorrect practice is to fail to push down with the feet in the descending and rising parts of the grand plié. Under this light, the grand plié should be viewed more as an extension of the demi-plié. The pressure of the whole feet on the floor helps to keep balance, especially in the descending part of the plié. Reaching the lowest level of the demi-plié with the whole feet down while coming down and up will cause the feet to be more actively involved in the whole process, making the exercise easier and safer.

Application. The grand plié is a challenging movement, especially for the control of the back, the hip flexors, the knee joints, and the alignment of the body while keeping the necessary turn-out. It should be introduced much later in a recreational program.

Exercise 3

Battement tendu en croix, in 1st, four counts:

Students repeat Exercise 3 of the Fifth Class of the Seventh Week.

Exercise 4

Preparation for chassé à terre 2nd, with transfer, stretch the legs, in 1st, four counts, facing the barre.

Students repeat Exercise 4 of the Fifth Class of the Seventh Week.

Exercise 5

Battement tendu 2nd, start and close in plié, in 1st, four counts, facing the barre.

Students repeat Exercise 5 of the Fifth Class of the Seventh Week.

Exercise 6

Preparation for battement jeté en croix, in 1st, eight counts, facing the barre.

Students repeat Exercise 5 of the Fourth Class of the Seventh Week.

Exercise 7

Demi-rond de jambe à terre en dehors and en dedans (start derrière), with port de bras, in 1st, eight counts.

Students repeat Exercise 6 of the Fourth Class of the Seventh Week.

Exercise 8

Preparation for battement frappé 2nd, without closing, in 1st, four counts, facing the barre.

On 1, bring the foot on the cou-de-pied

devant, turning the head slightly toward the right side; on 2, hold the position; on 3, extend with vigor the leg 2nd pointing the foot onto the floor, straightening the head; on 4, hold the position; on 5, bring the foot on the cou-de-pied derrière, turning the head slightly toward the left side; on 6, hold the position; on 7, extend the leg 2nd, straightening the head; on 8, hold the position. Repeat the exercise one more time devant and derrière. At the end, close 1st and bring the foot on the cou-de-pied devant and hold balance, with the head held straight. To close from the cou-de-pied position, students extend their leg 2nd and close 1st. Repeat the whole exercise one more time.

Explanation. Students are repeating Exercise 9 of the Second Class of the Seventh Week, except they do not close 1st after each extension. The working foot must strike the supporting leg with energy and briskness before sharply extending 2nd with vigor. The sharp bending and stretching of the working leg must be given equal musical time for now. Students are reminded of the proper head positions when the working foot moves from one position to another. Notice that the head remains straight so that it is easier to keep balance at the end of the exercise.

Music. The tempo is fairly slow, but the music has sharp beats.

Exercise 9

Adagio: lift the leg in 4th position derrière, cambré, in 1st, eight counts, facing the barre.

On 1 and 2, battement tendu derrière, keeping the head straight; on 3 and 4, lift the leg; on 5 and 6, lower the leg, and bring the pointed foot onto the floor; on 7 and 8, close 1st. On 1 and 2, lift the torso and bend back; on 3 and 4, straighten up; on 5, plié; on 6, stretch the knees; on 7 and 8, hold the position. At the end, roll up and hold balance.

Explanation. This is a preparatory exercise for the arabesque, which is the position of one leg stretched in the back, usually held à la hauteur. At this early stage of training, students are not expected to hold the leg à la hauteur, as in a true arabesque. For now, correct placement and the quality of the lift more than the height itself, is important. The arabesque, which is a position, must not be confused with the movement of lifting the leg derrière, which of course comes first to bring the leg in arabesque. Until students can achieve correctly a height close to at least à la hauteur, the expression of lifting the leg derrière

The impact of the lifting of the leg is minimal when the leg remains low.

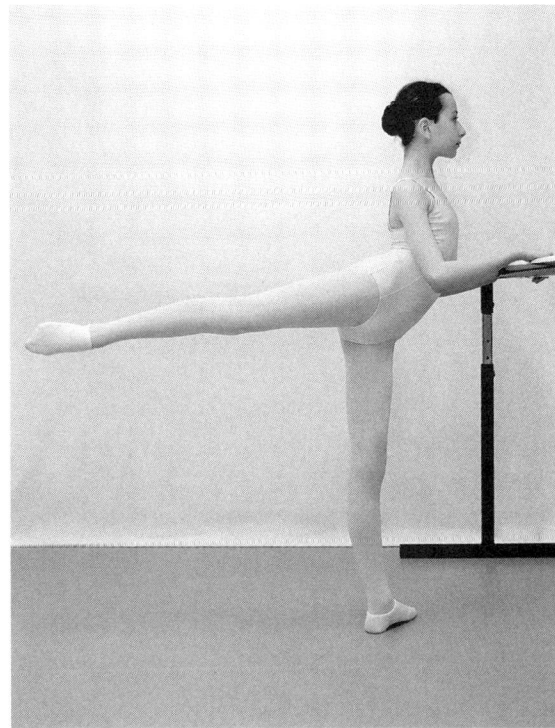

As the leg goes up, the torso inclines forward.

The leg is out of alignment with the supporting leg.

will be used to emphasize more the movement (how to get to the position) than the position itself.

The shoulders must remain low and level during the exercise. The lifting of the leg derrière has a definite impact on the torso (the higher the working leg, the greater the impact). As the lift of the leg increases, the torso inclines forward more and more. In this introductory exercise to raise the leg derrière, the torso should not move forward much at all, since the leg remains fairly low. In order to minimize this tilting of the torso, before lifting the leg, it is important that students lengthen the torso and lift their lower abdomen. The working leg is very stretched in the back. Since this exercise is in preparation for the arabesque position, in which the head is generally held straight, students will not rotate their head in this exercise. Students are also practicing the cambré in 1st. When bending back, the legs remain tightly together without any release of the adductor muscles as it is sometimes seen in beginners. In both movements, the abdominal muscles are strongly activated to help support the lengthened spine and maintain the stretch of

the iliopsoas.[13] In lifting the leg derrière, careful alignment of the leg with the heel of the supporting leg should be aimed for.

Application. As a general rule, all beginner ballet students are better off facing the barre when being introduced to lifting the leg derrière. Students will have studied the battement tendu and the battement jeté derrière sufficiently before practicing this exercise.

Exercise 10

Petits battements sur le cou-de-pied, in 1st, one count hold after each movement, facing the barre.

Students repeat Exercise 10 of the Fifth Class of the Seventh Week.

Exercise 11

Preparation for the 5th position: battement tendu 2nd, start in 1st, close 5th devant and derrière, four counts, facing the barre.

Students repeat Exercise 11 of the Second Class of the Seventh Week.

Exercise 12

Preparation for the 5th position: battement tendu devant, start in 1st, close 5th, four counts, facing the barre.

Students repeat Exercise 12 of the Fifth Class of the Seventh Week.

Exercise 13

Preparation for the 5th position: battement tendu derrière, start in 1st, close 5th, four counts, facing the barre.

Students repeat Exercise 13 of the Fifth Class of the Seventh Week.

Exercise 14

Preparation for the 5th position: preparation for battement jeté 2nd, start in 1st, close 5th, eight counts, facing the barre.

Students repeat Exercise 9 of the Fourth Class of the Seventh Week.

Exercise 15

Preparation for grand battement 2nd [grand battement jeté—Vaganova], plié, in 1st, facing the barre.

13   Grieg, *Inside Ballet Technique*, 24.

On 1 and 2, battement tendu 2nd; on 3, battement 2nd; on 4, lower the leg, and point the foot onto the floor; on 5 and 6, close 1st; on 7 and 8, plié and stretch. Repeat three more times, alternating legs. At the end, relevé in 1st and hold balance.

Explanation. Students are introduced to the grand battement 2nd, facing the barre. Unlike with the battement jeté, students do not hold the working leg but throw it lightly. When coming down, the leg does not collapse but is lowered quickly, with control, the toes touching the floor first. The leg is thrown without lifting the hip excessively. In order to avoid this lifting, students must use their turn-out muscles to lift the leg. The knee of the supporting leg must remain fully stretched at all times during the grand battement. Students should not be directed to throw the leg beyond their flexibility level to avoid picking up wrong habits such as bending knees, raising shoulders, swinging the torso, and turning in the leg. The energy of the throw, the correctness of the alignment, and the turn-out are the most important aspects of this exercise. Students have plenty of time to execute the battement tendu before the throw as precisely as they have practiced so far.

Music. A dynamic 6/8 march is an appropriate choice.

Application. Like for the battement derrière, the battement 2nd will be first practiced facing the barre to keep the body as straight as possible. For beginning students in a recreational program, the grand battement comes later in the training.

Exercise 16

Roll-up and relevé in 1st, plié, four counts, facing the barre, review.
    Students repeat Exercise 15 of the Fifth Class of the Seventh Week.

Exercise 17

Pied sur la barre in 2nd, plié, facing the barre.
    Students repeat Exercise 16 of the Fifth Class of the Seventh Week.

Exercise 18

Battement tendu 2nd, bring the foot down, point the foot, with transfer, with port de bras, in 1st.
    Students repeat Exercise 13 of the Fourth Class of the Seventh Week.

Exercise 19

Battement tendu devant, 2nd, derrière, plié, in 1st, four counts.
    Students repeat Exercise 18 of the Fifth Class of the Seventh Week.

Exercise 20

Adagio: lift the leg 2nd, in 1st, eight counts.
    Students repeat Exercise 20 of the Fifth Class of the Seventh Week.

Exercise 21

Preparation for glissade 2nd, in 1st, four counts, facing the barre.
    On 1, plié in 1st; on 2, battement tendu 2nd with the right foot; on 3, transfer the weight onto the right leg in plié, stretch the left leg and point the left foot; on "and" 4, close 1st in plié and stretch. Repeat the glissade one more time to the right.

Explanation. This is a very basic step to learn the mechanics of the glissade, in which students transfer their weight from one leg onto another. Students must have been already introduced to the battement tendu in plié before executing such an exercise, with the working foot brushing the floor to a fully pointed foot. The arms must move along on the barre so that they remain in front of the shoulders when students finish the glissade. The movement is performed softly as a gliding movement, with a flowing transfer from one leg to another. Yet, softness does not mean that the step should appear as if the legs are dragging. The sharp pointing of each foot and the brisk closing of the second leg increase the impression of lightness and liveliness of the step.

The French approach to the glissade is that of a gliding movement, performed softly, with a wave-like motion between the opening and the closing. It has remained true to the root of the glissade, which is a traveling step à terre, whereas other schools approach it more as a jump. Like Marc Hertsens argues, "the glissade . . . has been deteriorating as it has changed from a lower level horizontal step to an upper level vertical step. Instead of a lovely flowing, elongated movement, it has become close to a jeté, making a combination like glissade/grand jeté redundant."[14]

Music. A medium-tempo 3/4 waltz or a 4/4 works well.

Application. This broken down version of the French style glissade is a good introduction to the step. Most beginners will appreciate and understand the simple approach to this exercise.

Exercise 22

Soubresaut in 2nd and 1st, two counts, one count hold, review.

Students repeat Exercise 21 of the Fifth Class of the Seventh Week.

Exercise 23

Échappé 2nd, in 1st, with port de bras, four counts.

Students repeat Exercise 22 of the Fifth Class of the Seventh Week.

Exercise 24

Preparation for déboulés, in 1st, arms in low 1st, each half turn on one count, hold one count, review.

Students repeat Exercise 17 of the Fifth Class of the Fourteenth Week.

Exercise 25

Curtsey.

THIRD CLASS

Students repeat the material of the Second Class of this week.

FOURTH CLASS

Exercise 1

Battement tendu 2nd, bring the foot down in 2nd, battement tendu 2nd, turn the leg in and out, in 1st, facing the barre.

Students repeat Exercise 1 of the Second Class of this week.

Exercise 2

Plié and grand plié in 2nd and 1st, facing the barre.

Students repeat Exercise 2 of the Second Class of this week.

Exercise 3

Battement tendu en croix, in 1st, four counts.

Students repeat Exercise 3 of the Fifth Class of the Seventh Week.

Exercise 4

Battement tendu 2nd, start and close in plié, in 1st, four counts, facing the barre.

Students repeat Exercise 5 of the Fifth Class of the Seventh Week.

Exercise 5

Preparation for chassé à terre 2nd, with transfer, stretch the legs, in 1st, four counts, facing the barre.

Students repeat Exercise 4 of the Fifth Class of the Seventh Week.

Exercise 6

Preparation for battement jeté en croix, in 1st, eight counts, facing the barre.

Students repeat Exercise 5 of the Fourth Class of the Seventh Week.

Exercise 7

Preparation for battement jeté piqué 2nd [battement tendu jeté pointé—Vaganova], in 1st, eight counts, facing the barre.

On 1 and 2, battement tendu 2nd; on 3, battement à la demi-hauteur; on 4, lower the leg, and point the foot onto the floor; on 5, bring the leg again à la demi-hauteur; on 6, lower the leg; on 7 and 8, close 1st. Repeat one more time with the right foot. Repeat the whole exercise one more time.

Explanation. For now the lifting and the lowering of the working leg is performed evenly, unlike the final version of the battement jeté piqué that students will practice later this year. The working foot comes down with the toes very

---

14   Hertsens, *Ballet Technique*, 39.

The working foot is in 2nd position.

The turn-out of the working leg is maintained as much as possible as the leg moves to the back.

taut. When the leg goes up, it always reaches the same height in the air à la demi-hauteur with a slight hold. By now students should have enough control of the working leg so it does not wobble when it is held in the air.

Exercise 8

Rond de jambe à terre en dehors and en dedans, in 1st, eight counts, facing the barre.

On 1 and 2, battement tendu devant, turning the head slightly toward the right side; on 3 and 4, rond de jambe en dehors to 2nd position, straightening the head; on 5 and 6, rond de jambe to the back, turning the head slightly toward the left side; on 7 and 8, close 1st, straightening the head. On 1 and 2, battement tendu derrière, turning the head slightly toward the left; on 3 and 4, rond de jambe to 2nd position, straightening the head; on 5 and 6, rond de jambe to the front, turning the head slightly toward the right; on 7 and 8, close 1st, straightening the head. Repeat the whole exercise one more time. At the end, roll up and hold balance.

Explanation. Students are now performing the full rond de jambe à terre en dehors and en

dedans. The working leg must remain turned out as long as possible, and this without moving the supporting hip forward, from the 2nd to the 4th position derrière. Turning in the working leg too soon can compromise the benefit of the exercise, which is to increase the range of hip rotation. Students are reminded of the proper head positions.

Exercise 9

Preparation for battement frappé 2nd, without closing, in 1st, four counts, facing the barre.

Students repeat Exercise 8 of the Second Class of this week.

Exercise 10

Adagio: lift the leg derrière, cambré, in 1st, eight counts, facing the barre.

Students repeat Exercise 9 of the Second Class of this week.

Exercise 11

Petits battements sur le cou-de-pied, in 1st, one count hold after each movement, facing the barre.

Students repeat Exercise 10 of the Fifth Class of the Seventh Week.

Exercise 12

Battement tendu en croix en dehors, directly in 5th, four counts, facing the barre.

Start directly in 5th, right foot front: the weight spread equally on both feet, the turn-out equal on both legs, feet flat without rolling in, the hips parallel to the barre and a correct alignment of the body. The head is slightly turned toward the right side. From now on, students will turn their head to the same side as the one of their front foot when positioned in 5th.

On 1 and 2, battement tendu devant; on 3 and 4, close 5th; on 5 and 6, battement tendu 2nd, straightening the head; on 7 and 8, close 5th derrière, with the head turning slightly toward the left; on 1 and 2, battement tendu derrière; on 3 and 4, close; on 5 and 6, battement tendu 2nd, straightening the head; on 7 and 8, close 5th devant, turning the head slightly toward the right. Repeat the exercise one more time with the right foot.

Explanation. Students are starting this exercise directly in 5th. To avoid confusion about the closing of the 5th for battements tendus 2nd when the exercise is en croix en dehors, a good rule of thumb can be remembered: when the number of closings in 2nd is odd, the first one closes back; when the number is even, the first one closes front. Students are reminded of the proper head positions. In this exercise in 5th, the head straightens only when the leg comes out in 2nd and not before, like it did when the exercise is performed in 1st.

Exercise 13

Preparation for grand battement 2nd, with plié, in 1st, facing the barre.

Students repeat Exercise 15 of the Second Class of this week.

Exercise 14

Roll-up and relevé in 1st, plié, four counts, facing the barre, review.

Students repeat Exercise 15 of the Fifth Class of the Seventh Week.

Exercise 15

Pied sur la barre in 2nd, plié, facing the barre.

Students repeat Exercise 16 of the Fifth Class of the Seventh Week.

CENTER

Exercise 16

Battement tendu 2nd, arms in 6th, in 1st, four counts.

In the preparatory port de bras, on 1, bring the arms 1st; on 2, hold the position; on 3, open the left arm to 2nd while the right arm stays in 1st, the head turning slightly toward the right; on 4, hold the position.

On 1 and 2, battement tendu 2nd with the right foot; on 3 and 4, close. Repeat three more times with the right foot. Switch arm position when repeating the exercise with the left foot.

Explanation. Students are introduced to a new arm position that is common to accompany some ballet moves, even though it is not one of the five principal arms positions. The arm that is in 1st must not sag or move during the exercise. It stays softly curved. The tips of the fingers are

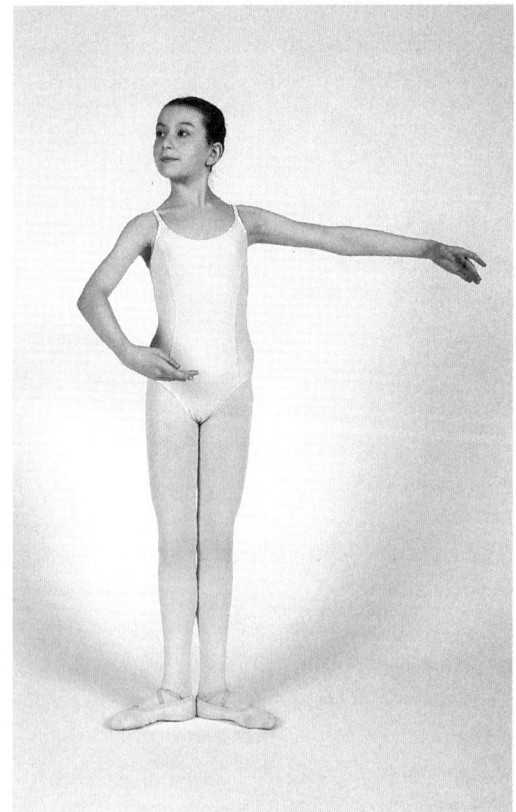

The arms are in preparatory 6th position.

centered to the middle of the torso. The head is turned at about 45° toward the side of the arm in 1st.

Music. The tempo is dynamic and slightly accelerated for this exercise. A tango or other lively music would work well.

Exercise 17

Battement tendu devant, 2nd, derrière, plié, in 1st, four counts.

Students repeat Exercise 18 of the Fifth Class of the Seventh Week.

Exercise 18

Adagio: lift the leg 2nd, in 1st, eight counts.

Students repeat Exercise 20 of the Fifth Class of the Seventh Week.

Exercise 19

Preparation for glissade 2nd, in 1st, four counts, facing the barre.

Students repeat Exercise 21 of the Second Class of this week.

Exercise 20

Soubresaut in 2nd and 1st, on two counts, one count hold, review.

Students repeat Exercise 21 of the Fifth Class of the Seventh Week.

Exercise 21

Échappé 2nd, in 1st, with port de bras, four counts.

Students repeat Exercise 22 of the Fifth Class of the Seventh Week.

Exercise 22

Preparation for the assemblé: brush forward in plié, jump to assemble both legs, two counts, one count hold, in 6th, facing the barre.

On "and," plié; on 1, still in plié, brush the right foot forward and extend the leg off the floor à la demi-hauteur, while pushing off the floor with the supporting leg, both legs fully stretched in the air; on 2, land on *both* feet in 6th; on 3, stretch both knees; on 4, hold the position. Repeat three more times, alternating legs.

Explanation. The formal assemblé is studied later. In this exercise, however, the main mechanisms of the assemblé apply: the brushing of the

working foot before lifting the leg, the bringing of the feet together before the landing, and the landing on both feet. The assemblé does not travel, that is, the body stays at the same place from the beginning to the end of the jump. The body stays erect. The brushing of the working foot before the jump gives stability before the working leg does the battement and the supporting leg springs off the floor. The barre or the wall should not be an obstacle for the working leg to extend forward.

Music. A medium-tempo waltz may be the best here.

Application. Since the exercise is done in parallel, it can be practiced by pre-ballet and all beginners to prepare for the assemblé.

Exercise 23

Introduction to balancé, in 6th, traveling sideways, four counts, hands on the waist.

In the preparatory port de bras, bring both hands on the waist as performed in Exercise 13 of the Third Class of the Second Week.

On "and" 1, extend the right leg sideways; on 2, step onto the right foot in plié, bending the left leg and bringing the left foot pointed next to the right ankle; on 3, directly out of the plié, step onto demi-pointe with the left foot, stretching the left leg, while stretching the right leg and raising the pointed right foot slightly off the floor; on 4, come down into plié onto the right foot with the left foot pointed next to the right ankle; on "and" 5, extend the left leg toward the left side; on 6, step onto the left foot in plié, bending the right leg and bringing the right foot pointed next to the left ankle; on 7, go up onto demi-pointe on the right foot, stretching the right leg, while stretching the left leg and pointing the foot slightly off the floor; on 8, come down into plié onto the left foot with the right foot pointed next to the left ankle. Repeat the exercise at least six more times.

Explanation. Students are repeating the exercise done earlier in Exercise 19 of the Fifth Class of the Sixth Week, but this time it is performed sideways, alternating sides, with the extension done on the count. They are also stepping on the foot onto demi-pointe each time they switch legs and transfer the weight from one leg onto another. This is an informal introduction of holding on one foot on demi-pointe; the foot must be straight when stepping onto demi-pointe.

Exercise 24

Curtsey.

FIFTH CLASS

Exercise 1

Battement tendu 2nd, bring the foot down in 2nd, battement tendu 2nd, turn the leg in and out, in 1st, facing the barre.

Students repeat Exercise 1 of the Second Class of this week.

Exercise 2

Plié and grand plié in 2nd and 1st, facing the barre.

Students repeat Exercise 2 of the Second Class of this week.

Exercise 3

Battement tendu 2nd, close in plié, in 1st, four counts, facing the barre.

On 1 and 2, battement tendu 2nd; on "and" 3, close in plié; on 4, stretch the knees. Repeat three more times with the right foot. At the end, roll up in 1st and hold balance.

Explanation. As the foot closes, both knees bend at the same time. The plié occurs not too soon: only when the working foot comes down sliding into a close 2nd position. Students stretch their knees before they resume the battement tendu.

Exercise 4

Battement tendu en croix, in 1st, four counts, facing the barre.

Students repeat Exercise 3 of the Fifth Class of the Seventh Week.

Exercise 5

Preparation for battement jeté en croix, directly in 5th, eight counts, facing the barre.

On 1 and 2, battement tendu devant; on "and," lift the leg à la demi-hauteur; on 3, hold the position; on "and," lower the leg and point the foot onto the floor; on 4, hold the position; on 5 and 6, close 5th; on 7 and 8, hold the position. Repeat the exercise en croix en dehors.

Explanation. After having been introduced to the battement tendu performed en croix in 5th, in Exercise 12 of the Fourth Class of this week, students are now practicing the preparatory exercise for the battement jeté en croix also directly in 5th. Both exercises are similar, for they start and finish the same way. Here, however, students lift their leg à la demi-hauteur. Notice that the leg comes up more quickly, freezes, and comes down quickly as well. Students will apply the same head positions that they have learned in performing an exercise en croix.

Music. A 2/4 tango would work here.

Exercise 6

Preparation for battement jeté piqué 2nd, in 1st, eight counts, facing the barre.

Students repeat Exercise 7 of the Fourth Class of this week.

Exercise 7

Rond de jambe à terre en dehors and en dedans, in 1st, eight counts, facing the barre.

Students repeat Exercise 8 of the Fourth Class of this week.

Exercise 8

Preparation for battement frappé 2nd, without closing, in 1st, four counts, facing the barre.

Students repeat Exercise 8 of the Second Class of this week.

Exercise 9

Adagio: lift the leg 2nd, directly in 5th, eight counts, facing the barre.

On 1 and 2, battement tendu 2nd; on 3 and 4, lift the leg 2nd; on 5 and 6, lower the leg and point the foot onto the floor; on 7 and 8, close 5th devant. Repeat the exercise closing 5th derrière.

Explanation. Students are practicing the exercise in 5th, facing the barre.

Exercise 10

Adagio: lift the leg derrière, cambré, in 1st, eight counts, facing the barre.

Students repeat Exercise 9 of the Second Class of this week.

Exercise 11

Petits battements sur le cou-de-pied, in 1st, one count hold after each movement, facing the barre.

Students repeat Exercise 10 of the Fifth Class of the seventh Week.

Exercise 12

Preparation for grand battement 2nd, with plié, in 1st, facing the barre.

Students repeat Exercise 15 of the Second Class of this week.

Exercise 13

Roll-up and relevé in 1st, plié, four counts, facing the barre, review.

Students repeat Exercise 15 of the Fifth Class of the Seventh Week.

Exercise 14

Pied sur la barre in 2nd, plié, facing the barre.

Students repeat Exercise 16 of the Fifth Class of the Seventh Week.

CENTER

Exercise 15

Battement tendu 2nd, arms in 6th, in 1st, four counts.

Students repeat Exercise 16 of the Fourth Class of this week.

Exercise 16

Battement tendu 2nd, directly in 5th, four counts.

On 1 and 2, battement tendu 2nd with the right foot, straightening the head; on 3 and 4, close 5th derrière, with the head turning slightly toward the left; on 5 and 6, battement tendu 2nd, still with the right foot, straightening the head; on 7 and 8, close 5th devant, turning the head slightly toward the right; on 1 and 2, battement tendu 2nd, straightening the head; on 3 and 4, close 5th derrière, turning the head slightly toward the left; from 5 to 8, port de bras to 1st and 2nd.

Explanation. Students are introduced to the battement tendu 2nd in 5th in the center. Students apply the same head movements learned in Exercise 11 of the Second Class of the Seventh Week. The same principles apply as in the exercise at the barre, especially the brushing of the foot out of and into position. Students must be reminded not to draw the toes out over the line that the foot has in 5th in the battement tendu 2nd when coming out, and to transfer the weight onto both legs when closing. When performing an exercise in 5th at the barre and in the center, at the end of the preparatory port de bras where the arms remain 2nd, at the beginning of the exercise itself, the head turns de face when the following movement is performed in 2nd or it is a plié followed by a movement in 2nd. Unless otherwise specified, this rule will apply from now on.

Exercise 17

Preparation for battement jeté en croix, in 1st, eight counts.

On 1 and 2, battement tendu devant; on "and," lift the leg with vigor à la demi-hauteur; on 3, hold the position; on "and," bring it down, and point the foot onto the floor; on 4, hold the position; on 5 and 6, close 1st; on 7 and 8, plié and stretch. Repeat the exercise en croix.

Explanation. Students are performing the exercise en croix en dehors in the center.

Exercise 18

Demi-rond de jambe à terre en dehors and en dedans (start derrière), with port de bras, in 1st, eight counts.

Following the preparatory port de bras, bring the arms down.

On 1 and 2, battement tendu devant, bringing the arms in 1st; on 3 and 4, rond de jambe to 2nd, opening the arms 2nd; on 5 and 6, close 1st, closing the arms down; on 7 and 8, hold the position.

On 1 and 2, battement tendu derrière, bringing the arms in 1st; on 3 and 4, rond de jambe en dedans to the 2nd position, while the arms open 2nd; on 5 and 6, close 1st, closing the arms down; on 7 and 8, hold the position. Repeat the exercise one more time with the right foot.

Explanation. The port de bras is added to this

rond de jambe exercise. Students pull themselves up on their supporting leg for the battement tendu derrière and for the rond de jambe en dedans to keep balance. The weight should be on the supporting leg at all times.

Exercise 19

Preparation for chassé à terre 2nd, with transfer, stretch the legs, in 1st, with port de bras, four counts.

Following the preparatory port de bras, bring the arms down.

On 1, plié; on 2, slide the right foot on the floor to 2nd position in plié, bringing the arms in 1st; on 3, stretch both legs, transferring the weight onto the right leg, while pointing the left foot 2nd, and opening the arms 2nd; on 4, close 1st, bringing the arms down. Repeat three more times, alternating legs each time.

Explanation. After practicing the preparation for the chassé à terre at the barre, students are now performing it in the center with a port de bras. When stretching out of the 2nd position, students activate their turn-out muscles to hold balance on their supporting leg, while maintaining a strong back. The torso remains straight.

Application. This exercise can be practiced by most beginners to work the coordination of arms and legs.

Exercise 20

Adagio: lift the leg devant and 2nd, in 1st, eight counts.

On 1 and 2, battement tendu devant; on 3 and 4, lift the leg à la demi-hauteur; on 5 and 6, lower the leg, and point the foot onto the floor; on 7 and 8, close in 1st. On "and" 1 and 2, bring the arms down, on 3 and 4, bring the arms 1st, on 5 and 6, bring the arms 5th, on 7 and 8, open the arms 2nd. On 1 and 2, battement tendu 2nd; on

3 and 4, lift the leg à la demi-hauteur; on 5 and 6, lower the leg; on 7 and 8, close in 1st. Repeat the port de bras.

Explanation. Students are now adding the lifting of the leg devant in this adagio exercise.

Exercise 21

Preparation for glissade 2nd, in 1st, four counts, facing the barre.

Students repeat Exercise 21 of the Second Class of this week.

Exercise 22

Soubresaut in 2nd and 1st, two counts, one count hold, review.

Students repeat Exercise 21 of the Fifth Class of the Seventh Week.

Exercise 23

Échappé 2nd, in 1st, with port de bras, four counts.

Students repeat Exercise 22 of the Fifth Class of the Seventh Week.

Exercise 24

Preparation for the assemblé:, brush forward in plié, jump to assemble both legs, two counts, one count hold, in 6th, facing the barre.

Students repeat Exercise 22 of the Fourth Class of this week.

Exercise 25

Introduction to balancé, in 6th, traveling sideways, four counts, hands on the waist.

Students repeat Exercise 23 of the Fourth Class of this week.

Exercise 26

Curtsey.

Ninth Week

§

Students repeat the material of the Fifth Class of the Eighth Week.

SECOND CLASS

Exercise 1

Close and open legs in 1st, battement tendu 2nd, in 1st, facing the barre.

On 1, close the feet in 6th; on 2, open in 1st; on 3 and 4, repeat; on 5 and 6, battement tendu 2nd; on 7 and 8, close 1st. Repeat the exercise with the right foot.

Explanation. Students are revisiting the movement for the rotation of the hips performed at the beginning of the program.

Application. All beginners and even more advanced students will benefit from this type of exercise requiring both legs to turn out at the same time.

Exercise 2

Plié and grand plié in 2nd and 1st, facing the barre.

Students repeat Exercise 2 of the Second Class of the Eighth Week.

Exercise 3

Battement tendu 2nd, close in plié, in 1st, four counts, facing the barre.

Students repeat Exercise 3 of the Fifth Class of the Eighth Week.

Exercise 4

Battement tendu 2nd, plié when pointing, in 1st, facing the barre.

On 1 and 2, battement tendu 2nd; on 3, plié on the supporting leg, with the working toes sliding out; on 4, stretch the supporting leg, with the working toes sliding in; on 5 and 6, close 1st; on 7 and 8, hold the position. Repeat one more time

with the right foot. At the end, roll up in 1st and hold balance.

Explanation. A plié follows the extension of the leg 2nd in this exercise. Students must not crush their toes and must keep their weight on the supporting leg. The toes slide out and in with the plié and the stretch actions of the supporting leg. The knee is pushed to the side, lining up with the toes in the plié.

Exercise 5

Battement tendu en croix, in 1st, four counts, facing the barre.

Students repeat Exercise 3 of the Fifth Class of the Seventh Week.

Exercise 6

Preparation for battement jeté en croix, eight counts, facing the barre.

Students repeat Exercise 5 of the Fifth Class of the Eighth Week.

Exercise 7

Preparation for battement jeté piqué 2nd, in 1st, facing the barre.

Students repeat Exercise 7 of the Fourth Class of the Eighth Week.

Exercise 8

Rond de jambe à terre en dehors and en dedans, in 1st, eight counts, facing the barre.

Students repeat Exercise 8 of the Fourth Class of the Eighth Week.

Exercise 9

Preparation for battement frappé 2nd, without closing, directly in 5th, four counts, facing the barre.

On 1, bring the foot on the cou-de-pied devant; on 2, hold the position; on 3, extend the leg 2nd, pointing the foot onto the floor; on 4, hold the position; on 5, bring the foot on the cou-de-pied derrière; on 6, hold the position; on

7, extend the leg 2nd; on 8, hold the position; on 1, bring the foot on the cou-de-pied devant; on 2, hold the position; on 3, extend the leg 2nd; on 4, hold the position; on 5 and 6, close in 5th derrière; on 7 and 8, hold the position. Repeat the exercise starting with the right foot derrière. At the end, bring the working foot on the cou-de-pied derrière and hold balance.

Explanation. The battement frappé is performed in 5th, but it is otherwise similar to Exercise 8 of the Second Class of the Eighth Week. The knee is pushed to the side right away when the foot is on the cou-de-pied. Even though the exercise is done in 5th, it must not lose sharpness, especially in the extension of the foot from the cou-de-pied to the pointed position. Students apply the same head positions as the ones performed in Exercise 8 of the Second Class of the Eighth Week.

Exercise 10

Adagio: lift the leg 2nd, eight counts, facing the barre.

Students repeat Exercise 9 of the Fifth Class of the Eighth Week.

Exercise 11

Preparation for grand battement 2nd, facing the barre.

On 1 and 2, battement tendu 2nd; on 3, battement 2nd; on "and," lower the leg and point the foot onto the floor; on 4, hold the position; on 5 and 6, close 5th devant; on 7 and 8, hold the position. Repeat one more time with the right leg. Repeat the whole exercise one more time.

Explanation. Students are repeating the grand battement exercise in 5th. Notice the lowering of the leg is done more rapidly to activate the adductors and gain strength in closing the working leg; this practice will prove very useful in the future performance of grand allegro exercises.

Exercise 12

Pied sur la barre in 2nd and 4th position devant, plié.

Place the leg in 2nd on the barre, with both hands resting on the barre.

On "and" 1, plié; on 2, stretch; on 3 and 4, repeat; on 5, bring the arms in 1st; on 6, open 2nd; on 7 and 8, rest the left hand on the barre

and rotate so that the working leg is in front of the hips and the supporting foot is perpendicular to the working leg, the right arm remaining 2nd. The left hand adjusts so that the elbow is relaxed and the arm is slightly forward. Repeat the pliés with the right arm 2nd, bring both arms in 5th at the end and hold the position for eight counts.

Explanation. In the plié the knee must be above the toes. The back remains very erect and both hips face the working leg when performing the exercise in 4th position devant. By turning out the working leg, the supporting leg does not turn in and the supporting hip must not be pushed forward or out.

Application. Most beginners in a recreational program will find the 4th position devant in this exercise more awkward because of the croisé (crossed) position and would benefit more by still practicing the pied sur la barre only in 2nd for now.

CENTER

Exercise 13

Battement tendu 2nd, arms in 6th, in 1st, four counts.

Students repeat Exercise 16 of the Fourth Class of the Eighth Week.

Exercise 14

Battement tendu 2nd, start and close in plié, in 1st, four counts.

On 1, plié; on 2, battement tendu 2nd, staying in plié; on 3, close in 1st; on 4, stretch the knees. Repeat the exercise three times, alternating legs.

Explanation. Students are repeating the exercise as performed in Exercise 5 of the Fifth Class of the Seventh Week.

Exercise 15

Battement tendu 2nd, four counts.

Students repeat Exercise 16 of the Fifth Class of the Eighth Week.

Exercise 16

Preparation for battement jeté en croix, in 1st, eight counts.

Students repeat Exercise 17 of the Fifth Class of the Eighth Week.

Exercise 17

Preparation for chassé à terre 2nd, with transfer, stretch the legs, in 1st, with port de bras, four counts.

Students repeat Exercise 19 of the Fifth Class of the Eighth Week.

Exercise 18

Demi-rond de jambe à terre en dehors and en dedans (start derrière), in 1st, eight counts, with port de bras.

Students repeat Exercise 18 of the Fifth Class of the Eighth Week.

Exercise 19

Adagio: lift the leg devant and 2nd, in 1st, eight counts.

Students repeat Exercise 20 of the Fifth Class of the Eighth Week.

Exercise 20

Preparation for glissade 2nd, in 1st, four counts.

On 1, plié in 1st; on 2, battement tendu 2nd with the right foot; on 3, transfer the weight onto the right leg in plié, stretch the left leg and point the left foot; on "and" 4, close 1st in plié and stretch. Repeat three more times traveling toward the right.

Explanation. Students are practicing the exercise in the center with the arms 2nd.

Exercise 21

Soubresaut in 1st, on the count, two count hold in 1st, facing the barre.

On "and," plié and push off the floor; on 1, land in plié; on 2, stretch both knees; on 3 and 4, hold the position. Repeat three more times. After a pause, repeat the exercise.

Explanation. Students are performing the jump with a sharper plié on the upbeat and landing on the count. There is still a hold after each jump. The heels are pressed firmly onto the floor in the plié.

Music. A not too fast 2/4 march, a 3/8, or a 6/8 can be used. The tempo must be slow enough for students to have enough time to be able to stretch the legs and the feet fully in the air before landing.

Exercise 22

Preparation for the assemblé: brush forward in plié, jump to assemble both legs, two counts, one count hold, in 6th, facing the barre.

Students repeat Exercise 22 of the Fourth Class of the Eighth Week.

Exercise 23

Introduction to balancé, in 6th, traveling sideways, four counts, hands on the waist.

Students repeat Exercise 23 of the Fourth Class of the Eighth Week.

Exercise 24

Curtsey.

THIRD CLASS

Students repeat the material of the Second Class of this week.

FOURTH CLASS

Exercise 1

Close and open legs in 1st, battement tendu 2nd, in 1st, facing the barre.

Students repeat Exercise 1 of the Second Class of this week.

Exercise 2

Plié and grand plié in 2nd and 1st, facing the barre.

Students repeat Exercise 2 of the Second Class of the Eighth Week.

Exercise 3

Battement tendu 2nd, close in plié, in 1st, four counts, facing the barre.

Students repeat Exercise 3 of the Fifth Class of the Eighth Week.

Exercise 4

Battement tendu 2nd, plié when pointing, in 1st, facing the barre.

Students repeat Exercise 4 of the Second Class of this week.

Exercise 5

Battement tendu devant and 2nd, start and close in plié, in 1st, four counts, facing the barre.

On 1, plié; on 2, battement tendu devant in plié; on 3, close in 1st; on 4, stretch the knees. Repeat the exercise in 2nd. Repeat the whole exercise one more time. At the end, roll up in 1st and hold balance.

Explanation. Students are performing the exercise adding a battement tendu devant. When brushing out in plié, the working foot goes through a small 4th position devant before the heel comes up and the foot points fully. In doing so, the hips remain level. The heel is strongly pushed forward when the leg comes out.

Exercise 6

Battement tendu en croix, en dehors and en dedans (derrière, 2nd, devant, 2nd), four counts, facing the barre.

On 1 and 2, battement tendu devant; on 3 and 4, close 5th; on 5 and 6, battement tendu 2nd; on 7 and 8, close 5th derrière; on 1 and 2, battement tendu derrière; on 3 and 4, close; on 5 and 6, battement tendu 2nd; on 7 and 8, close 5th derrière.

On 1 and 2, battement tendu derrière; on 3 and 4, close 5th; on 5 and 6, battement tendu 2nd; on 7 and 8, close 5th devant; on 1 and 2, battement tendu devant; on 3 and 4, close; on 5 and 6, battement tendu 2nd; on 7 and 8, close 5th devant.

Explanation. Students are introduced to the concept of en croix en dedans. So far, except for the rond de jambe exercise, they have executed movements in a clockwise direction (devant, side, derrière). Here they do so in counterclockwise motion (derrière, side, devant).

Application. Students in a recreational program will be introduced to the concept of en croix en dedans much later, for this may confuse them, especially when closing the battement tendu 2nd in 5th.

Exercise 7

Preparation for battement jeté en croix, eight counts, facing the barre.

Students repeat Exercise 5 of the Fifth Class of the Eighth Week.

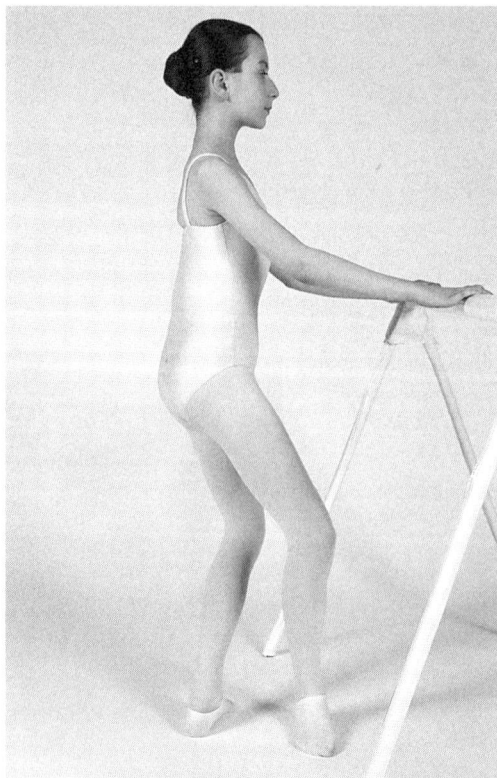

The foot is sliding out in plié, through a small 4th position, with the head held straight.

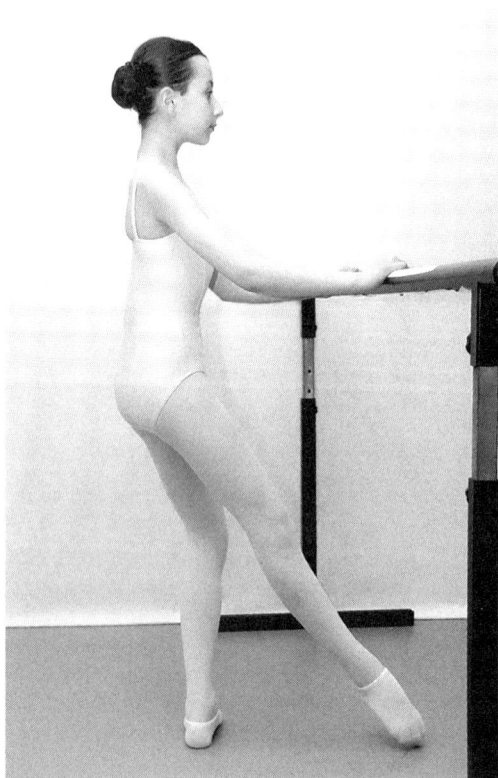

The leg is fully extended devant, still in plié, with the head held straight.

Exercise 8

Rond de jambe à terre en dehors and en dedans, directly in 5th, eight counts, facing the barre.

On 1 and 2, battement tendu devant; on 3 and 4, rond de jambe en dehors to 2nd position; on 5 and 6, rond de jambe to 4th derrière; on 7 and 8, close 5th. On 1 and 2, battement tendu derrière; on 3 and 4, rond de jambe to 2nd position; on 5 and 6, rond de jambe to 4th position devant; on 7 and 8, close 5th. Repeat one more time.

Explanation. Students are practicing the same rond de jambe exercise than the one performed in Exercise 8 of the Fourth Class of the Eighth Week, in 5th this time.

Exercise 9

Preparation for battement frappé 2nd, without closing, four counts, facing the barre.

Students repeat Exercise 9 of the Second Class of this week.

Exercise 10

Adagio: lift the leg 2nd, facing the barre.

Students repeat Exercise 9 of the Fifth Class of the Eighth Week.

Exercise 11

Preparation for grand battement 2nd, facing the barre.

Students repeat Exercise 11 of the Second Class of this week.

Exercise 12

Pied sur la barre in 2nd and 4th position devant, plié.

Students repeat Exercise 12 of the Second Class of this week.

CENTER

Exercise 13

Battement tendu 2nd, close in plié, in 1st, four counts.

On 1 and 2, battement tendu 2nd; on "and" 3, close in plié; on 4, stretch the knees. Repeat three more times, alternating legs.

Explanation. Students are repeating the exercise done at the barre earlier in Exercise 3 of the Fifth Class of the Eighth Week.

Exercise 14

Battement tendu 2nd, start and close in plié, in 1st, four counts.

Students repeat Exercise 14 of the Second Class of this week.

Exercise 15

Battement tendu 2nd, four counts.

Students repeat Exercise 16 of the Fifth Class of the Eighth Week.

Exercise 16

Preparation for battement jeté en croix, in 1st, eight counts.

Students repeat Exercise 17 of the Fifth Class of the Eighth Week.

Exercise 17

Preparation for chassé à terre in 2nd, with transfer, stretch the legs, in 1st, with port de bras, four counts.

Students repeat Exercise 19 of the Fifth Class of the Eighth Week.

Exercise 18

Demi-rond de jambe à terre en dehors and en dedans (start derrière), with port de bras, in 1st, eight counts.

Students repeat Exercise 18 of the Fifth Class of the Eighth Week.

Exercise 19

Adagio: lift the leg devant and 2nd, in 1st, eight counts.

Students repeat Exercise 20 of the Fifth Class of the Eighth Week.

Exercise 20

Preparation for glissade 2nd, in 1st, four counts.

Students repeat Exercise 20 of the Second Class of this week.

Exercise 21

Relevé in 6th and 1st, plié, four counts.

Following the preparatory port de bras, bring the arms down.

On 1, plié; on 2, relevé directly from the plié, bringing the arms in low 1st; on 3, come down into plié; on 4, stretch both knees. Repeat three times more. Open the legs in 1st and repeat the exercise.

Explanation. Students are practicing the relevé with plié in the center. Students are starting in 6th, which is the easiest position. A strong back, the heels pressed onto the floor in the plié, stability in the ankles, and straight feet are required to execute this exercise in the center. Like at the barre, no adjustment is made once the feet come down into plié. The heels come down each time, pressing onto the floor. Students must not shuffle with their feet while on demi-pointes. The knees are fully taut in the relevé.

Application. It goes without saying that the relevés in the center can be practiced only when students can perform them well enough at the barre and their ankles have acquired enough strength to keep the feet straight and elevated on demi-pointes.

Exercise 22

Soubresaut in 1st, on the count, two count hold in 1st, facing the barre.

Students repeat Exercise 21 of the Second Class of this week.

Exercise 23

Preparation for the assemblé: brush forward in plié and jump to assemble both legs, two counts, one count hold, in 6th.

Following the preparatory port de bras, bring the arms down.

On "and," plié; on 1, brush the right foot devant off the floor and extend the leg, while pushing off the floor with the supporting leg, bringing both legs stretched together in 6th in the air, with the arms in low 1st; on 2, land on both feet in 6th; on 3, stretch both knees; on 4, hold the position. Repeat the exercise, alternating right and left legs.

Explanation. Students are repeating the exercise in the center with a slightly faster tempo. They must press their working foot firmly on the floor when brushing it, starting jumping *just* as the working leg stretches out, not later, for otherwise the momentum would be broken. Both legs and feet are stretched in the air. The arms do not bounce in the jump.

Application. Students in a recreational pro-

gram may hold their hands on the waist for this exercise, without the hands sliding up and down.

Exercise 24

Curtsey.

FIFTH CLASS

Exercise 1

Close and open legs in 1st, battement tendu 2nd, facing the barre.

Students repeat Exercise 1 of the Second Class of this week.

Exercise 2

Plié in 2nd and 1st, arm in low 1st, port de bras performed separately.

Following the preparatory port de bras, open both feet 2nd, as learned earlier, and bring the arm down.

On 1 and 2, plié, bringing the arm in low 1st; on 3 and 4, stretch; from 5 to 8, repeat; on 1 and 2, bring the arm in full 1st; on 3 and 4, open 2nd; on 5 and 6, bring the arm down; on 7 and 8, close in 1st. Repeat the exercise in 1st.

Explanation. Students are practicing the plié exercise sideways again, as performed in Exercise 2 of the Fifth Class of the Fifth Week. This time the working arm is held in low 1st. A port de bras performed separately is included in the exercise. The elbow of the arm does not sag.

Exercise 3

Battement tendu 2nd, bring the foot down 2nd with plié, point the foot and close, with transfer, in 1st, eight counts, facing the barre.

On 1 and 2, battement tendu 2nd; on 3, bring the foot down in 2nd; on 4, plié on both legs in 2nd; on 5, stretch both legs; on 6, point the left foot while transferring the weight onto the right leg; on 7 and 8, close 1st. Repeat three more times, alternating legs. At the end, roll up and hold the position.

Explanation. Students are practicing the exercise with a plié and a transfer of weight from one leg onto another. This is a very broken down preparatory exercise for a simple temps lié (linked step), starting with a stretched leg. In the temps lié, smoothness of execution, stability, and a deep plié to transfer from one leg onto another are essential. The maintaining of the turn-out, especially in the passage through plié from one position to another, is also required. This type of exercise will help students to develop these skills and to avoid common errors in the temps lié such as rolling the feet with the knees pushed forward in the passage from one leg to another, executing a shallow plié, bending the first leg before the heel touches the floor, and insufficiently transferring weight from one leg to another.

Music. A medium-tempo 3/4 waltz would be a good choice for this exercise.

Application. Like the preparation for the chassé, this exercise will benefit most beginners, no matter how often they take ballet a week, for it sensitizes students to the transfer of weight in a broken down manner.

Exercise 4

Battement tendu en croix, close in plié, in 1st, four counts.

On 1 and 2, battement tendu devant; on "and" 3, close in plié; on 4, stretch the knees. Repeat the exercise en croix en dehors. At the end, roll up in 1st and hold the position.

Explanation. Students are performing the exercise en croix sideways.

Exercise 5

Battement tendu 2nd, plié when pointing, in 1st, facing the barre.

Students repeat Exercise 4 of the Second Class of this week.

Exercise 6

Battement tendu devant and 2nd, start and close in plié, in 1st, four counts, facing the barre.

Students repeat Exercise 5 of the Fourth Class of this week.

Exercise 7

Battement tendu en croix, en dehors and en dedans, four counts, facing the barre.

Students repeat Exercise 6 of the Fourth Class of this week.

Exercise 8

Preparation for battement jeté en croix, en dehors and en dedans, eight counts, facing the barre.

On 1 and 2, battement tendu devant; on "and," lift the leg with vigor à la demi-hauteur; on 3, hold the position; on "and," lower the leg, and point the foot onto the floor; on 4, hold the position; on 5 and 6, close 5th; on 7 and 8, hold the position. Repeat the exercise en croix en dehors, the last one closing 5th derrière.

On 1 and 2, battement tendu derrière; on "and," lift the leg with vigor à la demi-hauteur; on 3, hold the position; on "and," lower the leg and point the foot onto the floor; on 4, hold the position; on 5 and 6, close 5th; on 7 and 8, hold the position. Repeat the exercise en croix en dedans, the last one closing 5th devant.

Explanation. The exercise is now performed en dehors and en dedans.

Exercise 9

Preparation for battement jeté piqué en croix, eight counts, facing the barre.

On 1 and 2, battement tendu devant; on "and," lift the leg; on 3, hold the position; on "and," lower the leg, and point the foot onto the floor; on 4, hold the position; on "and," lift the leg; on 5, hold the position; on "and," lower the leg; on 6, hold the position; on 7 and 8, close 5th. Repeat en croix en dehors.

Explanation. Students are repeating the exercise en croix in 5th, as performed in Exercise 7 of the Fourth Class of the Eighth Week. Both the lifting and the lowering are done more quickly with less holding.

Music. A tango with clear beats would work well here.

Exercise 10

Position on the cou-de-pied, pointed, devant and derrière, extension of the leg 2nd, eight counts, facing the barre.

On "and," bring the foot on the cou-de-pied devant; on 1 and 2, hold the position; on 3, extend the leg 2nd, pointing the foot onto the floor; on 4, hold the position; on 5 and 6, close 5th derrière; on 7 and 8, hold the position. Repeat the exercise with the foot on the

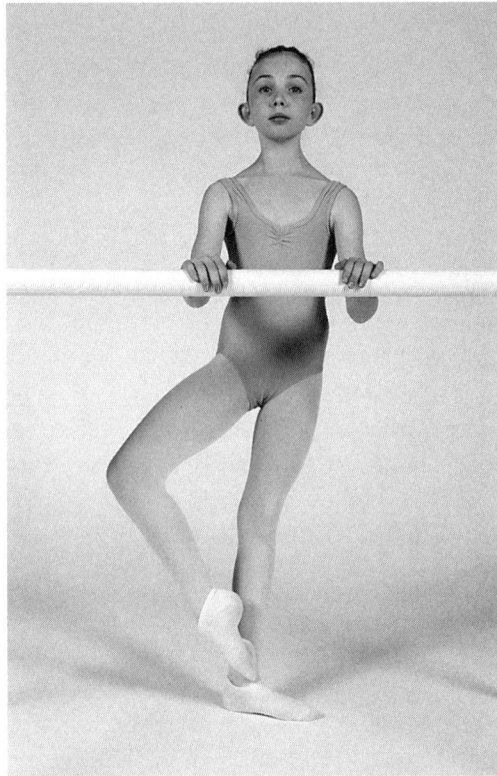

The foot is pointed on the cou-de-pied devant; the head is held straight.

The foot is sickled against the cou-de-pied; the head is held straight.

cou-de-pied derrière. Repeat the exercise alternating devant and derrière.

Explanation. The exercise introduces the pointed—in contrast to the wrapped—position of the foot on the cou-de-pied devant and derrière in 5th position. In the position devant, the side of the small toe touches the supporting leg just above the ankle joint, while the heel is pushed forward; in the back, the position of the foot is the same as the one students learned earlier in the training. The movement of the working foot coming onto the cou-de-pied is sharp, but, unlike the vigorous extension movement in the battement frappé, the extension here is smooth, since it is used only to be able to close and change feet. When extending 2nd, both legs must be kept very turned out, pushing forward the inside muscles of the thighs as much as possible, but without turning the hips one way or the other.

Application. The instructor will watch for students pushing their working heel against the supporting ankle (the banana-like position!) when the foot is on the cou-de-pied devant.

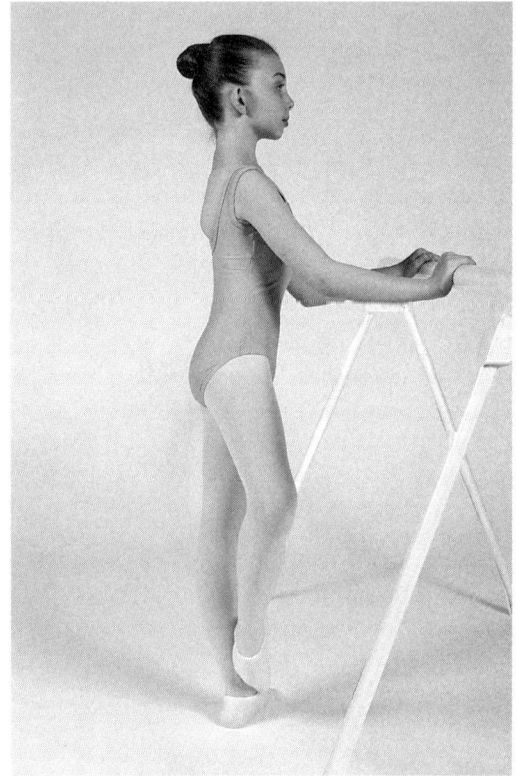

Exercise 11

Rond de jambe à terre en dehors and en dedans, eight counts, facing the barre.

Students repeat Exercise 8 of the Fourth Class of this week.

Exercise 12

Preparation for battement frappé 2nd, without closing, four counts, facing the barre.

Students repeat Exercise 9 of the Second Class of this week.

Exercise 13

Adagio: lift the leg devant, sideways, 2nd and derrière facing the barre.

In 4th position devant, sideways: on 1 and 2, battement tendu devant; on 3 and 4, lift the leg; on 5 and 6, lower the leg and point the foot onto the floor; on 7 and 8, close in 5th devant. Repeat one more time.

In 2nd position, facing the barre: on 1 and 2, battement tendu 2nd; on 3 and 4, lift the leg; on 5 and 6, lower the leg; on 7 and 8, close 5th devant. Repeat one more time closing 5th derrière.

In 4th position derrière, facing the barre: on 1 and 2, battement tendu derrière; on 3 and 4, lift the leg; on 5 and 6, lower the leg; on 7 and 8, close 5th derrière. Repeat one more time.

Explanation. Students are introduced to lifting their leg devant performed sideways of the barre. Lifting the leg 2nd and derrière is still done facing the barre to keep the body as straight as possible. The working leg is fully stretched in the position derrière. A slight allowance is permitted for a tilt of the pelvis, without which the leg is not able to be lifted with turn-out. In the position of the leg at 90°, the pelvis is almost horizontal.[15] As the leg goes higher, the opening of the hip position is necessarily increased.

Exercise 14

Relevé in 2nd and 1st, plié and relevé on one count, roll down, four counts, facing the barre.

Following the preparatory position, battement tendu 2nd and bring the foot down.

On "and," plié; on 1, relevé; on 2, hold the position; on 3, roll down; on 4, hold the position. Repeat the exercise twice more and close 1st. Repeat the exercise in 1st. Repeat the exercise with a battement tendu with the left foot.

Explanation. This time the plié and the relevé are performed on the count, making it much sharper. Students are coming down by rolling the feet down onto the floor with control and resistance.

Exercise 15

Preparation for grand battement 2nd, facing the barre.

Students repeat Exercise 11 of the Second Class of this week.

Exercise 16

Pied sur la barre in 2nd and devant, plié.

Students repeat Exercise 12 of the Second Class of this week.

CENTER

Exercise 17

Battement tendu 2nd, close in plié, in 1st, four counts.

Students repeat Exercise 13 of the Fourth Class of this week.

Exercise 18

Battement tendu 2nd, start and close in plié, in 1st, four counts.

Students repeat Exercise 14 of the Second Class of this week.

Exercise 19

Battement tendu 2nd, en descendant, with head rotation, four counts.

On 1 and 2, battement tendu 2nd with the left foot, turning the head slightly toward the left side without tilting it back; on 3 and 4, close 5th devant, keeping the head turned to the left; on 5 and 6, battement tendu 2nd with the right foot, turning the head toward the right; on 7 and 8, close 5th devant. Repeat the exercise one more time, always closing front. After a pause, repeat the exercise.

Battement tendu 2nd position en descendant; the head is tilted slightly back.

---

15   Grieg, *Inside Ballet Technique*, 44.

Explanation. Students are closing their working foot always front in this exercise, thus causing students to move forward. Here students coordinate their head and leg movements. As a general rule, the head is de face when the working leg is 2nd. However, in exercises as this one, the head anticipates the closing, turning toward the same side as the working foot closes on. Here, the head turns toward the working leg when moving forward (by closing devant). The head does not move to the other direction before the working leg comes out.

Exercise 20

Preparation for glissade 2nd, in 1st, four counts.

Students repeat Exercise 20 of the Second Class of this week.

Exercise 21

Relevé in 6th and in 1st, plié four counts.

Students repeat Exercise 21 of the Fourth Class of this week.

Exercise 22

Soubresaut in 1st, on the count, two count hold in 1st, facing the barre.

Students repeat Exercise 21 of the Second Class of this week.

Exercise 23

Preparation for the assemblé: brush forward in plié and jump to assemble both legs, two counts, one count hold, in 6th.

Students repeat Exercise 23 of the Fourth Class of this week.

Exercise 24

Curtsey.

Tenth Week

𝄞

FIRST CLASS

Students repeat the material of the Fifth Class of the Ninth Week.

SECOND CLASS

Exercise 1

Battement tendu 2nd, flex the foot, in 1st, eight counts, facing the barre.

On 1 and 2, battement tendu 2nd; on 3, flex the toes; on 4, flex the rest of the foot; on 5, point the foot, except for the toes; on 6, point the toes, bringing the pointed foot onto the floor; on 7 and 8, close 1st. Repeat the whole exercise. At the end, roll up and hold balance.

Explanation. Students are reviewing the flexion of the working foot. The flexion is still done broken down for the articulation of the foot. The foot when flexing must be flat, and both legs remain turned out.

Application. For all beginning students, it is difficult to overdo exercises involving flexing the foot, which gently increase the flexibility of the whole foot and ankle.

Exercise 2

Plié in 2nd and 1st, arm in low 1st, port de bras performed separately.

Students repeat Exercise 2 of the Fifth Class of the Ninth Week.

Exercise 3

Battement tendu 2nd, bring the foot down 2nd with plié, point the foot and close, with transfer, in 1st, eight counts, facing the barre.

Students repeat Exercise 3 of the Fifth Class of the Ninth Week.

Exercise 4

Battement tendu en croix, close in plié, in 1st, four counts.

Students repeat Exercise 4 of the Fifth Class of the Ninth Week.

Exercise 5

Battement tendu en croix, en dehors and en dedans, four counts, facing the barre.

Students repeat Exercise 6 of the Fourth Class of the Ninth Week.

Exercise 6

Preparation for battement jeté en croix, en dehors and en dedans, eight counts, facing the barre.

Students repeat Exercise 8 of the Fifth Class of the Ninth Week.

Exercise 7

Preparation for battement jeté piqué en croix, eight counts, facing the barre.

Students repeat Exercise 9 of the Fifth Class of the Ninth Week.

Exercise 8

Position on the cou-de-pied, pointed, devant and derrière, extension of the leg 2nd, eight counts, facing the barre.

Students repeat Exercise 10 of the Fifth Class of the Ninth Week.

Exercise 9

Rond de jambe à terre en dehors and en dedans, eight counts, facing the barre.

Students repeat Exercise 8 of the Fourth Class of the Ninth Week.

Exercise 10

Preparation for battement frappé en croix, without closing, four counts, facing the barre.

On "and," the front foot comes on the cou-de-pied devant; on 1 and 2, hold the position; on 3, extend the leg devant pointing the foot with sharpness onto the floor; on 4, hold the position; on 5, bring the foot on the cou-de-pied devant; on 6, hold the position; on 7, extend the leg 2nd, pointing the foot onto the floor; on 8, hold the position; on 1, bring the front foot on the cou-de-pied derrière; on 2, hold the position; on 3, extend the leg derrière, pointing the foot onto the floor; on 4, hold the position; on 5, bring the foot on the cou-de-pied derrière; on 6, hold the position; on 7, extend the leg 2nd; on 8, hold the position. Repeat the exercise one more time. At the end, bring the foot on the cou-de-pied devant and hold balance.

Explanation. Students are now performing the battement frappé exercise en croix, still on four counts, and still facing the barre to keep the hips square, with a hold on the cou-de-pied and a hold when the foot is pointed on the floor. The working knee is pushed to the side when the foot comes on the cou-de-pied and remains so as much as possible when extending out. Students are reminded of the different head positions they have learned for this type of exercise.

Exercise 11

Adagio: lift the leg devant, sideways, 2nd, and derrière facing the barre.

Students repeat Exercise 13 of the Fifth Class of the Ninth Week.

Exercise 12

Relevé in 2nd and 1st, plié and relevé on one count, roll down, four counts, facing the barre.

Students repeat Exercise 14 of the Fifth Class of the Ninth Week.

Exercise 13

Preparation for grand battement 2nd, facing the barre.

Students repeat Exercise 11 of the Second Class of the Ninth Week.

Exercise 14

Pied sur la barre in 2nd and devant, plié.

Students repeat Exercise 12 of the Second Class of the Ninth Week.

CENTER

Exercise 15

Battement tendu 2nd, close in plié, in 1st, four counts.

Students repeat Exercise 13 of the Fourth Class of the Ninth Week.

Exercise 16

Battement tendu 2nd, en descendant, with head rotation, four counts.

Students repeat Exercise 19 of the Fifth Class of the Ninth Week.

Exercise 17

Preparation for battement jeté 2nd, eight counts.

On 1 and 2, battement tendu 2nd with the right foot, straightening the head; on "and," lift the leg a la demi-hauteur; on 3, hold the position; on "and," lower the leg and point the foot onto the floor; on 4, hold the position; on 5 and 6, close 5th devant, turning the head slightly toward the right; on 7 and 8, hold the position. Repeat the exercise one more time closing 5th derrière. Repeat the whole exercise one more time.

Explanation. Students are practicing the preparatory exercise for the battement jeté 2nd in 5th.

Music. A 4/4 polka with sharp beats would work well.

Exercise 18

Adagio: lift the leg 2nd, eight counts.

On 1 and 2, battement tendu 2nd with the right foot, straightening the head; on 3 and 4, lift the leg; on 5 and 6, lower the leg and point the foot onto the floor; on 7 and 8, close 5th derrière. Repeat the whole exercise one more time.

Explanation. Students are practicing the exercise in 5th. The elbows do not scoop and the back remains very erect.

Exercise 19

Relevé in 6th and in 1st, plié, four counts.

Students repeat Exercise 21 of the Fourth Class of the Ninth Week.

Exercise 20

Soubresaut in 1st, on the count, two count hold in 1st, facing the barre.

Students repeat Exercise 21 of the Second Class of the Ninth Week.

Exercise 21

Preparation for the assemblé: brush forward in plié and jump to assemble both legs, two counts, one count hold, in 6th.

Students repeat Exercise 23 of the Fourth Class of the Ninth Week.

Exercise 22

Preparation for déboulés, in 1st, arms in low 1st, each half turn on one count, hold two counts after two half turns.

Start the exercise in the back of the studio.

On "and" 1, transfer the weight onto the right foot, raising the right heel very slightly and rotating it toward the right, rotate a half turn toward the right, keeping the arms in low 1st, turning the head so that, by the end of the half turn, it is now toward the left shoulder with the eyes focused on a particular point; on "and" 2, transferring the weight onto the left foot, rotate a half turn toward the right, keeping the eyes still focused on the particular point as the body starts rotating, and the head snapping so that the head precedes the end of the rotation of the body with the eyes still focused on the same spot; on 3 and 4, hold the position. Repeat a few more times. Repeat the exercise rotating toward the left.

Explanation. Students are performing two half turns on two counts and holding two counts.

Exercise 23

Curtsey.

THIRD CLASS

Students repeat the material of the Second Class of this week.

FOURTH CLASS

Exercise 1

Battement tendu 2nd, flex the foot, in 1st, eight counts, facing the barre.

Students repeat Exercise 1 of the Second Class of this week.

Exercise 2

Plié in 2nd and 1st, arm in low 1st, port de bras performed separately.

Students repeat Exercise 2 of the Fifth Class of the Ninth Week.

Exercise 3

Battement tendu 2nd, bring the foot down 2nd with plié, point the foot and close, with transfer, in 1st, eight counts, facing the barre.

Students repeat Exercise 3 of the Fifth Class of the Ninth Week.

Exercise 4

Battement tendu en croix, close in plié, in 1st, four counts.

Students repeat Exercise 4 of the Fifth Class of the Ninth Week.

Exercise 5

Battement tendu en croix, en dehors and en dedans, four counts, facing the barre.

Students repeat Exercise 6 of the Fourth Class of the Ninth Week.

Exercise 6

Preparation for battement jeté en croix, en dehors and en dedans, eight counts, facing the barre.

Students repeat Exercise 8 of the Fifth Class of the Ninth Week.

Exercise 7

Preparation for battement jeté piqué en croix, facing the barre.

Students repeat Exercise 9 of the Fifth Class of the Ninth Week.

Exercise 8

Position on the cou-de-pied, pointed, devant and derrière, extension of the leg 2nd, eight counts, facing the barre.

Students repeat Exercise 10 of the Fifth Class of the Ninth Week.

Exercise 9

Rond de jambe à terre en dehors and en dedans, with port de bras, eight counts, bending forward.

Following the preparatory port de bras, bring the arm down and turn the head slightly toward the right.

On 1 and 2, battement tendu devant, bringing the arm to 1st; on 3 and 4, rond de jambe to 2nd position while the arm opens 2nd; on 5 and 6, rond de jambe to 4th position derrière, keeping the arm 2nd; on 7 and 8, close 5th derrière, bringing the arm down. On 1 and 2, battement tendu derrière, bringing the arm to 1st; on 3 and 4, rond de jambe to 2nd position, while the arm opens 2nd; on 5 and 6, rond de jambe to 4th position devant, keeping the arm 2nd; on 7 and 8, close 5th devant while bringing the arm down, keeping the head slightly turned toward the right. Repeat the exercise one more time and close in 5th.

On 1 and 2, bring the arm to 5th, with the head turned slightly toward the arm; on 3 and 4, bend forward keeping the back flat with the arm still in 5th; on 5 and 6, straighten up, starting by lengthening the lower back, and keeping the back flat; on 7 and 8, hold both arms in 5th, the head turned de face.

Explanation. Students are practicing the exercise sideways with a port de bras. The head turns slightly toward the side of the barre when closing 5th derrière. Students are also introduced to the bending forward performed sideways. When bringing the arm in 5th, the shoulder remains down. When bending, students must not push backward or move their hand too far forward on the barre. Such adjustment would result in their being off balance.

Exercise 10

Preparation for battement frappé en croix, without closing, four counts, facing the barre.

Students repeat Exercise 10 of the Second Class of this week.

Exercise 11

Petits battements, each movement on the count, facing the barre.

On "and," bring the foot on the cou-de-pied devant; on 1, hold the position; on 2, unbend the leg halfway to 2nd, with a slight hold, straightening the head; on 3, transfer to the cou-de-pied derrière, turning the head slightly toward the left; on 4, open the leg halfway to 2nd, straightening the head; on 5, transfer the foot on the cou-de-pied devant, turning the head slightly toward the right; on 6, extend the leg 2nd, the pointed toes touching the floor, straightening the head; on 7 and 8, close 5th derrière, turning the head slightly toward the left. Repeat the exercise starting on the cou-de-pied derrière. At the end, hold the cou-de-pied position devant, bringing the arms in low 1st, keeping the head straight.

Explanation. Students are resuming the study of petits battements. This time, each transfer is on the count with no hold. There is only a slight hold after each movement, with the leg freezing into position. When the foot is on the cou-de-pied, students press their working foot firmly against the ankle. Before closing, students extend their leg 2nd first. Students are reminded of the

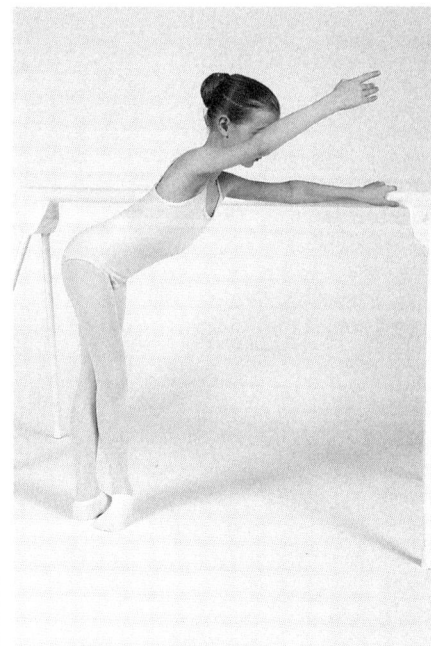

Bending forward with the arm 5th position. Bending forward, pushing too far backward. Bending forward, pushing too far forward.

head positions as learned in Exercise 10 of the Fifth Class of the Seventh Week.

Music. A coda with clear and sharp beats works well for this type of exercise.

Exercise 12

Adagio: lift the leg devant, sideways, 2nd and derrière, facing the barre.

Students repeat Exercise 13 of the Fifth Class of the Ninth Week.

Exercise 13

Preparation for grand battement 2nd, facing the barre.

Students repeat Exercise 11 of the Second Class of the Ninth Week.

Exercise 14

Relevé in 2nd and 1st, plié and relevé on one count, roll down, four counts, facing the barre.

Students repeat Exercise 14 of the Fifth Class of the Ninth Week.

Exercise 15

Pied sur la barre in 2nd, plié and bend.

On "and" 1, plié; on 2, stretch; on "and" 3 and 4, repeat; on 5 and 6, bring the left arm 1st and open it 2nd, with the head following the left hand; on 7 and 8, bring it in 5th, and turn the head toward the right; on 1 and 2, bend sideways toward the right side; on 3 and 4, straighten up; on 5 and 6, open the left arm 2nd, with the head following the opening of the arm movement; on 7, rest the left hand on the barre; on 8, hold the position; on 1 and 2, bring the right arm in 1st and open it 2nd; on 3 and 4, bring it in 5th, and turn the head toward the left side; on 5 and 6, bend sideways toward the left; on 7 and 8, straighten up and bring both arms in 5th and hold the position.

Explanation. Students are adding bending to the sides in this exercise. In each port de bras, students follow the movement of the hand with the head and the eyes. Before even bending, the head turns toward the same side as the bending. When the head is turned, the chin does not come down toward the shoulder. The hip of the working leg stays down during the bending, especially when bending away from the working leg. The shoulders stay down, and while bending,

the distance between the top of the head and the hand of the arm in 5th is respected. When bending toward the leg that is on the barre, the opposite shoulder of the raised arm must slide slightly down so that the working shoulder is not an obstacle for the student to really stretch the side of the torso. During the exercise, the working foot does not relax but remains pointed and turned out at all time.

Application. There is a tendency to relax the muscles of the whole working leg when it rests on the barre in the exercise of pied sur la barre, especially for students taking ballet recreationally; therefore, the instructor will remind them often to keep the muscles tightened throughout the exercise.

CENTER

Exercise 16

Battement tendu 2nd, bring the foot down 2nd with plié, point the foot and close, with port de bras, in 1st, eight counts.

On 1 and 2, battement tendu 2nd; on 3, bring the foot down, bringing the arms in 1st; on 4, plié on both legs; on 5, stretch both legs; on 6, point the left foot, opening the arms 2nd, while transferring the weight onto the right leg; on 7 and 8, close 1st. Repeat the whole exercise one more time.

Explanation. Students are repeating Exercise 3 of the Fifth Class of the Ninth Week performed at the barre. A port de bras accompanies the leg movement. The second foot should be very active in pointing off the floor to transfer the weight onto the first leg.

Exercise 17

Battement tendu 2nd, start and close in plié, in 1st, four counts, review.

On 1, plié; on 2, battement tendu 2nd in plié; on 3, close in 1st; on 4, stretch the knees. Repeat the exercise three more times, alternating legs.

Explanation. Students are repeating Exercise 14 of the Second Class of the Ninth Week.

Exercise 18

Battement tendu 2nd, en descendant, with head rotation, four counts.

Students repeat Exercise 19 of the Fifth Class of the Ninth Week.

Exercise 19

Preparation for battement jeté 2nd, eight counts.
Students repeat Exercise 17 of the Second Class of this week.

Exercise 20

Adagio: lift the leg 2nd, eight counts.
Students repeat Exercise 18 of the Second Class of this week.

Exercise 21

Relevé in 6th and in 1st, plié, four counts.
Students repeat Exercise 21 of the Fourth Class of the Ninth Week.

Exercise 22

Preparation for déboulés, in 1st, arms in low 1st, each half turn on one count, hold two counts after two half turns.
Students repeat Exercise 22 of the Second Class of this week.

Exercise 23

Curtsey.

FIFTH CLASS

Exercise 1

Battement tendu 2nd, flex the foot, in 1st, eight counts, facing the barre.
Students repeat Exercise 1 of the Second Class of this week.

Exercise 2

Plié in 2nd and 1st, arm in 1st, separate port de bras.
Students repeat Exercise 2 of the Fifth Class of the Ninth Week.

Exercise 3

Preparation for passé à terre: battement tendu devant and derrière, in 1st, four counts, facing the barre.
On 1 and 2, battement tendu devant with the right foot; on 3 and 4, close 1st; on 5 and 6, battement tendu derrière, still with the right foot; on 7 and 8, close 1st. Repeat the exercise one more time. Repeat the whole exercise starting back. At the end, roll up and hold balance.

Explanation. This battement tendu exercise involves a new pattern. It prepares for the brushing through 1st (passé à terre) from front to back and vice versa. There is a hold in the closing so that students bring their foot flat each time it is in 1st and avoid, later on in the passé, rolling in their working foot when it slides through 1st from back to front and turning in their working leg in every brush.

Application. The introduction of this new pattern will come later for recreational ballet beginners who may get confused with the change of direction.

Exercise 4

Battement tendu en croix, en dehors and en dedans, four counts.
On 1 and 2, battement tendu devant; on 3 and 4, close 5th; on 5 and 6, battement tendu 2nd; on 7 and 8, close 5th derrière; on 1 and 2, battement tendu derrière; on 3 and 4, close 5th derrière; on 5 and 6, battement tendu 2nd; on 7 and 8, close 5th derrière.
On 1 and 2, battement tendu derrière; on 3 and 4, close 5th; on 5 and 6, battement tendu 2nd; on 7 and 8, close 5th devant; on 1 and 2, battement tendu devant; on 3 and 4, close 5th devant; on 5 and 6, battement tendu 2nd; on 7 and 8, close 5th devant.

Explanation. Students are practicing Exercise 6 of the Fourth Class of the Ninth Week, this time performed sideways. The tempo is even with the same speed opening up and closing. Students close 5th derrière at the end of the first series to be able to start en croix en dedans.

Exercise 5

Battement tendu 2nd, start and close in plié, four counts, facing the barre.
On 1, plié; on 2, battement tendu 2nd, still in plié; on 3, close 5th devant still in plié; on 4, stretch both knees; on 5, plié; on 6, battement tendu 2nd; on 7, close 5th derrière; on 8, stretch the knees. Repeat the exercise one more time with the right foot, closing the last battement tendu 5th derrière.

Explanation. Students are now practicing the exercise in 5th instead of 1st. Since closing the feet in 5th is easier in plié, students may be tempted to over turn their feet in that position in plié. When it is time to stretch the knees, the discrepancy between the over turning of the feet in 5th in plié and the real turn-out out of the hips may cause serious injury in the knees and ankles. Therefore, the angle of the feet in 5th should be kept consistent throughout the exercise. Students may have to adjust the distance from the barre, as they perform the exercise with the right foot and the left foot.

Exercise 6

Preparation for battement jeté en croix, en dehors and en dedans, eight counts, facing the barre.

Students repeat Exercise 8 of the Fifth Class of the Ninth Week.

Exercise 7

Rond de jambe à terre en dehors and en dedans, with port de bras, eight counts, bending forward.

Students repeat Exercise 9 of the Fourth Class of this week.

Exercise 8

Preparation for battement frappé en croix, without closing, four counts, facing the barre.

Students repeat Exercise 10 of the Second Class of this week.

Exercise 9

Adagio: retiré devant and derrière [passé—Cecchetti], extension of the leg 2nd, facing the barre.

On 1, bring the foot pointed on the cou-de-pied devant, straightening the head; on 2, hold the position; on 3 to 4, slide the side of the small toe up against the supporting leg; on 5 and 6, slide down to the cou-de-pied position, following the same trajectory as on the way up; on 7 and 8, extend the leg 2nd, and point the foot onto the floor, close 5th devant. Repeat the exercise, closing derrière.

On 1, bring the foot on the cou-de-pied derrière; on 2, hold the position; on 3 to 4, slide the inner side of the heel and then progressively open the foot slightly out so that now the side of the big toe slides up against the back of the supporting leg to knee level; on 5 and 6, slide down to the cou-de-pied position; on 7 and 8, extend the leg 2nd, and point the foot onto the floor, close 5th derrière. Repeat the exercise, closing devant.

Explanation. This exercise introduces the retiré 2nd with turn-out. Students extend their leg 2nd so that they can close 5th from the open position; the direct closing into 5th will come later. The hamstrings should be very active in holding the leg up in retiré. The weight of the working leg is in no way supported by the foot, especially in the retiré devant. For the retiré derrière, when the foot comes onto the cou-de-pied, only the heel touches the back of the ankle, as students have practiced in the exercises of battements frappés and petits battements; as it slides up, the foot opens up so that by the time the leg is in retiré, only the inner side of the metatarsals touches the back of the knee. This change of position is necessary so that the thigh of the working leg is as perpendicular as possible to the supporting leg, with part of the working foot still against the supporting leg. The adjustment of the foot when sliding up also prevents the toes from being seen across the supporting leg, a condition that would break the aesthetic line of the supporting leg. For now, the head remains straight.

In the French school of ballet, even in adagio exercises, the foot comes up pointed sharply against (devant or derrière) the cou-de-pied. It forces students to control their balance right

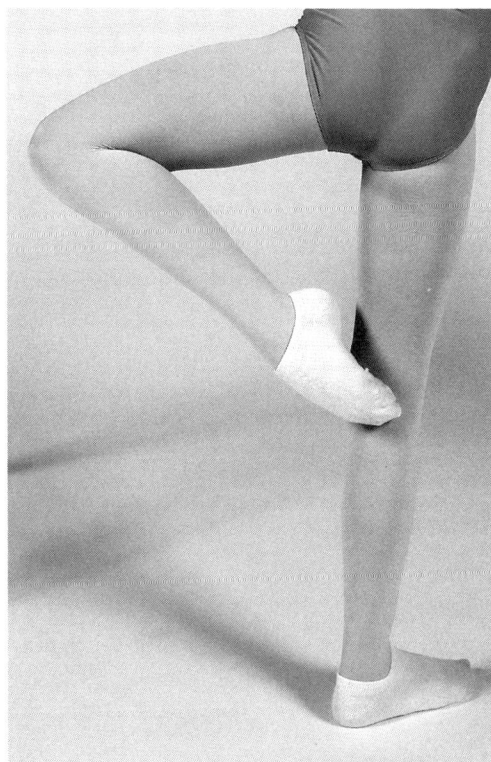

Executing the retiré derrière; the working hip is slightly lifted.

away, as soon as the weight is on one foot; it also gets to the final position of the foot on the supporting leg more quickly for a lasting impression. How the foot gets there should be imperceptible to the audience. As the leg goes up to the retiré position, students must pull up the opposite side of the torso to compensate for the lift of the working leg. This pulling up is important to help balancing, and its practice will be reflected in the performance of pirouettes and extensions practiced later in the center. In the retiré, the working hip is not raised, and both hips remain as straight as possible.

For the retiré devant, the heel never touches the supporting leg; the side of the small toe slides up to knee level. Once at knee level, the side of the pointed toes is nested between the kneecap and the side of the knee (along the side of the supporting leg at the knee level), a soft spot next to the patella. This particular spot of the knee offers a nesting place for the toes of the working foot so that the position is more stable, especially when it is time to perform pirouettes. The foot is fully pointed with the heel aimed forward during this exercise. A common error is for students to let their working foot sickle with the heel pushing back against the supporting leg.

The retiré is an important part of the développé but also of the pirouette, both of them studied later during the year. Students will practice the retiré regularly throughout the year.

There is much confusion and many mistakes are made regarding the correct linguistic designation for this important position in ballet technique.[16] Here are a few clarifications to help with the confusion:

Retiré: withdrawn. The term describes the action of the working leg bending from a closed position (1st, 3rd, or 5th) on the floor. In the retiré, the working foot in the pointed position slides along the supporting leg and points against the supporting leg, usually at knee level for a full retiré.

Raccourci: shortened. In many ballet schools, a raccourci is a synonym of retiré, whereas a raccourci actually means that the working leg bends

from a position in the air, such as when following a battement.

Passé: passed. This term is commonly used in American ballet schools. Actually a passé is a movement in which the working leg goes from one position to another in the air or à terre with the foot passing the knee of the supporting leg or the stretched working leg passing the side of the supporting leg by brushing the foot on the floor.

Application. Most beginners will tend to bring the weight of the working leg on the knee of the supporting leg, instead of using their inner thigh muscles to hold the leg, more so students who have not developed enough strength yet in those muscles. This tendency will likely cause the working foot to turn into a banana-like shape and the working hip to push backward. Those students will be better off keeping the bent leg lower, either on the cou-de-pied or against the calf.

Exercise 10

Petits battements, each movement on the count, facing the barre.

Students repeat Exercise 11 of the Fourth Class of this week.

Exercise 11

Preparation for grand battement 4th position devant, sideways, preparation for grand battement 2nd and 4th position derrière, facing the barre, in 1st, eight counts.

In 4th devant sideways: on 1 and 2, battement tendu devant; on 3, battement devant; on "and," lower the leg, and point the foot onto the floor; on 4, hold the position; on 5 and 6, close 1st; on 7 and 8, hold the position. Repeat three more times.

In 2nd facing the barre: on 1 and 2, battement tendu 2nd; on 3, battement 2nd; on "and," lower the leg; on 4, hold the position with the pointed foot onto the floor; on 5 and 6, close 1st; on 7 and 8, hold the position. Repeat three more times, alternating legs.

In 4th derrière facing the barre: on 1 and 2, battement tendu derrière; on 3, battement derrière; on "and," lower the leg, and point the foot onto the floor; on 4, hold the position; on 5 and 6, close 1st; on 7 and 8, hold the position. Repeat the exercise three times, alternating legs.

---

16   De Soye, *Les Verbes de la Danse*, 170.

Explanation. Students are introduced to the grand battement devant and derrière. The exercise is performed in 1st for greater stability. The battements 2nd and derrière are performed facing the barre. The opening and the closing of the grand battement are still carefully monitored to make sure students brush the floor up to the pointed position. The throw must be energetic and light with no hold in the air. In the return to the pointed position, the leg must not be dropped but should be lowered with control. Notice again that the lowering of the leg is quick, the purpose being to engage fully the adductors in bringing down the leg. This approach will help achieve the quick closing of the working leg often required in the big jumps (such as the temps de flèche) later on in the training. The body remains erect, pulled up in the middle without rounding the upper back. The knee of the supporting leg must not bend at all. At this level, the emphasis should be on the mastery of the correct execution of the grand battement so that later, everything will be in place to apply extension to the battement. An incorrect throw (overly using the external thigh muscles) can build bulk on the upper portion of the thighs. In the battement 2nd, students must not swing their torso at all in the throw or raise their working hip along with the leg. Introducing the practice of the grand battement with a battement tendu may seem tenuous, since there is no momentum to throw the leg; however, it helps students to control the throw of the leg as well as assure the use of the turn-out muscles to throw the leg with the toes pointed to the maximum. The working leg is fully stretched in the battement derrière.

Music. The music will be an energetic, medium-tempo 2/4 march.

Exercise 12

Relevé in 2nd and 1st, plié and relevé on one count, roll down, four counts, facing the barre.

Students repeat Exercise 14 of the Fifth Class of the Ninth Week.

Exercise 13

Pied sur la barre in 2nd, plié and bend.

Students repeat Exercise 15 of the Fourth Class of this week.

Exercise 14

Battement tendu 2nd, bring the foot down 2nd with plié, point the foot and close, with port de bras, in 1st, eight counts.

Students repeat Exercise 16 of the Fourth Class of this week.

Exercise 15

Battement tendu 2nd, start and close in plié, in 1st, four counts, review.

Students repeat Exercise 17 of the Fourth Class of this week.

Exercise 16

Battement tendu 2nd, en remontant, with head rotation, four counts.

On 1 and 2, battement tendu 2nd with the right foot, turning the head slightly toward the left side; on 3 and 4, close 5th derrière, keeping the head at the same place; on 5 and 6, battement tendu 2nd with the left foot, turning the head toward the right; on 7 and 8, close 5th derrière. Repeat the exercise one more time, always closing back. After a pause, repeat the exercise.

Explanation. Students are practicing the exercise en remontant; that is, the front leg closes back after each battement tendu. Notice the head turns to the opposite direction of the working leg. Many students tend to turn in their working leg when extending it 2nd out of the 5th devant. Brushing the foot thoroughly out and keeping the toes on the floor will help to avoid turning in.

Exercise 17

Preparation for battement jeté 2nd, eight counts.

Students repeat Exercise 17 of the Second Class of this week.

Exercise 18

Adagio: lift the leg 2nd, eight counts.

Students repeat Exercise 18 of the Second Class of this week.

Exercise 19

Relevé in 2nd and 1st, plié on one count, four counts.

Following the preparatory port de bras, battement tendu 2nd, bring the foot down.

On 1, plié; on 2, relevé; on 3, come down in plié; on 4, stretch both knees. Repeat the exercise twice more. Point the right foot, close 1st, and bring the arms down. Repeat the exercise in 1st, holding the arms in low 1st.

Explanation. Even though students have started to practice the relevé with a sharper plié, for review and more stability while performing the exercise in the center, students are still using a full count for the plié and a hold to stretch the knees after each relevé.

Exercise 20

Soubresaut in 1st, on the count, two count hold in 1st.

Following the preparatory port de bras, bring the arms down.

On "and," plié and push off the floor; on 1, land in plié; on 2, stretch both knees; on 3 and 4, hold the position. Repeat three more times. Repeat the exercise.

Explanation. Students are performing the jump in the center.

Exercise 21

Preparation for chassé sauté 2nd [pas chassé—Vaganova], in 1st, four counts, facing the barre.

On "and," plié; on 1, brush the right foot and extend the leg 2nd; on 2, step onto the right foot in a deep plié, and push off the floor, with the left leg joining the right one in the air in 1st position, both legs stretching in the air, traveling to the right; on 3, come down in 1st, in plié; on 4, stretch the knees. Repeat one more time with the right foot. Repeat the whole exercise one more time.

Explanation. Students have already practiced the chassé à terre 2nd in which the working foot slides onto the floor without jumping. Here they are performing a preparatory exercise for the chassé sauté (jumped), in which, in its final version, the second leg pushes the first one out. Here students close in 1st after each chassé sauté to secure a proper landing. The second leg has to catch up with the other at the high point of the jump. The second leg remains turned out and does not drag; it is pulled beside the first leg quickly in the air. The chassé is widely used in ballet and should be practiced regularly.

Music. A medium-tempo 2/4 polka works well for chassés sautés.

Application. The easy propulsive movement involved in the jump makes it a favorite among ballet students and a staple of the ballet class, especially for youngsters who can use the jump to move around without too much difficulty. In a pre-professional program, it is necessary to break down the elements of the step to perform the jump properly with precision, height and turn-out maintained at all times. Many beginners in a recreational program are better off practicing this exercise in 1st.

Exercise 22

Preparation for déboulés, in 1st, arms in low 1st, each half turn on one count, hold two counts after two half turns.

Students repeat Exercise 22 of the Second Class of this week.

Exercise 23

Curtsey.

Eliventh Week

𝄐

FIRST CLASS

Students repeat the material of the Fifth Class of the Tenth Week.

SECOND CLASS

Exercise 1

Battement tendu 2nd, broken down, bend the head, in 1st, four counts, facing the barre.

On "and" 1, battement tendu 2nd, stretching the instep up; on 2, point the toes; on 3, bring the toes down; on "and" 4, close 1st; on 5 and 6, bend the head toward the right shoulder; on 7 and 8, straighten the head. Repeat the whole exercise one more time. At the end, roll up and hold balance.

Explanation. Students are reviewing the broken down version of the battement tendu and the bending of the head.

Exercise 2

Plié and grand plié in 2nd and 1st, four counts, facing the barre, review:

Following the preparatory port de bras, battement tendu with the right leg and bring the foot down.

On 1 and 2, plié; on 3 and 4, stretch; on 5 and 6, deeper plié, keeping the heels down; on 7 and 8, come back up into demi-plié and stretch; on 1, point the right foot; on 2, hold the position; on 3 and 4, close 1st; from 5 to 8, hold the position.

On 1 and 2, plié; on 3 and 4, stretch; on 5 and 6, deep plié, at the end of which the heels go off the floor to allow the bending of the knees further into a grand plié; on 7 and 8, bring the heels down into a demi-plié and stretch the legs; on 1 and 2, roll up onto demi-pointes; hold balance from 3 to 4; on 5 and 6, come down; on 7 and 8, battement tendu 2nd with the left foot and bring it down 2nd. Repeat the whole exercise one more time.

Explanation. Students are reviewing the

grand plié in 2nd and 1st, facing the barre, as performed in Exercise 2 of the Second Class of the Eighth Week.

Exercise 3

Preparation for passé à terre: battement tendu devant and derrière, in 1st, four counts, facing the barre.

Students repeat Exercise 3 of the Fifth Class of the Tenth Week.

Exercise 4

Battement tendu 2nd, hold the position when the foot is pointed and when the foot is closed, in 1st, four counts, facing the barre.

On "and" 1, battement tendu 2nd; on 2, hold the position; on 3, close 1st; on 4, hold the position; on "and" 5, battement tendu 2nd; on 6, hold the position; on 7, close 1st; on 8, hold the position. Repeat the whole exercise one more time. At the end, plié and relevé in 1st.

Explanation. Until now, students have executed the battement tendu with the opening and the closing actions performed evenly on two counts each. Here such actions are performed more rapidly with a hold at the end of each movement to ease the transition. This exercise prepares for the battement tendu being performed on two counts. By now, students must perform the brushing of the working foot satisfactorily so that they can still apply the same cleanness of execution with a more dynamic tempo. The tempo is sharper, but still not too fast. The exercise is simple and done in 1st so that students can concentrate on the new rhythm.

Exercise 5

Battement tendu en croix en dehors and en dedans, four counts.

Students repeat Exercise 4 of the Fifth Class of the Tenth Week with a slightly accelerated tempo.

Exercise 6

Battement tendu 2nd, start and close in plié, four counts, facing the barre.

Students repeat Exercise 5 of the Fifth Class of the Tenth Week.

Exercise 7

Preparation for battement jeté 2nd, in 1st, four counts, facing the barre.

On "and" 1, battement tendu 2nd; on "and," sharply lift the leg 2nd; on 2, hold the position; on "and," lower the leg, and bring the pointed toes down onto the floor; on 3, hold the position; on 4, close 1st. Repeat three more times with the right foot. After a pause, repeat the whole exercise one more time. At the end, roll up and hold balance.

Explanation. Here the starting battement tendu is on one count instead of two counts. The whole exercise is sharper, still with a slight freeze when the leg goes up and down.

Exercise 8

Rond de jambe à terre en dehors and en dedans, with port de bras, eight counts, bending forward.

Students repeat Exercise 9 of the Fourth Class of the Tenth Week.

Exercise 9

Preparation for battement frappé en croix en dehors and en dedans, without closing, four counts, facing the barre.

On "and," the front foot comes on the cou-de-pied devant; on 1 and 2, hold the position; on 3, extend the leg devant pointing the foot with sharpness onto the floor; on 4, hold the position; on 5, bring the foot on the cou-de-pied devant; on 6, hold the position; on 7, extend the leg 2nd; on 8, hold the position; on 1, the front foot comes on the cou-de-pied derrière; on 2, hold the position; on 3, extend the leg derrière; on 4, hold the position; on 5, bring the foot on the cou-de-pied derrière; on 6, hold the position; on 7, extend the leg 2nd; on 8, hold the position.

On "and," the front foot comes on the cou-de-pied derrière; on 1 and 2, hold the position; on 3, extend the leg derrière, pointing the foot onto the floor; on 4, hold the position; on 5, bring the foot on the cou-de-pied derrière; on 6, hold the position; on 7, extend the leg 2nd; on 8, hold the position; on 1, the front foot comes on the cou-de-pied devant; on 2, hold the position; on 3, extend the leg devant; on 4, hold the position; on 5, bring the foot on the cou-de-pied devant; on 6, hold the position; on 7, extend the leg 2nd; on 8, hold the position. Bring the foot on the cou-de-pied devant and hold balance.

Explanation. Students are adding the battement frappé en croix en dedans to this exercise, which is otherwise similar to Exercise 10 of the Second Class of the Tenth Week. The tempo is slightly accelerated.

Exercise 10

Adagio: retiré devant and derrière, extension of the leg 2nd, facing the barre.

Students repeat Exercise 9 of the Fifth Class of the Tenth Week.

Exercise 11

Petits battements, each movement on the count, facing the barre.

Students repeat Exercise 11 of the Fourth Class of the Tenth Week.

Exercise 12

Preparation for grand battement 4th position devant, sideways, preparation for grand battement 2nd and 4th position derrière, facing the barree, in 1st, eight counts.

Students repeat Exercise 11 of the Fifth Class of the Tenth Week.

Exercise 13

Pied sur la barre in 2nd, plié and bend.

Students repeat Exercise 15 of the Fourth Class of the Tenth Week.

CENTER

Exercise 14

Battement tendu 2nd, bring the foot down 2nd with plié, point the foot and close, with port de bras, in 1st, eight counts.

Students repeat Exercise 16 of the Fourth Class of the Tenth Week.

Exercise 15

Battement tendu 2nd, start and close in plié, four counts.

On 1, plié; on 2, battement tendu 2nd with the right foot still in plié; on 3, close 5th devant, still in plié; on 4, stretch both knees. Repeat the exercise with the right foot closing derrière. Repeat the whole exercise one more time.

Explanation. This exercise is similar to Exercise 5 of the Fifth Class of the Tenth Week. Students are reminded to turn the head de face when the exercise starts, since the battement tendu that follows the plié is in 2nd.

Exercise 16

Battement tendu 2nd, en remontant, with head rotation, four counts.

Students repeat Exercise 16 of the Fifth Class of the Tenth Week.

Exercise 17

Adagio: lift the leg devant and 2nd, eight counts.

On 1 and 2, battement tendu devant; on 3 and 4, lift the leg; on 5 and 6, lower the leg, bringing the pointed foot onto the floor; on 7 and 8, close 5th devant. Repeat the exercise in 2nd, closing 5th derrière.

Explanation. Students are also lifting their leg devant in this exercise. Maximum turn-out is maintained in both legs.

Exercise 18

Preparation for glissade 2nd, en descendant (glissade derrière) toward the back foot, four counts, four repetitions.

On 1, plié; on 2, battement tendu 2nd with the left foot in plié; on 3, transfer the weight onto the left leg in plié, while the right leg stretches and the right foot points; on "and" 4, close 5th right foot front and stretch. Repeat the glissade three more times to the left. After a pause to relax the arms, repeat the exercise traveling to the right, starting with the left foot front.

Explanation. This exercise is similar to the one practiced in 1st. The exercise of battement tendu in plié in 5th must be performed prior to this exercise, which involves the same movement at the beginning and at the end of the glissade. The brushing of the foot coming out is important, for it helps to create the flowing aspect of the step, instead of the staccato aspect of the jump-like glissade. It also assures that the working foot comes out with a good turn-out. The working foot must come out and close with the heel pushed forward (without moving the hips), so that the turn-out is maintained from the beginning to the end. Students must refrain from adjusting, turning in, or moving their front foot, just before brushing the back foot to start the glissade.

Exercise 19

Relevé in 2nd and 1st, plié on one count, four counts.

Students repeat Exercise 19 of the Fifth Class of the Tenth Week.

Exercise 20

Soubresaut in 1st, on the count, two count hold in 1st.

Students repeat Exercise 20 of the Fifth Class of the Tenth Week.

Exercise 21

Preparation for chassé sauté 2nd, in 1st, four counts, facing the barre.

Students repeat Exercise 21 of the Fifth Class of the Tenth Week.

Exercise 22

Curtsey.

THIRD CLASS

Students repeat the material of the Second Class of this week.

FOURTH CLASS

Exercise 1

Battement tendu 2nd, broken down, bend the head, in 1st, four counts, facing the barre.

Students repeat Exercise 1 of the Second Class of this week.

Exercise 2

Plié and grand plié in 2nd and 1st, four counts, facing the barre, review.

Students repeat Exercise 2 of the Second Class of this week.

Exercise 3

Preparation for passé à terre: battement tendu devant and derrière, in 1st, four counts, facing the barre.

Students repeat Exercise 3 of the Fifth Class of the Tenth Week.

Exercise 4

Battement tendu 2nd, hold position when the foot is pointed and when the foot is closed, in 1st, four counts, facing the barre.

Students repeat Exercise 4 of the Second Class of this week.

Exercise 5

Battement tendu en croix, flex the foot, facing the barre.

On "and" 1, battement tendu devant; on 2, flex the toes; on 3, flex the rest of the foot; on 4, point the foot, except for the toes; on 5, point the toes, bringing the pointed foot onto the floor; on 6, close 5th devant, on 7 and 8, hold the position. Repeat the exercise en croix.

Explanation. The flexion of the foot is still broken down. Students are keeping their hips straight and the working leg very stretched throughout.

Music. A medium-tempo waltz would be a good musical choice for what has become a familiar exercise.

Exercise 6

Preparation for battement jeté 2nd, in 1st, four counts, facing the barre.

Students repeat Exercise 7 of the Second Class of this week.

Exercise 7

Rond de jambe à terre en dehors and en dedans, with port de bras, eight counts, bending forward.

Students repeat Exercise 9 of the Fourth Class of the Tenth Week.

Exercise 8

Preparation for battement frappé en croix en dehors and en dedans, four counts, facing the barre.

Students repeat Exercise 9 of the Second Class of this week.

Exercise 9

Adagio: lift the leg devant, sideways, lift the leg 2nd and derrière, facing the barre, eight counts, two count hold in the air.

In 4th devant sideways: on "and" 1, battement tendu devant; on 2, hold the position; on 3, lift the leg; on 4 and 5, hold the position; on 6, lower the leg, and point the foot onto the floor; on "and" 7, close in 5th devant; on 8, hold the position. Repeat the exercise one more time.

In 2nd facing the barre: on "and" 1, battement tendu 2nd; on 2, hold the position; on 3, lift the leg; on 4 and 5, hold the position; on 6, lower the leg and point the foot onto the floor; on "and" 7, close 5th devant; on 8, hold the position. Repeat the exercise one more time, closing 5th derrière.

In 4th derrière facing the barre: on "and" 1, battement tendu derrière; on 2, hold the position; on 3, lift the leg; on 4 and 5, hold the position; on 6, lower the leg; on "and" 7, close 5th derrière; on 8, hold the position. Repeat the exercise one more time.

Explanation. This is a review of the adagio performed a few weeks ago. However, the timing of the movement is different; this exercise involves a slightly faster lifting and longer holding when the leg is in the air. This is to gain strength in holding the leg up. Students may be able to bring their working leg close to à la hauteur by now. À la hauteur means that the leg is held at least at 90°. However, holding the leg between the demi-hauteur and the hauteur is also quite acceptable for less flexible students, as long as proper placement, stretched knees, and the turnout of both legs are maintained.

Exercise 10

Petits battements, each movement on the count, facing the barre.

Students repeat Exercise 11 of the Fourth Class of the Tenth Week.

Exercise 11

Preparation for grand battement 4th position devant, sideways, preparation for grand battement 2nd and 4th derrière, facing the barre, in 1st, eight counts.

Students repeat Exercise 11 of the Fifth Class of the Tenth Week.

Exercise 12

Relevé in 6th and 1st, plié and relevé on one count, four counts, four repetitions, facing the barre.

On "and" 1, plié and relevé; on 2 and 3, hold the position; on 4, come down in plié; on 5, directly out of the plié, relevé; on 6 and 7, hold the position; on 8, come down; on 1, relevé; on 2 and 3, hold the position; on 4, come down in plié; on 5, relevé; on 6 and 7, hold the position; on 8, roll down. Open the feet in 1st and repeat the exercise. Repeat the exercise one more time, holding balance on the last one.

Explanation. Students are not stretching the knees when coming down between each relevé, as they did before. They perform each relevé directly from the plié, pressing the feet down on the floor.

Exercise 13

Bending forward, back to the barre, cambré, facing the barre, in 1st.

Following the preparatory port de bras, rest both hands on the barre.

On 1 and 2, bend forward, keeping the back as flat as possible, still holding the barre; on 3 and 4, relax the back, and bring the torso closer to the knees to stretch further; from 5 to 7, starting with the head, straighten up, while lengthening the back; on 8, hold the position. Repeat one more time. Turn toward the barre to face it. From 1 to 4, lift the upper back and bend back, keeping the head straight; from 5 to 8, straighten up. Repeat the cambré one more time. Repeat the whole exercise one more time.

Explanation. Students are repeating the exercise in 1st. When bending forward, the legs remain turned out with the knees tight. The shoulders do not tense up when trying to bring the head closer to the knees. In the cambré, the legs stay together, the feet do not roll in, and the knees remain taut.

Exercise 14

Pied sur la barre in 2nd, plié and bend.

Students repeat Exercise 15 of the Fourth Class of the Tenth Week.

Exercise 15

Battement tendu en croix, close in plié, in 1st, four counts.

On 1 and 2, battement tendu devant; on "and" 3, close in 1st in plié; on 4, stretch both legs. Repeat the exercise en croix en dehors.

Explanation. Students are repeating the exercise en croix in the center.

Exercise 16

Battement tendu 2nd, en remontant, with head rotation, four counts.

Students repeat Exercise 16 of the Fifth Class of the Tenth Week.

Exercise 17

Battement tendu 2nd, start and close in plié, four counts.

Students repeat Exercise 15 of the Second Class of this week.

Exercise 18

Adagio: lift the leg devant and 2nd, eight counts.

Students repeat Exercise 17 of the Second Class of this week.

Exercise 19

Preparation for glissade 2nd, en descendant, toward the back foot, four counts, four repetitions.

Students repeat Exercise 18 of the Second Class of this week.

Exercise 20

Relevé in 2nd and 1st, plié on one count, four counts.

Students repeat Exercise 19 of the Fifth Class of the Tenth Week.

Exercise 21

Échappé 2nd, in 1st, with port de bras, four counts, review.

Following the preparatory port de bras, bring the arms down.

On "and," plié; on 1, spring off the floor, stretching the legs and feet, bringing the arms to 1st, and opening the legs and the arms 2nd; on 2, land in plié in 2nd; on "and," directly out of the plié, spring off the floor, stretching the whole legs and feet; on 3, land in plié in 1st, with the arms closing in preparatory position; on 4, stretch both legs. Repeat three more times. After a pause, repeat the exercise.

Explanation. Students are repeating the échappé performed in Exercise 22 of the Fifth Class of the Seventh Week, still using a full count to execute the first part of the jump.

Exercise 22

Soubresaut in 1st, on the count, two count hold in 1st.

Students repeat Exercise 20 of the Fifth Class of the Tenth Week.

Exercise 23

Preparation for chassé sauté 2nd, in 1st, four counts, facing the barre.

Students repeat Exercise 21 of the Fifth Class of the Tenth Week.

Exercise 24

Assemblé 2nd [petit pas assemblé—Vaganova], without changing feet, start with the front foot, two counts, one count hold, facing the barre.

On "and," plié; on 1, brush the right foot and extend the right leg 2nd à la demi-hauteur, stretching the knee, the instep, and the toes, while pushing off the floor with the other leg, and stretch both legs in the air; on 2, land on both feet in plié in 5th, right foot front; on 3, straighten up the knees; on 4, hold the position. Repeat three more times with the right foot front. After a pause, repeat the whole exercise one more time.

Explanation. Students are introduced to the assemblé 2nd with turn-out. The jump starts on one foot and lands on two feet. Joining the legs in 5th in the air before landing is the objective; it is a difficult movement, and will take much practice to achieve it, for it takes more strength in the adductors to close quickly in the air. However, at this stage, students are expected to at least straighten their knees and point their feet in each jump, and to land in 5th on both feet with a deep plié, keeping the knees to the sides. Students must take off *as* they extend their working leg 2nd, not later; otherwise, the momentum for the spring is lost. For now, the assemblé does not change feet. The working leg must not extend too

Both legs are stretched in the air in the assemblé in 2nd position.

high in 2nd (not higher than à la demi-hauteur), for it would be otherwise difficult to assemble both legs before landing without traveling.

The assemblé is taught fairly early in the first year. It is one of the first jumps to study, since it lands on two feet, involves familiar elements, and is relatively easy to break down. However, as tempting as it may be, even in this introduction, there should not be any hold between the battement and the spring. Breaking down the brush and the spring would fail to teach one of the most important aspects of the jump: the coordination between both legs that helps attain height in the jump.

Music. A medium-tempo waltz would well accommodate this exercise.

Application. This exercise can be easily practiced in 1st position for those students who do not have enough turn-out to perform in 5th.

Exercise 25

Curtsey.

FIFTH CLASS

Exercise 1

Battement tendu 2nd, broken down, bending the head, in 1st, four counts, facing the barre.

Students repeat Exercise 1 of the Second Class of this week.

Exercise 2

Plié and grand plié in 2nd and 1st, four counts, facing the barre, review.

Students repeat Exercise 2 of the Second Class of this week.

Exercise 3

Battement tendu 2nd, hold the position when the foot is pointed and when the foot is closed, in 1st, four counts, facing the barre.

Students repeat Exercise 4 of the Second Class of this week.

Exercise 4

Battement tendu en croix, flex, eight counts, facing the barre.

Students repeat Exercise 5 of the Fourth Class of this week.

Exercise 5

Preparation for battement jeté 2nd, in 1st, four counts, facing the barre.

Students repeat Exercise 7 of the Second Class of this week.

Exercise 6

Rond de jambe à terre en dehors and en dedans, with port de bras, eight counts, bending forward.

Students repeat Exercise 9 of the Fourth Class of the Tenth Week.

Exercise 7

Preparation for battement frappé en croix, en dehors and en dedans, without closing, four counts, facing the barre.

Students repeat Exercise 9 of the Second Class of this week.

Exercise 8

Adagio: lift the leg devant, sideways, lift the leg 2nd and derrière, facing the barre, eight counts, two count hold in the air.

Students repeat Exercise 9 of the Fourth Class of this week.

Exercise 9

Petits battements, each movement on the count, facing the barre.

Students repeat Exercise 11 of the Fourth Class of the Tenth Week.

Exercise 10

Preparation for grand battement 4th position devant, sideways, grand battement 2nd and 4th position derrière, facing the barre, in 1st, eight counts.

Students repeat Exercise 11 of the Fifth Class of the Tenth Week.

Exercise 11

Relevé in 6th and 1st, plié and relevé on one count, four counts, four repetitions, facing the barre.

Students repeat Exercise 12 of the Fourth Class of this week.

Exercise 12

Bending forward, back to the barre, cambré, facing the barre, in 1st.

Students repeat Exercise 13 of the Fourth Class of this week.

Exercise 13

Pied sur la barre in 2nd, plié and bend.

Students repeat Exercise 15 of the Fourth Class of the Tenth Week.

CENTER

Exercise 14

Battement tendu en croix, close in the plié, in 1st, four counts.

Students repeat Exercise 15 of the Fourth Class of this week.

Exercise 15

Battement tendu en croix, four counts.

On 1 and 2, battement tendu devant; on 3 and 4, close 5th devant; on 5 and 6, battement tendu 2nd; on 7 and 8, close 5th derrière; on 1 and 2, battement tendu derrière; on 3 and 4, close 5th; on 5 and 6, battement tendu 2nd; on 7 and 8, close 5th derrière. After a pause, repeat the whole exercise.

Explanation. Students are now practicing the exercise in the center, with a slightly faster tempo.

Exercise 16

Preparation for battement jeté 2nd, in 1st, four counts.

On "and" 1, battement tendu 2nd; on "and," lift the leg sharply 2nd; on 2, hold the position; on "and," lower the leg, and point the toes down onto the floor; on 3, hold the position; on 4, close 1st. Repeat three more times. A small plié and stretch ends the whole exercise.

Explanation. Like at the barre, the disengaging and the closing of the foot in the battement tendu is on the count instead of two counts. Students are keeping both legs turned out.

Exercise 17

Rond de jambe à terre en dehors and en dedans, in 1st, with port de bras, eight counts.

Following the preparatory port de bras, bring the arms down.

On 1 and 2, battement tendu devant, bringing the arms 1st; on 3 and 4, rond de jambe to 2nd position, opening the arms 2nd; on 5 and 6, rond de jambe to 4th position derrière, keeping the arms 2nd; on 7 and 8, close 1st, closing the arms. On 1 and 2, battement tendu derrière, bringing the arms 1st; on 3 and 4, rond de jambe to 2nd position, opening the arms 2nd; on 5 and 6, rond de jambe to 4th devant; on 7 and 8, close 1st, closing the arms.

Explanation. Students are practicing the full rond de jambe à terre in the center, in 1st position to be more stable.

Exercise 18

Adagio: lift the leg devant and 2nd, eight counts.

Students repeat Exercise 17 of the Second Class of this week.

Exercise 19

Preparation for glissade 2nd, en descendant, four counts, four repetitions.

Students repeat Exercise 18 of the Second Class of this week.

Exercise 20

Relevé in 6th and 1st, in plié, eight counts, facing the barre.

On 1, plié; on "and" 2, relevé still in plié; on 3 and 4, stretch the knees, still on demi-pointes; on 5 and 6, hold the position; on 7 and 8, come down with stretched knees. Repeat three more times. Open the feet in 1st and repeat the exercise.

Explanation. This relevé involves bringing the feet up while still in plié to force the instep out so that students are as high as they can be on their demi-pointes. Both feet must be perfectly straight and next to each other with a slight space between them while in 6th. When stretching the knees, students must keep their instep above the toes without shifting their weight back.

Music. The music is fairly slow with a soft beat, for students need to perform each stage of this exercise thoroughly.

Application. This is usually an exercise performed on pointes. However, it is a good exercise for all beginners and even more advanced dancers to perform on demi-pointes to bring their demi-pointes as high as possible, while keeping the feet straight.

Exercise 21

Échappé 2nd, in 1st, with port de bras, four counts, review.

Students repeat Exercise 21 of the Fourth Class of this week.

Exercise 22

Assemblé 2nd, without changing feet, start with the front foot, two counts, one count hold, facing the barre.

Students repeat Exercise 24 of the Fourth Class of this week.

Exercise 23

Curtsey.

Twelfth Week

§

FIRST CLASS

Students repeat the material of the Fifth Class of the Eleventh Week.

SECOND CLASS

Exercise 1

Lift the foot, extend the leg devant and 2nd, in 6th and 1st, facing the barre.

On 1, bring the heel of the right foot up, keeping the foot straight; on 2, push off the floor with the toes; on 3, extend the leg devant, pointing the toes onto the floor; on 4, hold the position; on 5, close 6th; on 6, open both legs in 1st; on 7 and 8, hold the position. Repeat the exercise in 1st.

Explanation. Students are revisiting part of Exercise 3 of the First Class of the First Week. Students must push the instep of the working foot out, without sickling it. They stretch their toes vigorously, pushing off the floor, and freeze the leg. This is a good exercise for the articulations of the foot and its flexibility.

Exercise 2

Plié, two counts, grand plié in 2nd and 1st, four counts, port de bras performed separately, facing the barre.

Following the preparatory port de bras, battement tendu 2nd and bring the foot down.

On 1 and 2, plié and stretch; on 3 and 4, repeat; on 5 and 6, deeper plié, keeping the heels down; on 7 and 8, come back up into demi-plié and stretch the legs; on 1 and 2, bring the arms in 1st; on 3 and 4, open the arms 2nd; on 5, point the right foot; on 6, close in 1st, bringing the arms down; on 7, bring the arms in 1st; on 8, bring the hands on the barre. Repeat the exercise in 1st. Repeat the whole exercise starting with a battement tendu 2nd with the left foot, and closing the left leg in 1st.

Explanation. Students are performing the demi-plié on two counts each in this otherwise familiar exercise. Students will observe the pressing of the heels onto the floor in the descending and ascending parts of the grand plié in 1st, before and after the heels are off the floor. Notice the port de bras that accompanies the change of feet position from 2nd to 1st, requiring students to release the barre and test their balance.

Music. Since the demi-plié is on two counts, the adagio music will be particularly legato.

Exercise 3

Battement tendu en croix, hold the position when the foot is pointed and when the foot is closed, in 1st, four counts.

On "and" 1, battement tendu devant; on 2, hold the position; on 3, close 1st; on 4, hold the position. Repeat the exercise en croix en dehors. Repeat the exercise one more time. At the end, roll up and hold balance.

Explanation. After performing the exercise 2nd in Exercise 4 of the Second Class of the Eleventh Week, students are practicing it en croix and sideways. Here students brush their foot out and in with more dynamism and hold the pointed and closing positions for one count. The working foot assumes the pointed position and closes in 1st with energy.

Music. A tango or other energetic music is appropriate here.

Exercise 4

Preparation for passé à terre: battement tendu devant and derrière, hold the position when the foot is pointed and when the foot is closed, in 1st, four counts, facing the barre.

On "and" 1, battement tendu devant; on 2, hold the position; on 3, close 1st; on 4, hold the position; on "and" 5, battement tendu derrière, with the right foot; on 6, hold the position; on 7, close 1st; on 8, hold the position. Repeat one more time. Repeat the whole exercise, starting back. At the end, roll up and hold the position.

Explanation. Students are repeating the same exercise performed in Exercise 3 of the Fifth Class of the Tenth Week, but this time with the opening and the closing of the battement tendu, each performed on one count.

Exercise 5

Battement tendu en croix, start and close in plié, in 1st, four counts, facing the barre.

On 1, plié; on 2, brush the leg out in plié devant; on 3, remaining in plié, brush the foot in and close 1st; on 4, stretch both legs. Repeat the exercise en croix en dehors. At the end, relevé in 1st and hold balance.

Explanation. Students are practicing the exercise en croix this time. For the battement tendu derrière, the coming out and in of the working foot derrière passes through a small open 4th position with the foot still flat on the floor, while keeping the weight on the supporting leg. Students must not raise the working heel too soon (or too late) when closing. The foot does not roll in when the exercise is performed derrière.

Exercise 6

Preparation for battement jeté en croix, in 1st, four counts, facing the barre.

On "and" 1, battement tendu devant; on "and," battement; on 2, hold the position; on "and," lower the leg, and point the foot onto the floor; on 3, hold the position; on 4, close 1st. Repeat the exercise en croix en dehors.

Explanation. Students are repeating the exercise en croix.

Exercise 7

Position on the cou-de-pied, pointed devant and derrière, in plié, extension of the leg 2nd, eight counts, facing the barre.

On "and," bring the front foot on the cou-de-pied devant, while the supporting leg does a sharp plié; on 1 and 2, hold the position; on 3, extend the leg 2nd, while stretching the supporting leg and pointing the foot onto the floor; on 4, hold the position; on 5 and 6, close 5th devant; on 7 and 8, hold the position. Repeat three more times with the right foot. Repeat the whole exercise one more time.

Explanation. Students are reviewing the exercise, adding a plié when the working leg bends.

Music. A sharp tango music would be well suited for this exercise.

Application. This is another exercise to increase the speed of the articulation of the knee. It can also be done easily in 1st.

Exercise 8

Rond de jambe à terre en dehors and en dedans, start in plié, in 1st, eight counts, facing the barre.

On 1, plié; on 2, battement tendu devant in plié; on 3 and 4, rond de jambe en dehors to 2nd, while stretching the supporting leg; on 5 and 6, rond de jambe to 4th derrière; on 7 and 8, close 1st. On 1, plié; on 2, battement tendu derrière in plié; on 3 and 4, rond de jambe en dedans to 2nd, stretching the supporting leg; on 5 and 6, rond de jambe to 4th devant; on 7 and 8, close 1st. Repeat the whole exercise one more time. At the end, roll up and hold the position.

Explanation. The rond de jambe starts with a plié, and the supporting leg stretches in the first demi-rond de jambe. Students have practiced the battement tendu in plié in this lesson. The same principles apply. Students must maintain the turn-out throughout the exercise—especially when coming out and in of the 1st and in the passage of the 2nd position in the rond de jambe en dedans. When drawing the leg 2nd out of the plié, both legs are pulled to opposite sides.

Exercise 9

Preparation for battement fondu 2nd, start with battement, demi-attitude, eight counts, facing the barre.

On "and" 1, battement tendu 2nd; on 2, lift the leg à la demi-hauteur; on 3 and 4, bend the leg in demi-attitude 2nd, while the supporting leg does a plié; on 5 and 6, stretch the leg 2nd, while the supporting leg stretches; on 7, lower the leg and point the foot down onto the floor; on 8, close 5th devant. Repeat the exercise one more time closing 5th derrière.

Explanation. This exercise prepares students for the battement fondu. Battements fondus are exercises to develop the softness and depth of the plié—especially in jumps and movements that require landing on one foot such as the ballonné. The instructor will explain to students the meaning of the word fondu to help them understand the quality of the movement demanded here. Fondu is translated as melted. Like the name suggests, the movement should be smooth, flowing, soft, and even.

Students are introduced to the demi-attitude in which the working leg is bent at about halfway between a close and an open position of the working leg at the calf level. The full attitude will be studied later.

This exercise helps students to learn to bend and stretch both knees at the same time. Neither leg must be stretched before the other. In the attitude, the thigh must be held well turned-out and the heel actively moved forward. In doing so, the hip of the supporting leg must not come forward. The body is erect and pulled up, especially in the plié. The thigh moves as little as possible when the leg bends and stretches.

Music. A barcarolle or soft flowing waltz would work well here.

Application. For beginning students in a recreational program, this exercise can be introduced with parallel legs, with the working leg extending forward to work the coordination of the legs in the plié and the stretching.

Exercise 10

Preparation for battement frappé 2nd, flexed position of the foot, four counts, facing the barre.

On "and," bring the front foot on the cou-de-pied devant in a flexed position; on 1 and 2, hold the position; on 3, extend the leg 2nd, pointing the foot onto the floor with sharpness; on 4, hold the position. Repeat seven more times, alternating derrière and devant.

Explanation. This exercise is similar to the one performed so far, except the working foot is in a flexed position on the cou-de-pied. To make the exercise most beneficial, students thoroughly flex their foot while keeping it flat. This is a good exercise for the articulation of the ankle. The pointing (plantar flexion) and flexing (dorsiflexion) actions strengthen very important muscles in the lower legs such as the deep posterior muscles, the lateral muscles of the lower leg, and the anterior muscles (such as the anterior tibialis of the lower leg).[1] It also strengthens the ligaments of the ankle and helps the foot flexibility.

1   Grieg, *Inside Ballet Technique*, 106–12.

The foot is flexed on the cou-de-pied devant.

Music. Each battement frappé is still on four counts, but the tempo is a bit faster.

Exercise 11

Adagio: lift the leg devant, sideways, lift the leg 2nd and derrière, facing the barre, eight counts, two count hold in the air.

Students repeat Exercise 9 of the Fourth Class of the Eleventh Week.

Exercise 12

Petits battements, each movement on the count, arm in low 1st.

Following the preparatory port de bras, bring the arm down.

On "and," bring the foot on the cou-de-pied devant, bringing the arm in low 1st; on 1, hold the position; on 2, unbend the leg halfway to 2nd, on 3, transfer to the cou-de-pied derrière; on 4, unbend the leg; on 5, transfer the foot on the cou-de-pied devant; on 6, extend the leg 2nd, the pointed toes touching the floor, while opening the arm 2nd; on 7, close 5th derrière, closing the arm; on 8, hold the position. Repeat starting on the cou-de-pied derrière. Repeat the whole exercise one more time. At the end, hold the position on the cou-de-pied position devant and balance with the arms in low 1st.

Explanation. Students are repeating the exercise sideways with the arm in low 1st. Students must avoid sagging on their supporting leg in this exercise. Students apply the head movements they have learned in Exercise 10 of the Fifth Class of the Seventh Week.

Exercise 13

Preparation for grand battement 2nd and derrière, facing the barre, preparation for grand battement devant, sideways, in 1st, four counts.

In 2nd facing the barre: on "and" 1, battement tendu 2nd; on 2, battement; on "and," lower the leg and point the foot onto the floor; on 3, hold the position; on 4, close 1st. Repeat three more times, alternating legs.

In 4th derrière facing the barre: on "and" 1, battement tendu derrière; on 2, battement; on "and," lower the leg and point the foot onto the floor; on 3, hold the position; on 4, close 1st. Repeat three more times alternating legs.

In 4th devant sideways: on "and" 1, battement tendu devant; on 2, battement; on "and," lower the leg and point the foot onto the floor; on 3, hold the position; on 4, close 1st. Repeat three more times with the right leg.

Explanation. Students are performing the grand battement exercise on four counts.

Music. A 2/4 march works well for this exercise.

Exercise 14

Relevé in 6th and 1st, plié and relevé on one count, four counts, four repetitions, facing the barre.

Students repeat Exercise 12 of the Fourth Class of the Eleventh Week.

Exercise 15

Bending forward, back to the barre, cambré, facing the barre, in 1st.

Students repeat Exercise 13 of the Fourth Class of the Eleventh Week.

Exercise 16

Battement tendu en croix, close in plié, in 1st, four counts.

Students repeat Exercise 15 of the Fourth Class of the Eleventh Week.

Exercise 17

Battement tendu 2nd, hold the position when the foot is pointed and when the foot is closed, in 1st, four counts.

On "and" 1, battement tendu 2nd; on 2, hold the position; on 3, close 1st; on 4, hold the position. Repeat three more times with the right leg. Repeat the whole exercise one more time.

Explanation. Students are repeating Exercise 4 of the Second Class of the Eleventh Week, this time performed in the center.

Exercise 18

Battement tendu en croix, four counts.

Students repeat Exercise 15 of the Fifth Class of the Eleventh Week.

Exercise 19

Preparation for battement jeté 2nd, in 1st, four counts.

Students repeat Exercise 16 of the Fifth Class of the Eleventh Week.

Exercise 20

Rond de jambe à terre en dehors and en dedans, in 1st, with port de bras, eight counts.

Students repeat Exercise 17 of the Fifth Class of the Eleventh Week.

Exercise 21

Position on the cou-de-pied, pointed, extension of the leg 2nd, in 1st, with port de bras, eight counts.

Following the preparatory port de bras, bring the arms down.

On "and," bring the foot pointed on the cou-de-pied devant, bringing the arms in 1st; on 1 and 2, hold the position; on 3, extend the leg 2nd, pointing the foot onto the floor, and opening the arms 2nd; on 4, hold the position; on 5 and 6, close 1st, closing the arms; on 7 and 8, hold the position. On "and," bring the foot on the cou-de-pied derrière, bringing the arms in 1st; on 1 and 2, hold the position; on 3, extend the leg 2nd, pointing the foot on the floor, and opening the arms 2nd; on 4, hold the position; on 5 and 6, close 1st, closing the arms; on 7 and 8, hold the position. Repeat the exercise twice more with the right foot.

Explanation. This exercise is now executed in the center with port de bras, in 1st to be more stable.

Music. A sharp-tempo tango music would be appropriate for this exercise.

Exercise 22

Preparation for glissade 2nd, en remontant (glissade devant), traveling toward the side of the front foot, arms in 6th, four counts, four repetitions.

In the preparatory port de bras, bring both arms in 1st, open the left arm 2nd, and keep the right arm in 1st, with the head turned slightly toward the right arm.

On 1, plié in 5th, inclining the torso very slightly toward the right; on 2, battement tendu 2nd with the right foot in plié; on 3, transfer the weight onto the right leg in plié, while the left leg stretches and the left foot points; on "and" 4, close 5th right foot front and stretch. Repeat the glissade three more times to the right. Switch the arms when performing the exercise toward the left.

Explanation. Students are traveling toward the side of the front foot in this glissade exercise. The arms are in 6th, which is a standard arm position for the glissade 2nd. The glissade is still broken down for proper habits to take place, but the tempo is slightly faster. When closing, the back leg does not turn in. Here the torso and the head are more engaged and slightly inclined toward the traveling side. The torso is lifted at all times.

Exercise 23

Relevé in 6th and 1st, in plié, eight counts, facing the barre.

Students repeat Exercise 20 of the Fifth Class of the Eleventh Week.

Exercise 24

Roll-up in 5th (pulling in the front foot), and relevé in 5th, plié, eight counts, facing the barre.

On 1 and 2, transfer the weight onto the back leg while pulling the front foot toward the back foot, as both feet come up onto demi-pointes; on 3 and 4, hold the position; on 5 and 6, come down, sliding the front foot out so that both feet are still in 5th (or close to 5th), and by the time both heels are down, plié on both feet; on 7, stretch the knees; on 8, hold the position. Repeat one more time with the right foot front.

On 1, plié; on 2, relevé in 5th; on 3 and 4, hold the position; on 5, come down in plié; on 6, stretch the knees; on 7 and 8, hold the position. Repeat one more time with the right foot front. Repeat the whole exercise with the left foot front.

Explanation. The dynamics of the two kinds of relevés in 5th are different. While the first one requires a soft rise, the second one asks for an energetic relevé out of the plié, with the toes of both feet coming under. In the first part of the relevé, one leg needs to move closer to the other to keep both feet in 5th on demi-pointes. As soon as students have pulled the front foot toward the other, the transfer of weight is again spread onto both feet with the knees tight. Coming down, as the front foot slides down, the weight is spread again onto both feet by the time both feet are down on the floor. Once the heels are down, without pause, the legs execute a plié and stretch.

To execute the relevé with plié, the weight remains on both feet, and both feet must very slightly spring onto demi-pointes, without actually jumping onto the balls. Coming down from the relevé, both feet slide out as softly as possible into 5th position in plié. Again it is important that the adductor muscles be used fully in this exercise. When the feet are on demi-pointes, the back leg does not turn in to favor the front leg. Students must keep their legs together but not tighten their legs so much in 5th that they have to bend the front knee. Practicing the relevé in 5th may feel awkward at first, especially on demi-pointes. However, once students can apply the proper momentum to have both feet come together onto demi-pointes, executing the step will

The legs are in 5th position on demi-pointes, front view.

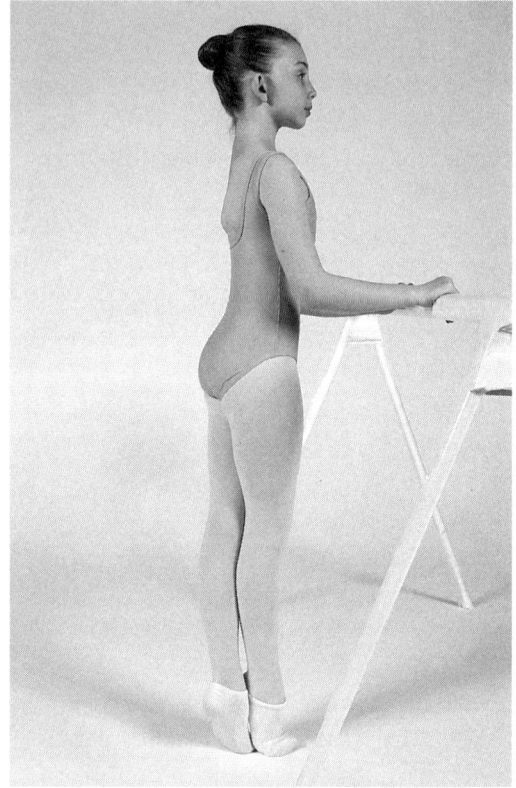

The legs are in 5th position on demi-pointes, side view.

become more comfortable. It will also help in the performance of the soubresaut in 5th, in that the work of the adductors is important in both movements. Note that the relevé in 5th position is also given several other names such as sous-sus, temps relevé en demi-pointes, and soutenu.

Exercise 25

Soubresaut in 5th [temps levé in 5th—Vaganova], two counts, one count hold, facing the barre.

On "and," plié, straightening the head; on 1, jump off equally with both feet, pointing them and stretching the knees, and keeping the legs in 5th tight in the air; on 2, land in plié; on 3, stretch the knees; on 4, hold the position. Repeat three more times with the right foot front.

Explanation. Students are introduced to the soubresaut in 5th at the barre. In the plié, the whole feet, especially the heels, push down onto the floor before taking off. Like in the jumps practiced so far, at the highest point of the jump, the knees, insteps, and toes must be taut and stretched to the maximum. The image of having the toes picking up dust from the floor as the feet

take off in the jump may help in pointing the feet to the fullest. Since the jump is new to students, it is done on two counts so that they have time to apply the correct position in the air.

Application. Performing this jump properly is challenging for most beginners, and much practice will be necessary to perfect it. Those taking ballet in a recreational program will lack sufficient control of the turn-out and strength in the adductors to keep the legs one in front of the other in 5th in the air; they will be introduced to this jump later in their training. In this exercise, one common flaw for beginners and even more advanced students is to fail to immobilize the front leg in the air in front of the back leg; it tends to wobble, cross excessively, or not cross enough. More work on the adductors (the muscles holding the position in the air) is needed. The image of holding the legs' 5th position in the air for a photo or trying to squeeze a sheet of paper between the thighs may also help students to achieve the proper position in the air. In the landing, the knees do not come forward, but remain above the toes in the plié.

Landing of the soubresaut in plié in 5th position, with the front knee slightly forward.

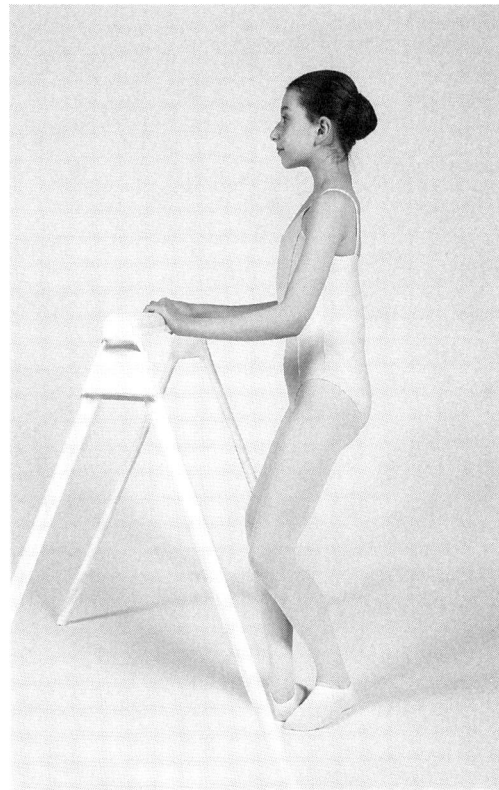

Landing of the soubresaut in 5th position, with the back leg turned in.

Exercise 26

Assemblé 2nd, without changing feet, start with the front foot, two counts, one count hold, facing the barre.

Students repeat Exercise 24 of the Fourth Class of the Eleventh Week.

Exercise 27

Preparation for chassé sauté 2nd, arms in 6th, four counts.

In the preparatory port de bras, bring the arms in 1st, open the left arm 2nd, and keep the right arm in 1st with the head slightly turned toward the right. The torso remains straight.

On "and," plié; on 1, brush the right foot and extend the leg 2nd; on 2, step onto the right foot with a plié and push off the floor, with the left leg joining the right one, both stretched in the air in 5th position, thus traveling to the right; on 3, land in 5th right foot front, in plié; on 4, stretch. Repeat three more times with the right leg. Switch arms when repeating the exercise to the left.

Explanation. After practicing the exercise at the barre, students now perform the exercise in the center in 5th with the arms in 6th. The second leg quickly pulls behind the front leg in the air.

Application. The exercise can still be done in 1st for students whose turn-out is not sufficient.

Exercise 28

Curtsey.

THIRD CLASS

Students repeat the material of the Second Class of this week.

FOURTH CLASS

Exercise 1

Lift the foot, extend the leg, in 6th and 1st, facing the barre.

Students repeat Exercise 1 of the Second Class of this week.

Exercise 2

Plié, two counts, grand plié in 2nd and 1st, four counts, port de bras performed separately, facing the barre.

Students repeat Exercise 2 of the Second Class of this week.

Exercise 3

Battement tendu en croix, hold the position when the foot is pointed and when the foot is closed, four counts.

Students repeat Exercise 3 of the Second Class of this week.

Exercise 4

Preparation for the passé à terre, battement tendu devant and derrière, hold the position when the foot is pointed and when the foot is closed, in 1st, four counts, facing the barre.

Students repeat Exercise 4 of the Second Class of this week.

Exercise 5

Battement tendu en croix, start and close in plié, in 1st, four counts, facing the barre.

Students repeat Exercise 5 of the Second Class of this week.

Exercise 6

Preparation for battement jeté en croix, in 1st, four counts, facing the barre.

Students repeat Exercise 6 of the Second Class of this week.

Exercise 7

Position on the cou-de-pied, pointed devant and derrière, in plié, extension of the leg 2nd, eight counts, facing the barre.

Students repeat Exercise 7 of the Second Class of this week.

Exercise 8

Rond de jambe à terre en dehors and en dedans, start in plié, in 1st, eight counts, facing the barre.

Students repeat Exercise 8 of the Second Class of this week.

Exercise 9

Preparation for battement fondu 2nd, start with a battement, demi-attitude, eight counts, facing the barre.

Students repeat Exercise 9 of the Second Class of this week.

Exercise 10

Preparation for battement frappé 2nd, flexed position of the foot, four counts, facing the barre.

Students repeat Exercise 10 of the Second Class of this week.

Exercise 11

Petits battements, each movement on the count, arm in low 1st.

Students repeat Exercise 12 of the Second Class of this week.

Exercise 12

Adagio: retiré devant and derrière, extension 2nd, with port de bras, eight counts.

Following the preparation, bring the arm down in preparatory position.

On "and," bring the foot pointed on the cou-de-pied devant; on 1 and 2, hold the position; on 3 and 4, slide the side of the pointed toes along the leg up to the knee, while the arm comes into 1st; on 5 and 6, slide the foot down to the cou-de-pied position; on 7, extend the leg 2nd, opening the arm 2nd; on 8, close 5th derrière with the arm coming down. Repeat the exercise with a retiré derrière, closing 5th devant. Repeat the exercise one more time.

Explanation. Students are repeating the exercise sideways with a port de bras. This is also in preparation for the développé that will be studied later. The working foot must not sickle and the knee is pushed to the side. In the retiré devant, the heel is pushed forward as soon as the foot comes off the floor. The leg extends 2nd before closing 5th.

Exercise 13

Preparation for grand battement 2nd and derrière, facing the barre, preparation for grand battement devant, sideways, in 1st, four counts.

Students repeat Exercise 13 of the Second Class of this week.

Exercise 14

Bending forward, back to the barre, cambré, facing the barre, in 1st.

Students repeat Exercise 13 of the Fourth Class of the Eleventh Week.

CENTER

Exercise 15

Battement tendu en croix, close in plié, in 1st, four counts.

Students repeat Exercise 15 of the Fourth Class of the Eleventh Week.

Exercise 16

Battement tendu 2nd, start and close in plié, en descendant and en remontant, four counts.

On 1, plié, straightening the head; on 2, battement tendu 2nd with the left foot in plié and with the head turning slightly toward the left; on 3, close 5th devant; on 4, stretch the knees; on 5, plié, straightening the head; on 6, battement tendu 2nd with the right foot in plié, turning the head toward the right; on 7, close 5th devant; on 8, stretch the knees.

On 1, plié, straightening the head; on 2, battement tendu 2nd with the right foot (front foot) in plié and with the head turning slightly toward the left; on 3, close 5th derrière; on 4, stretch the knees; on 5, plié, straightening the head; on 6, battement tendu 2nd with the left foot in plié, turning the head toward the right; on 7, close 5th derrière; on 8, stretch the knees. After a pause, repeat the whole exercise.

Explanation. This exercise is now executed in 5th, traveling forward and backward. Students are reminded of the different positions of the head.

Application. Performing this exercise in 1st is also a good option for students unable to attain a correct 3rd or 5th position. The head will then remain de face.

Exercise 17

Preparation for battement jeté 2nd, in 1st, four counts.

Students repeat Exercise 16 of the Fifth Class of the Eleventh Week.

Exercise 18

Rond de jambe à terre en dehors and en dedans, in 1st, with port de bras, eight counts.

Students repeat Exercise 17 of the Fifth Class of the Eleventh Week.

Exercise 19

Position on the cou-de-pied, pointed, extension of the leg 2nd, in 1st, with port de bras, eight counts.

Students repeat Exercise 21 of the Second Class of this week.

Exercise 20

Preparation for glissade 2nd, en remontant, toward the front foot, arms in 6th, four counts, four repetitions.

Students repeat Exercise 22 of the Second Class of this week.

Exercise 21

Relevé in 6th and 1st, in plié, eight counts, facing the barre.

Students repeat Exercise 20 of the Fifth Class of the Eleventh Week.

Exercise 22

Roll-up in 5th (pulling in the front foot) and relevé in 5th, plié, eight counts, facing the barre.

Students repeat Exercise 24 of the Second Class of this week.

Exercise 23

Soubresaut in 5th, two counts, one count hold, facing the barre.

Students repeat Exercise 25 of the Second Class of this week.

Exercise 24

Assemblé 2nd, without changing feet, start with the back foot, two counts, one count hold, facing the barre.

On "and," plié; on 1, brush the left foot and extend the leg 2nd, stretching the knee, the instep, and the toes while pushing off the floor with the supporting foot, and stretch both legs in the air; on 2, land on both feet in plié in 5th, right foot front; on 3, straighten up the knees; on 4, hold the position. Repeat three more times with the right foot front. Repeat the whole exercise one more time.

Explanation. This time the assemblé is executed by throwing the back leg and landing with the working foot derrière. The same rules applied in Exercise 24 of the Fourth Class of the Eleventh Week are also observed in this exercise. The working leg extends out of 5th position without losing the turn-out.

Exercise 25

Preparation for chassé sauté 2nd, arms in 6th, four counts.

Students repeat Exercise 27 of the Second Class of this week.

Exercise 26

Curtsey.

FIFTH CLASS

Exercise 1

Lift the foot, extend the leg, in 6th and 1st, facing the barre.

Students repeat Exercise 1 of the Second Class of this week.

Exercise 2

Plié, two counts, grand plié in 2nd and 1st, four counts, port de bras performed separately, facing the barre.

Students repeat Exercise 2 of the Second Class of this week.

Exercise 3

Battement tendu en croix, hold the position when the foot is pointed and when the foot is closed, in 1st, four counts.

Students repeat Exercise 3 of the Second Class of this week.

Exercise 4

Preparation for the passé à terre, battement tendu devant and derrière, hold the position when the foot is pointed and when the foot is closed, in 1st, four counts, facing the barre.

Students repeat Exercise 4 of the Second Class of this week.

Exercise 5

Battement tendu en croix, start and close in plié, in 1st, four counts, facing the barre.

Students repeat Exercise 5 of the Second Class of this week.

Exercise 6

Preparation for battement jeté en croix, in 1st, four counts, facing the barre.

Students repeat Exercise 6 of the Second Class of this week.

Exercise 7

Position on the cou-de-pied, pointed devant and derrière, in plié, extension of the leg 2nd, eight counts, facing the barre.

Students repeat Exercise 7 of the Second Class of this week.

Exercise 8

Rond de jambe à terre en dehors and en dedans, start in plié, in 1st, eight counts, facing the barre.

Students repeat Exercise 8 of the Second Class of this week.

Exercise 9

Preparation for battement fondu 2nd, start with battement, demi-attitude, eight counts, facing the barre.

Students repeat Exercise 9 of the Second Class of this week.

Exercise 10

Preparation for battement frappé 2nd, flexed position of the foot, four counts, facing the barre.

Students repeat Exercise 10 of the Second Class of this week.

Exercise 11

Petits battements, each movement on the count, arm in low 1st.

Students repeat Exercise 12 of the Second Class of this week.

Exercise 12

Adagio: retiré devant and derrière, extension 2nd, with port de bras, eight counts.

Students repeat Exercise 12 of the Fourth Class of this week.

Exercise 13

Preparation for grand battement 2nd and derrière, facing the barre, preparation for grand battement devant, sideways, in 1st, four counts.

Students repeat Exercise 13 of the Second Class of this week.

Exercise 14

Preparation for quick retiré, in 6th, four counts, facing the barre.

On "and," bring the foot sharply against the supporting ankle; on 1, hold the position; on "and," lift the leg to bring it to the knee level; on 2, hold the position; on "and," lower the foot to rest against the ankle again; on 3, hold the position; on "and" 4, close in 6th. Repeat one more time with the right leg.

Explanation. This exercise is designed to perform sharp bendings of the knee and freeze the position of the working leg. When closing, the foot remains pointed until the toes touch the floor. Students should be asked to release the barre at times to maintain balance.

Music. A quick polka or even a not-too-fast tarantella music would be appropriate.

Application. This exercise can be included in most beginners' classes and will contribute to increase the speed of the knee's articulation.

CENTER

Exercise 15

Battement tendu en croix, hold the position when the foot is pointed and when the foot is closed, in 1st, four counts.

On "and" 1, battement tendu devant; on 2, hold the position; on 3, close 1st; on 4, hold the position. Repeat the exercise en croix en dehors. Repeat the whole exercise one more time. A small plié and stretch will end the exercise.

Explanation. Students are repeating the exercise en croix.

Exercise 16

Battement tendu 2nd, start and close in plié, en descendant and en remontant, four counts.

Students repeat Exercise 16 of the Fourth Class of this week.

Exercise 17

Preparation for battement jeté en croix, in 1st, four counts.

On "and" 1, battement tendu devant; on "and," battement devant; on 2, hold the position; on "and," bring the toes pointed onto the floor; on 3, hold the position; on 4, close 1st. Repeat the exercise en croix en dehors. Repeat the whole exercise one more time.

Explanation. After practicing the exercise in 2nd, students are performing it en croix.

Exercise 18

Position on the cou-de-pied, pointed, extension of the leg 2nd, in 1st, with port de bras, eight counts.

Students repeat Exercise 21 of the Second Class of this week.

Exercise 19

Adagio: lift the leg devant, 2nd, and derrière, in 1st, hold two counts, with port de bras, eight counts.

On "and" 1, battement tendu devant; on 2, hold the position; on 3, lift the leg; on 4 and 5, hold the position; on 6, lower the leg and point the foot onto the floor; on "and" 7, close 1st; on 8, hold the position. Repeat the exercise 2nd and derrière. On "and" 1 and 2, bring the arms down, on 3 and 4, bring the arms 1st, on 5 and 6, open the arms 2nd, on 7 and 8, hold the position. A small plié and stretch ends the whole exercise.

Explanation. Students are adding the lifting of the leg derrière in the center. The exercise is done in 1st for greater stability. Students must lift their abdomen before raising their leg derrière and keep pulling up during the lift.

Application. For most recreational ballet students who are beginning training, lifting the leg in the back will have to wait, for keeping the turn-out in this position can be quite a challenge, even à la demi-hauteur.

Exercise 20

Preparation for glissade 2nd, en remontant, toward the front foot, arms in 6th, four counts, four repetitions.

Students repeat Exercise 22 of the Second Class of this week.

Exercise 21

Relevé in 6th and 1st, in plié, eight counts, facing the barre.

Students repeat Exercise 20 of the Fifth Class of the Eleventh Week.

Exercise 22

Soubresaut in 5th, two counts, one count hold, facing the barre.

Students repeat Exercise 25 of the Second Class of this week.

Exercise 23

Assemblé 2nd, without changing feet, start with the back foot, one count hold, two counts, facing the barre.

Students repeat Exercise 24 of the Fourth Class of this week.

Exercise 24

Preparation for chassé sauté 2nd, arms in 6th, four counts.

Students repeat Exercise 27 of the Second Class of this week.

Exercise 25

Introduction to balancé 2nd, traveling sideways, four counts.

On "and" 1, extend the right leg 2nd; on 2, step onto the right foot in plié, while the left leg bends and the left foot comes on the cou-de-pied derrière of the right leg; on "and" 3, go up onto demi-pointe with the left foot, stretching both legs, while raising the pointed right foot slightly off the floor; on 4, come down into plié onto the right foot with the left foot on the cou-de-pied derrière; on "and" 5, extend the left leg 2nd; on 6, step onto the left foot in plié, bending the right leg and bringing the right foot on the cou de pied derrière of the left foot; on "and" 7, go up onto demi-pointe with the right foot, stretching both legs, while pointing the left foot slightly off the floor; on 8, come down in plié on the left foot. Repeat three more times, alternating traveling to the right and to the left.

Explanation. Earlier in the training, students practiced the balancé informally in 6th. Here they are performing it with turn-out. The exercise is still very broken down so that students learn the precise mechanism. When students go up onto demi-pointe, the front leg stretches with the foot pointing down; the working leg does not just hang down, as is often seen in ballet students. When going onto demi-pointe, both legs are stretched and turned out.

Exercise 26

Curtsey.

Thirteenth Week

§

FIRST CLASS

Students repeat the material of the Fifth Class of the Twelfth Week.

SECOND CLASS

Exercise 1

Port de bras, battement tendu 2nd, roll-up, in 1st, facing the barre.

On "and" 1, bring the right arm in 1st; on 2, open the arm 2nd; on 3, bring the right arm 5th; on "and" 4, bring it in 1st, and rest the hand on the barre, straightening the head; from 5 to 8, repeat with the left arm; on 1 and 2, battement tendu 2nd; on 3 and 4, close; on 5 and 6, roll up; on 7 and 8, come down. Repeat the whole exercise one more time, starting the port de bras with the left arm and performing the battement tendu with the left leg this time.

Explanation. Students are revisiting the port de bras en dedans from 5th to 1st, done earlier in Exercise 6 of the Third Class of the Fourth Week. Students are reminded of the movements of the head accompanying the port de bras. The shoulders remain straight during the port de bras.

Exercise 2

Plié, two counts, grand plié in 2nd and 1st, four counts, port de bras performed separately, facing the barre.

Students repeat Exercise 2 of the Second Class of the Twelfth Week.

Exercise 3

Battement tendu devant, passé à terre [passé par terre—Vaganova], battement tendu derrière, hold when pointing, no hold in 1st, battement tendu 2nd, bring the foot down, in 1st, facing the barre.

On "and" 1, battement tendu devant; on 2, hold the position; on 3 and 4, brush the working foot through 1st and battement tendu derrière; on 5 and 6, brush the foot through 1st and battement tendu devant; on 7, close 1st; on 8, hold the position. On "and" 1, battement tendu 2nd; on 2, hold the position; on 3, bring the foot down; on 4, hold the position; on 5, point the right foot; on 6, hold the position; on 7, close in 1st; on 8, hold the position. Repeat the whole exercise one more time. At the end, plié, relevé, and hold balance.

Explanation. Students are now brushing through 1st without holding. When doing so, the working foot is flat. The turn-out of the foot is fully applied, with the toe leading the foot in the brushing from the pointed position devant to the one of the battement tendu derrière, and the heel leading the action of the foot in the brushing of the foot from back to front.

Music. A medium-to-slow flowing waltz is appropriate for this exercise.

Exercise 4

Battement tendu en croix, hold the position of the foot when it is pointed and when it is closed, with port de bras, in 1st, four counts.

On "and" 1, battement tendu devant; on 2, hold the position; on 3, close in 1st, while the arm comes in 1st; on 4, hold the position, still with the arm in 1st. Repeat the exercise en croix en dehors. Except for the first battement tendu, the arm opens at the same time as the leg extends out in each direction, and the arm closes when the leg closes in 1st. At the end, roll up and balance with the arms in 1st.

Explanation. Students coordinate their arm and leg in this plain battement tendu exercise, logically bringing the arm in 1st as the foot closes.

Music. The tempo is fairly slow for this first battement tendu exercise with port de bras.

Exercise 5

Battement tendu en croix en dehors and en dedans, hold the position of the foot when it is pointed and when it is closed, four counts.

On "and" 1, battement tendu devant; on 2, hold the position; on 3, close 5th devant; on 4, hold the position. Repeat the exercise en croix en dehors, the last one closing 5th derrière. Repeat the exercise en croix en dedans. At the end, roll up in 5th, bringing the front foot toward the back foot and hold position.

Explanation. This time, the exercise is done in 5th, but with no port de bras. Notice the roll-up in 5th at the end of the exercise, now that students have practiced it separately for a few classes. To be more stable, students can also turn toward the barre and execute the roll-up in 5th facing the barre. The position on demi-pointes will have to be steady (without the ankles wobbling) before students let go of the barre. The back leg does not turn in.

Exercise 6

Preparation for battement en cloche à la demi-hauteur, hold the position when the foot is closed, in 1st, facing the barre.

On "and" 1, battement tendu; on "and," battement devant à la demi-hauteur; on 2, hold the position; on "and," lower the leg and point the foot onto the floor; on 3, hold the position; on 4, close 1st; on "and" 5, battement tendu derrière; on "and," battement; on 6, hold the position; on "and," lower the leg; on 7, hold the position; on 8, close 1st. Repeat three more times, alternating legs. At the end, plié and relevé in 1st and hold balance.

Explanation. Students are introduced to the preparatory exercise for the battement en cloche, which, in its final form, involves a brush through 1st between a battement devant and derrière. Here students hold in 1st each time.

Application. It is advisable for all beginners to precede the final version of the battement en cloche with this exercise that forces students to bring their foot en dehors flat in 1st after each battement, with the pelvis correctly placed.

Exercise 7

Preparation for battement jeté en croix, four counts, facing the barre.

On "and" 1, battement tendu devant; on "and," battement devant; on 2, hold the position; on "and," lower the leg, and pointing the foot onto the floor; on 3, hold the position; on 4, close 5th. Repeat the exercise en croix en dehors, closing the last battement 5th derrière to be able to perform the exercise with the left foot front.

Explanation. Students are performing the battement jeté exercise in 5th en croix en dehors. The working leg assumes its position in the air quickly and holds the position briefly.

Music. A staccato 4/4 works well here.

Exercise 8

Demi-rond de jambe en dehors and en dedans à la demi-hauteur, eight counts, facing the barre.

On "and" 1, battement tendu devant; on 2, lift the leg à la demi-hauteur; on 3 and 4, demi-rond de jambe to 2nd, keeping the leg at the same height; on 5, bring the foot pointed onto the floor; on 6, hold the position; on 7, close 5th derrière; on 8, hold the position. On "and" 1, battement tendu derrière; on 2, lift the leg derrière; on 3 and 4, demi-rond de jambe to 2nd, keeping the leg at the same height; on 5, bring the foot pointed onto the floor; on 6, hold the position; on 7, close 5th devant; on 8, hold the position. Repeat one more time. At the end, bring the front leg into retiré devant and hold balance with arms 1st.

Explanation. Students are introduced to the demi-rond de jambe performed off the floor. Ideally they perform this exercise facing the barre, if there is enough room in front of the barre to bring their leg devant à la demi-hauteur. In the rond de jambe, the working leg remains at the same height, fully turned-out. As in the rond de jambe à terre, the leg, circling from back to side, is turned out as soon as possible without turning the hips sideways.

Exercise 9

Preparation for battement fondu en croix, start with battement, eight counts, facing the barre.

On "and" 1, battement tendu devant; on 2, lift the leg à la demi-hauteur; on 3 and 4, bend the leg in demi-attitude devant, while the supporting leg bends; on 5 and 6, stretch the leg fully devant, while the supporting leg stretches; on 7, lower the leg, and point the foot onto the floor; on 8, close 5th devant. Repeat the exercise en croix en dehors, the last one closing 5th derrière.

Explanation. After practicing the exercise 2nd, students are performing it en croix. There should not be any space restriction to perform it in front of the barre. Like before, students coordinate the bend and the stretch of both legs.

Exercise 10

Preparation for battement frappé en croix, en dehors and en dedans, flexed position of the foot, four counts.

On "and," bring the front foot flexed on the cou-de-pied devant; on 1 and 2, hold the position; on 3, extend the leg devant, pointing the foot onto the floor with sharpness; on 4, hold the position. Repeat the exercise en croix en dehors and en dedans. At the end, roll up in 5th and hold.

Explanation. Students are repeating the exercise en croix sideways, with the foot in a flexed position.

Exercise 11

Petits battements, double, extend 2nd, bring the foot down in 2nd, facing the barre.

On "and," bring the working foot on the cou-de-pied devant; on 1, hold the position; on 2, unbend the leg halfway to 2nd; on 3, bring the foot on the cou-de-pied derrière; on 4, extend the leg 2nd, pointing the foot onto the floor; on 5, bring the foot down; on 6, point the foot again; on 7, close 5th derrière; on 8, hold the position. Repeat the exercise starting on the cou-de-pied derrière. Repeat three more times with the right foot. At the end, plié and relevé in 5th and hold.

Explanation. In this exercise, students are performing a double petit battement before extending 2nd. The double battement frappé, which will be studied later, is actually composed of two petits battements such as in this exercise. But, unlike the double battement frappé, the extension here is not as sharp. Upon extending, students bring their foot down, with a consequent transfer of weight to the center of both legs. When pointing again 2nd, the working foot must actively push off the floor. The hands slide when the working foot comes down 2nd. Students bring

both feet under for the relevé in 5th, making sure that both legs remain turned-out.

Exercise 12

Adagio: retiré devant and derrière, extension 2nd before closing, with port de bras, eight counts.

Students repeat Exercise 12 of the Fourth Class of the Twelfth Week.

Exercise 13

Preparation for grand battement 2nd and derrière, facing the barre, preparation for grand battement devant, sideways, in 1st, four counts.

Students repeat Exercise 13 of the Second Class of the Twelfth Week.

Exercise 14

Preparation for quick retiré in 6th, four counts, facing the barre.

Students repeat Exercise 14 of the Fifth Class of the Twelfth Week.

Exercise 15

Pied sur la barre 2nd and devant, plié and bend forward,

On "and" 1, plié; on 2, stretch; on 3 and 4, repeat; on 5 and 6, bring the left arm 1st and open it 2nd; on 7 and 8, bring it in 5th and turn the head toward the right; on 1 and 2, bend sideways toward the right side; on 3 and 4, straighten up; on 5 and 6, open the left arm 2nd; on 7, rest the left hand on the barre; on 8, hold the position; on 1 and 2, bring the right arm 1st and open it 2nd; on 3 and 4, bring the arm in 5th and turn the head toward the left side; on 5 and 6, bend sideways toward the left; on 7 and 8, straighten up, opening the arm 2nd and rotating the legs so that the working leg is in 4th position devant. The right arm is 2nd and the left arm is slightly forward, with the hand resting on the barre. On 1 and 2, plié and stretch; on 3 and 4, repeat; on 5 and 6, bring the arm 5th; on 7 and 8, bend forward keeping the arm 5th; on 1 and 2, straighten up; on 3 and 4, bring both arms in 5th and hold the position from 5 to 8.

Explanation. Students are adding bending forward with the leg in 4th devant. The cambré will come later. The bending forward should initiate from the lower back so that the back

Pied sur la barre devant, with bending forward.

remains as flat as possible, keeping the arm in 5th. The head is turned toward the arm in 5th.

CENTER

Exercise 16

Battement tendu en croix, hold the position when the foot is pointed and when it is closed, in 1st, four counts.

Students repeat Exercise 15 of the Fifth Class of the Twelfth Week.

Exercise 17

Battement tendu 2nd, start and close in plié, en descendant and en remontant, four counts.

Students repeat Exercise 16 of the Fourth Class of the Twelfth Week.

Exercise 18

Preparation for battement jeté en croix, in 1st, four counts.

Students repeat Exercise 17 of the Fifth Class of the Twelfth Week.

Exercise 19

Adagio: lift the leg devant, 2nd, derrière, in 1st, hold two counts, with port de bras, eight counts.

Students repeat Exercise 19 of the Fifth Class of the Twelfth Week.

Exercise 20

Roll-up in 5th (pulling in the back foot), eight counts, relevé in 5th, plié, 8 counts, facing the barre.

On 1 and 2, pull the back foot toward the front foot, as both feet come up onto demi-pointes; on 3 and 4, hold the position, on 5 and 6, come down, sliding the back foot out so that both feet are still in 5th (or close to 5th) by the time both feet are down, plié on both feet; on 7, stretch the knees; on 8, hold the position. Repeat one more time with the right foot front.

On 1, plié; on 2, relevé in 5th; on 3 and 4, hold the position, on 5, come down in plié; on 6, stretch, on 7 and 8, hold the position. Repeat one more time with the right foot front. Repeat the whole exercise one more time with the left foot front.

Explanation. Students are repeating the exercise done two weeks ago, in Exercise 24 of the Second Class of the Twelfth Week, except this time it is the back leg that moves toward the front one in the roll-up, keeping full turn-out.

Exercise 21

Pas de bourrée dessous, changing feet, four counts, facing the barre.

On "and," bring the back foot on the cou-de-pied derrière, while the supporting leg does a plié; on 1, hold the position; on 2, step onto the back foot onto demi-pointe behind the supporting foot, and stretch both legs; on "and," open the right leg 2nd; on 3, step onto the right foot on demi-pointe, transferring the weight onto the right leg; on "and," close 5th, left foot front in plié; on 4, stretch both knees. Repeat three more times, alternating legs.

Explanation. Students are introduced to the pas de bourrée dessous, which is one of the most common pas de bourrée. Pas de bourrées are widely used in ballet. It is a very old step with folkloric origins and is still widely used in many countries' ethnic dances, such as in Greece and Spain.

It may be performed without changing feet, but this present version is more frequently used, since it allows the dancer to change feet during the exercise. It must be lightly executed but with precision. This step brings a slight travel to the side.

Both heels must be pushed forward with stretched knees on demi-pointes. The bringing of the foot on the cou-de-pied is sharp, with the foot pressed against it. The stepping onto demi-pointe is performed in plié, with both legs stretching, still on demi-pointe. The hips remain parallel to the barre. The pas de bourrée can be initiated from an open position with the foot pointed 2nd. However, starting with the foot on the cou-de-pied makes it easier to get the first foot onto demi-pointe.

When transferring the weight onto the working leg (the first leg), the toes of the second leg are slightly off the ground. When stepping onto the first leg, students must not bring it too close to the second leg; the stepping should occur where the toes are pointed down.

In the Vaganova school, the bourrée is performed by bringing each foot on the cou-de-pied position at each transfer.[2] The pas de bourrée on the cou-de-pied (as the French school calls it) because of its difficulty, is studied later in the French school. The present version is perhaps less elegant but more simple in that the feet stay pointing down to ease balance.

Music. A large waltz with a slow tempo is best for this introduction.

Application. All beginners will benefit by studying this step at the barre first, so each element is properly executed. The closing after each pas de bourrée is important, for it allows students to re-center between each pas de bourrée. For those students who are not comfortable with the 5th position, the step can also be easily performed in 1st.

Exercise 22

Soubresaut in 5th, two counts, one count hold, facing the barre.

---

2   Kostrovitskaya and Pisarev, *School of Classical Dance*, 167.

Students repeat Exercise 25 of the Second Class of the Twelfth Week.

Exercise 23

Assemblé 2nd, without changing feet, start with the back foot, one count hold, two counts, facing the barre.

Students repeat Exercise 24 of the Fourth Class of the Twelfth Week.

Exercise 24

Introduction to balancé 2nd, traveling sideways, four counts.

Students repeat Exercise 25 of the Fifth Class of the Twelfth Week.

Exercise 25

Curtsey.

THIRD CLASS

Students repeat the material of the Second Class of this week.

FOURTH CLASS

Exercise 1

Port de bras, battement tendu 2nd, roll-up, facing the barre.

Students repeat Exercise 1 of the Second Class of this week.

Exercise 2

Plié in 2nd and 1st, with port de bras.

Following the preparatory port de bras, battement tendu 2nd and bring the feet down in 2nd.

On 1 and 2, plié and stretch; on 3 and 4, repeat; on "and" 5, turn the hand so that the palm faces down, and with the head turned toward the working hand, plié with the arm coming down; on 6, keep the heels down in the plié, rounding the arm by bringing the lower arm inward (at the deepest level of the plié); on 7, stretch both knees, bringing the arm 1st; on 8, open the arm 2nd. Close 1st. Repeat the exercise in 1st. At the end, bring both arms in 5th and hold the position.

Explanation. Students are introduced to the port de bras accompanying the plié. The back

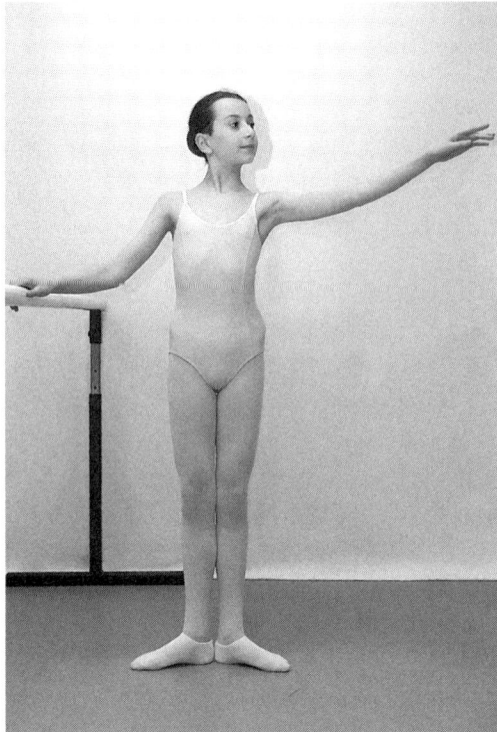

The arm turns slightly to start the port de bras accompanying the plié.

remains straight during the exercise. The shoulder of the working arm must not come forward when bringing the arm down. When the arm is in 1st, the tips of the fingers must be lined up with the centerline of the torso and must not cross over that line; crossing over this middle line tends to bring the shoulder forward, a bad habit that could affect the stability of the dancer in the center. Students must breathe in and raise the fingers ever so slightly before bringing the arm down.

Application. The proper coordination between the arm movement and the plié is difficult to achieve; most beginners in a recreational program will benefit from still practicing each part independently before putting the movement of the legs and arms together in this particular exercise.

Exercise 3

Battement tendu devant, passé à terre, battement tendu derrière, hold when pointing, no hold in 1st, battement tendu 2nd, bring the foot down, in 1st, facing the barre.

Students repeat Exercise 3 of the Second Class of this week.

Exercise 4

Battement tendu en croix, hold the position of the foot when it is pointed and when it is closed, with port de bras, in 1st, four counts.

Students repeat Exercise 4 of the Second Class of this week.

Exercise 5

Battement tendu en croix en dehors and en dedans, hold the position when the foot is pointed and when it is closed, four counts.

Students repeat Exercise 5 of the Second Class of this week.

Exercise 6

Preparation for battement en cloche à la demi-hauteur, hold the position when the foot is closed, in 1st, facing the barre.

Students repeat Exercise 6 of the Second Class of this week.

Exercise 7

Preparation for battement jeté en croix, four counts, facing the barre.

Students repeat Exercise 7 of the Second Class of this week.

Exercise 8

Demi-rond de jambe en dehors and en dedans à la demi-hauteur, eight counts, facing the barre.

Students repeat Exercise 8 of the Second Class of this week.

Exercise 9

Preparation for battement fondu en croix, start with battement, demi-attitude, eight counts, facing the barre.

Students repeat Exercise 9 of the Second Class of this week.

Exercise 10

Preparation for battement frappé en croix, en dehors and en dedans, flexed position of the foot, four counts.

Students repeat Exercise 10 of the Second Class of this week.

Exercise 11

Petits battements, double, extend 2nd, bring the foot down in 2nd, facing the barre.

Students repeat Exercise 11 of the Second Class of this week.

Exercise 12

Adagio: plié in 5th and cambré, facing the barre.

On 1 and 2, plié in 5th, straightening the head; on 3 and 4, stretch the knees; on 5 and 6, cambré keeping the head straight; on 7 and 8, straighten up the torso. Repeat the exercise one more time with the right foot front.

Explanation. Like with other pliés with turn-out, students will avoid stretching their knees with their feet rolling in and opening beyond the angle of the outward rotation of their hips. The body must be erect and pulled up, the back held without caving in. The action of bending and straightening the knees is smooth without jerking so that the movement is flowing. The back leg should not come out of alignment, as it often does, especially in students who do not have a sufficient turn-out. The weight should be equally distributed on both feet. The tempo is a little bit faster than the one used in previous plié exercises.

Exercise 13

Preparation for grand battement 2nd and derri-ère, facing the barre, preparation for grand batte-ment devant, sideways, in 1st, four counts.

Students repeat Exercise 13 of the Second Class of the Twelfth Week.

Exercise 14

Preparation for quick retiré, in 6th, four counts, facing the barre.

Students repeat Exercise 14 of the Fifth Class of the Twelfth Week.

Exercise 15

Pied sur la barre 2nd and devant, plié and bend forward.

Students repeat Exercise 15 of the Second Class of this week.

CENTER

Exercise 16

Battement tendu en croix, hold the position of the foot when it is pointed and when it is closed, in 1st, four counts.

Students repeat Exercise 15 of the Fifth Class of the Twelfth Week.

Exercise 17

Preparation for battement jeté en croix, in 1st, four counts.

Students repeat Exercise 17 of the Fifth Class of the Twelfth Week.

Exercise 18

Adagio: lift the leg devant, 2nd, and derrière, in 1st, hold two counts, with port de bras, eight counts.

Students repeat Exercise 19 of the Fifth Class of the Twelfth Week.

Exercise 19

Roll-up in 5th (pulling in the back foot), eight counts, relevé in 5th, plié, four counts, facing the barre.

Students repeat Exercise 20 of the Second Class of this week.

Exercise 20

Pas de bourrée dessous, changing feet, four counts, facing the barre.

Students repeat Exercise 21 of the Second Class of this week.

Exercise 21

Soubresaut in 5th, on the count, two count hold, facing the barre.

On "and," plié and jump off equally with both feet, pointing them and stretching the knees, and keeping the legs in 5th position tight in the air; on 1, land in plié; on 2, stretch the knees; on 3 and 4, hold the position. Repeat three more times with the right foot front.

Explanation. Students are practicing the sou-bresaut in 5th on the count at the barre, still with a hold between each jump. This exercise should be practiced only at the barre if students are not performing it well enough.

Music. Since the landing is on the count, the tempo should not be too fast so that students have time to get some height during the jump. A march or a music usually used for grand allegro would be suitable for this exercise.

Exercise 22

Assemblé 2nd, en descendant and en remontant, with head rotation, two counts, one count hold, facing the barre.

En descendant: on "and," plié, straightening the head; on 1, brush the left foot and extend the leg 2nd, stretching the knee, the instep, and the toes, with the head directed slightly toward the left, while pushing off the floor with the right leg, and stretch both legs in the air; on 2, land in plié in 5th, left foot front; on 3, straighten up the knees; on 4, hold the position.

On "and," plié, straightening the head; on 1, brush the right foot and extend the leg 2nd, stretching the whole leg, with the head directed slightly toward the right, while pushing off the floor with the left leg, and stretch both legs in the air; on 2, land in plié in 5th, right foot front; on 3, straighten up the knees; on 4, hold the position.

En remontant: on "and," plié, straightening the head; on 1, brush the right foot and extend the leg 2nd, stretching the whole leg, with the head directed slightly toward the left, while pushing off the floor with the left leg, and stretch both legs in the air; on 2, land in plié in 5th, left foot front; on 3, straighten up the knees; on 4, hold the position.

On "and," plié, straightening the head; on 1, brush the left foot and extend the left leg 2nd, stretching the whole leg, with the head directed slightly toward the right, while pushing off the floor with the right leg, and stretch both legs in the air; on 2, land in plié in 5th, right foot front; on 3, straighten up the knees; on 4, hold the position. Repeat the whole exercise one more time.

Explanation. Here students are changing feet in the assemblé: en descendant, the back foot closes front and en remontant, the front foot closes back. They also rotate their head (as they did in the battement tendu exercise), so that the head is turned toward the working leg when the working foot closes front and opposite of the working leg when the working foot closes back. Students must not stand too close to the barre so that they have room to perform both assemblés en descendant. The plié of the landing must be deep with both feet pressed firmly onto the floor. The working foot brushes firmly onto the floor when coming out of the 5th, with the heel pushed forward.

Exercise 23

Preparation for déboulés, in 1st, arms in low 1st, each half turn on one count, hold two counts after two half turns, review.

Students repeat Exercise 22 of the Second Class of the Tenth Week.

Exercise 24

Curtsey.

FIFTH CLASS

Exercise 1

Port de bras, battement tendu 2nd, roll-up in 1st, facing the barre.

Students repeat Exercise 1 of the Second Class of this week.

Exercise 2

Plié in 2nd and 1st, with port de bras.

Students repeat Exercise 2 of the Fourth Class of this week.

Exercise 3

Battement tendu devant, passé à terre, battement tendu derrière, no hold in 1st, battement tendu 2nd, bring the foot down, in 1st, facing the barre.

Students repeat Exercise 3 of the Second Class of this week.

Exercise 4

Battement tendu en croix, hold the position when the foot is pointed and when the foot is closed, in 1st, with port de bras, four counts.

Students repeat Exercise 4 of the Second Class of this week.

Exercise 5

Battement tendu en croix, en dehors and en dedans, hold the position when the foot is pointed and when the foot is closed, four counts.

Students repeat Exercise 5 of the Second Class of this week.

Exercise 6

Preparation for battement en cloche à la demi-hauteur, hold the position when the foot is closed, in 1st, facing the barre.

Students repeat Exercise 6 of the Second Class of this week.

Exercise 7

Preparation for battement jeté en croix, four counts, facing the barre.

Students repeat Exercise 7 of the Second Class of this week.

Exercise 8

Demi-rond de jambe en dehors and en dedans à la demi-hauteur, eight counts, facing the barre.

Students repeat Exercise 8 of the Second Class of this week.

Exercise 9

Preparation for battement fondu en croix, start with battement, demi-attitude, eight counts, facing the barre.

Students repeat Exercise 9 of the Second Class of this week.

Exercise 10

Preparation for battement frappé en croix, en dehors and en dedans, flexed position of the foot, four counts.

Students repeat Exercise 10 of the Second Class of this week.

Exercise 11

Preparation for rond de jambe soutenu 2nd [rond de jambe en l'air 45°—Vaganova], no rotation, in 1st, facing the barre.

On "and" 1, battement tendu 2nd; on 2, lift the leg à la demi-hauteur; on 3, bend the working leg without moving the thigh so that the tips of the toes touch the back of the supporting leg; on 4, stretch the leg 2nd again; on 5, bend the working leg again; on 6, stretch the leg 2nd again; on 7, lower the leg, and point the foot onto the floor; on 8, close 1st.

Explanation. This is a very basic exercise that introduces the bending and stretching involved in the rond de jambe soutenu 2nd. The working thigh must not move at all during the bending and the stretching of the leg. The working foot does not sickle, and the hips remain parallel to the barre. The rond de jambe is performed à la demi-hauteur in this preparatory exercise.

Application. It is a good idea to start with this introductory exercise before actually practicing the rond de jambe 2nd with rotation, which is difficult to execute properly. For now, students just need to learn to isolate the movement of the lower leg from the thigh that should remain still.

Exercise 12

Petits battements, double, extend 2nd, bring the foot down in 2nd, facing the barre.

Students repeat Exercise 11 of the Second Class of this week.

Exercise 13

Adagio: plié in 5th and cambré, facing the barre.

Students repeat Exercise 12 of the Fourth Class of this week.

Exercise 14

Preparation for grand battement 2nd and derrière, facing the barre, preparation for grand battement devant, sideways, four counts.

In 2nd facing the barre: on "and" 1, battement tendu 2nd; on 2, battement; on "and," lower the leg and point the foot onto the floor; on 3, hold the position; on 4, close 5th devant. Repeat three more times, alternating closing devant and derrière.

In 4th derrière facing the barre, left foot front: on "and" 1, battement tendu derrière; on 2, battement; on "and," lower the leg and point the foot onto the floor; on 3, hold the position; on 4, close 5th. Repeat three more times.

In 4th devant sideways: on "and" 1, battement tendu devant; on 2, battement; on "and," lower the leg and point the foot onto the floor; on 3, hold the position; on 4, close 5th. Repeat three more times.

Explanation. Students are repeating Exercise 13 of the Second Class of the Twelfth Week, performed this time in 5th.

Exercise 15

Pied sur la barre 2nd and devant, plié and bend forward.

Students repeat Exercise 15 of the Second Class of this week.

CENTER

Exercise 16

Battement tendu en croix, hold the position of the foot when it is pointed and when it is closed, in 1st, four counts.

Students repeat Exercise 15 of the Fifth Class of the Twelfth Week.

Exercise 17

Battement tendu en croix, hold the position of the foot when it is pointed and when it is closed, four counts.

On "and" 1, battement tendu devant; on 2, hold the position; on 3, close 5th devant; on 4, hold the position. Repeat the exercise en croix en dehors, with the last battement tendu 2nd closing 5th derrière. Repeat the whole exercise one more time.

Explanation. Students are repeating Exercise 5 of the Second Class of this week.

Exercise 18

Adagio: grand plié in 2nd, port de bras performed separately.

Start in 1st, battement tendu 2nd and bring the foot down.

On 1, plié; on 2, stretch the knees; on 3 and 4, repeat the plié; on 5 and 6, deeper plié, keeping the heels down; on 7 and 8, come back up into demi-plié and stretch the knees; on "and" 1 and 2, bring the arms down; on 3, bring the arms in 1st; on 4, bring the arms to 5th; on 5 and 6, hold the position; on "and" 7 and 8, open the arms 2nd. Repeat the exercise one more time. Point the foot and close 1st after the last port de bras to end the exercise.

Explanation. Students are starting to work on the grand plié in the center. For now, the port de bras is independent of the leg movement. The exercise starts with a demi-plié to prepare for the grand plié, which, at this stage, is in fact a notch lower than the demi-plié. The heels do not come off the floor, and the space between the feet remains the same as the one in the demi-plié.

Application. A good control of the back and the turn-out is required to practice the grand plié

in the center, especially when practiced later in 1st position.

Exercise 19

Relevé in 6th and 1st, plié and relevé on one count, two counts, three repetitions, facing the barre and in the center.

On "and" 1, plié and relevé; on 2, come down in plié; on 3, directly out of the plié, relevé; on 4, come down; on 5, relevé; on 6, come down in plié; on 7, stretch the knees; on 8, open the feet in 1st and repeat the exercise. Repeat the exercise one more time. Repeat the whole exercise in the center with the arms in low 1st.

Explanation. There is no holding on demi-pointes in this exercise. In order not to fall backward in the relevé, especially when it is performed in the center, students must shift their weight onto their toes and keep their lower abdomen held tight, with the upper torso very slightly forward.

Exercise 20

Pas de bourrée dessous, changing feet, four counts, facing the barre.

Students repeat Exercise 21 of the Second Class of this week.

Exercise 21

Soubresaut in 5th, on the count, two count hold, facing the barre.

Students repeat Exercise 21 of the Fourth Class of this week.

Exercise 22

Assemblé 2nd, en descendant and en remontant, with head rotation, two counts, one count hold, facing the barre.

Students repeat Exercise 22 of the Fourth Class of this week.

Exercise 23

Preparation for déboulés, in 1st, arms in low 1st, each half turn on one count, hold two counts after two half turns, review.

Students repeat Exercise 22 of the Second Class of the Tenth Week.

Exercise 24

Curtsey.

Fourteenth Week

𝔰

FIRST CLASS

Students repeat the material of the Fifth Class of the Thirteenth Week.

SECOND CLASS

Exercise 1

Bending and rotation of the head, battement tendu 2nd, in 1st, facing the barre.

On 1 and 2, bend the head to the right and straighten it; on 3 and 4, repeat to the left; from 5 to 8, move the head in a circle (bending the head to the right, bringing it down, to the left, to the back, and to the right again before straightening it up). On 1 and 2, battement tendu 2nd; on 3 and 4, close 1st; on 5 and 6, battement tendu 2nd with the left foot; on 7 and 8, close 1st. Repeat the whole exercise bending and rotating the head to the left and starting the battement tendu with the left leg.

Explanation. When bending and rotating the head, the shoulders do not move and remain pushed down to get maximum stretching of the neck. This is not a ballet move but an exercise to loosen up and stretch the neck muscles. As said before, the stiffness of the neck can affect the quality and aesthetic effect of the dancing; it can also have a negative effect on ballet turns, when the head fails to spot properly.

Exercise 2

Plié in 2nd and 1st, with port de bras.

Students repeat Exercise 2 of the Fourth Class of the Thirteenth Week.

Exercise 3

Battement tendu devant, passé à terre, battement tendu derrière, hold when pointing, no hold in 1st, battement tendu 2nd, bring the foot down, with port de bras, in 1st.

On "and" 1, battement tendu devant; on 2, hold the position; on 3 and 4, brush the working foot through 1st and battement tendu derrière; on 5 and 6, brush the foot through 1st and battement tendu devant; on 7, close 1st; on 8, hold the position. On "and" 1, battement tendu 2nd; on 2, hold the position; on 3, bring the foot down 2nd, bringing both arms in 1st; on 4, hold the position; on 5, point the foot, opening the arms 2nd, with the hand holding the barre again; on 6, hold the position; on 7, close in 1st; on 8, hold the position. Repeat the exercise one more time starting back. At the end plié, relevé, and hold balance.

Explanation. Students are repeating the exercise sideways with a port de bras. The head moves accordingly when the working leg moves from front to back and vice versa. The torso remains straight.

Exercise 4

Battement tendu 2nd, hold the position of the foot when it is pointed and when it is closed, four counts, battement tendu 2nd, without holding, two counts, plié, in 1st, facing the barre.

On "and" 1, battement tendu 2nd; on 2, hold the position; on "and" 3, close 1st; on 4, hold the position; on "and" 5, battement tendu 2nd; on 6, close 1st; on 7 and 8, plié and stretch. Repeat three more times with the right foot. At the end, roll up and hold balance.

Explanation. Students are introduced to the battement tendu 2nd on two counts without holding. A battement tendu with holding, on four counts, starts each series to smooth the transition.

Application. The mixing of different counts for the battement tendu comes later for beginners who take ballet recreationally, especially those taking ballet once a week.

Exercise 5

Battement tendu 2nd, four counts, two counts, facing the barre.

On 1 and 2, battement tendu 2nd; on 3 and 4, close 5th derrière; on "and" 5, battement tendu 2nd; on 6, close 5th devant, on 7 and 8, hold the position. Repeat three more times with the right foot. At the end, roll up and hold balance.

Explanation. Unlike in the previous exercise, students will use two counts each way for the first battement tendu, since the movement is more challenging when performed in 5th. Instead of plié and stretch when closing, students just hold the position. Students are reminded, if needed, of the correct head movements when performing exercises in 5th.

Exercise 6

Preparation for battement jeté en croix en dehors and en dedans, four counts.

On "and" 1, battement tendu devant; on "and," battement devant; on 2, hold the position; on "and," lower the leg and point the foot onto the floor; on 3, hold the position, on 4, close 5th. Repeat the exercise en croix en dehors, the last one closing 5th derrière. Repeat the exercise en croix en dedans.

Explanation. Students are repeating Exercise 7 of the Second Class of the Thirteenth Week, executed this time sideways, en croix en dehors and en dedans.

Exercise 7

Battement jeté 2nd, broken down and direct, in 1st, four counts, facing the barre.

On "and" 1, battement tendu 2nd; on "and," battement; on 2, hold the position; on "and," lower the leg; on 3, hold the position; on 4, close 1st; on "and" 5, direct battement 2nd; on 6, hold the position; on "and," point the foot onto the floor; on 7, hold the position; on 8, close 1st. Repeat the exercise one more time with the right foot. Repeat the whole exercise one more time. At the end, relevé in 1st and hold balance.

Explanation. Students are introduced to the direct battement 2nd. To make the transition easier, the exercise starts with the broken down version of the battement that students have studied so far. In the direct battement, the foot brushes all the way to the pointed position before taking off, without a pause. At the end of the dégagé on the floor, the pointed toes must be the last part to take off. When performing the battement directly, students actively press down their working foot before lifting the leg.

Music. A 2/4 tango would work well here.

Exercise 8

Position on the cou-de-pied, pointed, extension of the leg en croix, with a stretched supporting leg and in plié, four counts, facing the barre.

On "and," bring the foot on the cou-de-pied devant; on 1, hold the position; on 2, extend the leg devant, pointing the foot onto the floor; on 3, hold the position; on 4, close 5th devant. Repeat the exercise en croix en dehors.

On "and," bring the foot on the cou-de-pied devant, with a sharp plié on the supporting leg; on 1, hold the position; on 2, extend the leg devant, pointing the foot onto the floor, and stretching the supporting leg; on 3, hold the position; on 4, close 5th devant. Repeat the exercise en croix en dehors, with the last extension closing 5th derrière.

Explanation. Students are now practicing the exercise on four counts, bringing the foot on the cou-de-pied with a stretched supporting leg and also with a plié on the supporting leg.

Music. A 2/4 tango or a sharp 4/4 would be appropriate musical choices.

Exercise 9

Demi-rond de jambe en dehors and en dedans à la demi-hauteur, eight counts, facing the barre.

Students repeat Exercise 8 of the Second Class of the Thirteenth Week.

Exercise 10

Battement fondu 2nd, start with a fondu, eight counts, facing the barre.

On 1 and 2, bring the foot pointed on the cou-de-pied devant, with a deep plié on the supporting leg; on 3 and 4, extend the leg in demi-attitude in 2nd, still in plié; on 5 and 6, stretch both legs at the same time à la demi-hauteur; on 7, lower the leg and point the foot onto the floor; on 8, close in 5th devant. Repeat the exercise with a battement fondu closing 5th derrière. For the last fondu, students hold the working leg in 2nd and release the barre to check balance with the arms 2nd. After a pause, repeat the exercise starting left foot front.

Explanation. Here students are starting the fondu by bringing the foot pointed directly against the cou-de-pied. The foot comes up directly, without wrapping around the ankle as it is done in some other schools. Either starting with a fondu or a battement, the exercise is commonly called a battement fondu—even though there is no real battement initiating the movement in the present version. Notice that the plié of the fondu takes two counts to seek the maximum depth of the plié; unlike the sharp plié required in some exercises when the foot comes onto the cou-de-pied, the plié in the fondu is more continuous so that the movement looks smooth and flowing. The bending and the stretching of both legs occur at the same time when students extend the leg 2nd. Like other exercises requiring students to extend their leg 2nd, they should be asked to release the barre often or, at least, at the end of the exercise, to check balance. The whole movement must appear continuous, filling up the music as much as possible, without pausing between the first plié to the pointing of the foot onto the floor before closing.

Exercise 11

Battement tendu 2nd, bring the foot on the cou-de-pied, eight counts, facing the barre.

On "and" 1, battement tendu 2nd; on 2, hold the position; on "and," bend the knee sharply and bring the foot pointed on the cou-de-pied derrière; on 3 and 4, hold the position; on 5, extend the leg 2nd; on 6, hold the position; on "and" 7, close 5th devant; on 8, hold the position. Repeat the exercise closing derrière.

Explanation. This is another exercise in which the foot comes sharply in a pointed position on the cou-de-pied. It is similar to the battement frappé, except the focus here is on the bending inward of the working leg. The leg extends 2nd before closing 5th. Whereas the battement tendu and the extension are fairly smooth, the bending of the knee should be sharp, with the foot freezing on the cou-de-pied.

It is a good exercise for the control of the knee and keeping the foot straight as the leg bends; when bending from the 2nd position to the one on the cou-de-pied, the foot must not sickle as many ballet students tend to do. The thigh of the working leg hardly moves during the bending. Students keep their knee to the side when they bend the working leg.

Application. This is another exercise to increase the speed of the bending and also to strengthen the adductors.

Exercise 12

Preparation for rond de jambe soutenu 2nd, no rotation, in 1st, facing the barre.

Students repeat Exercise 11 of the Fifth Class of the Thirteenth Week.

Exercise 13

Petits battements, double, extend 2nd, bring the foot down in 2nd.

On "and," bring the working foot on the cou-de-pied devant; on 1, hold the position; on 2, unbend the leg halfway to 2nd; on 3, bring the foot on the cou-de-pied derrière; on 4, extend the leg 2nd, pointing the foot onto the floor; on 5, bring the foot down in 2nd and close the arms 1st; on 6, point the foot again, opening the arms 2nd, and the left hand resting again on the barre; on 7, close 5th derrière; on 8, hold it. Repeat the exercise starting on the cou-de-pied derrière. Repeat three more times with the right foot. At the end, plié and relevé in 5th and hold balance.

Explanation. The exercise is now done sideways, with a port de bras when the working foot comes down. Otherwise the arm remains 2nd during the petits battements. Students need to shift their center of gravity to the middle of both legs when they bring their foot down and shift their weight again onto their supporting leg when they point their foot.

Exercise 14

Adagio: plié in 5th and cambré, facing the barre.

Students repeat Exercise 12 of the Fourth Class of the Thirteenth Week.

Exercise 15

Preparation for grand battement 2nd and derrière, facing the barre, preparation for grand battement devant, sideways, four counts.

Students repeat Exercise 14 of the Fifth Class of the Thirteenth Week.

Exercise 16

Pied sur la barre 2nd and devant, plié and bend forward.

Students repeat Exercise 15 of the Second Class of the Thirteenth Week.

Exercise 17

Battement tendu en croix, hold the position when the foot is pointed and when the foot is closed, in 1st, four counts.

Students repeat Exercise 15 of the Fifth Class of the Twelfth Week.

Exercise 18

Battement tendu en croix, hold the position when the foot is pointed and when the foot is closed, four counts.

Students repeat Exercise 17 of the Fifth Class of the Thirteenth Week.

Exercise 19

Preparation for battement jeté 2nd, en descendant, four counts.

On "and" 1, battement tendu 2nd with the left foot; on "and," battement 2nd; on 2, hold the position; on "and," lower the leg and bring the pointed toes down onto the floor; on 3, hold the position; on 4, close 5th devant. Repeat three more times, always closing 5th devant. Repeat the exercise one more time.

Explanation. Students are practicing the battement tendu 2nd in 5th en descendant.

Exercise 20

Adagio: grand plié in 2nd, port de bras performed separately.

Students repeat Exercise 18 of the Fifth Class of the Thirteenth Week.

Exercise 21

Pas de bourrée dessous, with head rotation, four counts, facing the barre.

On "and," bring the back foot on the cou-de-pied derrière, while the supporting leg does a plié, with the head still turned toward the right; on 1, hold the position; on 2, step onto the back foot onto demi-pointe behind the supporting foot, and stretch both legs; on "and," open the right leg 2nd, with the head straightening; on 3, step onto the right foot on demi-pointe, and transfer the weight onto the right leg; on "and," close 5th, left foot front in plié, with the head turned toward the left; on 4, stretch both knees. Repeat the exercise three more times, alternating legs.

Explanation. The movement of the head now accompanies the pas de bourrée.

Exercise 22

Relevé in 6th and 1st, plié and relevé on one count, two counts, three repetitions, facing the barre and in the center.

Students repeat Exercise 19 of the Fifth Class of the Thirteenth Week.

Exercise 23

Soubresaut in 1st, on the count, two count hold, review.

Following the preparatory port de bras, bring the arms down.

On "and," plié and push off the floor; on 1,

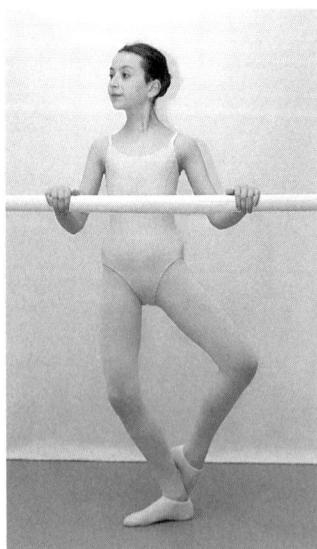

The back leg bends to start the pas de bourrée.

The first leg opens briefly 2nd position on demi-pointe.

The second leg extends 2nd position, once the weight is transferred onto the first leg.

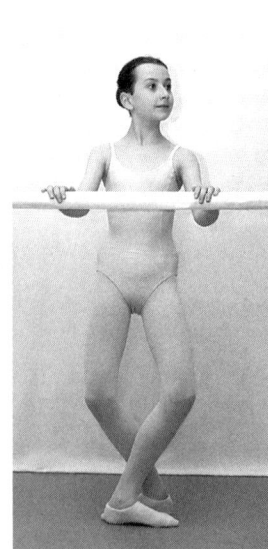

Both feet close and are in 5th position in plié.

land in plié; on 2, stretch both knees; on 3 and 4, hold the position. Repeat three more times. Repeat the exercise.

Explanation. Students are reviewing Exercise 20 of the Fifth Class of the Tenth Week.

Exercise 24

Assemblé 2nd, en descendant and en remontant, with head rotation, two counts, one count hold, facing the barre.

Students repeat Exercise 22 of the Fourth Class of the Thirteenth Week.

Exercise 25

Preparation for déboulés, in 1st, arms in low 1st, each half turn on one count, hold two counts after two half turns, review.

Students repeat Exercise 22 of the Second Class of the Tenth Week.

Exercise 26

Preparation for grand battement 2nd, en descendant, four counts.

On "and" 1, battement tendu 2nd with the left foot; on 2, battement; on 3, lower the leg, pointing the foot onto the floor; on 4, close 5th, left foot front. Repeat three more times, alternating the legs, always closing front. Repeat the exercise one more time.

Explanation. Students are performing the grand battement 2nd in the center, closing 5th devant. The hips do not swing along with the leg in the battement. The focus of this exercise is to control the back and the turn-out in the battement. Notice that the descent of the leg is not performed as quickly as at the barre, since students need to balance at the same time. The head remains straight so that students are not destabilized by rotating the head as they lift their working leg.

Application. The exercise can be done very well in 1st, changing the working leg for each battement.

Exercise 27

Curtsey.

THIRD CLASS

Students repeat the material of the Second Class of this week.

FOURTH CLASS

Exercise 1

Bending and rotation of the head, battement tendu 2nd, in 1st, facing the barre.

Students repeat Exercise 1 of the Second Class of this week.

Exercise 2

Plié in 2nd and 1st, with port de bras.

Students repeat Exercise 2 of the Fourth Class of the Thirteenth Week.

Exercise 3

Battement tendu devant, passé à terre, battement tendu derrière, battement tendu 2nd, bring the foot down in 2nd, with port de bras, in 1st.

Students repeat Exercise 3 of the Second Class of this week.

Exercise 4

Battement tendu 2nd, hold the position when the foot is pointed and when it is closed, plié, in 1st, four counts, two counts, facing the barre.

Students repeat Exercise 4 of the Second Class of this week.

Exercise 5

Battement tendu 2nd, four counts, two counts, facing the barre.

Students repeat Exercise 5 of the Second Class of this week.

Exercise 6

Preparation for battement jeté en croix en dehors and en dedans, four counts.

Students repeat Exercise 6 of the Second Class of this week.

Exercise 7

Battement jeté 2nd, broken down and direct, in 1st, four counts, facing the barre.

Students repeat Exercise 7 of the Second Class of this week.

Exercise 8

Position on the cou-de-pied, pointed, extension of the leg en croix, with a stretched supporting leg and in plié, four counts, facing the barre.

Students repeat Exercise 8 of the Second Class of this week.

Exercise 9

Demi-rond de jambe en dehors and en dedans à la demi-hauteur, eight counts, facing the barre.

Students repeat Exercise 8 of the Second Class of the Thirteenth Week.

Exercise 10

Battement fondu 2nd, start with a fondu, eight counts, facing the barre.

Students repeat Exercise 10 of the Second Class of this week.

Exercise 11

Battement tendu 2nd, bring the foot on the cou-de-pied, eight counts, facing the barre.

Students repeat Exercise 11 of the Second Class of this week.

Exercise 12

Preparation for rond de jambe soutenu 2nd, no rotation, in 1st, facing the barre.

Students repeat Exercise 11 of the Fifth Class of the Thirteenth Week.

Exercise 13

Petits battements, double, extend 2nd, bring the foot down in 2nd.

Students repeat Exercise 13 of the Second Class of this week.

Exercise 14

Preparation for grand battement 2nd and derrière, facing the barre, preparation for grand battement devant, sideways, four counts.

Students repeat Exercise 14 of the Fifth Class of the Thirteenth Week.

Exercise 15

Attitude devant, plié, facing the barre.

Bend the leg and rest the lower part of the leg on the barre, in front of the torso, with the external side of the heel resting on the barre, pointing the foot with the toes aiming down against the barre. Both hands rest on the barre. The supporting leg is turned out and stretched.

On 1 and 2, plié and stretch. Repeat three more times. At the end, release the barre and hold the position with the arms 2nd. Moving the supporting leg backward, stretch the working leg and bend forward while holding the barre, with both legs parallel.

Explanation. This is another stretching exercise for the articulation of the hip joint. For this exercise, the barre should be at an adequate height (usually at hip level of the student). In the attitude position, the lower back is pulled up. To avoid sickling the foot at the barre, students slide their toes slightly down the side of the barre so that the heel is kept up. In the second part of the exercise, students stretch the hamstrings by pulling the barre while the working leg is stretched forward, with the heel resting on the barre.

CENTER

Exercise 16

Battement tendu 2nd, bring the foot down, point the foot, with transfer, with port de bras, in 1st, eight counts, review.

On "and" 1, battement tendu 2nd; on 2, hold the position; on 3, bring the foot down 2nd in plié, bringing the arms in 1st; on 4, point the left foot while transferring the weight onto the right foot and opening the arms 2nd; on 5, hold the position; on "and" 6, close 1st; on 7 and 8, hold the position. Repeat the whole exercise one more time.

Explanation. Students are reviewing a version of Exercise 16 of the Fourth Class of the Tenth Week. The tempo is accelerated.

Exercise 17

Battement tendu en croix, hold the position when the foot is pointed and when it is closed, four counts.

Students repeat Exercise 17 of the Fifth Class of the Thirteenth Week.

Exercise 18

Preparation for battement jeté 2nd, en descendant, four counts.

Students repeat Exercise 19 of the Second Class of this week.

Exercise 19

Adagio: grand plié in 2nd, port de bras performed separately.

Students repeat Exercise 18 of the Fifth Class of the Thirteenth Week.

Exercise 20

Pas de bourrée dessous, with head rotation, four counts, facing the barre.

Students repeat Exercise 21 of the Second Class of this week.

Exercise 21

Relevé in 6th and 1st, plié and relevé on one count, two counts, three repetitions, facing the barre and in the center.

Students repeat Exercise 19 of the Fifth Class of the Thirteenth Week.

Exercise 22

Soubresaut in 1st, on the count, two count hold, review.

Students repeat Exercise 23 of the Second Class of this week.

Exercise 23

Échappé 2nd, without changing, two counts, one count hold, facing the barre.

On "and," plié, straightening the head, spring off the floor, opening the legs 2nd; on 1, land in plié in 2nd; on "and," directly out of the plié, spring off the floor again; on 2, land in plié right foot front; on 3, stretch the knees; on 4, hold the position. Repeat three more times.

Explanation. Students are returning to the barre to perform the petit échappé 2nd in 5th, performed on two counts this time. The first plié of the jump is sharper. In the second jump of the échappé, the legs do not open wider than when the feet are in 2nd on the floor. Again, considerable attention is given to the plié in both jumps; the knees remain above the toes throughout and the legs and feet are fully stretched. The head remains de face.

Music. The musical choice must reflect the change in counts for this échappé exercise. Both jumps are performed more evenly than in the échappé exercise that was practiced on four counts, (which emphasizes the first jump). Yet, students must have enough time for the first plié and the takeoff, and still land on the count. A music used normally for grand allegro would be the best choice for this exercise.

Exercise 24

Preparation for grand battement 2nd, en descendant, four counts.

Students repeat Exercise 26 of the Second Class of this week.

Exercise 25

Marche with passé à terre, in 1st, arms in 1st, in diagonal.

Start in 1st in the upper left corner facing the lower right corner of the studio. Following the preparatory port de bras, bring the arms down, with the head turned toward the front of the studio.

On "and" 1, battement tendu devant with the right foot, bringing the arms in low 1st; on 2, hold the position; on "and" 3, step onto the right foot, brush the left foot in 1st from back to front, pointing the left foot devant; on 4, hold the position; on "and" 5, step onto the left foot, brush the right foot through 1st, pointing the right foot; on 6, hold the position; on "and" 7, step onto the right foot, brush the left foot through 1st, pointing the left foot devant; on 8, hold the position. Repeat the exercise to the end of the diagonal.

Explanation. Since students have already practiced the brushing of the foot through 1st, they can start practicing this marche with a direct brushing forward. If the marche itself is hardly used in ballet for its intrinsic value, it is a good exercise to develop rhythm and style during which the student achieves an elegant bearing

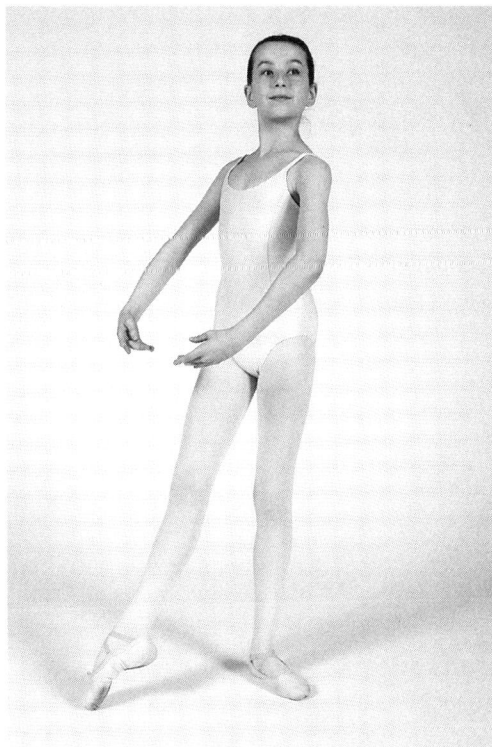

The leg is stretched in 4th position devant with the arms in low 1st position.

in the carriage of the upper body. The heel is actively pushed forward in each battement tendu. The back is pulled up.

Exercise 26

Curtsey.

FIFTH CLASS

Exercise 1

Bending and rotation of the head, battement tendu 2nd, in 1st, facing the barre.

Students repeat Exercise 1 of the Second Class of this week.

Exercise 2

Plié in 2nd, 1st, and 4th, facing the barre.

Following the preparatory port de bras, battement tendu 2nd with the right foot and bring it down.

On 1 and 2, plié; on 3 and 4, stretch; on 5 and 6, plié; on 7 and 8, stretch and close the right foot in 1st.

On 1 and 2, plié; on 3 and 4, stretch; on 5 and 6, plié; on 7 and 8, stretch. On 1 and 2, battement tendu devant; on 3, bring the foot down in 4th position; on 4, hold the position; on 5 and 6, point the back foot; on 7, bring it down; on 8, hold the position.

On 1 and 2, plié; on 3 and 4, stretch; on 5 and 6, plié; on 7 and 8, stretch. On 1 and 2, point the front foot and close; on 3 and 4, point the back foot and bring it into 1st; from 5 to 8, battement tendu 2nd with the left foot and bring the foot down to repeat the exercise. In 4th position, the left foot will come forward.

Explanation. This exercise introduces students to the plié in 4th position. As for the 2nd position performed sideways of the barre, students have to adjust their position to be in 4th facing the barre so that they remain at a proper distance from the barre. If no adjustment were made, they would be either too close or too far. The introduction of the 4th follows the 5th position, for it is more difficult to keep the hips in a proper place and the weight centered between both legs, especially when a plié is involved.

The 4th position is an important position, especially for the pirouette preparation. For students with sufficient turn-out, this position should not present much difficulty. The instructor must make sure that the knees are above the toes in the plié, the thighs remain turned-out, and the hips are properly aligned. The feet do not roll in, and the back hip does not come out. The weight is spread equally on both legs. The space between both feet is about one foot, but no more than one and a half feet; the wider the 4th position, the more difficult it is to keep the turn-out in the plié. The hips are parallel to the barre. In the ideal version of the 4th, the heel of the front foot must be aligned with the toes of the back foot, and the toes of the front foot must be aligned with the heel of the back foot. However, at this stage, it is acceptable to open the back leg a bit off the alignment to ease the demand on the turn-out, as long as the weight is spread equally on both legs.

Exercise 3

Battement tendu devant, passé à terre, battement tendu derrière, battement tendu 2nd, bring the foot down 2nd, with port de bras, in 1st.

Students repeat Exercise 3 of the Second Class of this week.

Exercise 4

Battement tendu 2nd, hold the position when the foot is pointed and when it is closed, plié, in 1st, four counts, two counts, facing the barre.

Students repeat Exercise 4 of the Second Class of this week.

Exercise 5

Battement tendu 2nd, start in plié, stretch when pointing, in 1st, four counts, facing the barre.

On 1, plié; on "and" 2, battement tendu 2nd starting in plié and both knees stretching by the time the foot is pointed; on 3, hold the position; on 4, close 1st. Repeat three more times, alternating legs. At the end, roll up in 1st and hold balance.

Explanation. Students are introduced to a useful exercise to perform many ballet movements that involve the stretching of the working leg out of the plié, like an assemblé. Again, coordination of the stretching is the most challenging aspect of this exercise, for, by the time the foot is pointed, the supporting leg must be stretched.

The difficulty lies in the fact that the movement of the working leg is of a greater range of motion than the one of the supporting leg, which means that the working leg must stretch faster.

Music. An energetic tango would work well here.

Application. This is a useful preparatory exercise for ballet dancers to coordinate the stretching of the knees. This exercise can be toned down by being performed in parallel with the leg stretching forward.

Exercise 6

Battement tendu 2nd, four counts, two counts, facing the barre.

Students repeat Exercise 5 of the Second Class of this week.

Exercise 7

Preparation for battement jeté en croix en dehors and en dedans, four counts.

Students repeat Exercise 6 of the Second Class of this week.

Exercise 8

Battement jeté 2nd, broken down and direct, in 1st, four counts, facing the barre.

Students repeat Exercise 7 of the Second Class of this week.

Exercise 9

Position on the cou-de-pied, pointed, extension of the leg en croix, with a stretched supporting leg and in plié, four counts, facing the barre.

Students repeat Exercise 8 of the Second Class of this week.

Exercise 10

Demi-rond de jambe en dehors and en dedans à la demi-hauteur, eight counts, facing the barre.

Students repeat Exercise 8 of the Second Class of the Thirteenth Week.

Exercise 11

Battement fondu 2nd, start with a fondu, eight counts, facing the barre.

Students repeat Exercise 10 of the Second Class of this week.

Exercise 12

Battement tendu 2nd, bring the foot on the cou-de-pied, eight counts, facing the barre.

Students repeat Exercise 11 of the Second Class of this week.

Exercise 13

Petits battements, double, extend 2nd, bring the foot down in 2nd.

Students repeat Exercise 13 of the Second Class of this week.

Exercise 14

Preparation for grand battement devant and 2nd, sideways, preparation for grand battement derrière, facing the barre, four counts.

In 4th devant and 2nd sideways: on "and" 1, battement tendu devant; on 2, battement; on "and," lower the leg, and point the foot onto the floor; on 3, hold the position; on 4, close 5th devant; on "and" 5, battement tendu 2nd; on 6, battement; on "and," lower the leg and point the foot onto the floor; on 7, hold the position; on 8, close 5th devant. Repeat one more time.

In 4th derrière facing the barre, left foot front: on "and" 1, battement tendu derrière; on 2, battement; on "and," lower the leg and point the foot onto the floor; on 3, hold the position; on 4, close 5th derrière. Repeat three more times.

Explanation. Students are repeating the exercise, except they are performing the battement 2nd sideways. When doing so, they must not pull the barre, swing the torso, or raise the inside shoulder in an attempt to bring the leg higher.

Exercise 15

Attitude devant, plié, facing the barre.

Students repeat Exercise 15 of the Fourth Class of this week.

CENTER

Exercise 16

Battement tendu 2nd, bring the foot down, point the foot, with transfer, with port de bras, in 1st, eight counts, review.

Students repeat Exercise 16 of the Fourth Class of this week.

Exercise 17

Battement tendu 2nd, hold the position when the foot is pointed and when it is closed, plié, in 1st, four counts, two counts.

On "and" 1, battement tendu 2nd; on 2, hold the position; on "and" 3, close; on 4, hold the position; on "and" 5, battement tendu 2nd; on 6, close 1st; on 7 and 8, plié and stretch. Repeat the exercise three more times, alternating legs.

Explanation. Students are repeating Exercise 4 of the Second Class of this week.

Exercise 18

Preparation for battement jeté 2nd, en descendant, four counts.

Students repeat Exercise 19 of the Second Class of this week.

Exercise 19

Position of the foot on the cou-de-pied, pointed, extend the leg 2nd, with port de bras, four counts.

Following the preparatory port de bras, bring the arms down.

On "and," bring the front foot on the cou-de-pied devant, bringing the arms in 1st; on 1, hold the position; on 2, extend the leg 2nd with the foot pointed on the floor, opening the arms 2nd; on 3, hold the position; on 4, close 5th devant, bringing the arms down. Repeat one more time closing 5th derrière. Repeat the whole exercise one more time.

Explanation. Students are practicing the exercise in the center in 5th, on four counts.

Exercise 20

Pas de bourrée dessous, with head rotation, four counts, facing the barre.

Students repeat Exercise 21 of the Second Class of this week.

Exercise 21

Roll-up relevé and relevé in 1st, with plié, two counts, three repetitions, facing the barre.

On 1, roll up; on 2, roll down; on 3, roll up; on 4, roll down; on 5, roll up; on 6, roll down; on 7 and 8, hold the position.

On "and," plié; on 1, relevé; on 2, come down in plié; on 3, relevé; on 4, come down in plié; on 5, relevé; on 6, come down in plié; on 7, stretch the knees; on 8, hold the position. Repeat the exercise one more time.

Explanation. The roll-up relevé is also practiced on two counts, with no hold in between. In rolling up and down, the feet must not roll in, and the adductor muscles are rotating actively outward.

Music. The tempo is fairly slow with clear beats.

Exercise 22

Soubresaut in 1st, on the count, two count hold.

Students repeat Exercise 23 of the Second Class of this week.

Exercise 23

Échappé 2nd, without changing, two counts, one count hold, facing the barre.

Students repeat Exercise 23 of the Fourth Class of this week.

Exercise 24

Preparation for grand battement 2nd, en descendant, four counts.

Students repeat Exercise 26 of the Second Class of this week.

Exercise 25

Marche with passé à terre, in 1st, arms in 1st, in diagonal.

Students repeat Exercise 25 of the Fourth Class of this week.

Exercise 26

Curtsey.

This ends the first part of the year. If there is more time, students will review some of the exercises they have already studied since the beginning of the year.

Application. Beginning students in a recreational program taking ballet once, twice, or three times a week will not have achieved as much; but many exercises of this first part can be applied to them or even to students with more experience to improve their technique. It is the role of the instructor to gauge whether such and such exercise can be properly introduced to students, and to make sure they are exposed to new ballet steps progressively and gradually.

Fifteenth Week

§

When students come back from midyear break (usually around Christmas time), the instructor should not introduce anything new during the first week. They repeat exercises that have been studied in the first part of the year to recondition muscles after time off.

Sixteenth Week

§

Students pick up the training as they left it in the Fourteenth Week of the first part of the training.

FIRST CLASS

Exercise 1

Warm up.

From now on, the instructor will select the elements of the first exercise at the barre. The exercise will be at a fairly slow tempo, performed in 1st or 6th. It will include elements already known, and it will be performed preferably facing the barre.

Exercise 2

Plié in 2nd, 1st, and 4th, facing the barre.

Students repeat Exercise 2 of the Fifth Class of the Fourteenth Week.

Exercise 3

Battement tendu en croix, plié, hold when pointing and when closing, in 1st, four counts, two counts.

On "and" 1, battement tendu devant; on 2, hold the position; on "and" 3, close 1st; on 4, hold the position; on "and" 5, battement tendu devant; on 6, close 1st; on 7 and 8, plié and stretch. Repeat the exercise en croix en dehors. At the end, roll up and hold balance.

Explanation. Students are repeating Exercise 4 of the Second Class of the Fourteenth Week, except this time the exercise is performed en croix.

Exercise 4

Battement tendu 2nd, start in plié, stretch when pointing, in 1st, four counts, facing the barre.

Students repeat Exercise 5 of the Fifth Class of the Fourteenth Week.

Exercise 5

Battement tendu devant, passé à terre in plié, hold when pointing, in 1st, facing the barre.

On "and" 1, battement tendu devant; on 2, hold the position; on "and" 3, brush through 1st in plié and battement tendu derrière while stretching both legs; on 4, hold the position; on "and" 5, brush through 1st in plié and battement tendu devant, stretching the legs; on 6, hold the position; on 7, close 1st; on 8, hold the position. Repeat the exercise one more time.

Explanation. Students have to coordinate the bending and the stretching of the knees so that the whole movement is smooth. Before practicing the exercise, they should have performed the battement tendu closing in plié and the battement tendu starting in plié and stretching out.

Music. A slow-to-medium waltz would work well for this exercise.

Exercise 6

Battement tendu en croix, hold when pointing and when closing, four counts, two counts.

On "and" 1, battement tendu devant; on 2, hold the position; on 3, close 5th devant; on 4, hold the position; on "and" 5, battement tendu devant; on 6, close 5th devant; on 7 and 8, hold the position. Repeat the exercise en croix en dehors. At the end, roll up and hold balance.

Explanation. The exercise is now performed en croix. The first battement tendu 2nd closes devant, since there is an even number of battements tendus.

Exercise 7

Battement jeté 2nd, broken down and direct, four counts, facing the barre.

On "and" 1, battement tendu 2nd; on "and," battement; on 2, hold the position; on "and," lower the leg and point the foot onto the floor; on 3, hold the position; on 4, close 5th devant; on "and" 5, direct battement 2nd; on "and," lower the leg and point the foot onto the floor; on 6, hold the position; on 7, close 5th derrière; on 8, hold the position. Repeat the exercise one more time with the right foot, closing 5th devant and derrière. Repeat the whole exercise one more time.

Explanation. This exercise is similar to Exercise 7 of the Second Class of the Fourteenth Week, except this time the second battement is not held in the air as long, and the whole exercise is performed in 5th. Even though the second

battement is direct, when lowering the leg, students still hold the position of the foot onto the floor before closing.

Exercise 8

Demi-rond de jambe à la demi-hauteur, en dehors, with port de bras, eight counts.

Following the preparatory port de bras, bring the arm down.

On "and" 1, battement tendu devant, bringing the arm in 1st; on 2, lift the leg; on 3 and 4, demi-rond de jambe en dehors, opening the arm 2nd; on 5, hold the position; on 6, lower the leg and point the foot onto the floor; on 7, close 5th devant, closing the arm down; on 8, hold the position. Repeat three more times. At the end, plié and relevé in 5th.

Explanation. This time students are practicing the demi-rond de jambe off the floor sideways, with a port de bras. The one en dedans will be practiced later.

Exercise 9

Battement fondu 2nd, start with a fondu, eight counts, facing the barre.

Students repeat Exercise 10 of the Second Class of the Fourteenth Week.

Exercise 10

Battement tendu 2nd, bring the foot on the cou-de-pied, four counts, facing the barre.

On "and" 1, battement tendu 2nd; on "and," bend the knee sharply and bring the foot pointed on the cou-de-pied derrière; on 2, hold the position; on "and" 3, extend the leg 2nd, pointing the foot down onto the floor; on 4, close 5th devant. Repeat three more times with the right foot.

Explanation. Students are repeating Exercise 11 of the Second Class of the Fourteenth Week, except the exercise is performed on four counts this time.

Music. The tempo is not too fast so that the closing is performed correctly.

Exercise 11

Petits battements, double, extend 2nd, bringing the foot down in 2nd.

Students repeat Exercise 13 of the Second Class of the Fourteenth Week.

Exercise 12

Adagio: retiré devant and derrière, close directly in plié, without changing and changing feet, eight counts, facing the barre.

Without changing feet: on "and," bring the front foot pointed onto the cou-de-pied devant; on 1, hold the position; on 2 and 3, slide the side of the small toe along the leg to the knee level; on 4, hold the position; on 5 and 6, slide the foot down; on 7, close 5th devant in plié; on 8, stretch. Repeat the exercise.

On "and," bring the back foot onto the cou-de-pied derrière; on 1, hold the position; on 2 and 3, slide the side of the heel, and then progressively open the foot slightly out so that the side of the big toe slides up against the back of the supporting leg to the knee level; on 4, hold the position; on 5 and 6, slide the foot down; on 7, close 5th derrière in plié; on 8, stretch. Repeat one more time.

Changing feet: on "and," bring the front foot pointed onto the cou-de-pied devant; on 1, hold the position; on 2 and 3, slide the side of the small toe along the leg to the knee level; on 4, hold the position; on 5 and 6, graze the pointed toes around the supporting leg to transfer the pointed foot to the back of the leg, slide the foot down; on 7, close 5th derrière in plié; on 8, stretch.

On "and," bring the back foot onto the cou-de-pied derrière; on 1, hold the position; on 2 and 3, slide the side of heel and then progressively open the foot slightly out so that now the side of the big toe slides up against the back of the supporting leg to the knee level; on 4, hold the position; on 5 and 6, graze the pointed toes around to the front of the knee, and slide the foot down; on 7, close 5th devant in plié; on 8, stretch.

Explanation. In this exercise, students are closing their working foot directly into 5th position. The movement of the working leg is gradual, except for the foot that comes up sharply onto the cou-de-pied. There is less holding on the cou-de-pied. The knee must be actively pushed to the side. The knee goes up slightly so that the bending at the hip level forms a 90° angle (or close), when the toes graze around the back of the supporting leg. The closing in 5th is done in plié to make it easier. However, as said

before, the closing in the plié can be deceiving, for students can turn out their feet more in plié than they can with stretched knees. Therefore, the angle of the feet in 5th in plié will be consistent with the one of the feet when the knees are stretched.

Exercise 13

Preparation for grand battement devant and 2nd, sideways, preparation for grand battement derrière, facing the barre, four counts.

Students repeat Exercise 14 of the Fifth Class of the Fourteenth Week.

Exercise 14

Attitude devant, plié, facing the barre.

Students repeat Exercise 15 of the Fourth Class of the Fourteenth Week.

Exercise 15

Pied sur la barre 2nd and devant, plié, bend, cambré.

On "and" 1, plié; on 2, stretch; on 3 and 4, repeat; on 5 and 6, bring the left arm 1st and open it 2nd; on 7 and 8, bring it in 5th, and turn the head toward the right; on 1 and 2, bend sideways toward the right side; on 3 and 4, straighten up; on 5 and 6, open the left arm 2nd; on 7, rest the left hand on the barre; on 8, hold the position; on 1 and 2, bring the right arm in 1st and open it 2nd; on 3 and 4, bring it in 5th, and turn the head toward the left side; on 5 and 6, bend sideways toward the left; on 7 and 8, straighten up, open the right arm, and rotate the legs so that the working leg is 4th position devant. The right arm is 2nd, and the left hand rests on the barre, slightly forward of the left shoulder.

On "and" 1, plié; on 2, stretch; on 3 and 4, repeat; on 5 and 6, bring the arm 5th, turning the head slightly toward the arm; on 7 and 8, bend forward keeping the arm 5th; on 1 and 2, straighten up; on 3 and 4, cambré, keeping the head turned slightly toward the right arm; on 5 and 6, straighten up; on 7 and 8, bring both arms in 5th, and hold the position.

Explanation. Students are repeating Exercise 15 of the Second Class of the Thirteenth Week, except they are adding a cambré when the working leg is 4th position devant. The cambré in this exercise follows the same principles as the ones learned in the previous cambré exercises: the lengthening of the lumbar spine, the control of the neck, and the tightening of the abdomen muscles.

CENTER

Exercise 16

Battement tendu 2nd, hold the position when the foot is pointed and when the foot is closed, plié, in 1st, four counts, two counts.

Students repeat Exercise 17 of the Fifth Class of the Fourteenth Week.

Exercise 17

Preparation for battement jeté 2nd, en remontant, four counts.

On "and" 1, battement tendu 2nd with the right leg; on "and," battement; on 2, hold the position; on "and," bring the toes down onto the floor; on 3, hold the position; on 4, close 5th derrière. Repeat three more times, always closing 5th derrière. Repeat the exercise one more time.

Explanation. Students are practicing the exercise en remontant. Students must brush their working foot carefully in 2nd before lifting the leg so that the battement does not start with a leg turned inward. Students must refrain from drawing the leg too much to the side, as it is often the case. Doing so would make them lose balance if they actually had to hold the leg 2nd.

Exercise 18

Position on the cou-de-pied, pointed, extend the leg 2nd, with port de bras, four counts.

Students repeat Exercise 19 of the Fifth Class of the Fourteenth Week.

Exercise 19

Adagio: port de bras, all positions, in 1st, four counts each, review.

Port de bras to 2nd: on "and" 1, bring the arms down; on 2, bring the arms 1st; on 3 and 4, open the arms 2nd.

Port de bras to 3rd: on "and" 5, bring the arms down; on 6, bring the arms 1st; on 7, bring the right arm 5th and open the left arm 2nd; on "and" 8, open the arms 2nd.

Port de bras to 4th: on "and" 1, bring the arms down; on 2, bring the arms 1st; on 3, bring the right arm in 5th while the left arm stays in 1st; on "and" 4, open both arms 2nd.

Port de bras to 5th: on "and" 5, bring the arms down; on 6 and 7, bring the arms 5th through the 1st; on "and" 8, open the arms 2nd.

Repeat the whole exercise with the left arm going up in 3rd and 4th arms positions.

Explanation. Students are reviewing the different port de bras learned so far; this time each of the port de bras is performed more flowingly on four counts. Like in previous port de bras exercises, the head accompanies the arm movement. It is a good idea to include in class work a port de bras exercise regularly throughout the year.

Exercise 20

Adagio: retiré devant, extension of the leg 2nd, with port de bras, eight counts.

Following the preparatory port de bras, bring the arms down.

On "and," bring the pointed foot on the cou-de-pied devant; on 1 and 2, hold the position; on 3 to 4, slide the side of the pointed toes up against the supporting leg to knee level, with the arms coming 1st; on 5 and 6, slide down to the cou-de-pied position; on 7 and 8, extend the leg 2nd, and point the foot onto the floor, while the arms open 2nd, and close 5th devant bringing the arms down. Repeat the exercise, closing 5th derrière.

Explanation. Students are practicing the retiré devant exercise in the center. This is a more challenging exercise for balance. Again a strong back and proper contraction of the turn-out muscles, especially of the supporting leg, are requisites. Students must actively pull up the side opposite of the one of the working leg to compensate for the movement of the leg going up. In seeking balance at the beginning of the exercise, students must not cheat by resting the ball of the working foot before raising the whole foot off the floor; the foot points on the cou-de-pied right away, and balance should be attained by the time the foot is off the floor. The hips remain straight. The arms come gradually into 1st when the working leg comes up into retiré, but they stay in 1st when the foot comes down until they open 2nd. Even though it is an adagio, the tempo is accelerated.

Application. The exercise can be done with the working foot on the cou-de-pied instead of the knee level for greater stability for those students who do not have enough control of the turn-out.

Exercise 21

Roll-up relevé and relevé in 1st, with plié, two counts, three repetitions, facing the barre.

Students repeat Exercise 21 of the Fifth Class of the Fourteenth Week.

Exercise 22

Pas de bourrée dessous, with port de bras, four counts.

Following the preparatory port de bras, bring the arms down.

On "and," plié and bring the back foot on the cou-de-pied derrière, bringing the arms in 1st, and keeping the head still turned toward the right; on 1, hold the position; on 2, step onto the left foot on demi-pointe behind the supporting foot and stretch both legs; on "and," open the right leg 2nd, with the head turning straight, and opening the arms 2nd; on 3, step onto the right foot on demi-pointe in 2nd, transferring the weight onto the right leg, with still both legs stretched; on "and," close 5th, left foot front in plié, the head turned toward the left, and closing the arms down; on 4, stretch both knees, keeping the head turned to the left. Repeat three more times, alternating legs.

Explanation. The exercise is performed in the center with a port de bras and the movement of the head. Whereas this port de bras is quite standard for the pas de bourrée, others can accompany it.

Exercise 23

Échappé 2nd, without changing, two counts, one count hold, facing the barre.

Students repeat Exercise 23 of the Fourth Class of the Fourteenth Week.

Exercise 24

Assemblé 2nd, en descendant and en remontant, with head rotation, two counts, one count hold, facing the barre.

Students repeat Exercise 22 of the Fourth Class of the Thirteenth Week.

Exercise 25

Marche with passé à terre, arms in 1st, in 1st, in diagonal.

Students repeat Exercise 25 of the Fourth Class of the Fourteenth Week.

Exercise 26

Curtsey.

SECOND CLASS

Students repeat the material of the First Class of this week.

THIRD CLASS

Exercise 1

Warm up.

Exercise 2

Plié in 2nd, 1st, and 4th, facing the barre.

Students repeat Exercise 2 of the Fifth Class of the Fourteenth Week.

Exercise 3

Battement tendu en croix, hold when pointing and when closing, plié, in 1st, four counts, two counts.

Students repeat Exercise 3 of the First Class of this week.

Exercise 4

Battement tendu devant, passé à terre in plié, hold when pointing, in 1st, facing the barre.

Students repeat Exercise 5 of the First Class of this week.

Exercise 5

Battement tendu en croix, hold when pointing and when closing, four counts, two counts.

Students repeat Exercise 6 of the First Class of this week.

Exercise 6

Battement jeté 2nd, broken down and direct, four counts, facing the barre.

Students repeat Exercise 7 of the First Class of this week.

Exercise 7

Demi-rond de jambe à la demi-hauteur, en dehors, with port de bras, eight counts.

Students repeat Exercise 8 of the First Class of this week.

Exercise 8

Battement fondu 2nd, start with a fondu, eight counts, facing the barre.

Students repeat Exercise 10 of the Second Class of the Fourteenth Week.

Exercise 9

Preparation for battement frappé en croix en dehors and en dedans, four counts, review.

On "and," bring the foot on the cou-de-pied devant; on 1 and 2, hold the position; on 3, extend the leg devant, pointing the foot onto the floor; on 4, hold the position; on 5, bring the foot on the cou-de-pied devant; on 6, hold the position; on 7, extend the leg 2nd; on 8, hold the position; on 1, bring the foot on the cou-de-pied derrière; on 2, hold the position; on 3, extend the leg derrière; on 4, hold the position; on 5, bring the foot on the cou-de-pied derrière; on 6, hold the position; on 7, extend the leg 2nd; on 8, hold the position.

On 1, bring the foot on the cou-de-pied derrière; on 2, hold the position; on 3, extend the leg derrière, pointing the foot onto the floor; on 4, hold the position; on 5, bring the foot on the cou-de-pied derrière; on 6, hold the position; on 7, extend the leg 2nd; on 8, hold the position; on 1, bring the foot on the cou-de-pied devant; on 2, hold the position; on 3, extend the leg devant; on 4, hold the position; on 5, bring the foot on the cou-de-pied devant; on 6, hold the position; on 7, extend the leg 2nd; on 8, hold the position.

Explanation. This is essentially review material performed sideways.

Music. The tempo is accelerated to a brisker 4/4.

Exercise 10

Battement tendu 2nd, bring the foot on the cou-de-pied, four counts, facing the barre.

Students repeat Exercise 10 of the First Class of this week.

Exercise 11

Petits battements, each on one count, facing the barre.

On "and," bring the working foot on the cou-de-pied devant; on 1, hold the position; on "and," unbend the leg halfway to 2nd; on 2, bring the foot on the cou-de-pied derrière; on "and," unbend the leg; on 3, bring the foot on the cou-de-pied devant; on "and," unbend the leg; on 4, bring the foot on the cou-de-pied derrière; on "and," unbend the leg; on 5, bring the foot on the cou-de-pied devant; on "and," unbend the leg; on 6, bring the foot on the cou-de-pied derrière; on 7, close in 5th in plié; on 8, stretch the knees. Repeat one more time, holding the last position of the cou-de-pied devant and balance on one foot.

Explanation. Each transfer between the petits battements devant and derrière is done faster.

Exercise 12

Adagio: retiré devant and derrière, changing and without changing side, close directly in plié, eight counts, facing the barre.

Students repeat Exercise 12 of the First Class of this week.

Exercise 13

Preparation for grand battement devant and 2nd, sideways, preparation for grand battement derrière, facing the barre, four counts.

Students repeat Exercise 14 of the Fifth Class of the Fourteenth Week.

Exercise 14

Pied sur la barre 2nd and devant, plié, bend, cambré.

Students repeat Exercise 15 of the First Class of this week.

CENTER

Exercise 15

Battement tendu 2nd, hold the position when the foot is pointed and when it is closed, plié, in 1st, four counts, two counts.

Students repeat Exercise 17 of the Fifth Class of the Fourteenth Week.

Exercise 16

Preparation for battement jeté 2nd, en remontant, four counts.

Students repeat Exercise 17 of the First Class of this week.

Exercise 17

Adagio: port de bras, all positions, in 1st, four counts each, review.

Students repeat Exercise 19 of the First Class of this week.

Exercise 18

Adagio: retiré devant, extension of the leg 2nd, with port de bras, eight counts.

Students repeat Exercise 20 of the First Class of this week.

Exercise 19

Roll-up relevé and relevé in 1st, with plié, two counts, three repetitions, facing the barre.

Students repeat Exercise 21 of the Fifth Class of the Fourteenth Week.

Exercise 20

Pas de bourrée dessous, with port de bras, four counts.

Students repeat Exercise 22 of the First Class of this week.

Exercise 21

Échappé 2nd, changing feet, two counts, one count hold, facing the barre.

On "and," plié, spring off the floor, opening the legs 2nd; on 1, land in plié in 2nd; on "and," directly out of the plié, spring off the floor; on 2, land in plié left foot front; on 3, stretch the knees; on 4, hold the position. Repeat three more times. After a pause, repeat one more time.

Explanation. Students are repeating Exercise 23 of the Fourth Class of the Fourteenth Week, this time changing feet when closing.

Exercise 22

Assemblé 2nd, en descendant and en remontant, with head rotation, two counts, one count hold, facing the barre.

Students repeat Exercise 22 of the Fourth Class of the Thirteenth Week.

Exercise 23

Curtsey.

FOURTH CLASS

Exercise 1

Warm up.

Exercise 2

Plié in 2nd, 1st, and 4th, port de bras performed separately.

Following the preparatory position, bring the feet in 2nd.

On 1 and 2, plié; on 3 and 4, stretch; on "and" 5 and 6, bring the arm down; on 7, bring the arm 1st; on 8, open the arm 2nd; from 1 to 4, repeat the plié; from 5 to 8, close both feet in 1st.

On 1 and 2, plié; on 3 and 4, stretch; on "and" 5 and 6, bring the arm down; on 7, bring the arm 1st; on 8, open the arm 2nd; from 1 to 4, repeat the plié; from 5 to 8, battement tendu devant and bring the foot down in 4th.

On 1 and 2, plié; on 3 and 4, stretch; from 5 to 8, point the front foot and close 1st, roll up and hold balance.

Explanation. Students are practicing the plié exercise sideways, with the port de bras performed independently. They slide their hand along the barre when the front foot comes down in 4th so that the arm on the side of the barre is not left behind. This time only the front foot moves for the opening of the feet in 4th, since the barre is not an obstacle to bringing the legs in 4th. The hips remain perpendicular to the barre. Performing the plié in 4th position sideways of the barre sometimes leads students to be off center and crooked. If unchecked, an incorrect position may cause problems later on in the performance of pirouettes in 4th position. The instructor will be particularly vigilant to correct students whose position is incorrect. For those students, practicing the exercise still facing the barre or having them perform the plié while releasing the barre with their hand are good alternatives.

Exercise 3

Battement tendu en croix, hold when pointing and when closing, plié, in 1st, four counts, two counts.

Students repeat Exercise 3 of the First Class of this week.

Exercise 4

Battement tendu devant, passé à terre in plié, hold when pointing, in 1st, facing the barre.

Students repeat Exercise 5 of the First Class of this week.

Exercise 5

Battement tendu en croix, hold when pointing and when closing, four counts, two counts.

Students repeat Exercise 6 of the First Class of this week.

Exercise 6

Battement jeté 2nd, broken down and direct, four counts, facing the barre.

Students repeat Exercise 7 of the First Class of this week.

Exercise 7

Demi-rond de jambe à la demi-hauteur, en dehors, with port de bras, eight counts.

Students repeat Exercise 8 of the First Class of this week.

Exercise 8

Battement fondu 2nd, start with a fondu, eight counts, facing the barre.

Students repeat Exercise 10 of the Second Class of the Fourteenth Week.

Exercise 9

Preparation for battement frappé en croix en dehors and en dedans, four counts.

Students repeat Exercise 9 of the Third Class of this week.

Exercise 10

Battement tendu 2nd, bring the foot on the cou-de-pied, four counts, facing the barre.

Students repeat Exercise 10 of the First Class of this week.

Exercise 11

Petits battements, each on one count, facing the barre.

Students repeat Exercise 11 of the Third Class of this week.

Exercise 12

Adagio: retiré devant and derrière, without changing and changing side, closing directly in plié, eight counts, facing the barre.

Students repeat Exercise 12 of the First Class of this week.

Exercise 13

Preparation for grand battement devant and 2nd, sideways, preparation for grand battement derrière, facing the barre, four counts.

Students repeat Exercise 14 of the Fifth Class of the Fourteenth Week.

Exercise 14

Pied sur la barre 2nd and devant, plié, bend, cambré.

Students repeat Exercise 15 of the First Class of this week.

CENTER

Exercise 15

Battement tendu 2nd, hold the position when the foot is pointed and when it is closed, plié, in 1st, four counts, two counts.

Students repeat Exercise 17 of the Fifth Class of the Fourteenth Week.

Exercise 16

Preparation for battement jeté 2nd, en remontant, four counts.

Students repeat Exercise 17 of the First Class of this week.

Exercise 17

Battement jeté 2nd, broken down and direct, in 1st, four counts.

On "and" 1, battement tendu 2nd; on "and," battement jeté; on 2, hold the position; on "and," lower the leg and point the toes onto the floor; on 3, hold the position; on 4, close 1st; on "and" 5, direct battement 2nd; on 6, hold the position; on "and," lower the leg and point the foot onto the floor; on 7, hold the position; on 8, close 1st. Repeat one more time with the right foot. Repeat the whole exercise.

Explanation. Students are repeating Exercise 7 of the Second Class of the Fourteenth Week, this time performed in the center. Students must push their shoulders down and keep the back very erect to help hold balance when the leg is off the floor.

Music. The tempo is accelerated for a quick 4/4.

Exercise 18

Adagio: port de bras, all positions, in 1st, four counts each, review.

Students repeat Exercise 19 of the First Class of this week.

Exercise 19

Relevé in 1st, two counts, three repetitions, facing the barre, review.

On "and," plié; on 1, relevé; on 2, come down in plié; on 3, relevé; on 4, come down in plié; on 5, relevé; on 6, come down in plié; on 7, stretch the knees; on 8; hold the position. Repeat the whole exercise twice more and hold balance on the last eight counts.

Explanation. This is mostly review material with a sharper tempo. Notice the balance at the end of the exercise.

Exercise 20

Pas de bourrée dessous, with port de bras, four counts.

Students repeat Exercise 22 of the First Class of this week.

Exercise 21

Échappé 2nd, changing feet, two counts, one count hold, facing the barre.

Students repeat Exercise 21 of the Third Class of this week.

Exercise 22

Assemblé 2nd, en descendant and en remontant, with head rotation, two counts, one count hold, facing the barre.

Students repeat Exercise 22 of the Fourth Class of the Thirteenth Week.

Exercise 23

Preparation for grand battement 2nd, en remontant, four counts.

On "and" 1, battement tendu 2nd with the right foot; on 2, battement 2nd, with the right leg; on 3, lower the leg and point the foot onto the floor; on 4, close 5th right foot derrière. Repeat three more times, alternating legs, always closing back. Repeat the exercise one more time.

Explanation. Students are performing the grand battement exercise en remontant this time. They press down their working foot in the battement tendu, keeping maximum turn-out in the whole leg. Elbows do not scoop in the effort to turn out the working leg.

Exercise 24

Curtsey.

FIFTH CLASS

Exercise 1

Warm up.

Exercise 2

Plié in 2nd, 1st, and 4th, port de bras performed separately.

Students repeat Exercise 2 of the Fourth Class of this week.

Exercise 3

Battement tendu en croix, hold when pointing and when closing, plié, in 1st, four counts, two counts.

Students repeat Exercise 3 of the First Class of this week.

Exercise 4

Battement tendu en croix, plié when pointing, in 1st, four counts, facing the barre.

On "and" 1, battement tendu devant; on 2, plié with the foot still pointed; on 3, stretch the supporting leg; on 4, close 1st. Repeat the exercise en croix en dehors. At the end, plié and relevé in 1st and hold balance with the arms in low 1st.

Explanation. Students are revisiting Exercise 4 of the Second Class of the Ninth Week, this time performed en croix and on four counts.

Exercise 5

Battement tendu 2nd, in 1st, two counts, three repetitions, facing the barre.

On "and" 1, battement tendu 2nd; on 2, close 1st; on "and" 3, battement tendu 2nd; on 4, close; on "and" 5, battement tendu 2nd; on 6, close; on 7 and 8, plié and stretch. Repeat the exercise one more time with the right foot. Repeat the whole exercise one more time. At the end, roll up and hold balance.

Explanation. Students are practicing the battement tendu 2nd, on two counts, three at a time with no hold.

Music. A medium tempo and sharp 4/4 is appropriate for this exercise.

Exercise 6

Battement tendu en croix, hold when pointing and when closing, four counts, two counts.

Students repeat Exercise 6 of the First Class of this week.

Exercise 7

Battement jeté 2nd, broken down and direct, four counts, facing the barre.

Students repeat Exercise 7 of the First Class of this week.

Exercise 8

Preparation for battement jeté piqué 2nd, direct battement, in 1st, facing the barre.

On "and" 1, battement 2nd; on "and," lower the leg and bring the pointed foot down onto the floor; on 2, hold the position; on "and," lift the leg 2nd again at the same height than previously; on 3, hold the position; on "and," bring the pointed foot down; on 4, hold the position; on "and," lift the leg one more time; on 5, hold the position; on "and," bring the foot down; on 6, hold the position; on 7, close 1st; on 8, hold the position. Repeat the exercise one more time with the right foot. At the end, roll up and hold balance.

Explanation. Students are revisiting this preparatory exercise for the battement jeté piqué, except they are doing so with a direct battement 2nd. In this exercise, students have to sharply bring the working foot down onto the floor and lift the leg à la demi-hauteur. The foot must be fully pointed with tight toes. When lifting the leg both times, the working leg freezes in the air at the same height. Students must avoid using the quadriceps excessively to bring the leg up; they must use their turn-out muscles to lift the leg. The lift need not be à la demi-hauteur; but the leg needs to be lifted and lowered quickly. Students do not lean their torso away from their working leg.

Music. A tango with a snappy tempo or a coda would be appropriate musical choices here.

Application. This exercise can be practiced by most beginners to prepare for the actual battement jeté piqué.

Exercise 9

Demi-rond de jambe à la demi-hauteur en dedans, eight counts, facing the barre, review.

Start with the left foot front.

On "and" 1, battement tendu derrière with the right foot; on 2, lift the leg à la demi-hauteur; on 3 and 4, demi-rond de jambe en dedans; on 5, lower the leg and point the foot onto the floor; on 6, hold the position; on 7, close 5th derrière, on 8, hold the position. Repeat twice more, holding the leg 2nd at the end of the last demi-rond de jambe.

Explanation. Students are reviewing the demi-rond de jambe en dedans as performed in Exercise 8 of the Second Class of the Thirteenth Week. Students are still facing the barre for this exercise, since the passage of the leg from back to 2nd can be challenging, especially when performed off the floor. The turning out of the leg must occur as soon as possible, without letting the supporting hip move forward, so that the working leg is turned out by the time it is in 2nd.

Exercise 10

Battement fondu, en croix, eight counts, facing the barre.

On 1 and 2, bring the foot on the cou-de-pied devant with a deep plié on the supporting leg; on 3 and 4, extend the leg in demi-attitude devant, still in plié; on 5 and 6, stretch both legs at the same time à la demi-hauteur; on 7 and 8, bring the foot down onto the floor, and close in 5th devant. Repeat the exercise en croix en dehors. In the last battement fondu 2nd, students hold their leg 2nd and balance with the arms in 2nd.

Explanation. After practicing the exercise 2nd, students perform it en croix, still facing the barre, if space allows. The tempo is slightly accelerated for a more flowing movement. The first plié is ongoing, filling up both counts.

Exercise 11

Preparatory exercise for battement frappé en croix, en dehors and en dedans, four counts.

Students repeat Exercise 9 of the Third Class of this week.

Exercise 12

Battement tendu 2nd, bring the foot on the cou-de-pied, four counts, facing the barre.

Students repeat Exercise 10 of the First Class of this week.

Exercise 13

Petits battements, each on one count, facing the barre.

Students repeat Exercise 11 of the Third Class of this week.

Exercise 14

Adagio: lift the leg devant and 2nd, sideways, lift the leg derrière, facing the barre, open and close on the count, hold two counts in the air.

In 4th devant and 2nd sideways: on "and" 1, battement tendu devant; on 2, lift the leg; on 3 and 4, hold the position; on 5, lower the leg and point the toes onto the floor; on 6, hold the position; on 7, close in 5th devant; on 8, hold the position. Repeat the exercise 2nd. Repeat one more time.

In 4th derrière facing the barre: on "and" 1, battement tendu derrière; on 2, lift the leg; on 3 and 4, hold the position; on 5, lower the leg and point the toes onto the floor; on 6, hold the position; on 7, close 5th derrière; on 8, hold the position. Repeat one more time.

Explanation. This is essentially review material. But the whole movement is performed more flowingly and continuously by now. The instructor will gauge whether students are ready to perform lifting the leg 2nd sideways. If the movement is done sideways, students must not pull the barre or bend their knees. Lifting the leg derrière is still done facing the barre to keep the torso and the shoulders as straight as possible.

Exercise 15

Preparation for grand battement devant and 2nd, sideways, preparation for grand battement derrière, facing the barre, four counts.

Students repeat Exercise 14 of the Fifth Class of the Fourteenth Week.

Exercise 16

Pied sur la barre 2nd and devant, plié, bend, cambré.

Students repeat Exercise 15 of the First Class of this week.

CENTER

Exercise 17

Battement tendu en croix, hold when pointing and when closing, in 1st, four counts, two counts.

On "and" 1, battement tendu devant; on 2, hold the position; on 3, close 1st; on 4, hold the position; on "and" 5, battement tendu devant; on 6, close 1st; on 7 and 8, plié and stretch. Repeat the exercise en croix en dehors.

Explanation. Students are repeating Exercise 3 of the First Class of this week, this time performed in the center.

Exercise 18

Battement tendu 2nd, hold when pointing and when closing, four counts, two counts.

On "and" 1, battement tendu 2nd; on 2, hold the position; on 3, close 5th devant; on 4, hold the position; on "and" 5, battement tendu 2nd; on 6, close 5th derrière; on 7 and 8, hold the position. Repeat one more time with the right foot. Repeat the whole exercise one more time.

Explanation. Students are repeating Exercise 5 of the Second Class of the Fourteenth Week, performed this time in the center. There is no plié and stretch in this exercise, just a holding for students to re-center themselves without further adjustment.

Exercise 19

Battement jeté 2nd, broken down and direct, in 1st, four counts.

Students repeat Exercise 17 of the Fourth Class of this week.

Exercise 20

Adagio: port de bras, all positions, in 1st, four counts each.

Students repeat Exercise 19 of the First Class of this week.

Exercise 21

Relevé in 1st, two counts, three repetitions, facing the barre, review.

Students repeat Exercise 19 of the Fourth Class of this week.

Exercise 22

Pas de bourrée dessous, with port de bras, four counts.

Students repeat Exercise 22 of the First Class of this week.

Exercise 23

Échappé 2nd, changing feet, two counts, one count hold, facing the barre.

Students repeat Exercise 21 of the Third Class of this week.

Exercise 24

Assemblé 2nd, en descendant and en remontant, with head rotation, two counts, one count hold, facing the barre.

Students repeat Exercise 22 of the Fourth Class of the Thirteenth Week.

Exercise 25

Preparation for grand battement 2nd, en remontant, four counts.

Students repeat Exercise 23 of the Fourth Class of this week.

Exercise 26

Curtsey.

Seventeenth Week

§

FIRST CLASS

Students repeat the material of the Fifth Class of the Sixteenth Week.

SECOND CLASS

Exercise 1

Warm up.

Exercise 2

Plié in 2nd, 1st, and 4th, port de bras performed separately.

Students repeat Exercise 2 of the Fourth Class of the Sixteenth Week.

Exercise 3

Battement tendu 2nd, in 1st, two counts, three repetitions, facing the barre.

Students repeat Exercise 5 of the Fifth Class of the Sixteenth Week.

Exercise 4

Battement tendu en croix, plié when pointing, in 1st, four counts, facing the barre.

Students repeat Exercise 4 of the Fifth Class of the Sixteenth Week.

Exercise 5

Battement jeté en croix en dehors, broken down and direct, four counts, facing the barre.

On "and" 1, battement tendu devant; on "and," battement; on 2, hold the position; on "and," lower the leg and point the foot onto the floor; on 3, hold the position; on 4, close 5th; on "and" 5, battement devant; on "and," lower the leg and point the foot on the floor; on 6, hold the position; on 7, close 5th devant; on 8, hold the position. Repeat the exercise en croix en dehors; the first battement 2nd closes devant. At the end, roll up and hold balance.

Explanation. Students are repeating Exercise 7 of the First Class of the Sixteenth Week, except it is now performed en croix. The closings into

5th are done as tightly as possible without bending the knees. Students do not turn their hips toward the working leg in order to keep it on the side in the battement 2nd.

Exercise 6

Preparation for battement jeté piqué 2nd, direct battement, in 1st, facing the barre.

Students repeat Exercise 8 of the Fifth Class of the Sixteenth Week.

Exercise 7

Demi-rond de jambe à la hauteur en dedans, eight counts, facing the barre, review.

Students repeat Exercise 9 of the Fifth Class of the Sixteenth Week.

Exercise 8

Battement fondu, en croix, eight counts, facing the barre.

Students repeat Exercise 10 of the Fifth Class of the Sixteenth Week.

Exercise 9

Battement frappé 2nd, two counts, facing the barre.

On "and," bring the front foot on the cou-de-pied devant; on 1, hold the position; on 2, extend the leg 2nd, pointing the foot onto the floor; on 3, bring the foot on the cou-de-pied derrière; on 4, extend the leg 2nd; on 5, bring the foot on the cou-de-pied devant; on 6, extend the leg; on 7, close 5th derrière; on 8, hold the position. Repeat three more times with the right foot. At the end, roll up and hold balance.

Explanation. In this exercise, the movement is much less broken down and looks more like the plain battement frappé. The battement frappé is performed on two counts. The extension is sharp but controlled.

Exercise 10

Adagio: lift the leg devant and 2nd, sideways, lift the leg derrière, facing the barre, open and close on the count, hold two counts in the air.

Students repeat Exercise 14 of the Fifth Class of the Sixteenth Week.

Exercise 11

Petits battements, each on one count, arm in low 1st.

Following the preparatory port de bras, bring the arm down.

On "and," bring the working foot on the cou-de-pied devant, bringing the arm in low 1st; on 1, hold the position; on "and," unbend the leg halfway to 2nd; on 2, bring the foot on the cou-de-pied derrière; on "and," unbend the leg; on 3, bring the foot on the cou-de-pied devant; on "and," unbend the leg; on 4, bring the foot on the cou-de-pied derrière; on "and," unbend the leg; on 5, bring the foot on the cou-de-pied devant; on "and," unbend the leg; on 6, bring the foot on the cou-de-pied derrière; on 7, close in 5th in plié; on 8, stretch the knees. Repeat the exercise one more time, holding the last position of the cou-de-pied devant and balance on one foot.

Explanation. Students are repeating Exercise 11 of the Third Class of the Sixteenth Week, except it is performed sideways with the arm in low 1st.

Exercise 12

Preparation for grand battement devant and 2nd, sideways, preparation for grand battement derrière, facing the barre, four counts.

Students repeat Exercise 14 of the Fifth Class of the Fourteenth Week.

Exercise 13

Bending forward, back to the barre, cambré, facing the barre, in 1st, review.

Following the preparatory port de bras, rest the hands on the barre.

On 1 and 2, bend forward keeping the back as flat as possible still holding the barre; on 3 and 4, relax the back, to bring the torso closer to the knees to stretch the hamstrings further; from 5 to 8, starting with the head, straighten up, while lengthening the back. Repeat three more times. Turn toward the barre to face it. From 1 to 4, lift the upper back and bend back, keeping the head straight; from 5 to 8, straighten up. Repeat three more times.

A cambré in 1st position.

Explanation. Students are repeating Exercise 13 of the Fourth Class of the Eleventh Week, this time adding more repetitions.

Exercise 14

Pied sur la barre 2nd and 4th devant, plié, bending with cambré.

Students repeat Exercise 15 of the First Class of the Sixteenth Week.

CENTER

Exercise 15

Battement tendu en croix, hold the position when pointing and when closing, in 1st, four counts, two counts.

Students repeat Exercise 17 of the Fifth Class of the Sixteenth Week.

Exercise 16

Battement tendu 2nd, hold the position when pointing and when closing, four counts, two counts.

Students repeat Exercise 18 of the Fifth Class of the Sixteenth Week.

Exercise 17

Battement jeté 2nd, broken down and direct, in 1st, four counts.

Students repeat Exercise 17 of the Fourth Class of the Sixteenth Week.

Exercise 18

Preparation for battement en cloche, broken down, in 1st, four counts.

On "and" 1, battement tendu devant; on "and," battement; on 2, hold the position; on "and," lower the leg and point the foot onto the floor; on 3, hold the position; on 4, close 1st; on "and" 5, battement tendu derrière; on "and," battement; on 6, hold the position; on "and," lower the leg and point the foot onto the floor; on 7, hold the position; on 8, close 1st. Repeat the whole exercise one more time.

Explanation. Students are revisiting the preparatory exercise for the battement en cloche that was performed in Exercise 6 of the Second Class of the Thirteenth Week, except that it is now performed in the center. When closing 1st, the working foot must be flat.

Exercise 19

Preparation for rond de jambe soutenu 2nd, no rotation, in 1st.

On "and" 1, battement tendu 2nd; on 2, lift the leg à la demi-hauteur; on 3, bend the working leg without moving the thigh so that the tips of the toes touch the supporting leg; on 4, stretch the leg 2nd again; on 5, lower the leg and point the foot onto the floor; on 6, hold the position; on 7, close 1st; on 8, hold the position. Repeat the whole exercise one more time.

Explanation. Students are practicing the exercise to prepare for the rond de jambe soutenu 2nd, executed earlier at the barre in Exercise 11 of the Fifth Class of the Thirteenth Class. To keep balance, students must particularly lift the side of the torso opposite of the working leg and activate their turn-out muscles. The foot does not sickle when the leg bends, and when it stretches, the heel aims forward.

Exercise 20

Preparation for glissade 2nd, en descendant, toward the back foot, arms in 6th, four counts, four repetitions, review.

In the preparatory port de bras, bring the arms in 1st, then open the right arm 2nd and keep the left arm in 1st, with the head slightly turned toward the left arm.

On 1, plié in 5th, inclining the torso very slightly toward the left; on 2, extend the left leg 2nd in plié; on 3, transfer the weight onto the left leg in plié, while the right leg stretches and the right foot points; on "and" 4, close 5th, right foot front, and stretch. Repeat the glissade three more times to the left. Repeat the exercise to the right, starting with the left foot front, the head turned toward the right elbow, the right arm closed in 1st, and the left arm opened 2nd.

Explanation. Students are repeating the glissade exercise performed in Exercise 22 in the Second Class of the Twelfth Week, except here students are traveling toward the back foot. The whole movement must be smoother and more flowing, with less holding between each position. The tempo is accelerated.

Exercise 21

Relevé in 1st, two counts, three repetitions, facing the barre, review.

Students repeat Exercise 19 of the Fourth Class of the Sixteenth Week.

Exercise 22

Soubresaut in 1st, on the count, one count hold, two repetitions, facing the barre.

On "and," plié and push off the floor, pointing the feet and stretching the legs in 1st; on 1, land in plié in 1st; on "and," directly out of the plié, push off the floor again; on 2, land in plié; on 3, stretch the knees; on 4, hold the position. Repeat three more times. At the end, roll up and hold the position.

Explanation. Students are performing two soubresauts in a row, without holding in between. Students use the plié of the landing of the first jump to take off for the second jump. Even though the tempo is faster, the correct position and cleanness of execution must apply. The heels come down each time in the plié. The jump is vertical, without coming forward over the barre. A pause between each series allows students to stretch their legs and stabilize balance.

Exercise 23

Assemblé 2nd, en descendant, two counts, one count hold.

On "and," plié, straightening the head; on 1, brush the left foot and extend the leg 2nd, while pushing off the floor with the supporting leg, stretch both legs in the air, the head turning slightly toward the left; on 2, land in plié in 5th, left foot front; on 3, straighten up the knees; on 4, hold the position. Repeat three more times bringing the back foot front each time. After a pause, repeat one more time.

Explanation. This time students are performing the assemblé in the center with the arms 2nd. Like at the barre, the leg must not be thrown too high (not higher than the demi-hauteur) so that students can bring their legs together as soon as possible before the landing. At this stage, the stretching of both legs and feet in the air is expected. Again the jump and the throw of the leg must coincide so that the momentum for the jump is not lost. The sitting in the plié is to be avoided. The step does not travel. Students are reminded of the head positions.

Exercise 24

Preparatory exercise for grand battement 2nd en remontant.

Students repeat Exercise 23 of the Fourth Class of the Sixteenth Week.

Exercise 25

Curtsey.

THIRD CLASS

Students repeat the material of the Second Class of this week.

FOURTH CLASS

Exercise 1

Warm up.

Exercise 2

Plié in 2nd and 1st, with port de bras, bending to the side.

Following the preparatory port de bras, bring both feet in 2nd.

On "and" 1, turn the hand so that the palm faces down, with the head turned toward the working hand, and plié with the arm coming down; on 2, deepen the plié, keeping the heels down in the plié, rounding the arm by bringing the lower arm inward (in the deepest level of the plié); on 3, stretch the knees, bringing the arm to 1st; on 4, open the arm 2nd; from 5 to 8, repeat, and close 1st. Repeat the exercise in 1st. On 1 and 2, bring the arm 5th and turn the head toward the left shoulder; on 3 and 4, bend toward the barre, without dropping the chin; on 5 and 6, straighten up; on 7 and 8, straighten the head, bring the other arm in 5th, and hold the position.

Explanation. Students are reviewing the plié exercise as performed in Exercise 2 of the Fourth Class of the Thirteenth Week. They are also practicing the bending to the side, performed sideways of the barre. The arm remains in 5th during the bending without dropping. When bending to the sides, the weight must remain on both legs without bending the knees.

Exercise 3

Battement tendu 2nd, in 1st, two counts, three repetitions, facing the barre.

Students repeat Exercise 5 of the Fifth Class of the Sixteenth Week.

Exercise 4

Battement tendu en croix, in 1st, two counts, two repetitions.

On "and" 1, battement tendu devant; on 2, close 1st; on "and" 3, battement tendu devant; on 4, close 1st. Repeat the exercise en croix en dehors. At the end, roll up in 1st and hold balance.

Explanation. Students are performing two battements tendus in a row in each direction in this exercise.

Exercise 5

Battement tendu en croix, plié when pointing, in 1st, four counts, facing the barre.

Students repeat Exercise 4 of the Fifth Class of the Sixteenth Week.

Exercise 6

Battement jeté en croix en dehors, broken down and direct, four counts, facing the barre.

Students repeat Exercise 5 of the Second Class of this week.

Exercise 7

Preparation for battement jeté piqué 2nd, direct battement, in 1st, facing the barre.

Students repeat Exercise 8 of the Fifth Class of the Sixteenth Week.

Exercise 8

Demi-rond de jambe à la demi-hauteur, en dedans, eight counts, facing the barre, review.

Students repeat Exercise 9 of the Fifth Class of the Sixteenth Week.

Exercise 9

Battement fondu, en croix, eight counts, facing the barre.

Students repeat Exercise 10 of the Fifth Class of the Sixteenth Week.

Exercise 10

Battement frappé 2nd, two counts, facing the barre.

Students repeat Exercise 9 of the Second Class of this week.

Exercise 11

Adagio: lift the leg devant and 2nd, sideways, lift the leg derrière, facing the barre, open and close on the count, hold two counts in the air.

Students repeat Exercise 14 of the Fifth Class of the Sixteenth Week.

Exercise 12

Petits battements, each on one count, arm in low 1st.

Students repeat Exercise 11 of the Second Class of this week.

Exercise 13

Preparation for grand battement devant and 2nd, sideways, preparation for grand battement derrière, facing the barre, four counts.

Students repeat Exercise 14 of the Fifth Class of the Fourteenth Week.

Exercise 14

Bending forward, back to the barre, cambré facing the barre, in 1st, review.

Students repeat Exercise 13 of the Second Class of this week.

CENTER

Exercise 15

Battement tendu en croix, in 1st, hold the position when pointing and when closing, four counts, two counts.

Students repeat Exercise 17 of the Fifth Class of the Sixteenth Week.

Exercise 16

Battement jeté 2nd, broken down and direct, four counts.

On "and" 1, battement tendu 2nd with the right leg; on "and," battement; on 2, hold the position; on "and," lower the leg and point the foot onto the floor; on 3, hold the position; on 4, close 5th devant; on "and" 5, direct battement 2nd; on 6, hold the position; on "and," lower the leg and point the foot onto the floor; on 7, hold the position; on 8, close 5th derrière. Repeat the exercise one more time with the right foot.

Explanation. Students are repeating Exercise 17 of the Fourth Class of the Sixteenth Week in the center, this time performed in 5th.

Exercise 17

Preparation for battement en cloche, broken down, in 1st, four counts.

Students repeat Exercise 18 of the Second Class of this week.

Exercise 18

Preparation for rond de jambe soutenu 2nd, no rotation, in 1st.

Students repeat Exercise 19 of the Second Class of this week.

Exercise 19

Preparation for glissade 2nd, en descendant, toward the back foot, arms in 6th, four counts, four repetitions, review.

Students repeat Exercise 20 of the Second Class of this week.

Exercise 20

Relevé in 6th and 1st, in plié, four counts, facing the barre.

On 1, plié; on "and" 2, relevé still in plié; on 3, stretch the knees; on 4, roll down with stretched knees. Repeat three more times. Open the feet in 1st and repeat the exercise.

Explanation. Students are repeating Exercise 20 of the Fifth Class of the Eleventh Week, except each relevé is now performed on four counts each.

Music. The music is not too fast so that students have time to force the instep out and stretch their knees, while keeping their instep as much as possible above the toes.

Exercise 21

Soubresaut in 1st, on the count, one count hold, two repetitions, facing the barre.

Students repeat Exercise 22 of the Second Class of this week.

Exercise 22

Assemblé 2nd, en descendant, two counts, one count hold.

Students repeat Exercise 23 of the Second Class of this week.

Exercise 23

Preparation for grand battement 2nd, en descendant and en remontant, four counts.

On "and" 1, battement tendu 2nd with the left foot; on 2, battement, with the left leg; on 3, lower the leg and point the foot onto the floor; on 4, close 5th left foot front. Repeat three more times, alternating legs. Repeat one more time.

On "and" 1, battement tendu 2nd with the right foot; on 2, battement with the right leg; on 3, lower the leg and point the foot onto the floor; on 4, close 5th, right foot back. Repeat three more times, alternating legs. Repeat the exercise one more time.

Explanation. Students are mixing the grand battement en descendant and en remontant. The head remains straight.

Exercise 24

Curtsey.

FIFTH CLASS

Exercise 1

Warm up.

Exercise 2

Plié in 2nd and 1st, with port de bras, bending to the side.

Students repeat Exercise 2 of the Fourth Class of this week.

Exercise 3

Battement tendu en croix, in 1st, two counts, two repetitions.

Students repeat Exercise 4 of the Fourth Class of this week.

Exercise 4

Battement tendu en croix, two counts.

On "and" 1, battement tendu devant; on 2, close 5th devant; on "and" 3, battement tendu 2nd; on 4, close 5th derrière; on "and" 5, battement tendu derrière; on 6, close 5th derrière; on "and" 7, battement tendu 2nd; on 8, close 5th devant. Repeat the exercise en croix en dehors. At the end, roll up in 5th and hold balance.

Explanation. Students are practicing battements tendus en croix on two counts, sideways.

Exercise 5

Battement tendu 2nd, start in plié and stretch when pointing, facing the barre.

On 1, plié; on "and" 2, battement tendu 2nd, starting in plié and stretching both knees by the time the foot is pointed; on 3, hold the position; on 4, close 5th devant. Repeat one more time with the right foot, closing 5th derrière. Repeat the whole exercise.

Explanation. Students are repeating Exercise 5 of the Fifth Class of the Fourteenth Week, this time performed in 5th.

Exercise 6

Battement jeté en croix en dehors, broken down and direct, four counts, facing the barre.

Students repeat Exercise 5 of the Second Class of this week.

Exercise 7

Preparation for battement jeté piqué en croix, eight counts.

On "and" 1, battement devant; on "and," lower the leg, and bring the pointed foot onto the floor; on 2, hold the position; on "and," lift the leg devant at the same height; on 3, hold the position; on "and," bring the pointed foot down; on 4, hold the position; on "and," lift the leg devant; on 5, hold the position; on "and," bring the pointed foot down; on 6, hold the position; on 7, close 5th; on 8, hold the position. Repeat the exercise en croix. At the end, roll up in 5th and hold balance.

Explanation. Students are repeating Exercise 8 of the Fifth Class of the Sixteenth Week en croix and sideways. The toes are fully stretched.

Exercise 8

Rond de jambe à terre en dehors and en dedans, in plié, eight counts, facing the barre.

On 1, plié; on 2, still in plié, battement tendu devant; on 3 and 4, rond de jambe to 2nd, still in plié; on 5 and 6, rond de jambe en dehors to derrière, still in plié; on 7, stretch the supporting leg; on 8, close 5th.

On 1, plié; on 2, still in plié, battement tendu derrière; on 3 and 4, rond de jambe to 2nd, still in plié; on 5 and 6, rond de jambe en dedans to devant, still in plié; on 7, stretch the supporting leg; on 8, close 5th. At the end, relevé in 5th and hold balance.

Explanation. This is a full rond de jambe à terre in plié. Since it is on eight counts, the music should not be too slow, to avoid putting too much pressure on the supporting leg. The exercise is practiced facing the barre to keep the hips straight. The head follows the same pattern learned so far in the rond de jambe exercises; however, the head is straight in the relevé in 5th.

Exercise 9

Battement fondu, en croix, eight counts, facing the barre.

Students repeat Exercise 10 of the Fifth Class of the Sixteenth Week.

Exercise 10

Battement frappé 2nd, two counts, facing the barre.

Students repeat Exercise 9 of the Second Class of this week.

Exercise 11

Adagio: preparation for small fendu, with port de bras, facing the barre.

On "and" 1, battement tendu derrière with the left foot, straightening the head; on 2, hold the position; on 3 and 4, bring the foot down in 4th position, with a plié on the front leg and the back leg stretched, with the foot flat, release the barre and bring the arms 2nd, holding the head straight; on 5 and 6, bring the arms down; on 7 and 8, bring them to 1st position and then to 5th; on 1 and 2, open the arms 2nd; on 3, pull up, transferring the weight onto the front leg, and pointing the back foot while the front leg stretches; on 4, hold the position; on 5 and 6, close 5th derrière, bringing the arms down; on 7, bring the arms 1st; on 8, rest the hands on the barre. Repeat one more time with the right foot front.

Explanation. This is a preparatory exercise for the small fendu, which is used not only in adagio

A small fendu in 4th position.

but also in preparation for certain pirouettes en dedans. This is a position of stability in which both feet are parallel and flat on the floor (even the back one), with the weight of the body being mostly on the front leg. The knee of the front leg must be above the toes and not pushed forward. Facing the barre helps students to keep their hips straight. The knee of the back leg in fendu must be very taut to properly stretch the iliopsoas. When straightening the body, students must not raise their buttocks but actively use the back of their thigh muscles while pulling up the torso.

Different wordings have developed to describe the position of the fendu. Some people confuse it with the fondu, which is a very soft and smooth kind of a plié. In the United States, it is often called a lunge. The fendu originates from the French verb *fendre*, which means to divide or cut lengthwise. It is a position also used in fencing and gymnastics. Later, students will do a large fendu, which is a more challenging position.

Application. The practice of the fendu offers a good stretch of the iliopsoas, but only if the back leg is totally stretched.

Exercise 12

Petits battements, each on one count, arm in low 1st.

Students repeat Exercise 11 of the Second Class of this week.

Exercise 13

Preparation for grand battement devant and 2nd, sideways, preparation for grand battement derrière, facing the barre, four counts.

Students repeat Exercise 14 of the Fifth Class of the Fourteenth Week.

Exercise 14

Demi-détourné, eight counts.

Following the preparatory port de bras, bring the arm down.

On "and" 1, plié and relevé in 5th, bringing the arm in 1st; on 2, hold the position; on 3 and 4, remaining on demi-pointes, turn a half turn toward the barre, with the right hand resting now toward the left on the barre (during the turn, students allow the feet to change, and in the last part of the turn, they raise the left foot to open it

ever so slightly to adjust the feet in 5th on demi-pointes, so that the feet are not locked in by the time the half turn is done), and bring the left arm in 1st; on 5 and 6, hold the position; on 7 and 8, come down in plié in 5th, opening the left arm 2nd, stretch the legs, bringing the arm down. Repeat with the left foot front, turning toward the right. Repeat three more times.

Explanation. Students are introduced to the demi-détourné, a useful step to change sides at the barre, among other things. It is practiced slowly so that students understand the mechanism. They must apply spotting, with the head being the last part of the body to turn and the first one to arrive. As a rule, in a détourné, students turn toward the back foot. The change in feet position is done automatically during the turn; however, students must adjust their front foot (that was in the back before the turn) with a slight transfer onto the back foot in order to do the adjustment. If such adjustment were not done, the feet would cross excessively in 5th. However, at the end of the détourné, the weight is spread on both feet again. This exercise prepares for the temps de pointe détourné (full détourné) that is practiced in the center later on in the training. Students must grab the barre at the right place and not too far back to avoid losing balance and raising the shoulder, the one closest to the barre.

Exercise 15

Pied sur la barre 2nd and devant, plié and bend, 4th derrière, plié.

Facing the barre, rest the right foot on the barre with the leg 2nd.

On 1 and 2, plié and stretch; on 3 and 4, repeat; on 5 and 6, bring the left arm in 1st and open it 2nd; on 7 and 8, bring it in 5th, and turn the head toward the right; on 1 and 2, bend sideways toward the right side; on 3 and 4, straighten up; on 5 and 6, open the left arm 2nd; on 7, rest the left hand on the barre; on 8, hold the position; on 1 and 2, bring the right arm 1st and open it 2nd; on 3 and 4, bring it in 5th, and turn the head toward the left side; on 5 and 6, bend sideways toward the left; on 7 and 8, straighten up; on 1 and 2, open the right arm 2nd; from 3 to 8, rotate the legs so that the working leg is 4th position devant. The right arm is 2nd with the left hand resting on the barre, slightly forward of the left shoulder.

On 1 and 2, plié and stretch; on 3 and 4, repeat; on 5 and 6, bring the right arm 5th; on 7 and 8, bend forward keeping the arm 5th; straighten up on 1 and 2; on 3 and 4, cambré; on 5 and 6, straighten up; on 7, rotate to be facing the barre, bringing both hands resting on the barre in front of the shoulders; on 8, bring the right arm slightly forward, open the left arm 2nd, while rotating to be facing the left side with the working leg now in the back.

On 1 and 2, plié and stretch; on 3 and 4, repeat; on 5, release the leg from the barre; on 6, hold the position; on 7, lower the leg and point the foot onto the floor; on 8, close in 5th back, bringing the arm down.

Explanation. Students are now performing the pied sur la barre derrière, a position that is much more demanding than the 2nd and 4th devant. The barre should not be too high, for the pelvis would otherwise be tilted too much backward and students could not pull up their torso correctly. For this introductory position, students are performing only the plié. They must remain balanced on their supporting leg without pushing back. The working leg does not turn in during the plié, and the working foot remains pointed. The shoulders are straight, and students avoid pulling the barre. When properly executed, it is a good exercise for the flexibility of the back.

Application. For those students with a tight back, stiff hamstrings and hip ligaments, they will particularly benefit from the exercise, assuming the barre is at a proper height. However, for recreational beginning students, the 4th position derrière will come later.

CENTER

Exercise 16

Battement tendu 2nd, in 1st, two counts, three repetitions.

On "and" 1, battement tendu 2nd; on 2, close 1st; on "and" 3, battement tendu 2nd; on 4, close; on "and" 5, battement tendu 2nd; on 6, close; on 7 and 8, plié and stretch. Repeat the whole exercise one more time.

Explanation. Students are repeating Exercise 5 of the Fifth Class of the Sixteenth Week, this time performed in the center.

Exercise 17

Battement jeté 2nd, broken down and direct, four counts.

Students repeat Exercise 16 of the Fourth Class of this week.

Exercise 18

Preparation for battement en cloche, broken down, in 1st, four counts.

Students repeat Exercise 18 of the Second Class of this week.

Exercise 19

Preparation for rond de jambe soutenu, no rotation, in 1st.

Students repeat Exercise 19 of the Second Class of this week.

Exercise 20

Adagio: grand plié in 2nd, port de bras performed separately, review.

Start in 1st, battement tendu 2nd and bring the foot down.

On 1, plié; on 2, stretch the knees; on 3 and 4, repeat the plié and stretch; on 5 and 6, deeper plié, keeping the heels down; on 7 and 8, come back up into demi-plié and stretch the knees; on "and" 1 and 2, bring the arms down; on 3, bring the arms in 1st; on 4, bring the arms to 5th; on 5 and 6, hold the position; on "and" 7 and 8, open the arms 2nd. Repeat the exercise one more time. Point the foot and close 1st after the last port de bras to end the exercise.

Explanation. Students are reviewing the grand plié in 2nd that was performed in Exercise 18 of the Fifth Class of the Thirteenth Week.

Exercise 21

Preparation for glissade 2nd, en descendant, toward the back foot, arms in 6th, four counts, four repetitions, review.

Students repeat Exercise 20 of the Second Class of this week.

Exercise 22

Relevé in 6th and 1st, in plié, four counts, facing the barre.

Students repeat Exercise 20 of the Fourth Class of this week.

Exercise 23

Soubresaut in 1st, on the count, one count hold, two repetitions, facing the barre.

Students repeat Exercise 22 of the Second Class of this week.

Exercise 24

Échappé in 2nd, with port de bras, two counts, one count to hold.

Following the preparatory port de bras, bring the arms down.

On "and" 1, plié and push off the floor, bringing the arms in 1st and opening the legs and the arms 2nd, land in 2nd; on "and," deepen the plié and jump again; on 2, close in 5th, left foot front, closing the arms down; on 3, stretch the knees; on 4, hold the position. Repeat three more times.

Explanation. Here students are practicing the échappé 2nd on two counts in the center with a port de bras. The exercise can also be toned down by performing it in 1st.

Music. A march with a slow-to-medium tempo would work well here.

Exercise 25

Assemblé 2nd, en descendant, two counts, one count hold.

Students repeat Exercise 23 of the Second Class of this week.

Exercise 26

Preparation for grand battement 2nd, en descendant and en remontant, four counts.

Students repeat Exercise 23 of the Fourth Class of this week.

Exercise 27

Curtsey.

Eighteenth Week

§

FIRST CLASS

Students repeat the material of the Fifth Class of the Seventeenth Week.

SECOND CLASS

Exercise 1

Warm up.

Exercise 2

Plié in 2nd and in 1st, with port de bras, bending to the side.

Students repeat Exercise 2 of the Fourth Class of the Seventeenth Week.

Exercise 3

Battement tendu en croix, flex the foot, plié, in 1st, eight counts, review.

On "and" 1, battement tendu devant; on 2, flex the toes; on 3, flex the rest of the foot; on 4, stretch the instep out, with the toes still flexed; on 5, point the toes, pointing the foot onto the floor; on 6, close 1st; on 7 and 8, plié and stretch. At the end, plié and relevé in 1st.

Explanation. This is essentially review, with the opening and closing of the battement tendu on one count each.

Exercise 4

Battement tendu en croix, two counts.

Students repeat Exercise 4 of the Fifth Class of the Seventeenth Week.

Exercise 5

Battement tendu 2nd, start in plié and stretch when pointing, facing the barre.

Students repeat Exercise 5 of the Fifth Class of the Seventeenth Week.

Exercise 6

Battement jeté 2nd, direct, four counts, facing the barre.

On "and" 1, battement 2nd; on "and," lower the leg and point the foot onto the floor; on 2, hold the position; on 3, close 5th devant; on 4, hold the position. Repeat the exercise one more time closing 5th derrière. Repeat the exercise one more time with the right foot. Hold the last battement 2nd and release the barre to check balance.

Explanation. Students are increasing the number of direct battements performed with each leg. There is no hold of the leg à la demi-hauteur. There is still a hold before closing though. The exercise can also be performed in 1st.

Exercise 7

Preparation for battement jeté piqué en croix, eight counts.

Students repeat Exercise 7 of the Fifth Class of the Seventeenth Week.

Exercise 8

Rond de jambe en dehors and en dedans, in plié, eight counts, facing the barre.

Students repeat Exercise 8 of the Fifth Class of the Seventeenth Week.

Exercise 9

Battement fondu en croix, eight counts.

On 1 and 2, bring the foot pointed on the cou-de-pied devant with a deep plié on the supporting leg; on 3 and 4, extend the leg in demi-attitude devant, still in plié; on 5 and 6, stretch both legs at the same time à la demi-hauteur; on 7 and 8, lower the leg down, point the foot down, and close 5th devant. Repeat the exercise en croix en dehors. At the end, hold the leg 2nd and balance with arms in 2nd.

Explanation. Students are practicing the exercise sideways with the arm 2nd. The hips remain straight. When stretching the working leg out of the attitude devant and 2nd, the lower leg is actively pushed forward. When stretching the leg in the back, the thigh remains turned out, with the heel pushed down.

Exercise 10

Battement frappé en croix, two counts, facing the barre.

On "and," bring the front foot on the cou-de-pied devant; on 1, hold the position; on 2, extend the leg devant, pointing the foot onto the floor; on 3, bring the foot on the cou-de-pied devant; on 4, extend the leg 2nd; on 5, bring the foot on the cou-de-pied derrière; on 6, extend the leg derrière; on 7, bring the foot on the cou-de-pied derrière; on 8, extend the leg 2nd. Repeat the exercise one more time. At the end hold the cou-de-pied devant position and hold balance.

Explanation. After practicing the exercise 2nd, students are performing it en croix en dehors, still facing the barre. When extending forward, the thigh remains to the side as much as possible while the lower leg moves forward. In the battement frappé derrière, the thigh also remains thoroughly turned out, with the heel pushed down.

Exercise 11

Preparation for rond de jambe soutenu 2nd, direct battement, no rotation, facing the barre.

On "and" 1, battement 2nd à la demi-hauteur; on 2, hold the position; on 3, bend the working leg without moving the thigh so that the tips of the toes touch the back of the supporting leg; on 4, stretch the leg 2nd; on 5, bend the working leg; on 6, stretch the leg 2nd, again; on 7, lower the leg, and point the foot onto the floor; on 8, close 5th devant. Repeat the exercise one more time, closing 5th derrière. Repeat the whole exercise one more time.

Explanation. This is essentially review, except the exercise is in 5th, starting with a direct battement 2nd. There is still no rotation. The thigh keeps as still as possible. Ideally the exercise is performed with the working leg à la hauteur. But the height here is not as important as the bending and the stretching of the lower leg without moving the thigh, and keeping the turn-out.

Exercise 12

Adagio: preparation for small fendu, with port de bras, facing the barre.

Students repeat Exercise 11 of the Fifth Class of the Seventeenth Week.

Exercise 13

Adagio: lift the leg devant, 2nd, and derrière, arabesque, eight counts, hold three counts in the air.

On "and" 1, battement tendu devant; on 2, lift the leg; from 3 to 5, hold the position; on 6, lower the leg and point the toes onto the floor; on 7, close 5th devant; on 8, hold the position. Repeat the exercise in 2nd and derrière. Perform a battement tendu 2nd to close 5th, right foot front. At the end, relevé in 5th and hold balance.

Explanation. Students are practicing lifting the leg devant, 2nd, and derrière, sideways, holding the position for three counts. They do not perform the last lift 2nd, for the exercise would require too much muscle tension, especially in the upper part of the legs, in this first exercise in which the lifting is done in each direction sideways. There is still a slight pause at the end of the battement tendu before lifting the leg so that students find themselves more stable. By now, students must have gained more strength and flexibility to lift the leg higher without bending the knees. The lifting of the leg back looks more like a true arabesque by now. Students need to stretch their working toes when the leg is lifted, for there is a tendency to release them in such movement. The elbow does not scoop down and the torso remains straight. Students do not use strength in their shoulders. In the lifting of the leg 2nd, they do not pull the barre. As they lift their leg in the back, students must bring the hand slightly forward at the barre to allow for the shift of the torso, but only if the height of the leg requires it. They pull up their back and keep the turn-out in both legs. The shoulders are straight. When the leg is at the highest level, students will be asked to briefly release the barre.

Exercise 14

Preparation for grand battement devant and 2nd, sideways, preparation for grand battement derrière, facing the barre, four counts.

Students repeat Exercise 14 of the Fifth Class of the Fourteenth Week.

Exercise 15

Demi-détourné, eight counts.

Students repeat Exercise 14 of the Fifth Class of the Seventeenth Week.

Exercise 16

Pied sur la barre 2nd and devant, plié and bend, 4th derrière, plié.

Students repeat Exercise 15 of the Fifth Class of the Seventeenth Week.

CENTER

Exercise 17

Battement tendu 2nd, in 1st, two counts, three repetitions.

Students repeat Exercise 16 of the Fifth Class of the Seventeenth Week.

Exercise 18

Battement tendu 2nd, start in plié and stretch when pointing, in 1st.

On 1, plié; on "and" 2, battement tendu 2nd starting in plié, with both knees stretching by the time the foot is pointed; on 3, hold the position; on 4, close 1st. Repeat the exercise one more time. Repeat the whole exercise one more time.

Explanation. Students are reviewing the exercise, which has already been performed several times. They must keep their weight on the supporting leg when brushing out. The tempo is accelerated.

Exercise 19

Battement jeté 2nd, broken down and direct, four counts.

Students repeat Exercise 16 of the Fourth Class of the Seventeenth Week.

Exercise 20

Position on the cou-de-pied, pointed, extension of the leg en croix, with port de bras, four counts.

Following the preparatory port de bras, bring the arms down.

On "and," bring the front foot pointed on the cou-de-pied devant, bringing the arms in 1st; on 1, hold the position; on 2, extend the leg devant, pointing the foot onto the floor and opening the arms 2nd; on 3, hold the position; on 4, close 5th

devant, closing the arms. Repeat the exercise en croix en dehors, the last one closing 5th derrière.

Explanation. Students are repeating Exercise 8 of the Second Class of the Fourteenth Week, this time performed en croix in the center.

Exercise 21

Adagio: grand plié in 2nd, port de bras performed separately, review.

Students repeat Exercise 20 of the Fifth Class of the Seventeenth Week.

Exercise 22

Relevé in 6th and 1st, in plié, four counts, facing the barre.

Students repeat Exercise 20 of the Fourth Class of the Seventeenth Week.

Exercise 23

Soubresaut in 1st, on the count, one count hold, two repetitions, facing the barre.

Students repeat Exercise 22 of the Second Class of the Seventeenth Week.

Exercise 24

Échappé in 2nd, with port de bras, two counts, one count hold.

Students repeat Exercise 24 of the Fifth Class of the Seventeenth Week.

Exercise 25

Piqué 2nd (temps de pointe) [glissade—Vaganova], eight counts, facing the barre.

On 1, plié; on 2, battement tendu 2nd, with the right foot, and the head still slightly turned toward the right side; on 3, step onto the right foot on demi-pointe, bringing the left foot derrière in 5th, with a stretched leg; from 4 to 5, hold the position; on 6, come down into plié; on 7, stretch; on 8, hold the position. Repeat three more times with the right foot front. The head is turned toward the direction of travel.

Explanation. This is the first formal exercise of piqué in the training. Here the second foot joins the other in 5th on demi-pointes before coming down. Students must start the piqué with a good plié, since it is the supporting leg that can propulse the whole body onto the leg that is doing the piqué. It is also crucial that the first leg be totally stretched. It is unfortunate that so many ballet students bend their knee, even slightly, to go up. This action kills the sharp character of the step. It also places too much pressure on the quadriceps. Once in place, the habit is very difficult to eradicate. The piqué is actually the action of the stepping of the working foot onto demi-pointe. It occurs where the toes are pointing on the floor: not further, not shorter. Introducing the piqué with a battement tendu helps to keep from doing the piqué too far or too close, since the toes are already touching the floor exactly at the place where the piqué should occur. The piqué is an energetic movement in which the working foot looks as if it is pricking the floor while transferring the weight onto that same leg. The second leg joins the other into a tight 5th with energy and without dragging in or turning in. The hips are parallel to the barre in the piqué, and the knee remains above the toes in the plié.

Music. A waltz would be a good musical choice for this exercise.

Exercise 26

Preparation for pas de bourrée couru (pas de bourrée suivi), relevé in 6th and tiptoes run, in diagonal.

Start at the left upper corner of the studio, traveling in diagonal. Following the preparatory port de bras, bring the arms down.

On "and" 1, plié and relevé in 6th, bringing the arms to 1st; from 2 to 6, run on demi-pointes with small shuffling steps, opening the arms 2nd gradually; on 7, come down in plié with the arms coming down; on 8, stretch the knees. Repeat the exercise one more time. Repeat the exercise in the other diagonal.

Explanation. This is an informal exercise in preparation for the pas couru, which is introduced formally later in the training. The pas couru is a run on tiptoes, keeping the feet close to each other in small scurry steps. The knees are not locked but should be allowed to slightly bend and stretch (to avoid the penguin-like walk!). It is important that the legs do not precede the torso, which would make the movement look pompous. The upper torso is very slightly bent forward, from the middle of the torso, as if it leads the movement of the feet. Note the use of the 6th position so that students become familiar with the action of the knees and the feet in the couru, before adding the turn-out.

Music. A quick and light 3/4 waltz or even a coda would work well here.

Application. To be beneficial, the steps should be small and almost imperceptible. The hands can also be held on the waist for an easier version.

Exercise 27

Curtsey.

THIRD CLASS

Students repeat the material of the Second Class of this week.

FOURTH CLASS

Exercise 1

Warm up.

Exercise 2

Plié in 2nd and 1st, with port de bras, bending to the side.

Students repeat Exercise 2 of the Fourth Class of the Seventeenth Week.

Exercise 3

Battement tendu en croix, flex, plié, in 1st, eight counts, review.

Students repeat Exercise 3 of the Second Class of this week.

Exercise 4

Battement tendu en croix, two counts.

Students repeat Exercise 4 of the Fifth Class of the Seventeenth Week.

Exercise 5

Battement tendu 2nd, start in plié and stretch when pointing, facing the barre.

Students repeat Exercise 5 of the Fifth Class of the Seventeenth Week.

Exercise 6

Battement jeté 2nd, direct, four counts, facing the barre.

Students repeat Exercise 6 of the Second Class of this week.

Exercise 7

Preparation for battement jeté piqué en croix, eight counts.

Students repeat Exercise 7 of the Fifth Class of the Seventeenth Week.

Exercise 8

Rond de jambe à terre en dehors and en dedans, in plié, eight counts, facing the barre.

Students repeat Exercise 8 of the Fifth Class of the Seventeenth Week.

Exercise 9

Battement fondu en croix, eight counts.

Students repeat Exercise 9 of the Second Class of this week.

Exercise 10

Battement frappé en croix, two counts, facing the barre.

Students repeat Exercise 10 of the Second Class of this week.

Exercise 11

Preparation for rond de jambe soutenu 2nd, direct battement, no rotation, facing the barre.

Students repeat Exercise 11 of the Second Class of this week.

Exercise 12

Adagio: lift the leg devant, 2nd, and derrière, arabesque, eight counts, hold three counts in the air.

Students repeat Exercise 13 of the Second Class of this week.

Exercise 13

Grand battement devant, sideways, grands battements 2nd and derrière, facing the barre, three counts, one count hold.

In 4th position devant: on "and" 1, battement devant; on "and," bring the leg down with the pointed foot onto the floor; on 2, hold the position; on 3, close 5th; on 4, hold the position. Repeat three more times.

In 2nd, facing the barre: on "and" 1, battement 2nd; on "and," bring the leg down with the pointed foot onto the floor; on 2, hold the position; on 3, close 5th devant; on 4, hold the position. Repeat three more times, alternating closing devant and derrière.

In 4th position derrière, facing the barre: on "and" 1, battement derrière; on "and," bring the leg down with the pointed foot; on 2, hold the position; on 3, close 5th; on 4, hold the position. Repeat three more times.

Explanation. Students are now performing the grand battement directly, without breaking it down in the ascending part. Students face the barre again for the direct battement 2nd for more stability in the direct throwing of the leg. There is still one count holding in the descending part of the leg to make sure that the foot is fully pointed before closing 5th.

Exercise 14

Demi-détourné, eight counts.

Students repeat Exercise 14 of the Fifth Class of the Seventeen Week.

Exercise 15

Pied sur la barre 2nd and devant, plié and bend, 4th derrière, plié.

Students repeat Exercise 15 of the Fifth Class of the Seventeen Week.

CENTER

Exercise 16

Battement tendu 2nd, in 1st, two counts, three repetitions.

Students repeat Exercise 16 of the Fifth Class of the Seventeenth Week.

Exercise 17

Battement tendu 2nd, start in plié and stretch when pointing, in 1st.

Students repeat Exercise 18 of the Second Class of this week.

Exercise 18

Position on the cou-de-pied, pointed, extension of the leg en croix, with port de bras, four counts.

Students repeat Exercise 20 of the Second Class of this week.

Exercise 19

Adagio: plié in 1st, port de bras done separately.

On 1 and 2, plié; on 3 and 4, stretch the knees; on "and" 5 and 6, bring the arms down; on 7, bring the arms in 1st; on 8, open the arms 2nd.

Repeat the exercise twice more. At the end, bring the arms in 5th and hold the position for eight counts.

Explanation. In preparation for the grand plié in 1st, students are practicing the demi-plié in 1st in the center. The knees remain to the sides in the plié. The music is still adagio, but the tempo is slightly accelerated. A very deep plié is expected; there is no pause in the lowest part of the plié before coming back up.

Exercise 20

Relevé in 6th and 1st, in plié, four counts, facing the barre.

Students repeat Exercise 20 of the Fourth Class of the Seventeenth Week.

Exercise 21

Relevé in 1st, two counts, three repetitions.

Following the preparatory port de bras, bring the arms down.

On "and," plié; on 1, relevé, bringing the arms in low 1st; on 2, come down in plié; on 3, relevé; on 4, come down in plié; on 5, relevé; on 6, come down in plié; on 7, stretch the knees; on 8, hold the position. Repeat three more times.

Explanation. Students are repeating Exercise 19 of the Fourth Class of the Sixteenth Week, this time performed in the center. The arms do not bounce. The upper torso is held very slightly forward to help balancing.

Exercise 22

Soubresaut in 1st, on the count, one count hold, two repetitions.

Following the preparatory port de bras, bring the arms down.

On "and," plié and push off the floor, pointing the feet and stretching the legs in 1st; on 1, land in plié; on "and," directly out of the plié, push off the floor again; on 2, land in plié; on 3, stretch the knees; on 4, hold the position. Repeat three more times. After a pause, repeat the exercise.

Explanation. Students are now practicing the exercise in the center, with still two jumps at a time.

Exercise 23

Piqué 2nd, eight counts, facing the barre.

Students repeat Exercise 25 of the Second Class of this week.

Exercise 24

Preparation for pas de bourrée couru: relevé in 6th and tiptoes run, in diagonal.

Students repeat Exercise 26 of the Second Class of this week.

Exercise 25

Curtsey.

FIFTH CLASS

Exercise 1

Warm up.

Exercise 2

Plié in 2nd and 1st, with port de bras, bending to the side.

Students repeat Exercise 2 of the Fourth Class of the Seventeenth Week.

Exercise 3

Battement tendu en croix, flex the foot, plié, in 1st, eight counts, review.

Students repeat Exercise 3 of the Second Class of this week.

Exercise 4

Battement tendu en croix, two counts.

Students repeat Exercise 4 of the Fifth Class of the Seventeenth Week.

Exercise 5

Battement tendu 2nd, close in plié, bring the foot on the cou-de-pied, eight counts, facing the barre.

On "and" 1, battement tendu 2nd; on 2, close 5th devant in plié; on "and," bring the foot on the cou-de-pied devant, stretching the supporting leg; on 3 and 4, hold the position; on 5, extend the leg 2nd, pointing the foot onto the floor; on 6, hold the position; on 7, close 5th devant; on 8, hold the position. Repeat three more times with the right foot, the last one closing 5th derrière.

Explanation. Students are mixing the battement tendu and bringing the foot onto the cou-de-pied out of the 5th position. The bringing of the foot onto the cou-de-pied is sharp. Students must really press firmly onto the floor while closing 5th in plié and use the working foot to push off the floor. Students should be asked to release the barre ever so briefly to make sure they are on their supporting leg when the foot comes onto the cou-de-pied. This type of exercise prepares students well for the preparation for pirouettes that comes later this year, since they are asked to balance quickly on one leg with the other leg bending sharply against the supporting leg, as it is done in pirouettes.

Exercise 6

Battement jeté 2nd, direct, no hold à la demi-hauteur, four counts, facing the barre.

Students repeat Exercise 6 of the Second Class of this week.

Exercise 7

Battement jeté piqué 2nd, bouncing on the count, in 1st, four counts, facing the barre.

On "and" 1, battement 2nd; on "and," bring the pointed foot down; on 2, battement; on "and," bring the pointed foot down onto the floor; on 3, hold the position; on 4, close 1st. Repeat three more times with the right foot. Repeat the whole exercise one more time. At the end, roll up and hold balance.

Explanation. In this battement jeté piqué exercise, the toes look as if they are bouncing off the floor lightly and sharply, with the toes very taut before lifting the leg à la demi-hauteur again. After the bounce, the leg comes back up and briefly freezes à la demi-hauteur.

Exercise 8

Rond de jambe à la demi-hauteur en dehors and en dedans, eight counts, facing the barre.

On "and" 1, battement devant; on 2, hold the position; on 3 and 4, demi-rond de jambe en dehors to 2nd; on 5 and 6, demi-rond de jambe en dehors to 4th derrière; on 7, lower the leg and point the foot onto the floor; on 8, close 5th derrière. On "and" 1, battement derrière; on 2, hold the position; on 3 and 4, demi-rond de jambe en dedans to 2nd; on 5 and 6, demi-rond de jambe

en dedans to 4th devant; on 7, lower the leg and point the foot onto the floor; on 8, close 5th devant. Repeat the exercise one more time with the right foot. At the end, retiré derrière with the left leg and balance.

Explanation. To practice the full rond de jambe à la demi-hauteur for the first time, students are facing the barre. As in the demi-rond de jambe, in the full rond de jambe the working leg remains at the same height, fully turned-out. The working foot must remain stretched throughout the exercise, like it leads the leg around.

Music. Since there are eight counts for each rond de jambe, the music is preferably a medium-tempo waltz.

Exercise 9

Battement fondu en croix, eight counts.

Students repeat Exercise 9 of the Second Class of this week.

Exercise 10

Battement frappé en croix, two counts, facing the barre.

Students repeat Exercise 10 of the Second Class of this week.

Exercise 11

Preparation for rond de jambe soutenu 2nd, direct battement, no rotation, facing the barre.

Students repeat Exercise 11 of the Second Class of this week.

Exercise 12

Adagio: lift the leg devant, 2nd, and derrière, arabesque, eight counts, hold three counts in the air.

Students repeat Exercise 13 of the Second Class of this week.

Exercise 13

Grand battement devant, sideways, battements 2nd and derrière, facing the barre, three counts, one count hold.

Students repeat Exercise 13 of the Fourth Class of this week.

Exercise 14

Pied sur la barre 2nd and devant, plié and bend, 4th derrière, plié.

Students repeat Exercise 15 of the Fifth Class of the Seventeenth Week.

CENTER

Exercise 15

Battement tendu 2nd, start in plié and stretch when pointing, in 1st.

Students repeat Exercise 18 of the Second Class of this week.

Exercise 16

Battement tendu en croix, in 1st, two counts.

On "and" 1, battement tendu devant; on 2, close 1st. Repeat the exercise en croix en dehors. After a pause, repeat the whole exercise one more time.

Explanation. This exercise is similar to Exercise 4 of the Fifth Class of the Seventeenth Week, performed this time in the center.

Exercise 17

Battement jeté 2nd, en descendant and en remontant, four counts.

On "and" 1, battement 2nd, with the left leg; on "and," lower the leg, and point the foot onto the floor; on 2, hold the position; on 3, close 5th devant; on 4, hold the position; on "and" 5, battement 2nd, with the right leg; on "and," lower the leg and point the foot onto the floor; on 6, hold the position; on 7, close 5th devant; on 8, hold the position. Repeat the exercise one more time.

On "and" 1, battement 2nd, with the right leg; on "and," lower the leg and point the foot onto the floor; on 2, hold the position; on 3, close 5th derrière; on 4, hold the position; on "and" 5, battement 2nd with the left leg; on "and," lower the leg and point the foot onto the floor; on 6, hold the position; on 7, close 5th derrière; on 8, hold the position. Repeat the exercise one more time.

Explanation. Students are practicing the battement jeté 2nd, changing legs each time, traveling forward and backward. There is still a slight hold when the foot is pointed on the floor before closing it in 5th.

Exercise 18

Position on the cou-de-pied, pointed, extension of the leg en croix, with port de bras, four counts.

Students repeat Exercise 20 of the Second Class of this week.

Exercise 19

Adagio: lift the leg devant and derrière, separate port de bras, eight counts, hold three counts in the air.

On "and" 1, battement tendu devant; on 2, lift the leg; from 3 to 5, hold the position; on 6, lower the leg and point the toes onto the floor; on 7, close 5th devant; on 8, hold the position. Repeat with the left leg derrière. From 1 to 8, bring the arms down, to 1st, to 5th, and open them 2nd. From 1 to 4, battement tendu 2nd with the left foot, closing 5th devant to perform the exercise with the left foot front. Hold the position for four counts.

Explanation. Students are revisiting lifting the leg devant and derrière in this adagio. The time that the student must hold the leg has increased. To make the exercise easier, the lift is performed only devant and derrière.

Exercise 20

Relevé in 1st, two counts, three repetitions.

Students repeat Exercise 21 of the Fourth Class of this week.

Exercise 21

Relevé in 5th, plié and relevé on the count, four counts, three repetitions, facing the barre.

On "and," plié; on 1, relevé; on 2 and 3, hold the position; on 4, come down in plié; on 5, directly out of the plié, relevé; on 6 and 7, hold the position; on 8, come down in plié; on 1, relevé; on 2 and 3, hold the position; on 4, come down in plié; from 5 to 8, stretching the knees, battement tendu 2nd with the back foot and close 5th left foot devant.

Explanation. This time students are performing the relevé in 5th on four counts, with a two count holding on demi-pointes. Notice the battement tendu 2nd to change feet to perform the exercise with the left foot front. Only a very slight spring is allowed to bring both feet under.

Exercise 22

Soubresaut in 1st, on the count, one count hold, two repetitions.

Students repeat Exercise 22 of the Fourth Class of this week.

Exercise 23

Assemblé 2nd, en descendant and en remontant, two counts, one count hold.

On "and," plié; on 1, brush the back foot and extend the leg 2nd, while pushing off the floor with the supporting leg, stretching both legs in the air; on 2, land in plié in 5th, left foot front; on 3, straighten up the knees; on 4, hold the position. Repeat three more times, bringing the back foot front each time.

On "and," plié; on 1, brush the front foot and extend the leg 2nd, while pushing off the floor with the supporting leg, stretching both legs in the air; on 2, land in plié in 5th, left foot front; on 3, straighten up the knees; on 4, hold the position. Repeat three more times, bringing the front foot back each time.

Explanation. Students are reviewing the assemblé en descendant and en remontant in this exercise in the center. The arms remain 2nd.

Exercise 24

Piqué 2nd, eight counts, facing the barre.

Students repeat Exercise 25 of the Second Class of this week.

Exercise 25

Preparation for pas de bourrée couru, relevé in 6th and run on tiptoes, in diagonal.

Students repeat Exercise 26 of the Second Class of this week.

Exercise 26

Curtsey.

Nineteenth Week

§

Students repeat the material of the Fifth Class of the Eighteenth Week.

SECOND CLASS

Exercise 1

Warm up.

Exercise 2

Plié in 2nd and 1st, with port de bras, bending to the side.

Students repeat Exercise 2 of the Fourth Class of the Seventeenth Week.

Exercise 3

Battement tendu en croix en dehors and en dedans, turn the leg in and out, in 1st, four counts.

On "and" 1, battement tendu devant; on 2, turn in the working leg; on 3, turn out; on 4, close 1st. Repeat the exercise en croix en dehors and en dedans. At the end, roll up in 1st and hold balance.

Explanation. The turning in and out of the working leg has already been practiced earlier in the training. In this exercise, there is no holding. As a reminder, the turning out of the leg occurs in the hip socket and not by swinging the hips.

Application. This is a good exercise to practice throughout the year—even for more advanced students, especially at the beginning of the barre.

Exercise 4

Battement tendu en croix, two counts, three repetitions.

On "and" 1, battement tendu devant; on 2, close 5th devant; on 3, battement tendu devant; on 4, close 5th devant; on 5, battement tendu devant; on 6, close 5th devant; on 7 and 8, hold the position. Repeat the exercise en croix en dehors, with the first battement tendu 2nd closing derrière. At the end, roll up and hold the position.

Explanation. The battement tendu on two counts is practiced further in this exercise with three repetitions in each direction.

Exercise 5

Battement tendu 2nd, close in plié, position on the cou-de-pied, eight counts, facing the barre.

Students repeat Exercise 5 of the Fifth Class of the Eighteenth Week.

Exercise 6

Battement jeté en croix en dehors and en dedans, four counts.

On "and" 1, battement jeté devant; on "and," lower the leg and point the foot onto the floor; on 2, hold the position; on 3, close 5th devant; on 4, hold the position. Repeat the exercise en croix en dehors and en dedans. The last battement 2nd of the first series closes derrière, and the last battement of the second series closes devant. At the end, relevé in 5th and hold balance.

Explanation. Students are performing the exercise en croix in this otherwise familiar exercise.

Music. The tempo is accelerated with a sharper beat.

Exercise 7

Battement jeté piqué 2nd, bouncing on the count, in 1st, four counts, facing the barre.

Students repeat Exercise 7 of the Fifth Class of the Eighteenth Week.

Exercise 8

Rond de jambe à la demi-hauteur en dehors and en dedans, eight counts, facing the barre.

Students repeat Exercise 8 of the Fifth Class of the Eighteenth Week.

Exercise 9

Battement fondu en croix, with port de bras, eight counts.

Following the preparatory port de bras, bring the arm down.

On 1 and 2, bring the foot on the cou-de-pied devant with a deep plié on the supporting leg, bringing the arm in low 1st; on 3 and 4, extend the leg in demi-attitude devant, still in plié, with the arm coming to full 1st; on 5 and 6, stretch both legs at the same time à la demi-hauteur, opening the arm 2nd; on 7 and 8, lower the leg down, and point the foot onto the floor, close in 5th devant, bringing the arm down. Repeat the exercise en croix en dehors.

Explanation. Students are adding a port de bras, which is quite standard: the arm coming in 1st as the leg bends and opening 2nd when the leg stretches. The opening of the arm and the stretching of the leg have to be synchronized so that the movement looks smooth and flowing in the final version of the battement fondu. Students should avoid pulling the barre and should be asked to release it from time to time.

Exercise 10

Battement frappé en croix, two counts.

On "and," bring the front foot on the cou-de-pied devant; on 1, hold the position; on 2, extend the leg devant, pointing the foot onto the floor; on 3, bring the foot on the cou-de-pied devant; on 4, extend the leg 2nd; on 5, bring the foot on the cou-de-pied derrière; on 6, extend the leg derrière; on 7, bring the foot on the cou-de-pied derrière; on 8, extend the leg 2nd. Repeat the exercise one more time. At the end, hold the cou-de-pied devant position and hold balance.

Explanation. Students are repeating Exercise 10 of the Second Class of the Eighteenth Week, this time performed sideways.

Exercise 11

Petits battements, each on one count, arm in low 1st, review.

Following the preparatory port de bras, bring the arm down.

On "and," bring the working foot on the cou-de-pied devant, bringing the arm in low 1st; on 1, hold the position; on "and," unbend the leg halfway to 2nd, straightening the head; on 2, bring the foot on the cou-de-pied derrière, turning the head slightly toward the barre; on "and,"

unbend the leg, straightening the head; on 3, bring the foot on the cou-de-pied devant, turning the head toward the right; on "and," unbend the leg, straightening the head; on 4, bring the foot on the cou-de-pied derrière, turning the head toward the barre; on "and," unbend the leg, straightening the head; on 5, bring the foot on the cou-de-pied devant, turning the head toward the right; on "and," unbend the leg, straightening the head; on 6, bring the foot on the cou-de-pied derrière, turning the head toward the barre; on 7, close in 5th in plié; on 8, stretch the knees. Repeat one more time, holding the last position of the cou-de-pied devant, holding the head straight, and balance on one foot.

Explanation. Students are revisiting Exercise 11 of the Second Class of the Seventeenth Week. Students are reminded of the different head positions that accompany the exercise.

Exercise 12

Grand battement devant, sideways, battements 2nd and derrière, facing the barre, three counts, one count hold.

Students repeat Exercise 13 of the Fourth Class of the Eighteenth Week.

Exercise 13

Pied sur la barre 2nd and devant, plié and bend, 4th derrière, plié.

Students repeat Exercise 15 of the Fifth Class of the Seventeenth Week.

CENTER

Exercise 14

Battement tendu en croix, in 1st, two counts.

Students repeat Exercise 16 of the Fifth Class of the Eighteenth Week.

Exercise 15

Battement tendu en croix, two counts.

On "and" 1, battement tendu devant; on 2, close 5th devant. Repeat the exercise en croix en dehors, with the last battement tendu 2nd closing derrière.

Explanation. Students are repeating Exercise 4 of the Fifth Class of the Seventeenth Week, this time performed in the center.

Exercise 16

Battement jeté 2nd, en descendant and en remontant, four counts.

Students repeat Exercise 17 of the Fifth Class of the Eighteenth Week.

Exercise 17

Adagio: lift the leg devant and derrière, arabesque, separate port de bras, eight counts, hold three counts in the air.

Students repeat Exercise 19 of the Fifth Class of the Eighteenth Week.

Exercise 18

Relevé in 1st, two counts, three repetitions.

Students repeat Exercise 21 of the Fourth Class of the Eighteenth Week.

Exercise 19

Relevé in 5th, plié and relevé on the count, four counts, three repetitions, facing the barre.

Students repeat Exercise 21 of the Fifth Class of the Eighteenth Week.

Exercise 20

Soubresaut in 1st, on the count, one count hold, two repetitions.

Students repeat Exercise 22 of the Fourth Class of the Eighteenth Week.

Exercise 21

Assemblé 2nd, en descendant and en remontant, two counts, one count hold.

Students repeat Exercise 23 of the Fifth Class of the Eighteenth Week.

Exercise 22

Piqué 2nd, four counts, facing the barre.

On "and," plié; on 1, battement tendu 2nd; on 2, step onto the right foot on demi-pointe, with the other leg joining immediately the first one into 5th, right foot front; on 3, come down in plié; on 4, stretch. Repeat three more times toward the right. Repeat toward the left.

Explanation. Students are repeating Exercise 25 of the Second Class of the Eighteenth Week, except this time it is performed on four counts. Like before, students are turning their head toward the traveling side.

Exercise 23

Preparation for déboulés, in 1st, arms in low 1st, each half turn on one count.

Start the exercise in the back of the studio, facing the left side. Following the preparatory port de bras, bring the arms down.

On "and" 1, transfer weight onto the right foot, slightly raising and pushing the right heel outward, rotate toward the right, keeping the arms in low 1st in front of the torso, and turning the head so that, by the end of the half turn, it is turned toward the left shoulder with the eyes focused on a particular point; on "and" 2, transferring the weight onto the left foot, rotate a half turn toward the right, keeping the eyes focused on the particular point as the body starts rotating, and the head snapping so that the head precedes the end of the rotation of the body with the eyes still focused on the same spot. Repeat at least six more times. Repeat the exercise rotating toward the left.

Explanation. Students are reviewing Exercise 22 of the Second Class of the Tenth Week, except this time there is no hold after rotation.

Exercise 24

Curtsey.

THIRD CLASS

Students repeat the material of the Second Class of this week.

FOURTH CLASS

Exercise 1

Warm up.

Exercise 2

Plié in 2nd and 1st, with port de bras, bending to the side.

Students repeat Exercise 2 of the Fourth Class of the Seventeenth Week.

Exercise 3

Battement tendu en croix en dehors and en dedans, turn the leg in and out, in 1st, four counts.

Students repeat Exercise 3 of the Second Class of this week.

Exercise 4

Battement tendu en croix, two counts, three repetitions.

Students repeat Exercise 4 of the Second Class of this week.

Exercise 5

Battement tendu en croix, close in plié, bring the foot on the cou-de-pied, with extension, eight counts, facing the barre.

On "and" 1, battement tendu devant; on 2, close 5th in plié; on "and," bring the foot pointed on the cou-de-pied devant, stretching the supporting leg; on 3 and 4, hold the position; on 5, extend the leg devant, pointing the foot onto the floor; on 6, hold the position; on 7, close 5th devant; on 8, hold the position. Repeat the exercise en croix en dehors.

Explanation. Students are practicing the exercise en croix, still facing the barre. When bringing the foot on the cou-de-pied out of the plié, the working foot must actively push off the floor. Students should be asked to release the barre as soon as their foot is on the cou-de-pied.

Exercise 6

Battement jeté en croix en dehors and en dedans, four counts.

Students repeat Exercise 6 of the Second Class of this week.

Exercise 7

Battement jeté piqué 2nd, bouncing on the count, in 1st, four counts, facing the barre.

Students repeat Exercise 7 of the Fifth Class of the Eighteenth Week.

Exercise 8

Rond de jambe à la demi-hauteur en dehors and en dedans, eight counts, facing the barre.

Students repeat Exercise 8 of the Fifth Class of the Eighteenth Week.

Exercise 9

Battement fondu en croix, eight counts, with port de bras.

Students repeat Exercise 9 of the Second Class of this week.

Exercise 10

Battement frappé en croix, two counts.

Students repeat Exercise 10 of the Second Class of this week.

Exercise 11

Adagio: grand plié in 2nd and 1st, with port de bras.

Following the preparatory port de bras, bring both feet down in 2nd.

On "and" 1, turning the hand so that the palm faces down, with the head turned toward the working hand, plié with the arm coming down; on 2, deepen the plié, keeping the heels down in the plié, and bringing the arm down, rounding it by curving the lower arm inward (in the deepest level of the plié); on 3 and 4, come up into demi-plié, bringing the arm to 1st, stretch the knees and open the arm 2nd; from 5 to 8, repeat the grand plié, and close 1st.

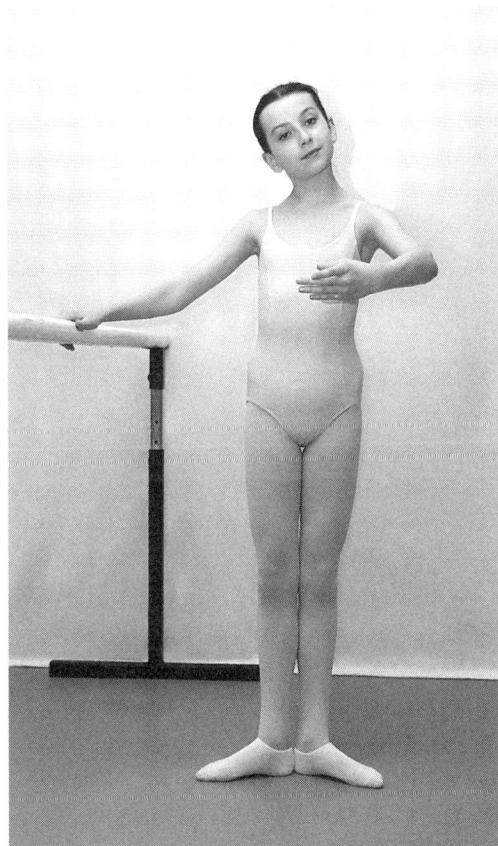

The head inclines toward the shoulder and the eyes are focused on the left hand, before the arm opens 2nd position at the end of the grand plié.

On "and" 1, turning the hand so that the palm faces down, with the head turned toward the working hand, plié with the arm coming down; on 2, deepen the plié, allowing the heels to rise into a grand plié, bringing the arm down, rounding it by curving the lower arm inward (in the deepest level of the plié); on 3 and 4, bring the heels down into a demi-plié, bringing the arm to 1st, and stretch the knees, opening the arm 2nd; from 5 to 8, repeat. Roll up in 1st and hold balance.

Explanation. Students are accompanying the arm with the grand plié in 2nd and 1st. Students are now familiar with the port de bras executed with the demi-plié. Here the port de bras is similar, except that its timing is slightly different, since it has to accompany a leg movement with more amplitude. The arm does not come down as fast as the legs bend; otherwise, it looks like the movement collapses. Students must keep the arm slightly suspended before it comes down. The elbow must initiate the descent of the arm in the port de bras, but without the elbow drooping. The head is turned toward the arm. When initiating the port de bras, the head is held up slightly and the eyes follow the movement of the arm. Like with any other plié, the back is erect, the knees above the toes, and the thighs well turned out. The heels should touch the floor

as soon as possible as they rise from the grand plié in 1st.

Students should inhale as the palm turns down; exhale when the arm comes down; inhale when the arm comes 1st; and exhale when the arm opens 2nd.

There are five common errors in this exercise to avoid:

1. Keeping the arm curved in on the side (as if holding a basket on the forearm) and not centering the arm in front of the torso when it comes down from the 2nd.

2. The working arm coming down too much during the plié in 1st, with the shoulder of the working arm coming forward: it then looks like students are picking up something on the floor. Instead, the elbow must lead the arm down with the forearm following; the elbow then stops when the forearm can round into the preparatory position. The hand must follow naturally this movement, without flexing or curving excessively.

3. The elbow being overly stretched when the arm comes down; this gives a standoff-ish attitude.

4. The arm coming down too soon; the arm must not be at the lowest point by the time

The arm comes down too low and the shoulder is too much forward in the port de bras.

The arm lowers more slowly than the body in the grand plié.

students reach first the lowest point of the demi-plié. Students must look like they are suspending themselves as the body lowers. Similarly, the head keeps up with the speed of the arm, which is again slightly slower than the one of the movement of the legs.

5. The shoulder of the working arm coming forward as the arm comes down and the arm crossing over the centerline of the torso.

Application. The quality of this coordination is difficult to achieve, especially for students who do not take ballet regularly during the week. This exercise should not be attempted if students are not executing this exercise with a deep enough demi-plié.

Exercise 12

Petits battements, each on one count, arm in low 1st, review.

Students repeat Exercise 11 of the Second Class of this week.

Exercise 13

Grand battement devant and 2nd, sideways, grand battement derrière, facing the barre, three counts, one count hold.

In 4th devant and 2nd sideways: on "and" 1, battement devant; on "and," bring the leg down and point the foot onto the floor; on 2, hold the position; on 3, close 5th; on 4, hold the position. Repeat the exercise 2nd, closing the foot 5th devant. Repeat three more times.

In 4th derrière facing the barre: on "and" 1, battement derrière; on "and," bring the leg down and point the foot onto the floor; on 2, hold the position; on 3, close 5th; on 4, hold the position. Repeat three more times.

Explanation. Students are performing the direct grand battement 2nd and devant sideways. Like with every other grand battement exercise, the energy of the battement must come from under with the activation of the turn-out muscles. The weight stays on the supporting leg at all times. Students do not pull the barre. They are expected to put as much energy in the throw as in bringing the leg down. This practice helps to give the impression of lightness that should be seen in the grand battement exercise.

Exercise 14

Attitude devant, plié, attitude derrière, facing the barre.

Bend the leg and place the lower part of the leg on the barre in front of the torso, resting the outer aspect of the heel on the barre, and point the foot so that the toes aim down at the side of the barre. Both hands rest on the barre on each side of the working leg. The supporting leg is turned out and stretched.

On 1 and 2, plié and stretch. Repeat twice more. At the end, release the barre and hold the position with the arms 2nd for a few counts. Move the supporting leg backward to be able to stretch the front leg completely, and bend forward while still holding the barre, with both legs in parallel. Hold the position for a few counts.

Bring the leg into retiré derrière, grab the working foot with the opposite hand, and pull the working leg up, while trying to keep the torso upright. Hold the position for a few seconds and release.

Explanation. Students are repeating the stretching exercise for attitude, this time adding the attitude derrière. When stretching the

Stretching of the back leg, facing the barre.

working leg on the barre, both legs are parallel. In the attitude derrière, students have to grab the foot with the opposite hand, while keeping the torso as straight as possible. It is a good exercise for back flexibility and stretching the quadriceps; it also helps to maintain the back leg behind the shoulders in this difficult position. For full benefit, the weight must remain on the supporting leg.

CENTER

Exercise 15

Battement tendu en croix, in 1st, two counts.

Students repeat Exercise 16 of the Fifth Class of the Eighteenth Week.

Exercise 16

Battement tendu en croix, two counts.

Students repeat Exercise 15 of the Second Class of this week.

Exercise 17

Battement jeté 2nd, en descendant and en remontant, four counts.

Students repeat Exercise 17 of the Fifth Class of the Eighteenth Week.

Exercise 18

Adagio: lift the leg devant and derrière, separate port de bras, eight counts, hold three counts in the air.

Students repeat Exercise 19 of the Fifth Class of the Eighteenth Week.

Exercise 19

Relevé in 5th, plié and relevé on the count, four counts, three repetitions, facing the barre.

Students repeat Exercise 21 of the Fifth Class of the Eighteenth Week.

Exercise 20

Relevé in 6th, hold on one foot, eight counts, facing the barre.

On "and," plié; on 1, relevé; on 2, hold the position; on 3, transfer the weight onto the left foot, bringing the right foot up pointed against the left ankle; on 4 and 5, hold the position; on 6, bring

the right foot onto demi-pointe again next to the other; on 7, come down into plié; on 8, stretch the knees. Repeat three more times, alternating feet.

Explanation. Students are introduced to the holding on one foot on demi-pointe. If they have mastered all the previous relevé exercises, this exercise should not present much difficulty, especially in 6th. The instructor will watch for any weakness of the ankle and sickling of the foot. Students will be asked to release the barre briefly to make sure their weight is on the supporting leg when holding on one foot.

Exercise 21

Soubresaut in 5th, on the count, two count hold, facing the barre and in the center, review.

On "and," plié, and jump off the floor equally with both feet, pointing them and stretching the knees, and keeping the legs in 5th position tight in the air; on 1, land in plié; on 2, stretch the knees; on 3 and 4, hold the position. Repeat three more times with the right foot front. Repeat the exercise in the center.

Explanation. Students are repeating Exercise 21 of the Fourth Class of the Thirteenth Week.

Exercise 22

Assemblé 2nd, en descendant and en remontant, two counts, one count hold.

Students repeat Exercise 23 of the Fifth Class of the Eighteenth Week.

Exercise 23

Piqué 2nd, four counts, facing the barre.

Students repeat Exercise 22 of the Second Class of this week.

Exercise 24

Preparation for déboulés, in 1st, arms in low 1st, each half turn on one count.

Students repeat Exercise 23 of the Second Class of this week.

Exercise 25

Curtsey.

FIFTH CLASS

Exercise 1

Warm up.

Exercise 2

Plié in 2nd and 1st, with port de bras, bending to the side.

Students repeat Exercise 2 of the Fourth Class of the Seventeenth Week.

Exercise 3

Battement tendu en croix en dehors and en dedans, turn the leg in and out, in 1st, four counts.

Students repeat Exercise 3 of the Second Class of this week.

Exercise 4

Battement tendu en croix, two counts, three repetitions.

Students repeat Exercise 4 of the Second Class of this week.

Exercise 5

Battement tendu en croix, close in plié, bring the foot on the cou-de-pied, with extension, eight counts, facing the barre.

Students repeat Exercise 5 of the Fourth Class of this week.

Exercise 6

Battement jeté en croix en dehors and en dedans, four counts.

Students repeat Exercise 6 of the Second Class of this week.

Exercise 7

Battement jeté piqué 2nd, bouncing on the count, in 1st, four counts, facing the barre.

Students repeat Exercise 7 of the Fifth Class of the Eighteenth Week.

Exercise 8

Rond de jambe à terre en dehors and en dedans, four counts, facing the barre.

On "and" 1, battement tendu devant; on 2, rond de jambe en dehors to 2nd; on 3, rond de jambe en dehors to 4th derrière; on 4, close 5th derrière; on "and" 5, battement tendu derrière; on 6, rond de jambe en dedans to 2nd; on 7, rond de jambe en dehors to 4th devant; on 8, close 5th devant. Repeat the exercise one more time. At the end, bring the front leg into retiré devant and balance with the arms in 5th.

Explanation. Students are performing the rond de jambe on four counts, still with a brief hold in each direction. The music is slightly slower than usual so that students have time to complete the full rond de jambe.

Exercise 9

Battement fondu en croix, with port de bras, eight counts.

Students repeat Exercise 9 of the Second Class of this week.

Exercise 10

Battement frappé en croix, two counts.

Students repeat Exercise 10 of the Second Class of this week.

Exercise 11

Adagio: grand plié in 2nd and 1st, with port de bras.

Students repeat Exercise 11 of the Fourth Class of this week.

Exercise 12

Petits battements, each on one count, arm in low 1st, review.

Students repeat Exercise 11 of the Second Class of this week.

Exercise 13

Grand battement devant and 2nd, sideways, grand battement derrière, facing the barre, three counts, one count hold.

Students repeat Exercise 13 of the Fourth Class of this week.

Exercise 14

Attitude devant, plié, attitude derrière, facing the barre.

Students repeat Exercise 14 of the Fourth Class of this week.

Exercise 15

Battement tendu en croix, in 1st, two counts.

Students repeat Exercise 16 of the Fifth Class of the Eighteenth Week.

Exercise 16

Battement tendu en croix, two counts.

Students repeat Exercise 15 of the Second Class of this week.

Exercise 17

Battement jeté 2nd, en descendant and en remontant, four counts.

Students repeat Exercise 17 of the Fifth Class of the Eighteenth Week.

Exercise 18

Adagio: retiré devant and derrière, close directly in plié, without changing sides, eight counts.

Following the preparatory port de bras, bring the arms down.

On "and," bring the foot pointed on the cou-de-pied devant; on 1, hold the position; on 2 and 3, slide the side of the small toe along the leg to the knee level, while the arms come up to 1st; on 4, hold the position; on 5 and 6, slide the foot down; on 7, close 5th devant in plié; on "and" 8, stretch, opening the arms and bringing them down again.

On "and," bring the foot on the cou-de-pied derrière (left foot); on 1, hold the position; on 2 and 3, slide the inner side of the heel along the supporting leg, and then progressively open the foot slightly out so that the side of the big toe slides up against the back of the supporting leg to the knee level, while the arms come up to 1st; on 4, hold the position; on 5 and 6, slide the foot down; on 7, close 5th derrière in plié; on "and" 8, stretch, opening the arms and bringing them down again. Repeat the whole exercise one more time.

Explanation. Students are performing the slow retiré in the center without changing feet and closing directly into 5th. The knee must be actively pushed to the side. The foot does not sickle in. The exercise requires a good control of the turn-out to hold balance. The activation of the turn-out muscles, mostly the adductors, keeping the hips straight and a strong back, and lifting the opposite side of one of the working legs will help balancing.

Exercise 19

Relevé in 6th, hold on one foot, eight counts, facing the barre.

Students repeat Exercise 20 of the Fourth Class of this week.

Exercise 20

Relevé in 1st, two counts, three repetitions, review.

Following the preparatory port de bras, bring the arms down.

On "and," plié; on 1, relevé, bringing the arms in low 1st; on 2, come down in the plié; on 3, relevé; on 4, come down in the plié; on 5, relevé; on 6, come down in the plié; on 7, stretch the knees; on 8, hold the position. Repeat three more times.

Explanation. Students are reviewing Exercise 21 of the Fourth Class of the Eighteenth Week. Whereas the relevé is sharp, the coming down is smoother with a deep plié.

Exercise 21

Soubresaut in 5th, on the count, two count hold, facing the barre and in the center.

Students repeat Exercise 21 of the Fourth Class of this week.

Exercise 22

Soubresaut in 5th, landing on the front foot, with the other foot on the cou-de-pied derrière (soubresaut volé [flown]) [sissonne simple—Vaganova], four counts, facing the barre.

On "and," plié, straightening the head; on 1, push off the floor and jump, bringing the legs together in 5th, one leg in front of the other, knees and toes strongly stretched; on 2, land in plié onto the right foot, with the back leg bent and the foot on the cou-de-pied derrière, turning the head slightly toward the right; on 3, the left foot joins the other in 5th derrière, in plié; on 4, stretch both knees. Repeat three more times with the right foot front.

Explanation. This exercise involves a soubresaut landing on one leg; it prepares for jumps landing on one foot, like the sissonnes that will be studied later this year. Unlike sissonnes though, this jump does not travel. It goes without saying that the study of the plain soubresaut in 5th should precede this exercise. The bending of the leg must not occur too soon, but just before landing. The knees are turned out and directly in alignment with the toes in the plié. The whole feet press down onto the floor to push for the jump. The body is erect with a pulled up back. The abdominal muscles are lifted during the jump. Even though, the French term soubresaut volé is not commonly used, technically, the landing on one leg following the hold of the legs together in the air (with or without beats) qualifies this jump for being volé.[3] When well performed, this jump should give the impression that the dancer flies, before landing softly onto one leg.

Exercise 23

Piqué 2nd, four counts, facing the barre.

Students repeat Exercise 22 of the Second Class of this week.

Exercise 24

Preparation for déboulés, in 1st, arms in low 1st, each half turn on one count.

Students repeat Exercise 23 of the Second Class of this week.

Exercise 25

Curtsey.

---

3   Guillot and Prudhommeau, *Grammaire de la Danse Classique*, 105.

Twentieth Week

§

FIRST CLASS

Students repeat the material of the Fifth Class of Nineteenth Week.

SECOND CLASS

Exercise 1

Warm up.

Exercise 2

Plié in 2nd and 1st, with port de bras, bending to the side.

Students repeat Exercise 2 of the Fourth Class of the Seventeenth Week.

Exercise 3

Battement tendu en croix, in 1st, four counts, two counts, two repetitions.

On "and" 1, battement tendu devant; on 2, hold the position; on 3, close 1st; on 4, hold the position; on "and" 5, battement tendu devant; on 6, close 1st; on "and" 7, battement tendu devant; on 8, close 1st. Repeat the exercise en croix en dehors. At the end, relevé and hold balance.

Explanation. Students have already performed a version of this exercise. It is always good practice to review different tempos in one exercise so that students can translate it into the quality of the movement, even early on in the training.

Application. Changes in musical phrases and tempos within one exercise should be applied regularly to the ballet class, especially for more advanced students and pre-professional beginning students. The variation sensitizes students to the different qualities of movement and the use of different muscles, even while performing the same step, like the battement tendu here.

Exercise 4

Battement tendu en croix, four counts, two counts, two repetitions.

On "and" 1, battement tendu devant; on 2, hold the position; on 3, close 5th; on 4, hold the position; on "and" 5, battement tendu devant; on 6, close 5th; on "and" 7, battement tendu devant; on 8, close 5th devant; on "and" 1, battement tendu 2nd; on 2, hold the position; on 3, close 5th derrière; on 4, hold the position; on "and" 5, battement tendu 2nd; on 6, close 5th devant; on "and" 7, battement tendu 2nd; on 8, close 5th derrière; on "and" 1, battement tendu derrière; on 2, hold the position; on 3, close 5th; on 4, hold the position; on "and" 5, battement tendu derrière; on 6, close; on "and" 7, battement tendu derrière; on 8, close 5th derrière; on "and" 1, battement tendu 2nd; on 2, hold the position; on 3, close 5th devant; on 4, hold the position; on "and" 5, battement tendu 2nd; on 6, close 5th derrière; on "and" 7, battement tendu 2nd; on 8, close 5th devant. At the end, roll up in 5th and hold the position.

Explanation. Students are repeating the exercise in 5th. Like in the preceding exercise, the battement tendu on two counts comes out more sharply with the accent out.

Exercise 5

Battement tendu en croix, close in plié, bring the foot on the cou-de-pied, eight counts, facing the barre.

Students repeat Exercise 5 of the Fourth Class of the Nineteenth Week.

Exercise 6

Battement jeté 2nd, start in plié and stretch out, hold à la demi-hauteur, facing the barre.

On "and" 1, plié, brush the right foot, and extend the leg out in 2nd, starting in plié, stretching both legs at the same time; on 2, hold the position; on "and," lower the leg and point the foot onto the floor; on 3, hold the position; on 4, close 5th devant. Repeat three more times with the right foot. Repeat the whole exercise one more time.

Explanation. After practicing the exercise with a battement tendu, students are performing the exercise with a battement 2nd. It not only prepares for the assemblé, in particular, but also for many other exercises in which the working foot comes out of a closed position in plié and both legs stretch at the end of the throw.

Exercise 7

Preparation for battement en cloche à la demi-hauteur, direct battement, hold in the closing, in 1st.

On "and" 1, battement devant; on "and," point the foot down onto the floor; on 2, hold the position; on 3, close the foot in 1st; on 4, hold the position; on "and" 5, battement derrière; on "and," point the foot; on 6, hold the position; on 7, close 1st; on 8, hold the position. Repeat three more times. At the end of the exercise, balance with the working leg à la demi-hauteur devant with the arms in 1st.

Explanation. Students are revisiting the preparation exercise for battement en cloche, except the battement is direct and quick with a slight hold in the air. There is still a hold when pointing and in 1st. The hips remain as straight as possible. They are perpendicular to the barre and do not swing with the working leg. The torso remains very still during the exercise. The arm is 2nd. The head changes position whether the leg is devant or derrière.

Exercise 8

Rond de jambe à terre en dehors and en dedans, four counts, facing the barre.

Students repeat Exercise 8 of the Fifth Class of the Nineteenth Week.

Exercise 9

Preparation for chassé à terre, forward and backward, four counts.

On 1, plié; on "and" 2, still in plié, slide the front foot forward so that both feet are in 4th position; on 3, stretch both legs with the right leg becoming the supporting leg and the left leg becoming the working leg, pointing the left foot back; on 4, close 5th derrière.

On 5, plié; on "and" 6, still in plié, slide the back foot backward so that both feet are in 4th position; on 7, stretch both legs with the left leg becoming the supporting leg and the right leg becoming the working leg, pointing the right foot front; on 8, close 5th devant. Repeat one more time.

Explanation. Students are practicing the preparatory exercise for the chassé à terre forward and backward. The hand at the barre must slide as students move forward and backward. In the chassé backward, the hip of the back leg does not come out. The sliding out must be done with the whole foot, without rolling in. Students do not slide their working foot further than the 4th position to avoid rolling in and losing balance. Eventually students will widen the traveling distance in the chassé. For now, to maintain balance, they must keep the distance of about one and a half feet (a standard 4th position) when they slide their foot out. The pelvis does not swing back when sliding the foot forward or backward.

Exercise 10

Battement fondu en croix, with port de bras, eight counts.

Students repeat Exercise 9 of the Second Class of the Nineteenth Week.

Exercise 11

Battement frappé en croix en dehors and en dedans, with the foot in a flexed position, two counts.

On "and," the front foot comes flexed on the cou-de-pied devant; on 1, hold the position; on 2, extend the leg devant, pointing the foot onto the floor; on 3, bring the foot in flexed position on the cou-de-pied devant; on 4, extend the leg 2nd; on 5, bring the foot on the cou-de-pied derrière; on 6, extend the leg derrière; on 7, bring the foot on the cou-de-pied derrière; on 8, extend the leg 2nd. Repeat the exercise en croix en dedans. At the end, relevé in 5th and hold the position with the arms in low 1st.

Explanation. Students are repeating Exercise 10 of the Second Class of the Nineteenth Week, performed now en croix en dehors and en dedans, and with the foot in flexed position.

Exercise 12

Petits battements, two on the count, accent devant, hold on the cou-de-pied, facing the barre.

On "and," bring the foot on the cou-de-pied devant; on 1 and 2, hold the position; on "and," bring the foot on the cou-de-pied derrière; on 3, bring the foot on the cou-de-pied devant; on 4, hold the position; on "and," bring the foot on the cou-de-pied derrière; on 5, bring the foot on the cou-de-pied devant; on 6, hold the position; on "and," bring the foot on the cou-de-pied derrière; on 7, bring the foot on the cou-de-pied devant; on 8, hold the position. Repeat the exercise one more time. At the end, perform the demi-dé-tourné that students have learned previously and hold balance in 5th on the left side before starting the exercise on the left side.

Explanation. After practicing the petits battements on an even tempo, students are practicing them with the accent devant; that is, the foot is on the cou-de-pied derrière on the musical upbeat. Here there is no hold à la demi-seconde when switching from back to front and vice versa, but there is one when the foot is on the cou-de-pied devant. The action of bending and unbending of the leg is still done through the half 2nd. Performing petits battements accentuated, such as this one, will prove particularly useful when it is time to perform the entrechats three and four later on in training.

Music. The music is a medium tempo 4/4 with a sharp beat, so students have the time to unbend and bend their working leg to change sides for each petit battement.

Exercise 13

Adagio: grand plié in 2nd and 1st, with port de bras.

Students repeat Exercise 11 of the Fourth Class of the Nineteenth Week.

Exercise 14

Grand battement devant and 2nd, sideways, grand battement derrière, facing the barre, three counts, one count hold.

Students repeat Exercise 13 of the Fourth Class of the Nineteenth Week.

Exercise 15

Attitude devant, plié, attitude back, facing the barre.

Students repeat Exercise 14 of the Fourth Class of the Nineteenth Week.

Exercise 16

Battement tendu devant, passé à terre, hold when pointing, battement tendu derrière, in 1st.

On "and" 1, battement tendu devant; on 2, hold the position; on "and" 3, brush through 1st, battement tendu derrière; on 4, hold the position; on "and" 5, brush through the 1st and battement tendu devant; on 6, hold the position; on 7, close 1st; on 8, hold the position. Repeat the exercise one more time.

Explanation. Students are revisiting the passé à terre in the center, this time with the passé performed faster. Since there is no hold in 1st during the passé, the transfer of weight onto both feet should be just enough to be able to brush the working foot with the whole foot. If the weight were equally spread on both feet, the working foot would not be able to slide through. Students must hold their torso erect, especially when brushing back.

Exercise 17

Battement tendu en croix, two counts.

Students repeat Exercise 15 of the Second Class of the Nineteenth Week.

Exercise 18

Battement jeté en croix, direct, four counts.

On "and" 1, battement jeté devant; on "and," lower the leg and point the foot onto the floor; on 2, hold the position; on 3, close 5th devant; on 4, hold the position. Repeat the exercise en croix en dehors, the last battement 2nd closing derrière.

Explanation. Students are repeating Exercise 6 of the Second Class of the Nineteenth Week, performed this time only en croix en dehors and in the center.

Exercise 19

Adagio: retiré devant and derrière, close directly in plié, without changing sides, eight counts.

Students repeat Exercise 18 of the Fifth Class of the Nineteenth Week.

Exercise 20

Relevé in 1st, two counts, three repetitions, review.

Students repeat Exercise 20 of the Fifth Class of the Nineteenth Week.

Exercise 21

Preparation for relevé on the cou-de-pied devant, pointed position, eight counts, facing the barre.

On "and" 1, plié and relevé 5th; on 2, hold the position; on 3, bring the front foot pointed on the cou-de-pied devant; on 4, hold the position; on 5, bring the foot into 5th on demi-pointe; on 6, hold the position; on 7 and 8, come down into plié and stretch. Repeat three more times.

Explanation. Students are now holding on demi-pointe on one foot with turn-out in this very broken down exercise. The torso must remain straight and the supporting knee very stretched. The working foot on the cou-de-pied does not sickle, but the heel is pushed forward while the foot is still pointing. It is important to transfer the weight from two feet onto one foot, and again from one foot onto both feet, with the hands adjusting their position on the barre to accommodate these transfers.

Exercise 22

Soubresaut in 5th, on the count, two count hold, facing the barre and in the center, review.

Students repeat Exercise 21 of the Fourth Class of the Nineteenth Week.

Exercise 23

Soubresaut in 5th, landing on the front foot, and the other foot on the cou-de-pied derrière, four counts, facing the barre.

Students repeat Exercise 22 of the Fifth Class of the Nineteenth Week.

Exercise 24

Chassé sauté 2nd, arms in 6th, four counts, two repetitions.

In the preparatory port de bras, bring the arms in 1st, open the left arm 2nd and keep the right arm in 1st, with the head turned slightly toward the right.

On "and," plié and extend the right leg 2nd pointing the foot; on 1, step onto the right foot in plié, immediately pushing off the floor and bringing the left leg into 5th derrière in the air; on "and," land on the left foot in plié, releasing the right leg 2nd, with the leg then reaching out

to the side with the pointed foot just above the floor; on 2, step onto the right foot in plié, and again jump, bringing the legs together in the air in 5th, left foot derrière; on 3, land in plié; on 4, stretch the knees. Repeat three more times. Repeat the exercise one more time.

Explanation. Students are practicing two chassés in a row in the center. It is now easier to see the chasing action of the legs and the second leg taking the place of the first leg. The jump must be as high as possible with tight legs in 5th in the air. The plié between the jumps is not held; the break away from the floor is short and quick. The second leg, kept well turned out, does not drag behind, but is brought energetically behind the first one. Both legs must ideally join in 5th in the air before landing. The hips stay straight during the exercise and do not turn toward the working leg. Before stepping onto the first foot, students must not flex their foot at all; the foot still pointed must reach out before stepping down with a deep plié.

Music. A medium-tempo march would work well for this exercise so that students have time to get some height.

Application. The chassé sauté can be performed by almost all beginners, even pre-ballet students. However, performing it properly is more challenging, especially keeping the turn-out of both legs throughout the movement and the feet pointed when the chassés are performed in a row, like in this exercise; beginning students tend to attack this step incorrectly with the heel, flexing their foot prematurely before stepping onto it for the jump.

Exercise 25

Piqué 2nd, arms in 6th, four counts.

In the preparatory port de bras, bring the arms 1st then open the left arm and keep the right arm in 1st, with the head slightly turned toward the right arm.

On "and," plié; on 1, battement tendu 2nd; on 2, step onto the right foot on demi-pointe, with the other leg joining immediately the first one into 5th, right foot front, still on demi-pointes; on 3, come down in plié; on 4, stretch. Repeat three more times toward the right.

Explanation. Students are now performing the exercise in the center with a standard port de bras. The head is turned toward the traveling side.

Application. It is recommended that students keep practicing this exercise at the barre if the execution is still shaky. The arms do not bounce.

Exercise 26

Curtsey.

THIRD CLASS

Students repeat the material of the Second Class of this week.

FOURTH CLASS

Exercise 1

Warm up.

Exercise 2

Plié, review.

From now on, the instructor will select the elements of the plié exercise. Demi-pliés should always be included. There are, of course, no strict rules regarding this exercise. Common sense prevails. If grands pliés are performed in the plié exercise of the beginning of the barre, they will be only in 2nd and 1st, which are less demanding positions. It is better to use the 5th and 4th positions no earlier than in the fourth or fifth exercise of the barre; but if demi-pliés in 5th and in 4th are at all practiced at the beginning of the barre, they are preceded by the ones in 2nd and 1st so that the demand on the turn-out is gradual. Students can repeat the different port de bras and the bendings practiced so far. It is always a good idea for all beginners to execute the plié exercise facing the barre on a regular basis.

Exercise 3

Battement tendu en croix, in 1st, four counts, two counts, two repetitions.

Students repeat Exercise 3 of the Second Class of this week.

Exercise 4

Battement tendu en croix, four counts, two counts, two repetitions.

Students repeat Exercise 4 of the Second Class of this week.

Exercise 5

Battement tendu en croix, bring the foot on the cou-de-pied, with extension, eight counts, facing the barre.

On "and" 1, battement tendu devant; on 2, hold the position; on "and," bend the supporting leg sharply and bring the foot pointed on the cou-de-pied devant; on 3 and 4, hold the position; on 5, extend the leg devant, stretching the supporting leg; on 6, hold the position; on 7, close 5th; on 8, hold the position. Repeat the exercise en croix en dehors. At the end, roll up and hold the position. Repeat with the left foot.

Explanation. Versions of this exercise have been studied. In this one, students are bringing their working foot directly from the pointed position. This exercise should not be confused with the battement frappé in which the extension is sharp. This exercise aims mostly at bending the working leg sharply and freezing the position on the cou-de-pied. When they bend their leg to bring the foot on the cou-de-pied position, students must push their knee to the side, keeping the foot from sickling.

Music. The tempo is fairly quick since the movement in each direction is done on eight counts. A sharp tango, for instance, would accompany this exercise well.

Exercise 6

Battement jeté 2nd, start in plié and stretch out, hold à la demi-hauteur, facing the barre.

Students repeat Exercise 6 of the Second Class of this week.

Exercise 7

Preparation for battement en cloche à la demi-hauteur, direct battement, in 1st, hold in closing, facing the barre.

Students repeat Exercise 7 of the Second Class of this week.

Exercise 8

Rond de jambe à terre à terre en dehors and en dedans, four counts, facing the barre.

Students repeat Exercise 8 of the Fifth Class of the Nineteenth Week.

Exercise 9

Preparation for chassé à terre, forward and backward, four counts.

Students repeat Exercise 9 of the Second Class of this week.

Exercise 10

Battement fondu en croix, with port de bras, eight counts.

Students repeat Exercise 9 of the Second Class of the Nineteenth Week.

Exercise 11

Battement frappé en croix en dehors and en dedans, with the foot in a flexed position, two counts.

Students repeat Exercise 11 of the Second Class of this week.

Exercise 12

Petits battements, two on the count, accent devant, hold on the cou-de-pied, facing the barre.

Students repeat Exercise 12 of the Second Class of this week.

Exercise 13

Adagio: plié in 5th, with port de bras, bending forward.

On "and" 1 and 2, plié with the arm coming down; on 3, stretch the legs, bringing the arm in 1st; on 4, open the arm 2nd; on 5 and 6, bring the arm 5th; on 7 and 8, hold the position; on 1 and 2, bend forward; on 3 and 4, straighten up; on 5 and 6, bring the arm in 1st; on 7 and 8, open the arm 2nd. Repeat the exercise one more time.

Explanation. Students are practicing the plié in 5th with port de bras. When bending forward, the space between the head and the arm in 5th must not change, and the working shoulder remains down. When bending, the back is flat as far down as possible, then it is released to stretch further. To initiate the ascending part, students lengthen their back, keeping it flat as they straighten it up. In the port de bras, notice the arm coming down in 1st from the 5th to finally open 2nd.

Exercise 14

Grand battement en croix, three counts, one count hold.

On "and" 1, battement devant; on "and," bring the leg down with the pointed foot; on 2, hold the position; on 3, close 5th; on 4, hold the position. Repeat the exercise en croix en dehors. At the end, demi-détourné and hold balance on demi-pointes.

Explanation. Students now practice the grand battement exercise en croix, sideways. This exercise is appropriate only if the grand battement derrière is performed correctly facing the barre.

Application. Practicing the grand battement 2nd and derrière still facing the barre is recommended for beginners and even intermediate students taking ballet recreationally.

Exercise 15

Attitude devant, plié, attitude back, facing the barre.

Students repeat Exercise 14 of the Fourth Class of the Nineteenth Week.

CENTER

Exercise 16

Battement tendu devant, passé à terre, hold when pointing, battement tendu derrière, in 1st.

Students repeat Exercise 16 of the Second Class of this week.

Exercise 17

Battement jeté en croix, direct, four counts.

Students repeat Exercise 18 of the Second Class of this week.

Exercise 18

Rond de jambe à terre en dehors, four counts.

On "and" 1, battement tendu devant; on 2, demi-rond de jambe to 2nd; on 3, demi-rond de jambe to 4th derrière; on 4, close 5th. Repeat the whole exercise one more time.

Explanation. Students are repeating the rond de jambe exercise done at the barre earlier, only en dehors for now. Students keep their weight on their supporting leg throughout the rond de jambe, with a very taut working foot. They alternate the right and left legs.

Exercise 19

Adagio: retiré devant and derrière, close directly in plié without changing sides, eight counts.

Students repeat Exercise 18 of the Fifth Class of the Nineteenth Week.

Exercise 20

Relevé in 1st, two counts, three repetitions, review.

Students repeat Exercise 20 of the Fifth Class of the Nineteenth Week.

Exercise 21

Preparation for relevé on the cou-de-pied devant, pointed position, eight counts, facing the barre. Students repeat Exercise 21 of the Second Class of this week.

Exercise 22

Changement de pied, two counts, one count hold, facing the barre.

On "and," plié; on 1, push off the floor with pointed feet, opening slightly the legs in the air; on 2, land in plié in 5th, left foot front; on 3, stretch both legs; on 4, hold the position. Repeat three more times.

Explanation. Students are introduced to the changement de pied. Whereas in the soubresaut both legs are held tightly together, in the changement, the legs open enough in the air to change feet and land with the opposite foot front in the landing.

The study of the soubresaut in 5th is the first step studied in the field of the batterie. It is technically an entrechat one, but the term is rarely used.[4] The changement de pied usually comes next, and it is also called less commonly entrechat two. It is the first movement of the batterie à croisement (beating with crossing). These jumps are the only entrechats studied during the first year of training. A good performance of these simple jumps is essential for performing the more difficult entrechats and other beat jumps.

The changement is a jump taking off and landing on both feet. The legs must not be separated widely to the side but moved apart only so far as

to make it possible to change them from front to back in the air to land with the other foot in 5th position. As with the jumps learned so far, the legs must be strongly stretched in the knees, the insteps, and the toes. While jumping, students do not lower their chin and must push straight up. When they land, they keep the knees to the sides without crossing their feet over in 5th, as it is often seen, especially when several changements are performed.

Music. A medium 2/4 is used.

Application. Like most jumps, the introduction of the changement is to be done at the barre first for all ballet students. Some instructors introduce the changement before the soubresaut in 5th. However, practicing the soubresaut before the changement eases the performance of the changement; the tight and sharp holding of the legs as required in the soubresaut in 5th leads students to force more the stretch of the knees and the pointing of the toes to prepare for the changement. Finally, in the soubresaut, there is no worry about changing feet!

Exercise 23

Soubresaut in 5th landing on the front foot, the other foot on the cou-de-pied derrière, four counts, facing the barre.

Students repeat Exercise 22 of the Fifth Class of the Nineteenth Week.

Exercise 24

Chassé sauté 2nd, arms in 6th, four counts, two repetitions.

Students repeat Exercise 24 of the Second Class of this week.

Exercise 25

Piqué 2nd, arms in 6th, four counts.

Students repeat Exercise 25 of the Second Class of this week.

Exercise 26

Curtsey.

---

4 Guillot and Prudhommeau, *Grammaire de la Danse Classique*, 101.

FIFTH CLASS

Exercise 1

Warm up.

Exercise 2

Plié.

Exercise 3

Battement tendu en croix, in 1st, four counts, two counts, two repetitions.

Students repeat Exercise 3 of the Second Class of this week.

Exercise 4

Battement tendu en croix, four counts, two counts, two repetitions.

Students repeat Exercise 4 of the Second Class of this week.

Exercise 5

Battement tendu en croix, bring the foot on the cou-de-pied, with extension, eight counts, facing the barre.

Students repeat Exercise 5 of the Fourth Class of this week.

Exercise 6

Preparation for battement en cloche à la demi-hauteur, direct battement, in 1st, hold in 1st, facing the barre.

Students repeat Exercise 7 of the Second Class of this week.

Exercise 7

Rond de jambe à terre, en dehors and en dedans, with port de bras, four counts.

Following the preparatory port de bras, bring the arm down.

On "and" 1, battement tendu devant, bringing the arm in 1st; on 2, rond de jambe en dehors to 2nd, opening the arm 2nd; on 3, rond de jambe en dehors to 4th derrière, keeping the arm 2nd; on 4, close 5th derrière, bringing the arm down, the head turning slightly toward the barre. On "and" 5, battement tendu derrière, bringing the arm 1st; on 6, rond de jambe en dedans to 2nd, opening the arm 2nd; on 7, rond de jambe en dehors to 4th devant, keeping the arm 2nd; on 8,

close 5th devant, closing the arm down. Repeat the exercise one more time. At the end, bring the back leg into retiré derrière and balance with the arms in 5th.

Explanation. Students are repeating the exercise sideways with port de bras to accompany the movement of the leg. Notice the balancing with a retiré derrière holding the back leg this time.

Exercise 8

Preparation for chassé à terre, forward and backward, four counts.

Students repeat Exercise 9 of the Second Class of this week.

Exercise 9

Battement fondu en croix, with port de bras, eight counts.

Students repeat Exercise 9 of the Second Class of the Nineteenth Week.

Exercise 10

Battement frappé en croix en dehors and en dedans, with the foot in a flexed position, two counts.

Students repeat Exercise 11 of the Second Class of this week.

Exercise 11

Petits battements, two on the count, accent devant, hold on the cou-de-pied, facing the barre.

Students repeat Exercise 12 of the Second Class of this week.

Exercise 12

Adagio: plié in 5th, with port de bras, bending forward.

Students repeat Exercise 13 of the Fourth Class of this week.

Exercise 13

Grand battement en croix en dehors, three counts, one count hold.

Students repeat Exercise 14 of the Fourth Class of this week.

Exercise 14

Attitude devant, plié, attitude back, facing the barre.

Students repeat Exercise 14 of the Fourth Class of the Nineteenth Week.

Exercise 15

Battement tendu devant, passé à terre, hold when pointing, battement tendu derrière, in 1st.

Students repeat Exercise 16 of the Second Class of this week.

Exercise 16

Battement jeté en croix, direct, four counts.

Students repeat Exercise 18 of the Second Class of this week.

Exercise 17

Rond de jambe à terre en dehors, four counts.

Students repeat Exercise 18 of the Fourth Class of this week.

Exercise 18

Adagio: lift the leg devant, 2nd, and derrière, arabesque, with port de bras, eight counts, hold three counts in the air.

On "and" 1 and 2, brush the foot devant and lift the leg; from 3 to 5, hold the position; on 6, lower the leg and point the toes onto the floor; on 7, close 5th devant; on 8, hold the position. Repeat the exercise in 2nd and in arabesque. From 1 to 8, perform a port de bras to 1st, 5th, and 2nd.

Explanation. Students are repeating Exercise 19 of the Fifth Class of the Eighteenth Week, except this time students perform the exercise devant, 2nd, and derrière in 5th. Notice that there is no holding at the end of the dégagé before lifting the leg; that means that students must be balanced right away to be able to lift their leg. Retaining the practice of holding too long when the foot is pointed will lead students to rely too much on the working foot for balancing before actually lifting the leg. By not holding when the foot is pointed, the movement is now more flowing and continuous.

Exercise 19

Échappé 2nd on demi-pointes, without changing feet, hold on demi-pointes, four counts, facing the barre.

On "and," plié; on 1, slide the balls of the feet out along the floor, opening equally both feet in 2nd onto demi-pointes while stretching the knees; on 2, hold the position; on 3, bring both feet into 5th in plié, right foot front; on 4, stretch both knees. Repeat three more times with the right foot front.

Explanation. This kind of échappé is usually practiced on pointes; performing it on demi-pointes may seem awkward at first, but learning the mechanisms on demi-pointes will make the pointe version easier for students. Like in the échappé sauté, both legs must open and close at the same time. In this échappé, this coordination is more difficult to achieve because the platform for landing (on the balls of the feet and on the toes) is not as large as it is for the échappé sauté (on the whole feet), and the landing is performed on stretched legs instead of a landing in plié. Both feet must open sharply at the same time. In the closing, both feet must close under simultaneously. The simultaneous opening and closing make the échappé look sharp and precise. Students must not jump or hop when opening their legs, but graze the floor to bring their feet onto demi-pointes. The width of the échappé does not exceed one foot or one and a half foot.

Exercise 20

Preparation for relevé, cou-de-pied devant, pointed position, eight counts, facing the barre.

Students repeat Exercise 21 of the Second Class of this week.

Exercise 21

Changement de pied, two counts, one count hold, facing the barre.

Students repeat Exercise 22 of the Fourth Class of this week.

Exercise 22

Soubresaut in 5th, landing on the back foot with the other foot on the cou-de-pied devant, four counts, facing the barre.

On "and," plié; on 1, push off the floor and jump, bringing the legs together in 5th, one in front of the other, with the knees and toes strongly stretched; on 2, land in plié onto the left foot, bending the front leg with the foot pointed on the cou-de-pied devant; on 3, the right foot joins the other in 5th devant in plié; on 4, stretch both knees. Repeat three more times with the right foot front.

Explanation. This exercise is similar to Exercise 22 of the Fifth Class of the Nineteenth Week, except this time students bring their front foot on the cou-de-pied devant when landing. The external side of the small toe will be pressed against the cou-de-pied devant with the heel pushed forward, without sickling or bouncing against the supporting ankle.

Exercise 23

Chassé sauté 2nd, arms in 6th, four counts, two repetitions.

Students repeat Exercise 24 of the Second Class of this week.

Exercise 24

Piqué 2nd, arms in 6th, four counts.

Students repeat Exercise 25 of the Second Class of this week.

Exercise 25

Curtsey.

Twenty-First Week

§

FIRST CLASS

Students repeat the material of the Fifth Class of the Twentieth Week.

SECOND CLASS

Exercise 1

Warm up.

Exercise 2

Plié.

Exercise 3

Battement tendu en croix, hold the position when the foot is pointed and when it is closed, with different ports de bras, in 1st, introduction of the arm allongé devant.

Following the preparatory port de bras, bring the arm 5th.

On "and" 1, battement tendu devant; on 2, hold the position; on 3, close 1st; on 4, hold the position; on "and" 5, battement tendu devant; on 6, hold the position; on 7, close 1st; on 8, hold the position; on "and" 1, battement tendu 2nd while the arm opens 2nd; on 2, hold the position; on 3, close 1st; on 4, hold the position; on "and" 5, battement tendu 2nd; on 6, hold the position; on 7, close 1st with the arm coming down; on 8, hold the position; on "and" 1, battement tendu derrière, bringing the arm in 1st and extending it forward to an allongé position, with the head slightly inclined toward the right shoulder; on 2, hold the position; on 3, close 1st; on 4, hold the position; on "and" 5, battement tendu derrière; on 6, hold the position; on 7, close 1st, while the arm comes into 1st, straightening the head; on 8, hold the position; on "and" 1, battement tendu 2nd, opening the arm 2nd; on 2, hold the position; on 3, close 1st; on 4, hold the position; on "and" 5, battement tendu 2nd; on 6, hold the position; on 7, close 1st; on 8, hold the position, bringing the arm down. Repeat the exercise one more time, with the arm coming to 1st and 5th in the battement tendu devant. At the end, plié and relevé in 1st, with the arms in 1st.

Explanation. This exercise introduces different arm positions in coordination with the leg movements. In the position of the arm allongé, the arm is extended forward, slightly ascending in front of the working shoulder and softly curved, the palm of the hand faces down, and the fingers are elongated; the head is a bit tilted toward the working shoulder and the eyes are focused on a direction just above the fingers.

Music. The music is a medium tempo 4/4, or even a waltz.

Application. This is a good exercise to introduce the arm allongé for all ballet students. It is the standard arm position for the arabesque. The battement tendu is performed evenly, with no accent, so that the changes in the ports de bras are executed softly.

Exercise 4

Battement tendu en croix, two counts, four repetitions.

On "and" 1, battement tendu devant; on 2, close 5th devant; on "and" 3, battement tendu devant; on 4, close 5th; on "and" 5, battement tendu devant; on 6, close 5th; on "and" 7, battement tendu devant; on 8, close 5th. Repeat the exercise en croix en dehors, the first battement tendu 2nd closing 5th devant, since there is an even number of battements tendus in each direction. At the end, roll up and hold balance.

Explanation. Students are increasing the number of battements tendus in each direction in this exercise.

Exercise 5

Battement tendu en croix, bring the foot on the cou-de-pied, with extension, with port de bras, eight counts.

On "and" 1, battement tendu devant; on 2, hold the position; on "and," bend the knee sharply and bring the foot pointed on the cou-de-pied devant, closing the arm in 1st; on 3 and 4, hold the position; on 5, extend the leg devant, opening the arm 2nd; on 6, hold the position; on 7, close 5th devant; on 8, hold the position. Repeat the exercise en croix en dehors.

Explanation. Students are repeating Exercise 5 of the Fourth Class of the Twentieth Week, this time performed with a port de bras accompanying the leg movement. The coordination between the arm and the leg follows the common pattern of closing the arm in 1st when the leg bends and opening the arm 2nd when the leg stretches. Whereas the leg movement is sharp when bending to place the foot on the cou-de-pied, the port de bras is smoother. Still, the arm and the leg must be in position at the same time. This is a difficult balance to achieve.

Exercise 6

Battement jeté en croix, start in plié and stretch out, hold à la demi-hauteur, four counts, facing the barre.

On "and" 1, plié, brush the right foot, still in plié, extend the leg out devant, and stretch both legs at the same time; on 2, hold the position; on "and," lower the leg and point the foot onto the floor; on 3, hold the position; on 4, close 5th devant. Repeat the exercise en croix en dehors, with the last battement 2nd closing back.

Explanation. Students are practicing the exercise en croix en dehors.

Exercise 7

Battement jeté piqué en croix, bouncing on the count, in 1st, four counts.

On "and" 1, battement devant; on "and," bring the pointed foot down onto the floor; on 2, lift the leg devant again at the same height as in the previous battement; on "and," bring the pointed foot down; on 3, hold the position; on 4, close 1st. Repeat the exercise en croix en dehors.

Explanation. Students are repeating Exercise 7 of the Fifth Class of the Eighteenth Week, this time performed en croix and sideways.

Exercise 8

Rond de jambe à terre en dehors and en dedans, with port de bras, four counts.

Students repeat Exercise 7 of the Fifth Class of the Twentieth Week.

Exercise 9

Battement fondu en croix, with port de bras, eight counts.

Students repeat Exercise 9 of the Second Class of the Nineteenth Week.

Exercise 10

Battement frappé 2nd, plié with the foot in flexed position, two counts, temps lié 2nd, facing the barre.

On "and," bring the foot on the cou-de-pied devant, flexing the working foot with a sharp plié on the supporting leg; on 1, hold the position; on 2, extend the leg 2nd, pointing the foot sharply onto the floor, while stretching the supporting leg; on 3, bring the foot, flexing it on the cou-de-pied derrière, with a plié on the supporting leg; on 4, extend the leg 2nd, stretching the supporting leg; on 5, bring the working foot down in 2nd with a plié on both legs; on 6, transfer the weight onto the right leg, pointing the left foot and stretching both legs; on 7, close 5th, left foot front; on 8, hold the position. Repeat the whole exercise one more time.

Explanation. Students are practicing bringing the foot on the cou-de-pied (flexing the foot here is easier than wrapping it), with a sharp plié on the supporting leg. Students must push both knees to the sides, while executing the plié with the working foot on the cou-de-pied. The working foot must freeze its position on the cou-de-pied. The exercise also includes a simple temps lié 2nd to change feet; whereas the plié in the frappé is sharp, the plié in the temps lié is smooth.

Music. The tempo will be medium-to-slow with sharp beats.

Exercise 11

Petits battements, two on the count, accent derrière, hold on the cou-de-pied, facing the barre.

Start with the right foot back.

On "and," bring the foot on the cou-de-pied derrière; on 1 and 2, hold the position; on "and," bring the foot on the cou-de-pied devant; on 3, bring the foot on the cou-de-pied derrière; on 4, hold the position; on "and," bring the foot on the cou-de-pied devant; on 5, bring the foot on the cou-de-pied derrière; on 6, hold the position; on "and," bring the foot on the cou-de-pied devant; on 7, bring the foot on the cou-de-pied derrière;

on 8, hold the position. Repeat the exercise one more time. At the end, hold the position on the cou-de-pied derrière and balance.

Explanation. Students are repeating Exercise 12 of the Second Class of the Twentieth Week, except the accent falls when the foot is on the cou-de-pied derrière.

Exercise 12

Adagio: lift the leg en croix, eight counts, hold three counts in the air, review.

On "and" 1 and 2, brush the front foot and lift the leg; from 3 to 5, hold the position; on 6, lower the leg and point the toes onto the floor; on 7, close 5th devant; on 8, hold the position. Repeat the exercise en croix en dehors. At the end, relevé in 5th and hold balance.

Explanation. This time students are performing the full exercise en croix en dehors.

Exercise 13

Grand battement en croix, three counts, one count hold.

Students repeat Exercise 14 of the Fourth Class of the Twentieth Week.

Exercise 14

Pied sur la barre 2nd, devant, and derrière, plié and bend.

Students repeat Exercise 15 of the Fifth Class of the Seventeenth Week and add the movement that follows when the working leg has rotated from 4th position devant to 4th position derrière.

On 1 and 2, plié and stretch; on 3 and 4, repeat; on 5 and 6, bring the arm in 5th; on 7 and 8, bend forward keeping the arm in 5th; on 1 and 2, straighten up; on 3 and 4, cambré, keeping the arm in 5th; on 5 and 6, straighten up; on 7 and 8, open the arm 2nd and release the leg from the barre and hold it in arabesque before closing 5th derrière, bringing the arm down.

Explanation. Students are adding the bending forward and backward when the working leg is in the back. As said before, the barre must be at a proper height so that students are able to pull up their torso. They must keep the turn-out of their working leg and the toes stretched at all times, even when they bend forward. The weight remains on the supporting leg.

Exercise 15

Battement tendu en croix, in 1st, four counts, two counts, two repetitions.

On "and" 1, battement tendu devant; on 2, hold the position; on 3, close 1st; on 4, hold the position; on "and" 5, battement tendu devant; on 6, close 1st; on "and" 7, battement tendu devant; on 8, close 1st. Repeat the exercise en croix en dehors. At the end, roll up in 1st and hold balance with the arms in low 1st.

Explanation. Students are repeating Exercise 3 of the Second Class of the Twentieth Week, this time performed in the center. Notice the ending of the exercise, which requires students to hold balance on demi-pointes with the arms in low 1st.

Exercise 16

Rond de jambe à terre en dehors, four counts.

Students repeat Exercise 18 of the Fourth Class of the Twentieth Week.

Exercise 17

Adagio: lift the leg devant, 2nd, and derrière, arabesque, with port de bras, eight counts, hold three counts in the air.

Students repeat Exercise 18 of the Fifth Class of the Twentieth Week.

Exercise 18

Échappé 2nd on demi-pointes, without changing feet, hold on demi-pointes, four counts, facing the barre.

Students repeat Exercise 19 of the Fifth Class of the Twentieth Week.

Exercise 19

Preparation for relevé, cou-de-pied derrière, eight counts, facing the barre.

On "and" 1, plié and relevé 5th; on 2, hold the position; on 3, bring the back foot (left) on the cou-de-pied derrière, keeping the head turned toward the right; on 4, hold the position; on 5, bring the foot into 5th on demi-pointes; on 6, hold the position; on 7 and 8, come down into plié and stretch. Repeat three more times with the right foot front.

Explanation. Students are repeating Exercise 21 of the Second Class of the Twentieth Week, this time bringing the back foot on the cou-de-pied. The position of the foot is just above the raised heel. The tempo is increased since the whole exercise is done on eight counts.

Exercise 20

Pas de bourrée dessous, with port de bras, four counts, review.

Following the preparatory port de bras, bring the arms down.

On "and," bring the back foot on the cou-de-pied derrière, with a plié on the supporting leg, bringing the arms in 1st; on 1, hold the position; on 2, step onto the left foot on demi-pointe, and then stretch both legs; on "and," open the right leg and the arms 2nd, with both legs still stretched; on 3, step onto the right foot on demi-pointe in 2nd, transferring the weight onto the right leg; on "and," close 5th, left foot front in plié, and close the arms down; on 4, stretch both knees. Repeat three more times, alternating legs.

Explanation. Students are repeating Exercise 22 of the First Class of the Sixteenth Week, applying the same head positions.

Exercise 21

Pas de bourrée dessus, without changing feet, four counts, facing the barre.

On "and," bring the front foot on the cou-de-pied devant, with a plié on the supporting leg; on 1, hold the position; on 2, step onto the front foot on demi-pointe and stretch both legs; on "and," open the left leg 2nd, with both legs still stretched; on 3, step onto the left foot on demi-pointe, transferring the weight onto the left leg; on "and," close 5th, right foot front in plié; on 4, stretch both knees. Repeat three more times toward the left. Repeat the exercise with the left foot front, traveling toward the right.

Explanation. This is a less common pas de bourrée, especially done by itself; it is often combined with the pas de bourrée dessous. In this pas de bourrée, the front foot comes onto the cou-de-pied and goes up onto demi-pointe, directly from the plié, in front of the supporting leg. The working foot does not sickle when it is on the cou-de-pied devant, with the side of the

little toe firmly pressed against the talus of the supporting foot.

Exercise 22

Changement de pied, two counts, one count hold, facing the barre.

Students repeat Exercise 22 of the Fourth Class of the Twentieth Week.

Exercise 23

Soubresaut in 5th landing on the back foot, and the other foot on the cou-de-pied devant, four counts, facing the barre.

Students repeat Exercise 22 of the Fifth Class of the Twentieth Week.

Exercise 24

Marche with passé à terre in plié, in 1st, arms in low 1st, in diagonal.

Start in the upper left corner of the studio facing the lower right corner. Bring the arms down following the preparatory port de bras; the head is turned de face.

On "and" 1, battement tendu devant with the right foot, bringing the arms in low 1st; on 2, hold the position; on "and" 3, step onto the right foot in plié, and brush the left foot in 1st from back to front still in plié, then extend the left foot devant, stretching both legs; on 4, hold the position; on "and" 5, step onto the left foot in plié, brush the right foot through 1st in plié, then extend the right foot devant, stretching both legs; on 6, hold the position. Repeat the same pattern to the end of the diagonal. Repeat the exercise in the other diagonal.

Explanation. The passé à terre is performed in plié in this exercise. Students initiate the stepping forward by actively pushing the front heel forward. As soon as the front foot comes down in plié, the other comes forward through 1st in plié, stretching both legs by the time the working foot is fully pointed onto the floor.

Exercise 25

Curtsey.

THIRD CLASS

Students repeat the material of the Second Class of this week.

FOURTH CLASS

Exercise 1

Warm up.

Exercise 2

Plié.

Exercise 3

Battement tendu en croix, with different ports de bras, in 1st, introduction of the arm allongé devant.

Students repeat Exercise 3 of the Second Class of this week.

Exercise 4

Battement tendu en croix, two counts, four repetitions.

Students repeat Exercise 4 of the Second Class of this week.

Exercise 5

Battement tendu en croix, bring the foot on the cou-de-pied, with extension, with port de bras, eight counts.

Students repeat Exercise 5 of the Second Class of this week.

Exercise 6

Battement jeté en croix, start in plié and stretch out, four counts, facing the barre.

Students repeat Exercise 6 of the Second Class of this week.

Exercise 7

Battement jeté piqué en croix, bouncing on the count, in 1st, four counts.

Students repeat Exercise 7 of the Second Class of this week.

Exercise 8

Battement jeté 2nd, accent out, in 1st, two counts, facing the barre.

On "and," battement jeté 2nd; on 1, hold the position; on "and," point the foot onto the floor; on 2, close in 1st. Repeat three more times with the right foot. Repeat the whole exercise one more time. At the end, plié and relevé in 1st.

Explanation. The lifting of the working leg is performed more rapidly in this exercise. There is a slight holding of the leg à la demi-hauteur, and when the foot is pointed on the floor before closing. The goal here is to bring the leg quickly in position in the air, hold it slightly, and then quickly bring it down. This exercise works the sharpness and vivacity of the movement, crucial qualities for small allegro and rapid pointe work.

Exercise 9

Rond de jambe à terre en dehors and en dedans, with port de bras, four counts.

Students repeat Exercise 7 of the Fifth Class of the Twentieth Week.

Exercise 10

Battement fondu en croix, with port de bras, eight counts.

Students repeat Exercise 9 of the Second Class of the Nineteenth Week.

Exercise 11

Battement frappé 2nd, plié with the foot in flexed position, two counts, temps lié 2nd, facing the barre.

Students repeat Exercise 10 of the Second Class of this week.

Exercise 12

Petits battements, two on the count, accent derrière, hold on the cou-de-pied, facing the barre.

Students repeat Exercise 11 of the Second Class of this week.

Exercise 13

Adagio: lift the leg en croix, eight counts, hold three counts in the air, review.

Students repeat Exercise 12 of the Second Class of this week.

Exercise 14

Grand battement en croix, three counts, one count hold.

Students repeat Exercise 14 of the Fourth Class of the Twentieth Week.

Exercise 15

Pied sur la barre 2nd, devant, and derrière, plié and bend.

Students repeat Exercise 14 of the Second Class of this week.

CENTER

Exercise 16

Battement tendu en croix, in 1st, four counts, two counts, two repetitions.

Students repeat Exercise 15 of the Second Class of this week.

Exercise 17

Rond de jambe à terre, en dehors and en dedans, with port de bras, four counts.

Following the preparatory port de bras, bring the arms down.

On "and" 1, battement tendu devant, bringing the arms in 1st; on 2, rond de jambe en dehors to 2nd, opening the arms 2nd; on 3, rond de jambe en dehors to 4th derrière, keeping the arms 2nd; on 4, close 5th derrière, bringing the arms down. On "and" 5, battement tendu devant with the left foot, bringing the arms 1st; on 6, rond de jambe en dehors to 2nd, opening the arm 2nd; on 7, rond de jambe en dehors to 4th derrière, keeping the arm 2nd; on 8, close 5th derrière, closing the arms down.

On "and" 1, battement tendu derrière with the left foot, bringing the arms in 1st; on 2, rond de jambe en dedans to 2nd, opening the arms 2nd; on 3, rond de jambe en dedans to 4th devant, keeping the arms 2nd; on 4, close 5th devant, bringing the arms down. On "and" 5, battement tendu derrière with the right foot, bringing the arms 1st; on 6, rond de jambe en dedans to 2nd, opening the arm 2nd; on 7, rond de jambe en dedans to 4th devant, keeping the arm 2nd; on 8, close 5th devant, closing the arms down.

Explanation. The rond de jambe exercise is performed en dehors and en dedans with a port de bras in the center. It is important to pull up onto the supporting leg in this exercise, especially to and from the 4th position derrière.

Exercise 18

Adagio: lift the leg devant, 2nd, and derrière, arabesque, with port de bras, eight counts, hold three counts in the air.

Students repeat Exercise 18 of the Fifth Class of the Twentieth Week.

Exercise 19

Échappé 2nd on demi-pointes, without changing feet, hold on demi-pointes, four counts, facing the barre.

Students repeat Exercise 19 of the Fifth Class of the Twentieth Week.

Exercise 20

Preparation for relevé, cou-de-pied derrière, eight counts, facing the barre.

Students repeat Exercise 19 of the Second Class of this week.

Exercise 21

Pas de bourrée dessous, with port de bras, four counts, review.

Students repeat Exercise 20 of the Second Class of this week.

Exercise 22

Pas de bourrée dessus, without changing feet, four counts, facing the barre.

Students repeat Exercise 21 of the Second Class of this week.

Exercise 23

Preparation for relevé retiré devant and derriére, without changing feet, eight counts, facing the barre.

On "and" 1, plié and relevé 5th; on 2, hold the position; on 3, bring the front leg to a retiré devant, with the head still turned toward the right; on 4, hold the position; on 5, bring the foot into 5th on demi-pointes; on 6, hold the position; on 7 and 8, come down into plié and stretch. Repeat three more times. Repeat the exercise, bringing the back leg into retiré derrière.

Explanation. The relevé retiré is still broken down into eight counts. When lifting the leg, students keep the working knee well to the side, without sickling the foot and without raising the hip. When closing the retiré derrière, especially, the knee is pulled to the side until closing 5th. Whereas students keep their head straight in the retiré they have practiced in adagio exercises in preparation for the developpé, they turn their head (always at about a 45° angle) for the retiré practiced in the relevé exercises, unless it is used in preparation for pirouettes. Basically, the movement follows the same pattern used in the petits battements and frappés exercises. For the retiré devant, the head is turned toward the side of the leg in retiré devant; for the retiré derrière, the head is turned toward the supporting leg. Notice, however, that the position of the head can vary according to the orientation of the dancer and the position of the arms: for instance, if the movement is performed de face in the center, the head in the retiré derrière will be turned toward the working leg; whereas, if it is done in croisé, the head will be turned away from the working leg. Furthermore, depending on the movement that follows the retiré, such pattern may vary to avoid too many turns of the head that could destabilize dancers.

Exercise 24

Changement de pied, two counts, one count hold, facing the barre.

Students repeat Exercise 22 of the Fourth Class of the Twentieth Week.

Exercise 25

Soubresaut in 5th landing on the back foot, the other foot on the cou-de-pied devant, four counts, facing the barre.

Students repeat Exercise 22 of the Fifth Class of the Twentieth Week.

Exercise 26

Marche with passé à terre in plié, in 1st, arms in low 1st, in diagonal.

Students repeat Exercise 24 of the Second Class of this week.

Exercise 27

Curtsey.

FIFTH CLASS

Exercise 1

Warm up.

Exercise 2

Plié.

Exercise 3

Battement tendu en croix, with different ports de bras, introduction of the arm allongé devant, in 1st.

Students repeat Exercise 3 of the Second Class of this week.

Exercise 4

Battement tendu en croix, two counts, four repetitions.

Students repeat Exercise 4 of the Second Class of this week.

Exercise 5

Battement tendu en croix, bring the foot on the cou-de-pied, with extension, with port de bras, eight counts.

Students repeat Exercise 5 of the Second Class of this week.

Exercise 6

Battement jeté piqué en croix, bouncing on the count, in 1st, four counts.

Students repeat Exercise 7 of the Second Class of this week.

Exercise 7

Battement jeté 2nd, accent out, in 1st, two counts, facing the barre.

Students repeat Exercise 8 of the Fourth Class of this week.

Exercise 8

Rond de jambe à terre en dehors and en dedans, passé à terre, four counts, facing the barre.

On "and" 1, battement tendu devant; on 2, rond de jambe to 2nd, without hold; on 3, rond de jambe en dehors to 4th derrière; on 4, hold the position; on "and" 5, brush through 1st and extend the leg devant, with the head turning slightly toward the right, repeating the rond de jambe en dehors and closing 5th derrière, turning the head slightly toward the left.

On "and" 1, battement tendu derrière; on 2, rond de jambe to 2nd, without hold; on 3, rond de jambe en dedans to 4th devant; on 4, hold the position; on "and" 5, brush through 1st and extend the leg derrière, with the head turning slightly toward the left, repeating the rond de jambe en dedans and closing 5th devant. Repeat the exercise one more time. At the end, roll up in 5th and balance with the arms in 5th.

Explanation. In this exercise, students are performing the ronds de jambe without closing, by just brushing the foot through 1st. Even though there is no pause, the working leg must still remain turned out, especially while going through 2nd. Again, to keep the hips in place, students are facing the barre.

Application. Before students are introduced to this exercise, all the preliminary rond de jambe exercises, practiced so far, should have prepared students to perform the proper brushing through 1st. This preparation is necessary to ensure the quality of the movement for all beginners.

Exercise 9

Battement fondu en croix, with port de bras, eight counts.

Students repeat Exercise 9 of the Second Class of the Nineteenth Week.

Exercise 10

Battement frappé 2nd, plié with the foot in flexed position, two counts, temps lié 2nd, facing the barre.

Students repeat Exercise 10 of the Second Class of this week.

Exercise 11

Petits battements, two on the count, accent derrière, hold on the cou-de-pied, facing the barre.

Students repeat Exercise 11 of the Second Class of this week.

Exercise 12

Adagio: lift the leg en croix, eight counts, hold three counts in the air, review.

Students repeat Exercise 12 of the Second Class of this week.

Exercise 13

Adagio: retiré devant and derrière, close directly in plié, without changing and changing feet, four counts, facing the barre.

Without changing feet: on "and," bring the front foot pointed on the cou-de-pied; on 1 and 2, slide the side of the small toe along the leg to the knee level; on "and" 3, slide the foot down,

still in front of the leg; on "and" 4, close 5th devant in plié and stretch.

Changing feet from back to front: on "and," bring the back foot onto the cou-de-pied; on 5 and 6, slide it up along the leg to the knee level; on "and," graze the toes around the supporting knee; on 7, slide the foot down; on "and" 8, close 5th devant in plié and stretch. Repeat one more time. After adjusting the distance from the barre if needed, repeat the exercise.

Explanation. Students are repeating Exercise 12 of the First Class of the Sixteenth Week, this time performed on four counts, alternating closing without changing feet and changing feet. The changing is done only from back to front here. As the leg bends and the foot slides up, the hip is not raised. The thigh of the working leg rises slightly (not the hip!) when transferring sides, since the toes are grazing against the back of the supporting leg. When coming down, the knee does not come forward and is kept to the side. Students start the exercise a bit further from the barre to allow the changing of feet closing devant.

Music. The tempo is slightly slower than the one used for prior exercises of retiré, since this time the retiré is performed on four counts.

Exercise 14

Grand battement en croix, three counts, one count hold.

Students repeat Exercise 14 of the Fourth Class of the Twentieth Week.

Exercise 15

Pied sur la barre 2nd, devant, and derrière, plié and bend.

Students repeat Exercise 14 of the Second Class of this week.

CENTER

Exercise 16

Battement tendu en croix, plié when pointing, in 1st, four counts, review.

On "and" 1, battement tendu devant; on 2, plié, with the foot still pointed; on 3, stretch the supporting leg; on 4, close 1st. Repeat the exercise en croix en dehors.

Explanation. This exercise is performed mainly for review. In the battement tendu derrière, students must not crush their toe, but must instead keep the foot lightly pointed on the floor. In each plié, the knee remains above the toes.

Exercise 17

Rond de jambe à terre en dehors and en dedans, with port de bras, four counts.

Students repeat Exercise 17 of the Fourth Class of this week.

Exercise 18

Échappé 2nd on demi-pointes, changing feet, hold on demi-pointes, four counts, facing the barre.

On "and" 1, plié and slide the balls of the feet along the floor, opening equally both feet in 2nd; on 2, hold the position; on 3, bring both feet into 5th in plié, left foot front; on 4, stretch both knees. Repeat three more times, changing feet at each closing.

Explanation. This exercise is similar to the one practiced in Exercise 19 of the Fifth Class of the Twentieth Week, except that this time students change feet when closing.

Exercise 19

Preparation for relevé, on the cou-de-pied derrière, eight counts, facing the barre.

Students repeat Exercise 19 of the Second Class of this week.

Exercise 20

Pas de bourrée dessous, with port de bras, four counts, review.

Students repeat Exercise 20 of the Second Class of this week.

Exercise 21

Pas de bourrée dessus, without changing feet, four counts, facing the barre.

Students repeat Exercise 21 of the Second Class of this week.

Exercise 22

Preparation for relevé retiré devant and derrière, without changing feet, eight counts, facing the barre.

Students repeat Exercise 23 of the Fourth Class of this week.

Exercise 23

Changement de pied, two counts, one count hold, facing the barre.

Students repeat Exercise 22 of the Fourth Class of the Twentieth Week.

Exercise 24

Soubresaut in 5th, landing on the front foot and the back foot, the working foot on the cou-de-pied derrière and devant, two counts, one count hold, facing the barre.

On "and," plié and push off the floor keeping the legs tight in 5th; on 1, land in plié, with the left foot on the cou-de-pied derrière; on 2, close in 5th in plié; on 3, stretch both legs, on 4, hold the position. Repeat the exercise bringing the right foot on the cou-de-pied devant when landing on the left foot. Repeat the exercise one more time with the right foot front.

Explanation. The jump is performed on the count this time, and students alternate the landing with the working foot on the cou-de-pied derrière and devant. Both legs are held tightly together in the soubresaut part of the jump, and the bending of the leg is sharp. In the landing, the foot on the cou-de-pied does not bounce.

Music. Music usually played for grand allegro would fit the exercise well, even though it is not a large allegro exercise. Students need time to get some height and tighten their legs in 5th before landing on one foot.

Exercise 25

Marche with passé à terre in plié, in 1st, arms in low 1st, in diagonal.

Students repeat Exercise 24 of the Second Class of this week.

Exercise 26

Curtsey.

Twenty-Second Week

𝄞

FIRST CLASS

Students repeat the material of the Fifth Class of the Twenty-First Week.

SECOND CLASS

Exercise 1

Warm up.

Exercise 2

Plié.

Exercise 3

Battement tendu en croix, plié when pointing, in 1st, with port de bras, four counts.

Following the preparatory port de bras, bring the arm down.

On "and" 1, battement tendu devant, bringing the arm in 1st; on 2, plié on the supporting leg, with the arm coming up in 5th; on 3, stretch both knees with the arm opening 2nd; on 4, close in 1st with the arm coming down. Repeat en croix en dehors.

Explanation. This is a more involved coordination between the arm and the leg: the port de bras changes for each movement of the leg. The head accompanies the movement of the arm accordingly. The hips remain straight.

Music. A slow-to-medium tempo waltz is a good musical choice so that students have time to adjust to these different ports de bras.

Exercise 4

Battement tendu en croix, bring the foot down, four counts.

On "and" 1, battement tendu devant; on 2, bring the foot down in 4th position, transferring the weight onto both legs; on 3, transfer the weight onto the back leg, pointing the right foot; on 4, close 5th devant. Repeat the exercise en croix en dehors. At the end, roll up and hold the position in 5th.

Explanation. Students are practicing the exercise en croix en dehors, bringing the foot flat on the floor in all positions. Since there is a transfer of weight in the movement forward and backward, the hand slides along accordingly. In putting down the foot in 4th devant and derrière, the foot, when coming down flat, is brought slightly closer to the supporting leg; otherwise, the 4th would be too wide, thus making it difficult to keep the turn-out and the hips straight. If needed, students may also have to open their working leg out a little bit so that the hips remain straight and both legs are turned out. The width of the 4th is no more than one and a half feet. Students release the barre to remain centered when doing the exercise 2nd. Releasing the barre often during the exercise helps to stay centered throughout the exercise.

Exercise 5

Battement jeté 2nd, accent out, in 1st, two counts, facing the barre.

Students repeat Exercise 8 of the Fourth Class of the Twenty-First Week.

Exercise 6

Battement jeté en croix, accent out, two counts, two count hold.

On "and," battement jeté devant direct; on 1, hold the position; on "and," bring the foot pointing on the floor; on 2, close 5th; on 3 and 4, hold the position. Repeat the exercise en croix en dehors. At the end, roll up and hold balance.

Explanation. Students are performing the exercise en croix in 5th. The same sharpness must be applied. However, there are two counts holding in the closing so that students have time to re-center and spread their weight onto both feet.

Music. The tempo is slightly accelerated. A sharp 2/4 rag would work well.

Application. The exercise can also be practiced facing the barre and in 1st.

Exercise 7

Rond de jambe à terre en dehors and en dedans, passé à terre, four counts, facing the barre.

Students repeat Exercise 8 of the Fifth Class of the Twenty-First Week.

Exercise 8

Preparation for rond de jambe soutenu 2nd, no rotation, with direct battement, facing the barre, review.

On "and" 1, battement 2nd; on 2, hold the position; on 3, bend the working leg without moving the thigh so that the tips of the toes touch the back of the supporting leg; on 4, stretch the leg in 2nd again; on 5, bend the working leg; on 6, stretch the leg 2nd again; on 7, lower the leg, and point the foot onto the floor; on 8, close 5th devant. Repeat the exercise one more time, closing derrière.

Explanation. Students are reviewing Exercise 11 of the Second Class of the Eighteenth Week one more time before adding the rotation. Students are reminded to keep the thigh from moving in the bending and unbending of the leg. Students should be able to keep their leg at the same height throughout the exercise, even if their leg is higher than the demi-hauteur.

Exercise 9

Battement frappé en croix, plié with the foot in flexed position, transfer of supporting leg, two counts, facing the barre.

On "and," bring the foot on the cou-de-pied devant, flexing it, with a sharp plié on the supporting leg; on 1, hold the position; on 2, extend the leg front, pointing the foot onto the floor, and stretching the supporting leg; on 3, bring the foot on the cou-de-pied devant in plié; on 4, extend 2nd; on 5, bring the foot on the cou-de-pied derrière; on 6, extend the leg derrière; on 7, bring the foot on the cou-de-pied derrière; on 8, extend the leg 2nd; on 1, bring the foot down in 2nd with stretched legs; on 2, hold the position in 2nd; on 3, point the left foot, while transferring the weight on the right foot; on 4, hold the position; on 5, close 5th, left foot front; from 6 to 8, hold the position.

Explanation. Students are practicing the exercise en croix, switching legs in between series

to change working leg, since performing this exercise with eight sharp pliés in a row would be quite demanding on the supporting leg.

Exercise 10

Petits battements, two on the count, accent devant and derrière, hold on the cou-de-pied, facing the barre.

Following the preparatory port de bras, battement tendu 2nd.

On "and," bring the foot on the cou-de-pied devant; on 1 and 2, hold the position; on "and," bring the foot on the cou-de-pied derrière; on 3, bring the foot on the cou-de-pied devant; on 4, hold the position; on "and," bring the foot on the cou-de-pied derrière; on 5, bring the foot on the cou-de-pied devant; on 6, hold the position; on 7, extend the leg 2nd; on 8, hold the position.

On "and," bring the foot on the cou-de-pied derrière; on 1 and 2, hold the position; on "and," bring the foot on the cou-de-pied devant; on 3, bring the foot on the cou-de-pied derrière; on 4, hold the position; on "and," bring the foot on the cou-de-pied devant; on 5, bring the foot on the cou-de-pied derrière; on 6, hold the position; on 7, extend the leg 2nd; on 8, hold the position. Repeat the exercise one more time.

Explanation. This time students are alternating series of petits battements with the accent devant and petits battements with the accent derrière. Like in the previous petits battements exercise with accent, the adductors are very active to bring the working foot on the cou-de-pied each time with the accent. Even though the tempo is sharper with a definite accent on the cou-de-pied, the same principles studied so far should apply, especially the immobility of the thigh and the passage through 2nd. Notice that the first beat is initiated from the 2nd position, with the lower limb bending sharply and the foot coming quickly into position.

Exercise 11

Adagio: retiré devant and derrière, close directly in plié, without changing and changing feet, four counts, facing the barre.

Students repeat Exercise 13 of the Fifth Class of the Twenty-First Week.

Exercise 12

Grand battement 2nd, two counts, two count hold, facing the barre.

On "and" 1, grand battement 2nd; on "and," point the foot onto the floor; on 2, close 5th devant; on 3 and 4, hold the position. Repeat three more times with the right foot. Repeat the whole exercise one more time.

Explanation. Students are introduced to the grand battement performed on two counts each, with two counts holding in the closing to give time to students to re-center with their weight on both feet. To introduce the new timing, students are performing the battement only 2nd.

Exercise 13

Pied sur la barre 2nd, devant, and derrière, plié and bend.

Students repeat Exercise 14 of the Second Class of the Twenty-First Week.

CENTER

Exercise 14

Battement tendu en croix, plié when pointing, in 1st, four counts, review.

Students repeat Exercise 16 of the Fifth Class of the Twenty-First Week.

Exercise 15

Battement tendu 2nd, en descendant and en remontant, two counts.

On "and" 1, battement tendu 2nd with the left foot; on 2, close 5th devant; on "and" 3, battement tendu 2nd with the right foot; on 4, close 5th devant. Repeat one more time.

On "and" 1, battement tendu 2nd with the right foot; on 2, close 5th derrière; on "and" 3, battement tendu 2nd with the left foot; on 4, close 5th derrière. Repeat one more time.

Explanation. Students are revisiting the battement tendu exercise that was introduced in Exercise 19 of the Fifth Class of the Ninth Week. This time each battement tendu is executed on two counts instead of four counts. The head moves accordingly and the arms remain 2nd.

Music. The tempo is not too fast, so that students have time to brush their foot out and in.

Exercise 16

Preparation for chassé à terre, forward and backward, with port de bras, four counts.

Following the preparatory port de bras, bring the arms down.

On 1, plié; on "and" 2, still in plié, slide the front foot forward so that both feet are in 4th position, with the arms in 1st; on 3, stretch both legs with the right leg becoming the supporting leg and the left leg becoming the working leg, the left foot pointing, and opening the arms 2nd; on 4, close 5th derrière, bringing the arms down.

On 5, plié; on "and" 6, still in plié, slide the back foot backward so that both feet are in 4th position, bringing the arms in 1st; on 7, stretch both legs with the left leg becoming the supporting leg and the right leg becoming the working leg, the right foot pointing, and opening the arms 2nd; on 8, close 5th devant, bringing the arms down. Repeat the exercise one more time.

Explanation. Students are repeating Exercise 9 of the Second Class of the Twentieth Week, this time performed in the center with a port de bras.

Exercise 17

Adagio: grand plié in 1st, port de bras performed separately.

On 1 and 2, plié and stretch; on 3 and 4, repeat the plié and stretch; on 5 and 6, deep demi-plié, at the end of which the heels go off the floor to allow the bending of the knees further into a grand plié; on 7 and 8, bring the heels down into a demi-plié, and stretch the legs; on "and" 1 and 2, bring the arms down; on 3, bring the arms in 1st; on 4, bring the arms to 5th; on 5 and 6, hold the position; on "and" 7 and 8, open the arms 2nd. Repeat the exercise one more time. After a pause, repeat the exercise.

Explanation. Students are practicing the grand plié in 1st in the center. The pressing down of the heels into the floor in the descending and ascending part of the grand plié, seeking depth of the demi-plié each time, must be observed. It will greatly help students to find balance in this challenging exercise. To make the exercise easier, the arms remain 2nd.

Exercise 18

Échappé 2nd on demi-pointes, changing feet, hold on demi-pointes, four counts, facing the barre.

Students repeat Exercise 18 of the Fifth Class of the Twenty-First Week.

Exercise 19

Pas de bourrée dessus, changing feet, with head rotation, four counts, facing the barre.

On "and," bring the front foot on the cou-de-pied devant with a plié on the supporting leg, and with the head still turned slightly to the right; on 1, hold the position; on 2, step onto the front foot onto demi-pointe in front of the supporting foot, and stretch both legs; on "and," open the left leg 2nd, with both legs stretched, straightening the head; on 3, step onto the left foot on demi-pointe and transfer the weight onto the left leg; on "and," close 5th, left foot front in plié, turning the head toward the left; on 4, stretch both knees. Repeat the exercise three more times, alternating legs.

Explanation. This time students are changing feet when closing the pas de bourrée. Like in previous pas de bourrée exercises, the head turns toward the side of the front foot and stays de face when the legs are 2nd.

Exercise 20

Preparation for relevé retiré devant and derrière, without changing feet, eight counts, facing the barre.

Students repeat Exercise 23 of the Fourth Class of the Twenty-First Week.

Exercise 21

Soubresaut in 2nd and 1st, on the count, five repetitions, facing the barre.

Following the preparatory port de bras, battement tendu 2nd, and bring the foot down.

On "and," plié and push off the floor, stretching the toes and knees; on 1, land in plié in 2nd; on "and," push off the floor again; on 2, land in plié in 2nd; on "and," push off the floor; on 3, land in plié; on "and," push off the floor; on 4, land in plié; on "and," push off the floor; on 5, land in plié; on 6, stretch the knees; on 7 and 8,

hold the position. Repeat three more times. After a pause, repeat the exercise in 1st.

Explanation. Students have already practiced the exercise with two jumps in a row. Here they are performing the exercise with five jumps in a row, with a holding to end the musical phrase. Students who have not learned to breathe properly will have difficulty catching their breath in this exercise. They may not be able to finish the exercise, or they may do so badly; the more out of breath students get, the shorter the plié becomes and the more offbeat students' jumps will be. The legs may also turn in more than they should in the landings.

Exercise 22

Soubresaut in 5th, landing on the front foot and the back foot, the working foot on the cou-de-pied derrière and devant, two counts, one count hold, facing the barre.

Students repeat Exercise 24 of the Fifth Class of the Twenty-First Week.

Exercise 23

Assemblé 2nd, en descendant and en remontant, two counts, one count hold, review.

On "and," plié; on 1, brush the back foot and extend the leg 2nd, while pushing off the floor with the supporting leg, stretch both legs in the air; on 2, land in plié in 5th, left foot front; on 3, straighten up the knees; on 4, hold the position. Repeat three more times bringing the back foot front each time.

On "and," plié; on 1, brush the front foot and extend the leg 2nd, while pushing off the floor with the supporting leg, stretch both legs in the air; on 2, land in plié in 5th, left foot front; on 3, straighten up the knees; on 4, hold the position. Repeat three more times bringing the front foot back each time.

Explanation. Students are reviewing the exercise of the assemblé that was practiced in Exercise 23 of the Fifth Class of the Eighteenth Week, applying the same head positions learned previously.

Exercise 24

Curtsey.

THIRD CLASS

Students repeat the material of the Second Class.

FOURTH CLASS

Exercise 1

Warm up.

Exercise 2

Plié.

Exercise 3

Battement tendu en croix, plié when pointing, in 1st, with port de bras, four counts.

Students repeat Exercise 3 of the Second Class of this week.

Exercise 4

Battement tendu en croix, bring the foot down, four counts.

Students repeat Exercise 4 of the Second Class of this week.

Exercise 5

Battement jeté en croix, accent out, two counts, two count hold.

Students repeat Exercise 6 of the Second Class of this week.

Exercise 6

Battement jeté 2nd, two counts, facing the barre.

On "and," battement jeté 2nd; on 1, hold the position; on "and," point the foot on the floor, on 2, close 5th devant. Repeat three more times with the right foot. Repeat the whole exercise one more time.

Explanation. Students are repeating Exercise 8 of the Fourth Class of the Twenty-First Week, this time performed in 5th. Each closing is as tight as possible. Students are not holding the pointing of the working foot on the floor before closing, but the touch down of the pointed foot must still be noticeable. The practice of observing the pointing of the working foot until the toes touch the floor, as tedious as it may seem, will be rewarding later on in practice, when it is time to perform faster movements like in small allegro and pointe work. Instead of releasing the pointing of the working foot prematurely when closing the leg, as it is often seen among ballet students, they will keep their foot pointed as long as possible, thus bringing sharpness and cleanness to the movement, no matter how fast it goes.

Music. The tempo is sharp and dynamic.

Exercise 7

Rond de jambe à terre en dehors and en dedans, passé à terre, four counts, facing the barre.

Students repeat Exercise 8 of the Fifth Class of the Twenty-First Week.

Exercise 8

Preparation for rond de jambe soutenu 2nd, no rotation, direct battement, facing the barre, review.

Students repeat Exercise 8 of the Second Class of this week.

Exercise 9

Battement frappé en croix, plié with the foot in flexed position, transfer of supporting leg, two counts, facing the barre.

Students repeat Exercise 9 of the Second Class of this week.

Exercise 10

Petits battements, two on the count, accent devant and derrière, hold on the cou-de-pied, facing the barre.

Students repeat Exercise 10 of the Second Class of this week.

Exercise 11

Adagio: retiré devant, close directly without plié, four counts, grand fendu, facing the barre.

On "and," bring the foot pointed on the cou-de-pied devant; on 1 and 2, slide the foot to the retiré position; on "and" 3, slide down to the cou-de-pied; on 4, close 5th devant. Repeat the exercise with the left leg in a retiré derriére.

On "and" 1, battement tendu derrière with the left foot; on 2, hold the position; on 3 and 4, slide the back foot further back with a plié on the front leg, keeping the back foot flat, and bring the arms 2nd, releasing the barre; on 5 and 6, bring both arms to 5th; on 7 and 8, open them 2nd; on "and" 1 and 2, pull up, transferring the weight onto the front leg, stretching the front leg and pointing the back foot; on 3, hold the position; on 4, close 5th position, on 5 and 6, battement tendu 2nd with the left leg and close 5th left foot front, bringing the arms down; on 7 and 8, bring the arms in 1st and rest the hands on the barre to repeat the exercise with the left foot front.

Explanation. Students have already practiced the retiré with the closing into 5th with a plié. Here they are closing without plié, which can be challenging, especially when closing 5th derrière. In order to keep the turn-out of the foot at all times, students bring their foot slightly off the cou-de-pied position, bringing the big toe first onto the floor, then sliding the whole foot flat, heel first, into 5th derrière. This helps to keep the back foot from turning in as it closes 5th, especially for beginners with less than ideal turn-out, until they can close 5th derrière directly. This practice is done keeping the hips parallel to the barre. Students are also introduced to the large fendu, in which the back leg comes down at least more than in the small fendu, thus stretching even more the iliopsoas. In the fendu, students keep most of their weight onto their front leg and the back foot flat on the floor. Coming back up can be difficult, for it requires a lot of strength; in order to so, students do not stick their buttocks out, but keep their pelvis down, with a very pulled-up back.

Exercise 12

Grand battement 2nd, two counts, two count hold, facing the barre.

Students repeat Exercise 12 of the Second Class of this week.

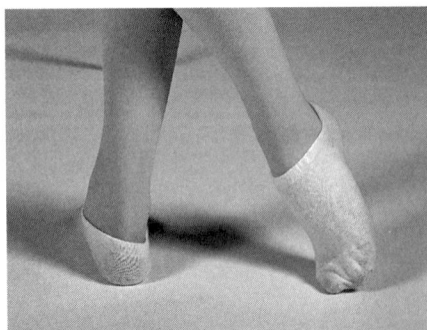

Exercise 13

Pied sur la barre 2nd, devant, and derrière, plié and bend.

Students repeat Exercise 14 of the Second Class of the Twenty-First Week.

CENTER

Exercise 14

Battement tendu en croix, plié when pointing, in 1st, four counts.

Students repeat Exercise 16 of the Fifth Class of the Twenty-First Week.

Exercise 15

Battement tendu 2nd, en descendant and en remontant, two counts.

Students repeat Exercise 15 of the Second Class of this week.

Exercise 16

Preparation for chassé à terre, forward and backward, with port de bras, four counts.

Students repeat Exercise 16 of the Second Class of this week.

Exercise 17

Adagio: grand plié in 1st, port de bras performed separately.

Students repeat Exercise 17 of the Second Class of this week.

Exercise 18

Échappé 2nd on demi-pointes, changing feet, hold on demi-pointes, four counts, facing the barre.

The toes are pushed toward the back with a slight opening of the foot.

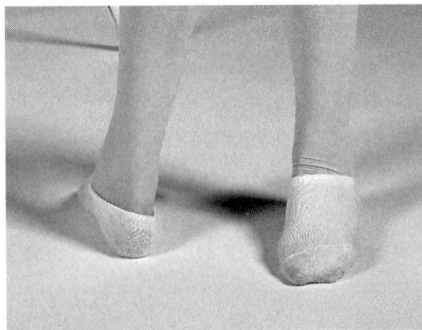

The foot slides in.

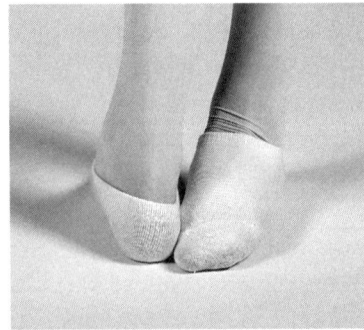

The foot closes into 5th position.

Students repeat Exercise 18 of the Fifth Class of the Twenty-First Week.

Exercise 19

Relevé in 1st, two counts, four repetitions, holding on demi-pointes six counts, facing the barre.

On "and," plié; on 1, relevé; on 2, come down with a plié; on 3, relevé; on 4, come down with a plié; on 5, relevé; on 6, come down with a plié; on 7, relevé; on 8, hold the position; from 1 to 6, hold the position on demi-pointes; on 7, roll down; on 8, hold the position. Repeat the exercise one more time, and at the end, hold balance.

Explanation. Students are reviewing Exercise 20 of the Fifth Class of the Nineteenth Week, except this time they return to the barre to execute the exercise in which they now hold the demi-pointe position for six counts in between series to gain strength in the ankles. The tempo is slightly faster.

Exercise 20

Pas de bourrée dessus, changing feet, with head rotation, four counts, facing the barre.

Students repeat Exercise 19 of the Second Class of this week.

Exercise 21

Relevé cou-de-pied devant and derrière, come down through 5th on demi-pointes, four counts, facing the barre.

On "and" 1, plié and relevé onto the left foot, bringing the right foot on the cou-de-pied devant; on 2, hold the position; on "and" 3, bring the working leg into 5th on demi pointes in front of the other; on "and" 4, come down into plié in 5th. Repeat three more times. Repeat the exercise, bringing the back foot on the cou-de-pied derrière.

Explanation. Students are finally performing the relevé on one foot directly. Coming down, they are still bringing both feet into 5th, making sure that both feet slide down into 5th in plié together. Following a good push on both feet (many students tend to anticipate the relevé by moving the weight onto their supporting leg even before the relevé itself), they bring their weight onto their supporting leg as quickly as possible. Students can test their balance by briefly releasing hands off the barre. Notice that, in the French school, the supporting foot does not get displaced at all, and dancers transfer their weight onto the supporting leg; it is not the leg that moves under in the relevé. The relevé is direct without any spring, with the working foot coming sharply on the cou-de-pied.

Exercise 22

Soubresaut in 2nd and 1st, on the count, five repetitions, facing the barre.

Students repeat Exercise 21 of the Second Class of this week.

Exercise 23

Soubresaut in 5th, landing on the front foot and the back foot, the working foot on the cou-de-pied derrière and devant, two counts, one count hold, facing the barre.

Students repeat Exercise 24 of the Fifth Class of the Twenty-First Week.

Exercise 24

Assemblé 2nd, en descendant and en remontant, two counts, one count hold, review.

Students repeat Exercise 23 of the Second Class of this week.

Exercise 25

Curtsey.

FIFTH CLASS

Exercise 1

Warm up.

Exercise 2

Plié.

Exercise 3

Battement tendu en croix, plié when pointing, with port de bras, four counts.

Students repeat Exercise 3 of the Second Class of this week.

Exercise 4

Battement tendu en croix, bring the foot down, four counts.

Students repeat Exercise 4 of the Second Class of this week.

Exercise 5

Battement jeté en croix, accent out, two counts, two counts hold.

Students repeat Exercise 6 of the Second Class of this week.

Exercise 6

Battement jeté 2nd, accent out, two counts, facing the barre.

Students repeat Exercise 6 of the Fourth Class of this week.

Exercise 7

Battement en cloche [Battement jeté balancé 45°—Vaganova], direct, in 1st, hold when pointing, three repetitions.

On "and," battement devant; on 1, hold the position; on "and," lower the leg, pointing the foot onto the floor; on 2, hold the position; on "and" 3, brush through the 1st, battement derrière; on "and," point the foot onto the floor; on 4, hold the position; on "and" 5, brush through 1st, battement devant; on "and," point the foot onto the floor; on 6, hold the position; on 7, close 1st; on 8, hold the position. Repeat the exercise one more time. At the end, relevé and hold balance.

Explanation. Students are now performing a direct battement en cloche, with no hold in 1st, but with still a slight holding when pointing. The brushing is done with the whole foot.

Exercise 8

Rond de jambe à terre en dehors and en dedans, passé à terre, four counts.

On "and" 1, battement tendu devant; on 2, rond de jambe to 2nd, without holding; on 3, rond de jambe en dehors to the back; on 4, hold the position; on "and" 5, brush through 1st, and extend the leg devant, repeat the rond de jambe en dehors, and close 5th derrière.

On "and" 1, battement tendu derrière; on 2, rond de jambe to 2nd, without hold; on 3, rond de jambe en dedans to devant; on 4, hold the position; on "and" 5, brush through 1st, extend the leg derrière, and repeat the rond de jambe en dedans and close 5th devant. At the end,

demi-détourné to the left side and hold balance with arms in 5th.

Explanation. Students are repeating Exercise 8 of the Fifth Class of the Twenty-First Week, this time performed sideways.

Exercise 9

Preparation for rond de jambe soutenu 2nd, direct battement, no rotation, facing the barre, review.

Students repeat Exercise 8 of the Second Class of this week.

Exercise 10

Battement frappé en croix, plié with the foot in flexed position, transfer of supporting leg, two counts, facing the barre.

Students repeat Exercise 9 of the Second Class of this week.

Exercise 11

Petits battements, two on the count, accent devant and derrière, hold on the cou-de-pied, facing the barre.

Students repeat Exercise 10 of the Second Class of this week.

Exercise 12

Adagio: retiré devant, close directly without plié, four counts, grand fendu, facing the barre.

Students repeat Exercise 11 of the Fourth Class of this week.

Exercise 13

Grand battement 2nd, two counts, two count hold, facing the barre.

Students repeat Exercise 12 of the Second Class of this week.

Exercise 14

Pied sur la barre 2nd, devant, and derrière, plié and bend.

Students repeat Exercise 14 of the Second Class of the Twenty-First Week.

CENTER

Exercise 15

Battement tendu en croix, close in plié, in 1st, with port de bras, two counts.

On "and" 1, battement tendu devant; on 2, close 1st; on "and" 3, battement tendu devant; on 4, close in 1st in plié, closing the arms in 1st; on "and" 5, battement tendu 2nd coming out of the plié, stretching the legs and opening the arms 2nd; on 6, close 1st; on "and" 7, battement tendu 2nd, opening the arms 2nd; on 8, close in 1st in plié, closing the arms in 1st; on "and" 1, battement tendu derrière, opening the arms 2nd; on 2, close 1st; on "and" 3, battement tendu derrière; on 4, close in 1st in plié, closing the arms in 1st; on "and" 5, battement tendu 2nd coming out of the plié and open the arms 2nd; on 6, close 1st; on "and" 7, battement tendu 2nd; on 8, close in 1st in plié, closing the arms in 1st.

Explanation. Students are practicing the battement tendu finishing in plié with port de bras. It is only in the closing of the second battement tendu that the arms close 1st. The arms open in the first battement tendu and the first battement tendu comes directly out of the plié (except for the first one). The exercise is particularly challenging when performing the battement tendu derrière and closing in plié; not to lose balance in the closing, students have to align their pelvis as soon as possible as the foot closes, with the weight spreading onto both feet as soon as possible.

Exercise 16

Battement tendu 2nd, en descendant and en remontant, two counts.

Students repeat Exercise 15 of the Second Class of this week.

Exercise 17

Preparation for chassé à terre, forward and backward, with port de bras, four counts.

Students repeat Exercise 16 of the Second Class of this week.

Exercise 18

Adagio: grand plié in 1st, port de bras performed separately.

Students repeat Exercise 17 of the Second Class of this week.

Exercise 19

Relevé in 1st, two counts, four repetitions, holding on demi-pointes six counts, facing the barre.

Students repeat Exercise 19 of the Fourth Class of this week.

Exercise 20

Pas de bourrée dessus, changing feet, with head rotation, four counts, facing the barre.

Students repeat Exercise 19 of the Second Class of this week.

Exercise 21

Relevé cou-de-pied devant and derrière, come down through 5th, on demi-pointes, four counts, facing the barre.

Students repeat Exercise 21 of the Fourth Class of this week.

Exercise 22

Soubresaut in 2nd and 1st, on the count, five repetitions, facing the barre.

Students repeat Exercise 21 of the Second Class of this week.

Exercise 23

Sissonne 2nd (sissonne ouverte de côté) [sissonne 2nd ouverte—Vaganova], traveling toward the front foot, without changing feet, four counts, facing the barre.

On "and" 1, plié and push off the floor, with a slight travel toward the right side (toward the side of the front foot), stretching the left leg 2nd à la demi-hauteur; on 2, land in plié on the right foot, with the left foot pointing 2nd onto the floor; on 3, close 5th, left foot back; on 4, stretch the knees. Repeat three more times toward the right.

Explanation. After practicing the soubresaut landing on one foot, students are now executing the real sissonne, landing on one leg, with the working foot pointing onto the floor in 2nd in plié. Both legs must be kept equally turned out, with the knees pushed to the sides. There is a slight traveling toward the side of the front leg. At a more advanced level, the dancer aims to hold legs held together at the beginning of the jump, especially in the sissonnes performed in grand allegro. For this introduction, what is most required is the quality of the plié, keeping the knees to the sides, stretching and turning out both legs during the jump, and landing softly on one leg, with the other foot pointing onto the floor. This holding in the pointed position is to make sure that the foot closes only after the pointed toes touch the ground. It also prevents students from bending their working leg prematurely (while the leg is still in the air) before closing, which is a common mistake among ballet students. Another bad habit to keep in check is the tendency to turn in the working leg in the sissonne 2nd, making it look more like a sissonne arabesque.

Music. So that students have the time to really push off with a deep plié and stretch both legs, a tempo usually used for grand allegro is more adequate for this introductory sissonne exercise. If the tempo is too quick, students will not have time to jump high enough to be able to stretch the knees.

Exercise 24

Assemblé 2nd, en descendant and en remontant, two counts, one count hold, review.

Students repeat Exercise 23 of the Second Class of this week.

Exercise 25

Curtsey.

Twenty-Third Week

ʃ

FIRST CLASS

Students repeat the material of the Fifth Class of the Twenty-Second Week.

SECOND CLASS

Exercise 1

Warm up.

Exercise 2

Plié.

Exercise 3

Battement tendu en croix, plié when pointing, in 1st, with port de bras, four counts.

Students repeat Exercise 3 of the Second Class of the Twenty-Second Week.

Exercise 4

Battement tendu en croix, start in plié and stretch when pointing, four counts.

On "and" 1, plié and battement tendu devant starting in plié and both knees stretched by the time the foot is pointed; on 2, hold the position; on 3, close 5th devant; on 4, hold the position. Repeat the exercise en croix en dehors. At the end, roll up and hold balance.

Explanation. Students are practicing this exercise en croix in 5th. The battement tendu coming out of the plié is performed more flowingly with the coordination of the stretching of both legs executed more precisely.

Exercise 5

Battement tendu en croix, bring the foot down in plié, point the foot, temps lié à terre forward and backward, four counts.

On "and" 1, battement tendu devant; on 2, transfer the weight onto both legs with a plié in 4th position; on 3, transfer the weight onto the back leg, stretching both legs and pointing the front foot; on 4, close 5th devant. Repeat the exercise en croix en dehors.

On "and" 1, battement tendu devant; on 2, transfer the weight onto both legs with a plié in 4th; on 3, transfer the weight onto the front leg, pointing the back foot, and stretching both legs; on 4, close 5th derrière. On "and" 5, battement tendu derrière; on 6, transfer the weight onto both legs with a plié in 4th; on 7, point the front foot stretching both legs; on 8, close in 5th devant. Repeat the exercise one more time.

Explanation. There are two series in this exercise, the first one preparing for the second one. Both start the same way, but in the second one, students transfer their weight onto the first leg each time. Like in the preparatory exercise for the chassé à terre, the hand at the barre must move along so that the shoulders remain straight. The working foot is brought a bit closer to the supporting leg when coming down in 4th; otherwise the distance between both legs would be too wide. In the second part of the exercise, students briefly go through 4th with both feet pressed down, without rolling the feet, especially the back one, and keeping the hips aligned. In the second series, students are practicing a very basic version of the temps lié en avant and en arrière, which requires that the movement be smooth and continuous, with each transfer from one leg to another performed flowingly. When performing the exercise backward, students should be particularly careful to bring their pelvis into alignment when the back leg comes into 4th position, since the pelvis is slightly tilted backward in the battement tendu derrière.

Exercise 6

Battement jeté 2nd, two counts, facing the barre.

Students repeat Exercise 6 of the Fourth Class of the Twenty-Second Week.

Exercise 7

Battement en cloche, direct, in 1st, hold when pointing, no hold in 1st.

Students repeat Exercise 7 of the Fifth Class of the Twenty-Second Week.

Exercise 8

Rond de jambe à terre en dehors and en dedans, passé à terre, four counts.

Students repeat Exercise 8 of the Fifth Class of the Twenty-Second Week.

Exercise 9

Rond de jambe soutenu 2nd en dehors, eight counts, facing the barre.

On "and" 1, battement 2nd; on 2, hold the position; on 3 and 4, bend the working leg, keeping the thigh still, whereas the toes describe an oval-like curve with the first arc toward the back, then grazing the calf (or the back of the knee if the leg is à la hauteur) of the supporting leg; on 5 and 6, through the forward arc, with the movement finishing in 2nd position with a stretched leg; on 7, lower the leg and point the foot onto the floor; on 8, close 5th devant. Repeat one more time with the right leg closing 5th derrière. Repeat the whole exercise one more time.

Explanation. Students are introduced to the rond de jambe soutenu 2nd with the rotation en dehors. As the lower leg draws both arcs, especially the back one, the thigh must be still and completely turned out. The working foot does not sickle. The circular movement is smooth, with no accent for now, since students are just learning the mechanisms. In this circular movement, the lower leg draws an elongated oblong-like shape that does not go too far either in front or in back of the line of the supporting leg. It is important that students fully stretch the leg 2nd at the end of the rond de jambe with a brief pause 2nd. Students keep their hands on the barre in front of the shoulders. The hips remain parallel to the barre.

Music. Since there are eight counts for each series, a medium-tempo lively waltz would be an appropriate musical choice. Too slow a tempo would put too much pressure on the working thigh.

Application. Students may find it difficult to perform the rotation without involving the thigh. To ease the understanding and the practice of this particular movement, students can hold their working knee with their hand to feel the independence of the movement from the knee joint—at least for a few lessons. The image of a thread holding the knee from the ceiling may also help keeping the thigh in place.

Exercise 10

Battement frappé 2nd, plié when pointing the foot, two counts, facing the barre.

On "and," bring the foot on the cou-de-pied devant; on 1, hold the position; on 2, extend the leg 2nd, in the plié, pointing the foot onto the floor; on 3, bring the foot on the cou-de-pied derrière, stretching the supporting leg; on 4, extend the leg 2nd on the plié; on 5, bring the foot on the cou-de-pied devant, stretching the supporting leg; on 6, extend the leg 2nd; on 7, stretch the supporting knee; on 8, close 5th devant. Repeat the exercise with the right foot one more time, closing 5th derrière. Repeat the whole exercise one more time. At the end, plié and relevé in 5th and hold the position.

Explanation. In this exercise, there is a plié when extending the leg. In the plié, students keep their weight on the supporting leg. When extending, by the time the leg stretches fully, the toes are pointed onto the floor; that is, the leg must not stretch in the air before the foot touches ground.

Exercise 11

Petits battements, two on the count, accent devant and derrière, hold on the cou-de-pied, arm in low 1st.

Following the preparatory port de bras, battement tendu 2nd and bring the arm down.

On "and," bring the foot on the cou-de-pied devant, and the arm in low 1st; on 1 and 2, hold the position; on "and," bring the foot on the cou-de-pied derrière; on 3, bring the foot on the cou-de-pied devant; on 4, hold the position; on "and," bring the foot on the cou-de-pied derrière; on 5, bring the foot on the cou-de-pied devant; on 6, hold the position; on 7, extend the leg and the arm 2nd; on 8, close 5th derrière, bringing the arm down.

On "and," bring the foot on the cou-de-pied derrière, bringing the arm in low 1st; on 1 and 2, hold the position; on "and," bring the foot on the cou-de-pied devant; on 3, bring the foot on the cou-de-pied derrière; on 4, hold the position; on "and," bring the foot on the cou-de-pied devant; on 5, bring the foot on the cou-de-pied derrière; on 6, hold the position; on 7, extend the leg 2nd and the arm is brought to 1st and 2nd; on 8, close 5th devant, bringing the arm down. Repeat the exercise one more time. At the end, relevé in 5th and hold balance.

Explanation. Students are repeating Exercise 10 of the Second Class of the Twenty-Second Week, except the exercise is now done sideways with the arm in low 1st. Notice the arm opening 2nd at the same time as the leg extends 2nd between each series.

Exercise 12

Adagio: retiré devant, close directly without plié, four counts, grand fendu, facing the barre.

Students repeat Exercise 11 of the Fourth Class of the Twenty-Second Week.

Exercise 13

Grand battement en croix, two counts, two counts hold, two repetitions.

On "and" 1, grand battement devant; on "and," point the foot on the floor; on 2, close 5th devant; on 3 and 4, hold the position. Repeat the exercise devant. Repeat the exercise en croix en dehors. At the end, roll up and hold balance.

Explanation. After practicing the exercise 2nd, students are performing it en croix, with two battements in each direction.

Exercise 14

Pied sur la barre 2nd, devant, and derrière, plié and bend.

Students repeat Exercise 14 of the Second Class of the Twenty-First Week.

CENTER

Exercise 15

Battement tendu en croix, close in plié, in 1st, with port de bras, two counts.

Students repeat Exercise 15 of the Fifth Class of the Twenty-Second Week.

Exercise 16

Battement tendu en croix, bring the foot down, with port de bras, four counts.

On "and" 1, battement tendu devant; on 2, bring the foot down in 4th position, transferring the weight onto both legs and bringing the arms 1st; on 3, transfer the weight onto the back leg, pointing the front foot, and opening the arms 2nd; on 4, close 5th devant. Repeat the exercise en croix en dehors, with the same port de bras, the last one closing 5th derrière.

Explanation. Students are repeating Exercise 4 of the Second Class of the Twenty-Second Week, this time performed in the center. When bringing their foot in 4th derrière, in particular, the lower abdomen is lifted, the hips remain de face, and the pelvis does not stick out. The 4th position is not too wide. The feet do not roll in, especially when the working foot comes down in 4th devant and derrière.

Exercise 17

Battement jeté 2nd, in 1st, arms in 6th, two counts.

In the preparatory port de bras, bring the arms in 1st and open the left arm 2nd. The head is directed toward the right.

On "and," battement jeté 2nd; on 1, hold the position; on "and," point the foot on the floor; on 2, close in 1st. Repeat three more times with the right foot. Repeat the whole exercise one more time. At the end, roll up and hold the position.

Explanation. Students are repeating Exercise 8 of the Fourth Class of the Twenty-First Week, this time performed in the center. The torso remains still, lifting the opposite side of the one of the working leg to help balancing.

Exercise 18

Rond de jambe à terre en dehors and en dedans, passé à terre, four counts.

On "and" 1, battement tendu devant; on 2, rond de jambe to 2nd, without hold; on 3, rond de jambe en dehors to the back; on 4, hold the position; on "and" 5, brush through 1st, extend the leg devant again, repeat the rond de jambe en dehors, and close 5th derrière. Repeat the exercise en dehors with the left leg, en dedans with the left leg and en dedans with the right leg.

Explanation. Students are performing the rond de jambe en dehors and en dedans with a passé in the center, switching sides between the ronds de jambe en dehors and en dedans.

Exercise 19

Battement fondu, 2nd, with port de bras, eight counts.

Following the preparatory port de bras, bring the arms down.

On 1 and 2, bring the foot on the cou-de-pied devant with a deep plié on the supporting leg, bringing the arms in 1st and straightening the head; on 3 and 4, extend the leg in demi-attitude 2nd, still in plié; on 5 and 6, stretch both legs at the same time, opening the arms 2nd; on 7 and 8, lower the leg down, point the foot down, and close 5th devant with the arms coming down. Repeat one more time with the right foot, closing 5th derrière.

Explanation. Students are practicing the battement fondu exercise in the center, only in 2nd for now and with a port de bras. When extending the leg, students must keep the working hip down and turn out the whole leg with the heel pushed forward. To help with balance, students lift the opposite side of the one of the working leg.

Music. The tempo is slightly accelerated for this exercise in the center.

Application. This is another challenging exercise to keep balance, while maintaining the turnout of both legs. For recreational ballet students, much more time may be needed to perform this kind of exercise comfortably.

Exercise 20

Relevé in 1st, two counts, four repetitions, holding on demi-pointes six counts, facing the barre.

Students repeat Exercise 19 of the Fourth Class of the Twenty-Second Week.

Exercise 21

Pas de bourrée dessus, changing feet, with port de bras, four counts.

Following the preparatory port de bras, bring the arms down.

On "and," bring the front foot on the cou-de-pied devant, with a plié on the supporting leg, with the head still turned to the right, and bringing the arms in 1st; on 1, hold the position; on 2, step onto the front foot on demi-pointe and stretch both legs; on "and," open the left leg 2nd, straightening the head, and opening the arms 2nd; on 3, step onto the left foot on demi-pointe, transferring the weight onto the left leg; on "and," close 5th, left foot front in plié, turning the head toward the left, and closing the arms down; on 4, stretch both knees. Repeat the exercise three more times, alternating legs.

Explanation. Students are practicing the pas de bourrée dessus in the center.

Exercise 22

Glissade 2nd, en descendant, toward the back foot, without changing feet, arms in 6th, two counts, one count hold, four repetitions.

In the preparatory port de bras, bring both arms in 1st, open the right arm 2nd keeping the left arm in 1st, with the head turned toward the left arm.

On "and," plié, inclining the torso very slightly toward the left; on 1, brush the back foot and extend the leg 2nd; on "and," transfer the weight onto the left leg in plié, while the right leg stretches and the right foot points; on 2, close 5th right foot front on the plié; on 3, stretch the knees; on 4, hold the position. Repeat the glissade three more times to the left. Repeat the exercise traveling to the right, starting with the left foot front, with the right arm 1st and the left arm 2nd.

Explanation. The glissade is now performed on two counts, which makes the movement smoother looking and much more flowing. Even though there is no pause when pointing the second foot (after the transfer), students must still point that foot before closing the leg in 5th. There is still a holding when closing. Both heels remain on the ground in the plié. The arms do not bounce during the exercise. The torso is slightly bent toward the direction of travel.

Exercise 23

Relevé cou-de-pied devant and derrière, come down through 5th, on demi-pointes, four counts, facing the barre.

Students repeat Exercise 21 of the Fourth Class of the Twenty-Second Week.

Exercise 24

Soubresaut in 2nd and 1st, on the count, five repetitions.

Following the preparatory port de bras, battement tendu 2nd, bring the foot and the arms down.

On "and," plié and push off the floor, stretching the toes and knees; on 1, land in plié in 2nd; on "and," directly out of the plié, push off the floor again; on 2, land in plié in 2nd; on "and," push off the floor; on 3, land in plié; on "and," push off the floor; on 4, land in plié; on "and," push off the floor; on 5, land in plié; on 6, stretch the knees; on 7 and 8, hold the position. Repeat three more times. After a pause, repeat the exercise in 1st.

Explanation. Students are repeating Exercise 21 of the Second Class of the Twenty-Second Week, this time performed in the center. Again proper breathing is crucial to build up stamina in this type of exercise. No jerking in the upper body should be allowed. If this is the case, it usually means that students are not pushing enough with their legs and feet, and thus try to use their upper body for strength; more practice is then required at the barre.

Exercise 25

Sissonne 2nd, traveling toward the front foot, without changing feet, four counts, facing the barre.

Students repeat Exercise 23 of the Fifth Class of the Twenty-Second Week.

Exercise 26

Curtsey.

THIRD CLASS

Students repeat the material of the Second Class of this week.

FOURTH CLASS

Exercise 1

Warm up.

Exercise 2

Plié.

Exercise 3

Battement tendu en croix, plié when pointing, in 1st, with port de bras, four counts.

Students repeat Exercise 3 of the Second Class of the Twenty-Second Week.

Exercise 4

Battement tendu en croix, start in plié and stretch when pointing, four counts.

Students repeat Exercise 4 of the Second Class of this week.

Exercise 5

Battement tendu en croix, bring the foot down in plié, point the foot, temps lié à terre forward and backward, four counts.

Students repeat Exercise 5 of the Second Class of this week.

Exercise 6

Battement jeté en croix, two counts, two repetitions.

On "and," battement jeté devant; on 1, hold the position; on "and," lower the leg and point the foot onto the floor; on 2, close 5th devant. Repeat the battement devant. Repeat the exercise en croix en dehors, closing the first battement 2nd 5th devant. At the end, plié, relevé in 5th, and hold the position.

Explanation. Students are repeating Exercise 6 of the Second Class of the Twenty-Second Week, with no holding in the closing.

Exercise 7

Battement en cloche, direct, hold when pointing, no hold in 1st, four counts.

Students repeat Exercise 7 of the Fifth Class of the Twenty-Second Week.

Exercise 8

Rond de jambe à terre en dehors and en dedans, passé à terre, four counts.

Students repeat Exercise 8 of the Fifth Class of the Twenty-Second Week.

The French School
of Classical Ballet

Exercise 9

Rond de jambe soutenu 2nd en dehors, eight
counts, facing the barre.

Students repeat Exercise 9 of the Second Class
of this week.

Exercise 10

Battement frappé 2nd, plié when pointing the
foot, two counts, facing the barre.

Students repeat Exercise 10 of the Second
Class of this week.

Exercise 11

Petits battements, two on the count, accent
devant and derrière, hold on the cou-de-pied,
arm in low 1st.

Students repeat Exercise 11 of the Second
Class of this week.

Exercise 12

Adagio: développé 2nd à la hauteur [battement
développé—Vaganova], eight counts, facing the
barre.

On "and," bring the foot pointed on the cou-
de-pied devant, straightening the head; on 1

and 2, slide the toes up the supporting leg to the
knee level; on 3, open the leg in attitude in 2nd;
on 4, stretch the leg fully 2nd; on 5 and 6, hold
the position; on 7, bring down the leg and point
the foot onto the floor; on 8, close 5th derrière.
Repeat the whole exercise one more time.

Explanation. This exercise is most appropriate if students are already comfortable lifting
their leg 2nd à la hauteur. However, as it was the
case in the direct lift of the leg practiced so far,
correct placement and application of the different parts of the movement are more important
than height. As the leg stretches from attitude
to full 2nd, the thigh is not lowered. Therefore,
the attitude must not be higher than the height
of the leg stretched 2nd. As for the introduction
of many steps, students start the full développé
facing the barre to keep the body as straight as
possible. The torso must not lean away from the
working leg as it extends 2nd. In raising the leg
from 5th devant, slide it along the front of the
supporting leg with a stretched foot; the heel
is moved well forward and does not touch the
supporting leg; the thigh must be turned out to
its maximum. In extending the leg 2nd, students
must maintain the turn-out of the thigh, actively

The leg is in attitude 2nd position.

The leg is fully stretched 2nd position.

moving forward the lower part of the leg without raising the working hip, as it is commonly observed among ballet students. The body remains pulled up and the back erect. The movement of the working leg must be very smooth, with even speed throughout.

Exercise 13

Grand battement en croix, two counts, two counts hold, two repetitions.

Students repeat Exercise 13 of the Second Class of this week.

Exercise 14

Pied sur la barre 2nd, devant, and derrière, plié and bend.

Students repeat Exercise 14 of the Second Class of the Twenty-First Week.

CENTER

Exercise 15

Battement tendu en croix, close in plié, in 1st, with port de bras, two counts.

Students repeat Exercise 15 of the Fifth Class of the Twenty-Second Week.

Exercise 16

Battement tendu en croix en dehors, bring the foot down, with port de bras, four counts.

Students repeat Exercise 16 of the Second Class of this week.

Exercise 17

Battement jeté 2nd, in 1st, with arms in 6th, two counts.

Students repeat Exercise 17 of the Second Class of this week.

Exercise 18

Rond de jambe a terre en dehors and en dedans, passé à terre, four counts.

Students repeat Exercise 18 of the Second Class of this week.

Exercise 19

Battement fondu, 2nd, with port de bras, eight counts.

Students repeat Exercise 19 of the Second Class of this week.

Exercise 20

Adagio: retiré, close directly in plié, without changing and changing feet, with port de bras, four counts.

Following the preparatory port de bras, bring the arms down.

Without changing feet: on "and," bring the front foot onto the cou-de-pied, straightening the head; on 1 and 2, slide the foot along the leg to the knee level, bringing the arms in 1st; on "and" 3, slide the foot down; on "and," close 5th devant in plié, opening the arms 2nd; on 4, stretch, bringing the arms down.

Changing feet from back to front: on "and," bring the back foot onto the cou-de-pied derrière; on 5 and 6, slide up the foot along the leg to the knee level, bringing the arms in 1st; on "and," the toes graze around the supporting leg; on 7, slide the foot down; on "and," close 5th devant in plié, opening the arms 2nd; on 8, stretch, bringing the arms down. Repeat one more time.

Explanation. Students are practicing Exercise 13 of the Fifth Class of the Twenty-First Week, this time performing it in the center. Without holding the retiré, the toes graze around the back of the knee to be against the front of the knee, without sickling the foot. Notice the port de bras at the end of each series.

Music. A slow waltz will work well here.

Exercise 21

Pas de bourrée dessus, changing feet, with port de bras, four counts.

Students repeat Exercise 21 of the Second Class of this week.

Exercise 22

Glissade 2nd, en descendant, toward the back foot, without changing feet, arms in 6th, two counts, one count hold, four repetitions.

Students repeat Exercise 22 of the Second Class of this week.

Exercise 23

Relevé in 1st, two counts, holding on demi-pointes six counts, facing the barre.

Students repeat Exercise 19 of the Fourth Class of the Twenty-Second Week.

Exercise 24

Relevé cou-de-pied devant and derrière, come down through 5th, on demi-pointes, four counts, facing the barre.

Students repeat Exercise 21 of the Fourth Class of the Twenty-Second Week.

Exercise 25

Soubresaut in 2nd and 1st, on the count, five repetitions.

Students repeat Exercise 24 of the Second Class of this week.

Exercise 26

Changement de pied, two counts, one count hold, facing the barre, review.

On "and," plié; on 1, push off the floor with pointed feet, opening the legs slightly in the air; on 2, land in plié in 5th with the left foot; on 3, stretch both legs; on 4, hold the position. Repeat three more times. Repeat the exercise one more time. Repeat the exercise in the center at the in-structor's discretion.

Explanation. Students are reviewing the exercise at the barre. The instructor will gauge whether students can execute the exercise in the center with a slightly accelerated tempo.

Exercise 27

Sissonne 2nd, traveling toward the front foot, without changing feet, four counts, facing the barre.

Students repeat Exercise 23 of the Fifth Class of the Twenty-Second Week.

Exercise 28

Curtsey.

FIFTH CLASS

Exercise 1

Warm up.

Exercise 2

Plié.

Exercise 3

Battement tendu en croix, plié when pointing, in 1st, with port de bras, four counts.

Students repeat Exercise 3 of the Second Class of the Twenty-Second Week.

Exercise 4

Battement tendu en croix, start in plié and stretch when pointing, four counts.

Students repeat Exercise 4 of the Second Class of this week.

Exercise 5

Battement tendu en croix, bring the foot down in plié, point the foot, temps lié à terre forward and backward, four counts.

Students repeat Exercise 5 of the Second Class of this week.

Exercise 6

Battement jeté en croix, two counts, two repetitions.

Students repeat Exercise 6 of the Fourth Class of this week.

Exercise 7

Rond de jambe à la demi-hauteur en dehors and en dedans, eight counts, facing the barre, review.

On "and" 1, battement devant; on 2, hold the position; on 3 and 4, rond de jambe en dehors to 2nd; on 5 and 6, rond de jambe en dehors to 4th back; on 7, lower the leg and point the foot onto the floor; on 8, close 5th derrière. On "and" 1, battement derrière; on 2, hold the position; on 3 and 4, rond de jambe en dedans to 2nd; on 5 and 6, rond de jambe en dedans to 4th devant; on 7, lower the pointed foot onto the floor; on 8, close 5th devant. Repeat the exercise one more time. At the end, retiré derrière with the left leg and balance with arms in low 1st.

Explanation. Students are reviewing this ex-ercise performed a few weeks ago. Students must keep the turn-out of their working leg as long as they can, without moving their supporting hip forward when the leg goes from 2nd to 4th der-rière. The shoulders remain straight.

Exercise 8

Rond de jambe soutenu 2nd, en dehors, eight counts, facing the barre.

Students repeat Exercise 9 of the Second Class of this week.

Exercise 9

Battement frappé 2nd, plié when pointing the foot, two counts, facing the barre.

Students repeat Exercise 10 of the Second Class of this week.

Exercise 10

Petits battements, two on the count, accent devant and derrière, holding on the cou-de-pied.

Students repeat Exercise 11 of the Second Class of this week.

Exercise 11

Adagio: développé 2nd, eight counts, facing the barre.

Students repeat Exercise 12 of the Fourth Class of this week.

Exercise 12

Grand battement en croix, two counts, two counts hold, two repetitions.

Students repeat Exercise 13 of the Second Class of this week.

Exercise 13

Stretching, review.

From now on, students will repeat one of the exercises of stretching practiced so far.

CENTER

Exercise 14

Battement tendu en croix, bring the foot down, four counts.

Students repeat Exercise 16 of the Second Class of this week.

Exercise 15

Battement jeté 2nd, in 1st, arms in 6th, two counts.

Students repeat Exercise 17 of the Second Class of this week.

Exercise 16

Battement jeté piqué 2nd, bouncing on the count, in 1st, four counts.

On "and," battement 2nd; on 1, hold the position; on "and," bring the pointed foot down 2nd; on 2, lift the leg 2nd again at the same height as

in the previous battement; on "and," lower the leg and point the foot onto the floor; on 3, hold the position; on 4, close 1st. Repeat the exercise one more time with the right foot. Repeat the whole exercise one more time.

Explanation. Students are performing the battement jeté piqué 2nd in the center. The working hip is not raised. The leg moves with lightness and vivacity. The leg remains low (around 25°) so that the work of the adductors can be better controlled.

Exercise 17

Rond de jambe à terre en dehors and en dedans, passé à terre, four counts.

Students repeat Exercise 18 of the Second Class of this week.

Exercise 18

Battement fondu, 2nd, with port de bras, eight counts.

Students repeat Exercise 19 of the Second Class of this week.

Exercise 19

Adagio: retiré close directly in 5th in plié, without changing and changing feet, with port de bras, four counts.

Students repeat Exercise 20 of the Fourth Class of this week.

Exercise 20

Pas de bourrée dessus, changing feet, with port de bras, four counts.

Students repeat Exercise 21 of the Second Class of this week.

Exercise 21

Glissade 2nd, en descendant, toward the back foot, without changing feet, arms in 6th, two counts, one count hold, four repetitions.

Students repeat Exercise 22 of the Second Class of this week.

Exercise 22

Relevé in 1st, two counts, three repetitions, review.

Following the preparatory port de bras, bring the arms down.

On "and," plié; on 1, relevé, bringing the arms

in low 1st; on 2, come down in the plié; on 3, relevé; on 4, come down in the plié; on 5, relevé; on 6, come down in the plié; on 7, stretch the knees; on 8, hold the position. Repeat three more times. At the end, hold balance.

Explanation. Students are reviewing Exercise 20 of the Fifth Class of the Nineteenth Week, with a slightly accelerated tempo.

Application. Even students who take ballet once or twice a week will greatly benefit from performing drills of relevés such as this one—even if this is only at the barre for students whose ankles are not strong enough.

Exercise 23

Soubresaut in 2nd and 1st, on the count, five repetitions.

Students repeat Exercise 24 of the Second Class of this week.

Exercise 24

Changement de pied, two counts, one count hold, facing the barre and in the center.

Students repeat Exercise 26 of the Fourth Class of this week.

Exercise 25

Sissonne 2nd, traveling toward the back foot, without changing feet, four counts, facing the barre.

On "and" 1, plié, and push off the floor with both feet, with a slight travel toward the left side (toward the back foot), stretching the right leg 2nd à la demi-hauteur; on 2, land in plié on the left foot with the right foot pointing 2nd onto the floor; on 3, close 5th, right foot front; on 4, stretch the knees. Repeat three more times

toward the left. Repeat the exercise toward the right with the left foot front.

Explanation. The hands move along during the jump.

Exercise 26

Marche with small développé, hold when pointing, in 1st, arms in 1st, in diagonal.

Start in the upper left corner facing the lower right corner. Following the preparatory port de bras, bring the arms down, with the head de face.

On "and" 1, battement tendu devant with the right foot, bringing the arms in 1st; on 2, hold the position; on "and" 3, step onto the right foot while the back leg bends, with the pointed foot passing through at the level of the cou-de-pied, stretch the leg forward with an actively turned-out foot, and point the foot onto the floor; on 4, hold the position; on "and" 5, step onto the left foot and bend the right leg forward extending it, and point the foot onto the floor; on 6, hold the position. Repeat the marche in diagonal traveling to the lower right corner.

Explanation. In this marche exercise, students bring their back leg forward with a small développé at a height of about 25°, before stepping onto the foot, freeing the other leg to move forward. The heel of the working leg leads the movement forward, with the pointed toes pushed down. When passing through 2nd, the pointed working foot comes by the back of the ankle of the supporting leg, keeping the leg turned out.

Exercise 27

Curtsey.

Twenty-Fourth Week

§

FIRST CLASS

Students repeat the material of the Fifth Class of the Twenty-Third Week.

SECOND CLASS

Exercise 1

Warm up.

Exercise 2

Plié.

Exercise 3

First Battement tendu exercise.

From now on, the instructor will select the elements of the first battement tendu exercise at the barre. The exercise is performed in 1st, which is a simpler and an easier position. The elements will be those already studied in the training, and the tempo will be fairly slow and even. It is a good time to review some of the simple battement tendu combinations already studied.

Exercise 4

Battement tendu devant, derrière, 2nd, four counts, facing the barre.

On 1 and 2, battement tendu devant; on 3 and 4, close 5th; on 5 and 6, battement tendu derrière with the left foot; on 7 and 8, close 5th; on 1 and 2, battement tendu 2nd with the right foot; on 3 and 4, close 1st; on 5 and 6, another battement tendu 2nd; on 7 and 8, close 5th devant. Repeat three more times.

Explanation. This exercise prepares students for a pattern of battement tendu usually done in 5th croisé in the center. Since it is a new pattern, each battement tendu takes more time, but with a fairly brisk tempo. For the battement tendu devant, the head is turned toward the side of the working leg, and for the battement tendu derrière, the head is turned toward the side of

the supporting leg. The head straightens for the battement tendu 2nd.

Exercise 5

Position on the cou-de-pied, pointed, extension of the leg en croix, with port de bras, four counts, review.

Following the preparatory port de bras, bring the arm down.

On "and," bring the front foot on the cou-de-pied devant, bringing the arm in 1st; on 1, hold the position; on 2, extend the leg devant with the foot pointed on the floor, opening the arm 2nd; on 3, close 5th, bringing the arm down; on 4, hold the position. Repeat the exercise en croix en dehors with the same port de bras. Repeat the whole exercise one more time. At the end, plié, relevé in 5th, bring the arm down, demi-détourné to the left side, and hold balance.

Explanation. Students are reviewing Exercise 8 of the Second Class of the Fourteenth Week, this time performed sideways, with a hold on the closing instead of on the pointing.

Exercise 6

Battement tendu en croix, bring the foot down in plié, point the foot, temps lié forward and backward, with port de bras, four counts, review.

On "and" 1, battement tendu devant; on 2, transfer the weight onto both legs with a plié in 4th position, bringing the arm in 1st; on 3, transfer the weight onto the back leg, stretching both legs and pointing the front foot, opening the arm 2nd; on 4, close 5th devant. Repeat the exercise en croix en dehors.

On "and" 1, battement tendu devant; on 2, bring the foot into 4th in plié, bringing the arm in 1st; on 3, transfer the weight onto the front leg, stretching both legs, pointing the back foot, and opening the arm 2nd; on 4, close 5th derrière. On "and" 5, battement tendu derrière; on 6, bring the foot in 4th in plié and the arm 1st; on 7, transfer the weight onto the back leg, point the front foot, while both legs stretch, opening the arm 2nd; on 8, close in 5th devant. Repeat the exercise one more time.

Explanation. Students are reviewing Exercise 5 of the Second Class of the Twenty-Third Week, this time adding a port de bras.

Exercise 7

Battement jeté en croix, two counts, two repetitions.

Students repeat Exercise 6 of the Fourth Class of the Twenty-Third Week.

Exercise 8

Rond de jambe à la demi-hauteur en dehors and en dedans, eight counts, facing the barre, review.

Students repeat Exercise 7 of the Fifth Class of the Twenty-Third Week.

Exercise 9

Battement frappé 2nd en l'air, two counts, three repetitions, facing the barre.

On "and," the front foot comes in wrapped-up position on the cou-de-pied devant; on 1, hold the position; on 2, extend the leg 2nd off the floor, with the toes grazing the floor before pointing the whole foot; on 3, bring the foot on the cou-de-pied derrière; on 4, extend the leg 2nd off the floor; on 5, bring the foot on the cou-de-pied devant; on 6, extend the leg 2nd; on 7, point the foot onto the floor; on 8, close the leg 5th derrière. Repeat the exercise with the right foot derrière. At the end, relevé in 5th, bring the front foot on the cou-de-pied devant, and hold the position.

Explanation. After practicing the battement frappé with the working foot pointing onto the floor, students are now learning the battement frappé en l'air. The working foot energetically strikes the cou-de-pied before the leg is sharply extended to 2nd, with the toes grazing the floor before full extension. The particular bent position of the foot on the cou-de-pied facilitates the action of the foot grazing the floor before full extension, and gives energy to the striking effect of the frappé and the stretching of the whole leg. If the foot were completely pointed on the cou-de-pied, the foot would have to slightly bend anyway to perform this action. It is important that the thigh not be lowered and the working

leg be kept turned out in the frappé. The height of the leg must be consistent in the extension, and need not be higher than 25°. Students do not kick their leg out, but stretch it sharply with control.

Music. The music, very staccato, must have strong beats.

Exercise 10

Rond de jambe soutenu 2nd, en dedans, eight counts, facing the barre.

On "and" 1, battement 2nd; on 2, hold the position; on 3 and 4, bend the working leg, with the tips of the toes describing an oval beginning with a forward arc, then grazing the calf (or the back of the knee if the leg is à la hauteur) of the supporting leg; on 5 and 6, through the arc toward the back, with the movement finishing 2nd position with a stretched leg; on 7, lower the leg and point the foot onto the floor; on 8, close 5th devant. Repeat the exercise one more time with the right leg, closing derrière. Repeat the whole exercise one more time.

Explanation. In the rond de jambe en dedans, the lower limb describes the reverse trajectory than in the one en dehors. Bringing the lower limb through the backward arc, the thigh must not turn in.

Exercise 11

Petits battements, accent devant, two on the count, no hold, facing the barre.

On "and," bring the foot on the cou-de-pied devant; on 1, hold the position; on "and," bring the foot on the cou-de-pied derrière; on 2, bring the foot on the cou-de-pied devant; on "and," bring the foot on the cou-de-pied derrière; on 3, bring the foot on the cou-de-pied devant; on "and," bring the foot on the cou-de-pied derrière; on 4, bring the foot on the cou-de-pied devant; on "and," bring the foot on the cou-de-pied derrière; on 5, bring the foot on the cou-de-pied devant; on "and," bring the foot on the cou-de-pied derrière; on 6, bring the foot on the cou-de-pied devant; on 7, extend the leg 2nd, pointing the foot onto the floor; on 8, close 5th devant. Repeat the exercise one more time with the right foot, closing 5th derrière.

Explanation. In this petits battements exercise, the accent is on the cou-de-pied devant, and there is no hold after each transfer. Even though the tempo has increased, each unbending must be precisely executed, keeping the knee on the side and the thigh as still as possible.

Exercise 12

Adagio: développé 2nd, raccourci, eight counts, facing the barre.

On "and," bring the foot pointed on the cou-de-pied devant; on 1 and 2, slide the toes up the supporting leg to the knee level; on 3, open the leg in attitude in 2nd; on 4, stretch the leg fully 2nd; on "and" 5, bend the leg so that the toes are against the knee; on 6, slide the foot down; on 7, close 5th devant in plié; on 8, stretch and hold the position. Repeat one more time.

Explanation. Instead of bringing the leg down after the développé, students are bending the knee to bring the leg into a raccourci before closing. When the leg starts bending, the knee remains suspended, dropping as little as possible when executing the raccourci, keeping it well turned out without sickling the working foot. Both hips are parallel to the barre and both hands are in front of the shoulders.

Music. The adagio music will be particularly legato to allow students to complete each part of the movement properly.

Exercise 13

Grand battement en croix, battement tendu, four counts.

On "and" 1, battement tendu devant; on 2, close 5th devant; on "and" 3, grand battement devant; on "and," point the foot on the floor; on 4, close 5th devant. Repeat the exercise en croix en dehors. At the end, plié and relevé in 5th and hold balance.

Explanation. Students are adding a battement tendu to the grand battement exercise, performed in each direction. The battement tendu comes before the grand battement, since the brushing action of the battement tendu prepares well for the brushing out involved in the grand battement.

Exercise 14

Stretching.

CENTER

243
Twenty-Fourth
Week

❧❧❧❧❧❧❧

SECOND CLASS

Exercise 15

Battement tendu en croix, bring the foot down, with port de bras, four counts.

Students repeat Exercise 16 of the Second Class of the Twenty-Third Week.

Exercise 16

Battement jeté piqué 2nd, bouncing on the count, in 1st, four counts.

Students repeat Exercise 16 of the Fifth Class of the Twenty-Third Week.

Exercise 17

Adagio: lift the leg 2nd, hold three counts in the air, small fendu, with port de bras.

On "and" 1 and 2, brush the foot 2nd and lift the leg; from 3 to 5, hold the position; on 6, lower the leg and point the foot onto the floor; on 7, close 5th devant; on 8, hold the position. On "and" 1, battement tendu derrière (with the left foot); on 2, hold the position; on 3 and 4, bring the foot down flat on the floor in a small fendu, with the arms still 2nd; on 5 and 6, bring the arms 5th; on 7, straighten up by stretching the front leg and pointing the back foot; on 8, close 5th and open the arms 2nd. Repeat the whole exercise one more time.

Explanation. Students are reviewing lifting the leg 2nd. The small fendu is also added to the exercise. The elbows do not scoop down and the torso remains straight. Both legs and the working foot are very stretched throughout. Shoulders do not rise when coming back up from the fendu.

Application. Even though students have started to work on the développé, they should still practice regularly just lifting the leg and holding it, which, in some aspects, is more difficult. The mechanics of the battement are simpler, but the lifting of the leg à la hauteur is more tedious, because there is the full weight of the leg to bring up, unlike the développé in which the leg can be brought up from the retiré into full extension.

Exercise 18

Relevé in 1st, two counts, three repetitions, review.

Students repeat Exercise 22 of the Fifth Class of the Twenty-Third Week.

Exercise 19

Relevé retiré devant and derrière, direct closing, four counts, facing the barre.

On "and," plié; on 1, relevé retiré devant; on 2, hold the position; on 3, both feet come down in plié and close 5th devant; on 4, stretch both knees. Repeat three more times. Repeat the exercise bringing the leg in a relevé retiré derrière.

Explanation. Students are now performing the exercise with a retiré closing directly into 5th. The working leg is sharply brought into retiré with the side of the toes pressing firmly against the front of the knee (retiré devant) and behind the supporting leg (retiré derrière). The working foot, when coming down, does not flex prematurely and must stay pointed as long as possible. Students must keep the knee well to the side until the working foot closes, especially when closing derrière. Students apply the same head positions as described in Exercise 23 of the Fourth Class of the Twenty-First Week.

Exercise 20

Soubresaut in 5th, on the count, two repetitions, facing the barre.

On "and," plié and push off the floor, keeping the legs in 5th; on 1, land in plié in 5th, right foot front; on "and," directly out of the plié, push off the floor; on 2, land in plié in 5th, right foot front; on 3, stretch the knees; on 4, hold the position. Repeat three times.

Explanation. Students are practicing the exercise with two jumps now. The same tightness of the legs in 5th in the air is expected in both jumps. The knees do not come forward in the plié of the landing, especially in the landing that is between both jumps.

Exercise 21

Sissonne 2nd, traveling toward the back foot, without changing feet, four counts, facing the barre.

Students repeat Exercise 25 of the Fifth Class of the Twenty-Third Week.

Exercise 22

Piqué with the foot on the cou-de-pied derrière, eight counts, facing the barre.

On "and," plié; on 1, battement tendu 2nd; on 2, step onto the right foot on demi-pointe, while the left leg bends with the foot coming onto the cou-de-pied derrière; on 3 and 4, hold the position; on 5, bring the back foot on demi-pointe in 5th behind the other; on 6, come down in plié, right foot front; on 7, stretch the knees; on 8, hold the position. Repeat three more times.

Explanation. Students are practicing the piqué with the foot on the cou-de-pied derrière. This exercise should be preceded by the exercise of relevé with a holding on one foot on demi-pointe so that students have enough strength to hold on one foot. The hands slide along so that they remain in front of the shoulders. A deep plié is essential to bring the body onto the supporting leg. The hips do not turn toward the working leg and remain facing the barre. Students must be balanced on their supporting leg as soon as possible. The turn-out muscles of the first leg (the one that does the piqué) will be particularly active to help keep balance.

Exercise 23

Marche with small développé, hold when pointing, in 1st, arms in 1st, in diagonal.

Students repeat Exercise 26 of the Fifth Class of the Twenty-Third Week.

Exercise 24

Curtsey.

THIRD CLASS

Students repeat the material of the Second Class of this week.

FOURTH CLASS

Exercise 1

Warm up.

Exercise 2

Plié.

Exercise 3

First battement tendu exercise.

Exercise 4

Battement tendu devant, derrière, 2nd, four counts, facing the barre.

Students repeat Exercise 4 of the Second Class of this week.

Exercise 5

Battement tendu en croix, start and close in plié, four counts, review.

On 1, plié; on 2, battement tendu devant; on 3, close 5th devant; on 4, stretch the knees. Repeat the exercise en croix en dehors, with the last battement tendu 2nd closing 5th devant. At the end, roll up and hold balance.

Explanation. Students are reviewing this exercise done earlier. As said before, the heel is pressed down as long as possible when extending the leg devant and derrière to help keep the foot turned out.

Exercise 6

Position on the cou-de-pied, pointed, extension of the leg en croix, with port de bras, four counts, review.

Students repeat Exercise 5 of the Second Class of this week.

Exercise 7

Battement tendu en croix, bring the foot down in plié, point the foot, temps lié forward and backward, with port de bras, four counts, review.

Students repeat Exercise 6 of the Second Class of this week.

Exercise 8

Battement jeté en croix, plié, two counts, three repetitions.

On "and," battement jeté devant; on 1, hold the position; on "and," point the foot on the floor; on 2, close in 5th. Repeat the battement devant twice more; on 7 and 8, plié and stretch. Repeat the exercise en croix. At the end, plié, relevé in 5th and hold balance.

Explanation. Students are reviewing Exercise 6 of the Fourth Class of the Twenty-Third Week, this time adding one more battement. A plié and

stretch complete each series. The first battement 2nd closes 5th derrière.

Exercise 9

Rond de jambe à la demi-hauteur en dehors and en dedans, eight counts, facing the barre, review.

Students repeat Exercise 7 of the Fifth Class of the Twenty-Third Week.

Exercise 10

Battement frappé 2nd en l'air, two counts, three repetitions, facing the barre.

Students repeat Exercise 9 of the Second Class of this week.

Exercise 11

Rond de jambe soutenu 2nd, en dedans, eight counts, facing the barre.

Students repeat Exercise 10 of the Second Class of this week.

Exercise 12

Petits battements, accent devant, two on the count, no hold, facing the barre.

Students repeat Exercise 11 of the Second Class of this week.

Exercise 13

Adagio: développé 2nd, raccourci, eight counts, facing the barre.

Students repeat Exercise 12 of the Second Class of this week.

Exercise 14

Grand battement en croix, battement tendu, four counts.

Students repeat Exercise 13 of the Second Class of this week.

Exercise 15

Stretching.

CENTER

Exercise 16

Battement jeté piqué 2nd, bouncing on the count, in 1st, four counts.

Students repeat Exercise 16 of the Fifth Class of the Twenty-Third Week.

Exercise 17

Adagio: lift the leg 2nd, hold three counts in the air, small fendu, with port de bras.

Students repeat Exercise 17 of the Second Class of this week.

Exercise 18

Relevé in 1st, two counts, three repetitions, review.

Students repeat Exercise 22 of the Fifth Class of the Twenty-Third Week.

Exercise 19

Relevé retiré devant and derrière, direct closing, four counts, facing the barre.

Students repeat Exercise 19 of the Second Class of this week.

Exercise 20

Soubresaut in 5th, on the count, two repetitions, facing the barre.

Students repeat Exercise 20 of the Second Class of this week.

Exercise 21

Sissonne 2nd, traveling toward the back foot, without changing feet, four counts, facing the barre.

Students repeat Exercise 25 of the Fifth Class of the Twenty-Third Week.

Exercise 22

Piqué with the foot on the cou-de-pied derrière, eight counts, facing the barre.

Students repeat Exercise 22 of the Second Class of this week.

Exercise 23

Marche with small développé, hold when pointing, in 1st, arms in 1st, in diagonal.

Students repeat Exercise 26 of the Fifth Class of the Twenty-Third Week.

Exercise 24

Curtsey.

FIFTH CLASS

Exercise 1

Warm up.

Exercise 2

Plié.

Exercise 3

First battement tendu exercise.

Exercise 4

Battement tendu devant, derrière, 2nd, four counts, facing the barre.

Students repeat Exercise 4 of the Second Class of this week.

Exercise 5

Position on the cou-de-pied, pointed, extension of the leg en croix, with port de bras, four counts.

Students repeat Exercise 5 of the Second Class of this week.

Exercise 6

Battement tendu en croix, start and close in plié, four counts, review.

Students repeat Exercise 5 of the Fourth Class of this week.

Exercise 7

Battement tendu en croix, bring the foot down in plié, point the foot, temps lié forward and backward, with port de bras, four counts.

Students repeat Exercise 6 of the Second Class of this week.

Exercise 8

Battement jeté en croix, plié, two counts, three repetitions.

Students repeat Exercise 8 of the Fourth Class of this week.

Exercise 9

Rond de jambe à terre en dehors and en dedans, start with the foot on the cou-de-pied, extend in plié, with port de bras, passé à terre, four counts.

Following the preparatory port de bras, bring the arm down.

On 1, bring the front foot on the cou-de-pied devant, and the arm in 1st; on 2, extend the leg

The foot is on the cou-de-pied devant on demi-pointe.

devant and point the foot onto the floor, with a plié on the supporting leg; on 3, rond de jambe en dehors to 2nd, stretching the supporting leg, while the arm opens 2nd; on 4, rond de jambe en dehors to the back, keeping the arm 2nd; on "and" 5, brush the foot in 1st, and extend the leg devant again, keeping the arm 2nd; on 6, rond de jambe to 2nd; on 7, rond de jambe to the back; on 8, close 5th derrière, bringing the arm down.

On 1, bring the back foot on the cou-de-pied derrière and the arm in 1st; on 2, extend the leg derrière and point the foot onto the floor, with a plié on the supporting leg; on 3, rond de jambe en dedans, stretching the supporting leg, while the arm opens 2nd; on 4, rond de jambe en dedans to the front, keeping the arm 2nd; on "and" 5, brush the foot in 1st to 4th position derrière, keeping the arm 2nd; on 6, rond de jambe to 2nd; on 7, rond de jambe to the front; on 8, close 5th devant, bringing the arm down. Repeat the exercise one more time. At the end, plié and relevé in 5th, bring the foot on the cou-de-pied devant, and hold the position.

Explanation. Students are starting each rond de jambe by bringing the working foot pointed on the cou-de-pied, with the knee pushed to the side, and without sickling the foot. They then extend the leg with a plié and stretch with the first demi-rond de jambe. The first rond de jambe is followed by another one in the same direction. When extending the working leg in plié, the knee of the supporting leg does not move forward and remains above the toes. The foot is wrapped on the cou-de-pied devant in the relevé at the end of the exercise; the working foot is positioned a bit higher against the supporting leg, since the length of the cou-de-pied on demi-pointe is shortened in the back.

Application. The exercise can be performed facing the barre. The holding on the cou-de-pied at the end of the exercise should be performed facing the barre for students who still need to keep both hands at the barre to hold balance on demi-pointe.

Exercise 10

Battement frappé 2nd en l'air, two counts, three repetitions, facing the barre.

Students repeat Exercise 9 of the Second Class of this week.

Exercise 11

Rond de jambe soutenu 2nd, en dedans, eight counts, facing the barre.

Students repeat Exercise 10 of the Second Class of this week.

Exercise 12

Petits battements, accent devant, no hold, two on the count, facing the barre.

Students repeat Exercise 11 of the Second Class of this week.

Exercise 13

Adagio: développé 2nd, raccourci, eight counts, facing the barre.

Students repeat Exercise 12 of the Second Class of this week.

Exercise 14

Grand battement en croix, battement tendu, four counts.

Students repeat Exercise 13 of the Second Class of this week.

Exercise 15

Stretching.

Exercise 16

Battement jeté piqué 2nd, bouncing on the count, in 1st, four counts.

Students repeat Exercise 16 of the Fifth Class of the Twenty-Third Week.

Exercise 17

Adagio: lift the leg 2nd, hold three counts in the air, small fendu, with port de bras.

Students repeat Exercise 17 of the Second Class of this week.

Exercise 18

Glissade 2nd, without and with changing feet, arms in 6th, two counts, one count hold, four repetitions.

In the preparatory port de bras, bring both arms in 1st, open the right arm 2nd and keep the left arm in 1st, and turn the head toward the left arm.

On "and," plié, inclining the torso very slightly toward the left; on 1, brush the left foot and extend the leg 2nd in plié; on "and," transfer the weight onto the left leg on the plié, while the right leg stretches and the right foot points; on 2, close 5th, right foot front, on the plié; on 3, stretch the knees; on 4, hold the position. Repeat the glissade three more times closing left foot front in the fourth glissade, at the end of which the left arm opens and the right arm closes in 1st. Repeat the exercise to the right, starting with the left foot front. Repeat the whole exercise one more time.

Explanation. Students are changing feet and arms in the last glissade of each series so that they do not stop the exercise to change feet.

Exercise 19

Échappé 2nd on demi-pointes, changing feet, two counts, one count hold when closing, facing the barre.

On "and" 1, plié and slide the balls of the feet along the floor, opening both feet equally in 2nd; on 2, bring both feet into 5th in plié, left foot front; on 3, stretch both knees; on 4, hold the position. Repeat three more times.

Explanation. Students are practicing the exercise on two counts, instead of four counts, with one count hold after each échappé.

Exercise 20

Relevé retiré devant and derrière, direct closing, four counts, facing the barre.

Students repeat Exercise 19 of the Second Class of this week.

Exercise 21

Soubresaut in 5th, on the count, two repetitions, facing the barre.

Students repeat Exercise 20 of the Second Class of this week.

Exercise 22

Sissonne 2nd, traveling toward the front foot, changing feet, four counts, facing the barre.

On "and" 1, plié and push off with both feet, with a slight travel toward the right side (toward the front foot), stretching the left leg 2nd à la demi-hauteur; on 2, land in plié, on the right foot, while the left foot points 2nd onto the floor; on 3, close 5th, left foot front; on 4, stretch the knees. Repeat three more times, alternating sides. After a pause, repeat the whole exercise one more time.

Explanation. This is the most commonly performed sissonne. Here students change feet in the sissonne and travel toward the direction of the front foot. The head turns slightly toward the leg that closes front.

Exercise 23

Piqué with the foot on the cou-de-pied derrière, eight counts, facing the barre.

Students repeat Exercise 22 of the Second Class of this week.

Exercise 24

Curtsey.

Twenty-Fifth Week

§

FIRST CLASS

Students repeat the material of the Fifth Class of the Twenty-Fourth Week.

SECOND CLASS

Exercise 1

Warm up.

Exercise 2

Plié.

Exercise 3

First battement tendu exercise.

Exercise 4

Battement tendu devant, derrière, 2nd, hold when pointing, four counts, two repetitions.

On "and" 1, battement tendu devant; on 2, hold the position; on "and" 3, close 5th; on 4, hold the position; on "and" 5, battement tendu derrière with the left leg; on 6, hold the position; on "and" 7, close 5th; on 8, hold the position; on "and" 1, battement tendu 2nd; on 2, hold the position; on "and" 3, close 1st; on 4, hold the position; on "and" 5, battement tendu 2nd; on 6, hold the position; on "and" 7, close 5th devant; on 8, hold the position. Repeat one more time. At the end, roll up and hold the position.

Explanation. Students are repeating Exercise 4 of the Second Class of the Twenty-Fourth Week, except it is performed sideways with a slightly more energetic beat. The positions of the head are the same as the ones applied in this exercise performed facing the barre.

Exercise 5

Battement tendu 2nd, followed by another battement tendu, start in plié and stretch when pointing, in 1st, facing the barre.

On "and" 1, battement tendu 2nd; on 2, close 1st with a plié; on "and" 3, battement tendu 2nd, starting in plié and stretching when pointing; on 4, close 1st. Repeat one more time with the right foot. Repeat the whole exercise one more time. At the end, roll up in 1st and hold balance.

Explanation. This is essentially review material in which students are mixing the battement tendu finishing in plié and the battement tendu coming out of the plié.

Exercise 6

Battement jeté en croix, plié, two counts, three repetitions.

Students repeat Exercise 8 of the Fourth Class of the Twenty-Fourth Week.

Exercise 7

Rond de jambe à terre en dehors and en dedans, start with the foot on the cou-de-pied, extend in plié, with port de bras, four counts.

Students repeat Exercise 9 of the Fifth Class of the Twenty-Fourth Week.

Exercise 8

Battement fondu 2nd, four counts, facing the barre.

On "and" 1, deep plié, while bringing the front foot pointed on the cou-de-pied devant; on 2, open the leg in attitude in 2nd; on 3, stretch both legs 2nd; on "and," lower the leg and point the foot onto the floor; on 4, close 5th devant. Repeat the exercise one more time, closing 5th derrière. Repeat the whole exercise one more time.

Explanation. Students are practicing the battement fondu on four counts each. Great care is brought to the closing and opening of the working foot. By now the movement must be more flowing and smoother, going from one position to another in a continuous manner.

Exercise 9

Quick retiré, with extension 2nd, four counts, facing the barre.

On "and," quick retiré devant; on 1 and 2, hold the position; on 3, extend the leg 2nd, pointing the foot onto the floor; on "and" 4, close 5th derrière; on "and," quick retiré derrière; on 5 and 6, hold the position; on 7, extend the leg 2nd, pointing the foot onto the floor; on 8, close 5th devant. Repeat the exercise one more time with the right foot, holding the last retiré for balance.

Explanation. Students are revisiting the exercise that requires a sharp bending of the knee in retiré. This time the exercise is performed with turned-out legs. The working foot remains straight and does not sickle. Students do not kick, but must control their leg in the extension. To bring the leg in retiré, the leg bends from under; that is, the pointed foot must go up along the supporting leg without deviating to the side and without raising the hip. The faculty to quickly zip up their leg into retiré will prove to be quite useful when students perform pirouettes. Students should be balanced right away when bringing their leg into retiré.

Music. The music, a 4/4, has a quick tempo.

Application. This exercise aims to develop the sharpness of the bending of the knee. It helps to acquire crisp and quick leg work in small allegro. It still can be practiced with legs in parallel. To help students bring their leg sharply, the instructor may clap hands to emphasize the quickness of the movement.

Exercise 10

Rond de jambe soutenu 2nd, en dehors and en dedans, in 1st, eight counts, facing the barre.

On "and" 1, battement 2nd; on 2, hold the position; on 3 and 4, bend the working leg, with the toes describing an arc toward the back, then grazing the calf (or the back of the knee if the leg is à la hauteur) of the supporting leg; on 5 and 6, through the arc toward the front, with the movement finishing 2nd position with a stretched leg; on 7, lower the leg and point the foot onto the floor; on 8, close 1st. Repeat three more times, alternating legs.

On "and" 1, battement 2nd; on 2, hold the position; on 3 and 4, bend the working leg, draw the forward arc, with the toes grazing the back of the supporting leg; on 5 and 6, through the backward arc, with the movement finishing 2nd position with a stretched leg; on 7, lower the leg; on 8, close 1st. Repeat three more times, alternating legs. At the end, relevé in 1st.

Explanation. Here students practice the rond de jambe soutenu en dehors and en dedans. The exercise is performed in 1st so that students can switch legs easily without having to adjust the distance from the barre when closing the rond de jambe. The tempo is slightly accelerated.

Exercise 11

Battement frappé 2nd, en l'air, two counts, seven repetitions, facing the barre.

On "and," bring the front foot on the cou-de-pied devant; on 1, hold the position; on 2, extend the leg 2nd off the floor, grazing the toes on the floor before full extension; on 3, bring the foot on the cou-de-pied derrière; on 4, extend the leg 2nd; on 5, bring the foot on the cou-de-pied devant; on 6, extend the leg 2nd; on 7, bring the foot on the cou-de-pied derrière; on 8, extend the leg 2nd; on 1, bring the front foot on the cou-de-pied devant; on 2, extend the leg 2nd; on 3, bring the foot on the cou-de-pied derrière; on 4, extend the leg 2nd; on 5, bring the foot on the cou-de-pied devant; on 6, extend the leg 2nd; on 7, lower the leg and point the foot onto the floor; on 8, close 5th derrière. Repeat the whole exercise one more time.

Explanation. This is the same exercise performed previously, except the number of frappés has increased from three to seven battements frappés 2nd in each series.

Exercise 12

Petits battements, accent derrière, no hold, two on the count, facing the barre.

Start the exercise with the right foot back.

On "and," bring the foot on the cou-de-pied derrière; on 1, hold the position; on "and," bring the foot on the cou-de-pied devant; on 2, bring the foot on the cou-de-pied derrière; on "and," bring the foot on the cou-de-pied devant; on 3, bring the foot on the cou-de-pied derrière; on "and," bring the foot on the cou-de-pied devant; on 4, bring the foot on the cou-de-pied derrière; on "and," bring the foot on the cou-de-pied devant; on 5, bring the foot on the cou-de-pied derrière; on "and," bring the foot on the cou-de-pied devant; on 6, bring the foot on the cou-de-pied derrière; on 7, extend the leg 2nd, pointing the foot onto the floor; on 8, close 5th derrière. Repeat the exercise one more time.

Explanation. Students are repeating the exercise with the working foot starting derrière.

Exercise 13

Adagio: plié in 5th, with port de bras, retiré, changing feet, eight counts.

On "and" 1 and 2, plié, bringing the arm down; on "and" 3, straighten up the knees, bringing the arm in 1st; on 4, open the arm 2nd; on 5 and 6, bring it 5th; on 7 and 8, open it 2nd and bring it down; on "and," bring the foot on the cou-de-pied devant; on 1 and 2, slide up the foot along the leg to the level of the knee, bringing the arm 1st; on 3 and 4, hold the position; on "and," the toes graze the back of the leg; on 5 and 6, slide down the foot; on 7, close 5th derrière in plié; on 8, stretch the knees, opening the arm 2nd. Repeat the exercise with the right foot back, bringing the retiré from back to front. At the end, hold the last retiré and balance with both arms in 1st.

Explanation. This is a review exercise mixing the plié in 5th with port de bras and the retiré. Here the retiré is on eight counts. The second time, the plié is done with the left foot front, even though students are still facing the same direction. The back leg remains well turned out. The working leg stays turned out and the foot does not sickle when closing 5th derrière. The port de bras from 5th to the preparatory position is performed in two stages: first, the arm comes down from 5th to 2nd, and then the palm turns to face down and the arm and the fingers are slightly raised to initiate the port de bras to bring the arm down. The distinction between both ports de bras should be observed, even though the movement is continuous.

Exercise 14

Preparation for grand battement jeté piqué 2nd, in 1st, four counts, facing the barre.

On "and" 1, grand battement 2nd; on "and," lower the leg and point the foot on the floor; on 2, hold the position; on 3, throw the leg 2nd from the pointed position; on "and," lower the leg and point the foot on the floor; on 4, close 1st. Repeat three more times, alternating legs.

Explanation. This is a preparatory exercise for the grand battement piqué performed on four counts. There is no brushing of the foot in the second battement, thus reducing the momentum to get height in the battement. However, students must not compensate by swinging their upper torso or shoulders to try to lift their leg higher. They have to use their adductor muscles as much as possible, trying to bring their leg up from under. They also have to feel that their highly stretched and pointed foot is leading their leg up, as if the pointed foot is trying to hit a ball hard in the air. This approach will alleviate the use of the quadriceps that, unfortunately, tends to be overly active in the lifting of the leg. The lengthening and lifting of the torso (not the shoulders though!) will help make the whole movement look light and effortless.

Exercise 15

Stretching.

CENTER

Exercise 16

Battement tendu 2nd, en descendant and en remontant, two counts, review.

On "and" 1, battement tendu 2nd with the left foot; on 2, close 5th devant; on "and" 3, battement tendu 2nd with the right foot; on 4, close 5th devant. Repeat the exercise one more time.

On "and" 1, battement tendu 2nd with the right foot; on 2, close 5th derrière; on "and" 3, battement tendu 2nd with the left foot; on 4, close 5th derrière. Repeat the exercise one more time. Repeat the whole exercise one more time.

Explanation. Students are repeating Exercise 15 of the Second Class of the Twenty-Second Week, trying to perfect the brushing of the foot out and in.

Exercise 17

Quick lift of the foot on the cou-de-pied and in retiré devant, close in plié.

Following the preparatory port de bras, bring the arms down.

On "and," bring the front foot pointed on the cou-de-pied devant, bringing the arms in low 1st; on 1 and 2, hold the position; on 3, close in 5th in plié; on 4, stretch the legs; on "and," bring the foot on the cou-de-pied devant; on 5 and 6, hold the position; on 7, close in 5th in plié; on 8, stretch the legs; on "and," bring the front foot in retiré devant; from 1 to 4, hold the position; on 5, bring the foot on the cou-de-pied devant; on 6, close in 5th in plié; on 7 and 8, stretch the legs, opening the arms 2nd and bring them down. Repeat the exercise one more time with the right foot front.

Explanation. Students are practicing bringing the foot sharply on the cou-de-pied and retiré in the center. It is similar to the quick retiré exercise done at the barre in this lesson. Notice that students are given plenty of time to hold balance each time they are on one foot. The activation of the turn-out muscles and a pulled-up back are essential to keep balance. The knee in the retiré is pushed to the side. The pelvis remains aligned in the plié.

Music. A 4/4 staccato music works well here. Even a coda could accommodate this exercise, if it is not too fast.

Exercise 18

Glissade 2nd, without and with changing feet, arms in 6th, two counts, one count hold, four repetitions.

Students repeat Exercise 18 of the Fifth Class of the Twenty-Fourth Week.

Exercise 19

Échappé 2nd on demi-pointes, changing feet, two counts, one count hold when closing, facing the barre.

Students repeat Exercise 19 of the Fifth Class of the Twenty-Fourth Week.

Exercise 20

Relevé retiré devant and derrière, direct closing, four counts, facing the barre.

Students repeat Exercise 19 of the Second Class of the Twenty-Fourth Week.

Exercise 21

Soubresaut in 5th, on the count, two repetitions, facing the barre.

Students repeat Exercise 20 of the Second Class of the Twenty-Fourth Week.

Exercise 22

Sissonne 2nd, traveling toward the front foot, changing feet, four counts, facing the barre.

Students repeat Exercise 22 of the Fifth Class of the Twenty-Fourth Week.

Exercise 23

Piqué retiré derrière [jeté on pointe—Vaganova], four counts, facing the barre.

On "and," plié; on 1, extend the leg 2nd; on 2, step onto the right foot on demi-pointe, while the working leg comes into retiré derrière; on 3, come down in 5th in plié; on 4, stretch. Repeat three more times toward the right.

Explanation. Students are practicing the piqué on four counts, with direct closing. This time, the working leg is extended off the floor—but not too high—to do the piqué.

Exercise 24

Déboulés: three relevés in 1st, two half turns, each half turn on one count.

Following the preparatory port de bras, bring the arms down.

On "and" 1, plié and relevé, bringing the arms in low 1st; on 2, come down in plié; on 3, relevé directly from the plié; on 4, come down in plié; on 5, relevé; on 6, transfer the weight onto the right foot still on demi-pointe, rotate one half turn toward the right, turning the head so that, by the end of the half turn, it is directed toward the left shoulder with the eyes focused on a particular point; on 7, shift the weight onto the left foot, rotate toward the right one a half turn, keeping the eyes focused on the particular point as the body starts rotating, and the head snapping so that the head precedes the end of the rotation of the body, with the eyes still focused on the same spot; on 8, come down. Repeat the exercise traveling toward the right.

Explanation. Students are now performing the déboulés on demi-pointes. Students should have practiced regularly the spotting exercise flat-footed. The exercise starts with relevés to help students get into the pattern. The relevés must be well controlled by now so that students do not wobble. The knees must not bend in the turns, and the arms stay controlled in front of the torso. Students do not perform many déboulés yet at a time so that there is no risk of stuttering after each rotation. The increase in the number of repetitions will occur gradually. When turning, students must keep the 1st position on demi-pointes, using their adductors to avoid losing the turn-out during the half turns. The whole body turns as a block. The shoulders do not rise or come forward, as it is often seen, even in professional ballet dancers.

Application. The déboulé is a very ancient step, with illustrations dating from ancient Greece.[1] As we have seen, this step can be practiced at different levels depending on the student's strength. For those who do not practice pirouettes yet, it is a very useful step to perform in class to become familiar with the effect of rotation.

Exercise 25

Curtsey.

THIRD CLASS

Students repeat the material of the Second Class of this week.

FOURTH CLASS

Exercise 1

Warm up.

Exercise 2

Plié.

Exercise 3

First battement tendu exercise.

Exercise 4

Battement tendu devant, derrière, 2nd, hold when pointing, four counts, two repetitions.

Students repeat Exercise 4 of the Second Class of this week.

Exercise 5

Battement tendu 2nd, followed by another battement tendu, start in plié and stretch when pointing, facing the barre.

Students repeat Exercise 5 of the Second Class of this week.

---

1   Guillot and Prudhommeau, *Grammaire de la Danse Classique*, 117, citing Prudhommeau.

Exercise 6

Battement jeté en croix, plié, two counts, three repetitions.

Students repeat Exercise 8 of the Fourth Class of the Twenty-Fourth Week.

Exercise 7

Rond de jambe a terre en dehors and en dedans, start with the foot on the cou-de-pied, extend in plié, with port de bras, four counts.

Students repeat Exercise 9 of the Fifth Class of the Twenty-Fourth Week.

Exercise 8

Battement fondu 2nd, four counts, facing the barre.

Students repeat Exercise 8 of the Second Class of this week.

Exercise 9

Quick retiré, with extension 2nd, four counts, facing the barre.

Students repeat Exercise 9 of the Second Class of this week.

Exercise 10

Rond de jambe soutenu 2nd, en dehors and en dedans, in 1st, eight counts, facing the barre.

Students repeat Exercise 10 of the Second Class of this week.

Exercise 11

Battement frappé 2nd en l'air, two counts, seven repetitions, facing the barre.

Students repeat Exercise 11 of the Second Class of this week.

Exercise 12

Petits battements, accent derrière, no hold, two on the count, facing the barre.

Students repeat Exercise 12 of the Second Class of this week.

Exercise 13

Adagio: plié in 5th, with port de bras, retiré, changing feet, eight counts.

Students repeat Exercise 13 of the Second Class of this week.

Exercise 14

Preparation for grand battement jeté piqué 2nd, in 1st, four counts, facing the barre.

Students repeat Exercise 14 of the Second Class of this week.

Exercise 15

Stretching.

CENTER

Exercise 16

Battement tendu 2nd, en descendant and en remontant, two counts, review.

Students repeat Exercise 16 of the Second Class of this week.

Exercise 17

Quick lift of the foot on the cou-de-pied and retiré devant, eight counts.

Students repeat Exercise 17 of the Second Class of this week.

Exercise 18

Glissade 2nd, without and with changing feet, arms in 6th, two counts, one count hold, four repetitions.

Students repeat Exercise 18 of the Fifth Class of the Twenty-Fourth Week.

Exercise 19

Échappé 2nd on demi-pointes, changing feet, two counts, one count hold when closing, facing the barre.

Students repeat Exercise 19 of the Fifth Class of the Twenty-Fourth Week.

Exercise 20

Relevé retiré devant and derrière, without changing feet, two counts, two repetitions, facing the barre.

On "and," plié; on 1, relevé on the left foot, bringing the right leg into retiré devant; on 2, come down into plié in 5th, right foot front; on "and" 3, directly out of the plié, relevé on the left foot, bringing the right leg in retiré devant; on 4, come down in plié in 5th, right foot front. Repeat the exercise bringing the left leg in retiré derrière.

Repeat the exercise one more time, right foot front.

Explanation. Students are getting closer to the final version of the relevé retiré that students will be studying this year in the center. There is no stretching in between the relevés. Students transfer their weight directly onto the supporting leg in the relevé. They must be balanced right away to be able to hold the position when it is time to perform the exercise in the center. The working leg comes sharply in retiré each time without sickling the foot. Both feet are equally pressed down onto the floor in the plié.

Music. The music is fairly slow but sharp with clear beats.

Application. The progression of the exercise of the relevé has been very gradual to allow for proper strengthening and cleanness of execution. This progression is applicable to all ballet students starting training. For those who take the activity recreationally, the progression will be, of course, much slower.

Exercise 21

Soubresaut in 5th, on the count, two repetitions, facing the barre.

Students repeat Exercise 20 of the Second Class of the Twenty-Fourth Week.

Exercise 22

Sissonne 2nd, traveling toward the front foot, changing feet, four counts, facing the barre.

Students repeat Exercise 22 of the Fifth Class of the Twenty-Fourth Week.

Exercise 23

Piqué retiré derrière, four counts, facing the barre.

Students repeat Exercise 23 of the Second Class of this week.

Exercise 24

Déboulés: three relevés in 1st, two half turns, each half turn on one count.

Students repeat Exercise 24 of the Second Class of this week.

Exercise 25

Curtsey.

FIFTH CLASS

Exercise 1

Warm up.

Exercise 2

Plié.

Exercise 3

First battement tendu exercise.

Exercise 4

Battement tendu devant, derrière, 2nd, four counts, two repetitions.

Students repeat Exercise 4 of the Second Class of this week.

Exercise 5

Battement tendu 2nd, followed by another battement tendu, start in plié and stretch when pointing, facing the barre.

Students repeat Exercise 5 of the Second Class of this week.

Exercise 6

Battement jeté devant, derrière, 2nd, two counts, two repetitions, facing the barre.

On "and," battement jeté devant; on 1, hold the position; on "and," point the foot onto the floor; on 2, close 5th; on "and," battement jeté devant; on 3, hold the position; on "and," point the foot onto the floor; on 4, close 5th; on "and," battement jeté derrière; on 5, hold the position; on "and," point the foot onto the floor; on 6, close 5th; on "and," battement derrière; on 7, hold the position; on "and," point the foot onto the floor; on 8, close 5th derrière; on "and," battement 2nd with the right leg; on 1, hold the position; on "and," point the foot onto the floor; on 2, close 1st; on "and," battement 2nd; on 3, hold the position; on "and," point the foot onto the floor; on 4, close 1st; on "and," battement 2nd; on 5, hold the position; on "and," point the foot onto the floor; on 6, close 5th devant; on 7 and 8, hold the position. Repeat the exercise one more time. At the end, relevé in 5th and hold the position.

Explanation. Students are applying the new pattern, as introduced in Exercise 4 of the Sec-

ond Class of the Twenty-Fourth Week, to the battement jeté exercise.

Exercise 7

Battement jeté en croix, start in plié and stretch out, hold à la demi-hauteur, four counts, review.

On "and," plié; on 1, brush the right foot and extend the leg devant starting in plié, stretching both legs; on 2, hold the position; on "and," lower the leg and point the foot on the floor; on 3, hold the position; on 4, close 5th devant. Repeat the exercise en croix en dehors. Repeat one more time.

Explanation. Students are repeating Exercise 6 of the Second Class of the Twenty-First Week, this time performed sideways. There is a hold à la demi-hauteur to make sure that both legs are fully stretched before bringing the working leg down. The stretching of the legs has to be coordinated.

Exercise 8

Rond de jambe à terre en dehors and en dedans, start on the cou-de-pied, extend in plié, with port de bras, four counts.

Students repeat Exercise 9 of the Fifth Class of the Twenty-Fourth Week.

Exercise 9

Battement fondu 2nd, four counts, facing the barre.

Students repeat Exercise 8 of the Second Class of this week.

Exercise 10

Quick retiré, with extension 2nd, four counts, facing the barre.

Students repeat Exercise 9 of the Second Class of this week.

Exercise 11

Rond de jambe soutenu 2nd, en dehors and en dedans, eight counts, facing the barre.

Students repeat Exercise 10 of the Second Class of this week.

Exercise 12

Battement frappé 2nd en l'air, two counts, seven repetitions, facing the barre.

Students repeat Exercise 11 of the Second Class of this week.

Exercise 13

Petits battements, accent derrière, no hold, two on the count, facing the barre.

Students repeat Exercise 12 of the Second Class of this week.

Exercise 14

Adagio: plié in 5th, with port de bras, retiré, changing feet, eight counts.

Students repeat Exercise 13 of the Second Class of this week.

Exercise 15

Preparation for grand battement jeté piqué 2nd, in 1st, four counts, facing the barre.

Students repeat Exercise 14 of the Second Class of this week.

Exercise 16

Stretching.

CENTER

Exercise 17

Battement tendu 2nd, en descendant and en re-montant, two counts, review.

Students repeat Exercise 16 of the Second Class of this week.

Exercise 18

Quick lifting of the foot on the cou-de-pied and in retiré, eight counts.

Students repeat Exercise 17 of the Second Class of this week.

Exercise 19

Adagio: introduction to the épaulement croisé (crossed) position, port de bras to 3rd and 5th positions, eight counts.

Turn the body one-eighth of a turn away from the position de face, facing now the left front corner of the room, with the right shoulder forward, and the head directed to the right without tilting it sideways. Start in 5th. Following the preparatory port de bras, bring the arms down.

On "and" 1 and 2, bring the arms 1st; on 3 and 4, bring the arms to 3rd (with the left arm

Preparatory position in croisé; the head is slightly tilted sideways.

opening 2nd and the right arm coming to 5th); on 5 and 6, open the left arm 2nd; on "and" 7 and 8, bring the arms down; on 1 and 2, the arms come to 1st; on 3 and 4, they come to 5th, with the head slightly turned to the right; on 5 and 6, open both arms 2nd; on 7 and 8, bring the arms down. Repeat the port de bras one more time.

Repeat the exercise with the left foot front, turning the body one-eighth of a turn away from the de face direction to face now the lower right corner. This time, the head is slightly rotated toward the left shoulder.

Explanation. Students are introduced to the épaulement croisé, in which the body faces the lower diagonal. The position refers to bringing the shoulder that is the closest to the audience forward, with a rotation of the body. In this position, the dancer shows only one side of the body to the audience. The body is placed at an oblique angle, facing the downstage diagonals. To obtain this position, students rotate one-eighth of a turn from de face position. They must avoid turning too much to the side, which would reveal their back side to the audience. Notice the position of the head is toward the right if the épaulement is toward the right (the right shoulder is forward), and it is toward the left if the épaulement is toward the left, even when the arms are in 5th.

This position is introduced little by little, first with very simple exercises like this one. The croisé position, as well as the effacé and écarté positions studied later, accompanied with the appropriate head and shoulders positions and the focus of the eyes, give volume and expression to ballet movements that would otherwise be flat. Students should be introduced early on to these different orientations.

Fixed points of the studio: The French school, unlike the Cecchetti and the Vaganova schools, which use a different numbering system to describe stage directions, uses mainly the right, left, up, and down terms to describe these directions. The older terms côté court (the right side of the stage) and côté jardin (the left side of the stage)—both from the audience perspective—are not as commonly used, especially in the dance studio.

Exercise 20

Relevé retiré devant and derrière, without changing feet, two counts, facing the barre.

Students repeat Exercise 20 of the Fourth Class of this week.

Exercise 21

Glissade 2nd, two counts, soubresaut in 5th, on the count, four repetitions.

In the preparatory port de bras, keep the left arm in 1st and open the right arm 2nd, turning the head slightly toward the left side.

On "and" 1, inclining the torso slightly toward the left, plié and extend the left leg 2nd in plié; on "and" 2, transfer the weight onto the left leg in plié, while the right leg stretches and the right foot points, and close right foot front; on "and," directly from the plié, push off the floor with both feet, keeping the legs tight in 5th, closing the right arm, and straightening the torso and the head; on 3, land in plié, right foot front; on 4, stretch the legs, opening the right arm, resuming the overall body position for the glissade.

Repeat three more times traveling toward the left. Repeat the exercise with the left foot front and traveling toward the right side.

Explanation. Students are practicing both elements together in this combination. The focus should be on the cleanness of execution and the energy of the movements, especially in the landing of the jump and the closing of the glissade. The feet do not cross over in 5th in the landing of the soubresaut, and the legs are turned out with the knees above the toes in plié. Notice the change of port de bras between the glissade and the soubresaut. This exercise forces students to close the glissade energetically and transfer the weight quickly onto both feet at the end of the glissade to be able to take off for the jump equally with both feet.

Exercise 22

Sissonne 2nd, traveling toward the back foot, changing feet, four counts, facing the barre.

On "and," plié; on 1, push off the floor with both feet, with a slight travel toward the left side (toward the side of the back foot), stretching the right leg 2nd à la demi-hauteur; on 2, land in plié, on the left foot, while the right foot points 2nd onto the floor; on 3, close 5th, left foot front; on 4, stretch the knees. Repeat the exercise three more times, alternating legs. After a pause, repeat the exercise.

Explanation. Students are practicing the sissonne traveling toward the back foot and changing feet. The head slightly turns toward the traveling direction.

Exercise 23

Piqué retiré derrière, four counts, facing the barre.

Students repeat Exercise 23 of the Second Class of this week.

Exercise 24

Déboulés: three relevés in 1st, two half turns, each half turn on one count.

Students repeat Exercise 24 of the Second Class of this week.

Exercise 25

Curtsey.

Twenty-Sixth Week

§

FIRST CLASS

Students repeat the material of the Fifth Class of the Twenty-Fifth Week.

SECOND CLASS

Exercise 1

Warm up.

Exercise 2

Plié.

Exercise 3

First battement tendu exercise.

Exercise 4

Battement tendu en croix, close in plié, followed by another battement tendu, two counts, facing the barre.

On "and" 1, battement tendu devant; on 2, close 5th devant in plié; on "and" 3, battement tendu devant, stretching both legs at the same time; on 4, close 5th devant. Repeat the exercise en croix en dehors, with the first battement tendu 2nd closing devant. At the end, relevé in 5th and hold the position.

Explanation. Students are practicing the exercise that is similar to the Exercise 5 of the Second Class of the Twenty-Fifth Week, except it is now performed en croix.

Exercise 5

Battement tendu devant, derrière, 2nd, bring the foot down, two counts.

On "and" 1, battement tendu devant; on 2, close 5th devant; on "and" 3, battement tendu derrière; on 4, close 5th derrière; on "and" 5, battement tendu 2nd; on 6, bring down the foot 2nd, closing the arms in 1st; on 7, point the foot again, opening the arms 2nd and resting the hand onto the barre; on 8, close 5th devant. Repeat three more times. At the end, roll up and hold the position.

Explanation. The exercise is similar to Exercise 4 of the Second Class of the Twenty-Fifth Week, except it is now performed sideways on two counts instead of four. Notice that both arms close in 1st and open 2nd when the foot comes down and points 2nd.

Exercise 6

Battement jeté devant, derrière, 2nd, two counts, two repetitions, facing the barre.

Students repeat Exercise 6 of the Fifth Class of the Twenty-Fifth Week.

Exercise 7

Battement jeté en croix, start in plié and stretch out, hold à la demi-hauteur, four counts, facing the barre.

Students repeat Exercise 7 of the Fifth Class of the Twenty-Fifth Week.

Exercise 8

Rond de jambe à terre en dehors and en dedans, passé à terre, four counts, review.

On "and" 1, battement tendu devant; on 2, rond de jambe to 2nd, without hold; on 3, rond de jambe en dehors to the back; on 4, hold the position; on "and" 5, brush through 1st, extend the leg devant, and repeat the rond de jambe en dehors and close 5th derrière. Repeat the exercise with two ronds de jambe en dedans. Repeat the whole exercise one more time. At the end, plié, relevé, hold balance with arms in 5th.

Explanation. Students are reviewing Exercise 8 of the Fifth Class of the Twenty-Second Week, with an increased number of repetitions.

Exercise 9

Battement fondu en croix, four counts, facing the barre.

On "and" 1, deep plié while bringing the foot on the cou-de-pied devant; on 2, bend the working leg into attitude with a plié on the supporting leg; on 3, stretch both legs at the same time; on "and," lower the leg and point the foot onto the floor; on 4, close 5th devant. Repeat the exercise en croix en dehors. At the end, plié and relevé retiré devant and hold the position.

Explanation. Students are practicing the exercise en croix, still facing the barre.

Exercise 10

Quick retiré, with extension en croix, four counts, facing the barre.

On "and," quick retiré devant; on 1 and 2, hold the position; on 3, extend the leg devant, pointing the foot onto the floor; on 4, close 5th devant. Repeat the exercise en croix en dehors. At the end, hold the last retiré and balance.

Explanation. Students are repeating Exercise 9 of the Second Class of the Twenty-Fifth Week, this time performed en croix.

Music. For this kind of exercise, a medium-tempo coda or a tango with a sharp beat would work well.

Exercise 11

Battement frappé 2nd en l'air, with the foot in a flexed position, two counts, seven repetitions, facing the barre.

On "and," the front foot comes on the cou-de-pied devant, in a flexed position; on 1, hold the position; on 2, extend the leg 2nd off the floor, grazing the toes on the floor before full extension; on 3, bring the foot on the cou-de-pied derrière; on 4, extend the leg 2nd off the floor; on 5, bring the foot on the cou-de-pied devant; on 6, extend the leg 2nd; on 7, bring the foot on the cou-de-pied derrière; on 8, extend the leg 2nd; on 1, bring the foot on the cou-de-pied devant; on 2, extend the leg 2nd; on "and" 3, bring the foot on the cou-de-pied derrière; on 4, extend the leg 2nd; on "and" 5, bring the foot on the cou-de-pied devant; on 6, extend the leg 2nd; on "and" 7, lower the leg and point the foot onto the floor; on 8, close 5th derrière. Repeat the whole exercise one more time.

Explanation. Students are repeating the exercise with the foot flexed on the cou-de-pied. The whole movement is performed with vigor and sharpness.

Exercise 12

Rond de jambe soutenu 2nd, en dehors and en dedans, two counts for bending and stretching, in 1st, two repetitions, facing the barre.

On "and" 1, battement 2nd; on 2, hold the position; on 3, bend the working leg, with the toes describing an oval, first with an arc toward the back, then grazing the calf (or behind the knee if the leg is à la hauteur) of the supporting leg; on 4, drawing the arc toward the front and stretching the leg 2nd; from 5 to 6, repeat the rond de jambe; on 7, lower the leg and point the foot onto the floor; on 8, close 1st.

On "and" 1, battement 2nd; on 2, hold the position; on 3, bend the working leg, with the toes describing an oval first with an arc toward the front and then grazing the back of the supporting leg; on 4, finish the oval by drawing the arc toward the back and stretching the leg 2nd; from 5 to 6, repeat the same rond de jambe; on 7, lower the leg and point the foot onto the floor; on 8, close 1st. At the end, roll up and hold balance.

Explanation. Here students are performing each rond de jambe on two counts instead of four. They are also adding one more rond de jambe in each series.

Exercise 13

Petits battements, accent devant and derrière, two petits battements on the count, no hold, arm in low 1st.

Following the preparatory port de bras, bring the arm down.

On "and," bring the foot on the cou-de-pied devant, bringing the arm in low 1st; on 1, hold the position; on "and," bring the foot on the cou-de-pied derrière; on 2, bring the foot on the cou-de-pied devant; on "and," bring the foot on the cou-de-pied derrière; on 3, bring the foot on the cou-de-pied devant; on "and," bring the foot on the cou-de-pied derrière; on 4, bring the foot on the cou-de-pied devant; on "and," bring the foot on the cou-de-pied derrière; on 5, bring the foot on the cou-de-pied devant; on "and," bring the foot on the cou-de-pied derrière; on 6, bring the foot on the cou-de-pied devant; on 7, extend the leg 2nd, pointing the foot onto the floor, and opening the arm 2nd; on 8, close 5th derrière, closing the arm.

On "and," bring the foot on the cou-de-pied derrière, bringing the arm in low 1st; on 1, hold the position; on "and," bring the foot on the cou-de-pied devant; on 2, bring the foot on the cou-de-pied derrière; on "and," bring the foot on the cou-de-pied devant; on 3, bring the foot on the cou-de-pied derrière; on "and," bring the foot on the cou-de-pied devant; on 4, bring the foot on the cou-de-pied derrière; on "and," bring the foot on the cou-de-pied devant; on 5, bring the foot on the cou-de-pied derrière; on "and," bring the foot on the cou-de-pied devant; on 6, bring the foot on the cou-de-pied derrière; on 7, extend the leg 2nd, pointing the foot onto the floor, and opening the arm 2nd; on 8, close 5th devant, bringing the arm down. Repeat the exercise one more time. At the end, turn to face the barre, relevé and bring the foot on the cou-de-pied derrière, and hold the position.

Explanation. Students are mixing the petits battements, accent devant and derrière, in this exercise performed sideways.

Exercise 14

Adagio: lift the leg en croix, four counts.

On "and" 1 and 2, brush the front foot devant, and lift the leg; on "and" 3, lower the leg, and point the foot onto the floor; on 4, close 5th devant. Repeat the exercise en croix en dehors. At the end, relevé and hold balance in 5th.

Explanation. Students are reviewing this plain exercise of lifting the leg, except the timing here is different with each lift performed on four counts and the exercise done en croix. There is obviously less holding à la hauteur, but the leg reaches its highest point more rapidly. There is more continuity and fluidity in the whole movement.

Music. The adagio music is fairly slow to allow full completion of each battement properly, still carefully drawing the foot out and in at the beginning and at the end of the movement.

Exercise 15

Preparation for grand battement jeté piqué en croix, four counts.

On "and" 1, grand battement devant; on "and," lower the leg and point the foot onto the floor; on 2, hold the position; on 3, battement devant, from the pointed position; on "and," point the foot onto the floor; on 4, close 5th devant. Repeat the exercise en croix en dehors. At the end, relevé in 5th and hold balance.

Explanation. Students repeat Exercise 14 of the Second Class of the Twenty-Fifth Week, this time performed in 5th en croix en dehors.

Exercise 16

Stretching.

CENTER

Exercise 17

Battement tendu en croix, bring the foot down in plié, point the foot, temps lié en croix, in 1st, with port de bras, four counts.

On "and" 1, battement tendu devant; on 2, bring the foot down in 4th with a plié on both legs, bringing the arms in 1st; on 3, transfer the weight onto the back leg, stretching both legs, pointing the front foot, and opening the arms 2nd; on 4, close 1st. Repeat the exercise en croix en dehors, always starting with the same foot.

On "and" 1, battement tendu devant with the right foot; on 2, bring the foot down in 4th with a plié on both legs, bringing the arms in 1st; on 3, transfer the weight onto the front leg, stretching both legs, pointing the back foot, and opening the arms 2nd; on 4, close 1st. Repeat the exercise en croix, always starting with the same foot. At the end, roll up and hold balance.

Explanation. Students are reviewing Exercise 6 of the Second Class of the Twenty-Fourth Week, this time performed in the center. The whole exercise is done in 1st so as not to confuse students about which foot comes devant in the closing of the 5th.

Exercise 18

Battement jeté 2nd, en descendant and en remontant, two counts.

On "and," battement 2nd, with the left foot; on 1, hold the position; on "and," lower the leg and point the foot onto the floor; on 2, close 5th devant; on "and," battement 2nd, with the right foot; on 3, hold the position; on "and," lower the leg and point the foot onto the floor; on 4, close 5th devant. Repeat the exercise one more time, always closing front.

On "and," battement 2nd, with the right foot; on 1, hold the position; on "and," lower the leg and point the foot onto the floor; on 2, close 5th derrière; on "and," battement 2nd with the left foot; on 3, hold the position; on "and," lower the leg and point the foot onto the floor; on 4, close 5th derrière. Repeat the exercise one more time, always closing derrière. After a pause, repeat the exercise one more time.

Explanation. Students are repeating Exercise 15 of the Second Class of the Twenty-Second Week, this time performed with battements. Great attention is still given to the brushing out and in of the working foot for each battement.

Exercise 19

Adagio: introduction to the épaulement croisé position, port de bras to 3rd and 5th positions, eight counts.

Students repeat Exercise 19 of the Fifth Class of the Twenty-Fifth Week.

Exercise 20

Battement fondu, en croix, with port de bras, four counts.

Following the preparatory port de bras, bring the arms down.

On "and 1, bring the foot pointed on the cou-de-pied devant with a deep plié on the supporting leg, with the arms in low 1st; on 2, bring the leg in attitude devant, still in plié, with the arms coming to 1st; on 3, stretch both legs at the same time, opening the arms 2nd; on "and" 4, lower the leg down, point the foot down, close in 5th devant, and bring the arms down. Repeat the exercise en croix, the last one closing 5th derrière.

Explanation. The battement fondu is now performed in the center en croix on four counts. The coordination of the arms and the legs will be closely observed. The working knee is pushed to the side immediately when the foot comes onto the cou-de-pied.

Music. A medium-tempo waltz or a barcarolle would be good musical choices for this exercise.

Exercise 21

Relevé retiré devant and derrière, without changing feet, two counts, facing the barre.

Students repeat Exercise 20 of the Fourth Class of the Twenty-Fifth Week.

Exercise 22

Glissade 2nd, two counts, soubresaut in 5th, on the count, four repetitions.

Students repeat Exercise 21 of the Fifth Class of the Twenty-Fifth Week.

Exercise 23

Échappé 2nd, with port de bras, soubresaut 2nd, each on the count, facing the barre and in the center.

On "and" 1, plié and push off the floor, stretching the legs, and come down in plié; on "and," deepen the plié and push off the floor; on 2, land in 2nd; on "and," deepen the plié and push off again; on 3, land in 5th, left foot front; on 4, stretch the legs. Repeat three more times, closing alternatively right and left foot front. Repeat the exercise in the center with port de bras, opening the arms 2nd in the échappé and closing them when closing the échappé.

Explanation. Students are mixing the échappé and the soubresaut in 2nd in this exercise. The knees do not come forward in the pliés. They apply the standard port de bras as practiced in Exercise 24 of the Fifth Class of the Seventeenth Week.

Application. This is another exercise that can easily be done interchangeably in 1st and only at the barre for an easier version.

Exercise 24

Sissonne 2nd, traveling toward the back foot, changing feet, four counts, facing the barre.

Students repeat Exercise 22 of the Fifth Class of the Twenty-Fifth Week.

Exercise 25

Piqué 2nd, arms in 6th, four counts, review.

In the preparatory port de bras, bring the arms 1st, then open the left arm and keep the right arm in 1st, with the head slightly turned toward the right arm.

On "and," plié; on 1, extend the leg 2nd; on 2, step onto the right foot on demi-pointe, with the left leg joining the first one in 5th, right foot front; on 3, come down in plié; on 4, stretch. Repeat three more times toward the right. Repeat toward the left.

Explanation. Students are repeating Exercise 25 of the Second Class of the Twentieth Week.

Exercise 26

Curtsey.

THIRD CLASS

Students repeat the material of the Second Class of this week.

FOURTH CLASS

Exercise 1

Warm up.

Exercise 2

Plié.

Exercise 3

First battement tendu exercise.

Exercise 4

Battement tendu en croix, closed in plié, followed by another battement tendu, two counts, facing the barre.

Students repeat Exercise 4 of the Second Class of this week.

Exercise 5

Battement tendu devant, derrière, 2nd, bringing the foot down, two counts.

Students repeat Exercise 5 of the Second Class of this week.

Exercise 6

Battement jeté devant, derrière, 2nd, two counts, two repetitions, facing the barre.

Students repeat Exercise 6 of the Fifth Class of the Twenty-Fifth Week.

Exercise 7

Battement jeté en croix, start in plié and stretch out, hold à la demi-hauteur, four counts.

Students repeat Exercise 7 of the Fifth Class of the Twenty-Fifth Week.

Exercise 8

Rond de jambe à terre en dehors and en dedans, passé à terre, four counts, review.

Students repeat Exercise 8 of the Second Class of this week.

Exercise 9

Battement fondu en croix, four counts, facing the barre.

Students repeat Exercise 9 of the Second Class of this week.

Exercise 10

Quick retiré, with extension en croix, four counts, facing the barre.

Students repeat Exercise 10 of the Second Class of this week.

Exercise 11

Battement frappé 2nd en l'air, with the foot in a flexed position, two counts, seven repetitions, facing the barre.

Students repeat Exercise 11 of the Second Class of this week.

Exercise 12

Rond de jambe soutenu 2nd, en dehors and en dedans, two counts for bending and stretching, in 1st, two repetitions, facing the barre.

Students repeat Exercise 12 of the Second Class of this week.

Exercise 13

Petits battements, accent devant and derrière, no hold, two petits battements on the count, arm in low 1st.

Students repeat Exercise 13 of the Second Class of this week.

Exercise 14

Adagio: lift the leg en croix, four counts.

Students repeat Exercise 14 of the Second Class of this week.

Exercise 15

Preparation for grand battement jeté piqué en croix, four counts.

Students repeat Exercise 15 of the Second Class of this week.

Exercise 16

Stretching.

CENTER

Exercise 17

Battement tendu en croix, bring the foot down in plié, point the foot, temps lié en croix, in 1st, with port de bras, four counts.

Students repeat Exercise 17 of the Second Class of this week.

Exercise 18

Battement tendu devant and derrière, four counts, with épaulement croisé.

Stand in 5th position in the position croisé.

On 1 and 2, battement tendu devant; on 3 and 4, close 5th; on 5 and 6, battement tendu devant; on 7 and 8, close 5th; on 1 and 2, battement tendu devant; on 3 and 4, close 5th; from 5 to 8, port de bras, bringing the arms down, then to 1st and 2nd. Repeat the exercise with a battement tendu derrière. Repeat the exercise one more time.

Explanation. Students are practicing the battement tendu in the croisé position. The arms remain 2nd, and each battement tendu is on four counts. The head is slightly directed toward the arm of the épaulement. Students do not crush their big toe in the battement tendu derrière. The torso and lower abdomen are lifted, and the weight remains on the supporting leg. When extending the leg forward in the position croisé, students tend to turn in their supporting leg somewhat to favor the turn-out of the working leg. This may be caused by watching themselves in the mirror, where students focus naturally on the front leg, since the back leg is partly hidden by the front leg. Even though students are now facing the lower diagonals, the correct position of the whole body should be like it is when it is de face and should not be adjusted.

Music. Since each battement tendu is on four counts, the tempo is accelerated.

Exercise 19

Battement jeté 2nd, en descendant and en remontant, two counts.

Students repeat Exercise 18 of the Second Class of this week.

Exercise 20

Adagio: introduction to the épaulement croisé position, with port de bras to 3rd and 5th positions, eight counts.

Students repeat Exercise 19 of the Fifth Class of the Twenty-Fifth Week.

Exercise 21

Battement fondu, en croix, with port de bras, four counts.

Students repeat Exercise 20 of the Second Class of this week.

Exercise 22

Relevé retiré devant, en descendant and en remontant, two counts, facing the barre.

On "and" 1, plié and relevé bringing the left foot (back foot) against the front of the supporting knee into retiré devant, with the head turning slightly toward the left, and hold the position; on 2, come down in plié closing 5th, left foot front; on "and" 3, directly out of the plié, relevé bringing the right foot (back foot) against the front of the supporting knee in retiré, turning the head toward the right, and hold the position; on 4, come down in plié closing 5th, right foot front.

On "and" 5, directly out of the plié, relevé on the left leg, bringing the right foot against the front of the supporting knee in retiré, with the head turning slightly toward the left side, and hold the position; on 6, bring the working foot behind the supporting leg, coming down in plié, and closing right foot back; on "and" 7, relevé, bringing the left foot against the front of the supporting knee in retiré, turning the head toward the right side, and hold the position; on 8, bring the working foot behind the supporting leg, come down in plié, and close 5th left foot back. Repeat the exercise one more time.

Explanation. The relevé with retiré changes feet when closing in this exercise. So that the barre is not an obstacle, students perform only two in each direction, since they move forward and backward in this exercise. It is important that the working foot reaches the knee as quickly as possible. The rapidity of the leg coming up into retiré will contribute to the sharp look of the pirouette, with the dancers getting into the retiré position quickly so that how they get there or how they come down becomes as minimal as possible to the audience. Students are reminded of the head positions, which are similar to the ones used for most exercises performed en descendant and en remontant. The working foot does not flex prematurely when closing 5th.

Music. To help students zip up their leg into a retiré as quickly as possible, the rhythm of the music should be clear and uncluttered by too many notes.

Exercise 23

Glissade 2nd, two counts, soubresaut in 5th, on the count, four repetitions.

Students repeat Exercise 21 of the Fifth Class of the Twenty-Fifth Week.

Exercise 24

Échappé 2nd, with port de bras, soubresaut 2nd, each on the count, facing the barre and in the center.

Students repeat Exercise 23 of the Second Class of this week.

Exercise 25

Sissonne 2nd, traveling toward the back foot, changing feet, four counts, facing the barre.

Students repeat Exercise 22 of the Fifth Class of the Twenty-Fifth Week.

Exercise 26

Piqué 2nd, arms in 6th, four counts, review.

Students repeat Exercise 25 of the Second Class of this week.

Exercise 27

Curtsey.

FIFTH CLASS

Exercise 1

Warm up.

Exercise 2

Plié.

Exercise 3

First battement tendu exercise.

Exercise 4

Battement tendu en croix, close in plié, followed by another battement tendu, two counts, facing the barre.

Students repeat Exercise 4 of the Second Class of this week.

Exercise 5

Battement tendu devant, derrière, 2nd, bring the foot down, two counts.

Students repeat Exercise 5 of the Second Class of this week.

Exercise 6

Battement jeté devant, derrière, 2nd, two counts, two repetitions, facing the barre.

Students repeat Exercise 6 of the Fifth Class of the Twenty-Fifth Week.

Exercise 7

Battement en cloche, direct, on the count, in 1st, three repetitions.

On "and" 1, battement devant; on 1, hold the position; on "and" 2, brush through 1st and extend the leg derrière; on "and" 3, brush through 1st and extend the leg devant; on 4, hold the position; on "and" 5, brush through 1st and extend the leg derrière; on "and" 6, brush through 1st and extend the leg devant; on "and" 7, brush through 1st and extend the leg derrière; on 8, hold the position. Repeat the exercise one more time. At the end, hold the position with the leg stretched derrière, releasing the barre with the arms 2nd.

Explanation. Students are now practicing the battement cloche on the count. The third battement preceding the hold should be very energetic, quickly going up and held in a freeze, like it hits a wall. Students brush through 1st with the whole foot. Students must not pull the barre during the exercise. Notice the pause after two battements, and the holding à la demi-hauteur of the leg derrière at the end to check balance.

Exercise 8

Rond de jambe à terre en dehors and en dedans, passé à terre, four counts, review.

Students repeat Exercise 8 of the Second Class of this week.

Exercise 9

Battement fondu, en croix, four counts, facing the barre.

Students repeat Exercise 9 of the Second Class of this week.

Exercise 10

Quick retiré, with extension en croix, four counts, facing the barre.

Students repeat Exercise 10 of the Second Class of this week.

Exercise 11

Battement frappé 2nd en l'air, with the foot in a flexed position, two counts, seven repetitions, facing the barre.

Students repeat Exercise 11 of the Second Class of this week.

Exercise 12

Rond de jambe soutenu 2nd, en dehors and en dedans, two counts for bending and stretching, in 1st, two repetitions, facing the barre.

Students repeat Exercise 12 of the Second Class of this week.

Exercise 13

Petits battements, accent devant and derrière, no hold, two petits battements on the count, arm in low 1st.

Students repeat Exercise 13 of the Second Class of this week.

Exercise 14

Adagio: lift the leg en croix, four counts.

Students repeat Exercise 14 of the Second Class of this week.

Exercise 15

Preparation for grand battement jeté piqué en croix, four counts.

Students repeat Exercise 15 of the Second Class of this week.

Exercise 16

Stretching.

CENTER

Exercise 17

Battement tendu en croix, bring the foot down in plié, point the foot, temps lié en croix, in 1st, with port de bras, four counts.

Students repeat Exercise 17 of the Second Class of this week.

Exercise 18

Battement tendu devant and derrière, four counts, with épaulement croisé.

Students repeat Exercise 18 of the Fourth Class of this week.

Exercise 19

Battement jeté 2nd, en descendant and en remontant, two counts.

Students repeat Exercise 18 of the Second Class of this week.

Exercise 20

Adagio: introduction to the épaulement croisé position, port de bras to 3rd and 5th positions, eight counts.

Students repeat Exercise 19 of the Fifth Class of the Twenty-Fifth Week.

Exercise 21

Battement fondu, en croix, with port de bras, four counts.

Students repeat Exercise 20 of the Second Class of this week.

Exercise 22

Relevé retiré devant, en descendant and en remontant, two counts, facing the barre.

Students repeat Exercise 22 of the Fourth Class of this week.

Exercise 23

Échappé 2nd, with port de bras, soubresaut 2nd, each on the count, facing the barre and in the center.

Students repeat Exercise 23 of the Second Class of this week.

Exercise 24

Sissonne 2nd, traveling toward the back foot, changing feet, four counts, facing the barre.

Students repeat Exercise 22 of the Fifth Class of the Twenty-Fifth Week.

Exercise 25

Piqué 2nd, arms in 6th, four counts, review.

Students repeat Exercise 25 of the Second Class of this week.

Exercise 26

Curtsey.

Twenty-Seventh Week

𝔰

FIRST CLASS

Students repeat the material of the Fifth Class of the Twenty-Sixth Week.

SECOND CLASS

Exercise 1

Warm up.

Exercise 2

Plié.

Exercise 3

First battement tendu exercise.

Exercise 4

Battement tendu en croix, close in plié, followed by another battement tendu, two counts.

On "and" 1, battement tendu devant; on 2, close 5th devant in plié; on "and" 3, battement tendu devant, stretching both legs at the same time; on 4, close 5th devant. Repeat the exercise en croix en dehors, with the first battement tendu 2nd closing devant. At the end, relevé in 5th and hold the position.

Explanation. Students are repeating Exercise 4 of the Second Class of the Twenty-Sixth Week, this time performed sideways.

Exercise 5

Battement tendu devant, derrière, 2nd, battement tendu derrière, devant, 2nd, two counts, facing the barre.

On "and" 1, battement tendu devant; on 2, close 5th devant; on "and" 3, battement tendu derrière; on 4, close 5th derrière; on "and" 5, battement tendu 2nd; on 6, bring down the foot 2nd; on 7, point the foot again; on 8, close 5th derrière. On "and" 1, battement tendu derrière; on 2, close 5th derrière; on "and" 3, battement tendu devant; on 4, close 5th devant; on "and" 5, battement tendu 2nd, still with the right foot; on 6, bring the foot down in 2nd; on 7, point the

foot; on 8, close 5th devant. Repeat the exercise one more time. At the end, relevé in 5th and hold balance.

Explanation. Students are introduced to the concept of reversing directions in this exercise, the first part of which is already familiar. Performing this exercise facing the barre is recommended. This is the most intricate combination of battements tendus to which students are exposed in this program. Students apply the head positions they have learned for this type of exercise.

Music. The tempo is fairly slow so that students have time to think about the directions.

Exercise 6

Preparation for battement tendu soutenu 2nd, two counts, two counts hold in closing, facing the barre.

On "and" 1, plié and battement tendu 2nd with the right foot in plié; on 2, close 5th devant while the supporting leg stretches; on 3 and 4, hold the position. Repeat three more times, alternating closing devant and derrière.

Explanation. This exercise is in preparation for the battement soutenu, in which the working leg joins the supporting leg on demi-pointes or pointes. For now, the foot remains on the floor and the closing is done flat-footed. What is important to accomplish is the squeezing of both legs joining each other in 5th with a stretch of the supporting leg. Students must not shift their weight away from the supporting leg when the working leg is stretched out in plié, for it would otherwise be difficult to bring back the working leg in. The closing must be energetic with both legs squeezing together, with the working leg being like vacuumed in against the other.

Application. Like with many exercises in this manual, this one has been highly broken down to facilitate the introduction of the battement soutenu and assure cleanness of the final product.

Exercise 7

Battement jeté, en croix, two counts, four repetitions.

On "and," battement jeté devant; on 1, hold the position; on "and," point the foot on the floor; on 2, close in 5th. Repeat the battement devant three more times. Repeat the exercise en croix en dehors, the first battement 2nd closing 5th devant. At the end, plié and relevé in 5th and hold balance.

Explanation. Students are reviewing the exercise with four battements in each direction.

Exercise 8

Battement en cloche, on the count, in 1st, three repetitions.

Students repeat Exercise 7 of the Fifth Class of the Twenty-Sixth Week.

Exercise 9

Rond de jambe à la demi-hauteur, en dehors and en dedans, passé à terre, four counts, facing the barre.

On "and" 1, battement devant; on 2, rond de jambe en dehors to 2nd; on 3, rond de jambe en dehors to back; on 4, hold the position; on "and" 5, brush through 1st and extend the leg devant à la demi-hauteur; on 6, rond de jambe to 2nd; on 7, rond de jambe to back; on "and," lower the leg and point the foot onto the floor; on 8, close 5th derrière. Repeat the exercise starting with a battement derrière and two ronds de jambe en dedans. At the end, hold the leg devant à la demi-hauteur and hold balance.

Explanation. Students are practicing the rond de jambe à la demi-hauteur on four counts instead of eight, and performing two in each direction. Facing the barre facilitates maintaining the hips straight throughout.

Exercise 10

Battement frappé en l'air, en croix en dehors and en dedans, two counts, facing the barre.

On "and," the front foot comes on the cou-de-pied devant; on 1, hold the position; on 2, extend the leg devant, off the floor, grazing the toes on the floor before extending fully; on 3, bring the foot on the cou-de-pied devant; on 4, extend the leg 2nd; on 5, bring the foot on the

cou-de-pied derrière; on 6, extend the leg derrière; on 7, bring the foot on the cou-de-pied derrière; on 8, extend the leg 2nd.

On 1, the front foot comes on the cou-de-pied derrière; on 2, extend the leg derrière, off the floor; on 3, bring the foot on the cou-de-pied derrière; on 4, extend the leg 2nd; on 5, bring the foot on the cou-de-pied devant; on 6, extend the leg devant; on 7, bring the foot on the cou-de-pied devant; on 8, extend the leg 2nd. Keeping the leg 2nd, hold balance, releasing the barre with the arms 2nd.

Explanation. Students are practicing the exercise en croix en dehors and en dedans, with the same energy in the striking of the foot on the cou-de-pied as in the extension of the leg off the floor. The leg freezes when extended out. When bending, the knee of the working leg is pushed to the side.

Exercise 11

Petits battements, accent devant and derrière, no hold, two petits battements on one count, arm in low 1st.

Students repeat Exercise 13 of the Second Class of the Twenty-Sixth Week.

Exercise 12

Adagio: développé 2nd, eight counts, facing the barre, review.

On "and," bring the foot pointed on the cou-de-pied devant; on 1 and 2, slide the foot up to retiré; on 3, open the leg in attitude in 2nd; on 4, stretch the leg fully 2nd; on 5 and 6, hold the position; on 7, bring down the leg and point the foot onto the floor; on 8, close 5th devant. Repeat the exercise closing 5th derrière.

Explanation. Students are reviewing Exercise 12 of the Fourth Class of the Twenty-Third Week, this time performing the développé twice in a row with the same leg.

Exercise 13

Grand battement devant, back to the barre, battement 2nd and derrière, facing the barre, in 1st, two counts.

Start the exercise with the back facing the barre. Following the preparatory port de bras, the hands rest on the barre, with the elbows softly curved.

On "and" 1, grand battement devant with the right leg; on "and," lower the leg and point the foot onto the floor; on 2, close 1st. Repeat three more times. After performing the exercise with the left leg, turn around to face the barre.

On "and" 1, grand battement derrière with the right leg; on "and," lower the leg and point the foot onto the floor; on 2, close 1st. Repeat three more times.

On "and" 1, grand battement 2nd with the right leg; on "and," lower the leg and point the foot onto the floor; on 2, close 1st. Repeat three more times.

Explanation. Students are introduced to a new pattern in this exercise of grand battement, in which the battement devant is performed with the back facing the barre. Working in this position can be done occasionally; this practice used to be more common in France than it is now. It helps students to keep the shoulders back; it also allows them to lift their leg without space limitation or obstacle. However, it may also encourage students to raise one shoulder over the other (or both). The position also tends to impede the transfer of weight from one leg onto the other, since it is more difficult to move the hands along the barre when the back faces the barre. It will thus be used sparingly. Before changing direction, students execute the exercise with both legs. The use of the 1st position facilitates this change of legs.

Exercise 14

Stretching.

CENTER

Exercise 15

Battement tendu devant and derrière, four counts, with épaulement croisé.

Students repeat Exercise 18 of the Fourth Class of the Twenty-Sixth Week.

Exercise 16

Battement jeté devant and derrière, two counts, two count hold in closing, with épaulement croisé.

On "and," battement devant; on 1, hold the position; on "and," point the foot onto the floor; on 2, close 5th; on 3 and 4, hold the position; on

"and," battement devant; on 5, hold the position; on "and," point the foot onto the floor; on 6, close 5th; on 7 and 8, hold the position. Repeat the exercise with the back leg. Repeat the exercise one more time.

Explanation. Students are now practicing the battement jeté in the croisé position. Notice the holding in the closing to make sure students are stable with the pelvis correctly aligned and that they are ready to change supporting legs when needed. The change of orientation can be indeed a little bit destabilizing for students who are not used to it. To be able to hold balance in the battement jeté derrière, students lift up their lower abdomen and upper torso, while minimizing the turning in of the supporting leg.

Exercise 17

Adagio: lift the leg devant and derrière, arabesque croisée with arms 2nd, four counts, with épaulement croisé.

On "and" 1 and 2, brush the front foot out, lift the leg, and hold the position; on "and" 3, lower the leg and point the foot onto the floor; on 4, close 5th devant; on "and" 5 and 6, brush the back foot, lift the leg derrière, with the arms still 2nd, but coming very slightly forward, and hold the position; on "and" 7, lower the leg; on 8, close 5th derrière. Repeat one more time.

Explanation. Students are now practicing lifting the leg devant and derrière in croisé position, with the arms 2nd. The same principles of execution apply as when performing the exercise de face. In the arabesque, the arms come very slightly forward in 2nd to compensate for the lifting of the leg in the back. A fully pointed foot is required and should give the impression that it leads the movement of the working leg. Even though the position is now croisé, the turn-out must not be neglected and should be applied without favoring one leg over the other. Students should refrain from holding the pointed position before lifting the leg so that the rise of the leg appears continuous.

So far, the arabesque has been practiced de face. Here it is performed with an épaulement. It is called an arabesque croisée, which is usually performed with one arm forward; the arms here remain 2nd to keep the upper torso straight. There are two basic arabesques in the

French school: the arabesque croisée, where the supporting leg is the closest to the audience and hides the working leg, and the arabesque ouverte, in which the working leg is the closest to the audience and is not hidden by the supporting leg. Not involved in this exercise, since the arms are 2nd, there are also two other kinds of arm positions for each of these arabesques, one of them will be studied later in the training.

Exercise 18

Relevé retiré devant, en descendant and en remontant, two counts, facing the barre.

Students repeat Exercise 22 of the Fourth Class of the Twenty-Sixth Week.

Exercise 19

Soubresaut in 1st, with a quarter of a turn, on the count.

Following the preparatory port de bras, the arms come down.

On "and," plié and push off the floor with pointed feet and stretched legs, while turning to face the right side of the studio; on 1, land into plié; on 2, stretch both knees. Repeat three more times, changing directions, turning toward the right, a quarter of a turn each time. Repeat the whole exercise one more time.

Explanation. Students are introduced to rotation while jumping. They must make a precise quarter of a turn with no adjustment once they land. Students sometimes cheat in the takeoff by turning in the foot that is opposite of the side to which they must rotate; just as they get ready to take off, students must not adjust their 1st position, but jump off directly out of it. Likewise, when they land, both feet should be in the position they started from. The whole body turns as a block, even the head. There is no spotting.

Music. A slow-to-medium tempo march would work well here so that students adjust to the new feature of the jump and can stretch the knees between each jump.

Exercise 20

Sissonne 2nd, traveling toward the back foot, changing feet, four counts, facing the barre.

Students repeat Exercise 22 of the Fifth Class of the Twenty-Fifth Week.

Exercise 21

Preparation for chassé à terre and sauté, traveling forward, arms in 6th, two counts each.

Start in the back of the studio, traveling forward. In the preparatory port de bras, bring the arms in 1st, open the left 2nd, and keep the right arm in 1st.

On "and," plié; on 1, slide the front foot forward, through 4th, transfer the weight onto the front foot, stretching both legs, with the back foot pointing onto the floor; on 2, close 5th derrière; on "and," plié; on 3, brush the front foot and extend the leg devant, pointing the foot, step onto the right foot in plié and immediately push off the floor, bringing the left leg into 5th derrière in the air; on 4, land in plié 5th position. Repeat the exercise several times. Switch arms when executing the exercise with the left leg. Repeat the whole exercise one more time.

Explanation. Students are combining the preparatory exercise for the chassé à terre and the chassé sauté traveling forward this time, with a brisker tempo for a more energetic attack in each step. When extending the front leg to prepare for the chasse sauté, the leg is turned out with the heel pushed forward. The working foot must not flex in anticipation of stepping down to push for takeoff.

Exercise 22

Piqué retiré derrière, arms in 6th, four counts.

In the preparatory port de bras, bring the arms in 1st, open the left arm and keep the right arm in 1st, with the head turned toward the right.

On "and," plié; on 1, extend the leg 2nd; on 2, step onto the right foot on demi-pointe while the working leg comes into retiré derrière; on 3, come down in 5th in plié; on 4, stretch. Repeat three more times toward the right. Repeat the whole exercise one more time.

Explanation. Students are practicing the piqué retiré in the center with the standard 6th position of the arms. The side of the torso opposite of the direction of travel must be particularly lifted, with the arm 2nd held in place. Since there is no barre to keep balance, students have to gauge how much momentum they have to bring onto the leg doing the piqué so that they can balance on it as much as possible. If not enough

Piqué with retiré derrière and arms in 6th position; the left hip is lifted.

momentum, they are not able to get their weight onto it, thus falling back onto the second leg; and if too much momentum, they go over their demi-pointe, thus losing balance. To ease this difficulty, students must learn to quickly transfer their weight onto the first leg so that balance is obtained as fast as possible and to do the piqué where the toes are pointing. To keep balance, it is necessary to keep a strong back and to maximize the use of the turn-out muscles of the first leg to keep the body de face with both legs turned out. In the piqué 2nd onto one leg, if there is no control of the turn-out, students tend to rotate onto their supporting leg, unable to maintain balance with both legs turned out.

Music. Since the exercise is very broken down, the music will be an energetic 4/4.

Exercise 23

Déboulés: relevé in 1st, four half turns, each half turn on one count.

Following the preparatory port de bras, bring the arms down.

On "and" 1, plié and relevé, bringing the arms in low 1st; on 2, hold the position; on 3, rotate one half turn toward the right; on 4, rotate one half turn; on 5, rotate one half turn; on 6, rotate one half turn; on 7 and 8, come down in plié and stretch. Repeat the exercise several times traveling toward the right.

Explanation. Students are now executing four half turns at a time. The same principles learned previously apply.

Exercise 24

Curtsey.

THIRD CLASS

Students repeat the material of the Second Class of this week.

FOURTH CLASS

Exercise 1

Warm up.

Exercise 2

Plié.

Exercise 3

First battement tendu exercise.

Exercise 4

Battement tendu en croix, close in plié, followed by another battement tendu, two counts.

Students repeat Exercise 4 of the Second Class of this week.

Exercise 5

Battement tendu devant, derrière, 2nd, battement tendu derrière, devant, 2nd, two counts, facing the barre.

Students repeat Exercise 5 of the Second Class of this week.

Exercise 6

Preparation for battement tendu soutenu 2nd, two counts, two count hold in closing, facing the barre.

Students repeat Exercise 6 of the Second Class of this week.

Exercise 7

Battement jeté en croix, two counts, four repetitions.

Students repeat Exercise 7 of the Second Class of this week.

Exercise 8

Rond de jambe à la demi-hauteur, en dehors and en dedans, passé à terre, four counts, facing the barre.

Students repeat Exercise 9 of the Second Class of this week.

Exercise 9

Battement frappé en l'air, en croix en dehors and en dedans, two counts, facing the barre.

Students repeat Exercise 10 of the Second Class of this week.

Exercise 10

Petits battements, accent devant and derrière, no hold, two petits battements on one count, arm in low 1st.

Students repeat Exercise 13 of the Second Class of the Twenty-Sixth Week.

Exercise 11

Adagio: développé 2nd, eight counts, facing the barre, review.

Students repeat Exercise 12 of the Second Class of this week.

Exercise 12

Grand battement devant, back to the barre, derrière and 2nd facing the barre, in 1st, two counts.

Students repeat Exercise 13 of the Second Class of this week.

Exercise 13

Stretching.

CENTER

Exercise 14

Battement tendu devant and derrière, with port de bras, two counts, three repetitions, with épaulement croisé.

In the preparatory port de bras, bring the arms in 1st, open the right arm 2nd, and keep the left

Battement tendu devant croisé with the arms in 6th position.

arm in 1st. The head is slightly turned toward the right arm.

On "and" 1, battement tendu devant; on 2, close 5th devant; on "and" 3, battement tendu devant; on 4, close 5th devant; on "and" 5, battement tendu devant; on 6, close 5th; on 7 and 8, the right arm closes 1st and the left arm opens 2nd. Repeat the exercise with a battement tendu derrière. Repeat the exercise one more time.

Explanation. The exercise is performed on two counts with port de bras. Notice the arm position in which the arm opposite of the working leg is brought in 1st. This is a standard arm position for this type of exercise. Students have two counts to change arms positions in between series. The battement tendu is more energetic, but the change of arm position is smooth.

Exercise 15

Battement jeté devant and derrière, two counts, two counts hold in closing, with épaulement croisé.

Students repeat Exercise 16 of the Second Class of this week.

Exercise 16

Adagio: lift the leg devant and derrière, arabesque croisée with arms 2nd, four counts, with épaulement croisé.

Students repeat Exercise 17 of the Second Class of this week.

Exercise 17

Relevé in 1st, with port de bras, two counts, four repetitions.

Following the preparatory port de bras, bring the arms down.

On "and," plié; on 1, relevé, bringing the arms in low 1st; on 2, come down in plié; on 3, relevé; on 4, come down in plié; on 5, relevé; on 6, come down in plié; on 7, relevé; on 8, come down in plié and stretch the knees. From 1 to 8, port de bras bringing the arms 5th, 2nd, and down. Repeat one more time.

Explanation. Students are revisiting the relevé exercise with a port de bras in between each series.

Exercise 18

Relevé in 5th, two counts, three repetitions.

Following the preparatory port de bras, bring the arms down.

On "and," plié; on 1, relevé in 5th, with the arms in low 1st; on 2, come down in plié; on 3, relevé; on 4, come down in plié; on 5, relevé; on 6, come down in plié; on 7, stretch the knees; on 8, hold the position.

Explanation. Students are practicing the relevé in 5th exercise in the center on two counts and without holding. Like at the barre, students must not jump onto demi-pointes when going up, but bring both feet under with a very slight hop onto the balls of the feet. The knees are fully stretched in the relevé.

Exercise 19

Soubresaut in 1st, with a quarter of a turn, on the count.

Students repeat Exercise 19 of the Second Class of this week.

Exercise 20

Sissonne 2nd, traveling toward the back foot, changing feet, four counts, facing the barre.

Students repeat Exercise 22 of the Fifth Class of the Twenty-Fifth Week.

Exercise 21

Preparation for chassé à terre and sauté traveling forward, arms in 6th, two counts each.

Students repeat Exercise 21 of the Second Class of this last week.

Exercise 22

Piqué retiré derrière, arms in 6th, four counts.

Students repeat Exercise 22 of the Second Class of this week.

Exercise 23

Déboulés: one relevé in 1st, four half turns, each half turn on one count.

Students repeat Exercise 23 of the Second Class of this week.

Exercise 24

Curtsey.

FIFTH CLASS

Exercise 1

Warm up.

Exercise 2

Plié.

Exercise 3

First battement tendu exercise.

Exercise 4

Battement tendu en croix, close in plié, followed by another battement tendu, two counts.

Students repeat Exercise 4 of the Second Class of this week.

Exercise 5

Battement tendu devant, derrière, 2nd, battement tendu derrière, devant, 2nd, two counts, facing the barre.

Students repeat Exercise 5 of the Second Class of this week.

Exercise 6

Preparation for battement tendu soutenu 2nd, two counts, two count hold in closing, facing the barre.

Students repeat Exercise 6 of the Second Class of this week.

Exercise 7

Battement jeté en croix, two counts, four repetitions.

Students repeat Exercise 7 of the Second Class of this week.

Exercise 8

Rond de jambe à la demi-hauteur, en dehors and en dedans, passé à terre, four counts, facing the barre.

Students repeat Exercise 9 of the Second Class of this week.

Exercise 9

Battement frappé en l'air, en croix en dehors and en dedans, two counts, facing the barre.

Students repeat Exercise 10 of the Second Class of this week.

Exercise 10

Petits battements, accent devant and derrière, no hold, two petits battements on one count, arm in low 1st.

Students repeat Exercise 13 of the Second Class of the Twenty-Sixth Week.

Exercise 11

Adagio: développé 2nd, eight counts, facing the barre, review.

Students repeat Exercise 12 of the Second Class of this week.

Exercise 12

Grand battement devant, back to the barre, battement 2nd and derrière, facing the barre, in 1st, two counts.

Students repeat Exercise 13 of the Second Class of this week.

Exercise 13

Stretching.

Exercise 14

Battement tendu devant and derrière, with port de bras, two counts, three repetitions, with épaulement croisé.

Students repeat Exercise 14 of the Fourth Class of this week.

Exercise 15

Battement jeté devant and derrière, two counts, two counts hold in closing, with épaulement croisé.

Students repeat Exercise 16 of the Second Class of this week.

Exercise 16

Adagio: lift the leg devant and derrière, arabesque croisée with arms 2nd, four counts, with épaulement croisé.

Students repeat Exercise 17 of the Second Class of this week.

Exercise 17

Relevé in 1st, with port de bras, two counts, four repetitions.

Students repeat Exercise 17 of the Fourth Class of this week.

Exercise 18

Relevé in 5th, two counts, three repetitions.

Students repeat Exercise 18 of the Fourth Class of this week.

Exercise 19

Soubresaut in 1st, with a quarter of a turn, on the count.

Students repeat Exercise 19 of the Second Class of this week.

Exercise 20

Sissonne 2nd, traveling toward the front foot and the back foot, changing feet, two counts, hold in closing, facing the barre and in the center.

On "and," plié and push off the floor, with a slight travel toward the right side (toward the front foot), stretching both legs, with the left leg 2nd à la demi-hauteur, and the head turning slightly toward the left; on 1, land in plié on the right foot, while the left foot points 2nd onto the floor; on 2, close 5th, left foot front, still in plié; on 3 and 4, stretch both knees and hold the position; on "and," plié and push off the floor, with a slight travel toward the left side, both legs stretched in the air and the right leg 2nd à la demi-hauteur, the head turning slightly toward the right; on 5, land in plié on the left foot, while the right foot points 2nd onto the floor; on 6, close 5th, right foot front; on 7 and 8, stretch both knees and hold the position. Repeat three more times.

On "and," plié and push off the floor, with a slight travel toward the left side (toward the back foot), with both legs stretched in the air and the right leg 2nd à la demi-hauteur, the head turned slightly to the left; on 1, land in plié on the left foot, while the right foot points 2nd on the floor; on 2, close 5th, left foot front, still in plié; on 3 and 4, stretch both knees and hold the position; on "and," plié and push off the floor, with a slight travel toward the right side, with both legs stretched in the air and the left leg 2nd à la demi-hauteur, the head turned slightly to the right; on 5, land in plié on the right foot, while the left foot points 2nd on the floor; on 6, close 5th, left foot back; on 7 and 8, stretch both knees and hold the position. Repeat three more times. Repeat the exercise in the center with the arms 2nd.

Explanation. After practicing the sissonne at the barre for a while, students are finally practicing the jump in the center. The tempo is faster with less holding when the foot points on the floor in the landing. There is a pause in between each jump to help re-center. When the exercise is first done at the barre, the hands move along on the barre. As said before, the sissonne is more complicated than the assemblé, especially in the first stages of learning it. Practicing it at the barre for a while (which may seem too long for many!) helps students to master the main elements of the jump so that by the time they perform it in the center, the mechanisms of the jump are in place.

Music. Music for grand allegro would work well here to give students time to get some height and close after each landing properly.

Exercise 21

Preparatory exercise for chassé à terre and sauté traveling forward, arms in 6th, two counts each.

Students repeat Exercise 21 of the Second Class of this week.

Exercise 22

Piqué retiré derrière, arms in 6th, four counts.

Students repeat Exercise 22 of the Second Class of this week.

Exercise 22

Déboulés: relevé in 1st, four half turns, each half turn on one count.

Students repeat Exercise 23 of the Second Class of this week.

Exercise 24

Curtsey.

Twenty-Eighth Week

§

FIRST CLASS

Students repeat the material of the Fifth Class of last week.

SECOND CLASS

Exercise 1

Warm up.

Exercise 2

Plié.

Exercise 3

First battement tendu exercise.

Exercise 4

Battement tendu en croix, bring the foot down in plié, with port de bras, four counts, review.

On "and" 1, battement tendu devant; on 2, transfer the weight onto both legs, coming down into plié in 4th, and bringing the arm in 1st; on 3, stretch both legs, transferring the weight onto the back leg, point the front foot, and opening the arm 2nd; on 4, close 5th devant. Repeat the exercise en croix. At the end, roll up and hold balance.

Explanation. Students are reviewing Exercise 4 of the Second Class of the Twenty-Second Week, this time performed with a port de bras. Students do not round their back when they are in plié in 4th position, with the arm coming in 1st. Only the head slightly inclines.

Exercise 5

Battement tendu 2nd, accent in, one count hold when closing, in 1st, on the count, three repetitions, facing the barre.

On "and," battement tendu 2nd; on 1, close 1st; on 2, hold the position; on "and," battement tendu 2nd; on 3, close 1st; on 4, hold the position; on "and," battement tendu 2nd; on 5, close 1st; on 6, hold the position; on 7 and 8, plié and stretch. Repeat the whole exercise one more time. At the end, relevé in 1st and hold the position with the arms in 5th.

Explanation. Students are introduced to the battement tendu performed on the count. This translates into a quick opening of the leg so that it closes quickly. Notice that there is one count hold at each closing to smooth the transition. This kind of exercise requires a strong involvement of the adductor muscles, which must work hard to bring the leg on time, but without kicking heels. The musical upbeat "and" in this kind of exercise is very important; it signals that the closing is to fall on the count. Students must therefore anticipate such closing and start the movement on time.

Exercise 6

Preparation for battement tendu soutenu en croix, two counts, two count hold when closing.

On "and," plié; on 1, battement tendu devant in plié; on 2, bring the working leg to 5th position devant, with a simultaneous stretching of the supporting leg; on 3 and 4, hold the position. Repeat the exercise en croix en dehors. At the end, roll up and hold the position.

Explanation. Students are repeating the exercise en croix, still with a two count pause in between. The closing is performed tightly and with energy using the adductors to squeeze in. When closing, students strongly lift their abdomen muscles.

Exercise 7

Battement jeté 2nd, start in plié and stretch out, in 1st, two counts, facing the barre.

On "and," plié; on 1, battement 2nd with the right leg, stretching both legs at the same time; on "and," point the foot onto the floor; on 2, close 1st. Repeat three more times with the right leg. Repeat the whole exercise one more time. At the end, plié and relevé and hold balance.

Explanation. Students are practicing the

exercise on two counts, in 1st, and facing the barre. The weight remains on the supporting leg.

Music. The music is a not too fast 4/4.

Exercise 8

Rond de jambe à terre en dehors and en dedans, passé à terre, four counts, four repetitions, review.

On "and" 1, battement tendu devant; on 2, rond de jambe to 2nd, without hold; on 3, rond de jambe en dehors to the back; on 4, hold the position; on "and" 5, brush through 1st, battement tendu devant, and repeat the rond de jambe en dehors. Repeat twice more and close 5th derrière. Repeat the exercise with the ronds de jambe en dedans. At the end, plié, demi-détourné to the left side, and hold balance with the arms in 5th.

Explanation. Students are reviewing Exercise 8 of the Fifth Class of the Twenty-Second Week, this time increasing the number of repetitions.

Exercise 9

Battement frappé en l'air, en croix en dehors and en dedans, two counts.

On "and," the front foot comes on the cou-de-pied devant; on 1, hold the position; on 2, extend the leg devant, off the floor, grazing the toes onto the floor before full extension; on 3, bring the foot on the cou-de-pied devant; on 4, extend the leg 2nd; on 5, bring the foot on the cou-de-pied derrière; on 6, extend the leg derrière; on 7, bring the foot on the cou-de-pied derrière; on 8, extend the leg 2nd.

On 1, the front foot comes on the cou-de-pied derrière; on 2, extend the leg derrière, off the floor, grazing the toes on the floor; on 3, bring the foot on the cou-de-pied derrière; on 4, extend the leg 2nd; on 5, bring the foot on the cou-de-pied devant; on 6, extend the leg devant; on 7, bring the foot on the cou-de-pied devant; on 8, extend the leg 2nd. Keeping the leg 2nd, hold balance, releasing the barre with the arms 2nd.

Explanation. Students are practicing the exercise sideways in this otherwise familiar exercise.

Exercise 10

Petits battements, accent devant and derrière, no hold, two petits battements on one count, arm in low 1st.

Students repeat Exercise 13 of the Second Class of the Twenty-Sixth Week.

Exercise 11

Adagio: développé 2nd, with port de bras, eight counts.

Following the preparatory port de bras, bring the arm down.

On "and," bring the front foot pointed on the cou-de-pied devant, straightening the head; on 1 and 2, slide the foot to retiré devant, bringing the arm in 1st; on 3, open the leg in attitude 2nd, keeping the arm in 1st; on 4, stretch the leg fully 2nd, opening the arm 2nd, and keeping the head straight; on 5 and 6, hold the position; on 7, bring down the leg and point the foot onto the floor; on 8, close 5th derrière, bringing the arm down. Repeat the exercise closing 5th devant.

Explanation. Students are now performing the exercise sideways with a port de bras. The arm opens only as the leg stretches from the attitude. The idea is to coordinate the stretching of the arm with the one of the leg. This coordination in the développé is difficult for students, especially as they start practicing it in the center. Even advanced students show reluctance to practice it. There is a tendency to bring the arms first then the leg, the assumption being that, with the arms already in place, it is easier to balance on one leg with the other one extending. However, the beauty of the whole movement lies in the lower and upper limbs working in perfect coordination. Therefore, this coordination should be strictly enforced, first in the développé at the barre and then in the center.

Exercise 12

Grand battement devant, back to the barre, battement 2nd and derrière, facing the barre, in 1st, two counts.

Students repeat Exercise 13 of the Second Class of the Twenty-Seventh Week.

Exercise 13

Stretching.

Exercise 14

Battement tendu devant and derrière, with port de bras, two counts, three repetitions, with épaulement croisé.

Students repeat Exercise 14 of the Fourth Class of the Twenty-Seventh Week.

Exercise 15

Temps lié, preparation for chassé à terre forward and backward, with port de bras, four counts, review.

On "and" 1, battement tendu devant; on 2, transfer the weight onto both legs in plié in 4th, and with the arms coming in 1st; on 3, transfer the weight onto the front leg, stretching both legs, pointing the back foot, and opening the arms 2nd; on 4, close 5th derrière.

On "and" 5, battement tendu derrière; on 6, transfer the weight onto both legs in plié in 4th, and the arms coming in 1st; on 7, transfer the weight onto the back leg, stretching both legs, pointing the front foot, and opening the arms 2nd; on 8, close 5th devant, bringing the arms down.

On "and," plié; on 1 and 2, slide forward the front foot in 4th position with both legs still in plié, bring the arms 1st, stretch both legs, and transfer the weight onto the front leg, pointing the back foot; open the arms 2nd; on 3, hold the position; on 4, close 5th derrière, bringing the arms down.

On "and," plié; on 5 and 6, slide backward the back foot in 4th position with both legs still in the plié, bring the arms in 1st, stretch both legs, and transfer the weight onto the back leg, pointing the front foot, open the arms 2nd; on 7, hold the position; on 8, close 5th devant, bringing the arms down. Repeat the whole exercise one more time.

Explanation. This is mostly review material, except the whole exercise is performed with a more flowing quality. Even though the tempo is slightly faster, the passage of the 4th is done properly.

Music. A slow-to-medium tempo waltz would work well here.

Position effacé with the arms in low 1st position; the head is slightly held back.

Exercise 16

Adagio: introduction to the épaulement effacé (shaded) position, port de bras.

Stand in 5th right foot front, at an oblique angle of the front of the room, with the right side of the body out of view. Like for the croisé position, students rotate one-eighth of a turn from the position de face, facing the lower right corner. The head, still held straight on its axis, is slightly turned toward the left shoulder.

On "and" 1 and 2, bring the arms down; on 3 and 4, bring the arms to 1st and open 2nd, turning the head toward the left arm; on 5 and 6, bring the arms 5th; on 7 and 8, open the arms 2nd, and perform a small plié and stretch. Repeat the exercise one more time. When performing the exercise with the left foot front, students face the lower left corner.

Explanation. After studying the croisé position, students are introduced to the effacé position (also called ouvert [open]). In this position, the body has the same orientation as in the croisé position, but the back leg is now in full view, with the opposite side of the whole body being shaded from the audience. Notice that here the head does not follow the general rule of turning toward the side of the front foot, for that would mean turning the head away from the audience, which is not acceptable.

Exercise 17

Relevé in 1st, with port de bras, two counts, four repetitions.

Students repeat Exercise 17 of the Fourth Class of the Twenty-Seventh Week.

Exercise 18

Relevé retiré devant and derrière, without changing feet, two counts.

Following the preparatory port de bras, bring the arms down.

On "and," plié; on 1, relevé on the left foot, bringing the right leg into retiré devant and the arms in 1st; on 2, come down into plié in 5th, right foot front; on 3, directly out of the plié, relevé on the left foot, bringing the right leg in retiré devant; on 4, come down in plié in 5th, right foot front. Repeat the exercise twice bringing the left leg in retiré derrière. Repeat the whole exercise one more time.

Explanation. Students are practicing the exercise in the center without holding in between each relevé. The arms remain in 1st and motionless during the exercise.

Exercise 19

Soubresaut in 1st, with a quarter of a turn, on the count, two repetitions.

Following the preparatory port de bras, the arms come down.

On "and," plié and push off the floor with pointed feet, while turning to face the right side of the studio; on 1, land into plié; on "and," directly out of the plié, push off the floor again, facing the same direction; on 2, land in plié; on 3, stretch the knees; on 4, hold the position. Repeat three more times, turning a quarter of a turn toward the right side each time. Repeat the whole exercise one more time.

Explanation. This exercise is similar to Exercise 19 of the Second Class of the

Twenty-Seventh Week. Students are practicing the exercise with two jumps in a row this time, in each direction. The rotation occurs only in the first jump. Each jump is on the count.

Exercise 20

Sissonne 2nd, traveling toward the front foot and the back foot, changing feet, two counts, hold in closing, at the barre and in the center.

Students repeat Exercise 20 of the Fifth Class of the Twenty-Seventh Week.

Exercise 21

Chassé sauté traveling forward, arms in 6th, four counts, two repetitions.

Start in the back of the studio, traveling forward. In the preparatory port de bras, bring the arms in 1st, open the left arm 2nd, and keep the right arm in 1st.

On "and," extend the back leg just above the floor, with a plié on the supporting leg, bring it back in, hop and land in plié onto the back foot while pushing the front leg forward as if the back leg were taking a swing to chase the front leg toward the front, with the front foot pointed just above the floor; on 1, step onto the front foot with a plié and push off the floor bringing the back leg against the front leg in 5th in the air; on "and," land on the back foot in plié, releasing the front leg that extends forward; on 2, step onto the front foot with a plié and push off the floor, bringing the back leg against the front leg in 5th in the air; on 3, land in 5th on both feet; on 4, stretch legs. Repeat several times.

Explanation. Students are adding one more chassé to each series of chassés traveling forward this time. The exercise starts with a small battement to give momentum to the first chassé. In fact, it is a small chassé itself, in which the student hops to switch legs and pushes the front leg forward. Once extended forward, the front leg reaches far forward, with the pointed foot gliding just above the floor; students then step onto the front foot with a deep plié to push off the floor so that both legs can be reunited into 5th in the air. The back leg remains turned-out when landing, and the knee does not come forward in the plié. In the landing and before stepping down to jump again, the front foot must not flex prematurely.

Exercise 22

Assemblé 2nd, en descendant and en remontant, with port de bras, two counts, one count hold.

Following the preparatory port de bras, bring the arms down.

On "and," plié, bringing the arms in 1st and straightening the head; on 1, brush the left foot and extend the leg 2nd, while pushing off the floor with the supporting leg, stretching both legs in the air, and opening the arms 2nd, with the left arm slightly higher than the right arm and both palms faced down, turning the head slightly toward the left arm; on 2, land in plié in 5th, left foot front, with the arms still in the same position in 2nd; on 3, straighten the knees, bringing the arms down, keeping the head turned to the left; on 4, hold the position. Repeat three more times bringing the back foot front each time.

On "and," plié, bringing the arms in 1st and straightening the head; on 1, brush the right foot and extend the leg 2nd, while pushing off the floor with the supporting leg, stretching both legs in the air, and opening the arms 2nd, with the right arm slightly higher than the left, and the head turned toward the left arm; on 2, land in plié in 5th, left foot front; on 3, straighten the knees, and bringing the arms down, keeping the head turned toward the left; on 4, hold the position. Repeat three more times, bringing the front foot back each time. After a pause, repeat the whole exercise one more time.

Explanation. Students are reviewing the assemblé en descendant and en remontant, but with a port de bras, which is quite standard for the assemblé. So that the arms movement fully contributes to the leg movement, it has to be precisely coordinated with the legs: the arms start opening as the working leg comes out of the 5th position and fully open during the jump; in the landing they remain in position to finally close as students stretch their knees at the end of jump. The arms must not come down right away in the landing, for it would give the impression of collapse instead of a light and controlled landing. In other words, in the plié of the landing, the arms are still 2nd with the head directed toward the higher arm when executing the exercise en descendant and directed toward the lower arm when executing the exercise en remontant. The position of the arms, with one arm higher than

In the landing of the assemblé, the student's right arm is held slightly too high. The right leg is more turned out than the left leg.

the other is a traditional arm position for the assemblé, one that enhances the elevation effect and helps the magnitude of the jump. The position of the hands also contributes to this effect, with the palms facing down, the whole arms' position thus giving the impression of a flight that does not end, even in the landing.

Application. Practicing the sissonne does not mean that the assemblé is forgotten. Both should be regularly performed.

Exercise 23

Demi-détourné, with port de bras, four counts.

On "and" 1, plié and relevé; on 2, rotate one half turn toward the left (the same direction as the back foot), the back foot becoming the front foot, with the arms closing in 1st; on 3, come down in plié in 5th, left foot front; on 4, stretch the knees, opening the arms 2nd; on "and" 5, plié and relevé; on 6, rotate one half turn toward the right (the same direction as the back foot), the back foot becoming the front foot, with the arms closing in 1st; on 7, come down in plié in 5th, right foot front; on 8, stretch the knees, opening the arms 2nd. Repeat one more time.

Explanation. Notice the movement of the arms, both of them closing in 1st at the same time. This is important to give momentum in the rotation, especially in the full detourné. During the turn, the arms must remain in front of the torso. In the more advanced level, students hop slightly when turning, and the relevé occurs as they start to rotate. In this introductory exercise, students perform first the relevé, then rotate. Students must spot when turning.

Music. A 3/4 waltz, with a brisk but not-too-fast tempo, will accommodate this exercise.

Exercise 24

Balancé 2nd, traveling sideways, with port de bras, two counts.

On "and" 1, straightening the head, extend the right leg 2nd, step onto the right foot in plié, bending the left leg and the left foot coming on the cou-de-pied derrière, while the left arm comes in 1st, and the head turns slightly toward the left arm; on "and," step onto demi-pointe on the left foot stretching both legs, while raising the right foot pointed slightly off the floor; on 2, come down into plié onto the right foot with the left foot derrière the cou-de-pied of the right foot.

On "and" 3, straightening the head, extend the left leg 2nd, opening the left arm 2nd, step onto the left foot in plié, with the right leg bending and the right foot coming on the cou-de-pied derrière, while the right arm comes in 1st, and the head turns toward the right arm; on "and," step onto demi-pointe on the right foot, while raising the left foot pointed off the floor; on 4, come down into plié onto the left foot, with the right foot on the cou-de-pied derrière.

On "and" 5, straightening the head, extend the right leg, opening the arms 2nd, step onto the right foot in plié, bending the left leg and the left foot coming on the cou-de-pied derrière, while the left arm comes in 1st and the head turns slightly toward the left; on "and," step onto demi-pointe on the left foot, while raising the right foot pointed off the floor; on 6, come down into plié onto the right foot, with the left foot on the cou-de-pied derrière; on 7, close the foot in 5th derrière in plié; on 8, stretch the knees. Repeat the whole exercise one more time.

Explanation. Students are performing the balancé on two counts. The tempo is fairly slow. Notice the change of arm position in the port de bras when the leg extends out. If this port de bras is fairly standard, other arm positions can also be used. The back leg does not turn in, especially when the foot comes up onto demi-pointe.

Exercise 25

Grand battement 2nd, in 1st, two counts.

On "and" 1, grand battement 2nd with the right leg; on "and," lower the leg and point the foot onto the floor; on 2, close 1st; on "and" 3, grand battement 2nd with the right leg; on "and," lower the leg and point the foot onto the floor; on 4, close 1st. Repeat the whole exercise one more time.

Explanation. Students are revisiting the grands battements in the center, on two counts each. As said before, a strong holding of the back is crucial for practicing grands battements in the center so that the trunk remains solid and still and does not go along with the swing of the leg. The shoulders stay low. It is a good idea to regularly practice the grands battements in the center to make sure students do not pull the barre to throw their leg up.

Exercise 26

Marche with small développé, in 1st, arms in low 1st, in diagonal.

Start in the upper left corner, facing the lower right corner, in 1st, with the arms down, and the head de face.

On "and" 1, battement tendu devant with the right foot, bringing the arms in low 1st; on "and" 2, step onto the right foot while the back leg bends, with the pointed foot passing through at the level of the cou-de-pied, stretch the working leg forward with the foot strongly turned out, and point the foot onto the floor; on "and" 3, step onto the left foot and bend the right leg, extending it forward, and point the foot onto the floor. Repeat the marche in diagonal traveling to the lower right corner.

Explanation. Students are performing the marche directly with no hold. In the passage of the working leg from back to front, the knee is pushed to the side, and the inside of the lower leg, led by the working heel, aims forward. The leg is extended well forward before stepping onto it.

Exercise 27

Curtsey.

THIRD CLASS

Students repeat the material of the Second Class of this week.

FOURTH CLASS

Exercise 1

Warm up.

Exercise 2

Plié.

Exercise 3

First battement tendu exercise.

Exercise 4

Battement tendu en croix, bring the foot down in plié, with port de bras, four counts, review.

Students repeat Exercise 4 of the Second Class of this week.

Exercise 5

Battement tendu 2nd, accent in, one count hold when closing, in 1st, on the count, three repetitions, facing the barre.

Students repeat Exercise 5 of the Second Class of this week.

Exercise 6

Preparation for battement tendu soutenu en croix, two counts, two counts hold when closing.

Students repeat Exercise 6 of the Second Class of this week.

Exercise 7

Battement jeté 2nd, start in plié and stretch out, in 1st, two counts, facing the barre.

Students repeat Exercise 7 of the Second Class of this week.

Exercise 8

Rond de jambe à terre en dehors and en dedans, passé à terre, four counts, four repetitions, review.

Students repeat Exercise 8 of the Second Class of this week.

Exercise 9

Battement frappé en l'air, en croix en dehors and en dedans, two counts.

Students repeat Exercise 9 of the Second Class of this week.

Exercise 10

Petits battements, accent devant and derrière, no hold, two petits battements on one count, arm in low 1st.

Students repeat Exercise 13 of the Second Class of the Twenty-Sixth Week.

Exercise 11

Adagio: développé 2nd, with port de bras, eight counts.

Students repeat Exercise 11 of the Second Class of this week.

Exercise 12

Grand battement devant, back to the barre, battement 2nd and derrière, facing the barre, in 1st, two counts.

Students repeat Exercise 13 of the Second Class of the Twenty-Seventh Week.

Exercise 13

Stretching.

CENTER

Exercise 14

Battement tendu devant and derrière, four counts, arms 6th, with épaulement effacé.

Stand in 5th position, with épaulement effacé, right foot front and the left shoulder forward. In the preparatory port de bras, bring both arms in 1st, the right arm opens 2nd, and the left arm stays in 1st. The head is turned toward the left shoulder.

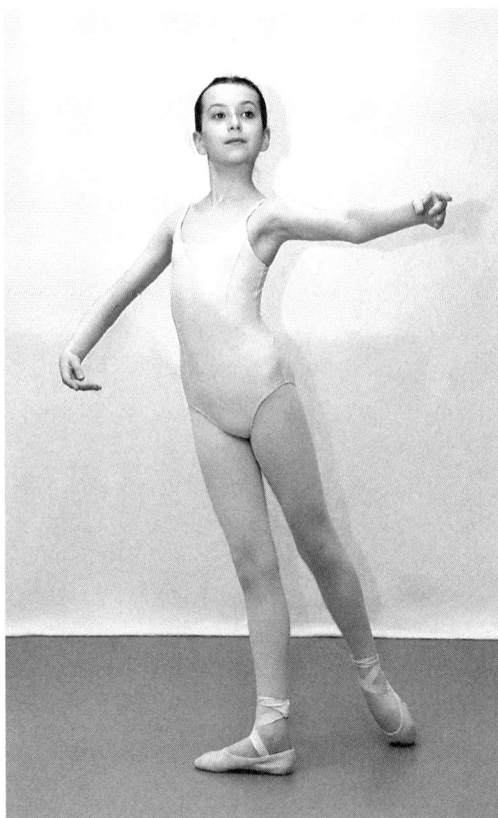

Battement tendu derrière, ouvert, in effacé. The rib cage is slightly held out.

On 1 and 2, battement tendu devant; on 3 and 4, close 5th; on 5 and 6, battement tendu devant; on 7 and 8, close 5th, closing the right arm in 1st and opening the left arm 2nd, the head still directed toward the left shoulder; on 1 and 2, battement tendu derrière; on 3 and 4, close 5th; on 5 and 6, battement tendu derrière; on 7 and 8, close 5th. Repeat the exercise one more time.

Explanation. The battements tendus are on four counts each, since the direction is new to students. Students are reminded to keep the turn-out of both legs.

Exercise 15

Temps lié, preparation for chassé à terre forward and backward, with port de bras, four counts, review.

Students repeat Exercise 15 of the Second Class of this week.

Exercise 16

Adagio: introduction to the épaulement effacé position, port de bras.

Students repeat Exercise 16 of the Second Class of this week.

Exercise 17

Relevé retiré devant and derrière, without changing feet, two counts.

Students repeat Exercise 18 of the Second Class of this week.

Exercise 18

Soubresaut in 1st, with a quarter of a turn, on the count, two repetitions.

Students repeat Exercise 19 of the Second Class of this week.

Exercise 19

Sissonne 2nd, traveling toward the front foot and the back foot, changing feet, two counts, hold in closing, facing the barre and in the center.

Students repeat Exercise 20 of the Fifth Class of the Twenty-Seventh Week.

Exercise 20

Chassé sauté traveling forward, arms in 6th, two counts, two repetitions.

Students repeat Exercise 21 of the Second Class of this week.

Exercise 21

Assemblé 2nd, en descendant and en remontant, with port de bras, two counts, one count hold.

Students repeat Exercise 22 of the Second Class of this week.

Exercise 22

Demi-détourné, with port de bras, four counts.

Students repeat Exercise 23 of the Second Class of this week.

Exercise 23

Balancé 2nd, traveling sideways, with port de bras, two counts.

Students repeat Exercise 24 of the Second Class of this week.

Exercise 24

Grand battement 2nd, in 1st, two counts.

Students repeat Exercise 25 of the Second Class of this week.

Exercise 25

Marche with small développé, in 1st, arms in low 1st, in diagonal.

Students repeat Exercise 26 of the Second Class of this week.

Exercise 26

Curtsey.

FIFTH CLASS

Exercise 1

Warm up.

Exercise 2

Plié.

Exercise 3

First battement tendu exercise.

Exercise 4

Battement tendu en croix, bring the foot down, with port de bras, four counts, review.

Students repeat Exercise 4 of the Second Class of this week.

Exercise 5

Battement tendu 2nd, accent in, one count hold when closing, in 1st, on the count, three repetitions, facing the barre.

Students repeat Exercise 5 of the Second Class of this week.

Exercise 6

Preparation for battement tendu soutenu en croix, two counts, two counts hold when closing.

Students repeat Exercise 6 of the Second Class of this week.

Exercise 7

Battement jeté 2nd, start in plié and stretch out, in 1st, two counts, facing the barre.

Students repeat Exercise 7 of the Second Class of this week.

Exercise 8

Rond de jambe à terre en dehors and en dedans, passé à terre, four counts, four repetitions, review.

Students repeat Exercise 8 of the Second Class of this week.

Exercise 9

Battement frappé en l'air, en croix en dehors and en dedans, two counts.

Students repeat Exercise 9 of the Second Class of this week.

Exercise 10

Petits battements, accent devant and derrière, no hold, two petits battements on one count, arm in low 1st.

Students repeat Exercise 13 of the Second Class of the Twenty-Sixth Week.

Exercise 11

Adagio: développé 2nd, with port de bras, eight counts.

Students repeat Exercise 11 of the Second Class of this week.

Exercise 12

Grand battement devant, back to the barre, battement 2nd and derrière, facing the barre, in 1st, two counts.

Students repeat Exercise 13 of the Second Class of the Twenty-Seventh Week.

Exercise 13

Stretching.

CENTER

Exercise 14

Battement tendu devant and derrière, four counts, arms in 6th, with épaulement effacé.

Students repeat Exercise 14 of the Fourth Class of this week.

Exercise 15

Temps lié and preparation for chassé forward and backward, with port de bras, four counts, review.

Students repeat Exercise 15 of the Second Class of this week.

Exercise 16

Relevé retiré devant and derrière, without changing feet, two counts.

Students repeat Exercise 18 of the Second Class of this week.

Exercise 17

Soubresaut in 1st, with a quarter of a turn, on the count, two repetitions.

Students repeat Exercise 19 of the Second Class of this week.

Exercise 18

Sissonne 2nd, traveling toward the front foot and the back foot, changing feet, two counts, hold in closing.

Students repeat Exercise 20 of the Fifth Class of the Twenty-Seventh Week.

Exercise 19

Assemblé 2nd, en descendant and en remontant, with port de bras, two counts, one count hold.

Students repeat Exercise 22 of the Second Class of this week.

Exercise 20

Chassé sauté traveling forward, arms in 6th, two counts, two repetitions.

Students repeat Exercise 21 of the Second Class of this week.

Exercise 21

Demi-détourné, with port de bras, four counts.

Students repeat Exercise 23 of the Second Class of this week.

Exercise 22

Balancé 2nd, traveling sideways, with port de bras, two counts.

Students repeat Exercise 24 of the Second Class of this week.

Exercise 23

Grand battement, in 1st, two counts.

Students repeat Exercise 25 of the Second Class of this week.

Exercise 24

Marche with small développé, in 1st, arms in low 1st, in diagonal.

Students repeat Exercise 26 of the Second Class of this week.

Exercise 25

Curtsey.

Twenty-Ninth Week

§

FIRST CLASS

Students repeat the material of the Fifth Class of the Twenty-Eighth Week.

SECOND CLASS

Exercise 1

Warm up.

Exercise 2

Plié.

Exercise 3

First battement tendu exercise.

Exercise 4

Battement tendu 2nd, small développé, eight counts, facing the barre.

On "and" 1, battement tendu 2nd; on 2, close 5th devant; on "and," bring the foot on the cou-de-pied devant; on 3, extend the leg out in 2nd, pointing the foot onto the floor; on 4, hold the position; on 5, close 5th derrière; from 6 to 8, hold the position. Repeat three more times, alternating closing devant and derrière.

Explanation. Students are combining the battement tendu and the small développé 2nd in this exercise. The holding on the cou-de-pied position is quick, but it still must be observed before it extends 2nd. The leg extends without kicking.

Music. The tempo is brisk, since each series is on eight counts.

Exercise 5

Battement tendu 2nd, in 1st, on the count, two repetitions, facing the barre.

On "and," battement tendu 2nd; on 1, close 1st; on "and," battement tendu 2nd; on 2, close 1st; on 3 and 4, hold the position. Repeat three more times. Repeat the whole exercise one more time. At the end, relevé in 1st and hold the position with the arms in 5th.

Explanation. Students are practicing the exercise with two battements tendus performed on the count each, with no hold in between. The working toes do not go off the floor in the battement tendu, and the heels do not kick in when closing.

Music. The tempo (4/4) is fairly quick.

Exercise 6

Battement tendu soutenu 2nd dessus, with rise onto demi-pointes, without changing feet, four counts, facing the barre.

On "and," plié; on 1, battement tendu 2nd with the right foot; on 2, bring the right leg in front of the supporting leg, with both feet coming onto demi-pointes in 5th, right foot front, and stretching both legs; on 3, come down in plié; on 4, stretch. Repeat the exercise with the right foot three more times, the last one closing derrière to change feet.

Explanation. Students are executing the battement tendu soutenu 2nd with a rise onto demi-pointes in 5th. Again the rise of the supporting foot must be coordinated with the working foot sliding in. The supporting heel does not rise prematurely; it goes off only when it becomes impossible for the working leg to slide in onto demi-pointe in 5th. This is a good exercise for the work of the adductors, with a tight fit of both legs in 5th.

Exercise 7

Battement jeté 2nd, two counts, two repetitions, battement jeté on the count, plié, in 1st, facing the barre.

On "and," battement 2nd; on 1, hold the position; on "and," lower the leg and point the foot onto the floor; on 2, close 1st; on "and," battement 2nd; on 3, hold the position; on "and," lower the leg and point the foot onto the floor; on 4, close 1st; on "and," battement jeté 2nd; on 5, close 1st directly; on 6, hold the position; on 7, plié; on 8, stretch the knees. Repeat three more times, alternating legs. At the end, relevé in 1st and hold the position.

Explanation. Students are mixing the battements on two counts and on the count. A plié ends each series. In the battement on two counts, there is a slight hold in the air. In the battement on the count, the first part of the battement is performed on the musical upbeat noted as "and"; there is no hold whatsoever in the pointed position on the floor; this translates into a quick opening of the leg so that it is back on the count. This kind of exercise requires an even stronger involvement of the adductor muscles, which must work hard to bring the leg on time. The torso does not swing at all.

Application. Students are exposed to more and more exercises involving greater use of the adductors now that they have spent a few months perfecting the different elements of these exercises.

Exercise 8

Rond de jambe à terre en dehors and en dedans, two counts, facing the barre.

On "and" 1, battement tendu devant; on "and," rond de jambe to 2nd; on 2, rond de jambe to derrière; on 3, hold the position; on 4, close 5th derrière; on "and" 5, battement tendu derrière; on "and," rond de jambe to 2nd; on 6, rond de jambe to devant; on 7, hold the position; on 8, close 5th. Repeat the exercise one more time. At the end, retiré devant and hold balance.

Explanation. Students are introduced to the rond de jambe à terre on two counts. The turnout is maintained throughout, especially through the passage of the 2nd to the 4th position derrière.

Music. The tempo is not too fast, since the rond de jambe is now performed on two counts.

Exercise 9

Battement frappé en l'air, en croix en dehors and en dedans, with the foot in a flexed position, two counts.

On "and," the front foot comes in flexed position on the cou-de-pied devant; on 1, hold the position; on 2, extend the leg devant, off the floor, grazing the toes on the floor before full extension; on 3, bring the foot on the cou-de-pied devant; on 4, extend the leg 2nd; on 5, bring the foot on the cou-de-pied derrière; on 6, extend the leg derrière; on 7, bring the foot on

the cou-de-pied derrière; on 8, extend the leg 2nd.

On 1, the foot comes in a flexed position on the cou-de-pied derrière; on 2, extend the leg derrière, off the floor, grazing the toes on the floor before full extension; on 3, bring the foot on the cou-de-pied derrière; on 4, extend the leg 2nd; on 5, bring the foot on the cou-de-pied devant; on 6, extend the leg devant; on 7, bring the foot on the cou-de-pied devant; on 8, extend the leg 2nd. At the end, relevé, bring the front foot wrapped on the cou-de-pied devant, and hold the position.

Explanation. Students are repeating Exercise 10 of the Second Class of the Twenty-Seventh Week, this time performed with the foot in a flexed position on the cou-de-pied and sideways.

Music. The tempo is accelerated.

Exercise 10

Rond de jambe soutenu 2nd, en dehors and en dedans, in 1st, two counts for each rond de jambe, facing the barre, review.

Students repeat Exercise 12 of the Second Class of the Twenty-Sixth Week.

Exercise 11

Petits battements, review.

From now on, the instructor will select the elements of the petits battements exercise. These elements must have already been studied. The petits battements must be included in the class very regularly to prepare students for the batterie, studied later in the training. The instructor will review the different exercises of petits battements: those done with an even tempo, and those performed with the accent devant and derrière. The composition of the exercise remains simple, though, so students can concentrate on the quality of the movement and the correct passage of the working foot from front to back and from back to front, each time unbending the working leg through 2nd.

Exercise 12

Adagio: développé devant and 2nd, with port de bras, eight counts.

Following the preparatory port de bras, bring the arm down.

On "and," bring the foot pointed on the

cou-de-pied devant; on 1 and 2, slide the foot up the supporting leg to retiré, bringing the arm in 1st; on 3, open the leg in attitude devant, keeping the arm in 1st; on 4, stretch the leg fully devant, opening the arm 2nd; on 5 and 6, hold the position; on 7, bring down the leg and point the foot onto the floor; on 8, close 5th devant, closing the arm.

On "and," bring the foot pointed on the cou-de-pied devant; on 1 and 2, slide the foot up the supporting leg to retiré, bringing the arm in 1st; on 3, open the leg in attitude 2nd; on 4, stretch the leg fully 2nd, opening the arm 2nd, keeping the head de face; on 5 and 6, hold the position; on 7, bring down the leg and point the foot onto the floor; on 8, close 5th devant, closing the arm. At the end, roll up and hold balance.

Explanation. Students are now performing the développé devant, sideways, with a port de bras. When the leg extends forward, the knee is pushed to the side as much as possible and the heel is pushed forward in the extension. Students remain balanced on their supporting leg and do not push backward. The head remains de face in the port de bras for the developpé 2nd.

Exercise 13

Grand battement en croix, two counts, three repetitions.

On "and" 1, grand battement devant; on "and," lower the leg and point the foot onto the floor; on 2, close 5th devant. Repeat the exercise twice more; on 7 and 8, hold the position. Repeat the exercise en croix en dehors, the first battement 2nd closing derrière. At the end, demi-détourné and hold the position.

Explanation. The number of battements has increased in each direction to gain stamina and strength in the throw of the leg.

Exercise 14

Stretching.

CENTER

Exercise 15

Battement tendu 2nd, hold when closing, in 1st, arms in 6th, on the count, four repetitions.

In the preparatory port de bras, bring the arms in 1st, open the left arm 2nd and keep the right

The leg is fully extended devant à la hauteur.

The leg is in attitude devant, with the weight slightly back.

arm in 1st, the head turned slightly toward the right arm.

On "and," battement tendu 2nd; on 1, close 1st; on 2, hold the position. Repeat three more times. Repeat with the left foot, switching arms. Repeat the whole exercise one more time.

Explanation. Students are repeating Exercise 5 of the Second Class of the Twenty-Eighth Week, this time performed in the center with four repetitions.

Exercise 16

Battement tendu devant and derrière, four counts, with épaulement effacé.

Students repeat Exercise 14 of the Fourth Class of the Twenty-Eighth Week.

Exercise 17

Glissade 2nd, two counts, two repetitions, without changing feet, pas de bourrée dessous, with port de bras, four counts.

Start with the left foot front, traveling to the right.

In the preparatory port de bras, bring both arms in 1st, open the left arm 2nd and keep the right arm in 1st, and turn the head slightly toward the right arm.

On "and," plié, inclining the torso slightly toward the right; on 1, extend the right leg 2nd in plié; on "and," transfer the weight onto the right foot in plié, while the left leg stretches and the left foot points 2nd; on 2, close 5th, left foot front, in plié; on 3, directly out of the plié, extend the right leg 2nd; on "and," transfer the weight onto the right foot in plié, while the left leg stretches and the left foot points; on 4, close 5th, left foot front.

On "and," bring the back foot on the cou-de-pied derrière in plié; on 5, step onto the right foot on demi-pointe and stretch both legs; on "and" 6, open the left leg 2nd, with both legs stretched 2nd and the head straightening, open the right arm 2nd, step onto the left foot, with still the right leg stretched 2nd; on 7, close 5th, right foot front, in plié, the head turning toward the left; on 8, stretch both knees, bringing the left arm in 1st and opening the right 2nd, and inclining the torso slightly toward the left. Repeat the exercise traveling to the left. Repeat the whole exercise one more time.

Explanation. This is a more complex exercise, mixing two elements that have been so far practiced separately. Students do not hold or stretch their legs in between the glissades, but they do so after the pas de bourrée. Notice the change of arms positions at the end of each series and the position of the head at the end of the pas de bourrée: it is turned toward the arm in 1st to resume the glissade and not toward the side of the front foot as it is usually done. The pas de bourrée, which has become a familiar element to students by now, is performed with more continuity and less holding when moving from one position to another. By the end of the pas de bourrée, students should be ready to resume the glissades.

Music. A medium-tempo waltz is used here.

Exercise 18

Relevé retiré devant and derrière, without changing feet, two counts.

Students repeat Exercise 18 of the Second Class of the Twenty-Eighth Week.

Exercise 19

Battement tendu 2nd, two counts, close in plié, retiré devant with port de bras, four counts.

Following the preparatory port de bras, bring the arms down.

On "and" 1, battement tendu 2nd, open the arms 2nd with the right arm held slightly higher than the left arm, palms turned down, and the head turning toward the right hand; on 2, close 5th devant in plié, bringing the right arm in 1st while the left arm remains 2nd, and turning the head de face; on 3, bring the right leg into a retiré devant while the left arm joins the right arm into 1st, stretching the supporting leg; on 4, bring the right foot down in 5th devant in plié. Repeat three more times, with the arms coming down slightly to open 2nd and the legs stretching out of the plié each time to perform the battement tendu.

Explanation. This type of exercise is a staple of the French ballet class to prepare for pirouettes in 5th en dehors that will come later in the training. The battement tendu precedes the retiré, for it prepares for the shift of weight that occurs when students are on both feet in the plié and transfer their weight onto one leg with the other coming off the floor. Notice the position of the arms in the battement tendu 2nd. It is a port de bras of preparation, giving more amplitude to the movement of the legs: the slightly higher arm accompanies the leg that does a battement tendu, and both palms are turned down. Unlike in the port de bras to 2nd that students have learned (in which the arms come to 1st before opening 2nd), the opening of the arms in this type of exercise starts with the arms hardly higher than the preparatory position. Since the arms are not rotated forward in the position accompanying the battement tendu, there is no need to bring the arms to 1st position. If students were to bring the arms 1st, the arms and hands would have to rotate much more, thus adding superfluous arms movements to the port de bras. The leg comes sharply into retiré so that the body is re-centered as quickly as possible to facilitate balance. The knee is pushed to the side in the retiré. Like in every exercise in which the working leg is off the floor in 2nd, the need for balancing requires that the turned-out muscles of the supporting leg be solidly held and the opposite side of the torso particularly be pulled up.

Application. The exercise should also be practiced at the barre for recreational students.

Exercise 20

Échappé 2nd, with quarter turn, in 1st, two counts, one count hold.

Following the preparatory port de bras, bring the arms down.

On "and," plié and push off the floor, bringing the arms in 1st, rotate a quarter turn toward the right, opening the legs and the arms 2nd; on 1, land in 2nd in plié; on "and," directly out of the plié, push off the floor; on 2, close in 1st in plié, closing the arms down; on 3, stretch the knees; on 4, hold the position. Repeat three more times with a quarter turn to the right each time.

Explanation. Students are performing a quarter rotation in the échappé. The échappé is in 1st to make the closing easier. There is still a pause in between each échappé. The rotation occurs only in the first part of the échappé; the second part is done in the same direction in which students land. As in many jump exercises that require a rotation in the air, there is a tendency among ballet students to cheat and start moving their feet

before the actual jump, whereas they must press down both feet in 1st position without moving or adjusting their feet. This practice will particularly pay off for male dancers to avoid turning their feet before executing their tour en l'air (turn in the air).

Exercise 21

Sissonne 2nd, traveling toward the back foot and the front foot, changing feet, two counts, three repetitions.

On "and," plié and push off the floor, with a slight travel toward the right side (toward the front foot), extending the left leg 2nd à la demi-hauteur, both legs stretched in the air, with the head turning slightly toward the left; on 1, land in plié, on the right foot, the left foot pointing 2nd onto the floor; on 2, close 5th, left foot front; on "and," directly out of the plié, push off, with a slight travel toward the left side, extending the right leg 2nd à la demi-hauteur, both legs stretched in the air, and turning the head slightly toward the right; on 3, land in plié on the left foot, the right foot pointing 2nd onto the floor; on 4, close 5th, right foot front; on "and," directly out of the plié, push off, with a slight travel toward the right side, extending the left leg 2nd à la demi-hauteur, both legs stretched in the air, and turning the head toward the left; on 5, land in plié on the right foot, the left foot pointing 2nd onto the floor; on 6, close 5th, left foot front; on 7 and 8, stretch both knees and hold the position. Repeat one more time.

On "and," plié and push off, with a slight travel toward the left side (toward the back foot), extending the right leg 2nd à la demi-hauteur, both legs stretched in the air, and with the head turning toward the left; on 1, land in plié on the left foot, the right foot pointing 2nd onto the floor; on 2, close 5th, left foot front; on "and," directly out of the plié, push off, with a slight travel toward the right side, extending the left leg 2nd à la demi-hauteur, both legs stretched, and with the head turning toward the right; on 3, land in plié on the right foot, the left foot pointing 2nd onto the floor; on 4, close 5th right foot front; on "and," directly out of the plié, push off, with a slight travel toward the left side, extending the right leg 2nd à la demi-hauteur, both legs stretched, and turning the head toward the left;

on 5, land in plié on the left foot, the right foot pointing 2nd onto the floor; on 6, close 5th, left foot front; on 7 and 8, stretch both knees and hold the position. Repeat one more time.

Explanation. The sissonnes are now performed on two counts each, three at a time. There is less holding in the different parts of the movement. As a general rule, when traveling toward the side of the front foot, the head turns toward the side of the working leg; when traveling toward the side of the back foot, the head turns away from the working leg.

Exercise 22

Assemblé 2nd, en descendant and en remontant, with port de bras, two counts, one count hold.

Students repeat Exercise 22 of the Second Class of the Twenty-Eighth Week.

Exercise 23

Petit jeté en descendant (dessous) [petit jeté—Vaganova], one count hold in closing, four counts, facing the barre.

On "and" 1, plié and throw the left leg 2nd, while simultaneously pushing off the floor with the supporting leg, and with both legs stretching in the air; on 2, land in plié on the left leg, while the right leg bends and the right foot comes on the cou-de-pied derrière; on 3, close in 5th derrière; on 4, stretch both legs. On "and" 5, plié and throw the right leg 2nd, while simultaneously pushing off the floor with the supporting leg, and with both legs stretching in the air; on 6, land in plié on the right leg, while the left leg bends and the left foot comes on the cou-de-pied derrière; on 7, close in 5th derrière; on 8, stretch both legs. Repeat three more times.

Explanation. Students are introduced to the petit jeté dessous, which involves a jump from one leg onto the other. It is the most common form of the petit jeté. During the jump, one leg is sharply thrown to the side. In the landing, the working foot becomes the supporting foot; the traveling is kept to a minimum between where the landing and the takeoff take place. Like in the assemblé, it is important to coordinate the throw of the leg with the spring of the other leg; the takeoff of the supporting leg starts before the working leg is fully stretched 2nd.

During the jump, both legs are stretched out in the air. When landing, the thigh of the working leg does not collapse but is maintained at about the same height, with the lower limb sharply bending, and the inner side of the metatarsals, not the heel, pressing against the external part of the cou-de-pied; this adjustment is recommended to avoid having the thigh drop, thus impeding the impression of lightness in the landing. In the landing, the working foot does not bounce but remains pressed against the supporting ankle, with the knee pushed to the side.

Exercise 24

Piqué retiré derrière, without hold, two counts, facing the barre.

On "and," plié and extend the right leg 2nd; on 1, step onto the right foot on demi-pointe, bringing the left leg into retiré derrière; on 2, come down in 5th in plié. Repeat three more times to the right.

Explanation. Students are going back to the barre to perform the piqué on two counts, without hold in between. Like in the previous piqué exercises, the head is slightly turned toward the traveling side and the hips remain parallel to the barre. To help with transferring the weight onto the supporting leg, the second leg quickly assumes its final position during the piqué. Since students travel, they must move the hands along the barre. Once students come down into plié, they brush their working foot 2nd to resume the piqué.

Exercise 25

Curtsey.

THIRD CLASS

Students repeat the material of the Second Class of this week.

FOURTH CLASS

Exercise 1

Warm up.

Exercise 2

Plié.

Exercise 3

First Battement tendu exercise.

Exercise 4

Battement tendu 2nd, small développé, eight counts, facing the barre.

Students repeat Exercise 4 of the Second Class of this week.

Exercise 5

Battement tendu 2nd, in 1st, on the count, two repetitions, facing the barre.

Students repeat Exercise 5 of the Second Class of this week.

Exercise 6

Battement tendu soutenu 2nd dessus, with rise onto demi-pointes, without changing feet, four counts, facing the barre.

Students repeat Exercise 6 of the Second Class of this week.

Exercise 7

Battement jeté 2nd, two counts, battement jeté, on the count, two repetitions, plié, in 1st, facing the barre.

Students repeat Exercise 7 of the Second Class of this week.

Exercise 8

Rond de jambe à terre en dehors and en dedans, two counts, facing the barre.

Students repeat Exercise 8 of the Second Class of this week.

Exercise 9

Battement frappé en l'air, en croix en dehors and en dedans, with the foot in a flexed position, two counts.

Students repeat Exercise 9 of the Second Class of this week.

Exercise 10

Rond de jambe soutenu 2nd, en dehors and en dedans, in 1st, two counts, facing the barre, review.

Students repeat Exercise 10 of the Second Class of this week.

Exercise 11

Petits battements.

Exercise 12

Adagio: développé devant and 2nd, with port de bras, eight counts.

Students repeat Exercise 12 of the Second Class of the Twenty-Fifth Week.

Exercise 13

Grand battement en croix, two counts, three repetitions.

Students repeat Exercise 13 of the Second Class of this week.

Exercise 14

Stretching.

CENTER

Exercise 15

Battement tendu 2nd, with hold when closing, in 1st, arms in 6th, on the count.

Students repeat Exercise 15 of the Second Class of this week.

Exercise 16

Battement tendu devant and derrière, with port de bras, two counts, with épaulement effacé.

Start right foot devant, facing the lower right corner. The head is turned toward the left shoulder. In the preparatory port de bras, bring both arms in 1st, open the right arm 2nd, and keep the left arm in 1st.

On "and" 1, battement tendu devant; on 2, close 5th devant; on "and" 3, battement tendu devant; on 4, close 5th devant; on "and" 5, battement tendu devant; on 6, close 5th devant; on 7 and 8, switch arms with the right arm closing 1st and the left arm opening 2nd. Repeat the exercise with three battements tendus with the back foot; then switch arms again before repeating the exercise.

Explanation. Students are repeating the exercise, except each battement tendu is done on two counts each. Since the battement tendu is on two counts, the change in the port de bras is performed on two counts to have time to place the arms correctly. The working leg must be really behind in the battement tendu derrière; the big toe is not crushed, and the lower abdomen remains lifted.

Exercise 17

Glissade 2nd, two counts, two repetitions, without changing feet, pas de bourrée dessous, with port de bras, four counts.

Students repeat Exercise 17 of the Second Class of this week.

Exercise 18

Preparatory exercise for the coupé (cut) dessous and dessus, four counts, facing the barre.

On "and," bring the back foot on the cou-de-pied derrière, with a sharp plié on the front leg; on 1, hold the position; on 2, the back foot steps onto demi-pointe, stretching the leg, while the front foot comes on the cou-de-pied devant; on 3, close 5th devant in plié; on 4, stretch both knees. Repeat one more time.

On "and," bring the front foot pointed on the cou-de-pied devant, with a sharp plié on the back leg; on 1, hold the position; on 2, the front foot steps onto demi-pointe, stretching the leg, while the back foot comes on the cou-de-pied derrière; on 3, close 5th derrière in plié; on 4, stretch both knees. Repeat one more time with the right foot front. Repeat the whole exercise one more time.

Explanation. Students are already familiar with stepping onto demi-pointe with the leg bent as it is done to initiate the pas de bourrée. In this coupé exercise, the second foot comes onto the cou-de-pied devant (dessus) and derrière (dessous) to take the place of the first foot. Both feet come into 5th in plié together. Here, the action of bringing the second foot on the cou-de-pied, thus cutting short the action of the first foot and taking its place, is called a coupé. It is usually performed at the lower level of the leg. The coupé can take several forms. It can be done flat-footed, with a jump, or on demi-pointe like here.

Music. The music is sharp with distinct counts, but not too fast, so that students can hold briefly the position in each part of the movement. The coupé is usually performed on the upbeat, but here the parts of the movement are performed evenly.

Exercise 19

Battement tendu 2nd, two counts, close in plié, retiré with port de bras, four counts.

Students repeat Exercise 19 of the Second Class of this week.

Exercise 20

Échappé 2nd, with a quarter turn, in 1st, two counts, one count hold.

Students repeat Exercise 20 of the Second Class of this week.

Exercise 21

Sissonne 2nd, traveling toward the back foot and the front foot, changing feet, two counts, three repetitions.

Students repeat Exercise 21 of the Second Class of this week.

Exercise 22

Petit jeté en descendant (dessous), one count hold in closing, four counts, facing the barre.

Students repeat Exercise 23 of the Second Class of this week.

Exercise 23

Piqué retiré derrière, without hold, two counts, facing the barre.

Students repeat Exercise 24 of the Second Class of this week.

Exercise 24

Curtsey.

FIFTH CLASS

Exercise 1

Warm up.

Exercise 2

Plié.

Exercise 3

First battement tendu exercise.

Exercise 4

Battement tendu 2nd, small développé, eight counts, facing the barre.

Students repeat Exercise 4 of the Second Class of this week.

Exercise 5

Battement tendu 2nd, in 1st, on the count, two repetitions, facing the barre.

Students repeat Exercise 5 of the Second Class of this week.

Exercise 6

Battement tendu soutenu 2nd dessus, with rise onto demi-pointes, without changing feet, four counts, facing the barre.

Students repeat Exercise 6 of the Second Class of this week.

Exercise 7

Battement jeté 2nd, two counts, two repetitions, battement jeté 2nd, on the count, plié, in 1st, facing the barre.

Students repeat Exercise 7 of the Second Class of this week.

Exercise 8

Rond de jambe à terre en dehors and en dedans, two counts, facing the barre.

Students repeat Exercise 8 of the Second Class of this week.

Exercise 9

Battement frappé en l'air, en croix en dehors and en dedans, with the foot in a flexed position, two counts.

Students repeat Exercise 9 of the Second Class of this week.

Exercise 10

Rond de jambe soutenu 2nd, en dehors and en dedans, in 1st, two counts, facing the barre, review.

Students repeat Exercise 10 of the Second Class of the Twenty-Fifth Week.

Exercise 11

Petits battements.

Exercise 12

Adagio: développé devant and 2nd, with port de bras, eight counts.

Students repeat Exercise 12 of the Second Class of this week.

Exercise 13

Grand battement en croix, two counts, three repetitions.

Students repeat Exercise 13 of the Second Class of this week.

Exercise 14

Stretching.

CENTER

Exercise 15

Battement tendu 2nd, hold when closing, in 1st, arms in 6th, on the count, four repetitions.

Students repeat Exercise 15 of the Second Class of this week.

Exercise 16

Battement tendu devant and derrière, with port de bras, two counts, with épaulement effacé.

Students repeat Exercise 16 of the Fourth Class of this week.

Exercise 17

Glissade 2nd, two counts, two repetitions, without changing feet, pas de bourrée dessous, with port de bras, four counts.

Students repeat Exercise 17 of the Second Class of this week.

Exercise 18

Preparatory exercise for the coupé dessous and dessus, four counts, facing the barre.

Students repeat Exercise 18 of the Fourth Class of this week.

Exercise 19

Battement tendu 2nd, two counts, closing in plié, retiré with port de bras, eight counts.

Students repeat Exercise 19 of the Second Class of this week.

Exercise 20

Échappé 2nd, with a quarter turn, in 1st, two counts, one count hold.

Students repeat Exercise 20 of the Second Class of this week.

Exercise 21

Sissonne 2nd, traveling toward the back foot and the front foot, changing feet, two counts, three repetitions.

Students repeat Exercise 21 of the Second Class of this week.

Exercise 22

Petit jeté en descendant (dessous), one count hold in closing, four counts, facing the barre.

Students repeat Exercise 23 of the Second Class of this week.

Exercise 23

Piqué retiré derrière, two counts, facing the barre.

Students repeat Exercise 24 of the Second Class of this week.

Exercise 24

Curtsey.

Thirtieth Week

§

FIRST CLASS

Students repeat the material of the Fifth Class of last week.

SECOND CLASS

Exercise 1

Warm up.

Exercise 2

Plié.

Exercise 3

First battement tendu exercise.

Exercise 4

Battement tendu en croix, small développé, hold in the pointing.

On "and" 1, battement tendu devant; on 2, close 5th devant; on "and," bring the foot on the cou-de-pied devant; on 3, extend the leg out devant, pointing the foot onto the floor; on 4, hold the position; on 5, close 5th devant; from 6 and 8, hold the position. Repeat the exercise en croix en dehors. At the end, roll up and hold the position.

Explanation. Students are repeating Exercise 4 of the Second Class of the Twenty-Ninth Week, this time performed en croix en dehors.

Exercise 5

Battement tendu 2nd, on the count, two repetitions, in 1st, facing the barre.

Students repeat Exercise 5 of the Second Class of the Twenty-Ninth Week.

Exercise 6

Battement tendu soutenu 2nd dessous, with rise onto demi-pointes, without changing feet, four counts, facing the barre.

On "and," plié; on 1, battement tendu 2nd with the left foot; on 2, bring the left leg behind the supporting leg, with both feet coming onto demi-pointes in 5th, right foot front, and the supporting leg stretching; on 3, come down in plié; on 4, stretch. Repeat the exercise with the left foot three more times, the last one closing 5th devant, to change feet.

Explanation. Students are repeating Exercise 6 of the Second Class of the Twenty-Ninth Week, this time bringing the back leg 5th derrière. That leg must be kept turned out at all times, with strongly activated turn-out muscles, especially when it comes into 5th.

Exercise 7

Battement jeté 2nd, direct closing, accent in, hold in the closing, on the count, three repetitions, plié, in 1st, facing the barre.

On "and," battement jeté 2nd; on 1, close 1st; on 2, hold the position; on "and," battement jeté 2nd; on 3, close 1st; on 4, hold the position; on "and," battement 2nd; on 5, close 1st; on 6, hold the position; on 7 and 8, plié and stretch. Repeat the exercise one more time. Repeat the whole exercise one more time. At the end, plié, relevé in 1st, and hold the position.

Explanation. The only holding is on the closing. The battement is otherwise direct.

Exercise 8

Preparation for battement soutenu 2nd, two counts, two counts hold in the closing, facing the barre.

On "and," plié; on 1, battement 2nd with the right leg in plié; on "and" 2, close 5th devant, stretching the supporting leg; on 3 and 4, hold the position. Repeat three more times with the right leg, closing the last one derrière. At the end, roll up and hold balance.

Explanation. Students are practicing the exercise with a battement this time, without a rise onto demi-pointes. They must not confuse this exercise with the one in which they must stretch their supporting leg by the time the working leg stretches à la demi-hauteur. The supporting leg does not stretch before the working leg joins the other in 5th. There is no pause to point the toes onto the floor before closing 5th; such a pause would break the energy of the closing of the working leg that is crucial in this exercise.

Music. A tango with sharp beats will work well here.

Exercise 9

Rond de jambe à terre en dehors and en dedans, two counts.

On "and" 1, battement tendu devant; on "and," rond de jambe to 2nd; on 2, rond de jambe to derrière; on 3, hold the position; on 4, close 5th derrière; on "and" 5, battement tendu derrière; on "and," rond de jambe to 2nd; on 6, rond de jambe to devant; on 7, hold the position; on 8, close 5th. Repeat three more times. At the end, retiré devant and hold balance.

Explanation. Students are now performing the exercise sideways. The tempo is slightly accelerated.

Exercise 10

Battement fondu en croix, start with a battement and start with a fondu, four counts, facing the barre.

On "and" 1, battement devant; on 2, bend the leg in attitude devant in plié, then without pausing, bring the foot on the cou-de-pied devant, keeping the knee well turned out; on 3, close in 5th in plié; on 4, stretch both knees; on "and" 5, bring the front foot on the cou-de-pied with a deep plié of the supporting leg; on 6, the leg comes into attitude devant; on 7, extend the leg devant, stretching the supporting leg; on "and," lower the leg and point the foot onto the floor; on 8, close 5th devant. Repeat the exercise en croix en dehors. At the end, plié and relevé in 5th, bring the front foot pointed on the cou-de-pied devant, and hold the position.

Explanation. Students are reviewing the battement fondu in this exercise where the second movement is the reverse of the first one. The movement is continuous and flowing.

Music. The tempo is slower since there are only four counts for each movement.

Exercise 11

Double battement frappé 2nd, alternating devant and derrière, four counts, facing the barre.

Following the preparatory port de bras, battement tendu 2nd.

On "and," bring the front foot on the cou-de-pied devant; on 1, hold the position; on "and" 2, perform a petit battement to bring the foot on the cou-de-pied derrière; on 3, extend the leg 2nd, pointing the foot onto the floor; on 4, hold the position; on "and," bring the foot onto the cou-de-pied derrière; on 5, hold the position; on "and" 6, bring the foot onto the cou-de-pied devant; on 7, extend the leg 2nd; on 8, hold the position. Repeat three more times, alternating bringing the foot on the cou-de-pied devant and derrière. Repeat the whole exercise one more time.

Explanation. Students are introduced to the double battement frappé. Students have practiced a similar exercise in Exercise 11 of the Second Class of the Thirteenth Week when studying the petits battements. A double battement frappé is in fact a petit battement going from back to front or front to back, followed by a sharp extension. Here the extension is performed in 2nd, pointing the foot onto the floor. Each movement is done energetically, especially when the leg bends to bring the foot onto the cou-de-pied and when extending 2nd.

Music. The tempo is fairly quick and tonic.

Exercise 12

Demi-rond de jambe en dehors à la demi-hauteur [preparation for petit temps relevé—Vaganova], start in plié, with port de bras, four counts.

Following the preparatory port de bras, bring the arm down.

On 1, plié; on 2, battement à la demi-hauteur devant, still in plié, bringing the arm 1st; on 3, rond de jambe 2nd, stretching the supporting leg, with the arm opening 2nd; on "and," bring the leg down, pointing the foot onto the floor; on 4, close 5th devant with the arm coming down. Repeat three more times. Students release the barre at the end of the last demi-rond de jambe, holding the leg 2nd with the arms 2nd.

Explanation. Students are practicing the demi-rond de jambe en dehors à la demi-hauteur, starting with a plié. This is another basic exercise to practice the coordination of the arm and the legs. The movement is similar to the one involved in the first part of a fouetté turn. Unlike the exercise of rond de jambe à la demi-hauteur practiced earlier, the movement here is dynamic with an energetic demi-rond de jambe while stretching the supporting leg. The difficulty in the performance of this movement is to abruptly stop in 2nd the momentum picked up in the rond de jambe, while keeping the turn-out in both legs. If the leg in the rond de jambe goes beyond the line of the 2nd position, the supporting hip has to move from its alignment, thus destroying the balance. Notice the coordination of the arm to closely fit the leg movement, with the arm opening 2nd when the leg opens 2nd. Like the working leg in the rond de jambe, the arm does not open past the 2nd position. Later on, the movement will be practiced with a relevé on demi-pointe in the demi-rond de jambe.

Music. A dynamic waltz music or even a tango would be appropriate.

Application. This is a good exercise to teach the first elements of the fouetté, and can be practiced early on at the barre in the training. It is, however, recommended that the rond de jambe en l'air in the regular rond de jambe exercise at the barre be practiced first.

Exercise 13

Petits battements.

Exercise 14

Adagio: développé 4th position derrière, arabesque, eight counts, facing the barre.

On "and," bring the left foot on the cou-de-pied derrière, straightening the head; on 1 and 2, slide it up along the supporting leg to retiré derrière; on 3, open the leg in attitude derrière; on 4, stretch the leg fully derrière; on 5 and 6, hold the position in arabesque; on 7, bring down the leg and point the foot onto the floor; on 8, close 5th derrière. Repeat the exercise one more time.

Explanation. Students are starting to work on the développé arabesque facing the barre. Like for the lift of the leg in arabesque, they start a bit further from the barre, since their torso comes slightly forward. As said before, an excessive bending of the torso forward in order to raise the working leg must be avoided. The torso must be lifted as the leg moves up. The working leg in arabesque must be aligned with the working shoulder and must not sway toward the side. The knee must be pressed well outward and must not drop when the working leg opens into attitude and stretches out. In the attitude, the knee must never be lower than the working foot; both must be aligned. The shoulders remain straight. By now, students should be able to raise the leg to à la hauteur or close to it, especially if regular conditioning has been a part of the program to increase back flexibility and strength; but no matter high the leg can go, students should strive to pull up their torso as the leg goes up.

The leg is in attitude derrière.

The leg is fully extended derrière.

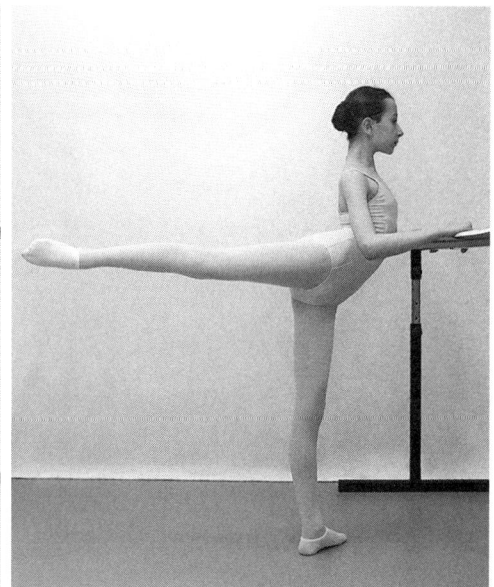

The leg is in arabesque à la hauteur.

Exercise 15

Grand battement en croix, two counts, three repetitions.

Students repeat Exercise 13 of the Second Class of the Twenty-Ninth Week.

Exercise 16

Stretching.

CENTER

Exercise 17

Battement tendu devant and derrière, with port de bras, two counts, with épaulement effacé.

Students repeat Exercise 16 of the Fourth Class of the Twenty-Ninth Week.

Exercise 18

Rond de jambe à terre en dehors and en dedans, passé à terre, with port de bras, four counts.

Following the preparatory port de bras, bring the arms down.

On "and" 1, battement tendu devant, bringing the arms in 1st; on 2, rond de jambe to 2nd, without holding, opening the arms 2nd; on 3, rond de jambe en dehors to the back; on 4, hold the position; on "and" 5, brush through 1st, battement tendu devant, keeping the arms 2nd; from 6 to 8, repeat the rond de jambe en dehors, and close 5th derrière, bringing the arms down. After repeating the exercise with the left foot front, repeat the exercise with ronds de jambe en dedans, starting with the left foot, with the same port de bras.

Explanation. Students are practicing the rond de jambe à terre with a port de bras and a passé à terre in the center. Notice the switch of the supporting leg for each series so that the supporting leg does not get overly tired. The port de bras is applied only in the first demi-rond de jambe, and the arms close at the end of the second rond de jambe.

Music. Since there are four counts for each rond de jambe, the tempo is slightly faster than the one used for the ronds de jambe à terre, now performed on two counts at the barre.

Exercise 19

Adagio: lift the leg devant and derrière, arabesque ouverte, four counts, with épaulement effacé.

Start in the effacé position, right foot front.

On "and" 1 and 2, brush the front foot out, lift the leg, and hold the position; on "and" 3, lower the leg and point the foot onto the floor; on 4, close 5th devant; on "and" 5 and 6, brush the back foot, lift the leg in arabesque, and hold the position; on "and" 7, lower the leg; on 8, close 5th derrière. Repeat one more time.

Explanation. Students are performing the adagio in the effacé position. The working leg front is turned out when lifted, keeping the turn-out equal on both legs (the tendency to favor one leg, especially the working leg, over the other tends to be unfortunately obvious in this exercise!). Here students are introduced to the arabesque ouverte, with both legs visible from the audience point of view. The arms remain 2nd to keep the shoulders straight for now.

Music. Since there are four counts for each lift, the adagio music is fairly slow.

Exercise 20

Rond de jambe soutenu 2nd, en dehors, in 1st, two counts.

On "and" 1, battement tendu 2nd; on 2, lift the leg à la demi-hauteur; on 3, bend the working leg, whereas the toes describe an oval beginning with a backward arc; on 4, through the forward arc and finishing in 2nd position with a stretched leg; on 5, lower the leg and point the foot onto the floor; on 6, hold the position; on 7, close 1st; on 8, hold the position. Repeat the whole exercise one more time.

Explanation. Students are performing the rond de jambe soutenu 2nd en dehors. This is a demanding exercise for balance and strength; they start the exercise with a battement tendu and in 1st to be more stable. For students who can raise their leg higher than à la demi-hauteur, the overall placement and the turn-out of both legs must not be neglected.

Music. A medium-tempo waltz with strongly accented beats will accompany the exercise.

Exercise 21

Relevé in 4th position, two counts, three repetitions, facing the barre.

Following the preparatory port de bras,

battement tendu devant and bring the foot down, then from that position, point the back foot and bring that foot down.

On 1, plié; on 2, relevé in 4th; on 3, come down in plié; on 4, relevé; on 5, come down in plié; on 6, relevé; on 7, come down in plié; on 8, stretch the knees and hold the position. Repeat the exercise one more time. To close, point the front foot and bring it in, and then the back foot closes in 5th against the front foot.

Explanation. Students are introduced to the relevé in 4th position. Notice the preparatory movement that was introduced in Exercise 2 of the Fifth Class of the Fourteenth Week so that students are not too close or too far from the barre. The feet are flat on the floor in 4th. Students must avoid to cross their feet over in 4th, especially if their turn-out is less than perfect, for it makes it difficult to keep the hips square and the knees above the toes in the plié. The back leg remains turned out with the heel pushed forward.

Application. The relevé in 4th is not very common, except in class work and some choreography. However, it is a useful exercise to better center oneself in this position, a skill that will help in the pirouette in 4th position introduced later on.

Exercise 22

Relevé in 1st, two counts, eight repetitions.

Following the preparatory port de bras, bring the arms down.

On "and," plié; on 1, relevé, bringing the arms in low 1st; on 2, come down in the plié; on 3, relevé; on 4, come down in the plié; on 5, relevé; on 6, come down in the plié; on 7, relevé; on 8, come down in plié. Repeat the exercise one more time.

Explanation. Students are performing eight relevés in each series. The exercise can also be performed at the barre.

Exercise 23

Relevé retiré devant, en descendant and en remontant, two counts.

Following the preparatory port de bras, bring the arms down.

On "and," plié; on 1, relevé on the right foot, bringing the left leg (the back leg) into a retiré devant sharply, with the arms in 1st, and the head turning slightly toward the left; on 2, close 5th devant in plié. Repeat three more times, bringing the back leg in retiré devant and closing 5th. Repeat three more times.

On "and," plié; on 1, relevé on the left foot, bringing the front leg in retiré devant, with the arms in 1st, and the head turning slightly toward the left; on "and" 2, bring the right foot back of the supporting leg and close 5th derrière in plié. Repeat three more times, closing 5th derrière each time. Repeat the exercise one more time.

Explanation. This time students are changing feet in the exercise. But the retiré is always devant with the working leg, either the front one or the back one, coming sharply into retiré devant. The hips stay straight, and the working foot remains pointed without sickling. The arms remain in 1st, without bouncing up and down during the exercise. When the working leg closes derrière, it does not flex prematurely, but must remain pointed as long as possible before closing 5th. Notice the movement of the head following the same pattern that was learned when practicing the battement tendu 2nd en descendant and en remontant. Later on in training, students will apply some épaulement to this type of exercise; for now, students should keep the body de face to maintain balance.

Exercise 24

Soubresaut in 1st, on the count, six repetitions, facing the barre and in the center.

On "and," plié and push off the floor; on 1, land in plié in 1st; repeat five more times (counts 2 to 6); on 7, stretch the knees; on 8, hold the position. Repeat three more times. Repeat the exercise in the center.

Explanation. Students are reviewing the soubresaut exercise, bouncing-type, increasing the number of jumps from five to six jumps in a row.

Exercise 25

Sissonne 2nd, traveling toward the back foot and the front foot, changing feet, two counts, three repetitions.

Students repeat Exercise 21 of the Second Class of the Twenty-Ninth Week.

Exercise 26

Curtsey.

THIRD CLASS

Students repeat the material of the Second Class of this week.

FOURTH CLASS

Exercise 1

Warm up.

Exercise 2

Plié.

Exercise 3

First battement tendu exercise.

Exercise 4

Battement tendu en croix, small développé, hold in the pointing.

Students repeat Exercise 4 of the Second Class of this week.

Exercise 5

Battement tendu 2nd, on the count, two repetitions, in 1st, facing the barre.

Students repeat Exercise 5 of the Second Class of the Twenty-Ninth Week.

Exercise 6

Battement tendu soutenu 2nd dessous, with rise onto demi-pointes, without changing feet, four counts, facing the barre.

Students repeat Exercise 6 of the Second Class of this week.

Exercise 7

Battement jeté 2nd, direct closing, accent in, hold in the closing, on the count, three repetitions, plié, in 1st, facing the barre.

Students repeat Exercise 7 of the Second Class of this week.

Exercise 8

Preparation for battement soutenu 2nd, two counts, two counts hold in the closing, facing the barre.

Students repeat Exercise 8 of the Second Class of this week.

Exercise 9

Rond de jambe à terre en dehors and en dedans, two counts.

Students repeat Exercise 9 of the Second Class of this week.

Exercise 10

Battement fondu en croix, start with a battement and start with a fondu, four counts, facing the barre.

Students repeat Exercise 10 of the Second Class of this week.

Exercise 11

Double battement frappé 2nd, alternating devant and derrière, four counts, facing the barre.

Students repeat Exercise 11 of the Second Class of this week.

Exercise 12

Demi-rond de jambe à la demi-hauteur en dehors, start in plié, with port de bras, eight counts.

Students repeat Exercise 12 of the Second Class of this week.

Exercise 13

Petits battements.

Exercise 14

Adagio: développé 4th position derrière, arabesque, eight counts, facing the barre.

Students repeat Exercise 14 of the Second Class of this week.

Exercise 15

Grand battement en croix, two counts, three repetitions.

Students repeat Exercise 13 of the Second Class of the Twenty-Ninth Week.

Exercise 16

Stretching.

CENTER

Exercise 17

Battement tendu 2nd, in 1st, arms in 6th, on the count, two repetitions.

In the preparatory port de bras, bring the arms in 1st, open the left arm 2nd, keep the right arm in 1st, and the head turned slightly toward the right arm.

On "and," battement tendu 2nd; on 1, close 1st; on "and," battement tendu 2nd; on 2, close 1st; on 3 and 4, hold the position. Repeat three more times. Repeat the whole exercise one more time. At the end, roll up in 1st and hold the position.

Explanation. Students are practicing the exercise with two battements tendus performed on the count each. The torso must not swing, and students lift their lower abdomen during the exercise.

Exercise 18

Battement jeté 2nd, two counts, battement jeté 2nd, one count, plié, in 1st.

On "and," battement 2nd; on 1, hold the position; on "and," lower the leg pointing the foot onto the floor; on 2, close 1st; on "and," battement 2nd; on 3, hold the position; on "and," lower the leg pointing the foot onto the floor; on 4, close 1st; on "and," battement jeté 2nd; on 5, close 1st; on 6, hold the position; on 7, plié; on 8, stretch the knees. Repeat the exercise one more time with the right leg. Repeat the whole exercise one more time.

Explanation. Students are repeating Exercise 7 of the Second Class of the Twenty-Ninth Week, this time performed in the center. The first two battements of each series prepare for the third one, which closes 1st directly. In these first two battements, the lowering of the leg is performed more quickly.

Exercise 19

Rond de jambe à terre en dehors and en dedans, passé à terre, with port de bras, four counts.

Students repeat Exercise 18 of the Second Class of this week.

Exercise 20

Adagio: lift the leg devant and derrière, arabesque ouverte, four counts, with épaulement effacé.

Students repeat Exercise 19 of the Second Class of this week.

Exercise 21

Rond de jambe soutenu 2nd, en dehors, in 1st, two counts.

Students repeat Exercise 20 of the Second Class of this week.

Exercise 22

Relevé in 4th position, four counts, facing the barre.

Students repeat Exercise 21 of the Second Class of this week.

Exercise 23

Relevé in 1st, two counts, eight repetitions.

Students repeat Exercise 22 of the Second Class of this week.

Exercise 24

Relevé retiré devant, en descendant and en remontant, two counts.

Students repeat Exercise 23 of the Second Class of this week.

Exercise 25

Soubresaut in 1st, on the count, six repetitions, facing the barre and in the center.

Students repeat Exercise 24 of the Second Class of this week.

Exercise 26

Sissonne 2nd, traveling toward the back foot and the front foot, changing feet, two counts, three repetitions.

Students repeat Exercise 21 of the Second Class of the Twenty-Ninth Week.

Exercise 27

Pas de basque en descendant [pas de basque par terre en avant—Vaganova], eight counts.

Following the preparatory port de bras, the arms come down.

On 1, plié; on 2, battement tendu devant in plié, with the arms coming to 1st; on 3, demi-rond de jambe à terre in 2nd en dehors, still in plié, opening the arms 2nd; on 4, transfer the weight onto the right foot, still in plié, stretching the left leg and pointing the left foot 2nd; on 5, bring the left foot into 1st in plié, bringing the arms in 1st; on 6, slide the left foot to

4th position front, still in plié; on 7, transfer the weight onto the front leg, stretching both legs, and pointing the right foot in the back, opening the arms 2nd; on 8, close the right foot in 5th derrière, bringing the arms down. Repeat the whole exercise one more time.

Explanation. The pas de basque is a very old ballet step that has been a staple of the classical French school. Its origin is ethnic, of the Basque country. The French school considers it as a step very much close to the floor, during which the transfer is operated from one leg to another. The pas de basque is usually performed from croisé to croisé position with the head movement accompanying it. For now, students remain de face, just to learn the mechanism in this very broken down version of the step. Going from the first leg onto the other in the first part of the exercise, the turn-out of both legs must be maintained before the second foot slides through 1st.

Music. A large waltz is appropriate for this exercise.

Application. The introduction of the pas de basque is reserved for students who already have a solid control of the turn-out and the different elements of this ballet step, such as brushing the foot out in plié.

Exercise 28

Curtsey.

FIFTH CLASS

Exercise 1

Warm up.

Exercise 2

Plié.

Exercise 3

First battement tendu exercise.

Exercise 4

Battement tendu en croix, small développé, hold in the pointing.

Students repeat Exercise 4 of the Second Class of this week.

Exercise 5

Battement tendu 2nd, on the count, two repetitions, in 1st, facing the barre.

Students repeat Exercise 5 of the Second Class of the Twenty-Ninth Week.

Exercise 6

Battement tendu soutenu 2nd dessous, with rise onto demi-pointes, without changing feet, four counts, facing the barre.

Students repeat Exercise 6 of the Second Class of this week.

Exercise 7

Battement jeté 2nd, direct closing, accent in, hold in the closing, plié, in 1st, on the count, three repetitions, facing the barre.

Students repeat Exercise 7 of the Second Class of this week.

Exercise 8

Preparation for battement soutenu 2nd, two counts, two counts hold on the closing, facing the barre.

Students repeat Exercise 8 of the Second Class of this week.

Exercise 9

Rond de jambe à terre en dehors and en dedans, two counts.

Students repeat Exercise 9 of the Second Class of this week.

Exercise 10

Battement fondu en croix, start with a battement and start with a fondu, four counts, facing the barre.

Students repeat Exercise 10 of the Second Class of this week.

Exercise 11

Double battement frappé 2nd, alternating devant and derriere, four counts, facing the barre.

Students repeat Exercise 11 of the Second Class of this week.

Exercise 12

Demi-rond de jambe en dehors à la demi-hauteur, start in plié, with port de bras, eight counts.

Students repeat Exercise 12 of the Second Class of this week.

Exercise 13

Petits battements.

Exercise 14

Adagio: développé 4th position derrière, arabesque, eight counts, facing the barre.

Students repeat Exercise 14 of the Second Class of this week.

Exercise 15

Grand battement en croix, two counts, three repetitions.

Students repeat Exercise 13 of the Second Class of the Twenty-Ninth Week.

Exercise 16

Stretching.

CENTER

Exercise 17

Battement tendu 2nd, in 1st, arms in 6th, on the count, two repetitions.

Students repeat Exercise 17 of the Fourth Class of this week.

Exercise 18

Battement jeté 2nd, two counts, battement jeté 2nd, one count, in 1st, plié.

Students repeat Exercise 18 of the Fourth Class of this week.

Exercise 19

Rond de jambe a terre en dehors and en dedans, passé à terre, with port de bras, four counts.

Students repeat Exercise 18 of the Second Class of this week.

Exercise 20

Adagio: lift the leg devant and derrière, arabesque ouverte, four counts, with épaulement effacé.

Students repeat Exercise 19 of the Second Class of this week.

Exercise 21

Relevé in 1st, two counts, eight repetitions.

Students repeat Exercise 22 of the Second Class of this week.

Exercise 22

Relevé retiré devant, en descendant and en remontant, two counts.

Students repeat Exercise 23 of the Second Class of this week.

Exercise 23

Preparation for pirouette in 5th en dehors: battement tendu 2nd, close in plié, relevé retiré devant, with port de bras.

Following the preparatory port de bras, bring the arms down.

On "and" 1, battement tendu 2nd, opening the arms 2nd, palms down with the right arm slightly higher than the left one, and the head turned toward the right arm; on 2, close 5th devant in plié, bringing the arms in 6th with the left arm 2nd and the right arm in 1st, straightening the head; on "and" 3, relevé with retiré devant, closing the left arm in 1st as well; on "and" 4, come down in plié in 5th, right foot front, keeping the arms in 1st. Repeat three more times, with the battement tendu coming out of the plié each time, bringing the arms slightly lower to open them 2nd with the battement tendu, with the head directed toward the higher arm.

Explanation. After practicing the exercise with the retiré, students are performing the same exercise with a relevé retiré, which brings us closer to the pirouette en dehors in 5th. Notice the important coordination of the arms: the arms must close in 1st as soon as students perform the relevé. This coordination is important when it is time to rotate. In the opening of the arms 2nd accompanying the battement tendu 2nd, the elbows do not scoop.

This year students have practiced many exercises that involved bringing sharply the leg into a retiré. This sharpness will limit the disturbing effect that the movement can have on balance. It will also help the timing between the relevé and the retiré. When it is time to perform the pirouette itself, if the leg is not in retiré 2nd quickly enough, it will have a difficult time to catch up with the supporting leg that is already in rotation, with the effect of shortening the rotation and compromising the overall turn-out position of both legs.

Following the battement tendu, students press their front foot down in a deep plié with the weight equal on both feet. Equalizing the weight on both legs helps to push vertically and consequently to balance better in the relevé. Being solely on the back leg tends to throw the weight backward in the relevé. Students must propulse themselves in a vertical line. The goal of this exercise is of course to hold balance as long as possible (within the musical accompaniment though), but it is also to bring together all the elements necessary for a correct pirouette: the arms in a proper position, the hips straight, a good retiré with the knee to the side and the pointed foot against the front knee of the supporting knee, a high demi-pointe, a plié and landing with the whole feet on the floor and the weight on both legs, the shoulders straight, a vertical push onto demi-pointe, and a pull of the torso of the opposite side of the one of the retiré. Students will spend some time practicing this exercise to firmly establish these good habits, before starting any rotation.

Exercise 24

Soubresaut in 1st, on the count, six repetitions, facing the barre and in the center.

Students repeat Exercise 24 of the Second Class of this week.

Exercise 25

Assemblé 2nd, without changing, on the count, facing the barre.

On "and," plié, brush the front foot and extend the leg 2nd, while pushing off the floor with the supporting leg, and stretching both legs in the air; on 1, land in plié in 5th, right foot front; on 2, stretch the knees; on "and," plié, brush the front foot and extend the leg 2nd, while pushing off the floor, and stretching both legs; on 3, land in plié in 5th, right foot front; on 4, stretch the knees. Repeat the exercise, extending the back leg 2nd this time and closing 5th, left foot back.

Explanation. Students are practicing each jump on the count, without changing feet for now. The throw of the leg is quicker, and the jump is closer to the floor than in previous assemblé exercises, for the landing is completed at the end of the count.

Music. A music usually played for grand allegro with a large tempo would be appropriate, for students need to have time to stretch their toes and knees during the jump itself and stretch their knees in between each jump.

Exercise 26

Petit jeté dessous, two counts, three repetitions, facing the barre.

On "and" 1, plié and throw the left leg 2nd, while the supporting leg springs from the floor, with both legs now stretched in the air; on 2, land in plié on the left foot, while the right leg bends and the right foot comes on the cou-de-pied derrière; on "and," brush the right foot into 5th; on 3, throw the right leg 2nd, while pushing off the floor with the supporting leg; on 4, land in plié on the right foot, while the left leg bends; on "and," brush the working foot into 5th; on 5, throw the left leg 2nd, while pushing off the floor with the supporting leg; on 6, land on the left foot in plié; on 7, close the foot in 5th plié; on 8, stretch both legs. Repeat three more times.

Explanation. Students are practicing the exercise with three petits jetés in a row. Even though students do not close in between jumps, they brush the working foot through the 5th each time before the throw. This practice helps to re-center, coordinate the throw of the working leg with the jump of the other leg, and maintain the pulling up of the thighs.

Music. The tempo is accelerated so that students do not sit in the plié in between the jumps.

Exercise 27

Pas de basque, en descendant, eight counts.

Students repeat Exercise 27 of the Fourth Class of this week.

Exercise 28

Curtsey.

Thirty-First Week

𝄞

FIRST CLASS

Students repeat the material of the Fifth Class of the Thirtieth Week.

SECOND CLASS

Exercise 1

Warm up.

Exercise 2

Plié.

Exercise 3

First battement tendu exercise.

Exercise 4

Battement tendu 2nd, in 1st, on the count, three repetitions, facing the barre.

On "and," battement tendu 2nd; on 1, close 1st; on "and," battement tendu 2nd; on 2, close 1st; on "and," battement tendu 2nd; on 3, close 1st; on 4, hold the position. Repeat three more times. Repeat the whole exercise one more time. At the end, relevé in 1st and hold the position with the arms in 5th.

Explanation. Students are repeating the exercise with three battements tendus in a row this time. Students must avoid to hit the heels when closing, by brushing their foot firmly on the floor and by using their adductors to bring the leg in with control, and yet with energy to close the leg in.

Exercise 5

Battement tendu en croix, with different port de bras, two counts, four repetitions, review.

Following the preparatory port de bras, bring the arm 5th.

On "and" 1, battement tendu devant; on 2, close 5th devant. Repeat three more times.

On "and" 1, battement tendu 2nd, opening the arm 2nd; on 2, close 5th devant. Repeat three

more times, bringing the arm down when closing the last battement tendu.

On "and" 1, battement tendu derrière, bringing the arm in 1st and in an allongé position; on 2, close 5th derrière. Repeat three more times, bringing the arm in 1st when closing the last one.

On "and" 1, battement tendu 2nd, opening the arm 2nd; on 2, close 5th derrière. Repeat three more times.

Explanation. Students are repeating Exercise 3 of the Second Class of the Twenty-First Week, except this time the battement tendu is performed on two counts, and the exercise is done in 5th. The music is not too fast so that there is time to change arm position.

Exercise 6

Battement tendu soutenu 2nd, with rise onto demi-pointes, changing feet, two counts, three repetitions, facing the barre.

On "and" 1, plié and battement tendu 2nd with the right foot still on the plié; on 2, bring the right foot back of the supporting leg, with both feet coming onto demi-pointes in 5th, and the supporting leg stretching; on "and," come down in plié in 5th; on 3, battement tendu 2nd with the right foot; on 4, bring the right foot devant, with both feet on demi-pointes in 5th, and the supporting leg stretching; on "and," come down in plié; on 5, battement tendu 2nd with the right foot; on 6, bring the right foot back of the supporting leg, with both feet going up on demi-pointes with stretched knees; on 7, come down in plié; on 8, stretch the knees. Repeat the whole exercise one more time.

Explanation. Students are repeating the exercise on two counts and changing feet. The head rotation follows the familiar pattern of turning toward the working leg when closing front and turning away from the working leg when closing back. After coming down into plié, students are brushing their whole foot carefully through the 5th, without holding, before extending the leg out in 2nd.

Music. A medium-tempo waltz is appropriate for this exercise. The tempo has to be slow enough to allow students to bring their foot into 5th before brushing it out.

Exercise 7

Battement jeté 2nd, on the count, no hold, two repetitions, in 1st, in plié, facing the barre.

On "and," battement jeté 2nd; on 1, close 1st; on "and," battement 2nd; on 2, close 1st; on 3 and 4, hold the position; on "and," battement jeté 2nd; on 5, close 1st; on "and," battement jeté 2nd; on 6, close 1st; on 7 and 8, plié and stretch. Repeat one more time with the right foot. Repeat the whole exercise one more time. At the end, directly from the plié, relevé in 1st and hold the position.

Explanation. Students are performing two battements jetés in a row, closing on the count. When closing, the foot closes in 1st with precision and resistance. The heels must not hit each other. The role of the adductor muscles and the resistance of the foot brushing in are equally important in the closing. Both legs must squeeze with control, with the brushing of the working foot acting as a brake before closing to avoid the heels kicking each other. The torso does not swing during the exercise but remains still.

Exercise 8

Battement jeté piqué en croix, bouncing on the count, two repetitions.

On "and" 1, battement devant; on "and," lower the leg, bringing the pointed foot onto the floor devant; on 2, lift the leg devant again at the same height than previously; on "and," lower the leg; on 3, lift the leg devant; on "and," lower the leg; on 4, close 5th devant. Repeat the exercise en croix en dehors. At the end, roll up and hold the position.

Explanation. Students are revisiting the battement jeté piqué, except the exercise is performed en croix in 5th. The leg should be bouncing very lightly onto the floor with taut toes.

Music. The tempo is very sharp, but not too fast, to allow for a slight hold à la demi-hauteur each time.

Exercise 9

Demi-rond de jambe à terre en dehors and en dedans, starting in 2nd, in 1st, four counts.

On "and" 1, battement tendu 2nd; on 2, rond de jambe en dedans to 4th position devant; on 3, rond de jambe en dehors to 2nd; on 4, close 1st.

On "and" 5, battement tendu 2nd; on 6, rond de jambe en dehors to the back; on 7, rond de jambe en dedans to 2nd; on 8, close 1st. Repeat the exercise one more time. At the end, grand plié in 1st with port de bras, roll up and hold balance.

Explanation. This exercise involves another pattern for the rond de jambe à terre, starting with a battement tendu 2nd. The hips do not swing and the head moves accordingly. Notice the grand plié with port de bras, as it was performed the first time in Exercise 11 of the Fourth Class of the Nineteenth Week.

Exercise 10

Battement fondu en croix, start with a battement and start with a fondu, four counts, facing the barre.

Students repeat Exercise 10 of the Second Class of the Thirtieth Week.

Exercise 11

Double battement frappé 2nd, alternating devant and derrière, arm in low 1st, four counts.

Following the preparatory port de bras, bring the arm down.

On "and," bring the front foot on the cou-de-pied devant, bringing the arm in low 1st; on 1, hold the position; on "and" 2, perform a petit battement to bring the foot back; on "and," extend the leg 2nd, pointing the foot onto the floor; on 3 and 4, hold the position; on "and," bring the foot onto the cou-de-pied derrière; on 5, hold the position; on "and" 6, bring the foot onto the cou-de-pied devant; on "and," extend the leg 2nd; on 7 and 8, hold the position. Repeat three more times, alternating bringing the foot on the cou-de-pied devant and on the cou-de-pied derrière, with the same arm position. At the end, relevé and bring the foot on the cou-de-pied devant and hold balance.

Explanation. Students are repeating Exercise 11 of the Second Class of the Thirtieth Week, this time performed sideways. The extensions and bendings are performed more quickly. The tempo is slightly accelerated.

Exercise 12

Demi-rond de jambe à la demi-hauteur, start in plié, en dedans, four counts, facing the barre.

Start with the right foot back.

On 1, plié; on 2, battement à la demi-hauteur derrière with the right leg, still in plié; on 3, demi-rond de jambe to 2nd, stretching the supporting leg; on "and," bring the leg down and point the foot onto the floor; on 4, close 5th derrière. Repeat three more times, holding the leg 2nd in the last demi-rond de jambe with the arms 2nd.

Explanation. Whereas the exercise for the demi-rond de jambe à la demi-hauteur en dehors performed in Exercise 12 of the Second Class of the Thirtieth Week was executed sideways, this one en dedans is still done facing the barre. The rotation of the working leg from back to 2nd makes the movement more difficult, leaving more room for incorrect movements to take place. The working leg does not drop down as it goes from back to 2nd, and the leg turns out in 2nd as soon as it is feasible, without turning the hips away from the barre.

Exercise 13

Adagio: grand plié in 1st, cambré, développé 2nd, facing the barre.

On 1 and 2, demi-plié going into grand plié; on 3 and 4, straighten up into demi-plié and stretch the legs; on 5 and 6, turning the head toward the right side, cambré; on 7 and 8, straighten up and turn the head de face; on "and," bring the front foot on the cou-de-pied devant; on 1 and 2, slide the side of the foot up the supporting leg to retiré; on 3, open the leg in attitude; on 4, stretch the leg 2nd; on 5 and 6, hold the position; on 7, bring down the leg and point the foot onto the floor; on 8, close 1st.

Explanation. Students are reviewing some of the elements studied so far in adagio in 1st. Notice that the head is now turned at a 45° angle for the cambré. Shoulders remain even. The grand plié can also be performed in 5th if the grand plié in 1st is correctly done.

Exercise 14

Grand battement jeté piqué 2nd, in 1st, four counts, facing the barre.

On "and" 1, grand battement 2nd; on "and,"

lower the leg and point the foot onto the floor; on 2, grand battement 2nd; on "and," lower the leg and point the foot onto the floor; on 3, hold the position; on 4, close 1st. Repeat three more times, alternating legs.

Explanation. This is the most difficult grand battement exercise students will be doing this year, and it can be left out if students are not ready for it, or if there is not enough time. The principles are the same as the ones for the battement jeté piqué à la demi-hauteur, except that the second battement does not hold in the air since the goal of the grand battement exercise is to bring the leg as high as possible. In this exercise, the working foot does not pause when pointing on the floor the first time, but it bounces to bring the leg à la hauteur again. The second battement is not as high as the first one since there is less momentum for the throw when it starts with the foot pointed on the floor. During the execution of this grand battement, the weight must be strongly maintained over the supporting side so that the working leg can be lifted lightly; otherwise the working leg appears heavy, as if unable to lift quickly and easily. The strongly pointed toes must never relax as they touch the floor. As said before, they must lead the movement as if to try to kick something in the air. The whole movement must appear effortless. Strong work of the adductors is required to bring the leg down in time. To make the exercise easier, students will not raise the leg too high.

Exercise 15

Stretching.

CENTER

Exercise 16

Battement tendu 2nd, in 1st, arms in 6th, on the count, two repetitions.

Students repeat Exercise 17 of the Fourth Class of the Thirtieth Week.

Exercise 17

Battement tendu 2nd, four counts, écarté devant.

Start in the croisé position.

On "and" 1, battement tendu 2nd with the right leg, with the head still turned slightly toward the right; on 2, hold the position; on "and"

3, close 5th derrière, keeping the head in the same direction; on 4, hold the position; on "and" 5, battement tendu 2nd; on 6, hold the position; on 7, close 5th devant; on 8, hold the position; on "and" 1, battement tendu 2nd; on 2, hold the position; on "and" 3, close derrière; on 4, hold the position; on "and" 5, battement tendu 2nd; on 6, hold the position; on 7, close 5th devant; on 8, hold the position. Repeat the whole exercise one more time.

Explanation. Students are introduced to a new orientation called écarté devant, which means drawn back, separated. In this position, the dancer faces one of the two front corners of the studio (like they did in the épaulement croisé), and the leg nearer to the audience is pointed 2nd. The head is turned toward the working leg, with the arms 2nd, even when the leg closes 5th derrière. This is to avoid looking away from the audience.

Exercise 18

Battement jeté 2nd, two counts, battement jeté, one count, in 1st, plié.

Students repeat Exercise 18 of the Fourth Class of the Thirtieth Week.

Exercise 19

Adagio: chassé à terre forward, arabesque ouverte with bras ouverts (open arms) [first arabesque—Vaganova/Cechetti], with port de bras.

Start in the upper left corner of the studio, facing the lower right corner, right foot front in effacé. Following the preparatory port de bras, bring the arms down.

On "and" 1, lift the stretched back leg slightly, bringing the arms in low 1st, and as the leg comes back into 5th in plié, the front leg slides forward still in plié, through 4th position devant; on 2, transfer the weight onto the front leg, stretching both legs, pointing the left foot, and bringing the arms in 1st; on 3, extend the right arm devant in allongé and the left arm 2nd, palms down, with the head facing the right arm; on 4, hold the position; on 5, lift the left leg in arabesque; on 6, hold the position; on 7, lower the leg and point the foot onto the floor; on 8, close the foot 5th derrière, bringing both arms down. Repeat at least several more times traveling in diagonal.

Explanation. This is one step closer to the final version of the chassé à terre, in which the back leg seems to push the front leg forward and the back foot takes the place of the front foot. Students are also introduced to the arabesque ouverte with open arms (bras ouverts). In this position, the placement of the arms is often referred to as bras arabesque (arm in arabesque) or arm allongé. Students have already been introduced to the bras allongé at the barre. Here the arm that is the opposite of the leg in arabesque is stretched forward with the elbow very slightly curved, in front of the shoulder, with the palm facing down and elongated fingers. The other arm is stretched at about 120° to no more than 150° from the other arm. A wider angle of the arms (unfortunately too common, even among professional dancers) creates a distortion of the shoulders and a rise of the shoulder that is on the same side of the leg in arabesque.

Notice that the port de bras is performed independently for proper execution. The head is facing the direction of travel. When the arm is in arabesque, the eyes are focused on an imaginary line on top of the fingers. Unlike in the allongé position that has been practiced previously, the head is held straight.

If a certain amount of cheating is allowed by turning in the supporting leg in the arabesque, students must still strive to keep their supporting foot turned out as much as possible when lifting the leg in arabesque. If there is an adjustment in the position of the supporting leg, it must be as little as possible—just necessary to achieve a proper balance between the turn-out of the working leg and the one of the supporting leg. The leg in arabesque does not shift to the side.

Exercise 20

Battement fondu 2nd, start with a fondu, four counts.

On "and" 1, bring the front foot on the cou-de-pied with a deep plié on the supporting leg; on 2, open the leg in small attitude in 2nd, still in plié; on 3, extend the leg 2nd, with a simultaneous stretch of the supporting leg; on "and," lower the leg, and point the foot onto the floor; on 4, close 5th devant. Repeat the exercise one more time, closing 5th derrière.

Explanation. Students are revisiting the battement fondu exercise on four counts.

Exercise 21

Preparation for pirouette in 5th en dehors: battement tendu 2nd, close in plié, relevé retiré devant, with port de bras.

Students repeat Exercise 23 of the Fifth Class of the Thirtieth Week.

Exercise 22

Changement de pied, on the count, two repetitions, facing the barre and in the center.

On "and," plié and push off the floor, stretching the legs and pointing the feet; on 1, land in 5th plié, left foot front; on "and," directly out of the plié, push off the floor again; on 2, land in 5th plié, right foot front; on 3 and 4, stretch the knees. Repeat three more times. Repeat in the center.

Explanation. Students are practicing the changement de pied on the count, two at a time.

Exercise 23

Assemblé 2nd, without changing, on the count, facing the barre.

Students repeat Exercise 25 of the Fifth Class of the Thirtieth Week.

Exercise 24

Petit jeté dessous, two counts, three repetitions, facing the barre.

Students repeat Exercise 26 of the Fifth Class of the Thirtieth Week.

Exercise 25

Pas de basque, en descendant, eight counts.

Students repeat Exercise 27 of the Fourth Class of the Thirtieth Week.

Exercise 26

Piqué 2nd and piqué retiré derrière, no hold, arms in 6th, two counts.

In the preparatory port de bras, bring both arms in 1st and then open the left arm 2nd, keeping the right arm in 1st, and turning the head slightly toward the right.

On "and," plié and extend the right leg 2nd; on 1, piqué onto the right foot on demi-pointe, bringing the left foot onto demi-pointe in 5th,

behind the right one, stretching both legs; on 2, come down in plié; on "and" 3, extend the right leg 2nd, piqué onto the right foot on demi-pointe, bringing the left leg in retiré derrière; on 4, come down into demi-plié in 5th position still with the right foot front. Repeat three more times to the right. Repeat the whole exercise one more time.

Explanation. Students are performing the exercise in the center on two counts each, without stretching the knees in between. Here both piqués that have been learned are combined for review. They close 5th each time. Students must not hold back in the piqué. As said before, gauging how much momentum to put onto that piqué takes much time and practice; performing the piqué where the toes are pointing down will help students control that momentum.

Exercise 27

Curtsey.

THIRD CLASS

Students repeat the material of the Second Class of this week.

FOURTH CLASS

Exercise 1

Warm up.

Exercise 2

Plié.

Exercise 3

First Battement tendu exercise.

Exercise 4

Battement tendu 2nd, in 1st, on the count, three repetitions, facing the barre.

Students repeat Exercise 4 of the Second Class of this week.

Exercise 5

Battement tendu en croix, with different port de bras, two counts, four repetitions.

Students repeat Exercise 5 of the Second Class of this week.

Exercise 6

Battement tendu soutenu 2nd, with rise onto demi-pointes, changing feet, two counts, three repetitions, facing the barre.

Students repeat Exercise 6 of the Second Class of this week.

Exercise 7

Battement jeté 2nd, on the count, no hold, two repetitions, in 1st, in plié, facing the barre.

Students repeat Exercise 7 of the Second Class of this week.

Exercise 8

Battement jeté piqué en croix, bouncing on the count, two repetitions.

Students repeat Exercise 8 of the Second Class of this week.

Exercise 9

Demi-rond de jambe à terre en dehors and en dedans, starting with battement tendu 2nd, in 1st, four counts.

Students repeat Exercise 9 of the Second Class of this week.

Exercise 10

Battement fondu en croix, start with a battement and start with a fondu, four counts, facing the barre.

Students repeat Exercise 10 of the Second Class of the Thirtieth Week.

Exercise 11

Double battement frappé 2nd, alternating devant and derrière, arm in low 1st, four counts.

Students repeat Exercise 11 of the Second Class of this week.

Exercise 12

Demi-rond de jambe en dedans à la demi-hauteur, à la demi-hauteur, start in plié, four counts, facing the barre.

Students repeat Exercise 12 of the Second Class of this week.

Exercise 13

Adagio: grand plié in 1st, cambré, développé 2nd, facing the barre.

Students repeat Exercise 13 of the Second Class of this week.

Exercise 14

Grand battement jeté piqué 2nd, in 1st, four counts, facing the barre.

Students repeat Exercise 14 of the Second Class of this week.

Exercise 15

Stretching.

CENTER

Exercise 16

Battement tendu 2nd, four counts, with épaulement écarté devant.

Students repeat Exercise 17 of the Second Class of this week.

Exercise 17

Battement jeté 2nd, in 1st, hold in 1st, on the count, three repetitions.

On "and," battement jeté 2nd; on 1, close 1st; on 2, hold the position; on "and," battement jeté 2nd; on 3, close 1st; on 4, hold the position; on "and," battement 2nd; on 5, close 1st; on 6, hold the position; on 7, plié; on 8, stretch. Repeat one more time with the right leg. Repeat the whole exercise one more time. At the end, roll up in 1st and hold the position.

Explanation. This exercise is similar to Exercise 7 of the Second Class of the Thirtieth Week, this time performed in the center.

Exercise 18

Adagio: chassé à terre forward, arabesque ouverte with bras ouverts, with port de bras.

Students repeat Exercise 19 of the Second Class of this week.

Exercise 19

Battement fondu 2nd, start with a fondu, four counts.

Students repeat Exercise 20 of the Second Class of this week.

Exercise 20

Preparation for pirouette in 5th en dehors:

battement tendu 2nd, close in plié, relevé retiré devant, with port de bras.

Students repeat Exercise 23 of the Fifth Class of the Thirtieth Week.

Exercise 21

Changement de pied, on the count, two repetitions, facing the barre and in the center.

Students repeat Exercise 22 of the Second Class of this week.

Exercise 22

Assemblé 2nd, without changing, on the count, facing the barre.

Students repeat Exercise 25 of the Fifth Class of the Thirtieth Week.

Exercise 23

Petit jeté dessous, two counts, three repetitions, facing the barre.

Students repeat Exercise 26 of the Fifth Class of the Thirtieth Week.

Exercise 24

Piqué 2nd and piqué retiré derrière, no hold, arms in 6th, two counts.

Students repeat Exercise 26 of the Second Class of this week.

Exercise 25

Déboulés: in 1st, six half turns, each half turn on one count, in diagonal.

Start the exercise in the upper left corner of the studio, in croisé position, traveling in a diagonal. Following the preparatory port de bras, bring the arms down, plié and relevé in 1st, with the arms coming to low 1st, and the head turning toward the lower right corner.

On 1, rotate one half turn toward the right; on 2, rotate one half turn; on 3, rotate one half turn; on 4, rotate one half turn; on 5, rotate one half turn; on 6, rotate one half turn; on 7 and 8, come down in demi-plié and relevé. Repeat the exercise several times, traveling toward the right. Repeat the exercise going from the right upper corner toward the lower left corner.

Explanation. Today students are executing six half turns starting with a relevé in the preparation. The pattern of execution must be very regular, holding the feet in 1st at all times. The rotation is performed slightly more rapidly for each half turn in this exercise.

Exercise 26

Curtsey.

FIFTH CLASS

Exercise 1

Warm up.

Exercise 2

Plié.

Exercise 3

First Battement tendu exercise.

Exercise 4

Battement tendu 2nd, in 1st, on the count, three repetitions, facing the barre.

Students repeat Exercise 4 of the Second Class of this week.

Exercise 5

Battement tendu en croix, with different port de bras, two counts, four repetitions.

Students repeat Exercise 5 of the Second Class of this week.

Exercise 6

Battement tendu soutenu 2nd, with rise onto demi-pointes, changing feet, two counts, three repetitions, facing the barre.

Students repeat Exercise 6 of the Second Class of this week.

Exercise 7

Battement jeté 2nd, on the count, no hold, two repetitions, in 1st, in plié, facing the barre.

Students repeat Exercise 7 of the Second Class of this week.

Exercise 8

Battement jeté piqué en croix, bouncing on the count, two repetitions.

Students repeat Exercise 8 of the Second Class of this week.

Exercise 9

Demi-rond de jambe à terre en dehors and en dedans, without closing, in 1st.

Students repeat Exercise 9 of the Second Class of this week.

Exercise 10

Battement fondu en croix, start with a battement and start with a fondu, four counts, facing the barre.

Students repeat Exercise 10 of the Second Class of the Thirtieth Week.

Exercise 11

Double battement frappé 2nd, alternating devant and derrière, arm in low 1st, four counts.

Students repeat Exercise 11 of the Second Class of this week.

Exercise 12

Demi-rond de jambe à la demi-hauteur en dedans, start in plié, four counts, facing the barre.

Students repeat Exercise 12 of the Second Class of this week.

Exercise 13

Adagio: grand plié in 1st, cambré, développé 2nd, facing the barre.

Students repeat Exercise 13 of the Second Class of this week.

Exercise 14

Grand battement jeté piqué 2nd, in 1st, four counts, facing the barre.

Students repeat Exercise 14 of the Second Class of this week.

Exercise 15

Stretching.

CENTER

Exercise 16

Battement tendu 2nd, four counts, with épaulement écarté devant.

Students repeat Exercise 17 of the Second Class of this week.

Exercise 17

Battement jeté 2nd, in 1st, hold in 1st, on the count, three repetitions.

Students repeat Exercise 17 of the Fourth Class of this week.

Exercise 18

Adagio: chassé à terre forward, arabesque ouverte, with bras ouverts, with port de bras.

Students repeat Exercise 19 of the Second Class of this week.

Exercise 19

Battement fondu 2nd, start with a fondu, four counts.

Students repeat Exercise 20 of the Second Class of this week.

Exercise 20

Pas de bourrée dessous and dessus, with port de bras, four counts.

Following the preparatory port de bras, bring the arms down.

On "and," bring the back foot on the cou-de-pied derrière with a plié on the supporting leg, the head still turned toward the right, bringing the arms in 1st; on 1, step onto demi-pointe on the back foot and stretch both legs; on "and," open the right leg 2nd, with both legs stretched and the head straightening, and opening the arms 2nd; on 2, step onto the right foot on demi-pointe, with the left leg still 2nd and the foot pointed down; on "and" 3, close 5th, left foot front in plié, with the head turning toward the left and closing the arms down; on 4, stretch both knees. Repeat three more times.

On "and," bring the front foot on the cou-de-pied devant with a plié on the supporting leg, with the head still turned toward the right, bringing the arms in 1st; on 1, step onto demi-pointe on the front foot, and stretch both legs; on "and," open the left leg 2nd, with both legs stretched and the head straightening, and opening the arms 2nd; on 2, step onto the left foot on demi-pointe, with the right leg still stretched 2nd; on "and" 3, close 5th, left foot front in plié, with the head turning toward the left and closing the arms down; on 4, stretch both knees. Repeat three more times.

Explanation. Students are reviewing the two pas de bourrée learned so far, with a slightly accelerated tempo.

Exercise 21

Preparation for pirouette in 5th en dehors: battement tendu 2nd, close in plié, relevé, retiré devant, with port de bras.

Students repeat Exercise 23 of the Fifth Class of the Thirtieth Week.

Exercise 22

Changement de pied, on the count, two repetitions, facing the barre and in the center.

Students repeat Exercise 22 of the Second Class of this week.

Exercise 23

Glissade 2nd, two counts, assemblé 2nd, en descendant, on the count, facing the barre.

On "and," plié; on 1, extend the left leg 2nd in plié; on "and," transfer the weight onto the left leg in plié while the right leg stretches and the right foot points; on 2, close 5th right foot front, still in plié; on "and," directly out of the plié, brush the left foot and extend the leg 2nd, while pushing off the floor with the supporting leg, and stretching both legs in the air; on 3, land in plié in 5th, left foot front; on 4, stretch the knees. Repeat three more times, with the assemblé closing devant each time.

Explanation. Students are practicing the glissade and the assemblé at the barre first. Students will be careful not to turn in their front foot as they close it in the glissade and as they transfer their weight onto that foot to extend the leg for the assemblé, as it is observed too often. There is no stretch of the knees after the glissade, only after the assemblé. The tempo is not too fast so that students have time to really brush their working foot out each time. Since students move slightly forward in this exercise, they have to adjust their glissade somewhat to avoid being too close to the barre.

Exercise 24

Petit jeté dessous, on the count, one count hold in the landing, three repetitions, facing the barre.

On "and," plié and throw the left leg 2nd, while the supporting leg springs off the floor, with both legs now stretched in the air; on 1, land in plié on the left foot, while the right leg bends and the right foot comes on the cou-de-pied derrière; on 2, hold the position in plié; on "and," brush the right foot into 5th, throw the leg 2nd; while the supporting leg pushes off the floor, stretching both legs in the air; on 3, land in plié on the right foot, while the left leg bends; on 4, hold the position; on "and," brush the left foot into 5th, and throw the leg 2nd, while the supporting leg pushes off the floor; on 5, land in plié on the left foot in plié; on 6, hold the position; on 7, close the foot in 5th plié; on 8, stretch both legs. Repeat three more times.

Explanation. The exercise is now done on the count, with one count hold in the plié. The initial plié is sharper, the throw is more rigorous, and the jump is closer to the floor. Like in the assemblé, the working leg should not extend too high in the battement so that students are able to bring the leg back under in the landing.

Music. A larghetto 2/4 march will be appropriate for this exercise. Since there is a hold in the plié, the music will be energetic for students to resume the jump following that hold, so that students do not sit in the plié. Coordination of the throw and the takeoff of the supporting leg, along with the brushing of the foot through 5th each time, will help students to get momentum to resume the jump starting on one foot.

Exercise 25

Piqué 2nd and piqué retiré derrière, no hold, arms in 6th, two counts.

Students repeat Exercise 26 of the Second Class of this week.

Exercise 26

Déboulés: in 1st, six half turns, each half turn on one count, in diagonal.

Students repeat Exercise 25 of the Fourth Class of this week.

Exercise 27

Curtsey.

Thirty-Second Week

§

FIRST CLASS

Students repeat the material of the Fifth Class of the Thirty-First Week.

SECOND CLASS

Exercise 1

Warm up.

Exercise 2

Plié.

Exercise 3

First battement tendu exercise.

Exercise 4

Battement tendu 2nd, on the count, hold in the closing, facing the barre.

On "and," battement tendu 2nd; on 1, close 5th derrière; on 2, hold the position; on "and," battement tendu 2nd; on 3, close devant; on 4, hold the position; on "and," battement tendu 2nd; on 5, close 5th derrière; on 6, hold the position; on "and," battement tendu 2nd; on 7; close 5th devant; on 8, hold the position. Repeat one more time. At the end, roll up and hold the position.

Explanation. This time students are closing in 5th, with one count holding. The tempo is not too fast so that students close 5th correctly, tightly against the supporting foot. The hips do not swing when closing.

Exercise 5

Battement tendu devant and derrière, passé à terre, battement tendu 2nd, on the count, in 1st, facing the barre.

On "and" 1, battement tendu devant; on "and" 2, brush the foot through 1st, and battement tendu derrière; on "and" 3, brush through 1st, and battement tendu devant; on 4, close 1st; on "and," battement tendu 2nd; on 5, close 1st; on

"and," battement tendu 2nd; on 6, close 1st; on 7 and 8, plié and stretch. Repeat three more times. At the end, roll up and balance.

Explanation. Students are combining some of the elements learned in previous battement tendu exercises. There is now much less holding in positions.

Exercise 6

Battement jeté 2nd, four counts, two counts, on the count, in 1st, facing the barre.

On "and" 1, battement jeté 2nd; on 2, hold the position; on 3, lower the leg and point the foot onto the floor; on 4, close 1st; on "and," battement jeté 2nd; on 5, hold the position; on "and," lower the leg and point the foot onto the floor; on 6, close 1st; on "and," battement 2nd; on 7, close 1st; on "and," battement 2nd; on 8, close 1st. Repeat the whole exercise one more time.

Explanation. This is a review of different tempos students have used in the battement jeté exercises performed previously. This type of exercise should be practiced often, for it involves different groups of muscles. Here the first part involves the abductor muscles of the thigh (the ones that lift the leg out). The second one involves the adductors (the ones that close the leg).[2] When bringing the leg out or in, the torso does not move and the hips do not swing.

Exercise 7

Battement soutenu 2nd, with rise onto demi-pointe, changing feet, four counts, facing the barre.

On "and," plié; on 1, battement 2nd with the left foot, still in plié; on 2, bring the foot in front of the supporting foot in 5th onto demi-pointes, with both legs stretched; on 3, come down in plié; on 4, stretch. Repeat the exercise with the right foot.

On "and," plié; on 1, battement 2nd with the

---

2   Howse and Hancock, *Dance Technique and Injury Protection*, 8.

right foot, still on the plié; on 2, bring it derrière of the supporting foot in 5th onto demi-pointes, with both legs stretched; on 3, come down in plié; on 4, stretch. Repeat the exercise with the left foot. Repeat the whole exercise one more time.

Explanation. Students are practicing the exercise with a relevé onto demi-pointes as the working leg closes into 5th.

Exercise 8

Rond de jambe à terre.

From now on, the instructor will select the elements of the rond de jambe à terre exercise. Students will review the different movements studied in this exercise throughout the year. The combination remains simple.

Exercise 9

Position on the cou-de-pied, close in plié, battement tendu 2nd, four counts, facing the barre.

On "and," bring the front foot on the cou-de-pied devant; on 1, hold the position; on 2, close in 5th in plié; on "and" 3, battement tendu 2nd out of the plié, stretching both legs; on 4, close 5th devant. Repeat three more times, alternating closing derrière and devant. At the end, roll up and hold balance.

Explanation. The foot comes onto the cou-de-pied position as quickly as possible with a sharp bend of the supporting leg. There is no holding when the foot brushes the foot through 5th in plié and extends the leg 2nd.

Music. A tango or a lively 4/4 will fit nicely this kind of exercise.

Exercise 10

Battement fondu en croix, with port de bras, four counts.

Following the preparatory port de bras, bring the arm down.

On "and" 1, bring the foot pointed on the cou-de-pied devant with a deep plié on the supporting leg, with the arm in low 1st; on 2, open the working leg into attitude devant still in plié, with the arm in 1st; on 3, stretch both legs at the same time, opening the arm 2nd; on "and," lower the leg and point the foot onto the floor; on 4, close 5th devant, bringing the arm down. Repeat the

exercise en croix en dehors. At the end, plié and relevé retiré devant and hold the position.

Explanation. Students are reviewing the exercise of fondu en croix on four counts with a port de bras, with a slightly slower tempo to accommodate the port de bras. Again, fluidity and coordination are the key qualities of this exercise.

Exercise 11

Double battement frappé 2nd, with the foot in a flexed position, alternating devant and derrière, arm in low 1st, four counts.

Following the preparatory port de bras, bring the arm down.

On "and," bring the front foot in a flexed position on the cou-de-pied devant, bringing the arm in low 1st; on 1, hold the position; on "and" 2, bring the foot onto the cou-de-pied derrière; on "and," extend the leg 2nd, pointing the foot onto the floor; on 3 and 4, hold the position; on "and," bring the foot onto the cou-de-pied derrière, flexing the foot; on 5, hold the position; on "and" 6, bring the foot onto the cou-de-pied devant; on "and," extend the leg 2nd; on 7 and 8, hold the position. Repeat three more times, alternating bringing the foot on the cou-de-pied devant and derrière, with the same arm position. At the end, relevé, bring the foot on the cou-de-pied devant, and hold balance.

Explanation. The exercise is performed now with the working foot in flexed position and sideways.

Exercise 12

Demi-rond de jambe à la demi hauteur, en dehors and en dedans, with port de bras, four counts.

Following the preparatory port de bras, bring the arm down.

On "and" 1, plié and battement devant, bringing the arm in 1st; on 2, demi-rond de jambe en dehors, stretching the supporting leg and opening the arm 2nd; on 3, point the foot down onto the floor; on 4, close 5th derrière, bringing the arm down. Repeat the exercise en dedans. Repeat the exercise one more time.

Explanation. Students are now performing the full exercise sideways.

Exercise 13

Adagio: développé devant, raccourci, with port de bras, preparation for passé en l'air, four counts.

Following the preparatory port de bras, bring the arm down.

On "and," bring the foot on the cou-de-pied devant; on 1 and 2, slide the foot up the supporting leg to retiré, bringing the arm in 1st; on 3, open the leg in attitude devant; on 4, stretch the leg fully devant, opening the arm 2nd; on "and" 5, bend the leg, pushing the knee to the side, and bring the foot against the knee devant into raccourci position, closing the arm in 1st, straightening the head; on 6, slide the foot down; on 7, close 5th devant in plié, opening the arm 2nd; on 8, stretch the knees, bringing the arm down. Repeat one more time.

Explanation. Students are practicing the raccourci from the 4th position devant to prepare for the passé en l'air in which the leg passes from one position en l'air to another one. The knee initiates the bending to bring the leg into raccourci, keeping the thigh as level as possible.

Exercise 14

Grand battement, review.

From now on, the instructor will select the elements of the grand battement exercise. Students will review the different movements studied in this exercise throughout the year. The combination remains simple.

Exercise 15

Stretching.

CENTER

Exercise 16

Battement tendu 2nd, with port de bras, two counts, écarté devant.

In the preparatory port de bras, bring the arms in 1st, and open the left arm 2nd with the right arm still in 1st. The head is turned slightly toward the right.

On "and" 1, battement tendu 2nd; on 2, close 5th derrière; on "and" 3, battement tendu 2nd; on 4, close 5th devant; on "and" 5, battement tendu 2nd; on 6, close derrière; on "and"

7, battement tendu 2nd; on 8, close 5th devant. Repeat the exercise one more time.

Explanation. In this exercise, students use an arm position that is fairly traditional for performing the battement tendu exercise in the écarté position. Like in every exercise involving a battement tendu 2nd, students are careful to brush their foot along the line of the 2nd position. The arm 2nd does not scoop and does not swing back.

Exercise 17

Battement en cloche, in 1st, on the count, four repetitions.

On "and" 1, battement devant; on "and" 2, brush through 1st and battement derrière; on "and" 3, brush through 1st and battement devant; on 4, hold the position; on "and" 5, brush through 1st and battement derrière; on "and" 6, brush through 1st and battement devant; on "and" 7, lower the leg, and point the foot onto the floor; on 8, close 1st. Repeat the whole exercise one more time.

Explanation. Students are practicing the exercise of battement en cloche in the center this time. This is a challenging exercise for balance. Students keep their working leg at around 25° to have better control of the movement. A strongly held back, a good brush through 1st, and a controlled turn-out will help students not to be destabilized by the swing of the leg.

Exercise 18

Adagio: lift the leg devant and arabesque, with épaulement croisé, lift the leg 2nd, écarté devant, four counts.

Start in the position croisé.

On "and" 1 and 2, battement tendu devant, lift the leg and hold the position; on 3, lower the leg and point the foot onto the floor; on 4, close 5th; on "and" 5 and 6, battement tendu derrière with the left leg, lift the leg in arabesque, and hold the position; on 7, lower the leg; on 8, close 5th; on "and" 1 and 2, battement tendu 2nd with the right leg, lift the leg, and hold the position; on 3, lower the leg; on 4, close 5th devant; from 5 to 8, port de bras, bringing the arms down, in 1st, 2nd, and down again to close the arms in preparatory position.

Explanation. Students are reviewing some of the different directions learned so far in this exercise.

Exercise 19

Pas de bourrée dessous and dessus, with port de bras, four counts.

Students repeat Exercise 20 of the Fifth Class of the Twenty-First Week.

Exercise 20

Preparation for pirouette in 5th en dehors: battement tendu 2nd, close in plié, relevé retiré devant, with port de bras.

Students repeat Exercise 23 of the Fifth Class of the Thirtieth Week.

Exercise 21

Preparation for pirouette in 4th: battement tendu 2nd, 4th position in plié, relevé retiré devant, eight counts, facing the barre.

On "and" 1, battement tendu 2nd; on 2, hold the position; on 3, close 1st; on 4, brush the working foot back in 4th position, with both legs in plié; on 5, relevé on the left foot, bringing the back leg in retiré devant; on 6, hold the position; on 7, close 5th devant on the plié; on 8, stretch both legs. Repeat three more times.

Explanation. This exercise is to prepare for the pirouette in 4th. Students may have to release the barre when they are in 4th position, since they transfer their weight slightly away from the barre. Notice the brush of the working leg through 1st position to re-center the weight onto both legs before spreading it in 4th position equally. Right now, students keep their weight in the middle of their feet in 4th position, very slightly favoring the front leg. All the toes are flat on the floor without rolling in, especially the toes of the back foot. The hips remain parallel to the barre, and the back knee is above the toes in the 4th position. In 4th position, the front foot, in particular, is pressed firmly onto the floor. The heel must not anticipate the relevé and be brought up too soon. This practice avoids the bad habit among many ballet students to turn their front foot prematurely in the pirouette en dehors.

Students must transfer their weight right away onto the supporting leg to be balanced immediately. They should test their balance by releasing their hands briefly off the barre. The working foot does not sickle when it is transferred to the front of the knee, and it remains pointed until it closes into 5th.

Exercise 22

Changement de pied, on the count, two repetitions, facing the barre and in the center.

Students repeat Exercise 22 of the Second Class of the Thirty-First Week.

Exercise 23

Glissade 2nd, two counts, assemblé 2nd, en descendant, on the count, facing the barre.

Students repeat Exercise 23 of the Fifth Class of the Thirty-First Week.

Exercise 24

Petit jeté dessous, on the count, one count hold in the landing, three repetitions, facing the barre.

Students repeat Exercise 24 of the Fifth Class of the Thirty-First Week.

Exercise 25

Piqué 2nd, piqué retiré derrière, no hold, arms in 6th, two counts, in diagonal, review.

Start in the upper left corner of the studio, in croisé position, traveling in diagonal.

In the preparatory port de bras, bring both arms in 1st, and then open the left arm 2nd, keeping the right arm in 1st, and turning the head slightly toward the right.

On "and," plié, extend the front leg 2nd; on 1, piqué onto demi-pointe, bringing the left foot on demi-pointe behind the right one, and stretching both legs; on 2, come down in plié; on "and" 3, directly out of the plié, extend the right leg 2nd, piqué onto demi-pointe, bringing the left leg in retiré derrière; on 4, come down in plié in 5th position, still with the right foot front. Repeat several times to the right.

Explanation. Students are repeating the exercise, except it is now performed in diagonal.

Music. The tempo is not too fast to allow students to come down into 5th and brush out the foot to execute the piqué.

Exercise 26

Déboulés: in 1st, six half turns, each half turn on one count, in diagonal.

Students repeat Exercise 25 of the Fourth Class of the Thirty-First Week.

Exercise 27

Curtsey.

THIRD CLASS

Students repeat the material of the Second Class of this week.

FOURTH CLASS

Exercise 1

Warm up.

Exercise 2

Plié.

Exercise 3

First battement tendu exercise.

Exercise 4

Battement tendu 2nd, on the count, hold in the closing, facing the barre.

Students repeat Exercise 4 of the Second Class of this week.

Exercise 5

Battement tendu devant and derrière, passé à terre, battement tendu 2nd, in 1st, on the count, facing the barre.

Students repeat Exercise 5 of the Second Class of this week.

Exercise 6

Battement jeté 2nd, four counts, two counts, on the count, in 1st, facing the barre.

Students repeat Exercise 6 of the Second Class of this week.

Exercise 7

Battement soutenu 2nd, with rise onto demi-pointe, changing feet, four counts, facing the barre.

Students repeat Exercise 7 of the Second Class of this week.

Exercise 8

Rond de jambe à terre.

Exercise 9

Position on the cou-de-pied, close in plié, battement tendu 2nd, four counts, facing the barre.

Students repeat Exercise 9 of the Second Class of this week.

Exercise 10

Battement fondu en croix, with port de bras, four counts.

Students repeat Exercise 10 of the Second Class of this week.

Exercise 11

Double battement frappé 2nd, with the foot in a flexed position, alternating devant and derrière, arm in low 1st, four counts.

Students repeat Exercise 11 of the Second Class of this week.

Exercise 12

Demi-rond de jambe à la demi-hauteur, en dehors and en dedans, start in plié, with port de bras, four counts.

Students repeat Exercise 12 of the Second Class of this week.

Exercise 13

Adagio: développé devant, raccourci, with port de bras, preparation for passé en l'air, four counts.

Students repeat Exercise 13 of the Second Class of this week.

Exercise 14

Grand battement.

Exercise 15

Stretching.

CENTER

Exercise 16

Battement tendu 2nd, with port de bras, two counts, écarté devant.

Students repeat Exercise 16 of the Second Class of this week.

Exercise 17

Battement en cloche, in 1st, on the count, four repetitions.

Students repeat Exercise 17 of the Second Class of this week.

Exercise 18

Adagio: lift the leg devant and derrière, with épaulement croisé, battement 2nd, with épaulement écarté devant, four counts.

Students repeat Exercise 18 of the Second Class of this week.

Exercise 19

Pas de bourrée dessous and dessus, with port de bras, four counts.

Students repeat Exercise 20 of the Fifth Class of the Thirty-First Week.

Exercise 20

Preparation for pirouette in 5th en dehors: battement tendu 2nd, close in plié, relevé retiré devant, with port de bras.

Students repeat Exercise 23 of the Fifth Class of the Thirtieth Week.

Exercise 21

Preparation for pirouette in 4th: battement tendu 2nd, 4th position in plié, relevé retiré devant, eight counts, facing the barre.

Students repeat Exercise 21 of the Second Class of this week.

Exercise 22

Changement de pied, on the count, two repetitions, facing the barre and in the center.

Students repeat Exercise 22 of the Second Class of the Thirty-First Week.

Exercise 23

Glissade 2nd, two counts, assemblé 2nd, en descendant, on the count, facing the barre.

Students repeat Exercise 23 of the Fifth Class of the Thirty-First Week.

Exercise 24

Petit jeté dessous, on the count, one count hold in the landing, three repetitions, facing the barre.

Students repeat Exercise 24 of the Fifth Class of the Thirty-First Week.

Exercise 25

Piqué 2nd in 5th, piqué retiré derrière, arms in 6th, two counts, in diagonal.

Students repeat Exercise 25 of the Second Class of this week.

Exercise 26

Curtsey.

FIFTH CLASS

Exercise 1

Warm up.

Exercise 2

Plié.

Exercise 3

First battement tendu exercise.

Exercise 4

Battement tendu 2nd, hold in the closing, on the count, facing the barre.

Students repeat Exercise 4 of the Second Class of this week.

Exercise 5

Battement tendu devant and derrière, passé à terre, battement tendu 2nd, in 1st, on the count, facing the barre.

Students repeat Exercise 5 of the Second Class of this week.

Exercise 6

Battement jeté 2nd, four counts, two counts, on the count, in 1st, facing the barre.

Students repeat Exercise 6 of the Second Class of this week.

Exercise 7

Battement soutenu 2nd, with rise onto demi-pointe, changing feet, four counts, facing the barre.

Students repeat Exercise 7 of the Second Class of this week.

Exercise 8

Rond de jambe a terre.

Exercise 9

Position on the cou-de-pied, close in plié, battement tendu 2nd, four counts, facing the barre.

Students repeat Exercise 9 of the Second Class of this week.

Exercise 10

Battement fondu en croix, with port de bras, four counts.

Students repeat Exercise 10 of the Second Class of this week.

Exercise 11

Double battement frappé 2nd, with the foot in a flexed position, alternating devant and derrière, arm in low 1st, four counts.

Students repeat Exercise 11 of the Second Class of this week.

Exercise 12

Demi-rond de jambe à la demi-hauteur, en dehors and en dedans, start in plié, with port de bras, four counts.

Students repeat Exercise 12 of the Second Class of this week.

Exercise 13

Adagio: développé devant, raccourci, with port de bras, preparation for passé en l'air, four counts.

Students repeat Exercise 13 of the Second Class of this week.

Exercise 14

Grand battement.

Exercise 15

Stretching.

CENTER

Exercise 16

Battement tendu 2nd, with port de bras, two counts, écarté devant.

Students repeat Exercise 16 of the Second Class of this week.

Exercise 17

Battement en cloche, in 1st, on the count, four repetitions.

Students repeat Exercise 17 of the Second Class of this week.

Exercise 18

Adagio: lift the leg devant and derrière, with épaulement croisé, battement 2nd, écarté devant, four counts.

Students repeat Exercise 18 of the Second Class of this week.

Exercise 19

Battement tendu 2nd, quarter of a pirouette en dehors (tour en dehors en 5th) [tour par terre en dehors—Vaganova], four counts.

Following the preparatory port de bras, bring the arms down.

On "and" 1, battement tendu 2nd, opening the arms 2nd, palms down with the right arm slightly higher than the left one and the head turned toward the right; on 2, close in 5th in plié with the right arm coming in 1st, straightening the head; on 3, relevé on the left foot, with the right leg coming into a retiré devant rotating a quarter turn toward the right, while the right arm slightly opens 2nd and the left arm joins the other in 1st, keeping the head de face at the beginning of rotation, then snapping it quickly so that it precedes the body by the end of the rotation; on 4, finish in 5th devant in plié, facing the right side of the studio, keeping the arms in place. Repeat three more times, starting with the same preparation, lowering the arms slightly and opening them 2nd with the battement tendu, and rotating a quarter turn each time. By the end of the fourth repetition, students will be de face again. Repeat the exercise turning toward the left, with the left foot front. Repeat the whole exercise one more time.

Explanation. This is the first taste of the actual pirouette for students, who are, by now, anxious to work on it. This exercise does not occur before the end of the year since, as this manual has described, many preparatory exercises must precede and be mastered beforehand. Starting the pirouette too soon is a common flaw of ballet training. In a commercial ballet school, even if the instructor has the best of intentions and starts preparing students for the turns methodically, students will often pressure the instructor to speed up the process, so anxious are they to experience the pirouette. Unfortunately, starting pirouettes too soon often results in maddening frustration, for students will have bypassed the basics that contribute to the quality of the pirouette and will have acquired some ineradicable bad habits. The result is turning all right, but turning in a sloppy way. Almost everybody can turn, but few can turn well.

The ballet pirouette is a very complex step that involves the application of many conditions for its success. The good news is that once students master the fundamentals of the pirouette, they have achieved its most difficult part. Patience and confidence are the keys. A good pirouette is not a matter of luck, but rather the result of the intelligent application of different movements, their coordination, and the holding of several parts of the body (the head and the eyes in the spotting; the foot in the relevé and the holding of the retiré; the arms in the opening and closing ports de bras in the turn; the strong holding of the back; the turn-out from the hips, et cetera).

Yet instructors will find that even if they devote equal attention to instructing their students in the fundamentals of pirouettes, some students will turn better than others. Is there a natural disposition for the turn? Obviously shorter dancers, with a lower center of gravity, have an easier time keeping their balance (which is essential in the pirouette). Some students are simply apprehensive about the turn; such fear can impede their performance. Students with little turn-out will have more difficulty maintaining balance during the pirouette. And even the best dancers in the world have bad days for turns, when their balance is off for unknown reasons.

Ballet training has a few general rules like "one must learn to hold still before moving." The important general rules in teaching the pirouette to beginners are to hold balance before turning and to think more about the relevé than rotation itself. The holding on one leg on demi-pointe with the working leg in a retiré is crucial. Students must hold, at a minimum, a few seconds in this position with the arms still, a strong back, both legs turned out, and the working leg in a correct retiré position. If the instructor has a crucial role in teaching the basics of the pirouette, students have to learn to feel what they must do to achieve such balance. The balance must be so good that, at the end of the turn, students still hold the relevé retiré position before closing, as if they are suspended on their demi-pointe. And yet, balance is not enough. Some students can hold balance very well but still fail to turn properly. The coordination of the arms in the rotation is also important, especially in gauging the amount of momentum the dancer needs to turn. The opening and the closing of the arms will differ if one seeks to perform only one half turn, as opposed to a double or triple pirouette. Whereas the first arm did not open 2nd in the exercise of the relevé retiré, when rotation is involved like here, it needs to open about half way through 2nd (even less for a quarter turn) before it is joined by the other into 1st. The coordination between the relevé and the retiré can also affect the quality of the turn. The timing of the relevé is important, for if it is performed too late, the coordination is broken, and the pirouette will not be balanced. Dancers tend to dislike performing pirouettes in 5th, because they do not have the momentum created by the spread of the legs on the floor to easily execute multiple pirouettes. Yet the natural limitation of the 5th makes it the best position to introduce the pirouette to beginners. For one thing, introducing the pirouette in 5th will force students to perform the relevé on time. The closeness of the feet makes it more difficult for students to rotate their feet too much before they actually execute the relevé. The legs and feet have to move in coordination to make the rotation possible. For the rotation to occur out of the 5th position, the relevé has to be snappy (a good habit to follow), since no rotation can occur before one foot is off the floor.

At this stage of learning, students do not want so much to turn than to be balanced while turning. The center of gravity is more easily found in 5th; fewer things can go wrong when the working leg comes into retiré since both legs are close to each other. Overall the 5th position encourages a sense of verticality that students need to acquire in order to succeed in pirouettes.

One aspect of the pirouette en dehors in 5th that can create problems is putting more weight on the back leg than on the front one. As said before, students must press both of their feet down, especially the front one, and not let their back leg carry all the weight before the relevé occurs. Putting too much weight on the back leg tends to throw students backward or toward the side of their supporting leg when they start rotating. Students must not cheat by moving out their front foot just before the relevé.

Unlike in the preparatory exercises that they have performed so far, in this exercise, students need to open the first arm, even if it is so slightly for a quarter turn rotation. This movement will become more obvious as students practice the half and full turns. Many students tend to make their arms do extra movements and jerks during the turn, especially when the arm 2nd joins the other in 1st. The arm 2nd must join the other along the same horizontal line. The hands must not do any flamenco-like gesture. Another bad habit to keep at bay is the tendency to allow the shoulder of the arm in 1st to come forward, to bring the arm in 1st over the centerline of the torso, and to bring the arm 2nd too far back in the preparation (as if to take more momentum). The shoulders remain back and low. For a quarter turn, the spotting and the opening of the first arm are kept to a minimum.

The working leg is pushed strongly to the side in the retiré; this action alone is nearly sufficient to perform less than one pirouette. The upper torso is held very slightly forward to help students remain above their legs, without, however, pushing the knees forward.

Exercise 20

Battement tendu 2nd, 4th position in plié, relevé retiré devant, eight counts, facing the barre.

Students repeat Exercise 21 of the Second Class of this week.

Exercise 21

Changement de pied, on the count, two repetitions, facing the barre and in the center.

Students repeat Exercise 22 of the Second Class of the Thirty-First Week.

Exercise 22

Glissade 2nd, two counts, assemblé 2nd, en descendant, with port de bras, on the count.

The front arm is crossed over and the shoulders are not straight in preparation for a pirouette en dehors.

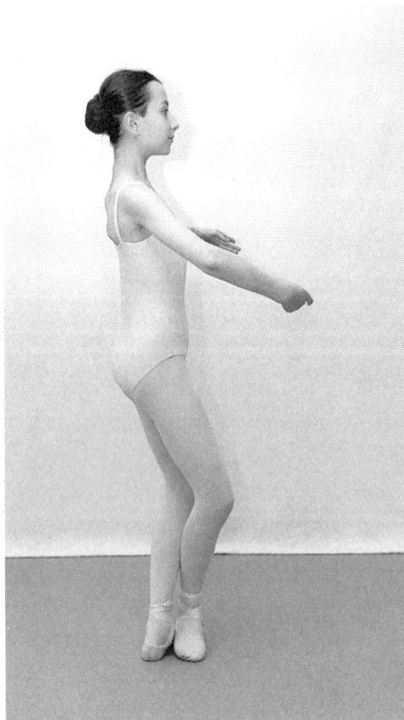

The weight is too far back.

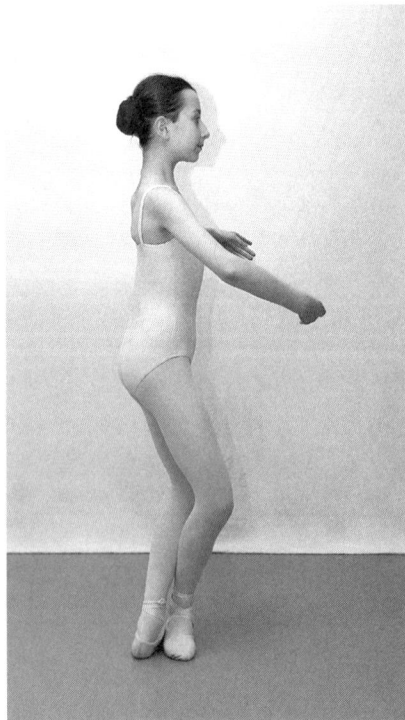

The weight is slightly forward, but the front knee is not aligned with the toes in the plié and the pelvis is tilted forward.

In the preparatory port de bras, bring the arms in 1st, keeping the left arm in 1st and opening the right 2nd, with the head turned slightly toward the left.

On "and," plié, inclining the torso slightly toward the left; on 1, extend the left leg 2nd in plié; on "and," transfer the weight onto the left leg on the plié, while the right leg stretches and the right foot points; on 2, close 5th, right foot front in plié; on "and," directly out of the plié, brush the left foot and extend the leg 2nd, pushing off the floor with the supporting leg, stretching both legs in the air, and opening the left arm 2nd (slightly higher than the right arm), turning the palms down, with the head still turned toward the left arm; on 3, land in plié in 5th, left foot front; on 4, stretch the knees, bringing the right arm in 1st and keeping the left arm 2nd, turning the head slightly toward the right arm and inclining the torso slightly toward the right. Repeat three more times, with the assemblé closing devant each time and switching arms to start the glissade.

Explanation. Students are practicing the glissade and assemblé in the center.

Exercise 23

Sissonne 2nd, traveling toward the front foot and the back foot, changing feet, two counts, three repetitions, review.

On "and," plié and push off the floor with both legs, with a slight travel toward the right side (toward the front foot), extending the left leg 2nd à la demi-hauteur, and stretching both legs in the air; on 1, land in plié on the right foot, while the left foot points 2nd onto the floor; on 2, close 5th, left foot front; on "and," directly out of the plié, push off again, with a slight travel toward the left side, extending the right leg 2nd à la demi-hauteur, and stretching both legs in the air; on 3, land in plié on the left foot, while the right foot points 2nd onto the floor; on 4, close 5th, right foot front; on "and," directly out of the plié, push off with both feet, with a slight travel toward the right side, extending the leg 2nd à la demi-hauteur, and stretching both legs in the air; on 5, land in plié on the right foot, while the left foot points 2nd onto the floor; on 6, close 5th, left foot front; on 7 and 8, stretch both knees and hold the position. Repeat one more time.

On "and," plié and push off the floor with both legs, with a slight travel toward the left side (toward the back foot), extending the right leg 2nd à la demi-hauteur, and stretching both legs in the air; on 1, land in plié on the left foot, while the right foot points 2nd onto the floor; on 2, close 5th left foot front; on "and," directly out of the plié, push off, with a slight travel toward the right side, extending the left leg 2nd à la demi-hauteur, and stretching both legs in the air; on 3, land in plié on the right foot, while the left foot points 2nd onto the floor; on 4, close 5th right foot front; on "and," directly out of the plié, push off, with a slight travel toward the left side, extending the right leg 2nd à la demi-hauteur, and stretching both legs in the air; on 5, land in plié on the left foot, while the right foot points 2nd onto the floor; on 6, close 5th left foot front; on 7 and 8, stretch both knees and hold the position. Repeat three more times.

Explanation. Students are reviewing Exercise 21 of the Second Class of the Twenty-Ninth Week. There is a hold with the knees stretching only after the third sissonne. The pointing of the foot in 2nd on the floor is not prolonged, but must still be observed at this elementary level.

Exercise 24

Petit jeté dessous, on the count, one count hold in the landing, three repetitions, facing the barre.

Students repeat Exercise 24 of the Fifth Class of the Thirty-First Week.

Exercise 25

Piqué 2nd in 5th, piqué with retiré derrière, arms in 6th, two counts, in diagonal.

Students repeat Exercise 25 of the Second Class of this week.

Exercise 26

Balancé 2nd, traveling sideways, on demi-pointe, with port de bras, two counts, review.

On "and" 1, extend the right leg 2nd, straightening the head, and step onto the right foot in plié, bending the left leg and the left foot coming derrière the cou-de-pied of the right foot, while the left arm comes in 1st, and the head turns slightly toward the left arm; on "and," step onto demi-pointe on the left foot, while raising the right foot pointed off the floor, stretching both legs; on 2, come down into plié onto the right foot, with the left foot on the cou-de-pied derrière.

On "and" 3, extend the left leg 2nd, opening the left arm 2nd and straightening the head, step onto the left foot in plié, bending the right leg and the right foot coming derrière the cou-de-pied of the left foot, while the right arm comes in 1st, and the head turns toward the right arm; on "and," step onto demi-pointe on the right foot, while pointing the left foot pointed off the floor; on 4, come down into plié onto the left foot, with the right foot on the cou-de-pied derrière.

On "and" 5, extend the right leg, opening the right arm and straightening the head, step onto the right foot in plié, bending the left leg and the left foot coming derrière the cou-de-pied of the right foot, while the left arm comes in 1st, and turning the head slightly toward the left; on "and," step onto demi-pointe on the left foot, while raising the right foot pointed off the floor; on 6, come down into plié onto the right foot with the left foot on the cou-de-pied derrière; on 7, close the foot in 5th derrière in plié; on 8, stretch the knees. Repeat the exercise one more time.

Explanation. Students are repeating Exercise 24 of the Second Class of the Twenty-Eighth Week.

Exercise 27

Curtsey.

Thirty-Third Week

§

FIRST CLASS

Students repeat the material of the Fifth Class of the Thirty-Second Week.

SECOND CLASS

Exercise 1

Warm up.

Exercise 2

Plié.

Exercise 3

First battement tendu exercise.

Exercise 4

Battement tendu 2nd, in 1st, four counts, two counts, on the count, facing the barre.

On 1 and 2, battement tendu 2nd; on 3 and 4, close 1st; on "and" 5, battement tendu 2nd; on 6, close; on "and," battement tendu 2nd; on 7, close; on "and," battement tendu 2nd; on 8, close. Repeat three more times with the right foot.

Explanation. Students are reviewing the battements tendus 2nd with different counts.

Exercise 5

Battement tendu devant and derrière, passé à terre, battement tendu 2nd, in 1st, on the count, review.

On "and" 1, battement tendu devant; on "and" 2, brush the foot through 1st and battement tendu derrière; on "and" 3, brush through 1st and battement tendu devant; on 4, close 1st; on "and," battement tendu 2nd; on 5, close 1st; on "and," battement tendu 2nd; on 6, close 1st; on 7 and 8, plié and stretch. Repeat three more times. At the end, relevé and balance.

Explanation. Students are repeating Exercise 5 of the Second Class of the Thirty-Second Week, except it is now performed sideways.

Music. A medium-tempo 3/4 waltz is suitable here.

Exercise 6

Battement jeté 2nd, in 1st, on the count, six repetitions, facing the barre.

On "and," battement jeté 2nd; on 1, close 1st; on "and," battement 2nd; on 2, close 1st; on "and," battement 2nd; on 3, close in 1st; on "and," battement jeté 2nd; on 4, close 1st; on "and," battement jeté 2nd; on 5, close 1st; on "and," battement jeté 2nd; on 6, close 1st; on 7, plié; on 8, stretch. Repeat the exercise one more time with the right foot. Repeat the whole exercise one more time. At the end, roll up and hold position.

Explanation. The number of battements jetés has increased in this otherwise familiar exercise.

Exercise 7

Battement jeté en croix, hold in the closing, on the count, two repetitions.

On "and," battement devant; on 1, close 5th devant; on 2, hold the position; on "and," battement devant; on 3, close 5th devant; on 4, hold the position. Repeat the exercise en croix en dehors with two battements in each direction.

Explanation. Students are starting to work on the battement jeté en croix performed on the count. Holding the pointed toes before closing in battement jeté exercises has been practiced almost systematically throughout the year. By now, students should perform the closing tightly without any holding whatsoever when the leg is lowered. However, if the foot starts bending—even a tiny bit—before the toes touch the floor in this type of exercise, the instructor will ask students to keep practicing the pointing of the toes with a slight pause before closing the foot.

Music. The tempo is not too fast so that the closing is done correctly.

Exercise 8

Rond de jambe à terre.

Exercise 9

Position on the cou-de-pied, close in 5th without plié, battement tendu 2nd, four counts, facing the barre.

On "and," bring the front foot on the cou-de-pied devant; on 1, hold the position; on 2, close in 5th; on "and" 3, battement tendu 2nd; on 4, close 5th derrière. Repeat twice more with the right foot and hold the position. At the end, roll up and hold balance. Repeat the exercise starting with the left foot.

Explanation. Students are repeating the exercise, closing the foot on the cou-de-pied without plié.

Application. Closing the foot on the cou-de-pied into 5th position without plié may still present difficulty, especially when the working leg and foot have to remain turned out when closing derrière. The exercise can also be still performed with a plié to close in 5th like in Exercise 9 of the Second Class of the Thirty-Second Week.

Exercise 10

Rond de jambe soutenu 2nd, en dehors and en dedans, in 1st, each rond de jambe on two counts, two repetitions, facing the barre, review.

On "and" 1, battement 2nd; on 2, hold the position; on 3, bend the working leg, whereas the toes describe an oval beginning with a backward arc; on 4, through the forward arc, and finishing in 2nd position with a stretched leg; on 5, bend the working leg, whereas the toes describe an oval beginning with a backward arc; on 6, through the forward arc, and finishing in 2nd position with a stretched leg; on 7, lower the leg, and point the foot onto the floor; on 8, close 1st. Repeat with the left leg.

On "and" 1, battement 2nd; on 2, hold the position; on 3, bend the working leg, whereas the toes describe an oval beginning with a forward arc; on 4, through the backward arc, and finishing in 2nd position with a stretched leg; on 5, bend the working leg, whereas the toes describe an oval beginning with a forward arc; on 6, through the backward arc, and finishing in 2nd position; on 7, lower the leg, and point the foot onto the floor; on 8, close 1st. At the end, roll up and hold balance.

Explanation. Students are repeating Exercise 12 of the Second Class of the Twenty-Sixth Week.

Exercise 11

Double battement frappé 2nd, two counts, two counts hold in 2nd, facing the barre.

On "and," bring the foot on the cou-de-pied devant; on 1, hold the position; on "and," bring the foot on the cou-de-pied derrière; on 2, bring the foot on the cou-de-pied devant; on "and," extend 2nd pointing the foot onto the floor; on 3 and 4, hold the position; on "and," bring the foot on the cou-de-pied derrière; on 5, hold the position; on "and," bring the foot on the cou-de-pied devant; on 6, bring the foot on the cou-de-pied derrière, on "and," extend the leg 2nd pointing the foot onto the floor; on 7 and 8, hold the position. Repeat three more times with the right foot. Repeat the whole exercise one more time.

Explanation. Students are introduced to the double battement frappé 2nd on two counts.

Application. The tempo is adjusted so that it is never too fast. The passage from one side to another must be clearly defined, always performed through the 2nd position.

Exercise 12

Demi-rond de jambe à la demi-hauteur, start in plié, en dehors and en dedans, with port de bras, four counts.

Students repeat Exercise 12 of the Second Class of the Thirty-Second Week.

Exercise 13

Adagio: développé devant and 2nd, sideways, with port de bras, développé arabesque, eight counts, facing the barre, review.

Following the preparatory port de bras, bring the arm down.

On "and," bring the foot on the cou-de-pied devant; on 1 and 2, slide the foot to retiré, bringing the arm in 1st; on 3, open the leg in attitude devant; on 4, stretch the leg fully devant, opening the arm 2nd; on 5 and 6, hold the position; on 7, bring down the leg and point the foot onto the floor; on 8, close 5th devant, bringing the arm down.

On "and," bring the foot on the cou-de-pied devant; on 1 and 2, slide the foot to retiré, bringing the arm in 1st; on 3, open the leg in attitude in 2nd; on 4, stretch the leg fully 2nd, opening the arm 2nd; on 5 and 6, hold the position; on 7, bring down the leg and point onto the floor; on 8, close 5th devant. Repeat the exercise one more time.

Turn toward the barre for développé arabesque, left foot front.

On "and," bring the foot on the cou-de-pied derrière; on 1 and 2, slide the foot to retiré derrière; on 3, open the leg in attitude derrière; on 4, stretch the leg fully derrière; on 5 and 6, hold the position in arabesque; on 7, bring down the leg and point the foot onto the floor; on 8, close 5th derrière.

Explanation. Students are reviewing the développés in all directions. For now, the développé arabesque is still practiced facing the barre.

Exercise 14

Grand battement.

Exercise 15

Stretching.

CENTER

Exercise 16

Battement tendu devant with épaulement croisé, battement tendu 2nd, écarté devant, battement tendu derrière in position ouvert, two counts.

On "and" 1, battement tendu devant; on 2, close 5th devant; on "and" 3, battement tendu 2nd; on 4, close 5th derrière; on "and" 5, battement tendu derrière; on 6, close 5th derrière; on "and" 7, battement tendu 2nd; on 8, close 5th devant. Repeat the exercise one more time.

Explanation. Students are reviewing some of the different directions they have learned so far in this exercise of battements tendus en croix en dehors.

Exercise 17

Battement jeté 2nd, in 1st, arms in 6th, on the count, three repetitions.

In the preparatory port de bras, bring the arms in 1st, open the left arm 2nd, keeping the right arm in 1st, and turning the head slightly toward the right.

On "and," battement jeté 2nd; on 1, close 1st; on "and," battement 2nd; on 2, close 1st; on

"and," battement 2nd; on 3, close in 1st; on 4, hold the position. Repeat one more time with the right foot. Repeat the whole exercise one more time. At the end, roll up in 1st and hold the position.

Explanation. Students are repeating the exercise with no hold in the closing. In this exercise, even though the closing brings both legs in 1st, most of the weight remains on the supporting leg so that students can release the working leg quickly out of the 1st and still be balanced. The transfer is transferred only slightly onto the working foot in 1st so that the foot can brush out and in.

Exercise 18

Adagio: retiré devant, four counts, small fendu, with port de bras, with épaulement croisé.

Following the preparatory port de bras, bring the arms down.

On "and," bring the front foot onto the cou-de-pied; on 1 and 2, slide the foot to retiré devant, bringing the arms in 1st; on "and" 3, slide it down; on 4, close 5th devant in plié, opening the arms 2nd and stretch.

On "and" 5, battement tendu derrière; on 6, hold the position; on 7, bring the back foot flat on the floor in small fendu; on 8, hold the position; on 1 and 2, bring the arms to 5th; on 3 and 4, open the arms 2nd; on 5, point the back foot, while stretching the supporting leg; on 6, hold the position; on 7, close 5th derrière, bringing the arms down; on 8, hold the position. Repeat the whole exercise one more time.

Explanation. This is essentially a review exercise, but performed in the position croisé.

Exercise 19

Battement tendu 2nd, quarter of a pirouette en dehors, four counts.

Students repeat Exercise 19 of the Fifth Class of the Thirty-Second Week.

Exercise 20

Battement tendu 2nd, 4th position in plié, relevé, retiré devant, four counts, facing the barre.

On "and" 1, battement tendu 2nd; on "and," close 1st; on 2, brush the working foot back in 4th position, with both legs in plié; on 3, relevé on the left foot while bringing the back leg in retiré devant; on 4, close 5th devant in plié. Repeat three more times, initiating the battement tendu 2nd out of the plié. In the last retiré, students hold balance.

Explanation. Students are repeating Exercise 21 of the Second Class of the Thirty-Second Week, this time performed on four counts. It is a more difficult exercise for balance and placement. There is more room for error, since the center of gravity is more spread out and the working leg has a longer trajectory to get to the supporting knee. The foot does not sickle and the hips remain straight.

Music. Since the exercise is on four counts, the tempo will be adjusted to allow proper placement through each position.

Exercise 21

Échappé 2nd, soubresaut 2nd, each on the count, facing the barre and in the center with port de bras, review.

On "and," plié and push off the floor, stretching the legs; on 1, come down in plié; on "and," directly out of the plié, push off; on 2, land in 2nd; on "and," directly out of the plié, push off the floor; on 3, land in 5th, left foot front; on 4, stretch the legs. Repeat three more times, closing alternatively left and right foot front. Repeat the exercise in the center with port de bras, opening the arms in the échappé and closing them with the last jump.

Explanation. Students are reviewing Exercise 23 of the Second Class of the Twenty-Sixth Week.

Exercise 22

Glissade 2nd, two counts, assemblé 2nd, en descendant, with port de bras, on the count.

Students repeat Exercise 22 of the Fifth Class of the Thirty-Second Week.

Exercise 23

Sissonne 2nd, traveling toward the front foot and the back foot, changing feet, two counts, three repetitions, review.

Students repeat Exercise 23 of the Fifth Class of the Thirty-Second Week.

Exercise 24

Petit jeté dessous, on the count, one count hold in closing.

On "and," plié, brush the left foot and throw the leg 2nd, with the supporting leg pushing off the floor and both legs stretching in the air; on 1, land in plié on the left foot, while the right leg bends and the right foot comes on the cou-de-pied derrière, and the right arm closes 1st, the head turned toward the right; on 2, close 5th; on 3, stretch the legs, and open the arm 2nd; on 4, hold the position; on "and," plié and brush the right foot into 5th, and throw the leg 2nd, with the supporting leg pushing off the floor; on 5, land in plié on the right foot while the left leg bends and the left arm closes 1st; on 6, close 5th; on 7, stretch the legs, and open the arm 2nd; on 8, hold the position. Repeat one more time. After a pause, repeat one more time.

Explanation. Students are now practicing the petit jeté in the center. They are closing each time for this first practice in the center so that they can coordinate better for the following jump. After a few repetitions, they will be able to perform the exercise, like at the barre, without closing in between the jumps. When landing, students avoid stutter steps. The plié should be deep and soft.

Music. The tempo is lively and brisk for this exercise so that students do not sit too long in plié in between the jumps. A medium-tempo coda would work well here.

Application. It is important for beginners to learn to control the plié of the landing with the foot softly coming down onto the floor, with the knee above the toes and without any part of the body wobbling. If the landing is still shaky, students remain at the barre for this exercise.

Exercise 25

Balancé 2nd, traveling sideways, with port de bras, two counts, three repetitions, review.

Students repeat Exercise 26 of the Fifth Class of the Thirty-Second Week.

Exercise 26

Curtsey.

THIRD CLASS

Students repeat the material of the Second Class of this week.

FOURTH CLASS

Exercise 1

Warm up.

Exercise 2

Plié.

Exercise 3

First battement tendu exercise.

Exercise 4

Battement tendu 2nd, in 1st, four counts, two counts, on the count, facing the barre.

    Students repeat Exercise 4 of the Second Class of this week.

Exercise 5

Battement tendu devant and derrière, passé à terre, battement tendu 2nd, in 1st, on the count.

    Students repeat Exercise 5 of the Second Class of this week.

Exercise 6

Battement jeté 2nd, in 1st, on the count, six repetitions, facing the barre.

    Students repeat Exercise 6 of the Second Class of this week.

Exercise 7

Battement jeté en croix, hold on the closing, on the count.

    Students repeat Exercise 7 of the Second Class of this week.

Exercise 8

Rond de jambe à terre.

Exercise 9

Position on the cou-de-pied, close in 5th without plié, battement tendu 2nd, four counts, facing the barre.

    Students repeat Exercise 9 of the Second Class of this week.

Exercise 10

Rond de jambe soutenu in 2nd, en dehors and en dedans, in 1st, each rond de jambe on two counts, two repetitions, facing the barre.

    Students repeat Exercise 10 of the Second Class of this week.

Exercise 11

Double battement frappé 2nd, two counts, two count hold in 2nd, facing the barre.

    Students repeat Exercise 11 of the Second Class of this week.

Exercise 12

Demi-rond de jambe à la demi-hauteur, start in plié, en dehors and en dedans, with port de bras, four counts.

    Students repeat Exercise 12 of the Second Class of the Thirty-Second Week.

Exercise 13

Adagio: développé devant and 2nd, with port de bras, sideways, développé arabesque, eight counts, two count hold, facing the barre.

    Students repeat Exercise 13 of the Second Class of this week.

Exercise 14

Grand battement.

Exercise 15

Stretching.

CENTER

Exercise 16

Battement tendu devant with épaulement croisé, battement tendu 2nd, écarté devant, battement tendu derrière in position ouvert, two counts.

    Students repeat Exercise 16 of the Second Class of this week.

Exercise 17

Battement jeté 2nd, in 1st, arms in 6th, on the count, three repetitions.

    Students repeat Exercise 17 of the Second Class of this week.

Exercise 18

Adagio: retiré devant, four counts, small fendu, with port de bras, with épaulement croisé.

Students repeat Exercise 18 of the Second Class of this week.

Exercise 19

Pas de bourrée dessous and dessus, start 2nd position, four counts, facing the barre.

On "and," plié; on 1, battement tendu 2nd with the left foot in plié, turning the head toward the left; on "and" 2, bring the left leg behind the right leg in 5th, with a simultaneous rise onto demi-pointes (like in a battement soutenu), stretching both legs; on "and," open the right leg 2nd, the pointed foot slightly off the floor, with both legs stretched, straightening the head; on 3, step onto the right foot on demi-pointe, transferring the weight onto the right leg; on "and," close 5th, left foot front in plié, the head turning toward the left; on 4, stretch the knees. Repeat three more times, alternating legs.

On "and," plié; on 1, battement tendu 2nd with the right foot in plié, the head still turned toward the right; on "and" 2, bring the right leg in front of the left leg in 5th with a simultaneous rise onto demi-pointes, stretching both legs; on "and," open the left leg 2nd, the pointed foot slightly off the floor, with both legs stretched, straightening the head; on 3, step onto the left foot on demi-pointe, transferring the weight onto the left leg; on "and," close 5th, left foot front in plié, with the head turning toward the left; on 4, stretch the knees. Repeat three more times, alternating legs.

Explanation. This is another way to initiate the pas de bourrée, in which there is no stepping onto demi-pointe on the plié but a soutenu onto demi-pointes. It is recommended to have studied the battement tendu soutenu in 2nd before practicing this exercise. Students should be reminded to keep their supporting heel down as long as possible as the working leg is brought into 5th on demi-pointes.

Exercise 20

Battement tendu 2nd, quarter of a pirouette en dehors, four counts.

Students repeat Exercise 19 of the Fifth Class of the Thirty-Second Week.

Exercise 21

Battement tendu, 4th position, relevé retiré devant, four counts, facing the barre.

Students repeat Exercise 20 of the Second Class of this week.

Exercise 22

Échappé 2nd, soubresaut 2nd, each on the count, facing the barre and in the center with port de bras, review.

Students repeat Exercise 21 of the Second Class of this week.

Exercise 23

Glissade 2nd, two counts, assemblé 2nd, en descendant, with port de bras, on the count.

Students repeat Exercise 22 of the Fifth Class of the Thirty-Second Week.

Exercise 24

Sissonne 2nd, traveling toward the front foot and the back foot, changing feet, two counts, three repetitions, review.

Students repeat Exercise 23 of the Fifth Class of the Thirty-Second Week.

Exercise 25

Petit jeté dessous, on the count, one count hold in closing.

Students repeat Exercise 24 of the Second Class of this week.

Exercise 26

Balancé 2nd, traveling sideways, with port de bras, two counts, three repetitions, review.

Students repeat Exercise 26 of the Fifth Class of the Thirty-Second Week.

Exercise 27

Curtsey.

FIFTH CLASS

Exercise 1

Warm up.

Exercise 2

Plié.

Exercise 3

First battement tendu exercise.

Exercise 4

Battement tendu 2nd, in 1st, four counts, two counts, on the count, facing the barre.

Students repeat Exercise 4 of the Second Class of this week.

Exercise 5

Battement tendu devant and derrière, passé à terre, battement tendu 2nd, in 1st, on the count.

Students repeat Exercise 5 of the Second Class of this week.

Exercise 6

Battement jeté 2nd, in 1st, on the count, six repetitions, facing the barre.

Students repeat Exercise 6 of the Second Class of this week.

Exercise 7

Battement jeté en croix, on the count, with hold on the closing.

Students repeat Exercise 7 of the Second Class of this week.

Exercise 8

Rond de jambe à terre.

Exercise 9

Position on the cou-de-pied, battement tendu 2nd, four counts, facing the barre.

Students repeat Exercise 9 of the Second Class of this week.

Exercise 10

Rond de jambe soutenu in 2nd, en dehors and en dedans, in 1st, two counts, two repetitions, facing the barre.

Students repeat Exercise 10 of the Second Class of this week.

Exercise 11

Double battement frappé 2nd, two counts, two count holding, facing the barre.

Students repeat Exercise 11 of the Second Class of this week.

Exercise 12

Demi-rond de jambe à la demi-hauteur, start in plié, en dehors and en dedans, with port de bras, four counts.

Students repeat Exercise 12 of the Second Class of the Thirty-Second Week.

Exercise 13

Adagio: développé devant and 2nd, with port de bras, sideways, développé arabesque, facing the barre.

Students repeat Exercise 13 of the Second Class of this week.

Exercise 14

Grand battement.

Exercise 15

Stretching.

CENTER

Exercise 16

Battement tendu devant with épaulement croisé, battement tendu 2nd, écarté devant, battement tendu derrière in position ouvert, two counts.

Students repeat Exercise 16 of the Second Class of this week.

Exercise 17

Battement jeté 2nd, in 1st, arms in 6th, on the count, three repetitions.

Students repeat Exercise 17 of the Second Class of this week.

Exercise 18

Adagio: retiré devant, four counts, small fendu, with port de bras, with épaulement croisé.

Students repeat Exercise 18 of the Second Class of this week.

Exercise 19

Pas de bourrée dessous and dessus, start in 2nd position, four counts, facing the barre.

Students repeat Exercise 19 of the Fourth Class of this week.

Exercise 20

Battement tendu 2nd, quarter pirouette en dehors, four counts.

Students repeat Exercise 19 of the Fifth Class of the Thirty-Second Week.

Exercise 21

Battement tendu 2nd, 4th position, relevé retiré devant, four counts, facing the barre.

Students repeat Exercise 20 of the Second Class of this week.

Exercise 22

Échappé 2nd, soubresaut 2nd, each on the count, facing the barre and in the center with port de bras, review.

Students repeat Exercise 21 of the Second Class of this week.

Exercise 23

Sissonne 2nd, traveling toward the front foot and the back foot, changing feet, two counts, three repetitions, review.

Students repeat Exercise 23 of the Fifth Class of the Thirty-Second Week.

Exercise 24

Assemblé 2nd, en descendant and en remontant, on the count, at the barre and in the center.

On "and," plié, brush the left foot and extend the leg 2nd, while pushing off the floor with the supporting leg, and stretch both legs in the air; on 1, land in plié in 5th, left foot front; on 2, stretch the knees. Repeat one more time.

On "and," plié, brush the right foot and extend the leg 2nd, while pushing off the floor with the supporting leg, and stretch both legs in the air;

on 5, land in plié in 5th, left foot front; on 6, stretch the knees. Repeat one more time. Repeat the whole exercise one more time. Repeat the exercise in the center.

Explanation. Students are reviewing the assemblé, both en descendant and en remontant. The jump is small and sharp, since it is on the count. Students must still pay attention to the brushing of the front foot when it comes out. The exercise can also be performed in the center with the arms in plain 2nd, depending on the students' quality of execution.

Music. A march would be a good musical choice for this exercise.

Exercise 25

Petit jeté dessous, on the count, one count hold in closing.

Students repeat Exercise 24 of the Second Class of this week.

Exercise 26

Balancé 2nd, traveling sideways, with port de bras, two counts, three repetitions, review.

Students repeat Exercise 26 of the Fifth Class of the Thirty-Second Week.

Exercise 27

Curtsey.

END OF THE FIRST YEAR

This is the end of the thirty-third week and the last week of training. Any time left will be spent reviewing the material of the year. The instructor will identify the elements that students need to practice most.

Conditioning Exercises

𝄞

With today's high demands on performers for more extension and considerable strength, ballet dancers need additional training outside of ballet class to improve their technique, since even regular class work is insufficient to develop and stretch certain muscles. Such training aims at strengthening and stretching certain muscles, which are generally used insufficiently in a regular ballet class. Proper conditioning should start early on in training and should include stretching, abdominal, and strengthening exercises. The conditioning exercises that follow are primarily designed to facilitate beginner students' acquisition of the placement and posture so essential in the first year. They seek to optimize muscle development in the application of basic ballet moves. The regular performance of floor exercises designed to work the turn-out, in particular, is highly recommended for beginner students. It permits them to feel and work their turn-out from the hips without cheating; that is, by using the pressure of the feet on the floor to open their feet at a wider angle than their real hip outward rotation permits.

The list of the present conditioning exercises is in no way exhaustive, and the number of repetitions is only illustrative. Numbers of repetitions can be increased at the teacher's discretion. To be effective in the first year of training, conditioning exercise should be practiced at least three times a week and should be conducted under proper supervision to make sure that the exercises are performed correctly and students do not get hurt. Proper breathing is important to get the full benefits from these exercises. The use of a mat may be necessary for some of them.

Ideally, conditioning exercises for posture, turn-out, and joints should precede a ballet class, and those for stretching and flexibility should be practiced after the barre or just after class, when students have sufficiently warmed up their muscles. Any kind of deep stretching should be avoided before warming up; even for naturally flexible students, merely sitting in a spilt before class will not be beneficial and may even be counterproductive for muscle elasticity.

POSTURE EXERCISES

Pelvis and Back

Stand sideways to the mirror with the arms relaxed at the sides and the legs slightly apart in parallel. The pelvis must be slightly tilted, keeping the hip bones lifted in front, while the lowest part of the spine is directed downward. The spine remains elongated without the pelvis tucking under and the rib cage sticking out. The abdominal and buttock muscles are tensed sufficiently to hold the pelvis in the proper alignment. Bring the arms 2nd. Breathe normally. Hold the position for ten counts and release. Repeat four times.

Explanation. This exercise acquaints students with the ballet posture of the upper body by practicing it in isolation. This posture should eventually become second nature to pre-professional students. In this exercise, students should feel as they are being pulled on both ends: the upper body pulling up and the legs and feet pushing down the floor. In this position, the upper torso is like being isolated from the rest of the trunk and held in suspension. Students can check their position in the mirror for visual feedback on what the posture looks like sideways. This exercise is particularly beneficial for students with a sharply curved lower back.

Pelvis and Back on the Floor

Lie down on the floor on the back, arms to the sides. Apply the same alignment as when standing in the previous exercise. Breathe normally. Hold the position for ten counts and release. Repeat four times.

Explanation. This exercise is similar to the preceding one, except it is performed on the floor. Gravity helps the alignment, without rounding the lower back or the pelvis tucking under. The position on the floor makes it easier to feel the opposite pulling of the legs and the torso. Shoulders should not tense.

Upper Back

Stand legs parallel, with the arms 2nd, applying the same alignment as when standing in the previous exercise, hold the upper back and contract the large back muscles (latissimus dorsi), while keeping the shoulders down. Hold the position for eight counts and release. Release the arms. Repeat the exercise one more time.

Explanation. Most of the holding of the arms in ballet positions should result from the contracting of the large upper back muscles so that the arms and the top of the shoulders do not tense up. In this exercise, students should be able to contract and release the correct muscles. When contracting the upper back, the shoulder blades do not stick out and the latissimus dorsi should feel tight when holding the correct position. The proper contraction of muscles holding the arms is important to avoid building tension and eventually bulk at the base of the neck and on the top of the shoulders. It allows fluidity and softness in the arm movement. It also helps to keep core strength for better balance and contributes to the majestic appearance of the dancer. A good holding of the upper back makes the torso function like a solid tree trunk, supporting the branches that are then free to move.

Upper Shoulders

Stand in front of the mirror, with legs parallel and the arms in 5th. Bring the shoulders up, trying to touch the ears with the shoulders; hold the position for four counts, and then push the shoulders down while pulling up the neck, holding for four counts. Repeat the exercise four times, alternating both positions. Release the arms. Repeat the exercise one more time.

Explanation. Working again with contrast, students bring the shoulders up and down keeping the arms in 5th. Beginning ballet students often associate the raising of the arms in 5th with the simultaneous lifting of the shoulders. This exercise helps them to dissociate the raising of the arms and the one of the shoulders.

ABDOMINALS

Crunches

Lie down on the back, knees bent, feet flat on the floor slightly apart, hands behind the neck and elbows to the sides. Bring the torso up four times in a row, keeping the neck as straight as possible and the elbows to the sides. Hold the last lift four times. Repeat the exercise ten times.

Explanation. The exercise results in the contraction of the rectus abdominis—the main abdominal muscle—working in isolation. To make the exercise more effective, students should not bend their neck and should keep their elbows to the sides when raising the upper torso. Strengthening abdominal muscles cannot be overemphasized; it develops the core strength that is so crucial to the performance of ballet, especially in the execution of jumps, which require the abdominal muscles to be lifted. It also helps the whole torso to remain in alignment.

Leg Lifts

Lie down on the back, with the hands under the lower part of the buttocks to keep the lower back on the floor. Bend the knees and lift the legs, turn them out and stretch them, keeping the feet pointed. Bring the legs slowly down to have the feet just above the ground and lift them to about 50°. Repeat the exercise a few times, increasing the number of repetitions over time. At the end of the exercise, bring the bent knees onto the chest to stretch the back, holding them with the hands for further stretching.

Explanation. This exercise, in addition to working the rectus abdominis, strengthens the transversus abdominis. The legs are held together in a turned-out position to avoid tensing the quadriceps excessively. The adductors, on the other hand, are quite active in holding the legs together. To avoid curving the lower back and to alleviate the pressure on the lower back, the hands are placed under the lower part of the buttocks.

Swing the Legs to the Sides

Lie down on the back, with the arms extended to the sides. Raise the legs stretched together.

Lower the legs to the right side, keeping the arms and the shoulders on the floor, and, without touching the floor with the feet, lift them back up to the center. Repeat the exercise, lowering the legs to the left side. Repeat the exercise several times.

Explanation. This is a more challenging exercise that works the internal and external obliques, in particular, which are involved in the rotation, and the lateral flexors of the spine, and which stabilizes the spine in the upright position. In order to resist rolling down with the legs, students should push their upper back and the arm down onto the floor for resistance, especially on the side of the torso that is the same as the side to which the legs are swung. When the legs are on the side, they are perpendicular to the torso and do not sway forward.

STRENGTHENING

Flexion of the Feet

Sit on the floor, legs in parallel, with the legs stretched forward together and feet pointed, holding the back straight. Hold the arms on the sides, with the tips of the fingers resting lightly on the floor. The shoulders are down. Flex the toes, keeping the instep stretched, and then flex both feet in their entirety. Stretch the instep, toes still flexed, and point the toes. Repeat five times and release. Repeat the whole exercise. Repeat the exercise with the legs turned out.

Lie on the back, legs lifted, with stretched knees and feet pointed, arms extended to the sides. Repeat the preceding flexing exercise, this time using only one foot at a time (while one foot flexes, the other stays pointed). Repeat four times. Bend the knees to release the legs and repeat the exercise one more time.

Explanation. These series of foot exercises are designed to improve foot flexibility. The knees remain taut, and each flex action should be performed to the maximum.

Knee and Quadriceps

Lie down on the back, raise the legs and stretch them, pointing the feet, arms extended to the sides. Bend the knees and stretch the legs. Repeat

the exercise four times and release. Repeat the exercise one more time.

Explanation. This easy exercise works the flexion and the stretching of the knee joints, without resistance for now, but with control. In the stretching, the back of the legs must be lengthened while the quadriceps pull on the patella.

Scissors for Adductors

Sit, and lift the legs stretched together and turned out, balancing on the buttocks, pointing the feet, with the arms 2nd. Rapidly cross and uncross the legs at the level of the upper calves, keeping the turn-out of both legs. Repeat ten times and release, bringing the legs down. Repeat one more time. Repeat the exercise lying down on the stomach, holding the front of the shoulders off the floor, with the arms bent and the hands flat on the floor, still keeping the turn-out of the legs.

Explanation. This exercise works mainly the adductors, but also the abdominals and the hip flexors (in the first part) and the back and the buttock muscles (in the second part). The legs are turned out as much as possible to avoid tensing excessively the quadriceps. The upper back is solidly held. It is a particularly effective exercise to strengthen the adductors, which are particularly utilized in ballet.

Back Extensors

Stand sideways to the mirror, with legs parallel and arms stretched up. Bend the torso forward with the arms aligned so that it is perpendicular to the legs. Hold the position ten counts. Release the back, bending the knees, and roll up the back slowly into a standing position.

Explanation. The exercise strengthens the back by using gravity. Students remain balanced on their legs, without pushing back. It can be made less difficult by holding the hands on the waist. Students can gain visual feedback by executing the exercise sideways to the mirror to check if the back remains flat.

Back Extensors and Gluteus

Lie down on the stomach, with the arms held against the torso and keeping the shoulders low, the feet held down by another student. Bend the torso back and bring it down ten times. After a pause, repeat ten more times. At the end, sit onto the heels and bend the torso forward to stretch the back with the arms forward.

Hip extensor

Lie prone, with the front of the shoulders off the floor and the arms bent and hands down, legs stretched together and turned out, and feet pointed. Raise the leg back, hold the position for two counts, and bring it down with control. Repeat six times, alternating legs. The torso remains on the floor, and the leg is lined up with the torso.

Back Hyperextension

Lie down on the stomach, arms stretched forward on the floor, raise the torso, with the arms and the legs together, and hold the position for five counts and then bring them down together. Repeat the exercise a few times. At the end, bring the hands on the floor to bend the back, pushing on the hands, and then sit on the heels and stretch the back with the arms forward on the floor.

Explanation. These back strengthening exercises work the back and the buttock muscles (except for the first exercise). The top of the shoulders must not tense. Proper warm up should precede these exercises.

Upper Back

Stand on a long cord and grab both ends with the hands on each side of the body so that the cord is stretched with the feet holding it in place. The arms are stretched to the sides at the level of the rib cage. Pull the cord up with the arms, while pushing down the shoulders. Hold the position for ten counts and release. Repeat the exercise one more time.

Explanation. This exercise results in the contraction of the upper back muscles (latissimus dorsi). Students, when performing the exercise, should feel the muscles tightening on the external sides of the upper back.

Squat Thrusts

Stand, with the arms stretched up and legs slightly apart. Bend the torso forward, bend the knees, bringing the arms down, and place the hands on the floor, while thrusting both legs backward and landing onto the flexed toes. Bring the legs back under, with bent knees, and straighten up the whole body with the arms up. Repeat the exercise ten times. Release and repeat the exercise.

Explanation. This is mostly an aerobic exercise to build up stamina and breathing capacity that ballet students need, especially for the performance of jumps. It also strengthens the back and the abdominal muscles in the plank-like position. Ideally, when the legs are stretched to the rear, the whole body should be lined up, resting only on hands and the flexed toes, with the back flat. Students must control their breathing: inhale just before bringing the legs down and exhale when coming down.

Ankle and Leg Strengthening For Jumps; Aerobic Exercise

Stand, with legs in parallel and hands on the waist. Perform two jumps on both feet, stretching the knees and feet in the air; without pause, transfer the weight to the right leg, bending the left leg so that it is not in the way, and perform two jumps; without pause, transfer the weight onto both legs and perform two jumps, transfer the weight onto the left leg, bending the right leg, and perform two jumps. Repeat the exercise at least one more time.

Explanation. This is an informal bouncing exercise to gain strength in the legs and feet. It is also an aerobic exercise for students to learn to breathe during the exercise: inhaling in the jump and exhaling in the landing. Unlike ballet jumps requiring the legs to be turned out, students can simply concentrate on the bouncing aspect of the jump. However, students should strive to stretch their legs and feet in the air, and land softly into plié, with the heels landing last. The exercise can be varied, and its difficulty increased, according to the students' level, by adding more jumps in each series. Proper warm-up should precede the exercise.

TURN-OUT

Hip Rotation

Lie on the back, legs stretched and held together, flexed feet, pelvis aligned, and arms extended to the sides while lengthening the back. Turn out the legs, hold the position for ten counts, and release. Repeat twice.

Hip Rotation, Hip Flexors, and Adductors

Keeping the legs turned out and the feet pointed, bend the knees into a frog position, keeping the feet pointed and the heels up, without curving the lower back. Stretch the legs to the sides, about three feet apart, turn in the legs, then turn them out, bend the knees into a frog position again, with the heels kept up, and stretch them slowly, keeping the turn-out to full stretch, with the legs coming tightly together again at the end. Repeat the exercise twice more. Repeat both exercises lying on the stomach, holding the front of the shoulders off the floor, with the arms bent and the hands flat on the floor. This time the heels are pushed down and the toes up.

Explanation. These exercises work mainly the hip rotation (when the hips are extended). When the frog position is involved, the exercises work the hip flexors. For the turn-out itself (that is, the outward rotation of the hips), the exercises require hip extension (as if students were standing in 1st position). Notice, however, the movement can involve both the rotators and the flexors when students have to flex their hips and stretch them, keeping the maximum turn-out. The lower back must not curve, and the back is lengthened throughout. In turning out their legs, students should activate all their turn-out muscles, as if they were trying to bring the internal side of the whole legs forward. These exercises are beneficial only if the pelvis and the whole back are held in a correct alignment. Thus careful monitoring by a knowledgeable instructor is particularly required.

STRETCHING

Hamstring (1)

Sit with a straight back and legs stretched forward and held together. Bend the torso forward, pushing the lower back forward and keeping the knees stretched. Pull the arms forward, with the hands holding the soles of the feet (if possible), for further stretch. Hold for ten counts. Release the back, straighten up the torso. Repeat four times. To also stretch the adductors, open the legs 2nd and stretch forward, keeping the back flat and the chin slightly up, without turning in the legs. Hold for ten counts and release. Repeat four times.

Hamstring (2)

Kneel down, and stretch the right leg forward flexing the foot, while kneeling on the left knee, the hands resting on the floor on each side of the front leg to keep balance. Bend the torso forward, pushing the lower back down as much as possible to keep the back flat. Hold the position for five counts and release. Repeat with the left leg. Repeat the exercise one more time.

Hamstring (3)

Kneel down, stretching one leg forward, keeping balance with the hands on the floor. Slide down the front leg with the hips straight and the front knee stretched. Repeat with the left leg.

Hamstring (4)

Lie on the back, with both legs stretched on the floor. Lift the right leg and hold it with the hands, keeping the back and the neck elongated on the floor and the shoulders down. Both buttocks remain on the floor. Hold the stretch for at least ten counts. Bend the knee to relax the hamstrings and stretch the leg again for ten counts, breathing normally. Repeat with the left leg.

Explanation. These exercises aim mainly to stretch the hamstrings needed for extension and bending in ballet technique. Tightness in the hamstrings will also tend to keep the knees bent, thus putting too much pressure on the lower legs and the thighs. Students will exhale when stretching and observe normal breathing when holding the stretching.

Hip Flexors, Hip Rotators

Sit, and then bend the knees in a frog position. Slowly bend the torso forward, lengthening the back and keeping it flat with the head aligned;

straighten the torso. Repeat the exercise three more times.

Hip Flexors Stretching, Back Flexion, Iliopsoas Stretching

Lie down on the stomach, legs stretched together, bring the torso up and arch the back, with the hands pushing down the floor, and keeping the shoulders low. Hold the position for ten counts and bring the torso down. Repeat one more time. Bend the legs, bringing the lower legs up, raise and arch the torso, keeping the legs together, while trying to reach the feet with the head. Hold the position for five counts, then release. Repeat one more time. To finish, sit on the heels and bring the torso and the arms forward to stretch the back. Hold the position for a few counts.

Calf and Hamstring Stretching, Feet Flexion

Stand sideways to the mirror, legs parallel and held slightly apart. Bend the torso forward, bringing the hands down onto the floor so that the whole body forms an upside down "V" with the heels touching the floor and the back flat. Roll up onto demi-pointes and bring the heels down, while pushing the lower back down. Repeat three times and roll up the back slowly. Students can check in the mirror the shape of their body when they are in the "V" position. Repeat the exercise one more time, facing the other side of the studio.

Explanation. The legs must be parallel, and the heels must come down each time, even if that means bringing the hands closer to the feet.

Calf Stretching, Quadriceps Strengthening, Foot, Knee, and Hip Flexion

Stand with legs parallel and with the pelvis and back aligned and stretch the arms forward. Bend the knees into a demi-plié and stretch. Repeat one more time. Bend the knees into a demi-plié, bend the knees further, allowing the heels to rise off the floor, and without pause, bring the heels down into demi-plié again, and stretch the legs. Release the arms. Bring the arms forward again and repeat the exercise, this time keeping the heels down in the deep plié, and stretching the arms forward to counterbalance.

Calf Stretching, Feet Flexion

Stand facing the barre, and place hands on the barre, legs in parallel and slightly apart. Draw the legs back, keeping the heels down. Roll up onto demi-pointes and bring the feet down, heels on the floor, and keeping the whole body lined up. Repeat three more times and release. Repeat the exercise one more time.

Explanation. It is a good idea to have students stretch their calf muscles often, even during ballet class, especially students who tend to have a shallow plié, and who fail to systematically bring their heels down in the plié. Over time, failing to bring the heels down can cause injuries such as cramps in the calf muscles and chronic tendinitis in the Achilles tendon. Like every other stretching exercise, the stretching is done gently and gradually after some warm-up.

Hands and Arms

Sit sideways to the mirror, with the legs and arms stretched forward, and the back held straight. Flex the hands at a 90° angle, hold it for four counts, and then bend the hands down. Repeat the exercise three more times. Release and repeat with the arms sideways, facing the mirror.

Step Progression Index
§

BATTEMENT JETÉ

BATTEMENT FONDU

BATTEMENT FRAPPÉ

ADAGIO

GRAND BATTEMENT

STRETCHING AT THE BARRE

POSITION ON THE COU-DE-PIED

RETIRÉ

RELEVÉ

PREPARATION FOR PIROUETTE

GLISSADE

DÉBOULÉS

MARCHE

DÉTOURNÉ

PAS DE BASQUE

GLOSSARY

༈༈༈༈༈༈༈༈༈༈༈༈༈

The vocabulary of classical ballet is fairly limited in scope. It is concentrated around some words, mainly verbs that describe basic actions and movements that the human body can perform. These verbs have given names to specific steps and positions of classical ballet. Yet the language is rich because of the astonishing numbers of combinations one can create with these steps and the different qualities a dancer can apply to a step, or a combination of steps; it is limited only by the physical restrictions of the human body. Exploring the verbal basis of ballet vocabulary and the etymology of its terms makes it easier to understand the dynamics of a particular ballet movement or step.

adage: adagio. The term derives from the Italian *ad agio* (with facility). It is a series of movements or positions executed slowly.

air, en l': in the air. The expression describes the position of the working leg that is off the floor.

allegro: the term originates from the Italian *allegro*, a musical word which means cheerful and gay. The expression designates an uplifting and energetic ballet move usually involving jumps.

allongé: stretched, lengthened. The verb *allonger* is often used in a French ballet class to mean to lengthen (without tensing) the back, the neck, the toes, or the arms. In the United States, by contrast, the term is often used to describe the slight rise of the working arm(s) to initiate the preparatory port de bras. It also describes the position of the arm extended in front of the shoulder, when the working leg is extended in the back.

arabesque: Moorish or Arabic ornamental design; from Italian *arabesco* and Arabic *arabo*. It is a position in which the body is supported on one leg, with the other leg stretched backward, and the arm forward, prolonging the line of the working leg. In the arabesque croisée, the supporting leg is the one closest to the audience and the working leg is partially hidden. In the arabesque ouverte, on the other hand, the

working leg is the closest to the audience and is not hidden by the supporting leg. There are also two other kinds of arabesques in the French school, which are variants of the arabesques croisée and ouverte, depending on which arm is extended forward.

arrière, en: backward, to the back. The term describes the direction of moving backward, away from the audience. It also describes the position of the foot that is behind the other.

assemblé: assembled. The verb *assembler* means to assemble or to bring together. In the assemblé, starting from a position à terre or en l'air, one jumps vertically on one foot, with both legs assembling in the air before landing on both feet in a closed position. It can be performed à la demi-hauteur, and it is then called petit; it can also be executed à la hauteur and is called grand.

assemblé, en descendant: it is an assemblé in which the back leg extends out 2nd and closes 5th position front. It is also called assemblé dessus or assemblé devant en changeant de pied.

assemblé, en remontant: it is an assemblé in which the front leg extends out 2nd and closes 5th position back. It is also called assemblé dessous or assemblé derrière en changeant de pied.

attitude: originally a technical term of art for the posture of a figure, it later generalized to indicate a position in which the body is supported on one leg, with the other leg bent (around 90°), and lifted to the side, in front or in back.

avant, en: forward. The term describes the direction of moving forward, toward the audience.

balancé: swung. The verb *balancer* means to rock slowly or swing from one side to another. The balancé is a rocking step in which one moves alternatively from one side to the other or from front to back. It can be performed in any direction, but always symmetrically around a central point. It is one version of the pas de valse (waltz step), except that the balancé has a more detached aspect, with a regular pattern of coming down and going up. It is also called pas de valse.

ballon: the term is named after Claude Ballon (1671–1744), a dancer famous for his lightness and grace. It is the faculty to jump high and to rebound lightly before landing as softly as possible.

ballonné: ball-like step. This term designates a jump in which the working leg extends in any direction with a spring off the floor with the supporting leg; the landing is in plié on the supporting leg, bending the working leg in retiré or against the cou-de-pied of the supporting leg.

battement: beaten movement of the leg. The verb *battre* means to beat repeatedly. A battement designates the movement of the working leg (usually en l'air) striking the supporting leg. Technically, to be called battement, the action must be performed with vigor, energy, and control.

battement en cloche: a battement performed as in a motion of a bell. The term refers to the movement of a stretched leg that moves from front to back and back to front, with the foot brushing through 1st each time. The repeated movement imitates the swinging motion of a ringing bell.

battement fondu: melting battement. The verb *fondre* means to melt. The battement fondu refers to an exercise in which both legs bend at the same time, with the working foot pointed against the cou-de-pied or the knee of the supporting leg. To finish the movement, both legs stretch at the same time, with the working leg extending out again front, side or back. See **fondu**.

battement frappé: struck battement. It is a movement in which the working leg bends, from a position à la demi-hauteur or à terre, and the foot strikes the cou-de-pied of the supporting leg with energy and control. It then extends out sharply in any direction. It is also less commonly called battement sur le cou-de-pied.

battement, grand: large battement. It is a battement that is executed à la hauteur or higher, in a sweeping manner.

battement jeté: thrown battement. It is a movement in which the working leg is lifted with vigor and control off the floor, without seeking height, and closes forcefully. It is also less commonly called battement tendu jeté, dégagé jeté, or dégagé en l'air. The battement is said to be grand battement jeté if it is executed à la hauteur or higher. See **jeté**.

battement jeté piqué: small pricked battement. The movement is similar to the battement jeté, except, instead of closing the working leg, the leg is lowered so that the pointed toes strike the ground sharply; then the leg is lifted to the same height it first assumed, before closing. When striking the floor and lifting, the working leg must be very light, with the foot bouncing off the floor.

battement soutenu: battement held from under. In the battement soutenu, the working leg is à la demi-hauteur or à la hauteur, with the supporting leg stretched or in plié, and closes with both feet rising onto pointes or demi-pointes. See **soutenu**.

battements sur le cou-de-pied, petits: small battements on the neck of the foot. It designates an exercise, usually performed at the barre, to prepare for batterie work. In this exercise, the working foot is positioned on the cou-de-pied devant. The working leg opens about halfway through 2nd and bends again to position the foot on the cou-de-pied derrière, without moving the thigh. It opens again and returns devant and so on.

battement tendu: stretched battement. It is the extension of the leg to the front, side, or back, with the foot sliding on the floor until it is fully stretched, with the toes still touching the floor. There are several other terms to designate this movement: dégagé, battement dégagé, battement glissé, or battement tendu jeté.

batterie: a group of steps in which one leg or both legs beat against the other while jumping.

batterie à croisement: beating with crossing. It is batterie in which the legs cross each other.

bras: arm.

bras en préparation: preparatory position of the arms. In this position, the slightly rounded arms are in front of the body, at about hip level, with the palms turned upward, thumbs in, the arms forming a soft oval curve. It is often shortened to préparation. It is less commonly called position de depart, position de repos, port de bras préparatoire, or bras au repos.

cambré: arched. The verb *cambrer* means to arch one's back or foot. In this position, the back is lifted and bent backward. In addition, the term refers to a foot with a high instep.

changement de pied: changing feet. The verb *changer* means to change. In ballet, the expression refers to a jump in 5th position, jumping with both feet, and changing feet in the air, before landing in 5th on both feet with the other foot front.

chassé à terre: chased on the floor. The verb *chasser* means to drive out or chase out. A chassé à terre is a traveling step in which the dancer moves the foot, sliding it on the floor on demi-plié, into an open position with the other foot taking the place of the first one. It is also called pas chassé.

chassé sauté: chassé with a spring. It is a traveling step in which one leg pushes the other away with a spring, with both legs stretched and held together underneath in the air before landing in plié.

côté jardin: it is the left side of the stage from the audience's perspective.

côte cour: it is the right side of the stage from the audience's perspective.

cou-de-pied: neck of the foot. The term designates the part of the body that is located between the lower calf and the ankle. In France, the term also refers to the arched instep, the tapered portion of the leg from the ankle to the mid foot. Not to confuse this term with *coup de pied,* which means a kick of the foot.

cou-de-pied, sur le: on the neck of the foot. The expression describes the position of the working foot that is placed just above the ankle, with the heel positioned against the inner aspect of the lower shin, the arch resting around the Achilles tendon and the tip of the toes, tautly stretched, aiming for the upper part of the heel bone, when the foot is on the cou-de-pied devant. The more common position of the working foot on the cou-de-pied is wrapped; but it also can be pointed or flexed.

coupé: cut. The verb *couper* means to cut, slice, break, or intersect. A coupé in ballet designates a sharp movement usually causing one foot to cut short the movement or position of the other foot, performed at the lower level of the leg. The term is also used to describe the position of the foot pointed on the cou-de-pied. Unlike the position on the cou-de-pied, the foot in the coupé is never wrapped.

couronne, en: in the shape of a crown. It describes the position of the arms in 5th position.

croisé: crossed. The verb *croiser* means to place two elements one over the other so that it forms a cross; to fold or cut across. In ballet, the term *croisé* refers to an épaulement of the dancer, who faces one of the front diagonals of the stage. In the position croisé, the leg that is closest to the audience hides part of the other leg. Croisé also refers to the position of the feet in the 5th and 4th positions, when the heel of the front foot properly lines up with the toes of the back foot.

croix, en: in the shape of a cross. It refers to the pattern of an exercise that is executed to the 4th position devant, 2nd, and 4th position derrière. It can be executed en dehors (starting 4th position devant) and en dedans (starting 4th position derrière).

déboulés: rolling like a ball. The verb *débouler* means to go down, rolling like a ball, or to bolt. A déboulé is a rotating and traveling movement usually performed in a series of half turns, switching weight from one foot onto the other, keeping the legs in 1st position throughout. The movement was formerly called tours chaînés or enchaînés. The term chaînés is still used widely in the United States.

dedans, en: inward. This term has three meanings, according to the context. It describes a circular counterclockwise movement that brings the working leg forward, starting from the back or from the side. It also refers to a style of pirouette in which the rotation is performed toward the side of the supporting leg. Finally, it describes a condition in which the legs are turned inward or are insufficiently turned out.

dégagé à terre: releasing step. The verb *dégager* means to free, to extricate, or to disengage. In ballet, a dégagé is a disengaging movement of the working leg, always fully stretched, away from the supporting leg by brushing the foot and pointing it in an open position with the toes pointing on the floor. The term is used interchangeably with battement tendu.

dehors, en: outward. The expression refers to the outward rotation of the leg from the hip that allows the leg and the foot to turn out. It increases flexibility and allows a greater range of motion in ballet technique. It also describes a circular clockwise movement that brings the working leg backward, starting from the front or from the side. It also refers to a style of pirouette in which the rotation is performed toward the side of the working leg.

demi: half.

demi-attitude: it is an attitude à la demi-hauteur.

demi-hauteur, à la: to half height. A position of the working leg that is halfway between the position of the leg closed in 1st or 5th position, and the leg situated à la hauteur (hip level).

demi-pointe: half point. The expression describes the position of the foot that is raised so that the heel is brought up and the weight is on the ball of the foot and part of the toes, with the instep being ideally perpendicular to the toes.

derrière: in the back, behind. The term describes the positioning or the movement performed in the back or behind the body. The term also refers to the position of the working leg or the arm in the back of or behind the body, or the foot closed back when the feet are in 5th, 4th or 3rd.

descendant, en: going down. The term originates from raked stages (a stage floor that rises from its front edge to the rear, which enables the audience to better see the performers at the rear of the stage) present in Italian-style theaters. It describes the action of the working leg closing from back to front, causing the dancer to move forward, toward the audience.

détourné: turned around. The verb *détourner* means to cause a change of direction. In ballet, the term refers to a change of direction executed usually by a sharp turn (or less than a turn), performed by whirling around on one foot or both feet. It can be performed by a pivot or even with a jump. It is also executed with a relevé in 5th, which allows changing feet, as in a relevé détourné. A true détourné is performed only en dehors, since the turning direction is usually toward the working leg or the back foot if the feet are in 5th.

devant: in front of. The term describes the positioning or the movement performed in front of the body. The term also refers to the position of the working leg or the arm in front of the body, or the foot closed front when the feet are in 5th, 4th or 3rd.

développé: developed. In ballet terminology, the word describes the action of the working leg that is drawn out along the supporting leg, either to the level of the ankle or to the knee, and then is extended out at any height and in any direction.

écarté: separated, moved away from a center point or a direction. The verb *écarter* means to separate, move apart or spread. In ballet terminology, the écarté position refers to the orientation of the dancer facing one of the front corners with the working leg extended out in 2nd, either à terre or en l'air.

échappé, sur les demi-pointes: escaping step on half points. The verb *échapper* means to escape, break out, or break free. The term échappé refers to the opening of the legs from a deep demi-plié in a closed position, with the feet sliding out evenly to the 2nd or 4th position. Both legs are fully stretched when on demi-pointes. To close, both legs, with a slight spring, close evenly in demi-plié. Also less commonly called pas échappé glissé.

échappé, sauté: jumped échappé. It is a jump in which both legs spring off the floor and land in 2nd in plié; out of the same plié, both legs spring off the floor and close in plié. The échappé can be called petit or grand, depending on its magnitude.

effacé: obscured, shaded. The verb *effacer* means to fade or to erase. In ballet, effacé is the opposite of épaulé. If one shoulder is épaulé, the other one is necessarily effacé. Effacé refers to an orientation of the dancer who faces one of the front corners (closest to the audience), at an oblique angle, so that only three-fourths of the body is visible to the audience. It is the same orientation as in the croisé position, except the supporting (back) leg is the closest one to the audience while the working leg is devant, either in a closed position or extended in 4th position devant à terre or en l'air.

entrechat: braiding. From the Italian *intrecciare*. In ballet, it is a jump in which the dancer rapidly beats the legs front and back of each other, with stretched knees and turned out legs.

épaulement: supported with the shoulder, shouldered. The verb *épauler* means to support or push with the help of the shoulder. In ballet, the term refers to bringing the shoulder that is the closest to the audience forward, while the torso rotates. More broadly, it describes the position of a dancer's body facing the diagonals (not necessarily with a twist of the torso); the dancer is not de face, but shows only part of the body to the audience. The main form of épaulement is croisé.

face, de: facing. It describes the orientation of the dancer who is facing the audience.

fendu: split, cracked. The verb *fendre* means to

split; slide through. A fendu is a position in which both legs are widely open in 4th or 2nd position, with the weight mostly on the front leg that is bent (in the case of the 4th position) and with the other leg stretched.

flexed: bent. The verb *fléchir* means to bend, to flex. Flex is short for flexion (bending). The term is especially used to designate the position of the working foot that is bent to form a 90° angle with the working leg.

fondu: melted. The verb *fondre* means to melt away, to shrink or to sink down. The fondu qualifies a particular plié, which is soft and deep in its execution. It also describes a position that requires bending on a leg with a soft and incremental plié.

fouetté: whipped. The verb *fouetter* means to hit with a whip. In ballet, it describes the sharp and vigorous action of the working leg passing around the supporting leg in back and forth motions like the ones done by the strip(s) of the whip.

glissade: slide, gliding. The verb *glisser* means to glide or to slide along. The glissade is a traveling step in which there is a transfer of weight from one leg onto another in plié as in a wave-like motion.

grand: large, tall. The term qualifies a ballet movement that is of large magnitude, high above the ground, or in which the working leg describes a large movement.

hauteur, à la: to the height. A position of the working leg that is at least perpendicular to the supporting leg.

jambe de terre: supporting leg.

jambe qui travaille: working leg.

jeté: thrown. The verb *jeter* means to throw something with force. In ballet, the term jeté, in general, refers to a jump taking off from one foot and landing onto the other. There are several kinds of jetés. In the petit jeté dessous, the first leg is thrown to the side, while jumping with the supporting leg, with a landing on the first leg, bending the second leg with the foot against the cou-de-pied derrière of the first leg. The jeté also serves to qualify a certain ballet move such as a battement or rond de jambe, which must be performed with force and vigor.

marche: walk, step march. The verb *marcher* means to step forward by successively bringing one foot in front of the other. In ballet, it is a traveling step in which the dancer generally walks on demi-pointes, with the toes instead of the heel of the foot touching the floor first when moving forward, keeping both legs turned out. There are, however, several variations of the marche, the most common being the one that consists of bringing the back leg forward with a small turned out développé through 2nd position. It is also less commonly called pas marché or pas allé.

milieu, au: in the center. The expression refers to the center of the studio. It is also called au centre.

Ouvert: open.

pas: step. It usually involves a movement that causes the dancer to travel.

pas de basque: basque step. Originally an ethnic dance step of the Basque country, the pas de basque is a traveling step à terre, moving forward or backward.

pas de bourrée: bourrée step. It designates a step performed on points or demi-pointes with transfers of weight from one foot onto another.

pas de bourrée couru: runs. The term comes from the verb *courir,* which means to run. It is a series of small steps on toes, keeping the feet close together. It is also called pas de bourrée suivi.

pas de valse: waltz step. It is not a classical ballet step, but a dance, whose origin comes from the German *walzer* (to turn in a circle). Of popular origin, it had entered the language of classical dance by the end of the eighteenth century. It is similar to the balancé, except for its flowing and smooth motion with an emphasis on the upward part of the movement.

passé: passed. The verb *passer* means to pass, to go from one place to another in a continuous manner. In ballet, it refers to the transfer of weight from one leg onto another or the passage from one position to another, often to prepare for another step. It is either performed with a brush through 1st position (passé à terre) or by bending the working leg à la hauteur into a high raccourci and followed by a développé to another direction (passé en l'air). It should not be confused with retiré (see **retiré**) or raccourci (see **raccourci**).

penché: leaned over, bent. The verb *pencher* means to bend or to lean over. The term penché describes the action of leaning the head from the level of the shoulders, the bust from the waist, or the whole torso from the level of the hips. It can be done to the side (sur le côté), forward (en avant), or backward (en arrière or cambré).

petit: small. The term qualifies a ballet move that is of low magnitude, or low above ground.

pied sur la barre: foot on the barre. The expression describes a stretching exercise in which the position of the working leg rests on the barre at the level of the ankle. In this position, the weight of the working leg rests on the barre with both legs in a turned-out position. It can be done with the leg 4th devant, 2nd, or 4th derrière. It is also called jambe sur la barre.

piqué: pricked. The verb *piquer* means to prick. The term piqué describes the action of stepping directly onto demi-pointe or pointe, thus transferring the weight onto it while the other leg is brought up into any position. When performed on pointe, without any rotation, the movement is also called temps de pointe. A piqué refers also to the movement of the working leg from a position à la demi-hauteur or à la hauteur, coming down so that the tips of the toes touch the floor very briefly (like bouncing off the floor) and is then brought up again to the same height. See **battement jeté piqué**.

pirouette: turn, spin. The term comes from Old French *pirouet* (spinning top), related to Italian *pirob* (peg, plug). It is a kind of turn that is performed on one foot on demi-pointe or on pointe. The pirouette can be executed with the working leg held in different positions; it also can be performed en dehors (the rotation is toward the working leg) or en dedans (the rotation is toward the supporting leg). Even though the pirouette is only one category of turn (tour), in practice, both terms (tour, pirouette) are often used interchangeably to designate one or the other. See **tour**.

placement: placement. It defines the fundamental condition of the classical ballet dancer in which he or she acquires ballet technique. It includes the proper alignment of each part of the body in relation to the other parts, and the correct turnout of the legs.

plié: bent. The verb *plier* means to bend. In ballet, the term plié refers to the bending of the knees. It can be smooth, fluid, and continuous, like in the plié exercise at the beginning of the barre.

When the plié is used as a spring, as in small allegro or pointe work, it is performed more energetically, but always with control.

plié, demi: half bent. In the demi-plié, the knees bend at 90°. The heels never rise from the floor, but rather push off the ground.

plié, grand: full bent. In the grand plié, the knees bend to a deep demi-plié, then the heels are raised to allow a deeper plié. Then, without interruption, the body straightens, bringing the heels down onto the floor as soon as possible, followed by a complete stretch of the knees. The heels are allowed to rise in the grand plié in all the positions, except in the grand plié in 2nd.

pointe: point. The verb *pointer* means to point. In general, it describes the tips of the toes. In ballet, it is the condition and the action of the whole foot being fully stretched, pointing down the toes, with the heel raised. When the dancer rests on the tips of her toes, she is also said to be on point (sur la pointe).

port de bras: bearing of the arms. This term denotes a series of graceful movements of the arms-or a passage of the arms-from one position to another, always keeping the arms softly curved, without tension or stiffness.

port de bras préparatoire: preparatory carriage of the arms. It is a specific port de bras that is performed just before an exercise, in which the dancer, usually, brings the arm(s) from the preparatory position to 1st position and then opens it or them to 2nd position or another arm position.

position de repos: resting position. This is yet another expression to designate the position of the arms in the preparatory position.

préparation: preparation. This term designates the position that the dancer must assume before starting an exercise.

raccourci: shortened. The verb *raccourcir* means to make shorter. In ballet, a raccourci is the reverse position of the développé. Each time the extended leg out bends, the line of the leg is therefore shortened. In the raccourci, the working leg is bent on the side, with the pointed working foot against the front, back, or side of the supporting leg, and the knee pushed to the side. It must not be confused with the retiré or the passé (see **retiré, passé**).

relevé: raised. The verb *relever* means to bring up. In ballet, a relevé describes the movement in which a dancer rises onto the tips of the toes (sur pointe) or onto the ball of the foot (sur demi-pointe). It can be executed in all the positions, starting with stretched legs or with a demi-plié.

remontant, en: going up. It describes the action of the working leg closing from front to back, causing the dancer to move backward, toward backstage. Again, both terms en descendant and en remontant originate from dancing on inclined stages in older Italian-style theaters.

retiré: taken out, removed. The verb *retirer* means to take out or bring out. In ballet, it refers to the upward movement of the foot, from a closed position of the feet (1st, 3rd or 5th), sliding along the supporting leg to the position of the retiré in which the leg is bent in 2nd position en l'air. It can be à la demi-hauteur (the level of the mid-calf) or à la hauteur (the level of the knee). It is the retiré that starts the movement of the développé. It must not be confused with the raccourci or the passé.

révérence: curtsey. The term comes from the verb *révérer*, which means to honor or to respect. In ballet, it is a short showing of respect to the teacher performed by students at the end of the class. It is also the curtsey performed by dancers at the end of their performance.

rond de jambe à terre: a circular movement of the leg on the floor. It can be done en dehors and en dedans. In the rond de jambe à terre en dehors, the toes of the working foot that is pointed on the floor devant, draws an arc passing through 2nd position and continues to draw the arc to the 4th position derrière (clockwise motion). For the rond de jambe en dedans, the action starts with the working foot pointed derrière, with the circular movement bringing the working foot through 2nd position, then to the 4th position devant (counterclockwise motion).

rond de jambe en l'air: circular movement of the leg en l'air. In the rond de jambe en l'air en dehors, the working leg, starting with a battement or a développé devant, is brought to 2nd position, then to the 4th position derrière. In the rond de jambe en dedans, the movement starts from the back and ends in the 4th position devant. If the leg is brought à la hauteur or higher, the movement is called grand rond de jambe en l'air. No matter what height is chosen, throughout the rond de jambe, the working leg

remains at the same height. The movement is also called rond de jambe soutenu.

rond de jambe soutenu 2nd: circular sustained movement in 2nd position. This rond de jambe starts with the working leg 2nd. When it is performed en dehors, only the lower part of the leg moves to describe half an oval curve toward the back, bringing the pointed toes against the side of the supporting leg, and drawing another half of the oval curve toward the front, finishing the movement by stretching the leg 2nd. When the movement is performed en dedans, the circular motion is counterclockwise. It is called, perhaps inaccurately, soutenu, since the thigh should be held still from under throughout the exercise. The movement is also called grand rond de jambe en l'air in 2nd.

sauté: jumped. The verb *sauter* means to jump. In ballet, it is the faculty to bring oneself off the floor, following certain principles. Before taking off, a good demi-plié is required, with both feet pushing firmly onto the floor to stretch the Achilles tendon. The dancer jumps by pushing off the floor, pointing the feet and the legs in the process, and lands with the feet (or one foot) touching the floor progressively, heels last, into a demi-plié. The term sauté qualifies a certain ballet move such as an échappé or a chassé, which is performed with a spring. Ballet jumps used to be referred to as temps levés or enlevés. See **temps levé**.

sautillements: hops, skips. The term is related to sauté (jump). The verb *sautiller* means to hop or to skip. The expression designates the small shuffling steps that the dancer performs to turn before some steps. The term also refers to the action of skipping from one leg onto another.

sissonne: a specialized jump that may have been named after the Count of Sissonne, a French nobleman of the early eighteenth century. It designates a jump, starting on both feet, like in a soubresaut, with one of the legs opening either stretched à la hauteur or à la demi-hauteur in any direction or even bent in retiré, at the height of the jump, and landing on one foot. The jump gives the opportunity to attain height, since both feet push off the floor, while the landing is as light as possible.

soubresaut: sudden jump with a start. In ballet, it describes a straight-legged jump from both feet with the toes pointed and feet together in 5th, one behind the other. The feet remain in the same position in the air, and land with the same foot in front. Even though the term traditionally designates a jump in 5th on both feet and landing with the same foot in front, the jump can be executed in most positions. In practice, many jumps, without a specific name are called soubresauts, especially those performed on both feet.

sous-sus: under over. It is another name for a relevé in 5th position, bringing both feet, on demi-pointes or pointes, tightly under. It is also less commonly called temps relevé en demi-pointes and soutenu.

soutenu: held from under. The term comes from the verb *soutenir,* which means to sustain or hold from under. It qualifies a certain step or movement that usually brings the whole body up, as if something were holding it, but without jumping. In a soutenu position, the legs are stretched. It can also designate a certain step in which the working leg, fully stretched, closes, either onto demi-pointe or pointe, an action that causes the body to rise slightly by bringing the leg under. See **battement soutenu**.

sur le côté: on the side, sideways. The expression is used to indicate that a movement or a step is performed sideways or to the side, such as pencher sur le côté (bend to the side).

sur place: in place, without traveling. The expression indicates that there is no traveling and that the dancer remains in the same place.

suivi: followed. The verb *suivre* means to accompany or to follow. In ballet terminology, the term indicates that a movement is repeated several times in succession, like in a series. It is also called less commonly en suite.

temps de fléche: movement of an arrow. The term designates a jump in which both legs stretched execute successively a battement 4th devant during the jump.

temps de pointe: a step on toes. The expression designates several steps or movements done on pointes or demi-pointes. It can refer to a piqué that makes the dancer travel forward (temps de pointe en descendant) or backward (temps de pointe en remontant) and that brings the

working leg in 5th or in a raccourci. Less commonly, it describes a relevé on both feet. In this case, the term relevé is more commonly used.

temps levé: raising step. The verb *lever* means to raise or to bring up. The expression temps levé traditionally referred to all the pas sautés. It now designates only certain jumps, especially those with no particular name, performed without traveling. See **sauté**.

temps lié: linking movement. The verb *lier* means to bring together without interruption or break, in a continuous manner. The temps lié includes a series of movements performed with fluidity to shift weight from one leg to another. The temps lié is usually a traveling step, accompanied by a specific port de bras.

tendu: stretched. The verb *tendre* means to stretch something that is bent. In ballet, tendu is the opposite of plié. It is the action of the legs stretching after having been bent, by pulling the quadriceps on the kneecap and stretching the back of the legs. As with the plié, the tendu is performed with control, by pushing the heels down onto the floor while pulling up the torso and the back. The term is also used to qualify a battement (e.g., battement tendu) in which the working leg, fully stretched, is extended out and is closed.

terre, à: on the ground. The term refers to a movement that is performed with the working toes pointed onto the floor, or to the position of the supporting foot resting entirely on the floor.

tour: turn. The verb *tourner* means to execute a movement in rotation or in a circle; to turn around. The term includes many kinds of turns, one of which is the pirouette that is executed on one foot. When the rotation occurs off the floor, it is called tour en l'air. See **pirouette**.

tour en l'air: turn in the air. The term designates a turn that is performed off the floor, mostly by male dancers.

volé: flown. The verb *voler* means to fly. The term in ballet refers to the entrechat or soubresaut starting or finishing on one foot. Not to be confused with a jump de volé, in which the beating is performed with the working leg already in the air.

BIBLIOGRAPHY

Attikov, Andréi. *La voie du Perfectionnement en Danse Classique*. Translated by Irina Balachova. Paris: Chiron, 1997.

Barringer, Janice, and Sarah Schlesinger. *The Pointe Book: Shoes, Training, and Technique*. Second edition. Hightstown, N.J.: Princeton Book Company, 2004.

Cass, Joan. *Dancing through History*. Englewood Cliffs, N.J.: Prentice Hall, 1993.

Cavalli, Harriet. *Dance and Music: A Guide to Dance Accompaniment for Musicians and Dance Teachers*. Gainesville: University Press of Florida, 2001.

Challet-Hass, Jacqueline. *La Danse Classique Enseignée aux Enfants*. Paris: Amphora, 1997.

De Soye, Suzanne. *Les Verbes de la Danse*. Paris: L'Arche, 1991.

Grant, Gail. *Technical Manual and Dictionary of Classical Ballet*. Third edition. New York: Dover, 1982.

Grieg, Valerie. *Inside Ballet Technique: Separating Anatomical Fact from Fiction*. Hightstown, N.J.: Princeton Book Company, 1994.

Guillot, Geneviève, and Germaine Prudhommeau. *Grammaire de la Danse Classique*. Paris: Librairie Hachette, 1969.

Hertsens, Marc. *Ballet Technique: Principles for the Horizontal Floor*. Saratoga, Calif.: R & E Publishers, 1989.

———. *Classical Ballet: A Review of Blasis and Cecchetti's Technique*. Bozeman, Mont.: Marc Hertsens, 1999.

Howse, Justin, and Shirley Hancock. *Dance Technique and Injury Protection*. London: A & C Black, 1988.

Kostrovitskaya, Vera, and Alexei Pisarev. *School of Classical Dance*. Translated by John Barker. 1978. Reprint, London: Dance Books, 1995.

Lifar, Serge. *Traité de Danse Académique*. Paris: Bordas, 1947.

Messerer, Asaf. *Classes in Classical Ballet*. Translated by Oleg Briansky. Garden City, N.Y.: Doubleday and Co., 1975.

Noverre, Jean-Georges. *Lettres sur la Danse et sur les Ballets*. Lyon, 1760.

Ward Warren, Gretchen. *Classical Ballet Technique*. Gainesville: University Press of Florida, 1989.

VANINA WILSON was trained in classical ballet at the Versailles Conservatory and by Paris Opera ballet masters Raymond Franchetti, Gilbert Mayer, Solange Golovine, and Claire Motte, the last of whom served as a personal coach. Her professional ballet experience ranged from ballet operettas to neoclassical ballet with the Varlan Compagnie, the Sally Amar Dance Ensemble, and the ballet company of the Toulon Opera. She won medals in international competitions, including Houlgate and Valenciennes. After retiring from the stage, she became Head of the Ballet Department at the Institute for the Performing Arts in Virginia. She taught at the Vermont Ballet Theater School before opening the New England Ballet Conservatory, where she developed a pre-professional program and trained students for international ballet competitions. She choreographed several shows and full-length productions of Coppelia and Beauty and the Beast. She also guest taught at the Lebanon Ballet School, Studio 260, and the Ballet School of Vermont. She now devotes her time to private coaching. Her articles on ballet-related subjects have been published in *Dance Europe*, *Dance Studio Life*, and the *Loyola Consumer Law Review*. She can be contacted via e-mail at vanina.wilson@aol.fr

A special thank you to my patient models!

Julicia Gherbaoui

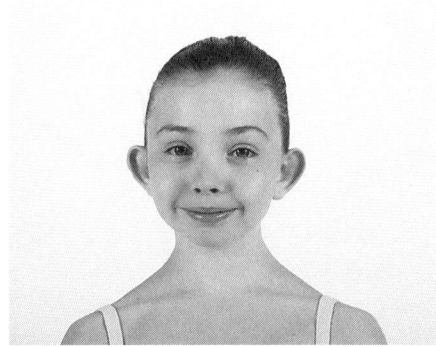

Anouk Varnier-Tchernia

Sylvia Wilson

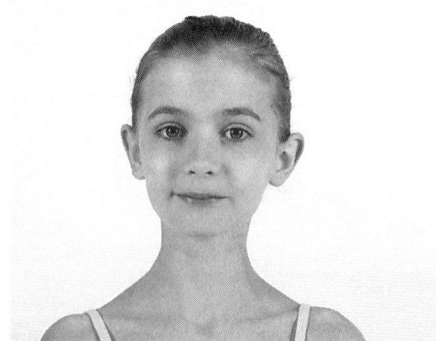

Cassandre Leblanc